Awakening the Ashes

-1—
0—
+1—

Awakening the Ashes

An Intellectual History of the Haitian Revolution

MARLENE L. DAUT

The University of North Carolina Press
Chapel Hill

© 2023 The University of North Carolina Press
All rights reserved

Set in Minion Pro by Westchester Publishing Services
Manufactured in the United States of America

Library of Congress Cataloging-in-Publication Data
Names: Daut, Marlene, author.
Title: Awakening the ashes : an intellectual history of the Haitian Revolution /
    Marlene L. Daut.
Description: Chapel Hill : The University of North Carolina Press, [2023] |
    Includes bibliographical references and index.
Identifiers: LCCN 2023029867 | ISBN 9781469674742 (cloth ; alk. paper) |
    ISBN 9781469676845 (paperback ; alk. paper) | ISBN 9781469674759 (ebook)
Subjects: LCSH: Haiti—Intellectual life—History—18th century. |
    Haiti—Intellectual life—History—19th century. | Haiti—History—Revolution,
    1791–1804. | BISAC: SOCIAL SCIENCE / Ethnic Studies / Caribbean &
    Latin American Studies | LITERARY CRITICISM / Caribbean & Latin American
Classification: LCC F1916 .D38 2023 | DDC 972.94038—dc23/eng/20230705
LC record available at https://lccn.loc.gov/2023029867

Cover illustration: Firelei Báez, *A motor with medicinal function* (2018).
Courtesy of the artist.

For Samy and Sébastien
Pou zansèt nou yo

-1—
0—
+1—

Contents

List of Illustrations, ix
Prologue, xi

Introduction, 1
    History

PART I Colonialism
Chapter 1 Indigenous, 31
Chapter 2 Slavery, 50
Chapter 3 Prejudice, 70

PART II Independence
Chapter 4 Revolution, 97
Chapter 5 Abolition, 130
Chapter 6 Freedom, 166

PART III Sovereignty
Chapter 7 Anti-colonialism, 211
Chapter 8 Antislavery, 247
Chapter 9 Anti-racism, 294

Epilogue, 326

Acknowledgments, 331
Notes, 333
Index, 393

-1—
0—
+1—

Illustrations

Figures

"Carte de la partie du milieu de l'île de St. Domingue" by Bailly Poulin, 1778, 28

"Parque de los Indios," Caonabo monument, San Juan de la Maguana, Dominican Republic, 37

Memorial to Queen Anacaona at Léogâne, Haiti, 48

Facsimile of André Rigaud's *Réponse du général de brigade André Rigaud, à l'écrit calomnieux du général Toussaint Louverture*, 1799, 155

Heroes Monument to Battle of Vertières, 204

Map of "Quartier de l'Artibonite," showing mountains called "Hayty," 233

Bust of Alexandre Pétion at Casa Museo Quinta de Bolívar, Bogotá, Colombia, 234

Paper gourde issued under President Jean-Pierre Boyer, 268

Citadelle Laferrière (Citadelle Henry) in northern Haiti, 292

Palace at Sans-Souci in Milot, Haiti, 293

Table

Number of enslaved people embarked by European slavers to the French Caribbean in the eighteenth century, 53

-1—
0—
+1—

Prologue

In 1814 in the city of Cap-Henry, King Henry Christophe's most prolific secretary, Baron de Vastey, published a striking testimonial against slavery, *Le Système colonial dévoilé* or *The Colonial System Unveiled*. Vastey's goal in publishing this book was to "unveil the heinous crimes" of the French colonists. His stated methodology was consulting the dead to share their stories from the grave. Vastey declared that bringing to light these damning testimonies against enslavers required him to "awaken the ashes" of the "numerous victims" whom the colonists "precipitated into the tomb" and to "borrow their voices."[1] By awakening these ashes, Vastey offered to tell the history of colonial slavery, and its many brutalities, from a Haitian perspective using a strategy today's historians might recognize as "history from below." Decades before Jules Michelet popularized this method with his nine-volume *Histoire de la révolution française* (History of the French Revolution, 1847–1853), one of Haiti's first professional historians established the tradition of talking to and/or for the dead to correct previous historical obfuscations. In Vastey's writing, awakening the ashes is not just a metaphor. Some of the testimony came from below the ground. Death was not an obstacle to accessing the experience of the deceased, hence the ashes that Vastey summoned and the graves he unearthed. Vastey also had living witnesses. He not only interviewed the still alive victims of slavery, but he said he interpellated their mutilated limbs and scars, as remnants of the tortures they experienced. His goal was to produce a history of the enslaved population of colonial Saint-Domingue from their own perspective, a novel method in the Atlantic World.

In a later publication, *Réflexions sur une lettre de Mazères* (Reflections on a letter by Mazères), evoking once more the "innumerable crimes of the ex-colonists," Vastey insisted that he was publicizing the "horrors of slavery" for political ends, not for personal aggrandizement. "Shall I [again] exhume the corpses of my unfortunate compatriots, whom they buried alive, to interrogate their souls and terrify humankind with the horrible account of the crimes of these monsters?" Vastey asked. Vastey imagined disturbing the peace of the dead solely to preserve the freedom of the living when he insisted that French crimes against the Black people they enslaved on Saint-Domingue formed a key part of Haiti's moral, legal, and spiritual claim to liberty and independence. "If injustice, bad faith, cruelties of all kinds, give rights to those who have experienced them, over those who have perpetrated them, what people have ever had more right to independence than the Haitian people?" he asked.[2] In 1816 Vastey expressed the principles of restitution, reparation, and compensation that form the backbone of modern claims for restorative justice after mass atrocities.[3]

To pursue the claim that Haitian independence was the humane and rightful l egal outcome of overthrowing the slave regime instituted and perpetuated by France, the French first needed to be found guilty, even if the only jurist in the court was public opinion. "Public opinion, that queen who rules over the civilized world, who calls kings and peoples to her tribunal, who dictates to them her impartial and irrevocable decrees . . . who extends her invisible empire over the whole universe, who submits to her judgment both the oppressed and the oppressor, who breathes into the trumpet of fame to publish good or bad deeds, who raises up or brings down, who dispenses glory or stigma; it is to the power of opinion that we appeal on earth, as in heaven, when we will be heard and judged by the Almighty," Vastey wrote.[4] For Vastey, condemnation by a public could precede the final day of judgment by a God. And the international community could hand down punishments every bit as severe as any court of law. A human rights trial of this nature required evidence and testimony, from survivors as equally as from the relatives and descendants of those treacherously killed by the French colonists and the French army. Averring that with this line of inquiry he was pursuing the "defense of humanity as a whole," Vastey concluded his *Réflexions* with this insistence: "Whites, yellows, and blacks, we are all brothers, all children of the Eternal Father, all interested in this cause: O man! Whatever the color of your skin! whatever your nation and whatever religion you profess! you are interested in the triumph of the Haitians."[5]

When Vastey published *Le Système* two years earlier, Haiti had only been i ndependent from France for ten years. Even though Vastey was never subjected to slavery in the colonial era, he used "we" pronouns to stress the collective nature of his writing and to emphasize the continuity of this history with the present day. The memory of slavery was as fresh and vivid for those who lived through it as it was for those who experienced firsthand the tumultuous revolutionary events that brought it down. This methodology of mixing enslaved testimony and memory with personal experience did not belong to Vastey alone. Other early nineteenth-century Haitian thinkers, like his predecessor, adjutant general and secretary to Jean-J acques Dessalines Louis-Félix Boisrond-Tonnerre, also turned to slavery's victims, both alive and dead, in pursuit of justifying Haitian i ndependence as a human right. When he published his *Mémoires pour servir à l'histoire d'Haïti* (Memoir to serve as the history of Haiti), immediately following independence, Boisrond-Tonnerre sought to document French crimes both for Haitian posterity and to evoke global outrage. As a member of the first Haitian state, under Emperor Jacques I (Dessalines), Boisrond-Tonnerre wanted to establish an official version of Haitian history. "I must state, first of all, that there is not a single fact, a single crime, or a single action mentioned in this work that does not carry with it the mark of the utmost veracity," he wrote.[6] Boisrond-Tonnerre's history undermined more dominant, European-authored accounts of the Haitian Revolution that, even when defending the rights of enslaved people to strive for freedom, were filled with prejudices against them. Boisrond-Tonnerre, who had also never been enslaved, argued that his task was to narrate not necessarily his individual memories of slavery and the revolution, but rather the collective facts he had access to as one of the revolutionaries. "One will not accuse this pen of vengeance, for it will not be guided by partiality," he wrote. "All the facts that this memoir contains must enter the domain of history that will contribute to our posterity. May it, being happier than we, only know of the French by name, and only have to read the history of our dissentions and problems as if it were a dream that its own happiness will erase!"[7] Boisrond-Tonnerre also used the language of the collective ("we") to poignantly evoke the memory of the revolution's dead, including his own family:

> Envision your cities shrouded in mourning; envision your property as a wasteland; envision the care you took upon yourself, night and day, to revive your companions; envision your children, your soldiers, the peaceful inhabitants of the countryside crippled by the French rifle, or mutilated by the dagger of the ferocious soldier who left him only one ear, only one hand . . . ; oh! think of the woman who wore the memory of a dead husband on her neck . . . what has become of her? . . . and the child who was unable to rip from his collar the golden rattle that hung there in order to give it to his executioner, where will you find him?

"Me, too, I weep for my relatives," Boisrond-Tonnerre finished.[8] The formerly enslaved and their ancestors, as well as all those who lived through the revolution and survived, did not forget all they suffered as they fought to end slavery and colonialism. How long would it take them to forget? Would their dead ancestors want them to forget? "We have seen our fellow citizens, our friends, our relatives, our brothers, men, women, children, the elderly, regardless of age or sex, subjected to the most horrible tortures by those monsters," Vastey recalled. "Those attached to the gibbets served as food for the birds of prey; some were delivered to dogs to be devoured, others, more fortunate, perished under the blows of daggers and bayonets," he concluded. "If it was necessary to recount all the injustices and cruelties the French have exercised on us, I would fill volumes."[9] More specifically railing against Napoléon Bo-

Prologue   xiii

naparte's role in sending a genocidal army to Saint-Domingue to reinstate slavery, Boisrond-Tonnerre wrote:

> And what, said I to myself a thousand times before undertaking this work, this repertory of French crimes, what being could add more veracity to the truths that I am recounting? What sensitive soul, especially after having lived during the storm of the revolution, will believe that the French improved upon their crimes in the most beautiful and the most unfortunate of their overseas possessions? How to persuade the nations of the world that the French contagion had not yet won, that a tyrant [Bonaparte] who ... even set himself up as the restorer of civilization and religion, decreed, in cold blood, the massacre of a million men, who only wanted liberty and equality for themselves; that they will defend against the entire universe?[10]

Both Boisrond-Tonnerre and Vastey were grappling with the politics of describing torture and terror as they tried to oppose the dominant, colonial perspective surging through European writings about the events of the Haitian Revolution and Haitian independence. What both authors consistently urged is that subsequent generations of Haitians never forget the violent history of colonialism and the tortures the French exacted upon the people of Haiti as they strove for freedom and independence. Vastey wrote, to that end, "Oh, you young Haitians who have had the good fortune to have been born under the reign of laws and of liberty! You, who do not remember these times of horror and barbarity; read this writing; never forget the misfortunes of your fathers, and teach yourselves to always defy and hate your enemies."[11] As two of Haiti's first historians, Boisrond-Tonnerre and Vastey helped create a framework of sovereign defiance against the colonial drive for oblivion. They derived their method directly from Haitian revolutionary thought.

The insistence that slavery and colonialism, revolution and sovereignty be meticulously documented by Haitians, and therefore discussed and not silenced, stretches back to the earliest days of independence. "Everything here calls forth the memory of the cruelties of that barbaric people; our laws, our mores, our cities, everything still carries the imprint of the French," reads Dessalines's January 1804 speech, which accompanied his presentation of Haiti's Declaration of Independence. "What am I saying? There are still Frenchmen on this island, and you believe yourselves to be free of this Republic that has made war against every nation." After reminding his audience of all they lost in their thirteen-year struggle for freedom—"your wives, your husbands, your brothers, your sisters, what I am saying ... your children, your suckling babes"—Dessalines asked, "What are you waiting for to appease their souls ... will you descend down into the tomb without having avenged them?"[12]

xiv Prologue

Obtaining "vengeance" was both material and discursive. In the final words of his memoir, Boisrond-Tonnerre explained the lesson Haitians and the still enslaved peoples of the Americas needed to draw from reading his history of the Haitian Revolution. "Haitians," he called out, "whom the bravery of a true hero has lifted out of the anathema of prejudice, in reading these memoirs, you will be able to see with your own eyes the abyss from which [Dessalines] has rescued you. And you, slaves of all countries, you will learn from this great man, that every person naturally carries liberty in his heart, and the keys to that liberty are in his own hands."[13]

Inspired by the visionary desire of early Haitian writers to revive the souls of their dead compatriots to tell the Haitian side of the story of Atlantic slavery and the revolution that heralded its end, the goal of *Awakening the Ashes* is both to emphasize the methodological innovations found in eighteenth- and nineteenth-century Haitian thought and to demonstrate the centrality of Haitian revolutionary thought within broader global intellectual currents. Eighteenth- and nineteenth-century Haitian revolutionaries, politicians, and other intellectuals both documented and theorized the Haitian Revolution and Haitian independence. I am interested in how Haitians who told the story of the revolution and independence, as it unfolded and in its immediate aftermath, influenced the development of anti-colonial, antislavery, and anti-racist approaches to historical writing, as equally as state governance. *Awakening the Ashes* documents the emergence of Haitian historiography in the nineteenth century and the various philosophies of history and politics articulated through it. Starting with Haitian independence in 1804, Haitian writers sought to craft a national historical narrative written by them rather than by white Europeans. They led the way in exploring enduring questions about historical bias—particularly those having to do with race and nationality—through their attempts to justify and defend the existence of Haiti within a world of slavery and colonialism. Conversations about point of view continue to be at the heart of historical methodology today. Questions about race and perspective in historical writing are also fundamentally questions about the politics of knowledge. The issue of the provenance of sources—who wrote them, where, and why—undergirds Vastey's and Boisrond-Tonnerre's suspicions that the majority of European and U.S. writers who wrote about Haiti, because they were from slaving empires, republics, and kingdoms, were inherently biased and prejudiced against Haitians.

Throughout the long nineteenth-century Haitian writers used meticulous record-keeping, including the kinds of oral testimonies that structure the writings of Boisrond-Tonnerre and Vastey, to document Haitian history, but also to directly refute various mythologies of slavery promoted by enslavers and their apologists. In addition to newspapers, personal letters, laws, and other decrees, Haitian authors posed questions to the dead, and offered to transmit their answers to the living. This allowed the deceased to become more than just vehicles of testimony. They were also interlocutors called upon to refute the many faulty logics used by proponents of slavery and colonialism to support their terror tactics. In *Le Cri de la nature* (The cry of nature, 1810), addressing the common argument that slavery was more humane than European day labor, Juste Chanlatte, secretary to Dessalines and then to Christophe, remonstrated, "Go ask the unfortunate people you condemned to the torments of hell? They will respond to you through my organ!"[14] After detailing the horrible crimes of the French during the Leclerc expedition, sent by Bonaparte to rid the island of Governor-General Toussaint Louverture and reinstate slavery, Chanlatte concluded, "Detractors of our cause! White men, both the deceitful and deceived! if you had caught a glimpse of that deboned breast, those scattered limbs, those palpitating shreds, that flesh mulled and dragged by carnivorous quadrupeds, you would no longer speak of your good treatments! You would no longer be surprised at our just right of reprisal!"[15]

What makes Haitian historical writing and political documentation of this time unique is the continued concern with detailing the history of slavery and colonialism as not a pure, objective science—a claim laden with white supremacy—but as a deeply moral one located in the experience of the Haitian Revolution and the fact of Haitian independence. Chanlatte wrote, "There had to exist in our souls a native virtue, an innate force above all human comprehension, for us to have suddenly sprung forth from within the bosom of nothingness, from the darkness of barbarism, to this august state of freedom and independence whose splendor increases every day!"[16] Even though he had his own experience of the Leclerc expedition as evidence, Chanlatte thought deeply about the kinds of documents that could support his narrative in a world biased against Haitians—for example, Christophe's letters to various French military officials, including Leclerc, which Chanlatte appended to the volume to prove Leclerc disguised his goal of restoring slavery to convince Christophe to join the French army—and the way they might be utilized by future historians. "Happy!" he would be, Chanlatte wrote, "If these materials, collected in haste, could be employed by a skilled hand to construct our historical edifice!"[17] This preservation work was necessary because of the systematic way the French absconded with the documentation of the colonial and revolutionary periods and the racist methods they used to catalog them in French archives.[18] Curating these collections, alongside narrating the history of the revolution, produced archiving in Haitian thought as an intellectual endeavor as much as a preservation project.

xvi Prologue

Eighteenth- and nineteenth-century Haitians were remarkable record-keepers. So much would be lost to us today if not for the painstaking efforts of Saint-Domingue/Haiti's earliest writers who were determined to archive and otherwise preserve written evidence of slavery, colonialism, and revolution in Saint-Domingue. The colonists were covering the earth in shrieking testimonials about the Haitian Revolution, which they usually referred to as an "insurrection." Saint-Dominguan pamphleteers like Julien Raimond exposed as lies the white French colonists' claims to victimhood by consistently documenting and publishing episodes that showed the colonists to be the aggressors and the people of color, especially the enslaved Africans, to be the victims of French colonial violence—discursive, material, and physical.[19] Perhaps because they kept these records under conditions of great duress Haitian writers learned to value not only their preservation but their world-historical significance. Nearly all of the earliest writers from Saint-Domingue and Haiti attached appendices of numerous documents (letters and often copies of official decrees) to their publications to support and prove the merits of Haitian interpretations of history. Later in the nineteenth century there were more formal attempts to create official printed documentary collections, as in Jean-Baptiste Symphor Linstant de Pradine's seven-volume *Recueil général des lois et actes du gouvernement d'Haïti* (General collection of laws and acts of the government of Haiti, 1851–88). The ethnologist and historian Anténor Firmin admired all three of nineteenth-century Haiti's best-known historians, Thomas Madiou, Beaubrun Ardouin, and Joseph Saint-Rémy, precisely for their contributions to historical thought and usage of dynamic documentation methods: oral, archival, manuscript, and print. Firmin reserved special praise, however, for Pradine's "arduous work" of archiving Haitian political proceedings for future generations: "Linstant Pradines [*sic*], who was educated in France, took care, with a spirit of consistency very rare in young countries, to edit and annotate the various laws of the young black republic . . . he defined their meaning and indicated the interpretation to be given to them."[20] Still, it was the "three historians," Ardouin, Madiou, and Saint-Rémy, whom Firmin clarified, "could have competed with their European counterparts, had they found themselves in more favorable circumstances," which is to say if they had the same resources as European historians.[21]

Yet, even without the resources of a Michelet or a François Guizot, Ardouin, Madiou, and Saint-Rémy are the most well known and highly referenced of nineteenth-century Haitian historians today. *Awakening the Ashes* locates their contributions to Haitian intellectual history alongside the eighteenth- and early nineteenth-century Saint-Dominguan and Haitian pamphleteers, revolutionaries, historians, and politicians who were the triumvirate's greatest sources of knowledge and interpretation. Just as much of

Prologue   xvii

contemporary Haitian historical writing is inflected by the work of Ardouin, Madiou, and Saint-Rémy, their histories are stamped by the writing of their predecessors, in Raimond, Vastey, Chanlatte, Charles Hérard-Dumesle (called Dumesle), and Julien Prévost (the Comte de Limonade), as well as the memoirs, newspapers, and other government documents produced under the administrations of Louverture, Dessalines, Christophe, Alexandre Pétion, and Jean-Pierre Boyer. Focusing on these eighteenth- and early nineteenth-century Haitian intellectuals underscores how the documents they gathered and the forms of discourse analysis they applied to interpret and explain them had as much impact as revolutionary actions and laid the groundwork for later nineteenth- and early twentieth-century Haitian historians who helped the revolutionary ideas of their predecessors to enter global streams of thought.

Along with preserving documents and testimony (including their own) from the revolution and early independence, these writers and thinkers presented Haiti's laws and constitutions as further immutable evidence of the Haitian state's deeper morality in comparison with ongoing colonial slavery in the Atlantic World and the dynamic forms of imperial domination that began to take slavery's place as the nineteenth century ended. Many debates animating international conversations about independence and sovereignty in the age of revolutions revolved in complex ways around Haiti's revolutionary past. It was the Haitian Revolution and Haitian independence that forced anti-colonial, antislavery, and anti-racist ideas into the modern political grammar of Western philosophy, and it was the early state(s) of Haiti that ensured they stayed there. All the first constitutions of Haiti contained anti-conquest and anti-colonial clauses, which barred Haiti's leaders from attempting to expand the boundaries of the new country. This made Haiti under Dessalines not only the first state to outlaw slavery and color prejudice, but to ban imperialism.

In the process of establishing their national existence in a hostile Atlantic World, Haitians were compelled to develop profoundly new ways of thinking about freedom and equality. The goal of *Awakening the Ashes* is to examine how the modern understanding of freedom and equality in operation today—often ritually yoked to the French Declaration of the Rights of Man or the U.S. Declaration of Independence—stems more acutely from Haitian revolutionary thought, or what we might think of as the 1804 Principle. The principles that undergird the 1804 Haitian Declaration of Independence were quite simple, yet wholly radical: no human being can ever be legitimately enslaved or colonized, and slavery, racism, and colonialism are the greatest evils of any time. The 1804 Principle, thus, marks less an origin, than it does an opening, an invitation for the rest of the world to humanity. The Haitian revolutionaries, with their *Acte d'Indépendance* in 1804,

xviii Prologue

and their descendants in the nineteenth century who carried it forward with their constitutions and decrees, provided us with this now seemingly *commonsense* understanding that slavery, racism, and colonialism are incompatible with liberty. After they made history by freeing themselves, Haitians developed a distinct philosophy of history and state governance. What I hope what will emerge from encounters with Haitian writers, thinkers, and politicians from a long nineteenth century that begins in eighteenth-century Saint-Domingue is that understanding the principles that undergird the development of freedom and equality as decolonial imperatives necessarily involves engaging with and recognizing the impact of Haitian revolutionary thought.

Consulting this robust historical, political, and literary output that spans the late eighteenth and nineteenth centuries, produced in a region no bigger than the U.S. state of Massachusetts, required me to reconfigure what I understood an intellectual history to be. This book has ended up being a history of ideas that regards both *acts* and *actes* (deeds and discourse) as intellectual. Haitian revolutionary thought is multivalent, and those who engaged in revolutionary acts contributed just as much to the intellectual history of the revolution as those who wrote *actes* during and after the freedom struggle. Here, Makandal, Grande Brigitte, Boukman Dutty, and Cécile Fatiman, along with mostly unidentified Saint-Dominguan "maroons," are as much considered Haitian thinkers as the revolutionaries turned statesmen, Louverture, Dessalines, Christophe, and Pétion; and independent Haiti's earliest chroniclers, most of whom lived through the revolution and used their memories as evidence, like Boisrond-Tonnerre, Vastey, Chanlatte, and Dumesle, are considered to be no less serious historians than Saint-Rémy, Ardouin, and Madiou, who were able to more readily access traditional archives.

There are different concerns and a different set of urgencies for those authors who lived and wrote long after the revolution ended, like Madiou, Ardouin, Saint-Rémy, Demesvar Delorme, Louis Joseph Janvier, and Firmin, and those who were documenting and participating in it as it was ongoing, like Louverture, Dessalines, André Rigaud, Raimond, and Boisrond-Tonnerre. There is also a third dynamic of those who lived through the revolution, and even participated in some way, but due to their young age, or prolonged absence from the colony, largely wrote about it only after the fact, like Vastey, Chanlatte, and Dumesle. We must keep in mind these dynamics, if only to analyze and reflect upon the different ways of knowing that might be brought to the fore.

The question of Haiti's national culture, which underlies each of the three main parts of this book—colonialism, independence, and sovereignty—is also intertwined with the much larger concept of history, the subject of the introduction. Each of the nine chapters in *Awakening the Ashes*, starting in the fifteenth century with the violent encounter between Christopher Columbus and the Indigenous Ayitians, details the precise historical moments that linked Haiti to the rest of the world. Despite international hostility to formal recognition of Haitian sovereignty, Haitian thinkers of the nineteenth century, like their twentieth-century counterparts, were in regular dialogue with politicians, intellectuals, and journalists in Europe, the United States, and throughout the Caribbean. During the Haitian Revolution, Louverture influenced the United States' trade policies (under the presidency of John Adams) with French Saint-Domingue. After independence Christophe had the ear of the British abolitionist Thomas Clarkson, who publicly argued for the recognition of Haitian sovereignty. Vastey's early nineteenth-century anti-slavery writings were frequently quoted in the U.S., British, and Dutch presses to advance the cause of abolition in these countries. Pétion and Simón Bolívar kept up a well-known correspondence, and in 1815 and 1816 the Haitian president provided refuge to the leader of Venezuelan independence, as well as weapons, ammunition, and money on the condition that Bolívar help liberate the enslaved Africans of South America. Decades later, Delorme published advice to the United States about how to institute a true racial democracy in the wake of the U.S. Civil War; while Janvier went further to claim that the independence of Haiti led directly to the liberation of the enslaved populations of Martinique, Guadeloupe, Puerto Rico, and the British Caribbean.

Awakening the Ashes explores the interplay among these Haitian thinkers and writers, politicians and activists, and their counterparts from around the Atlantic World. It shows how Haitian writers inspired those outside their country, even as they were sometimes energized by ideas from abroad. Chanlatte paid homage in his antislavery writings to the French abolitionist, the abbé Grégoire, for the latter's publication of writers of African descent, including Raimond; Ignace Nau once counseled Haitian writers to try to emulate the originality, described as a break with European style, of early national U.S. authors Edgar Allen Poe and James Fenimore Cooper; Firmin devoted numerous passages in his *De l'Égalité des races humaines* (On the equality of the human races) to analyzing the writings of Frederick Douglass whom Firmin exalted as "the finest individual of his race in the United States";[22] and Jean Price-Mars was influenced by W. E. B. Du Bois and Booker T. Washington, whose works Price-Mars creolized in *La Vocation de l'élite* (The vocation of the elite, 1919).

Adopting this explicitly intertextual and intercultural approach to documenting and analyzing Haitian revolutionary thought allows me to tell a story that is both local and global. Precisely because Haitians were primary actors in a revolutionary stage of the world, they were very aware of contemporary

xx Prologue

cultural and political movements and eagerly dialogued with those promoting them. There are rich debates about the relationship between monuments and history, a country's usage of European languages versus Indigenous African or creolized *American* ones, the establishment of democratic republics versus constitutional monarchies, and the ethics of representing violence (especially about the depredations of slavery) in fictional form. Haitian intellectuals also passionately debated whether race was a social construction or a biological fact. They argued about whether histories that relied on oral testimony were as valid as those that delved into written archives, and they wondered whether the culture of Haiti (and really all New World Afro-diasporans) was (or should be) at heart African, European, Amerindian, or some combination of all of these. At the same time, Haitian writers frequently deviated from political, historiographical, intellectual, scientific, artistic, and philosophical trends dominant outside the country to create something novel.

Ultimately, this book offers readers an encounter with a history of the Haitian Revolution and Haitian independence that is shaped by the interpretations and systems of knowledge of Haitian historians and other thinkers rather than by Haiti's "visitors," as Janvier referred to foreigners who meddled in Haitian politics.[23] Despite the relative obscurity today of most of the Haitian names that populate this study, in their own era, these eighteenth- and nineteenth-century pamphleteers, revolutionaries, historians, and politicians demonstrated to the world that the registers of Haiti's history did not contain empty pages waiting to be filled by artists and scholars from abroad. My goal with this book is in some ways quite simple, then. I hope readers will come to share in the enthusiasm of Émile Nau, who in the introduction to his 1855 Indigenous history of Haiti, *Histoire des Caciques* (History of the Caciques), exclaimed, "Voilà, all of Haitian history constructed by Haitian hands."[24] He further boasted, "The annals of Haiti, in spite of the little bit of space they appear to take up in those of the world, abound in teachings that are useful for the study and education of humanity."[25] The Haitian revolutionaries played an absolutely central role in the transatlantic abolitionist movement and the development of anti-racist ideologies and platforms. While fighting for their lives, these remarkable thinkers promoted the destruction of white supremacist colonialism and slavery as the political destiny of all true revolutions. *Awakening the Ashes* tells their stories.

-1—
0—
+1—

Awakening the Ashes

-1—
0—
+1—

Introduction

History

In 1977 in Brooklyn, New York, Haiti's best known historian, Michel-Rolph Trouillot, published his first book, *Ti difé boulé sou istoua Ayiti*, a slim volume of Haitian history written entirely in Haitian Creole.[1] In English we might literally translate the title as something like *Burning Debates in Haitian History*. "'Ti Dife Boule' is a common Haitian expression that can be translated to fanning the flames over a contentious issue; it connotes the image of an instigator," explains Nathalie Pierre, one of only a handful of scholars living outside Haiti to have analyzed the text. "The title, *Ti Dife Boule sou Istwa Ayiti*, then, suggests that someone is fanning the flames over Haitian history and seeks to provoke debate."[2] Trouillot's brother, Lyonel (or Lionel), who wrote the introduction to the 2012 revised edition, *Ti dife boule sou istwa Ayiti*, reminded readers that the original version of the book was produced in the wake of the Trouillot family's flight from the Jean-Claude Duvalier regime: "The dictatorship was in full swing.... It was in this context that . . . *Ti dife boule sou istwa Ayiti* appeared."[3]

Ti dife boule was published under the imprint of the Brooklyn-based publishing collective Kóleksion Lakansièl, whose bilingual activist arts journal *Lakansièl* ("rainbow," in Creole) was created by a New York Haitian diasporic intellectual community that included Jean Coulanges, Cauvin Paul, and three of the four Trouillot siblings, Lyonel, Michel-Rolph, and Évelyne.[4] Lakansièl's publication of Michel-Rolph's first book not only marked the start of his career as a scholar but was itself a "historic moment," since, as Lyonel observed, *Ti dife boule* was "the first work of social science to be published in Haitian Creole."[5]

Because of Haiti's legacy as a former French-controlled colony, coupled with the fact that in the nineteenth century Creole was primarily an oral rather than a written language, most written documents from Haiti have historically been produced in French. Most Haitians today, however, like their ancestors of the nineteenth century, are considered to be monolingual Haitian Creole speakers.[6] This linguistic situation has presented a conundrum for Haitian authors wanting to reach a Haitian audience.[7] The novelist Philippe Thoby-Marcelin characterized Haiti's relationship to French as an existential problem when in the early 1940s he wrote, "As long as language separates us from the people, there will exist no Haitian Literature."[8] With the publication of *Ti dife boule*, for the first time Haitians had a history of their country written by a Haitian in the language of the majority of the Haitian people.

Ti dife boule begins by exploring the colonial history of Saint-Domingue, moves through the revolutionary period, and finishes with episodes detailing what happened in the wake of independence, particularly during the reign of King Henry Christophe. This made *Ti dife boule*, as Trouillot acknowledged in *Silencing the Past*, the first history of the Haitian Revolution written and published in Haitian Creole.[9] For Trouillot, this longitudinal exploration of Haiti's revolutionary past in the language of the revolution itself was necessary for understanding the contemporary dictatorial politics of the Duvalier regime, the very one that exiled Trouillot and his family: "When you know where you came from the path forward that you must take becomes more clear."[10] Haitians living in Haiti at the time of its publication recognized the book's groundbreaking possibilities. Lyonel Trouillot revealed that the text was clandestinely passed around and shared by activists and students in Duvalierist Haiti. He remarked of the 2012 edition published by Inivèsite Karayib, thirty-five years after the original: "[It is] a wonderful gift . . . to us, to put back into circulation a classic of such importance to the history of intellectual production in Haiti."[11]

Yet, despite the historical, political, intellectual, social, and linguistic significance of *Ti dife boule*, Trouillot's first book has only recently been published in English by Liverpool University Press as *Stirring the Pot of Haitian History*, making it the first translation of the text in any language.[12] Lack of translation into multiple languages has precluded the book's ability to travel beyond a small subset of non-Haitians skilled enough to read Trouillot's powerfully poetic, but deliberately circuitous, analysis of Haitian history. One passage of *Ti dife boule* reads:

A contradiction of the Slave/Liberty
A contradiction of Dependency/Independence
A contradiction of the Commodity/Life
A contradiction of the Big House/the Little Garden.

(Yon kontradiskyon Esklav/Libète
Yon kontradiksyon Depandans/Endependans
Yon kontradiksyon Danre/Viv[13]
Yon kontradiksyon Gwo bitasyon/Ti jaden).[14]

While *Ti dife boule* is perhaps Trouillot's most significant book, precisely because of the language barrier it is probably his least known.

Ti dife boule has been overshadowed by *Silencing the Past* in Haitian revolutionary historiography, even though the latter does not actually provide a

-1—
0—
+1—

2   Introduction

history of the Haitian Revolution. In 1996, retired Webster University professor Bob Corbett, creator of the highly influential Corbett email list of Haiti, published a review of *Silencing the Past* that unwittingly captures how the book is both about the Haitian Revolution and not about the Haitian Revolution: "Without writing a book about Haiti, Michel-Rolph Trouillot has written one of the most interesting books about Haiti I've ever read."[15] Yet, in a 1995 post, Corbett acknowledged his own difficulty learning Haitian Creole.[16] In the over thirty-one thousand messages that appeared on the list from 1994 to 2007—which surely recorded the most comprehensive and sustained public conversation on Haiti in the world—Corbett does not appear to have ever contributed a post about Trouillot's *Ti dife boule*.

The problem that the lack of Haitian Creole literacy presents to the non-Haitian scholar of Trouillot's oeuvre is that it is difficult to truly comprehend the significance of *Silencing the Past* unless we understand where it came from. Laurent Dubois has acknowledged that *Ti dife boule* contains the "central themes that would guide and shape Trouillot's work over the coming decades: respect for multiple historical perspectives, the centrality of the Caribbean peasantry in the region's past, present, and future, the power of silence, and the power of breaking silence." It was meant, in Dubois's estimation, to act as a "bridge" between "French language historiography written by Haitian intellectuals" and the Haitian public.[17] Trouillot considered *Ti dife boule* to be not the beginning of his career but, paradoxically, the culmination of it: "The most lasting product of . . . [my intellectual and political] choices is my first book," he wrote in 1996, "*Ti dife boule sou istoua Ayiti*, a history of the Haitian Revolution of 1791–1804."[18]

Returning to *Ti dife boule*, then, on the one hand, permits me to explain how I arrived at the potentially displeasing provocation I announced at the outset of the preceding paragraph, and, on the other, gives me the opportunity to explain my interest in exploring the genealogy of Haitian revolutionary thought as it relates to broader trends in contemporary historical scholarship. It was through the acceptance and ascendance of *Silencing the Past* within the very academic "guild" that Trouillot said was his audience in both *Silencing the Past* and his 2003 *Global Transformations: Anthropology and the Modern World* that the ideas of eighteenth- and nineteenth-century Haitian revolutionaries, thinkers, and writers, including the Saint-Dominguan maroons, most of whose names we do not know, indelibly influenced the direction of historical scholarship published in the North Atlantic.[19] The stamp of eighteenth- and nineteenth-century Haitian revolutionaries, thinkers, and historians can be glimpsed in many realms of contemporary social history—from colonial and revolutionary historical and cultural analyses, to histories of slavery and abolitionist thought, to imperial and postcolonial studies—but most readily in the concept of history from below, even though the vast majority of historians in Europe and the United States will never have heard the names of many of the eighteenth- and nineteenth-century Haitian writers who animate and inform Trouillot's study.

To advance this associative rather than empirical claim, we can juxtapose Trouillot's writings with those of his Haitian predecessors. In so doing, we can question what it means to tie Trouillot's writings less to his acknowledged interests in the European intellectual traditions of "Karl Marx, Nicos Poulantzas, Louis Althusser, [and] Antonio Gramsci,"[20] and instead to contemplate the kinds of historical genealogies that emerge when we take into account his intellectual formation in Haiti, which included not just growing up in a "family where history sat at the dinner table," but also his readings of Haitian-produced historiography, much of which is cited in the bibliography to *Ti dife boule* and in footnotes throughout *Silencing the Past*.[21]

There are politics involved in the constant evocation of Trouillot as a Marxist rather than a Haitianist, particularly because Trouillot may be the one Haitian scholar that a non-Caribbeanist has ever read. The same uneven power dynamics inherent in the long-standing reading practices that silenced the Haitian Revolution in Western historiography—and which Trouillot deconstructed in *Silencing the Past*—have also produced Trouillot's greatest influence as Germany's Karl Marx rather than Haiti's Baron de Vastey or any other Haitian historian, philosopher, writer, or thinker.[22] In other words, when North Atlantic scholars, who routinely evoke the concept of "silencing the past," read and claim Trouillot as a Marxist *tout court*, they effectively extricate him from Haitian thought, and vice versa. If it has been possible to argue the influence of the Haitian Revolution on Hegel precisely because the nineteenth-century German philosopher lived in a world bathed in news of the Haitian Revolution,[23] I am now asking us to consider the effect of the massive circulation of eighteenth- and nineteenth-century Haitian writers' acts and deeds on a world system created in the wake of the age of revolutions. Haiti's Declaration of Independence, its first constitutions, and the works of its earliest historians (many of whom Trouillot cites) were read widely across the nineteenth-century Atlantic World, especially in the United States and Western Europe.[24]

European and U.S. historians also read and personally interacted with Haitian authors. The Haitian historian Thomas Madiou visited Jules Michelet in Paris, and an 1854 letter reveals the French historian received copies of Madiou's three-volume *Histoire d'Haïti* (1847–1848). Michelet, who extolled the beauty of Madiou's daughter in his *Journal* (published posthumously in 1959), also very publicly praised Haiti and, in particular, Haitian women, in his 1859 book, *La Femme*. Michelet's interactions with Madiou led Anténor Firmin to

4 Introduction

remark of the French historian that his words, which should be "engraved in gold," required him to be "loved by all the descendants of Africa."[25] Michelet was well acquainted with the works of the Haitian historian Beaubrun Ardouin, too, whose eleven-volume *Études sur l'histoire d'Haïti* (Studies of Haitian history), published from 1853 to 1860, the French historian mentioned in his published correspondence as well as in his *Journal*.[26] Alphonse de Lamartine also corresponded with Madiou and with the Haitian historian, playwright, poet, and politician Pierre Faubert. As with Michelet, many nineteenth-century Haitian authors admired Lamartine for his historical volumes, as well as for his contribution to the permanent abolition of slavery in the French colonies in 1848 and for his famous treatment of the Haitian Revolution, the 1850 tragic drama written in rhyming couplets, *Toussaint Louverture*.[27] Joseph Saint-Rémy, for his part, became known to a wider audience when his 1853 *Mémoires de Toussaint L'Ouverture, écrits par lui-même* (Memoirs of Toussaint L'Ouverture, written by himself) was translated into English and published in the United States by the abolitionist James Redpath.[28]

My aim is less to trace how Haitian writers appear in the works of European and U.S. authors and publishers, and vice versa, than it is to make visible the power dynamics inherent in long-standing reading practices that have led many scholars to believe that Trouillot's greatest influence could have been Germany's Karl Marx.[29] Trouillot could not have learned much about how to understand the Haitian Revolution from Marx's facile comparison of Haiti's Toussaint Louverture and Faustin Soulouque I to France's Napoléon and Louis Bonaparte in *The Class Struggle in France*, except, perhaps, how not to talk about Haiti. Moreover, in *Die deutsche Ideologie* (The German ideology), Marx and Engels painted as "comical" fellow German philosopher Max Stirner's observation that "the insurgent Negroes of Haiti and fugitive Negroes of all the colonies wanted to free not themselves, but 'man.'" Scholar Wulf D. Hund, who has studied Marx's sheer incomprehension of the world historical significance of the Haitian Revolution, noted that in another essay Marx refused to "concede" to the enslaved freedom fighters of Saint-Domingue "what he stressed concerning the 'class struggles in France'—that the 'popular masses' developed a 'new feature' of revolutionary struggles," which involved, in Marx's words, "tak[ing] the actual management of the [French] Revolution into their own hands."[30] For our purposes, the most pertinent question is not if Trouillot was aware of Marx's own silencing of the Haitian Revolution, but how and why the vast majority of Trouillot's readers have silenced the Haitian part of Trouillot's bookshelf. Ignoring, discounting, dismissing, downplaying, or outright failing to consult Haitian scholarship produced in Haiti by Haitians is a familiar dynamic in contemporary scholarship.[31] Its antecedent is in the very eighteenth- and nineteenth-century French attempts

History   5

to "silence" the Revolution that Trouillot described and deconstructed in *Silencing the Past* and that are emblematic of Marx's dismissal of the Haitian Revolution's ingenuity.

By putting forward a few cases in which eighteenth- and nineteenth-century Haitian thought clearly laid the groundwork for later writers, both inside and outside Haiti, I do not wish to insist that what is most important is being "first," thereby contributing to the primordial problem of seeking pure origins (the root of white supremacy) that I am, in fact, trying to disrupt. Instead, I aim to underscore some forms of thinking made possible by the fact (and the idea) of the Haitian Revolution and the military, intellectual, legal, and cultural contributions of the Haitian revolutionaries and their descendants to methods and theories of historical writing now dominant in the North Atlantic. Eighteenth- and nineteenth-century Haitian thinkers (broadly construed) contributed to many of the political and cultural theories that govern contemporary historical and literary study. Yet, it is the voices of Haiti's earliest historians and chroniclers that have ultimately been most excluded in North Atlantic scholarship during the present resurgence of interest in Haitian history, even, or perhaps especially, following on the heels of what Celucien Joseph has referred to as the "Haitian turn."[32] The continued silencing of the influence of Haitian thinkers, writers, and politicians on the development of Western intellectual practices is perhaps one of the clearest instances of the problematic that Trouillot laid out in the famous chapter of *Silencing the Past* called "The Three Faces of Sans Souci": they are "silences thrown against a superior silence."[33]

––––––––

Even though in his introduction Lyonel Trouillot referred to *Ti dife boule* as a fundamentally Marxist text, a characterization that has also been made of *Silencing the Past*, both works were clearly influenced by Haitian writers and historians, specifically of the nineteenth century.[34] These earlier Haitian historians markedly influenced Trouillot's ideas about silences in the historical record. This can be clearly seen if we take a closer look at the Haitian authors Trouillot cites in both *Silencing the Past* and *Ti dife boule*. Yet, what Trouillot quotes from or refers to from prior Haitian historians, with his extensive footnotes and bibliographic references, cannot encapsulate the entire story of his influences. There is a way of thinking about the Haitian past by simply writing and thinking in Creole that Trouillot is deeply engaged with and that marks both works.

In the bibliography for *Ti dife boule* Trouillot lists sixty-three different sources. Fourteen of them are in the English language, including C. L. R. James's *The Black Jacobins*. The rest of the publications are French-language

6   Introduction

works, twenty-two of these being publications or other documents from Haiti. Those writers listed from the nineteenth century include most of Haiti's earliest historians: Baron de Vastey, Beaubrun Ardouin, Louis-Félix Boisrond-Tonnerre, Thomas Madiou, and Joseph Saint-Rémy. Not a single work of history in the bibliography was written in the Haitian Creole language because before *Ti dife boule* they largely did not exist. The dominance of the French language in Haitian print culture is the precise phenomenon that drove the subsection "Silences in the Historical Narrative" in the Sans-Souci chapter of *Silencing the Past*. French-language publications have historically excluded most Haitian people not only from accessing the written documents that constitute the majority of written sources about colonial Saint-Domingue and the Haitian Revolution but also from contributing to Haitian revolutionary historiography. "First, the writing and reading of Haitian historiography," Trouillot wrote, "implies literacy and formal access to a Western—primarily French—language and culture, two prerequisites that already exclude the majority of Haitians from direct participation in its production." Exacerbating this situation is the fact that "the first published memoirs and histories of the revolution were written almost exclusively in French," as were "most of the written traces (letters, proclamations) that have become primary documents."[35] This dynamic continued well into the twentieth century, as Trouillot explained, and at the time of the publication of *Silencing the Past*, "the vast majority of history books about Saint-Domingue/Haiti" were still written and published in French.[36] "The first full-length history book (and for that matter the first full-length nonfiction book) written in Haitian Creole," Trouillot declared, "is my own work on the revolution, which dates from 1977."[37]

Ti dife boule, seen in the context of the linguistic scenario Trouillot described, emerged as a book deliberately written for the Haitian people in a style that, unlike *Silencing the Past*, did not need to conform to "the standards of the Western guild."[38] This lack of necessity to conform is reflected in several ways by the composition of *Ti dife boule*. As translators Mariana Past and Benjamin Hebblethwaite have pointed out, the original version of Trouillot's Haitian Creole-language history included unusual "typographical features" for a printed book, such as nonuniform font sizes and cursive, as well as "boldface" type, inventive "creation of paragraphs," and alternative "indentation."[39] The book is also organized around Haitian concepts, like the *kalfou* or crossroads of Papa Legba, famous songs such as the Vodou chant to Minis Azaka and the folk song "Twa Fey/Twa Rasin," along with the resonant concepts of *marasa* (twins), *vèvè* (sacred Vodou drawing), *rasanbleman* (gathering together), and *kalinda* (an Afro-Caribbean dance). This style of writing—replete with Haitian frames of reference rather than European ones—contrasts highly with that used in the English-language *Silencing the Past*, which

Trouillot acknowledged was in large part aimed not only at the so-called guild but at "North American undergraduates."[40] *Silencing the Past* was for the North Atlantic, but *Ti dife boule* was for the Haitians. Still, the two books, written in two different languages, composed in separate styles, and destined for two disparate audiences, stand in a mutually informing relationship.

The connection between the two texts, published almost two decades apart, is something that Trouillot's interest in Marx cannot fully explain but that the linguistic struggle between French and Haitian Creole in Haiti may very well. "Trouillot's decision to write *Ti dife boule* in Haitian Creole," Past and Hebblethwaite have written, "reflects a Marxist analytical framework that implicitly critiques the Haitian establishment's use of the minority language, French, to limit access to power just as they bind it to their families."[41] To understand how French language hegemony in Haiti has historically alienated the Haitian people from Haitian authors, politicians, educators, and other intellectuals, Trouillot did not need the famous German philosopher of class analysis. He had only to listen to the conversations in the streets of Port-au-Prince and to look outside his window onto the world in which he lived.

Even though the campaign to recognize Haitian Creole as the first and primary language of all Haitian people is ordinarily characterized as a mid- to late twentieth-century phenomenon, the roots of many arguments undergirding Creole linguistic politics stretch back to the earliest days of Haitian independence. Almost from the beginning, Haiti's first historians and government officials alike worried about the problematic relationship they saw developing between the French language/colonialism and Haitian Creole/independence. Recall that in his 1804 speech, which accompanied the reading of the Haitian Declaration of Independence, Jean-Jacques Dessalines lamented, "The French name makes our land sorrowful. Everything here calls forth the memory of the cruelties of that barbaric people: our laws, our mores, our cities, everything still carries the imprint of the French."[42] As a way to mitigate the dominance of *la francophonie*, one of Dessalines's successors, King Henry Christophe, proposed eliminating the French language from Haiti altogether: "It is by changing, with the help of time, even the very language that we speak, that we will have finally succeeded in undermining French power in Haiti by striking at its very source."[43] While Christophe, born in British-claimed Grenada, was partial to the English language, a prominent member of his court, Baron de Vastey, gestured toward creolization as a way to lessen the distance between the French-language-dominated Haitian kingdom and the Creole-speaking Haitian citizens. Vastey insisted that although constrained by a prison of linguistics, which he believed offered him little choice but to write in French, he planned to use a creolized syntax: "I find it necessary . . . to give my grammar, if I may say so, a Haitian turn." He fur-

8   Introduction

ther explained that while he assumed his works would reach an international audience, his ultimate goal was to reach the Haitian people. "I write only to enlighten all my fellow citizens," he insisted. "My foreign readers will please pardon me the method that I have adopted and the manner in which I express myself. . . . I find it necessary in my political writings, created to enlighten the people, to repeat myself, and to speak plainly and clearly so as to be intelligible."[44] In a more direct reference to the Haitian Creole language, the character Marguerite in Juste Chanlatte's 1818 opera *L'Entrée du roi en sa capitale* (The return of the king to his capital) complains that a song celebrating King Henry is not being sung in "criole."[45] Other Haitian authors who sought to promote the usage of Creole through their writings, even while primarily publishing in French, include mid-nineteenth-century Haitian fiction writer Ignace Nau and the later nineteenth-century poet Oswald Durand. The late nineteenth-century Haitian playwright Henri Chauvet also used Haitian Creole and Indigenous words in his theatrical productions, and his contemporary Paul Latortue's 1896 prose poem, *Un épisode de l'indépendance d'Haïti* (An episode of Haitian independence), contains numerous Haitian Creole phrases. Latortue not only footnoted the French translations of these words but went a step further to provide a glossary of meanings. Georges Sylvain engaged in simultaneous transculturation and creolization, too, with his Creole adaptations of the fables of Jean de Lafontaine in his book, *Cric?Crac!* (1901). Early twentieth-century Haitian novelists such as Fernand Hibbert, Justin Lhérisson, and Frédéric Marcelin used literary characters to deliberately argue that only in Creole could Haitians make themselves best and mutually understood.[46] When Trouillot published his 1977 *Ti dife boule* in Haitian Creole for the people of Haiti he was therefore operating in a field profoundly shaped by his intellectual predecessors.

Ti dife boule likewise emerged in the wake of a long-standing and concerted official effort in the twentieth century to turn Haitian Creole from a primarily oral language to a written one through the development of an orthography, and in the middle of an ongoing conversation about the politics of doing so. As Haitian scholar Maximilien Laroche wrote, "We had to wait for the adoption in 1944 of an orthographic system for the Haitian language and the beginning of a widespread literacy campaign in Haiti to see Haitian literature in Creole develop."[47] Even though Haitian Creole did not become more widely used in print documents in Haiti until after it was proclaimed one of the official languages of the country in the Haitian Constitution of 1987—and the Haitian Declaration of Independence was only recently translated into Haitian Creole by Jacques Pierre in 2011—the question was being hotly debated in the years preceding the publication of *Ti dife boule*.[48]

History   9

An early 1973 edition of the Haitian weekly *Le Petit Samedi Soir* was dominated by the theme that appeared on its title page, "A Language for the Development of Tolerance: Creole" ("Une langue pour le développement de la tolérance: Le Créole"). Among the articles therein we find the late Jean Dominique, of Radio Haïti-Inter, arguing unequivocally that the question of language in Haiti goes far beyond Marxist class politics. "Is not the development of the Creole language a problem that transcends the interests of any particular class of people?" Dominique asked. "Is it not instead a national question?"[49] The periodical then reported a debate about the usage of Creole that took place on Dominique's famous Radio Haïti-Inter station that February, and, in a November 1974 edition, the same journal published an article written entirely in Haitian Creole: Émile Célestin-Mégie's "Defense and Illustration of the Creole Language" ("Défense et illustration de la langue Créole: Koléksyon Koukouy").[50] The urgency of these discussions undoubtedly encouraged the Haitian novelist and poet Frankétienne to develop the first Haitian-Creole language novel, his 1975 *Dézafi*.

What we need to fully grasp the significance of Trouillot's concern in *Silencing the Past*—to call attention to the role of the masses whose lives were written out of the story of the Haitian Revolution in most foreign accounts—is the genealogy of this argument both in the narrative of Haitian revolutionary history contained in *Ti dife boule* and in the work of earlier Haitian intellectuals who paved the way for Trouillot to be able to make this argument in Creole. In *Silencing the Past*, Trouillot acknowledged that "historians build their narrative on the shoulders of previous ones."[51] *Silencing the Past* stands tall on the edifices of history created not only by the Haitian revolutionaries but by nineteenth- and early twentieth-century Haitian intellectuals such as Jean Price-Mars, who argued that Haitians needed to "draw the material of their works from the milieu where they live."[52]

Genealogies are about how people find themselves by looking for their ancestors. In *Ti dife boule* the Duvalier dictatorship becomes genealogically linked to the domination and exploitation that existed at the origins of the creation of Haitian society: "Today, we are in charge," Trouillot wrote, "but, we cannot do whatever we want. We alone are responsible for tomorrow, but yesterday evening is still coming after us. We alone have the right to choose, but the rules of this game were written beforehand, and they were not written by us."[53] This passage perhaps has a corollary in Marx's *Eighteenth Brumaire*—"Men make their own history, but they do not make it as they please; they do not make it under self-selected circumstances, but under circumstances existing already, given and transmitted from the past."[54] Yet the specific circumstances Trouillot references here have a much more immediate

-1—
0—
+1—

10   Introduction

and relevant genealogy in the works of nineteenth-century Haitian historians who linked the internecine conflicts of the revolutionary period to those of the four earliest iterations of Haiti—Dessalines's empire, Christophe's state, and then monarchy, which existed simultaneously with Pétion's, and later Boyer's, republic—to the conflicts of the era in which they lived. After all, it was Louis Joseph Janvier who in the preface to *Les Constitutions d'Haiti, 1801–1885* (The constitutions of Haiti) made the analogy, "The history of a nation narrates its existence from its earliest origins, just as a medical observation tells us when a disease was born."[55]

Trouillot explained how he saw the political struggles of Saint-Domingue, under Louverture, and then those of the various states of Haiti, first under Dessalines, then under Pétion and Christophe, and, finally, under Boyer, informing the Haitian dictatorial present under Duvalier:

> From 1789 to 1820, a crisis took hold in the bone marrow of Haiti. And it was during this crisis—that lasted for thirty long years—that the edifice of the entire society we raised up was built. Each generation that has passed, has left behind a weight of fifty pounds around our necks, weighing down the minds of the very men who are now here.
>
> From 1789 to 1820, the Haitian people enacted the only great slave revolution in the entire memory of humanity. But during those same thirty years or so, a native-born class turned its back on the people, they overturned the revolution. And if we really want to know what disease *we are suffering from today, we must retrace the path of this crisis. On* the left hand, a revolution, on the right hand, a coup d'état. And then when all the blood had cooled, when Boyer returned to Jérémie, me, myself . . . they, themselves . . . himself . . . you![56]

Here, in this final, poignant, mysterious phrase, Trouillot traced the origins of contemporary Haitian society to the moment when Boyer announced in Jérémie in February 1820 his plan to reunify the north and the south of Haiti under one government after thirteen years of estrangement.[57] The impetus for this proclamation was not an impending strike against Christophe (who would commit suicide eight months later). Instead, Boyer's confidence was related to the end of the thirteen-year-long maroon insurrection led by Jean-Baptiste Duperrier (known as Goman), who, in refusing to submit to either Haitian state, essentially held sovereign power over the region of Grand'Anse from 1807 until 1820 when Boyer's troops finally cornered him. The siege ended when Goman, surrounded in the Mamelles mountains by the southern army, leapt to his death from a mountaintop into the gulf below.[58] The references to blood in Trouillot's passage have so much to tell us about what he saw as the disease circulating in the Haitian republic that he left behind, in exile, and the cure that might have permitted him to return, in freedom.

For Trouillot's analysis of how Haitian leaders, for almost two centuries, alienated, impoverished, and compromised the sovereignty of *pèp ayisyen*—a power play of world historical significance—the celebrated Haitian philosopher of silencing did not need any German analysts of class; he did not need the famous French philosopher of power dynamics, either. He had only to look at two centuries of Haitian historiography sitting on his bookshelf.

––––––––

In the only passage of *Silencing the Past* referencing the French philosopher Michel Foucault, Trouillot wrote, "Power does not enter the story once and for all, but at different times and from different angles. It precedes the narrative proper, contributes to its creation and its interpretation. Thus, it remains pertinent even if we can imagine a totally scientific history, even if we relegate the historians' preferences and stakes to a separate, postdescriptive phase. In history, power begins at the source."[59] Trouillot argued that not only is "power constitutive of the story," but that "tracking power through various 'moments'" is to insist that "what history is matters less than how history works." "A warning from Foucault is helpful," Trouillot explained. "I don't believe that the question of 'who exercises power?' can be resolved unless that other question 'how does it happen?' is resolved at the same time."[60] The earliest Haitian historians, too, understood that there was power not only in sources but also in the ability to narrate history. In other words, they both demonstrated and theorized Trouillot's later point that "power itself works together with history."[61] Ardouin, for example, clarified that he was writing the history of his country to remind his compatriots of the importance of the revolutionary past for the sovereign present. In the first volume of *Études sur l'histoire d'Haïti*, Ardouin said, "In writing these pages, my goal is to excite in my compatriots, . . . the desire to understand under their true lights the events that brought the defenders of our rights to create a country for us."[62] Ardouin was living through the very historiographical dynamics of silencing that animate *Silencing the Past* and *Ti dife boule*, but as Trouillot wrote, "The production of a historical narrative cannot be studied . . . through a mere chronology of its silences." Ardouin—whom Trouillot argued "helped launch Haitian historiography on a modern path"[63]—insisted that one of his goals was to ensure that Haitian history would not become distorted or disfigured by documents and statements that were "sometimes dishonest."[64] Preceding by more than a century Foucault's observation that "if one controls people's memory one controls their dynamism,"[65] Ardouin argued, "The future of a

12 Introduction

people often depends on the manner in which their past is presented to them. If they bear a false judgment about the facts of their annals, about the principles that have guided their predecessors, their politicians, they will suffer in spite of themselves, the influence of this error, and they will be vulnerable to deviating from the route that they must follow in order to arrive at their prosperity."[66] Madiou likewise talked about the relationship between a country's history and the necessity it had to chronicle its past from a national point of view, including its past mistakes. In volume one of his three-volume *Histoire d'Haïti* (History of Haiti, published 1847–48), Madiou wrote: "It is impossible to steer a society towards the way of progress, to help them to avoid all the pitfalls into which have fallen so many . . . peoples, if we do not meditate on the events of the past of the entire world and in the country we would like to regenerate."[67]

That the past was informing, shaping, and even determining the present was also a concern of Trouillot's, particularly in the passages of *Silencing the Past* in which he references the Franco-Bulgarian historian Tzvetan Todorov. In *The Conquest of America: The Question of the Other*, a book that Trouillot cited twice in *Silencing the Past*, Todorov called the wars waged by Europeans against the Indigenous populations of the Americas "the greatest genocide in human history." Todorov explained his wish to contemplate the historical significance of this monumental claim by paradoxically stating, "The present is more important to me than the past."[68] Trouillot also claimed that the history he was setting forward was as much a history of the past as it was an analysis of the present: "We are never as steeped in history as when we pretend not to be, but if we stop pretending we may gain in understanding what we lose in false innocence." Trouillot went on to plainly declare, "This book is about history and power. . . . The ultimate mark of power may be its invisibility; the ultimate challenge, the exposition of its roots."[69] Trouillot's Haitian sources devoted their scholarly lives to exposing the roots of a Haitian history that could be developed outside of, or at least in contradistinction to, colonial European frameworks. Ardouin submitted that he had no aim other than to examine Haitian history "from the point of view natural to a Haitian, and in opposition to the myriad foreign authors who have themselves considered this history from their point of view."[70] Point of view is one of the most important elements of Trouillot's theorization of power. Acknowledging relations of power in historical storytelling led Trouillot to describe how the biases evident in Western historiography were inscribed in the sources European historians used. "Sources are thus instances of inclusion," he says, "the other face of which is, of course, what is excluded."[71] For Trouillot, the Haitian Revolution's significance was occluded, while it occurred and after the fact, not because no one was talking about these events in their era or beyond but rather because of the way they had been (and continued to be) discussed and because of whose voices were amplified in those discussions. "The contention that enslaved Africans and their descendants could not envision freedom—let alone formulate strategies for gaining and securing freedom—was based not so much on empirical evidence," Trouillot pointed out, "as on an ontology, an implicit organization of the world and its inhabitants."[72] What kinds of stories, then, did the colonists snuff out when they tried to silence—as a "silencer silences a gun"[73]—the ingenuity of the Haitian revolutionaries? Trouillot told us directly:

> The Haitian Revolution expressed itself mainly through its deeds, and it is through political practice that it challenged Western philosophy and colonialism. It did produce a few texts whose philosophical import is explicit, from Louverture's declaration of Camp Turel to the Haitian Act of Independence and the Constitution of 1805. But its intellectual and ideological newness appeared most clearly with each and every political threshold crossed, from the mass insurrection (1791) to the crumbling of the colonial apparatus (1793), from general liberty (1794) to the conquest of the state machinery (1797–98), from Louverture's taming of that machinery (1801) to the proclamation of Haitian independence with Dessalines (1804).[74]

If Laurent Dubois has urged study of an "enslaved enlightenment," Trouillot seemed to be calling for an embodied historiography of the Haitian Revolution.[75] In other words, focusing on what revolutionary actors *did* (their physical deeds) as the precursor to what was later *written* or *pronounced* (their discursive deeds). The doubleness of the word *deed* as both written receipt and material act captures the Haitian revolutionaries as both thinkers and doers of the revolutionary word—that is, what became the 1804 Principle of fighting for liberty from slavery and colonialism while promoting equality in the face of violent white supremacy.

Haiti's first historians left behind the best works for understanding the historical, political, and cultural import of the Haitian Revolution, and the orchestrated attempt of the French colonists to silence it. European writing on the revolution, according to Baron de Vastey, inevitably led to distortion because Europeans were incapable of seeing, literally and figuratively, certain elements of the revolution. They were especially incapable of understanding the role of the Haitian maroons. Haiti needed Haitian historians precisely to make visible what only those who had participated in the events from the Haitian side could see. Vastey explained this as the motivation for writing the first full-length history of Haiti written by a Haitian, his 1819 *Essai sur les causes de la révolution et des guerres civiles d'Hayti* (Essay on the

14 Introduction

causes of the revolution and civil wars of Haiti). He began by pointing out, "Haiti lacks a general history written by someone native to the country." The consequences of this lack were discursive, material, and longitudinal: "The majority of historians who have tried it have been Europeans who concerned themselves primarily with the part of our history that involves them; and when they were led, by the subject at hand, to speak of the natives, they did so with that spirit of prejudice and bias that they never seem to be able to abandon." Moreover, those Europeans who published histories of Haiti prior to his, "only had, to guide them, materials created by whites."[76] Vastey argued this dynamic led to an unevenness of discursive and material power between Haitians and Europeans, with the result being that "the scale has always tilted to [their] side" of the story. Vastey proposed to reveal a different perspective on Haiti's colonial and revolutionary history, the "indigenous" perspective, in his words, to distinctly challenge the dominance and prejudices of European narratives of Haiti.[77]

When Trouillot is paying attention to biases—racial and otherwise—to points of view, and to the way sources are being used, discounted, dismissed, or ignored, we might say with more than just a little insistence that he is operating in a field charted for him by nineteenth-century *Haitian* historians.

———————

There is a different methodological intervention that also links Vastey's writings to Trouillot. It is the question of the ancestors and how they could be brought back to life through historical research and excavation.

Who could forget the poignant statement from *Silencing the Past* in which Trouillot described modern-day attempts to scrub the conquest of the Americas and the much later massacre at the Alamo from narratives of U.S. history? "Yet even dead Indians can return to haunt professional and amateur historians," Trouillot wrote. "The Inter-Tribal council of American Indians affirms that the remains of more than a thousand individuals, mostly Native American Catholics, are buried in grounds adjacent to the Alamo."[78] That a dead history could be awakened by consulting, if not literally unearthing, those buried in the ground is directly related to a system of knowledge informed by the works of early Haitian historians. Recall Vastey's statement from *Le Système colonial dévoilé*: "Europeans, . . . Colonists who still exist, listen to me! I am going to awaken the ashes of the numerous victims whom you precipitated into the tomb, and borrow their voices to unveil your heinous crimes. I am going to exhume those unfortunates whom you buried alive. I am going to interrogate the souls of my unfortunate compatriots whom you have thrown alive into blazing ovens; those whom you have stabbed, roasted, impaled, and a thousand other diverse torments invented by hell!"

History   15

Vastey explained that "by tracing these horrors," he did not hope to "soften" the "hearts" of enslavers and colonialists—"we know all too well that they are harder than bronze and steel." Instead, he said to them, "if I hope nothing from you, at the very least I can make you tremble by revealing your crimes, and by recording your names here, consecrate them to contemporary and future scorn."[79]

Benedict Anderson, in his widely read and deeply influential *Imagined Communities*, traced such a method of talking to and for the dead to the French historian Jules Michelet, whom Anderson said was the first "to speak on behalf of large numbers of anonymous dead people," and who insisted, "with poignant authority, that he could say what they 'really' meant and 'really' wanted, since they themselves 'did not understand.'"[80] After Michelet, things shifted. "The silence of the dead was no obstacle to the exhumation of their deepest desires," Anderson wrote. "In this vein, more and more 'second-generation' nationalists, in the Americas and elsewhere, learned to speak 'for' dead people. . . . This reversed ventriloquism helped to open the way for a self-conscious *indigenismo*, especially in the southern Americas."[81] But if part of what made Michelet seem like the greatest historian was his ability to make the lives of the dead come to life for those still living, then Michelet was much more a beneficiary of *indigenismo* than one of its creators.[82] In 1814, long before Michelet, Vastey insisted that he could bring the world's attention to the ongoing tortures to which European and American enslavers were subjecting the Africans they were holding in bondage. To do so, he recited the tales of those who could only tell their stories through his organ because they were dead. "Listen to the story of the *colonial regime*, and form, if you can, an idea of the monsters capable of practicing such cruelties," Vastey challenged in *Le Système*, a work meant to be transmitted "to the Sovereigns of Europe and to the Tribunals of Nations" on behalf of "the cause of our oppressed Brothers."[83] Vastey's goal was to produce a history of the enslaved of colonial Saint-Domingue from their own perspective, something the French Atlantic World was not ordinarily accustomed to considering.[84] "The French have had the right to write and print thousands of volumes against us; their newspapers have poured out a thousand insults and calumnies against us," Vastey wrote. As a result, "we must therefore have the right, without offending anyone, to write a few pages for our just and legitimate defense."[85] While George Rudé's method of "history from below" is often cited to explain how to write a history *of* the oppressed,[86] Haiti's earliest historians offered us histories produced in collaboration *with* the oppressed.[87]

It is not enough to simply posit that Vastey's idea of thinking of the dead as sources predated Michelet's. We must examine the implications of Anderson's claim that Michelet could be the progenitor of so-called Indigenous history. Genetic sentences like Anderson's reflect a settler colonialist frame of mind, whereby a single origin story dominates rather than giving sway to the kinds of multiple, interlocking, and overlapping narratives of beginnings that Édouard Glissant called rhizomes.[88] Trouillot acknowledged as much when he noted, "If I write 'The history of the United States begins with the Mayflower,' a statement many readers may find simplistic and controversial, there will be little doubt that I am suggesting that the first significant event in the process that eventuated in what we now call the United States is the landing of the Mayflower."[89] The attention swirling around Nikole Hannah-Jones's "The 1619 Project" for *New York Times Magazine* demonstrates the messy simplicity of this type of origin-seeking, whether for radical or conservative aims. The thesis of "The 1619 Project" is that the true origins of the United States can be traced to the year 1619 when the first captive Africans were forcibly taken to Virginia by British enslavers.[90] Yet we might ask, like some critics, why not a date in the 1520s or '30s, which is when the Spanish forcibly transported captive Africans to Spanish-claimed Florida, now also a part of the United States?[91] Far more ardent detractors of the project have loudly decried its main argument, many reacting with outright racism, while others have denounced it using more clearly conservative ideology about the supposedly liberal origins of *America*. Several oppositional narratives briefly emerged as well.[92] One of them was the reactionary 1620 Project. The year 1620 is the year the *Mayflower* purportedly landed at Plymouth Rock. Both the dates 1619 and 1620 carry with them not just the kinds of problems with origins that Glissant theorized in *Caribbean Discourse*, and that Trouillot signals as problematic in *Silencing the Past*, but a heavy dose of the kind of mythology that always attends start dates when they are used as a stand-in for nationalism, rather than as potential indicators of ideology. Both these dates tell a story of the United States that might best be understood together. Put another way, the first date, 1619, marked less the beginning of the process that led to the creation of the United States, perhaps, than it foretold the slavery, racism, and violent white supremacy that would be constitutive to Black life in North America, regardless of who remained in control. The second date, 1620, helps to expose that contradiction: the British American colonists imposed a form of racial terror on the Black Africans they transported to the Americas right alongside the freedom they sought for themselves in the new to them world that they eventually constituted as the United States.[93]

Turning to the language with which historical ingenuity is described in national narratives, Trouillot further deconstructed what origins claims have to do with it: "Consider now a sentence grammatically identical to the preceding one and perhaps as controversial: 'The history of France starts with Michelet.' The meaning of the word 'history' has unambiguously shifted from the sociohistorical process to our knowledge of that process."[94] In other words, such a phrase "affirms that the first significant narrative about France was the one written by Jules Michelet."[95] It is worth insisting that genetic sentences, like Trouillot's hypothetical, are used by authors, even if unwittingly, to wield the power to decide who or what is historically important. To attribute to an individual the instantiation of an entire historical methodology can inexorably elide preceding or parallel developments across the world. The question then becomes: Who gets to be associated with, or recognition for, the big ideas that have shaped how we write history and how we think about the development of global historiography? To that end, in *A Global History of Historiography*, Georg G. Iggers, Q. Edward Wang, and Supriya Mukherjee have forcefully asserted, "Historical consciousness was not a privilege of the West, but existed in all cultures. The idea that only the West has a sense of history, as put forward in the late eighteenth century . . . and reiterated in the nineteenth century by thinkers as diverse as James Stuart Mill (1773–1836), Hegel, Ranke and Marx, a conception that dominated much Western thought until well past the middle of the twentieth century, cannot stand in the face of the rich historiographical traditions of other culture throughout the ages."[96] Even so, the authors still affirmed Michelet's own dominance in writing: "Michelet was without a doubt the most widely read French historian. He was generally revered by broad segments of the French population as the greatest historian."[97]

Nineteenth-century Haitians were not immune to singular exaltation of Michelet. Likening Madiou to Michelet, rather than the other way around, Firmin said of Madiou:

> Knowing how to breathe life into his heroes and color into his descriptions, he wrote above all with a spirited liveliness. He put his heart into it. With more accuracy, a deeper skill in the narration of facts, which is where the art of the historian restores life to things past, he could have, although from a respectful distance, followed the illustrious Michelet in this genre, whose charm, composed of ardent patriotism and vigorous reason, exalts the spirit of the reader and inspires him with an indescribable and vague regret of not having been able to take part in the struggles of which the historian paints such a moving portrait.[98]

Yet, looking deeper into Firmin's other mentions of Michelet produces a far more political cause for Firmin's admiration. The French historians that Firmin extolled, like the U.S. American writers he admired, namely Frederick Douglass, needed antislavery, if not anti-racism, credentials to earn the Haitian ethnographer's praise.

18   Introduction

Though his writing is peppered with some exoticism and flourishes of "Haitian exceptionalism,"[99] in *La Femme* Michelet expressed ardent support of Haitian independence and broadscale desire for the abolition of slavery. He also acknowledged the tendentious relationship of his country, France, to Haiti, its former colony, a past layered with Haitian suffering caused by the French people. "A thousand hopes for black France! I refer to Haiti like so, since this good people have so much love for the [country] that made their fathers suffer. Receive all my best wishes, young State!" Michelet wrote. "And may we protect you, in atonement for the past! May you develop your free genius, that of this great race, so cruelly calumniated, and of which you are the most civilizational representative on earth!—You are no less that of the genius of woman." While singing the praises of Haitian women, and Black women in general, Michelet did not fail to offer more concrete advice to the Haitian government: "It is through your charming women, so good and so intelligent, that you must cultivate yourself, organize your schools. They are such tender mothers that they will become, I am sure, admirable educators. A strong college to train teachers and schoolmistresses . . . is the first institution I would like to see in Haiti."[100] Haitian intellectuals read these statements as offering generosity, rather than customary French hostility. Even though Michelet's statements are clearly couched in paternalism, it was his support of the Haitian state, rather than his historical methodology, that earned him the highest praise from Firmin. "In a somewhat less refined expression of his ideas, the great historian clearly showed with what force his heart beats, when he traced these generous lines, so full of life that one would easily believe they could see in them the light and warm winds of the tropical breezes that quiver here. Haiti, on behalf of black women everywhere, has not forgotten it," Firmin declared. Firmin wanted to make it clear that he was not the only Haitian intellectual who revered Michelet for these lines, and because of his "sympathy" for the Haitian people, which led Firmin to call him "a most precious gift to the black race." "When France sought to pay the finest homage to this eminent writer, to that sympathetic philosopher, that a nation could pay to its great men, by erecting a statue to him, a black Haitian, Dr. Louis Joseph Janvier, worthy of his race and the immortal intellect of Michelet, hailed this name that all descendants of Africa must love and keep in their memory. Who knows, indeed, what miracles a good word can produce, when it comes from such a mouth?"[101] That Michelet's praise of Haitians could perform the work of anti-racism certainly cemented, if it was not entirely responsible for, his fame in Haiti. If Michelet had been an ardent white supremacist, Firmin, far from praising his prose, skill, and intellect, might have devoted an entire work to refuting him, as Firmin did with *De l'Égalité*, a long form refutation of Arthur de Gobineau's *De l'Inégalité des races humaines*, or *The Inequality of the Human Races*. Firmin said Gobineau had that "spirit made up of selfishness and pride, which has always led civilized peoples to believe that they are superior in nature to the nations that surround them."[102]

Let us now return to the notion of talking to the dead, or historical "resurrection," that is in large part responsible for Michelet's reputation as "the greatest historian." So famous is Michelet's maxim, "History is a resurrection," that it is inscribed on his tomb at Père Lachaise cemetery in France.[103] But in *Silencing the Past* Trouillot drew on two centuries of Haitian thought to explain how "dead bodies" could be resurrected by historical methodology. Haitian history could be "engraved in individual or collective bodies," Trouillot said. "What happened leaves traces, some of which are quite concrete—buildings, dead bodies, censuses, monuments, diaries [and] political boundaries."[104] Asking the dead to intervene to support a refutation of pro-colonial narratives of the revolution was a rhetorical tactic deeply rooted in a methodology employed by several of Haiti's first historians. Before Michelet could declare, "I defined history as *Resurrection*," Haitian historians were calling out to the dead in their graves.[105] In Vastey's *Le Cri de la conscience* (The cry of conscience, 1815), the dead are awakened to testify about the past and to celebrate the victories they never got to experience in their mortal lives. In so doing, the awakened dead were able to witness the joyous effects of life after Haitian independence. "We have avenged the spirits of our brave companions who died gloriously for liberty and independence; the ghosts of our fathers, our mothers, our brothers, our sisters, who were victims of the French, have arisen from the ashes of the pyres, from the depths of the seas, from the intestines of rapacious dogs, to applaud us and chant with us, vengeance! vengeance!" Vastey wrote.[106] Vengeance here becomes what Daina Ramey Berry might call one of the "soul values" of the formerly enslaved peoples of Saint-Domingue.[107] The human soul that lives after death and tells its own story, out of revenge for the intractable testimony of the colonists, oriented Haitian historical method toward justice as much as toward truth.

In *The Reaper's Garden*, Vincent Brown asked "how the dead affected the history of the living."[108] Drawing on nineteenth-century Haitian sources, we might ask different but related questions: How do we talk with the dead rather than solely about them? In a sense, all historians are engaged in a conversation with the dead that requires listening more than talking when they use archival documents to study the pre-twentieth century.[109] But it is not always clear what questions we should pose after listening to the fragmentary narratives of the real lives whose documentary remains rest in the archives. As Arlette Farge has written, "The archives [are] not lacking, but they created a

20   Introduction

void and emptiness that no amount of academic study can fill. Today, to use the archives is to translate this incompleteness into a question, and this begins by combing through them."[110] Alessandra Benedicty-Kokken, evoking the works of Ann Stoler, has similarly sought to bring attention to the "relationship, the codependency even, between on the one hand, the ideas, texts, and objects that we put into our archives; and, on the other hand, the questions that we ask." Benedicty-Kokken concluded, "What is important . . . is that we pose questions that are worth asking; and to do so we must put into our archive, objects, books, and ideas, that help us not so much to resolve the uncertainties that lead to the formulation of our questions, but rather that we construct our archives to help us better invite questions that interrogate the urgencies of our present human condition."[111] For early Haitian thinkers, a spiritual archive of the revolutionary past, one involving the evocation of memories, their own, and testimony, from the souls of the dead, was just as important as paper documents.

In *Le Cri de la nature* (1810), one of the first histories of Haiti, Chanlatte evoked the graves of Haiti's dead whose occupants had motivated Haiti's living to pursue the final ends of the Haitian Revolution: freedom and independence. "So many barbarities [and] unheard-of executions, forced us to throw ourselves into the forests, [that] the cry of vengeance resounded from all sides. At this noble resolution, the sepulchers of our ancestors opened, [and] their powdery bones trembled: vengeance! answered the tombs of all of nature."[112] Dessalines's speech pronounced in Gonaïves to the *armée indigène* on January 1, 1804, instantiated this hermeneutic of discursive justice, characterized in the language of vengeance, as the political and historical methodology of the new Haitian state. The future emperor of Haiti reminded his troops that attending to the living was only one of the duties of the victors of the revolution. Dessalines said that what Haitians needed to "appease" "the souls" of the victims of French colonialism was to avenge their lives: "Remember that you wanted your remains to rest beside your fathers' when you chased away tyranny; will you descend down into their graves without having avenged them? No, their bones would repel your own."[113] Four months later, in his famous April 28 proclamation, Dessalines played the role of historian to describe what that vengeance would partially entail. He reminded the Haitian people that while Leclerc and Bonaparte repeatedly promised not to bring back slavery, insisting that all people in Saint-Domingue, regardless of skin color, would remain free, the French turned around and directly reinstated slavery in neighboring Guadeloupe: "Guadeloupe, ransacked and destroyed; its ruins still fuming with the blood of children, of women, of old men run through with the sword." He continued by evoking the freedom fighter Louis Delgrès's failed opposition to French encroachments, which resulted in Delgrès's death by mass suicide: "The brave and immortal Delgresse [*sic*] . . . preferred to dissipate into the air along with the debris of his fort, rather than to accept chains once again." "Magnanimous warrior!" Dessalines called out to him in the grave, "your noble demise, far from shaking our courage, only encourages our thirst for revenge or to follow you." After referencing the awful fate experienced by Toussaint Louverture, one of "our brothers deported to Europe," Dessalines recalled how after the Peace of Amiens, instead of the French abolishing slavery in the newly reacquired Martinique, they maintained it and sought to extend it. This was "astonishing despotism, precursor of death," Dessalines said before issuing a call directly to the still enslaved people on that island: "Unfortunate Martinicans! If only I could fly to your aid and break your chains! Alas! An invincible obstacle stands between us . . . but perhaps a spark from the fire that ignites us, will alight in your soul; perhaps at the sound of this commotion, awakened with a start from your lethargy, you will claim, weapons in hand, your sacred and imprescriptible rights!"[114] By calling upon "ashes," "tombs," "graves," "bones," "shadows," and "souls," early Haitian historians and politicians not only offered to tell the history of French colonial slavery from the Haitian perspective using the strategy of "history from below," *way below*, but issued a pan-Caribbean call for antislavery, anti-racist, and anti-colonial action in the present.

The Haitian poet and statesmen Hérard Dumesle's 1824 *Voyage dans le nord d'Hayti: ou, Révélations des lieux et des monuments historiques* (Voyage to the north of Haiti: or, Revelations of historical sites and monuments) contains a concrete and sustained example of Dessalinean historical methodology.[115] The "shadows" of the Haitian revolutionaries revealed the terrible truths of the colonial era, wrote Dumesle, after explaining that he also planned to use monuments, specific locales of Haitian revolutionary battles, and the geography of the island, along with the spirits and remains of the ancestors buried there, as revelatory of the Haitian past.[116] In traveling throughout the country to gather material, Dumesle called for a history of the Haitian Revolution tied to the Haitian earth. The "geographical base" that Dumesle gave to his narration anticipated Michelet's much later exaltation of geography in history writing as both the "scene of the action" and the key to the motivation of the "historical actor," "influencing him in a hundred ways."[117] Dumesle associated every region and city in Haiti with specific leaders of the war of independence: General Pétion with Cul-de-Sac and Léogâne, General Lamarre with Petit-Goâve, General Capoix with Port-de-Paix and Cap-Haïtien, and Generals Clervaux, Dessalines, Jean-François, and a host of other revolutionaries with Fort Liberté and the valleys and rivers of the Artibonite. Earlier in *Voyage*, Dumesle spoke of how the city of Les Cayes was indelibly associ-

22 Introduction

ated in Haitian collective memory with the Haitian general André Rigaud. In each of these cities, which "has become famous due to this memorable war," the earth, too, could tell the story of how the Haitians defeated the French army there.[118] "Stones, mountains, and valleys, oh how your echoes resound!" the poet voyager exclaimed.[119] Later Dumesle not only listened to the earth's "resounding echoes," but he asked it to make public that to which its very existence attested. "Land that rent asunder proud despotism, and you, the imposing debris that testifies to its defeat, publish these feats in order to engrave them forever in the memory of man."[120] Dumesle continuously turned to the natural world, a distinct part of the "many monuments" that "flowed from these feats," as further proof of the "events of which they were the theater."[121]

Dead soldiers buried in the Haitian earth could also be conjured up to testify. Dumesle called on the ancestors, specifically the deceased generals of Haiti's revolution, to prove the treachery of the French colonists. Dumesle stated "all expression had escaped him" as he tried to record the many atrocities committed by the French soldiers during the Leclerc expedition, which made the French resemble "the first destroyers of the Americas."[122] To support this charge, Dumesle invoked the spirits of some of the less famous generals of the Haitian army. "Shadows of Maurepas, of Dommage, of Ferbos, of Bardet, of Braquehais . . . of Vendôme, of Desravines, of Vorbes and so many other illustrious victims, you will attest to these terrible truths."[123] Dumesle continued by suggesting that unearthing these men would make them "live until the most remote of ages," and that the memory of their names alone "will stand as depositions against the fury of the tyrants who have desolated this land."[124] By relying upon the testimonies of the dead, Dumesle exhibited continuous skepticism of official colonial documents used by foreign historians to write Haiti's history.

A will to correct the assumptions of the Haitian past promulgated by French colonial writers became one of the abiding hermeneutics of early nineteenth-century Haitian writing. In a footnote to a passage mentioning the former colonist Claude-Pierre-Joseph Le Borgne de Boigne's infamous screed urging the French to try to reconquer "Saint-Domingue," Dumesle wrote (with more than a hint of irony), "A profound ignorance of the circumstances surrounding our national emancipation, absurd and contrived facts, [and] views that all the art in the world would not be able to save from ridicule . . . distinguish the deep thoughts of this genius of reconstruction; to get a fair idea of this, we alert the reader to the refutation of it by M. Vastey."[125] This footnote speaks more generally to the way that certain passages of *Voyage*, echoing Vastey's writings, work simultaneously to refute the colonial histories of Saint-Domingue promulgated by foreign writers like Le Borgne de Boigne and to legitimate the political independence of Haiti. Dumesle wrote that "the impartial voice of history" could not but praise the Haitian revolutionaries for having "broken forever, the destructive scepter of an unjust metropole," but will "condemn, in the end, the silence that the governments of Europe have until now maintained with respect to our independence."[126]

Dumesle's lasting contributions to Haitian revolutionary historiography extend to other parts of his methodology as well. Although it is Vastey's phrase that Trouillot used to describe the palace at Sans-Souci and the Citadelle Laferrière in "The Three Faces of Sans Souci"—"These two structures, erected by descendants of Africans, show that we have not lost the architectural taste and genius of our ancestors who covered Ethiopia, Egypt, Carthage, and old Spain with their superb monuments"[127]—it is actually Dumesle's *Voyage dans le nord d'Hayti* to which this part of Trouillot's work is most genealogically connected. Trouillot began the chapter on Sans-Souci by referencing how different contemporary guides who took visitors to the palace at Sans-Souci would give them different stories; thus, different points of view about King Henry I, along with different attempts to silence his history of brutality, would come to light (or not). In *Ti dife boule* the guide has an altogether different function. "Grenn Pwomennen," the "Great Traveler," in the words of Nathalie Pierre, "functions simultaneously as our knowledgeable guide through Haiti's revolutionary past and as an instigator who intends to cause debate."[128] This latter kind of guide also appears in *Voyage* as Dumesle wanders through the ruins of King Henry I's palace and Citadelle.

Dumesle's methodology, for which he relied as equally on the spiritually evocative as on what Joan Scott has called the "evidence of experience," has produced a long genealogy of Haitian intellectual thought, one that inflects my exploration of the intellectual history of the Haitian Revolution, as much as it inflected Trouillot's.[129] Over many years of study, I have come to view nineteenth-century Haitian thinkers and doers as my guides. I rely on their eyes and ears, their acts and deeds, their poetics and their dreams, to gather the story of Black freedom and Black sovereignty marked by the Haitian Revolution against slavery, racism, and colonialism. Trouillot described why he used a similar range of elements as Dumesle—personal testimony, travelogue, monuments, reliance on prior historiography, and document retrieval—when he insisted, "We all need histories that no history book can tell, but they are not in the classroom—not the history classrooms, anyway. They are in the lessons we learn at home, in poetry and childhood games, in what is left of history when we close the history books with their verifiable facts."[130] I return to the histories, legacies, and interpretations, and yes, poetry, of the Haitian Revolution and Haitian independence written by Haitian authors, politicians, and journalists because I believe it is the key to demonstrating how scholars in the North Atlantic can go beyond simply *mentioning* Haiti as a pit stop on the way to extranational interests and imperatives.[131] What I have most learned from consulting this sometimes quixotic archive is the multiple ways eighteenth- and nineteenth-century Haitian revolutionaries, authors, and politicians made invaluable contributions to the world with their antiracist, antislavery, and anti-colonial revolutionary thought.

———

I began this introduction to the intellectual history of the Haitian Revolution with the argument that *Silencing the Past*'s ascendance, popularity, and ubiquity within the North Atlantic "guild" has paradoxically led to the silencing of eighteenth- and nineteenth-century Haitian thinkers and other intellectuals. I want to end with a final provocation from Dumesle about the term *silencing* and its relationship to Haiti's monumental history. In *Global Transformations*, Trouillot once again railed against the concept of silences/silencing by writing: "Silence to me seems a hasty abdication."[132] What I hear Dumesle saying is that not all silences are created equal. When imagining the former opulence of Sans-Souci palace and how King Henry's monarchy crumbled under the weight of the inequalities that reigned in the Kingdom of Haiti—and after sighing, "Oh, how this palace was so improperly named!"—Dumesle concluded, "I remembered how power stood up, by contemplating its ashes, and I meditated on this thought, *without a doubt the people did not have the right to speak up; but without a doubt, they did have the right to be silent, and their silence is the lesson of kings.*"[133] Sometimes the silences in the historical record are lessons from which we can learn more than in any text. That the people of Haiti appear to be largely absent in the voluminous print culture of the Kingdom of Haiti is highly suggestive since so many of King Henry's soldiers turned their backs on him to join Boyer's competing republic, immediately prior to the king's suicide on October 8, 1820.

Perhaps the real lesson is that if in discussing the concept of silencing, readers can think only of Trouillot's *Silencing the Past* and never of Dumesle's *Voyage*, they are engaged in yet another exercise of power, one that involves speaking often and rarely listening. Jean Casimir has written that the uneven dynamic between speakers and listeners is what drove the argument behind his *Une lecture décoloniale de l'histoire des Haïtiens* (A decolonial history of the Haitians): "This study is destined for those who wish to listen to the Haitian people in order to understand what they are saying," Casimir said. "Their speech is barely audible, because the modern world imprisons it within the dominant culture and its writing of the past, trying to make us believe it doesn't even exist."[134] Worse still are contemporary purveyors of "modernity" who operate under the hubris that they are the rightful stewards of culture, having inherited "the best which has been thought and said in the world" from their European ancestors.[135] It is so well established today to say that slavery is wrong that it is easy to forget that this was a wholly radical idea in the early modern world and remained so until the Black apotheosis in Haiti that inaugurated the age of abolition in 1804. To shrug off the momentousness of how the Haitian revolutionaries opened the age of abolition, a not at all inevitable historical event, is to shrug off history. The end of the Haitian Revolution marked a new normal for antislavery acts and deeds.

As such, Haiti did not owe its i ndependence to the French revolutionary principles of 1789. In the words of Haitian historian Alfred Nemours, "those Ideas of Liberty, Equality, Independence had long been known in Saint-Domingue. Well before 1789, there were tremendous explosions on the part of the Slaves, first, then the Free."[136] Nemours only had to consult the long arc of rebellion on the island of Ayiti, bending and stretching toward freedom, against great odds, since European colonizers arrived. "About twenty years after being disembarked in Hispaniola, they [the Africans] were revolting and encouraging the Indians to revolt," Nemours explained.[137] "Arriving in Saint-Domingue, in a more or less continuous current by 1666, they did not take long to rebel and from 1691 on engaged in a General Revolt, as in 1758, and continuously afterward until the General Revolt of 1791, which was Victorious." To say that slave revolts and rebellions, as much as the Haitian Revolution, were incited by white European principles, then, "is to lay waste to 260 years of history, during which many Revolts broke out, both in the Spanish Col-ony of Hispaniola and in the French Colony of Saint-Domingue. This long series of Revolts proves that it was only in their hearts and in their minds that the Slaves of Saint- Domingue found the power ful motor that made them con-stantly take action."[138] "Haiti owes its Name, its Freedom, its Independence, to itself alone," Nemours finished.[139] Nemours, who wrote these fervent, elo-quent words of wisdom more than sixty years before Trouillot, is hardly known or read outside of specialist circles.

The works of eighteenth- and nineteenth-century Haitian thinkers are even less well known. Janvier had hoped his *La République d'Haïti et ses visiteurs* (The Republic of Haiti and its visitors, 1883) might be capable of amplifying Haitian thought. He likened Haiti's threatened position in the Atlantic World, since the time of independence, to that of being on trial. For him, it had always been a trial in which the accused, Haitians, were never allowed by their accusers, the enslavers and colonialists, as much as the European and U.S. imperial powers, to testify on their own behalf. "Haiti has been on trial for eighty years," Janvier contended. "The accused was only ever able to respond at rare and short intervals. Almost always his voice was not heard. He asks to speak." Because of this uneven dynamic, Janvier insisted that his book was "current, timely, necessary."[140] Janvier believed there could be a world where Haitians spoke and were heard, rather than were silenced and mischaracterized, a Haiti capable of arguing on its own behalf rather than being argued about. Janvier offered a strikingly bold vision of his country as a central player in Atlantic World politics and the arbiter of its own destiny. In his account, the Haitian people are central to Caribbean, American, and especially Black political freedom. Janvier is hardly a household name either, his words having fallen silently into the abyss of time.

To understand the full import of what Trouillot accomplished with *Silencing the Past*, when he captivated the attention of global students, researchers, and readers—in essence, forcing them to listen to two hundred years of Haitian thought and to (unknowingly) encounter Haitian intellectuals as theorists of the world—we must go beyond him. *Silencing the Past* should be only the beginning of our encounter with Haitian thought and its enormous influence on Western historiography. Trouillot insisted that to do away with the "savage slot," we must be able to hear the rest of the world.[141]

Asking nonspecialists who may be newly interested in the history of Haiti to consult nineteenth-century Haitian-produced sources is an inconvenient argument. Practices of historical reading, whereby Haitians are seen as objects of study rather than as producers of studies, present inconveniences, too. The effects of this power play proliferate in the inconvenient silencing that occurs every time a scholar reads over the names of Ardouin, Vastey, or Dumesle in favor of claiming the influence of Marx, Michelet, or Foucault on Trouillot. More inconvenient still is for me to suggest that *Silencing the Past* must be read after (or at least alongside) *Ti dife boule*, the way the reading of a sequel ordinarily follows the reading of the original. This last argument requires that any scholar interested in tackling the vastness of Haitian history and literature become fluent not only in French but also in Haitian Creole. Yet the inconvenience of Haiti for the rest of the West is nothing new. In the 1883 words of Janvier, "Haiti is an argument . . . that is embarrassing and displeasing."[142] It is Haitian writing about those whom Nau referred to as "the first Haitians,"[143] and who suffered the ultimate consequences of being regarded as "inconvenient," to which we shall now turn.

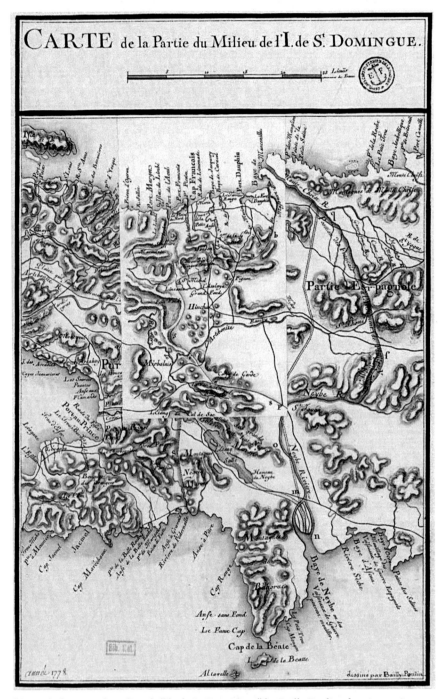

"Carte de la partie du milieu de l'île de St. Domingue," by Bailly Poulin, showing region where maroons are hiding, 1778. Courtesy of Bibliothèque Nationale de France.

PART I
Colonialism

-1—
0—
+1—

Chapter 1

Indigenous

The island called Haïti (Ayiti) by its original inhabitants was the first territory in the so-called new world to be un-settled by European invaders.[1] Inhabited by humans since at least 5000 B.C.E., this Caribbean land was the site of the initial battles between Spanish colonizers and the existing occupants, principally, those from the region called Xaragua. Xaragua, in the southwestern part of the island, soon to be renamed La Española by the Spanish crown, was home to the celebrated queen Anacaona, her late brother Bohechio, her ill-fated husband Caonabo (originally from the region called Maguana), their daughter Higuemota, and granddaughter Mencia, who eventually married the maroon chief Enrique, also known as Enriquillo and Henri. Nineteenth-century Haitians did not call the inhabitants of fifteenth-century Ayiti collectively by the erroneous name of "Taínos." Instead, they called them the "first Haitians."[2]

At the moment of Columbus's startling appearance on Ayiti in 1492, inhabitants of the five main principalities of the island, which spans more than seventy-five thousand square kilometers—Magua, Marien, Maguana, Xaragua, and Higuey[3]—do not appear to have understood themselves to be one people with a shared name. "A name was never with them an abstract and meaningless word, an arbitrary sound," wrote nineteenth-century Haiti's Émile Nau in his *Histoire des caciques* (1855), the most extensive Haitian chronicle of this period. "The names of their leaders [*caciques*], the names of their countries, rivers, mountains were combined words that painted the people or objects they named."[4] Cibao, one of the provinces of Maguana,[5] means "rocky mountain" (*montagne de pierre*). Further deconstructing the word shows how its meaning was assembled through combined utterances. "Ciba means rock," Nau said, "leaving the final o, which signifies . . . mountain."[6] Similarly, Tiburon, the name of one of the southernmost provinces of Xaragua, was named as such because sharks could be found swarming the waters near its coasts. "Ti" signified province or "country," while "buron" was the name of the "formidable fish."[7] The Spanish and then the English, who first encountered sharks in the Americas, still use the Ayitian word. "The Spanish borrowed the word *tiburón* from the Carib Indians, and, later, the English borrowed *tiburón* from the Spanish and used it for about 100 years," wrote José I. Castro in his brief study of the origins of the word.[8] Nau located the same "Ti" in Tiburon to be of significance in the word "Haï-ti," which "translates as elevated country or land." "Niti," he said, was a region of Maguana, meaning "populous province." The combination of these sounds formed the appellation Haïti, signifying mountainous, *populated* land.

In contrast, like the names the Spanish and the French later gave to the island and the constituent parts they claimed—La Española, Hispaniola, Santo Domingo, and Saint-Domingue—the appellations European colonizers used to refer to the Indigenous population—Taínos, Arawaks, and Caribs—were terms of pure European invention. Columbus seems to have dreamt up the idea of island Caribs out of pure fright to describe those he and the Spanish deemed "fierce and hostile natives"; what linguists refer to as the Taíno language group existed across South America and the Caribbean among people who were never to encounter nor even to conceive of each other's existence; and the term Arawak, which only gained use in the late nineteenth century after it was introduced by archeologist David Brinton, also refers to broad language systems spread out over large and distinct geographic territories.[9] Contemporary archeologists have thus drawn the same conclusion as Nau: "Caribbean social formations" before Columbus did not resemble European-style nomination, but instead "were assembled through the integration of previously distinct, albeit interacting, communities."[10]

From a metaphorical standpoint, the linguistic transformation of pre-Columbus Ayiti to post-colonial "Hayti" (under Dessalines, Christophe, and Pétion) to modern Haïti (or Ayiti, as it is pronounced and spelled in Haitian Creole orthography today) well encapsulates the forms of anti-colonial rebellion that historically link these two erroneously named peoples—"Africans" and "Indians"—whom Europeans "invented" as much as they alienated from the languages, cultures, and customs of their birth lands.[11] Their fates became indelibly intertwined when the Spanish forced colonial slavery and colonial racism on the people of the Americas, eventually destroying the "Indians" and replacing them with the "Africans." Nau perhaps said it best when he wrote, "The African and the Indian joined hands in chains. It is through this contra-fraternity of misfortune and a shared community of suffering that their destinies were yoked together." "To render a country free in this way was to avenge all who had been oppressed here, it was to avenge ourselves and at the same time to avenge the unfortunate Indians," he continued. "Having inherited their servitude, we also inherited their homeland."[12] This inescapable relationality structured Haitian national imaginings from the moment the state of Haiti was born. Making explicit connections between the Indigenous world, Spanish and French colonialism, the African slave trade, and Haitian independence, Nau explained:

32   Chapter 1

The first attempt at colonization which transformed this hemisphere and that succeeded was here. African slavery with its horrors began on this soil; but the first cries of freedom were also unleashed here; the first chains of bondage were broken here. The first free black people were formed here. From the discovery to the present day, so much suffering, so much murder, but so much heroism and so much martyrdom! It is the most beautiful island to have ever burst forth in the heart of the seas and under splendid skies, but it is also the land on the globe that has perhaps drunk the most human blood. Posterity must know.[13]

In Nau's retelling, the names, as equally as the stories, of the "Africans" and the "Indians" had a cosmological relationship, one that could be put into service for both historical and political purposes. "The fact of inhabiting today the country where they once lived," Nau wrote, "requires us, more than anyone else, to inquire into our predecessors."[14] A history of Haiti that began with the Indigenous period could explain and justify the Haitian people as the rightful, sovereign inheritors of the Ayitian earth. The Haitian Revolution, inspired by Ayitian anti-colonial rebellion, led to the "triumph of the *indigènes*, to liberty and the Haitian nationality, where Saint-Domingue rebecame Haiti," Nau declared.[15]

Nineteenth-century Haitian writers recognized the "first Haitians," or Ayitians, of the fifteenth century as organically anti-colonialist, because they used their bodies to oppose Spanish rule, often sacrificing their lives to remain independent and slavery free. Haitian writers, like Vastey, saw in Ayitian resistance, not a futile and unequivocal cautionary tale, but a logic and justification for their own independence. Early nineteenth-century Haitians and their ancestors of the late eighteenth century had not only similarly resisted and then overthrown the French colonists—who somehow managed to outdo the Spaniards in cruelty—but they followed the lead of the "first Haitians" when they became simultaneous resisters and theorists of colonialism.

In their voluminous writings on the state of slavery and color prejudice in the Atlantic World, especially as these topics related to the history of the Haitian Revolution, nineteenth-century Haitian authors developed a series of historical and political inquiries designed to disrupt the idea that colonialism was a harmless method of "settling" the so-called new world. Early modern anti-colonial resistance in Ayiti was instructive in this regard, since it proved that opposition to European encroachment on Ayitian territory existed from the beginning of the terrible encounter with the Spanish. This opposition carried a straight line into the kind of modern anti-colonialism expressed in the founding documents of Haiti and remained evident throughout nineteenth-century Haitian thought.

If we want to understand this, the relationship between "the first Haitians" and the philosophy of Haitian independence, we must begin with the process of *dis-settling* unleashed by Europeans against the Indigenous of the Americas. The story of how fifteenth- and sixteenth-century Ayitians by turns resisted Spanish encroachment, even while their communities were largely destroyed, is central to how colonialism began to be defined as unequivocally *bad* by nineteenth-century Haitians and remains key to understanding the revolution waged against it by the enslaved Africans and free people of color of late eighteenth-century Saint-Domingue. In exploring the impact of Haitian revolutionary thought on the two hemispheres of the Americas and Western Europe, we must not lose sight of this part of a deeply connective journey, one that illuminates how Ayiti became Haïti, by way of La Española, Hispaniola, Santo Domingo, and Saint-Domingue. This historical *process* will lead us back to today's Ayiti. The concept of indigeneity, or belonging to a land by birthright, and the fact of Indigenous resistance helped propel the twin fight to eliminate slavery and color prejudice from the colony of Saint-Domingue. These struggles—those of the "first Haitians" and their counterparts in suffering, the captive Africans—laid the foundations for the first antislavery, anti-colonial, and anti-racist state the world had ever seen to be constituted in Haiti.

After the start of the French Revolution of 1789, to oppose the color prejudices whereby the French colonists determined that a person was not a person if he or she was African or of African descent, or was born to someone who did not have "white" status, the free people of color of Saint-Domingue began to refer to themselves as the island's "new indigenous."[16] Soon after, as the island's enslaved population transformed the Haitian Revolution into a war of independence, the liberating army began to call itself the *armée indigène*. It was to be this Indigenous army that in the Haitian Declaration of Independence, issued on January 1, 1804, triumphantly proclaimed Saint-Domingue would henceforth be known as "Hayti," and that the occupants of this new nation would forever be called *des Haytiens*. "Haiti signified liberty, Saint-Domingue, slavery," explains the narrator in Émeric Bergeaud's 1859 posthumously published novel of the Haitian Revolution, *Stella*. "The heroes of 1803 restored to the country its first name, the name given to it by the Indians, whose heirs they became by the will of Providence, independently of any community of origin." "They named it Haiti," the narrator continues, "in memory of those same Indians who enjoyed independence and happiness here."[17] The Indigenous army's revolution against slavery, the transatlantic slave trade, racism, and, ultimately, colonialism was, in fact, the basis for Dessalines's radical claim that his actions in leading the *armée indigène* avenged all of America, not simply the island of Ayiti.

In the famous April 28, 1804, proclamation issued in Cap just four months after Haitian independence, Dessalines famously announced, "I have avenged America." "At last, the hour of vengeance has sounded, and the implacable enemies of the rights of man were subjected to the punishments due for their crimes," he said. "I raised my arm, which for so long had been held back, above their guilty heads. At this signal, provoked by a just God, your hands, sacredly armed, struck the axe against the ancient tree of slavery and prejudices." Just a little over a year later, in May 1805, Dessalines signed Haiti's first constitution, enshrining into law the renaming of the island. "The people inhabiting the island referred to previously as Saint-Domingue, here agree to form a free state, sovereign and independent of any other power in the universe, under the name of the Empire of Haiti."[18]

Haïti, the Ayitian word for mountainous, populated land could not have been a more fitting name for this newly free and sovereign state, whose soil was seemingly held together by an immense chain of peaks and valleys and the rivers that run through them.[19] Baron de Vastey explained the effect of renaming the island as further cementing the connection between those he likewise called "the first Haitians" and present-day Haitians: "The name of the island was changed, *the Saint-Domingue of the French* gave way to the former *Hayti*; and from this name, the Indigenous blacks and yellows adopted the generic denomination of *haytiens*."[20] What an intentionally bold discursive move of anti-colonialism! This reverse nomination—overturning European dis-settlement—has a direct relationship to the more organic resistance of the Ayitians. Let us now try to understand the history of colonial Ayiti through the people in whose very name independent Haïti's radical eruption out of colonialism and against slavery and color prejudice was inscribed.

The story of fifteenth- and sixteenth-century Ayitians is best understood for our purposes in the manner in which it was told by nineteenth-century Haitians. They are the ones who instrumentalized the struggle over colonial Ayiti to justify the creation of independent Haïti.

The Baron de Vastey was born in 1781 with free status in colonial Saint-Domingue to a free woman of color and a white Frenchman from Normandy. Vastey became one of independent Haiti's first professional historians when he published his widely reviewed and highly circulated pamphlet, *Le Système colonial dévoilé* (1814). The author of almost a dozen separate book-length works published between 1814 and 1820, Vastey drew his understanding of Ayitian resistance to Spanish domination, sometimes quoting large passages verbatim and without attribution, principally from the writings of Garcilaso de la Vega, Bartolomé de Las Casas, the Baron de Montesquieu, M. L. E. Moreau de Saint-Mery, Hilliard D'Auberteuil, and S. J. Ducoeurjoly. Even as

Indigenous   35

he repeated information based largely on the accounts of Spanish colonizers or French colonists, Vastey recontextualized the story to explain the importance of past Ayitian opposition for present Haitian independence. The Spaniard's love of gold was the sole and unique motivator of their interest in the Americas. "What's this? I cried, after finishing my reading?" Vastey exclaimed. "It has been three hundred years since these abominations were committed, uniquely to amass gold, and things have not changed at all today; we see the same outcome, it is to produce sugar and coffee that our oppressors have soiled themselves with similar atrocities."[21] Among the most execrable of these "atrocities," committed in the name of gold, was the execution of Anacaona, known as the poet of Ayiti, whose name—"Ana," the Ayitian word for flower, and "Caona," the word for gold—meant quite literally "golden flower."[22]

In 1503, along with 300 Xaraguans, Anacaona was tricked into attending a feast given by the new Spanish governor, Nicolás de Ovando. Once at the party she was accused of treason and then hanged at the gallows. Her execution was followed by six months of carnage, whereby the Spaniards massacred, nearly indiscriminately, the entire population of Xaraguans, leaving many orphans behind. One of those orphans was Anacaona's daughter, Higuemota. Caonabo, that brave Maguanan, Anacaona's husband and father to Higuemota, was previously arrested by the Spanish in 1496. In Haitian accounts, he later died on the ship by which he was being deported to Spain. "Unlucky man! he experienced the same fate as the unfortunate Toussaint Louverture," Vastey lamented.[23] Caonabo's sad demise here finds its corollary in Haitian thought to the wrongful death of Toussaint Louverture, who, after being tricked into a meeting where he was subsequently arrested by Bonaparte's army, was put on a ship to France and forever separated from his family. After months of torture and neglect at the hands of French authorities, Louverture died a cold, sad, and lonely death in a French prison in the Jura mountains. His official cause of death was pneumonia and complications from an untreated stroke. But his jailers' intentional withholding of medical care was murder, not accidental death.[24]

Later Haitian authors, clearly influenced by Vastey, also tied the history of Louverture to that of Caonabo, whose name, with "Bo" signifying "great leader" and "Caona" meaning gold, together indicated he was the "golden chief."[25] *Fille du Kacik* (The Kacik's daughter), published in Paris in 1894, was Haitian author Henri Chauvet's first play. He dedicated the drama to his par-ents and the Association du Centenaire de l'Indépendance, in honor of the impending hundredth anniversary of Haitian independence. The author of the unsigned preface compared Kaonabo (Caonabo), the leader of the Kaciks (Caciques) and the hero of Chauvet's play, to General Toussaint Louverture:

36 Chapter 1

Dominican Republic, Southwest, San Juan de la Maguana, "Parque de los Indios," Caonabo monument. Courtesy of Hackenberg-Photo-Cologne/Alamy Stock Photo.

"To we who are preparing the celebration of the centenary of our independence, [Chauvet] comes forward to here say: 'Do not forget that before your ancestors, another race fell, martyrs of their own generosity; Remember that this race, before disappearing entirely, saw rebel the first African slaves imported to Hispaniola!'"[26] As in the works of Nau and Bergeaud, Kaonabo's opposition, and that of the Kaciks, Enrique and Anacaona, are presented not merely as precursors to the Haitian Revolution, but as nodes along its longer teleology.

Kaonabo's speeches could easily be imagined coming from Louverture or any of the Haitian revolutionaries. "Wherever shall appear the stranger to Bohio," Kaonabo states,

> I will make war upon him, a war to the death!
> Eternal hate shall flow in my men's every breath
> Like that which overflows my heart.
> (*Pauses, then as if enlightened*)
> Yes, posterity
> Will grant my wish. In the name of liberty
> They shall all rise up, if out of your bondage

They suffer the fetters and outrage;
The cry of independence shall then carry over our green hills
Gloomy and solemn, and hearts wide open still
To this proud emotion within my soul stirring,
To make Haiti free shall sacrifice everything! . . .
Aya, aya bombé![27]

Chauvet, like Chanlatte before him, included Haitian Creole in his dramas. He also included words from the language of the Ayitians. The words above, *Aya, bombé*, famous utterances of Caliban in Aimé Césaire's *Une Tempête* (A tempest), are called by Chauvet "Indian words that mean, 'Let us die, let us die free.'"[28] Notably, Dessalines's "Independence or death," which is evoked elsewhere in the play, replaces the well-worn "Liberty or Death." In his *Histoire de la littérature haïtienne* (History of Haitian literature), the French critic Edgar La Selve included a transcription of what he said was the sole remaining record of a song from the Ayitians, namely, that of Caonabo chanting a version of liberty or death as a rallying cry for his men to fight the Spanish invaders. "Woe to him who, in the hour of common peril, does not raise his axe! . . . But he who dies to defend the sacred forests where the ancestors sleep, oh! he will live forever in the imperishable *areytos* [elegiac or epic songs celebrating warriors] of the *sambas* [bards or troubadours]," Caonabo sang. Dying for Ayitian freedom was the surest path to immortality. The "corpses, piously gathered by the *butios* [preachers and healers], after the fight, will be suspended from the high branches of the *mameys* [apricot trees] from which he will drink from the fruit at his leisure, and his *youanni* [soul] will go and savor the *ouicou* [victual], in the company of the Zémès [gods]."[29] Though La Selve's understanding of Ayitian poetics, and the vocabulary he included to explain the terminology, were largely derived from Nau's *Histoire des caciques*, sometimes even word for word without proper attribution, Nau did not include any sustained examples of Ayitian poetry. Nau, in fact, lamented that when the Ayitians were destroyed by the Spanish, their voluminous poetry, remnants of which he believed survived at least in cosmological form in Haitian thought, largely disappeared with them. "Their areytos were poems or songs sung at the funerals of caciques, nitaynos [important figures], or any other personage who deserved poetic regret, even a young girl or a child," Nau wrote. These were not simple funereal laments: "They were epic, lyrical, elegiac works, that is to say, they contained history and the mores and the feelings of the people from whom they emanated," he explained. Citing the example of Anacaona's poetry, Nau wrote that it "played a huge part in the ascendancy and fame of her throne." Nau's final condemnation of European invaders, beginning with Christopher Columbus, has the most to tell us about the sheer importance Haitian intellectuals attached to the concept of historical preservation. Nau observed that many of the island's first European voyagers spoke of the considerable poetic and melodic output of the Ayitians, but not even one of the Europeans seemed to have written down any of their songs for the sake of posterity, contrary to their usual custom. That the Ayitians did not write or transcribe their own melodies was, in contrast, understandable, since writing was simply not a part of their culture.[30] The Europeans, on the contrary, who destroyed that culture, as much with their words as with their deeds, were indefensible. "I have researched the causes of this culpable negligence, and I confess that I have not found a single valid excuse for this grave breach of the sacred duty of knowledge," Nau remonstrated. "To allow the thought of a people to perish, that which is the most imperishable, is an even more barbaric crime than to destroy every last vestige of a people."[31]

It was not just Ayitian warriors like Caonabo, Enrique/Henri, or Anacoana whose memorial ashes could be evoked in Haitian revolutionary thought to condemn the long history of colonialism and slavery and justify its destruction by the Haitians. French officials had corollaries in the European invaders from the era of Spanish colonialism on Ayiti. Nau likened the actions of the Spanish governor Ovando to that of the French general Donatien Rochambeau. In 1802, General Rochambeau arrived along with General Leclerc, both on the order of France's First Consul Napoléon Bonaparte, to reinstate slavery in Saint-Domingue. In Nau's words, "The memory of Ovando would have remained execrable for all of posterity among the Aborigines of Haiti, if they had not all perished, just as that of Rochambeau is to this day hateful to all Haitians."[32] Rochambeau, a name spoken with horror in nineteenth-century Haitian thought, augmented Leclerc's original wish to "destroy all the Negroes of the mountains, men and women, to only keep around children younger than twelve years old, to destroy the majority of those in the plain, and to not leave alive a single person of color who has ever worn an epaulette."[33] While the horrifically favorite move of Leclerc's troops was gassing people of color with sulfur in floating ships called *étouffoirs*,[34] another Haitian chronicler, Dumesle, focused on Rochambeau's usage of dogs to hunt the revolutionaries. Dumesle compared the French general to that infamous European killer, the Spaniard Hernán Cortés, responsible for the conquest of the Aztecs of Mexico. Dumesle recalled that when the man who was guarding the dogs Rochambeau imported from Cuba asked with what the French planned to feed them, Rochambeau, who had already ordered numerous drownings, hangings, and other atrocious executions, coolly responded: "With the flesh of negroes and mulattoes."[35] Connecting the French army under Rochambeau's multiple "crimes against humanity" to the earlier genocide of the Ayitians by the Spanish, Chanlatte opined: "In vain the cries of humanity at the sound of the barking invoked heaven and earth; in vain did a dying voice beg for pity; vain clamors! superfluous prayers! Pity! . . . it fled from this land with its original population, the Europeans discarded it when they passed into the tropics. Pity! . . . it would not know how to exist . . . in places where the thirst for gold has founded its empire; and it is not for the usurpers, the destroyers of Africa and the Indies to feel its sweet emotions, even after having been avenged."[36] Vengeance came from the revolutionaries and from destiny.

Nau drew a cosmological relationship between the death of Christopher Columbus and that of Napoléon Bonaparte. "Allow me, since we are talking about history, and the history of Haiti, to submit two terrible and striking examples of historical atonement," Nau wrote. "Christopher Columbus caused to be loaded with irons and put to death one of Haiti's most illustrious Caciques [Caonabo]; shortly afterwards, he himself [Columbus] was thrown into chains, and, on being released from captivity, soon thereafter died in abandonment, poverty and disgrace. Napoléon disloyally had Toussaint Louverture, the first of the blacks, arrested and sent him to die on an icy rock in the Jura mountains; twelve years later, the kings of Europe united to relegate him [Napoléon] to the burning rock of Saint Helena where he expired." It was not only the genocide perpetrated by Ovando against the Xaraguans that was meant to be instructive for nineteenth-century Haitians. There was also the constant response to Spanish violence and the ultimate outcome of *marronnage*, or fugitivity, by which some Xaraguans and other Ayitians did manage to escape the treacherous fate of the majority. "Such was the end of the last Chiefs of Haiti, whom the conquerors, upon their arrival, found reigning over free peoples," Nau wrote. "From then on, Spanish domination spread over the whole island, and the only independent Aborigines who existed thereafter were those, in small numbers, who, fleeing servitude, retired to the most inaccessible mountains of the interior. Clustering together as much as possible, they lived there free from all authority, but as fugitives, they found themselves ceaselessly wandering from retreat to retreat."[37] A tragedy forced to become a difficult miracle. Nau equated the fate of those fugitive Ayitians who opposed Spanish domination by fleeing and setting up maroon societies to the African revolutionaries who later fought to abolish French slavery in eighteenth-century Saint-Domingue.

Along with the terrible histories of Anacaona and Caonabo, Vastey connected the story of their great nephew Enrique, raised by Spanish priests in the wake of Ovando's war, directly to Haitian independence, and in particular to the reign of King Henry Christophe. In Vastey's account, after the death of his aunt, Higuemota, and the death of his benefactor, Valençuela, Enrique found himself mistreated at the convent where, from a young age, he learned to admire and revere the Spanish doctor Bartolomé de Las Casas. In 1519, following a dispute with the deceased Valençuela's son, Enrique escaped into the mountains. Having amassed arms, he convinced hundreds of other Ayitians, as well as dozens of enslaved Africans, to follow him.[38] From there, Enrique waged a fourteen-year war against the Spaniards, establishing a maroon state in the mountains of Bahoruco (present-day Dominican Republic). Of this, Ardouin concluded that the Indians and Africans of Ayiti "were the first to trace for others this honorable example."[39]

Nineteenth-century Haitian writers, who referred to Enrique with the French cognate, Henri, and sometimes with its Haitian counterpart, Henry, saw more than a coincidence between the maroon chief and their own king. Julien Prévost, the Comte de Limonade, explained that Enrique's ultimately victorious struggle against Spanish colonialism and slavery was the precursor to other maroon states in Haiti, as well the thirteen-year-long revolution that ended in Haitian independence:

> If in this long since gone epoch, some of the unfortunate Indians succeeded in establishing, in their own country a free and independent state, in the midst of their oppressors; if more recently (in 1785), Governor Bellecombe was forced to treat as independent the 125 inhabitants of Hayti living in the mountains of Doko [Docoëns]; what will become of us who have chased away the French; who have built impregnable fortresses in our mountains; who find in our climates various resources that the Europeans look for in vain? We, who are as similarly war-torn as them, but infinitely more robust in our lands, . . . we, who strongly feel our worth; and who are, to make use of an expression that to me seems quite just, *Children of the Sun*. How many reasons do we have to believe that we are the rightful claimants, truly independent and unable to be subjugated?

Prévost finished by making a much more solid link between European conquest of the Ayitian territory to Haitian recovery of it: "The first land discovered in the new world, was also the first to be conquered for independence."[40] For Prévost, the history of Enrique/Henri also justified the leadership of Haiti's King Henry I. "Heaven owed to its favorite children (for who would dare deny that we are) to give them as a present a hero, a magistrate, who, reinvigorating the features of the cacique Henry, whose name he bears, was born to deliver his people from the yoke of foreigners, calm the factions, and compel us to enjoy, in the shadow of peace and independence, the sweetness of liberty, civilization and prosperity, under his paternal administration!" "Of him we will say," Prévost concluded, "what they said of that other Henry, the model of kings, warriors and politicians, whose great qualities he possesses.

Indigenous   41

He was for his Subjects; the Victor and the Father."[41] According to La Selve, drawing on an anecdote from Nau's *Histoire des caciques*, when Christophe asked the members of his court which of the Ayitians was his "homologue," it was Vastey who, in shouting, "Aya bombé!" proposed the enduring connection to "the last defender of Indian independence," Enrique/Henri.[42]

In his own writings, Vastey used the history of the island's first Enrique/Henri to support the idea that Haïti's present King Henry I was the cosmological father of all Haitians:

> Let us rally round the great Henry, this good father, whose every care and solicitude is for the happiness of the Haytian family, all of whom are his children. He alone will guide the vessel of liberty and independence into port. Who could doubt it? From the correspondence of his name with that of the cacique Henry, who rescued the remnants of the first Haytians from shipwreck; from those extraordinary marks of distinction, his genius, his energy, the deep knowledge that he has of the world and the human heart: from signs such as these, let there be no doubt, it is he whom the All Powerful has singled out as the restorer and liberator of his people.[43]

At the end of *Le Système*, not unlike Prévost, Vastey drove home that there was more destiny in the relationship between the names of these two men than there was coincidence. Just as Enrique/Henri fled an oppressive situation, finding sovereignty and solace in building a separate and independent society, Vastey justified Christophe's abrupt creation of a separate state from the republic set up in Port-au-Prince in the wake of the assassination of the Emperor Jacques I in October 1806. Vastey ended his account of the Ayitians with Enrique/Henri's life story to point to what independent Haitians might learn from the history of colonial Ayiti. Warning that "little by little this race was entirely exterminated,"[44] Vastey told his fellow citizens what they needed to do to avoid the same fate: cherish the weapons that allowed Haitians to fight for their independence on the same terms as Enrique/Henri opposed the Spanish. "A race of exterminating men thus once passed through here?" Vastey asked, before musing upon how it was that the Spanish were able to perpetrate their earlier genocide against the Xaraguans despite being outnumbered.[45] "And had these unfortunate people no weapons? Could they not even defend themselves? At this thought, I seized my weapons, and I thanked the Heavens for having placed in our hands the instruments of our deliverance and our preservation."[46] The lesson and warning was that modern anticolonial resistance had to be carried out with the modern weapons that Enrique/Henri used to protect himself from the Spanish: "O precious weapons! Without you what would have become of my country, my compatriots,

42 Chapter 1

my relatives, my friends; from that moment forward, I considered my weapons as the greatest of all goods. Sons of the mountains, inhabitants of the forests, cherish your weapons, these precious keys to preserving your rights, never abandon them, transmit them to your children with the love of freedom and independence, and the hatred of tyrants, as the best inheritance you could ever give to them."[47] The first Haitians may have been gone, but according to Vastey, the material remains of their corporeal existence could still be accessed alongside the spiritual legacy they left behind.

Vastey forced Haitian material history of the "first Haitians" and their connection to contemporaneous Haitians into a global discursive sphere dominated by white European and North American accounts, which ordinarily erased or ignored these links. "The friends of slavery, those eternal enemies of the human race, have made all the presses of Europe groan for centuries in order to reduce the black man below the brute," Vastey proclaimed. "Now that we have Haitian printing presses, we can reveal the crimes of the colonists and respond to even the most absurd calumnies invented by the prejudice and greed of our oppressors."[48] It was not solely refutation that Vastey was after. He was also concerned with the recovery of memory, which entailed continuing to connect the past of Ayiti to the present of Haïti, even in absence of traditional narrative accounts from the Ayitians. "Wherever I place my feet, wherever I fix my gaze, I see the debris, pottery, utensils, and figures which bear in their forms the imprint and traces of art in its infancy," he wrote referring to the physical remains of the "first Haitians." "In remote and solitary places," he continued, "in the caves of inaccessible mountains, I have, trembling, discovered skeletons still intact, human bones scattered and whitened by time; and by allowing my thoughts to remain arrested on these sad remains, on these remnants that attest to the existence of a people who are no longer, my heart is moved."[49] These fragments, shards of bone, remnants of pottery and ceramics, became the basis of reconstructing the story of the Ayitians for nineteenth-century Haitian writers, just as they have been for twentieth- and twenty-first-century archeologists.[50]

Nau was careful to acknowledge that the history he was setting down would be only a fragmentary one, filled with voids, gaps, and a multitude of unanswered questions. There were also to be profound silences. Nau described his methodology, therefore, as a combination of folk history and traditional archival excavation:

It is impossible to go back even a day before the discovery, without giving into vagaries and conjecture. I have only gathered in one set of works related to Haiti the fragments of this history, sparse in the works of historians and the accounts of voyagers who embraced the discovery of the entire continent of America. I gave, or at least I tried to give, a little more consistency to the facts and actions of the aborigines, and to recount, during a short moment of their existence, according to fables handed down and traces of traditions, their character, their mores, and their lives.

Attention to the history of the Ayitians, Nau continued, would nevertheless ensure that all of Haiti's "annals would be conserved and transmitted by its proper citizens" and underscore the importance of "preventing [Haiti's] history from being forgotten."[51] Nau, like Vastey and Prévost, ended his history of Indigenous Ayiti with Enrique.[52] But in the penultimate chapter of *Histoire des caciques*, Nau described coterminous enslaved African resistance on the island, "whether owing to the example of the insurgents of Bahoruco, or whether they were pushed by their own will to break an already unbearable yoke." The first insurrection of enslaved Africans, Nau went on to explain, happened on a plantation owned by Diego Colón, son of Christopher Columbus and governor of the colony, when the Africans Diego was enslaving joined together with those from a neighboring plantation and took up arms. "They tried to do something like an African Vespers," Nau wrote. "They threw themselves at their masters, massacred them, and set fire to several plantations." When their actions did not spark general insurrection, as they hoped, those enslaved freedom fighters retreated to the mountains. After Diego, who was in the city of Santo Domingo at the time, learned of the insurrection, he gathered his troops in haste, put himself at their head, and led them in pursuit of "his rebelling slaves." Encountering them on the outskirts of a region called Nisao, Diego's troops beat and killed many of the freedom fighters, while the rest fled into the mountains of Ocoa, where other African fugitives were living, "the first to escape through their obstinate flight from the horrors of slavery."[53]

Immediately after this first recorded armed slave rebellion, the Spaniards, under Diego's directive, began to formally legislate punishments for slave rebellions and other accusations of breach of conduct. The Spaniards subsequently produced some of the first known "black codes." Turning for just a moment to the history of Spanish attempts to legislate and repress the strikes for freedom engaged in by enslaved Africans can help us to see the connection more plainly between Indigenous resistance on Ayiti and eighteenth- and nineteenth-century Haitian revolutionary thought. The earlier independence movements in Columbus-era Ayiti permeated the atmosphere on the island like ether, until an explosion, caused by that other "African vespers" known as the ceremony at Bois Caïman, occurred in August 1791. Although Nau did not give a date for the rebellion on Diego's plantation, the events he described are widely considered to be the first and largest struggle initiated by the en-

44   Chapter 1

slaved in sixteenth-century Ayiti. Known as the Christmastime rebellion, the freedom strike took place most likely on December 26, 1521.[54] We learn more about this uprising from the January 6, 1522, ordinance issued in response to the "rebellion" by Diego Colón. The Spanish were frustrated because, despite their earlier attempts to punish fugitives from slavery, "it has occurred that the Blacks and slaves that there are in this said island, without any fear and with devilish thoughts, have had the temerity of committing many crimes and excesses." Going on to describe what those "crimes" were, we read of the Christmastime rebellion:

> This last passed holiday of the Nativity of Our Redeemer, a certain number of them in quantity agreed to rebel and rebelled, with intention and purpose to kill all the Christians they could and to free themselves and take over the land, for which they took the arms they could find and made others out of sharpened rods and, on a night of the said holiday began to kill and wound the Christians they found in the province of the Nigua river bank, district of this city, and in other parts and roads of this said Island where they killed and wounded many Christians, stealing a lot of gold from the pedestrians they met and assaulting by night the farms and taking the jewels and garments they found in them.

The Spanish framed their response to this freedom struggle in the language of colonial violence. After characterizing the revolt as the result of "Blacks and slaves" "despising Christians" and having "little fear of God and of our Justice," Spanish authorities concluded, "If it had not been because of our said Viceroy and Governor [Diego Colón] with great diligence and gathering of people on foot and horses, after learning of the said uprising of the said Blacks, went in person to chase and apprehend and kill and bring them to justice, as he did . . . they would have done very great damages and deaths besides those they had done." The first article following the ordinance therefore mandated, "all Blacks and Whites and Canarians that are slaves who currently wander rebel in this island, be forced to come back and return to the service of their masters within twenty days." Twenty-two additional articles followed, spelling out what would happen to enslaved individuals who violated the first article, or who might "hereafter be absent from the service of their masters." Article 3 legislated the most severe punishment for fugitivity, one that carried over into other plantation societies. Any captured "slaves" were ordered to have "one foot be cut off them as per the first time." If the same individual were to flee and once more be caught for a second time the person "should die for it by hanging or by other type of crueler death," especially if it could be determined that the "slave" had "done a crime."[55]

Up until the late twentieth century, the only known surviving contemporaneous account of the Christmastime rebellion, and the "slave codes" Spanish colonizers issued in response, was the *Historia natural y general de las Indias* (Natural and general history of the Indies), published in Seville in 1535 by Gonzalo Fernández de Oviedo.[56] But "enslaved Africans," in the words of Anthony Stevens-Acevedo, "had been resisting their enslavement in La Española literally since [slavery] began in the early years of the sixteenth century, usually by fleeing their masters into the wilderness of the colony."[57] The forms of marronnage rampant on the island led not only to the first "slave codes," but also to the first known "maroon treaty," called a peace treaty at the time, to whose history we must now return. Enrique/Henri's treaty with the Spanish, so vaunted in early Haitian thought, was as problematic as many of the eighteenth- and nineteenth-century maroon treaties later struck between the British and maroons in eighteenth-century Jamaica.

Maroon treaties were complex and often contradictory "agreements" that might ensure freedom and protections for those living in particular maroon communities, but often mandated in exchange that "maroons" help white colonists capture other enslaved Africans and even engage in war against them. The March 1738 "Articles of Pacification with the Maroons of Trelawney Town" in Jamaica stand as a principal example. This British treaty pardoned Captain Cudjoe, the leader of a rebellion, and many of his men, stating they would be able to live in a "perfect state of freedom and liberty" in a limited area of the colony. At the same time, Cudjoe and "his successors" were required to "use their best endeavors to take, kill, suppress, or destroy, either by themselves, or jointly with any other number of men . . . all rebels, wheresoever they be, throughout this island," and to help the British suppress any invasions by a "foreign enemy." The ninth article has the most in common with Enrique/Henri's peace accord with the Spanish. It reads, "That if any negroes shall hereafter run away from their masters or owners, and shall fall into Captain Cudjoe's hands, they shall immediately be sent back to the chief magistrate of the next parish where they are taken." The Trelawney Town maroons were to be paid thirty shillings for each "fugitive" returned to enslavers under this agreement.[58] Many of these same contradictions—mandates for slavery found within decrees of liberty—distinctly characterized Enrique/Henri's peace treaty with the Spanish, and also came to stamp enslaved Africans' negotiations with white French colonial authorities in Saint-Domingue.

Despite Haitian veneration for his resistance and struggles, we cannot let Enrique/Henri's famed negotiations with the Spanish, which came to a head in 1533, pass without some remark. It was in that year that the Spanish crown sent an expedition of 187 men, led by Captain Francisco de Barrionuevo, to "pacify Enrique's rebellion." Once Barrionuevo and his men located Enrique

46   Chapter 1

in the Bahoruco mountains, the latter agreed to meet with the Spanish captain. In the official Spanish report given to the king, Enrique was handed a letter by Barrionuevo that offered a pardon, and, after a few hours, the meeting led to a preliminary peace agreement. To end the hostilities on both sides, Enrique would be required "from there onwards [to be] a friend of the Spanish Christians" and to send back "all the blacks and Indians that came to his pueblo."[59] In the words of scholar Ida Altman, "This meeting marked the beginning of the process by which Enrique was reconciled with his long-time adversaries."[60] In Nau's retelling, this compromise occurred in the European colonial language of extermination. Barrionuevo told Enrique/ Henri that if he "persisted in his rebellion," the Spanish would pursue him "at all costs."[61] Far from condemning the troubled Cacique, Nau sympathized with the difficult decision he faced and characterized his eventual submission as the ultimate mark of spiritual resignation. Enrique/Henri had previously resisted all Spanish attempts to negotiate. He insisted that the Spanish could not offer him and his followers "liberty." "We have already conquered it with our weapons," he insisted. "We cannot be freer than we are in our mountains." Yet, repeated attempts by the Spanish to root him out, proved to Enrique/Henri that he was going to have to spend the rest of his life fighting to maintain that freedom.[62] "What else could he gain by persevering in insurrection?" Nau wondered. "Haiti was irrevocably conquered on that land, forever to be colonized by a foreign population a hundred times larger than its small handful of Indians." "He could have, at most, remained independent in his mountains," Nau hypothesized. "But how long would that last? What would happen after he was gone?" Nau concluded, "He must have felt that his cause no longer had a future, that his race was going to die out, and that the wisest course was for it to end in peace and honor. . . . He preferred . . . to a doubtful and continuously fought independence, freedom and peace with submission."[63]

During a subsequent meeting with Spanish officials, Enrique reluctantly agreed to Spanish terms and, according to a colonial report written to the Crown, he finished by sending "a letter to this royal court expressing gratitude for the favor that your majesty had shown him in ordering that he be pardoned and that from here on he would be a very good friend of the Spaniards and that in order that they would have no suspicion of Indian rebels that he would travel all the sierras of the island and collect Indians and blacks in rebellion and would send them to the pueblos to which they belonged."[64] The peace accord, which required him to turn previously enslaved Africans and Ayitians over to the Spanish, was officially accepted and ratified by Enrique in the city of Santo Domingo in summer 1534.[65] "Despite lingering pockets of resistance," Altman concluded, "Enrique's reconciliation with Spanish authorities more or less brought to an end the era of Indigenous rebellion on the

Indigenous   47

Memorial to Queen Anacaona at Léogâne, Haiti. Courtesy of Malik W. Ghachem, 2016.

island."[66] But even with Enrique/Henri having died just one year later in September 1535, other forms of resistance endured. And nineteenth-century Haitians endowed fifteenth- and sixteenth-century Ayitian resistance to Spanish colonialism with triumphant, longitudinal meanings that transcended the difficult realities and complex compromises of those struggles. Nau mentioned only in passing, and without reference to the African maroons, the Spanish requirement that Enrique "return any subsequent Indians who ran away from them."[67] Still, Nau connected the Haïti founded in 1804 to the fifteenth- and sixteenth-century Ayiti of Anacaona, Caonabo, and Enrique/Henri to justify the new Haitians' claim to the land where the *armée indigène* staged the war of independence. "Their story ends here, along with their active lives. The trace of their existence fades, and we can no longer count each one that is snuffed out. They died out entirely," Nau wrote of the Ayitians. "Not one pure Indian lives here to this day."[68] The Haitian revolutionaries learned from and did not intend to share that destiny of extermination and effacement.

While traveling the length of Haiti to collect the stories that made up his *Voyage dans le nord d'Hayti* (1824), Dumesle mentioned visiting Anacaona's place of birth in what is now the Haitian city of Léogane.

Upon entering the city, Dumesle's imagination was suddenly forced into "retrograde toward an almost fabulous era" that "brought her closer to the circumstances of our own day, as if to bring that time back to life in thought."[69] After describing how Anacaona's marriage to the rival Maguanan Caonabo brought peace and stability to the island, Dumesle described the Spaniards as the interrupters of Ayitian tranquility. For Dumesle, the Spanish were nothing more than "greedy usurpers" who "crossed the Atlantic to sack and destroy [their] homeland." The French colonists of the late eighteenth century were similarly destructive and criminal. They invited the English to invade the island solely to help them (the white colonists) crush the rebellion of people of color and maintain slavery.[70]

To link colonial Ayiti to revolutionary Saint-Domingue, Vastey went back further than the French colonists' attempts to betray the French National Convention's 1794 unilateral abolition of slavery in French territory. Vastey saw the initial connection between these seemingly disparate epochs as hinging on the relationship between Spanish enslavement of the first Ayitians and the European, especially French, traffic in captive Africans. It is to the age of slavery that we must now therefore turn.

Chapter 2

Slavery

In 1501 the Spanish king and queen authorized Nicolás de Ovando, the governor of Ayiti (renamed by them Hispaniola), to transport African captives to the island for the purpose of chattel slavery. That same year, to fill the human void created through the wars and deportations they used to reduce the Ayitians into submission, the Spanish introduced the first captive, trafficked Africans onto the island of Ayiti.[1] "One crime always leads to another," said Vastey, before he issued a stinging condemnation of the Spanish and Portuguese invention of the transatlantic slave trade: "only the people who were accustomed to feasting on Indian tears and blood . . . could invent such a monstrosity."[2] Using his characteristically painful and sardonic rhetoric, he asked, "What means do they use to obtain slaves? The kidnapping and the theft of men; they kindle war by pitting one ruler against another . . . it is at their instigation that these rulers extend a despotic yoke over their unfortunate subjects."[3] The French invented new vocabulary to describe the primary instrument that facilitated their participation in this never before seen form of human commerce: "des négriers" or "negro slave ships" is what the French called the boats they used for their infamous traffic in human beings. Describing a disgusting scene from the Middle Passage (*la traversée*) drawn from the works of the French naturalist, Ducoeurjoly, Vastey painted a portrait of the slave ship as a death machine designed to instill in captive Africans a state of total submission and abjection. A putrid atmosphere of fear and terror, the chains that barely allowed those poor captives to physically move only added to the suffering caused when they were alienated from their own kin, he explained. "They will never see their parents, their friends again; all the bonds that could tie them to life are broken, destroyed forever."[4] Then, paraphrasing the French abolitionist abbé Grégoire's *De la Littérature des nègres* (On the literature of Negroes, 1808) to punctuate the slave ship as a site of human produced horror, Vastey recounted how one ship captain threw hundreds of his dead captives into the sea, while another threw overboard a baby, whose cries bothered him.[5]

Europeans depopulated Africa by way of chattel slavery (human trafficking they legalized!) and caused massive amounts of death and disease on the continent solely for the purposes of their own enrichment. For Vastey, this form of slavery indelibly linked Indigenous Africans to Indigenous Americans to Black Haitians. "Africa has seen torn from its womb, as we have just described, since the beginning of the slave trade until today, 20 million of its unfortunate children; its coasts, once so populous, have become deserted. The store of men has run out." Vastey's attentiveness to language and its many valences brought him to insist that "la traite," or "the trade," was not nearly a term strong enough to describe such an abominable human-created system of torture masquerading as commerce. "The trade!" Vastey exclaimed. "How this one word contains so many crimes! how many horrors and abominations are to be found in that one expression!"[6]

Vastey's compatriot, the intrepid Juste Chanlatte, unlikely member of three Haitian governments—he was secretary to Dessalines, Christophe, and Boyer—similarly declaimed against the word slavery: "Slavery! Oh how this word in and of itself is harsh and repulsive! So many bitter memories it recalls! So many turpitudes and attacks against the human race are captured with it alone!"[7] The words slavery and slave are ugly, dehumanizing terms that have fallen into descriptive disfavor by contemporary historians who prefer enslavement and enslaved.[8] But in nineteenth-century Haitian thought, the continued usage of the dehumanizing language of slavery and slave were necessary reminders of what the Europeans had done to the Africans they captured and forced to work the land in the Americas. "The French really believed that they could deceive us about the true meaning of words," Vastey complained. Going on to cite from the works of the white French colonist and former slaver the Baron de Malouet, Vastey opined, "that Nestor of the colonists wanted us to substitute for the word *slave*, the appellation of *unfree* [*non-libre*]; in order to distract from the idea of a man in chains, but to leave him that way."[9] Malouet had written, "Since the word slave represents to us a chained man, let the appellation of unfree be substituted! We buy the labor, the services, and not the legal person of the African."[10] In his earlier 1814 pamphlet, published as a direct response to Malouet's specious arguments about race, colonialism, and slavery, Vastey decried such illogic: "You had to have lost all common sense, or become quite blinded by your penchants and your love for slavery to dare to advance such nonsense." "For what do these expressions mean, slave or unfree? What does the name matter when the fact exists?" he finished.[11] Throughout the age of slavery the French colonists exhibited a poverty of expression that defied the French proverb pronounced by Antoine Rivaroli (called Rivarol), "ce qui n'est pas clair, n'est pas français," or, "that which is not clear is not French."[12] Using plain obfuscations of the French language was a tactic used by the white colonists to conceal, obscure, defend, and, in the end, justify the crimes against humanity they were committing against the Africans they were enslaving.

The French officially took over the western side of the island from Spain in 1697 at the Treaty of Ryswick and in so doing they pushed the territory they renamed Saint-Domingue fully into the heights of the plantation world, or a new world of African slavery, which had already been, albeit only feebly, inaugurated by Spanish dis-settlers two centuries before. The French accelerated the course of plantation slavery by leaps and bounds. Before the eighteenth century concluded, the French had forcibly transported nine hundred thousand captive Africans to use their very human hands to mechanically produce sugar, coffee, cotton, and indigo for the enrichment of the French crown as equally as the Saint-Dominguan "planteurs" or "habitants," French euphemisms for enslavers.

Those African captives who survived the journey from their continent to the Caribbean archipelago and/or who did not save themselves through suicide, ordinarily arrived on the island of Ayiti in a terrible state. Sold off to the highest bidders, their misfortunes only increased when their "masters" (their new enslavers) branded their names on their chests using hot irons. All too apparent evidence of the tyranny of the colonists, branding was an attempt by enslavers to establish discipline over the body and mind of the person they were forcing into captivity. "Perhaps the first letters learned by the unfortunate slaves . . . were the initials of the colonists," observed the eminent Haitian historian Jean Fouchard. "Their black chests stamped with red iron thus becoming their first syllabary."[13] Branding was meant to visibly produce the transformation of a human being into a commercial object. Those Africans forcibly transported to this new land by European human traffickers were now not merely captives but property. Subsequently forced by their white enslavers to lodge in "tiny and unsanitary huts," the enslaved slept on the ground on a "mat or a piece of leather." "A few rocks and calabashes made up all their furniture," Vastey explained.[14] The meager clothing and food the greedy enslavers afforded their captive Black laborers stood in stark contrast to the opulent mansions the white planters and their families erected for their own comfortable living.[15]

The gulf between those with free status and those with slave status could not have been larger. Such a fact was highlighted by the emergence of many self-styled "citoyens de couleur," or free people of color, who labored throughout the eighteenth century to ensure that they would never be "confused with *Slaves*," as they wrote in a December 1789 petition to the French government, whereby they demanded equal rights with the white colonists. The opposition of the free people of color to the kind of inhumanity associated with both *blackness* and slavery was earlier punctuated by a decree from the governor of Saint-Domingue, dated June 20, 1762, which stated that it was "nature" that "established three different classes of humans—*Whites, mixed-race and Free Mulattos or Negroes.*"[16] The enslaved do not even figure in this taxonomy of humanity, as they were considered *meubles* or household belongings.

52   Chapter 2

Number of enslaved people embarked by European slavers to the French Caribbean in the eighteenth century

		Flag under which they were transported						
		Spain/ Uruguay	Portugal/ Brazil	Great Britain	Netherlands	United States	France	Denmark/ Baltic	Totals
Their destination in French Caribbean	Saint-Domingue	616	603	6,500	680	449	898,825	3,469	911,142
	Martinique	0	381	48,097	7,365	3,284	201,659	257	261,043
	Guadeloupe	167	475	39,797	2,250	2,005	43,152	0	87,846
	French Guiana	0	1,170	4,587	1,137	217	29,707	0	36,818
	French Caribbean unspecified	0	285	8,823	4,289	1,659	16,517	0	31,573
	Totals	783	2,914	107,804	15,721	7,614	1,189,860	3,726	1,328,422

Source: Data from Slave Voyages Database, http://www.slavevoyages.org/estimates/ZE3viGhq.

Without using the word capitalism, Chanlatte explained that this new world of slavery involved "materializing humankind," an act contrary to the laws of nature, reason, and commerce.[17] Slavers alienated the human beings they enslaved by robbing them of that which was germane to being human, *personhood*. "How can alienating a thing [*un bien*] from that which is naturally inalienable from it, be admitted to the court of reason?" Chanlatte asked. "According to what jurisprudence, can a market in which everything is in the buyer's favor and nothing in the seller's have the force of law?" "If it is true that any contract of exchange can only be valid by the free consent of all parties and by the return of something of equal value to the price of the given object, we ask; where is the free consent of the person sold in Africa? Where is the compensation for the slave that is equivalent to the nature and duration of his suffering?"[18] Dumesle echoed Chanlatte's reading of the white colonists, whereby they became "merchants in human flesh," when he quoted a free man of color named Daguin who gave a speech before the provincial assembly in Port-au-Prince. Dumesle included this speech to support his contention that enslavers, known under the neologism of planters and *habitants*, were operating under laws that were contrary to both (divine) humanism and the market (logic). First, Daguin reminded the white colonists of their previous crimes against the Ayitians: "Torn from the shores of Africa because of ferocious greed, victims of a sacrilegious commerce, our ancestors and some of us even were transplanted to this soil which our arms fertilized, and which was so often watered with our sweat and our blood; we are the successors of the primitive races of this country who Europeans killed!" Locating the prejudices of the white colonists as an "aberration" of religious "logic," Daguin harangued the group of proslavery white colonists and Catholic clergymen before him:

> On what fallacies, on what abuses of thought have you not raised
> the scaffold of your system? What aberration of logic would allow the
> admission of ideas so incoherent; some claim slavery and dependence by
> divine right, yet you proclaim a just God who is the common father of all
> men; but, ascribing your passions to him, you paint him as a cruel tyrant
> who only reserves his benefits for a small portion of the chosen ones, and
> these chosen ones are the whites. . . . While strangers to his favors, like
> the scapegoat, we [men of color] are laden with the weight of the iniquities
> of his beloved children. Ah! if there was such a god, nature would disown
> him![19]

Daguin also remonstrated against Louis XIV's *Code Noir* (based on his royal edict of March 1685),[20] whose multipronged illogic of white supremacy is the most infamous set of laws to ever be established to legitimate slavery: "The law

-1—
0—
+1—

54   Chapter 2

that legitimates slavery is the code noir; its source is the slave trade; one section covers with an indelible stain the legislators who dictated its provisions and subjugated the slave for posterity, and the other consecrates to horror these immoral beings who, erecting their existence on a crime, have established themselves as merchants of human flesh. Can this infamous trade prohibited by philanthropy be lawful? Can a man be the object of commerce for another man?"[21] What Aimé Césaire called the "thingification" of various peoples of the world subjected to European colonialization was theorized in the eighteenth and nineteenth centuries by Saint-Dominguans of the time and later Haitians who reported that such "materialization" of humanity took on many forms in colonial Saint-Domingue.[22] The French colonists sought to "materialize the black man," specifically, in Vastey's words, by putting the Africans they were enslaving on par with farm animals.[23] "In public acts people forced into slavery were listed on the same line as cows, mules, pigs, etc . . . men were sold indistinctively."[24] Treating human beings as expendable, transferable, disposable, and ultimately saleable, led to all manner of "crimes against humanity" (*crime de lèse-humanité*),[25] a term used by Chanlatte to refer to the entire constellation of phenomena—colonialism, the slave trade, slavery, and color prejudice—that Europeans, in general, and the French colonists, in particular, used to justify their traffic in human beings. One of these phenomena involved slave patrols. The colonial government set up a system of what they called *maréchaussées*, originally designed to provide white people in the colony with compensation for hunting down fugitives from slavery, referred to by the colonists as "maroons." The white and *gens de couleur libres* militiamen who populated these *maréchaussées* often forced enslaved Black people to accompany them on their missions. Sometimes such efforts were fruitless. If the militias were unable to capture any fugitives from slavery, the white men killed the enslaved Africans and presented them as captured maroons to collect the monies anyway.[26]

Because of the system of slavery they created, the white French colonists were materialists of the highest order. Dumesle insisted, "A Colonist is unquestionably the most absurd materialist of the most revolting bad faith. He slanders nature by trying to erect the scaffold of his system of slavery on the differences between our skin colors, which serves as the basis for his ridiculous ideas about the differences in our physical constitution."[27] Dumesle made his own contribution to French vocabulary when he described what the French colonists were doing as practicing a form of "ultraracisme," or ultra racism, which he defined as the argument that Africans were naturally inferior to Europeans and therefore meant to be enslaved by them. It was with "ultraracisme" that the French repeated vis-à-vis Africans the Spanish destruction of the "Indians."[28] While for Vastey, the colonists were "ultra colons" who would

Slavery 55

never cease to explore ways to make slavery endure forever, Dumesle invented an altogether new term, racism, to describe the color prejudices undergirding the colonists' justifications for enslaving Africans in the Americas.[29] The full sentence of the passage from Dumesle's *Voyage* where he coined this extremely important concept involved the case of the two French commissioners, Léger-Félicité Sonthonax and Étienne Polverel, who were recalled back to France to account for their conduct in Saint-Domingue after the French National Convention formally abolished slavery in 1794. Polverel, who legislatively decreed the abolition of slavery in the western and southern departments in September and October 1793, respectively, perished before any judgment could be handed down. Sonthonax, who formally decreed the abolition of slavery in the northern department of the colony in August 1793, was eventually vindicated of wrongdoing. According to Dumesle, Sonthonax was the one who "emerged triumphant out of this perilous struggle in a time when the guillotine was everlasting in France, and [the French] were sailing here on the agitated sea of ultra racism."[30] In using differences in skin color to justify treating human beings as things or commodities, on the one hand, and to exclude them from citizenship, on the other, the Atlantic Ocean became the sign and symbol of European "ultraracism."

The first known usage in English of the term "racism" comes from 1902 or 1903.[31] The first recorded usage of the word in Spanish (*racismo*) dates from the early twentieth century as well. In French, in contrast, the word "racism" surfaced slightly earlier, at the end of the nineteenth century. One scholar has even gone so far as to claim, "French appears to be the first language to use the terms *racisme* and *raciste*." Scholar Nathan G. Alexander has argued, to that end, that Gaston Méry "coined the termed '*racisme*' in his novel called *Jean Révolte*, about a man who establishes an organization to preserve the integrity of the French 'Celtic' race against the supposedly dangerous influence of Jews and the 'Latin' race of southern France."[32] Dumesle's usage throws this genealogy into disarray. As the first Africans, and people of African descent, in the Americas to permanently break free from the systems of slavery and colonialism, it is natural that independent Haitians developed novel terminology and new epistemological frameworks to understand and describe the tortures they experienced at the hands of the European colonists, standing at the edge of humanity.

Conditions on the island under *ultraracist* French rule were as destructive to Black life as conditions on the island under Spanish rule were for the Ayitians. The tortures described in painstaking detail by nineteenth-century Haitian historians have a lot to tell us about the system of death, euphemistically called slavery, as it existed on the French island of Saint-Domingue in the eighteenth century. "Despite the introduction of 20 thousand black people

56   Chapter 2

each year," Vastey wrote, "the population of Haiti was struggling to grow; Oh! How could men multiply under the most awful tyranny that ever existed?"[33] Anticipating Orlando Patterson's theory of African "social death" under chattel slavery, Vastey observed that the people the French enslaved on Saint-Domingue had been "mort civilement" or "civilly dead" and "inhabited this earth as if they did not really inhabit it; . . . lived as if they were not really living."[34] A strikingly modern theory of slavery emerges out of Vastey's highly granular accounts of the torturous conditions on Saint-Domingue, making him the best chronicler and theorist of enslaved life and death of the period.

The accounts Vastey drew together in *Le Système*, which he gathered from formerly enslaved Haitians and their descendants, but also from French colonial documents, constitute the richest and most complete testimony of slave life on the French island of Saint-Domingue. Vastey named more than 120 French colonists responsible for the tortures he described. Eschewing the colonial European shorthand of referring to the victims of this traffic in human beings only with the term "slave," Vastey used the proper names of both the French colonists and the people they unjustly held in subjugation. Vastey's approach to the history of slavery and colonialism reminds us that one side of the story is the repression of enslaved Black people by white European enslavers, but the other side of the story is the near constant opposition that enslaved individuals engaged in to free themselves, as much to avenge the inhuman system of slavery to which enslavers were subjecting them.

According to Vastey, a white colonist named Poncet made his home a veritable prison, which no one could approach without horror. All that could be heard in the vicinity of his plantation was the clacking of chains and the cracking of the whip, along with the cries of those Poncet subjected to such abuses. All his "domestics," another French euphemism for enslaved people who resided in the home of their enslavers, were his natural born children, and even they were loaded with shackles. That "monster" "subjected to castration all his domestics and one of his quadroon children; after having committed incest with his own daughter, he killed her and her mother, dreadfully tormenting them by melting boiling wax in their ears," Vastey reported. The enslaved were not helpless victims in Vastey's account. As with the Ayitians, there was always struggle and always opposition. This story of rape, incest, and torture soon turned into one of resistance and rebellion: "That inhumane barbarian was strangled by his son and his domestics, all animated with righteous vengeance; they were burned alive for this murder, which would not have happened if Poncet, who had already outraged nature, had not experienced impunity for his crimes; the repressive laws [of the colony] were not made for the colonists, and even less so for the *grands planteurs*; everything was permitted to them."[35] Vastey included the entirety of the official decree from

Slavery   57

officials in Cap describing and naming the enslaved individuals who lived through Poncet's tortures and who ultimately paid with their lives for this attempt to reject the system of death that is slavery. In the decree we find the condemnation of "Sannon, quadroon, and the so-named Guillaume, negro, assassins of Sieur Poncet, inhabitant of Jacquezy." Their punishment was the following: "to have their knuckles cut off, and to be broken alive, their dead bodies were then to be exposed on wheels at the crossroads of the Poncet house, on the Chemin du Trou in Jacquezy . . . to remain facing their co-accused until after the execution."[36] The text of the actual decree named all the "assassins": Saintonge, *nègre commandeur* (negro driver), Boussole, *nègre moulinier* (negro textile laborer) and *cocher* (coachman). There was also Sannite, called Gogo, who was described using pseudoscientific terminology as a *quarteronne*. Her punishment read that she was to be strangled, hanged until death, and then put on the "gallows which will, for this purpose, be erected on the said public square of Fort-Dauphin." Before the white colonists could perpetrate this crime, a doctor was called to check to see if Gogo (Sannite) was pregnant, and if she was, the execution would not take place until after the birth of the baby. Profits, and profits, and more profits. Until she could be examined, Gogo was to be detained in the royal prison with the royal sacrament administered to her before her death. A forced conversion in the hour of her utmost misery. Others condemned alongside Gogo were Paul and Étienne, *nègres nouveaux* (African captives recently introduced on the island), who were to attend all the aforementioned executions with "a rope around their necks, after which they were to be stamped with a hot iron, imprinted with the letters G.A.L. on the right shoulder . . . and attached to the King's chain gang, to serve as convicts, in perpetuity."[37] Slavery's syllabary was sparse, and all its vocabulary led only to punishment and death.

The difference between Vastey's account of slavery and the precious few that were published before his is that, with the notable exception of Gustavus Vassa, also known as Olaudah Equiano, the majority of first-person testimonies about slavery were written by white "planters" or colonists. The account of Thomas Thistlewood from Jamaica remains a particularly notorious example of the important role that both perspective and positionality played in narrative descriptions of slavery in the age of slavery. From 1750 until his death in 1786, Thistlewood, an overseer in Westmoreland Parish, recorded the many tortures he exacted upon the Black people enslaved by John Cope on the Egypt plantation. Thistlewood described punishments for enslaved individuals who refused to comply. He also described raping (though he did not use that term) more than one hundred enslaved women and the crimes he enacted upon them if they attempted to resist.[38] While Thistlewood recorded these atrocities as the justified response to insolence, or worse, with the cold and calcu-

58 Chapter 2

lating indifference of a middle manager, Vastey brought the passion of Black perspective and the compassion of a true seeker of justice to his account. Vastey did not merely offer the kind of proof respected by historians of his own day—written documents, as well as first-person testimonies—but he insisted upon using the white colonists' own documentation against them. By reading against the grain of dispassion and indifference in the documents written by enslavers and white Saint-Dominguan officials, Vastey effectively pointed out the shameless violence they confessed to and their utter disregard for human life, which seemed to have no historical corollary.

One of the accounts that Vastey referred to from French colonial records tells the tale of Gabriel-Jean-Baptiste Larchevesque-Thibaud, a lawyer in the Conseil Supérieur in Cap, who purchased "a Martinican quadroon," named Sophie, from a Madame Lorsan, for the sum of one hundred portuguese (*portugaises*), or about four hundred gourdes.[39] Sophie was purchased by him to be the wetnurse to one of Larchevesque-Thibaud's two white children. After having nursed his first child, Sophie nursed the second one, and that is when Larchevesque-Thibaud's wife, Louise Catherine de Castonnet des Fosses, became suspicious and jealous.[40] Presuming that Sophie was having "an affair" with her husband, Castonnet des Fosses demanded that he provide her with proof to the contrary, which she explained meant shooting Sophie. Larchevesque-Thibaud, to appease the horrific demands of his wife, executed the order. The bullet hit Sophie in the hand when she tried to lift it up to avoid the shot. After this, Castonnet des Fosses seized Sophie and locked her away in a closet. Larchevesque-Thibaud's wife not only loaded her captive with irons, but she cut off Sophie's hair and ears, afterward throwing them into a *pot de nuit* like refuse. This was not enough torture and punishment to satisfy the rage-filled intentions of the government official's wife. In the end, she had Sophie burned with an iron, which she required her husband use to stamp Sophie "on each side of her body, from her ass to her face, which he did without hesitation." "That poor unfortunate woman languished for so long in this situation, until finally her punishers resolved to send her for sale to Charleston by way of one named Polony, a doctor from Cap," Vastey wrote. "She could not be sold, however," he continued, "because of the mutilations that disfigured her; this fact, known throughout Cap-[Français], is contained in the report of Garran Coulon [*sic*] on the colonies."[41] We will come back to Garran de Coulon in a moment. First, it must be acknowledged the great extent to which Larchevesque-Thibaud participated in the horrors of slavery. One fugitive slave notice in the *Affiches Américaines*, Saint-Domingue's most prominent newspaper, while designed to provide information about those captives questing for freedom solely for the purposes of their recapture, also revealed the desperation of individuals enslaved by Larchevesque-Thibaud, especially women. Consider the case of Fatine Diay, described as a "Griffone," who like Sophie previously belonged to Polony, the doctor. Fatine was the daughter of a woman named Fanchette, called "Fanchette à Doré," listed as a "Free negress, living in the savannah of Limonade." When Fanchette escaped the life of misery and torture that was slavery, Larchevesque-Thibaud, her new enslaver, offered five portugaises of compensation to anyone who could help return her to him. The ad for the return of Fanchette, perhaps one of the many forced concubines of Larchevesque-Thibaud described by Vastey, enu-merated the methods she engaged in to produce and perform freedom. "This *Griffone* is sometimes well, sometimes poorly dressed, sometimes walking barefoot, sometimes with shoes on," the notice reads. "She frequents, it is said, the colored peoples' balls, & it could be that to better escape our search for her, she calls herself free, perhaps even disguises herself as a man." Anyone who might glimpse Fanchette was warned, furthermore, that they should have her arrested "whether she has a *billet* [safe passage ticket] or not."[42] Freedom in mar-ronnage was precarious enough, but even a person with legally free status could find their liberty contested by powerful enslavers like Larchevesque-Thibaud.

Vastey used chronicles from colonial officials like Garran de Coulon, author of the famous *Rapport sur les troubles de Saint-Domingue, fait à l'Assemblée nationale* (Report on the troubles in Saint-Domingue, made to the National Assembly, 1797), to expose the brutality of various colonial family dynasties. Of the Desdunes family, drawing once more on Garran de Coulon's report, Vastey explained that Desdunes, *père*, an enslaver in the Artibonite, "had burned alive, successively, forty-five blacks, women and children." Several other members of the Desdunes family, Desdunes Lachicotte, Poincy, and Rossignol, "in fact, every member of that execrable family committed cruelties of every type." Vastey said it "would be hard to believe the number of cruelties that this family exercised in the Artibonite, if all these facts, which I collected on the spot, had not been confirmed to me by Mr. Jean Baptiste, judge, former inhabitant and proprietor in the Artibonite, currently Comte de Terre Neuve and Minister of Justice." This judge had "the kindness to share with me an infinity of notes concerning the crimes of the colonists, particularly, those of the colonists from the beautiful and rich plain of the Artibonite," Vastey said. Within these notes Vastey paused upon the account of "a certain naturalist, named Descourtiz [*sic*], relative of the Desdunes, who has, in several volumes, uttered a host of lies and calumnies about Haiti."[43] By the time Vastey published *Le Système*, the name Michel Étienne Descourtilz, a French naturalist and medical doctor, was already an infamous one. After having been held captive by the Haitian revolutionaries in the course of the war of independence, Descourtilz claimed in his *Voyages*

60   Chapter 2

d'un naturaliste (Voyages of a naturalist, 1809) that his life was spared by none other than the wife of General Jean-Jacques Dessalines, Marie-Claire Félicité Bonheur Heureuse.[44] Descourtilz also labored to portray enslaved resistance on the Desdunes plantations as innate vengeance and African savagery rather than the desperate opposition of enslaved Black people to the tortures they were endlessly subjected to by the white people who called themselves their masters. Vastey produced his *Le Système* precisely to counter such interpretations. Using armed violence against the system of death established by the colonists was a justified method for the enslaved to achieve freedom from slavery, which is to say salvation from suffering.

Violent and armed enslaved resistance on the plantation can only be understood within the context of the tortures and depredations of slavery. All else is excuse, obfuscation, and justification for white people torturing Black people. Arguments for nonviolent resistance in the age of slavery stemmed by turns from either outright ignorance of the conditions of slavery, blatant disregard for human suffering, and/or terrible indifference. "Colonialism is not a thinking machine, nor a body endowed with reasoning faculties," wrote Frantz Fanon in *The Wretched of the Earth*. "It is violence in its natural state, and it will only yield when confronted with greater violence."[45] Vastey awakened the ashes of the many victims that the white French colonists "sacrificed" and "slaughtered with [their] own hands," as if to prove this eternal truth. If the white colonists had the courage to confront the ghosts of the people they killed and tortured, then they could talk about "whether we have rights to the liberty and independence that we conquered at the price of our blood . . . !" Vastey exhorted.[46]

A colonist from the Artibonite named Dumontellier also used the highly popular form of the memoir, or personal essay, to unveil the crimes of the Desdunes family. What is important in this account, as told by Vastey, is how the colonists recognized that their own behavior deserved retribution to such an extent that their unconscious created the reality of slave vengeance they feared. "We are going to include here the extract that [Dumontellier] gave to us," Vastey wrote. "I would like my readers to please observe that this is a colonist who is speaking." The excerpt reveals that the elder Desdunes was haunted by the numerous Black people he sacrificed to his rageful imaginings: "He thought he saw everywhere and all the time those wandering shadows, sad fruits of his shameless ardor, inciting to vengeance their fathers, their brothers, their children, who still retained the memory of the torture of their relatives; and this terrible idea made him desire the apparatus of a protective force, capable of intimidating those wrathful slaves."[47] The brutal colonists brought their own worst nightmares to life—that the ancestors of the human beings they had killed after having forced them to live and labor in abjection would come back to haunt their torturers and eventually resurface from the tomb entirely. The white enslavers awakened the ashes themselves.

The enslaved Black people of Saint-Domingue suffered enormously from the dreadful imaginings of the white colonists. Welch, an inhabitant of Torbeck, together with his white manager, named Dehais, committed numerous crimes based on their fear that the people they were enslaving would one day seek revenge. Dehais complained often, in this regard, that Welch's *atelier* (enslaved people in workhouses) was given over to "magic and *sortilège* [spells]." Having lost one of the children he had out of wedlock, Dehais claimed that it was "the *macandals* of the *atelier*" who had committed the purported crime. "Welch and Dehais went to the spot, where the entire *atelier* was working on the hoe; unable to prove who or if anyone had killed Dehais's child, they coldly and indiscriminately chose twelve of those unfortunate men and women; they had the laborers dig . . . a large and deep pit, and then made them lower the twelve unfortunate victims into it and then forced them to kneel down; they started by throwing quicklime on them, and then afterwards the pit was filled with soil; thus, twelve human victims were buried alive, for an alleged crime."[48]

Vastey did not intend these accounts to be sensational, nor did he seek to be sentimental or gothic. The key to understanding Vastey's desire to unveil these histories is to see how he evoked these lives to justify the violence the enslaved used to achieve the independence of the very state (kingdom) to which Vastey belonged at the moment he composed *Le Système*. These descriptions proved that the definition of the "colonial system" was, as Vastey stated, "white domination" and "the massacre and enslavement of the blacks."[49] They also proved that the only viable response to the terrible system of death that is slavery was violent resistance. "Has any people ever had more right to independence than the Haitian people?" Vastey asked.[50] By naming the French planters and government officials involved in the "colonial system," Vastey produced them as real individuals rather than a faceless collective. In so doing, he showed clearly who were the victims and who were the perpetrators in an atmosphere where Haitians were regularly being described in the international press as brigands and villains out for white blood.[51] "If I were to hope for anything from you, at the very least I would like to make you tremble by unveiling your crimes," Vastey wrote. Further explaining the raison d'être for his exposé, Vastey said to the white French colonists directly that he hoped "by recording your names here," he could "doom them to contemporary and future scorn."[52]

In the twentieth century, the Holocaust incited Western European philosophers to question the place of fiction in a destructive and violent world of human torture. For example, Jean-Paul Sartre's musing on whether a depoliticized aesthetic could exist in *Qu'est-ce que la littérature?* (What is literature?, 1948) and Theodor Adorno's famous question about the ethics of creating art after Auschwitz when he wondered if in making art out of the Holocaust "something of its horror is removed."[53] For Haitians, their confrontation with French slavery, colonialism, and genocidal warfare incited similar questions. One hundred and fifty years before Adorno, Vastey wrote in *Le Système*: "It is not a novel that I am writing, it is an exposé of misfortunes, long sufferings and unheard of tortures."[54] As he went on to suggest, fiction might never be able to provide an adequate medium to describe the violence of colonial slavery: "Flowers and adornments suit those paintings of which man does not have to be ashamed," he wrote, "for such a somber subject, to sink into a cesspool of crimes, they are useless. I will do nothing but retell."[55] *Le Système* is more a collectively narrated chronicle of slavery than a slave narrative, which is ordinarily more novelistic like a *bildungsroman*. Vastey's choice not to compose this latter type of narrative of slavery is directly related to his philosophy of history. Even when Vastey used first-person pronouns, he made the choice not to tell his own story, with one notable exception. Without observing that he was speaking of his grandfather, Vastey told the tale of Pierre Dumas, an enslaver from Marmelade. Dumas tried to kill a sickly baby named Laurent, so the child's mother could return to the fields more quickly. Dumas's daughter, and Vastey's mother, Elisabeth "Mimi" Dumas prevented him from carrying out his murderous intentions in the name of profits.[56] "Oh, Mimi, virtuous and good, you are no longer with us! But you rejoice in the bosom of eternal beatitude, as compensation for your noble actions. Your friend here consecrates your name and your virtues, as a symbol of veneration and friendship for all kind and tender-hearted souls."[57] Vastey acknowledged the goodness of one family member, who stood in opposition to the system of death that is slavery, while exposing the crimes of another, who only sought to uphold it. Colonial Saint-Domingue was filled with such contradictions. Humanity existed alongside terrorism; and an enslaved person's own white family members could be their greatest torturer.

Like those Black writers who came before Vastey, such as Olaudah Equiano, and those who would come after, like Frederick Douglass and Harriet Jacobs, Vastey documented slavery to this extent with the goal of bringing attention to the many cruelties of the slave system. He wanted to indict the white French enslavers from Saint-Domingue, women and men, on a global scale for their crimes against humanity. By naming enslaved individuals and avoiding the tendency to make of them a nameless, faceless abstraction, "slaves," Vastey created a methodology capable of recognizing the humanity of individuals whom enslavers tried with all their might to divest of personhood. Even on those occasions where Vastey pointed to skin color and broad markers of identity, he almost always included the names of the people he

Slavery   63

described and t hose who tortured them. Dubuisson, inhabitant of Saint-Louis, whipped his "blacks" to death, and very often, he buried them alive, notably the "unfortunate Jean-Baptiste," Vastey wrote; Remoussin, a relative of the Desdunes f amily, "burned alive the unfortunate Nicole, wet-nurse to his children."[58] "There are not enough tears in the world to lament these horrors, and what tears we have are useless," Vastey concluded of the enslavers's many crimes.[59]

Since Ayitian resistance formed the basis for Haitian claims to independence through indigeneity, any account of slavery in French Saint-Domingue would be incomplete without a discussion of marronnage. *Petit marronnage* could be used for temporary flights of mind and short-lived fugitivity. *Grand marronnage*, in contrast, referred to running away with the intention of never returning. As responses to the pressures and tortures of the white colonists' atrocious behavi ors, both forms of marronnage were permanent fixtures i n the colony. "The unfortunate one who did not have the courage and the strength of spirit to support these cruel punishments, fled to the woods to avoid being tormented," Vastey wrote. "The barbaric master, furious to see his prey escape, pursued him there, which was the only asylum for a slave hoping to escape from tyranny." Whenever the enslaved developed new forms of marronnage, petit and grand, to resist slavery, the white colonists created new forms of organization to repress their resistance. The mission of the white French colonists of Saint-Domingue was to crush, destroy, or disappear any opposition to their domination. The colonists sought to eliminate g rand marronnage through the creation of the *maréchaussée*, "those famous hunters of men, who pursued and destroyed [the maroons] like carnivorous animals; the hunt was considered good when a dozen of t hose unfortunate people had been crushed."[60] Vastey supported this generalization with a decree from the Conseil of Cap, which granted to "five whites employed on the Carbon habitation, in the Bois de l'Anse, a sum of 1000 livres . . . f or having destroyed a band of maroon negroes, whose chiefs were the so-named Polydor and Joseph."[61] A 1789 letter from a ship captain in Cap-Français even more succinctly reveals how simultaneously valuable and expendable a slave life was to the white French colonists. Perhaps more importantly, the letter also indicates a diff erent relationship to the concept of life on the part of the enslaved. At times enslaved individuals preferred to turn grand marronnage into the eternal marronnage of death. "We have often butchered them," the author wrote, "but they recruit reinforcements easily."[62] Death in rebellion or in suicide was preferable for many enslaved people over a life lived under the tortures of slavery. This is, at the very least, the description of slave life supplied in the 1790 *Réflexions sur le code noir* (Reflections on the Code Noir), written collectively by members of the newly created abolitionist Société des Amis des

64 Chapter 2

Noirs (Society of the Friends of the Blacks). In this document, we learn that a white colonist named Mainguy was charged and convicted of having "beaten his slaves," "wounded them with scissors" and a machete. He also burned them with hot coals and irons. Taking his own life provided immediate deliverance for at least one of the men Mainguy was enslaving who could no longer "resist these agonies." A commonsense understanding of freedom as the liberty to move about and do as one pleased was consciously and repeatedly undermined in a world where "the spirit of freedom that is unfolding . . . only served to greater tighten the slaves' chains." To be human in such a world was suspect. The white authors of *Réflexions* lament, in the end, "we still perhaps fear being human."[63]

The colonial plantation was characterized by forms of sociality whereby death could be considered better than life and where bondage could be promoted as being preferable to freedom. "Is it any wonder if we resorted to suicide, to poisoning?" Vastey asked:

> And if our women extinguished in their hearts all the sweet feelings of motherhood, when with cruel pity they caused the deaths of the dear, sad fruits of their love? In fact, how do you support life when it has reached the final limits of degradation and misery? When you must die a thousand times in one life by undergoing the most cruel tortures, when you are reduced to this deplorable situation, without any hope of escaping from it; to want to go on living, would that not be the utmost symbol of cowardice? Oh, why give life to such unfortunate beings, whose entire existence would condemn them to lead a frail existence of torture and opprobrium in a long tissue of death without end; to extinguish such an odious life, was that such a great crime? it was compassion, humanity!!![64]

Vastey finished his punishing description of enslaved "life" by interrogating his imagined white interlocutors on this point. If the crimes the colonists imputed to the "blacks" who were in rebellion were so natural to *blackness*, why was it that since Haitian independence, when the *Blacks* had reclaimed their rights, and had at last rid the soil of Saint-Domingue of the "poisonous breath" (*souffle empoissoné*) of the enslavers, there were no longer any "suicides, nor poisonings, nor abortions; and that despite the bloody wars we were forced to undertake and our cruel misfortunes, our countryside swarms with brilliant youth?"[65] The Haitian Revolution transformed Saint-Domingue from what Michel- Rolph Trouillot called a "slave societ[y]"— because slavery de-fined the "economic, social and cultural organization" to such an extent that the "people who lived there, free or not, lived there because there were slaves"—to a living society.[66] The system of death, euphemistically called slavery, that

Slavery 65

existed on the island since the fifteenth century when the Spaniards instated colonialism, was bravely overthrown by the Haitian revolutionaries. They created a system of life with independence for Ayiti/Haïti in 1804.

Though his main object was to chronicle the horrors of slavery, Vastey was wholly attentive to the question of color prejudice (what we call racism today) and how white supremacy structured both the terribly violent regime of slavery that he so brazenly unfolded in *Le Système*, and the terrorism perpetrated by the white colonists against free people of color in its name. From the earliest days of their dis-settlement of the western third of Ayiti, the French used the maxim of what Vastey called "the supremacy of the white type, which is the palladium of our species" (*[la] suprématie de l'espèce blanche, qui est le palladium de notre espèce*) to support their genocidal "colonial system." White Europeans justified their enslavement of Black Africans in the name of whiteness. The colonists argued for and sought to protect the theory of white supremacy they created to support the economics of slavery by which they enriched themselves.[67] Let us not pass over in silence the fact that Vastey, Haiti's quintessential theorist of anti-colonialism, seems to have coined the phrase "white supremacy."

The first known known usage in English of the term "white supremacy" appears to be from 1824. In the *Oxford English Dictionary* T. S. Winn is credited with the first usage of the term in his *Emancipation: Or Practical Advice to British Slave-Holders: With Suggestions for the General Improvement of West India Affairs*: "It may be too late by any means, however wisely and honestly attempted, to reduce them to order and obedience under White supremacy, or even among themselves."[68] The next usage in English surfaced in 1839 with Henry Bevan's *Thirty Years in India*: "The security of our empire in the East would be greatly strengthened . . . if our functionaries would abandon, or at least conceal, those notions of White supremacy, which are frequently absurd, and always offensive."[69] The words appear even later in the French context, although the notion of "white supremacy" quite obviously already existed. The next usage in French after Vastey's seems to have been in an 1891 article titled, "La Question nègre aux Étas-Unis" (The Negro question in the United States) by Georges Pigeonneau. Under the guise of attempting to determine how the whites of the United States, and particularly, in the Southeast, were able to "keep the blacks in this subjection," even though they were vastly outnumbered by the latter, Pigeonneau exclaimed, "By what miracle, at last, could this illogical situation be indefinitely prolonged; or rather, what are the remedies to apply to it to prevent the disaster that will bring with it the ruin of white supremacy! [*la suprématie blanche*]."[70]

The term "white supremacy" was useful for Vastey to explain how the white French colonists, perpetuating another system of inequalities, like the kings

66   Chapter 2

of France back in the metropole, wanted to govern the colony not with the despotism of aristocracy, but racial hierarchy. "Those prideful beings lived in the midst of abundance and riches, leading a sensual and libidinous life," he wrote, "their days were passed in the heart of the most abominable prejudices that they themselves created": "Prejudice, barbaric genius! How powerful is your empire over the heart of man; it is you who leads him to disregard his brother, to hate him and to persecute him; it was you who was the soul and the motive of the ferocious colonists, when he exercised his cruelties on us; It was you who inspired him with this dreadful delirium, which led him at the same time to outrage the heavens and nature!"[71] These barbaric prejudices created an uncanny rapprochement between the enslaved and the free people of color, at least as far as Vastey was concerned: "We are now going to sketch the sad situation of those called, in these times of horror, impudently, the freed. We will not make any distinction between these so-called free people [and the slaves], because even if they didn't have distinct masters, the *white* public was their master, and by all counts, they suffered the same humiliations and the same infamies that the slaves did; we will consider them as such."[72] From the distance of the present, it is easy to question Vastey's comparison. It is also dangerous to completely dismiss it, based as it was on his own lived experiences. As usual, Vastey provided evidence, most of which he drew from the laws of the colony. He outlined the precise forms of violent prejudices (white supremacy) against the free people of color that reigned in the Saint-Domingue where he grew up.

Free people of color were prevented by various ordinances from dressing like the white colonists and from wearing certain hairstyles. According to a February 9, 1779 regulation, "The extreme luxury of the clothing and accessories by which the people of color, *ingénus* or *affranchis*, of both sexes indulge themselves, having also been brought to the attention of the magistrates, the public and our own, it has become necessary to temporarily put a brake on it."[73] Colonial administrators declared "this class of people" would be subject to the "protection of the king" only when they consented to remain within the bounds of "simplicity, decency, and respect." The decree urged the free people of color, therefore, to exercise the modesty "that many of them seem to have forgotten."[74] The first article of the regulation mandated that all the people of color, "ingénus or affranchis," of both sexes, observe the greatest respect for the whites, in general, including white women and children, "not just those who are their former masters." Breaching these regulations meant that the free people of color could be punished "according to the severity of the ordinances, by losing their liberty even, if the breach so merits." Let us pause for a moment to absorb this ridiculous proposition. A person of color not showing "respect" to a white person could be grounds for loss of liberty. The second article said the free people of color, in order to uphold the first article, had to dress in a manner to distinguish themselves from the whites. The third article decreed that they were forbidden from displaying any objects of "exterior luxuriousness" and, if they did, they could be imprisoned and have their possessions confiscated.[75] Vastey's biting sarcasm is never stronger than when he pointed out how these laws demonstrated the fragility of the white colonists' claims to racial superiority: "We can only read with pity the miserable ordinances written in this regard; we cannot help but to laugh today at these puerilities, which remain nonetheless great proof of the physical and moral inferiority of that species of men, of those colonists, who wanted to arrogate to themselves an alleged superiority over us."[76] Vastey further asserted that it was strange to glimpse how colonial officials seemed to have nothing better to do than to occupy themselves with "such frivolity," designed to satisfy the "unbraked passions of the colonists." There was irony and opportunity in the preoccupation of white people with asserting their superiority. "Without the vices of this administration, the revolution would never have taken place, and we would still be under the yoke of the colonists!" Vastey concluded. "Oh! Give thanks to their injustices, because it is that which brought us to break the chains of tyranny forever."[77]

The meaning of such an apostrophe is quite simple. Instead of "saving the colony" (which under the ancien régime in France meant the preservation of slavery) by instituting the reforms to the Code Noir contained in the edict of December 3, 1784, which were putatively designed by the French government to put a brake on slave punishments and other colonial abuses, these laws were trampled underfoot by the white colonists and the white administrators of the colony. Vastey believed the king's edict of 1784 was issued to repress the "unheard of cruelties that were committed on every habitation, from one extremity of the island to the other."[78] For, the edict opened with a statement from Louis XVI acknowledging the "abuses that have been introduced into the management of plantations in Saint-Domingue." Consequently, the edict required enslavers and their agents or overseers to record and report the number of deaths of enslaved people on their plantations while forbidding "all owners, agents, and overseers from treating their slaves inhumanely." The ordinance defined the inhumane treatment of an enslaved person as subjecting them to "more than fifty lashes of the whip," "beating them with a stick," "mutilating them," or "causing them to die in different ways." The law told on the colonists. There would have been no need for such prohibitions if such inhumanity were uncommon. The punishments for breaching these and other provisions were dramatic. An overseer found guilty of "excessive punishments, mutilation or murders," "nocturnal labors," and/or violating the "relief measures proscribed for pregnant negroes" would be declared "incapable of possessing slaves" and possibly even deported to France, or sentenced to death. Other punishments for "lesser" crimes involved the accused overseer or agent being "branded," not unlike the enslaved over whom they held power. Yet, instead of enforcing these laws, the white colonists at first ignored them and then delayed their approval for more than a year demanding and achieving various reforms from the French crown. In the subsequent 1785 ordinance, for example, enslaved individuals were required to show "respect and obedience" to those enslaving them, and failing this, overseers and enslavers were encouraged to punish them, especially in cases of "insubordination, neglect, relaxation of discipline and disobedience." The laws seem to have had the opposite effect. There are few records of any enslavers being punished for crimes against the people they enslaved, and no known records of an enslaver or overseer receiving capital punishment for abuses against people they enslaved.[79] "Such were the government, the mores and the character of the ex-colonists of Saint-Domingue before the revolution of 1789," Vastey concluded. "Any impartial man will be able to form a just idea of those dreadful times and of the deplorable situation in which we were plunged."[80] Vastey could only end his long recitation of human beings being tortured by other human beings with a profound sigh: "Prejudice! Barbaric genius! How your empire is powerful over the heart of man."[81]

The ideology of white supremacy structured life in colonial Ayiti and Spanish Hispaniola, as much as it did in French Saint-Domingue. The prejudices experienced by the free people of color, like slavery's tortures, had everything to do with how the French lost their most prized colony, which is to say how the system of death called slavery was destroyed by the Haitian revolutionaries to produce a system of life called independence. The legal framework the colonists instituted to support slavery has a distinct relationship to the color prejudices those same colonists conjured to justify excluding free men of color from citizenship. The perpetration of those prejudices by the French colonists ultimately encouraged the Indigenous army to strike not just for freedom but for independence. To unfold this history, we must consult a different set of laws from the ones Vastey placed in our purview—those emanating from revolutionary France—and we must let ourselves be guided by another brave pamphleteer, Julien Raimond. Although Raimond was an avowed anti-racist, he was certainly not an anti-colonialist, nor even at first an abolitionist. Yet he will find himself as a principal, and at times unwitting actor, in the events that eventually turned the Haitian Revolution against slavery, racism, and colonialism into a war of independence.

Slavery   69

Chapter 3

Prejudice

The French introduced the practice of kidnapping and enslaving Africans in territories they claimed under Louis XIII in the seventeenth century. But Dumesle believed "Louis XIII established slavery solely with a view to converting Africans and their descendants to Christianity." Rather than absolving the French king of blame, this fact indicted him. According to Dumesle, religion was simply one of the many illogics that white colonists and their home governments used to justify slavery. "But I ask all those who have the slightest knowledge of the heart of man, was this the way to make these new converts cherish worship? No; this means was more likely to make them hate it, to cause them to degenerate into superstition."[1] The Code Noir, issued under Louis XIV first as the edict of 1685, was meant to regulate France's growing slave system in the Americas, but enabled enslavers to practice some of the cruelest tortures to be found anywhere in the Atlantic World. The code also added to the religious illogics of slavery by mandating the expulsion of Jewish people from the colonies. But one of the code's sixty articles encouraged white men to marry African women and convert them to Catholicism, by which the Black woman would be "freed" from slavery. The result was that a large intermediary class of free people of color, almost as numerous as the white French colonists, rose up alongside the plantations.[2] Raimond provided historical context for the law to show that it was more ancient than the French colony itself (the Treaty of Ryswick not having been signed until 1697): "Louis XIV, in his edict of 1685, ordered a master to marry his slave, if he had children with her, and if he was not already married."[3] Later, Articles 56, 57, 58, and 59, of the revised and renamed Code Noir, also gave free people of color, no matter how or when they were "freed," equal rights with white Europeans, "granting to freedmen (*affranchis*) the same rights, privileges and immunities enjoyed by persons born free."[4] The status of these free(d) people, children of white men and Black women, transformed Saint-Domingue rapidly into a colony that had a nearly equal proportion of white people to free people of color. Initially, in Raimond's estimation, this had not posed a problem for the white inhabitants. Raimond insisted that color prejudice did not structure white relations with free people of color in the earliest days of French dis-settlement.

In 1703, a mere six years after Spain ceded the western third of the island to France with the Treaty of Ryswick, color prejudice did not exist in the colony, Raimond argued, and for this reason there were hardly any free people of color listed as such in the civil registers. When white men married women of color the notary did not mention the person's *racial* category, or color. Instead, all the free people of color were counted among the whites, which is why there can be found only about 150 people specifically listed as being "of color" in the earliest years of French "settlement" on the island.[5] At the time Raimond published his 1791 *Observations sur l'origine et les progrès du préjugé des colons blancs contre les hommes de couleur* (Observations on the origin and spread of the prejudices of the white colonists against the men of color) there were not even two hundred free men of color who had been enslaved at birth. In contrast there were nearly forty thousand free "citizens" of color. By asserting these statements as facts, Raimond was drawing what he considered to be an important distinction between the affranchis and the citizens of color. The affranchis were enslaved at some point and only later gained free status. Raimond explained in a later work, therefore, that the word affranchis referred to "a man who was a slave and then was freed," and, more specifically, the term designated "one who was born a slave, who lived as a slave, who was treated like a slave, brought up to remain a slave, and then was freed."[6] This ends up being crucial information for Raimond to include. His goal was to establish how it was that color prejudices, specifically, rather than enslaved or free status, came to structure life in the colony, on the one hand, and exploded into revolution, on the other.

It is easy to see now the blatant flaw in Raimond's thinking. Color prejudice always structured life in Saint-Domingue, from the moment the French stepped foot on the island's shores, just as it had on those parts of the island under Spanish rule. Only Black people, those classified as "nègre" or "noir" in some way, even by tiny degrees, were taken captive from Africa and sent to the colonies for the purposes of chattel, that is, hereditary slavery. It was the edict of 1685 that made slave status heritable through maternal lineage: "Article XIII . . . if a male slave has married a free woman, their children, either male or female, shall be free as is their mother, regardless of their father's condition of slavery. And if the father is free and the mother a slave, the children shall also be slaves."[7] It took Raimond some time to confront this realization. We shall follow him on his journey. Raimond's transformation from antiracist activist to antislavery advocate has everything to teach us about how independence from France went from being the goal of the white colonists to the raison d'être of the Black revolutionaries.

The edict of 1685 and later the Code Noir provided a path to freedom for a small number of captive African women in the early days of French control of the colony, but it did not eliminate the tyranny of rampant color prejudice and the violence of slavery. Only revolution would do that. The best person to explain to us how the prejudices against the free people of color—which were, in the end, the same prejudices that undergirded slavery and that destroyed the first Ayitians—seasoned Saint-Domingue for revolution is undoubtedly Julien Raimond, self-described *homme de couleur*, an "American colonist," and one of the richest planters (enslavers) in the French colony of Saint-Domingue.[8]

Raimond signed his first published pamphlet, *Observations adressées à l'Assemblée nationale, par un député des colons Amériquains* (Observations addressed to the National Assembly, by a deputy of the American colonists, 1789), using the moniker "An American colonist." Raimond defined American colonists, in contrast with white French colonists, as "free citizens of color" who owned property and who were born in the colony.[9] Raimond published this pamphlet to explain that the ongoing struggle between the French colonists and the "American colonists" was over how the rights of man, adopted in France in 1789, would be instituted in Saint-Domingue. Raimond's argument for the rights of the "American colonists" rested on what he styled as their singular claim to indigeneity. Though Raimond did not here use the so-called Indigenous status of the free people of color to argue for independence—quite the contrary, in fact—this claim eventually helped to support that outcome in 1804. "We were born in America, we have possessions here, therefore, we can and we must call ourselves American Colonists," Raimond wrote. Then, referring to the white French colonists' attempt to dispossess them of what Raimond implied was a kind of birthright citizenship, he asked, "Would they like still, after having robbed us of the sacred rights of man, to rob us even of the faculty of saying for ourselves which country gave birth to us?"[10] In nearly all his writings from 1789 forward Raimond sought to expose how racism, called color prejudice by him, undergirded the conflict between the two sets of colonists in Saint-Domingue. During the time of the French Revolution this conflict erupted over the meaning of the word "man," as well as defining those included in the category of "persons."

Julien Raimond, or Raymond, was born in October 1744 in the parish of Baynet in southern Saint-Domingue.[11] His father was a white Frenchman named Pierre Raymond from Gascogne, but his mother was a free woman of color named Marie Begasse.[12] She was considered a "fille légitime," or daughter of color born in wedlock, whose parents both enjoyed free status and were legally married at the time of her birth. Because of this genealogy, Raimond repeatedly rejected both the label "affranchis" and "mulâtre," insisting on their inaccuracy to describe him, since he was the "legitimate son and grandson of European fathers who were property owners in Saint-Domingue."[13] While not mentioning his mother in his remonstrations, Raimond claimed that since neither he nor any of his immediate family members were ever enslaved it was

72   Chapter 3

incorrect to refer to the family as "freed," per the term affranchis.[14] Yet, one of Raymond's female relatives must have been a captive African at some point. The only reason that Africans were taken to Saint-Domingue by Europeans was for slavery. Not having been enslaved himself, but nonetheless related and/or linked by marriage to enslaved African women, the Raimond family were, in the era of Julien Raimond's voluminous pamphleteering, also enslavers.[15] Like many free men of color, Raimond used his elite status, and ostensibly the money his family earned from enslaving others, to eventually go to France in 1784. He was still living there, in the city of Angoulême, at the time of the French Revolution of 1789.[16]

The 1789 Declaration of the Rights of Man and the Citizen at first thrilled Raimond. One of the reasons he moved to France was because of the increasing color prejudices he experienced in the colony, experiences that led him to develop a distinct theory about the relationship between color prejudice and the incoherence of the French Revolution. The Declaration of the Rights of Man, with its storied designation of the "natural and imprescriptible rights of man" to be "liberty, property, security, and resistance to oppression," gave Raimond reason to hope that things would change in Saint-Domingue. Raimond soon learned that the white colonists, aided by similarly racist agitators in the metropole, were willing to sacrifice everything at the pillar of the illogic of whiteness. They would stop at nothing to preserve what Vastey called the "atrocious privilege of being able to oppress a huge portion of humankind."[17]

According to Raimond, there were three key phases necessary for understanding how the French dis-settled Saint-Domingue for the purposes of slavery, and then used color prejudices to preserve it. In the first phase, there were few European women in the colony.[18] The white men therefore took up with African women, in concert with the provisions of the edict of 1685.[19] When white women started to come to Saint-Domingue several decades later, the second age began.[20] Raimond insisted, nevertheless, that there was still no color prejudice against the free people of color in the colony at that point. "There was no dishonor in seeing them, socializing with them, living with them, making alliances with their daughters, and men of color were even given [military] commissions."[21] It was toward the middle of the third age of the colony that color prejudices emerged. When white women began to come to Saint-Domingue with their daughters, they eventually sought to find rich white husbands for them. The white women often ended up being frustrated, because having little money themselves, the white colonists preferred to marry wealthy girls of color, "who brought dowries of land and slaves, which [the white men] claimed." "These preferences began to make white women jealous," Raimond said. These jealousies transformed into hatred and outright rage in the third age. "We saw at this time many young people . . . and a large number of the sons of nobles who passed through the colonies, marrying girls of color, whose parents had become wealthy," he continued.[22] Also during this epoch, the free men of color, many of whom were sent to France to be educated, came back to the colony and, suddenly, they could rival for the affections of the white women, occasioning the jealousy of white men, too. "They were reproached for their origins, because they could not be reproached for anything else," Raimond charged. The free people of color kept growing at the expense of the white population because so many white men preferred to live with Black women, either in legitimate marriage or in concubinage, rather than to marry white women.[23] "The talents, grace, and knowledge of these young people of color, was the cause of the aspersion that would eventually be cast upon them by the whites," concluded Raimond.[24]

To humiliate the free people of color, the white colonists used the favorite tactic of white supremacists: the law. The white French colonists created racist laws solely for the purpose of rationalizing their scornful behavior toward the *gens de couleur libres*. While free men of color previously enjoyed freedom of professions, suddenly, in 1773, they were prevented from practicing medicine, and it even became illegal for women of color to engage in midwifery.[25] On June 24, 1773, the French colonial government passed a decree that forbade free people of color from using the names of their white fathers, from dressing like whites (including wearing shoes in some instances), and from occupying any public function or profession such as priest, schoolteacher, surgeon, pharmacist, or doctor.[26] Furthermore, existing French colonial laws meant it was legally possible for a white person to commit a crime against a free person of color without any real punishment; other laws obliged free people of color to participate in *corvées* or forced labor. Years earlier, in 1769, a law was passed to forbid free men of color from serving as ranked officers in the military and, in March 1780, Saint-Domingue's acting governor, Jean-François Reynaud de Villevert, ordered the creation of the Chasseurs Royaux, a militia based on forced conscription of all men of color who had reached the age of majority or who could not present proper manumission papers.[27] Thus it was that the free people of color found themselves put fully into the service of not only the crime of slavery, but the ideology of whiteness.

These laws and their new applications, as reactions to the ascension to economic power of many wealthy free people of color in the middle part of the eighteenth century, sanctioned color prejudice and denied the rights that Louis XIV's 1685 edict granted to the affranchis. The original edict governing the status of the first enslaved Africans granted freedom through marriage with whites—who must therefore be understood to be the originators of essentially all Saint-Domingue's *gens de couleur libres*—and indicated that all free people, regardless of skin color had the same rights: "Article LIX. We grant to freed slaves the same rights, privileges and immunities that are enjoyed by freeborn persons. We desire that they are deserving of this acquired freedom, and that this freedom gives them, as much for their person as for their prop-erty, the same happiness that natural liberty has on our other subjects."[28]

Raimond documented how things changed. To avoid repressions and as-persions on their character, many of the white men began to abandon the f ree women of color who gave birth to their children in order to marry white women. In an effort to give their *mixed- race* children more legitimacy, some of them even took the children they had with women of color to met-ropolitan France.[29] The Martinican jurist and naturalist Médéric Louis-Élie Moreau de Saint-Méry was one such white colonist. He lived in a domestic partnership with a free woman of color named Marie-Louise Laplaine until 1778. In 1781, however, Moreau de Saint-Méry married Catherine Milhet, the white daughter of a Louisiana infantry captain. Moreau de Saint-Méry then became the l egal guardian over his daughter with Laplaine, Aménaïde, de-scribed as a "quadroon" in her parents' separation papers. Aménaïde was af-terward taken by her f ather to Paris where she was educated and raised by him and Milhet as a white woman.[30]

The entanglements of family structure with color politics and racial prej-udices had disastrous legal effects on those free people of color who remained in the colony. Anticipating Vastey's description, Raimond cited the numerous draconian laws that reigned. "It was then that the jealousy of whites against people of color was put on display with a fury without example," Raimond wrote. "We saw a host of ordinances published one after the other, each an attempt to outdo the previous one in tyranny, as much as in absurdity. Some of them forbade people of color to use a wheeled carriage; others forbade them to dress in the manner of whites, and to wear the same clothing, or to wear jewelry at all." For Raimond these last ordinances were both impolitic and impractical since they hurt the commerce of white people engaged in those industries, "but jealousy respects nothing and slits its own throat."[31] What Raimond called "jealousy" was actually the illogic of racist white settlers: forbade the registration of titles of nobility for white men who had married women of color; others argued against allowing people of color to go to France; even their children were forbidden from being sent there for education; others declared that those who married women of color had fallen from the rank of whites; still more enjoined the notaries and priests to write the word *libre* on the acts they recorded for people of color to remind them, they said, of their [African] origin, however remote it was; others sought to force them to abandon their European names and to take ones from the African idiom.[32]

There you have it. The fiction of whiteness laid bare in the law. In a world of slavery, what never existed, in fact—whiteness—could still be taken away, in practice.

On August 12, 1789, over a dozen white Saint-Dominguan colonists, who were in Paris at the time, signed a damning letter that Raimond says alone was responsible for the violence that ensued that year in Saint-Domingue.[33] Before we turn to this most consequential of letters, let us acknowledge that, for Raimond, each of the colonial laws passed after the revolution began in 1789, which he said sanctioned the draconian and abusive treatment of both the enslaved and the free people of color, had origins in revolutionary France, the supposed cradle of liberty and the rights of man. Revolutionary France was incoherent, and it is Raimond who was best positioned to show us how it became so. The confusion of principles contained in the Declaration of the Rights of Man, which did not pronounce on the condition of the enslaved Africans, nor on that of the free people of color—thus, permitting prejudice and oppression to exist right alongside declarations of liberty and equality— led to the creation of an incoherent French republic incapable of standing up to the racism of the colonists. This lasting and longitudinal incoherence, which persists in today's France, was summed up by Raimond's later admonition of the French National Assembly. Referring to the white French colonists' assertion that anyone with enslaved ancestry should only possess qualified liberty, Raimond wrote, "It is an atrocity to want to exercise such feudalism over men, when feudalism over inanimate things is revolting to every French person, and the very idea makes them shudder with horror; and it could only be proposed by one of those hard and fiscal-type souls, who breathe tyranny, while speaking of freedom."[34] We shall now follow Raimond to revolutionary France to see how in one breath the French exclaimed, "liberty, equality, fraternity," while in another they sought to ensure that these principles would never be applied to any subjects not considered to be "white." "Will the National Assembly be less just than a despot?" Raimond asked, referring to the French king's 1685 edict and its allowance of marriage between whites and Blacks, and therefore freedom and equal rights, at least in theory.[35]

In 1789, the French king, Louis XVI, invited the people of France to submit their grievances at a formal meeting of the Estates-General. Free men of color from the French colonies were prevented by angry planters (enslavers) from assembling with the white representatives from the colony, from attending the Estates-General, and from contributing to the *Cahiers des*

76   Chapter 3

doléances (Notebooks of grievances), which were presented to the French king in the hopes of encouraging necessary reforms. White colonists like Moreau de Saint-Méry gave spurious reasons, as if racism could ever be legally justified, for the lack of representation of the *gens de couleur libres*. The free men of color were a small and insignificant class of people who did not contribute monetarily to the colony, the white colonists argued. Raimond refuted this by observing that the "men of color" were not numerically inferior to the white colonists, nor were they socially, intellectually, or economically inferior. It was precisely because their numbers equaled that of the white colonists, if they did not surpass them entirely, that Raimond argued that the men of color needed to have their own representative at the National Assembly, recently formed in France to replace the Estates-General. "The white colonists have a deputation because of their numbers and their property. The American colonists, or the free citizens of color, must also have one as free citizens, owners and taxpayers; and an even greater reason is that all the free citizens of color belong to the land itself, by virtue of the fact that they were born there."[36] The free people of color repeatedly tied this kind of claim to Indigenous status to their demands for equal rights with the white colonists.

Under Raimond's guidance one hundred men of color from the colonies living in France convoked at the home of a French lawyer, Étienne de Joly, to compile their complaints.[37] The white French colonists later used the mere fact of this convocation as an excuse to further white prejudices and encourage violence against the free men of color. The white French colonists insisted that the gathering was evidence of a conspiracy underfoot. Prior to that, on August 12, 1789, a group of white colonists from Saint-Domingue in Paris issued their infamous letter, whereby they preemptively justified the violence and aggression that would soon be experienced by free people of color in Martinique, as Raimond lamented, and by hundreds of families of color in Saint-Domingue. The letter spoke of internal and external threats to the colony, the former being that the free people of color "seek to raise up our slaves." The white colonists painted themselves, because they were enslavers, as the victims of a freedom movement in France that could only end in the elimination of their livelihoods; that is, slavery. "We see it, and we are forced to remain silent: everyone is drunk on liberty. Men, a society of enthusiasts, who have taken the title of *Friends of the Blacks*, overtly write against us," the infamous August 1789 letter reads. "They are watching for the moment to become favorable for them to cause an explosion against slavery; it will perhaps suffice that we have the misfortune of even pronouncing the word, for them to seize the occasion to demand the emancipation of the negroes." The Haitian Revolution was not entirely unthinkable at this moment. The white colonists seemed to know it was coming. Perhaps they even already believed that it was inevitable. Yet, at the same time, they clearly thought that when revolution arrived in Saint-Domingue it would come from the free people of color, not the enslaved population. The white colonists as a whole rarely wavered from this assertion until it was too late. "We must warn you, the peril is great, it is coming soon," the letter reads. "*Let us not awaken the enemy.* Watch out, again, watch out; because the National Assembly is too preoccupied with the interior affairs of the kingdom to be capable of thinking about us. We are warning Americans from all sides to fly to the defense of their country."[38] The letter was not just fearmongering for the sake of casting further disdain on the free men of color; it actually asked the white colonists to take specific and determined *legal* action against them:

> Let us arrest suspicious people, let us seize any writings where the word liberty is even pronounced; redouble the watch of your plantations, in the towns, in the boroughs; *we must everywhere tie up all the free people of color*; beware of those coming to you from Europe. It is one of the greatest misfortunes that we were not able, in such a critical circumstance, to prevent the embarkation of the people of color who were in France . . . to prevent, at our very request, the embarkation of the slaves would be regarded as an act of violence denounced to the nation.[39]

The white French colonists back in the colony responded to the exhortations in the letter in murderous fashion. Raimond said the principle warning white Saint-Dominguans to "beware" of free people of color arriving from Europe was the cause of the first massacres in Saint-Domingue.[40] On November 15, 1789, the white colonists formed an assembly in Petit-Goâve to name electors to the provincial assemblies. In October of the same year, the free people of color had, with a petition, asked for the right to be able to join the colonial assemblies. A sympathetic white official, a seneschal from France named Ferrand de Baudière, printed the petition. Someone from the group of white colonists who knew the contents of the August 12 letter, "letting themselves be drawn into suspicion, spoke publicly against the free people of color, saying a plot had been formed by them and that the men of color wanted to revolt."[41] Five of the men of color were seized for having presented the petition. As they were questioned, they revealed that Ferrand de Baudière had transcribed the document. The men evidently outed Ferrand to defend themselves against the charge they sought to foment rebellion, arguing that because Ferrand was a white man he could not be suspected of participating in any supposed plot against the whites.[42] Still, the white colonists, without having obtained any official judgment against him, captured Ferrand de Baudière and cut off his head and put it on a pike. Afterward they paraded Ferrand de

78   Chapter 3

Baudière's head around the city as a warning. The white colonists then went into the neighboring parishes of Aquin and Jacmel and spread alarm throughout by showing excerpts of the fatal August 12 letter, which they used to argue that general scorn should be directed toward any man of color recently arrived from Europe.[43]

The colonists further spread a rumor that a large number of free people of color newly arrived in Saint-Domingue from France were hiding in the woods, like maroons. Unfounded fears and general alarm resulted from these rumors. More consequentially, the white planters used these allegations to encourage one another to arm themselves against the men of color. Anyone who objected was shamed into agreeing to go along with the plan to use viol ence to cow the *hommes de couleur* into submission. "Many of the inhabitants, honest plantation owners, truly objected that the plot was absurd and without foundation; they themselves were threatened, and were forced, by this class of vagrants (so considerable in the colonies) to withdraw."[44] Twenty-five white men from the quartier of Aquin subsequently "ransacked three of the dwellings of the richest men of color during the night. Two of the owners, my brother and Mr. Boisrond," Raimond wrote, "were absent from their homes; because they had been elected to go to the Cayes committee," where they were invited by the whites to putatively discuss their "common interests." In their absence, "their houses were pillaged by these brigands and their papers stolen. The whites purported to believe they would find evidence of the conspiracy in them," Raimond complained.[45]

Among the papers those "brigands" confiscated was a letter from a M. de Jarnac, written from his property in Jarnac to Raimond's brother, dated from the month of June 1789. Jarnac had asked Raimond's brother for a "memoir" or essay, which Julien Raimond wrote and sent to his brother from Angoulême, where the latter had been living. This was enough for the "brigands" to argue that M. de Jarnac was an "activist, [*philantrope*] friend of the blacks." There was also a letter from César Henri Guillaume de la Luzerne (comte de) to Raimond's brother asking to be informed about the contents of the essay that Julien Raimond sent to Charles Eugène Gabriel de la Croix, the marquis de Castries, and that the latter sent on to M. de la Luzerne, the former govenor-general of Saint- Domingue.[46] Taken together, the white colonists used these letters as evidence to arrest Raimond's brother for his supposed crimes. Soon after, Raimond's brother was sentenced to death.[47]

Raimond's brother was, in the end, protected by the Comité des Cayes, who appreciated the postscriptum in the August 12 letter, written by Gérard, deputy of that part of the colony.[48] Gérard, the only white colonial deputy to listen to the men of color, in Raimond's estimation, tried to mitigate the possible effect of t he A ugust 12 l etter w ith t his c ounsel: "It i s p oss ib le, a nd e ven probable, that the alarming rumors which have been spread, and which are the subject of this letter, are not founded; and in that case it would be unfortunate if it caused too much of a sensation in the colonies, which regardless of the fears it would inspire, could perhaps give rise to even more real dangers."[49] In the rest of the postscriptum Gérard counseled the whites to utilize circumspection and to keep their eyes open, less to ensure that the men of color would not rebel, but to ensure that the colonists did not end up allowing irrational fears to overwhelm them. Because Gérard was a white property owner from Saint-Domingue with a big plantation who had lived in the colony for thirty years, Raimond considered his words to be irreproachable and unimpeachable. Gérard also counseled that the *hommes de couleur* needed to be treated more humanely since they were the best avenue to maintaining the safety and security of the colony, which meant the preservation of slavery.[50] Raimond interjected after reprinting this part of the August 12 letter to say that far from having adhered to this sage council, the colonists took actions leading in the complete opposite direction.[51]

Soon after the letter was published, M. Labadie, a seventy-year-old man of color, and a plantation owner responsible for enslaving more than 150 individuals, was assailed by the white colonists in his home at midnight while he was sleeping: "The doors of the house were broken open with an axe, 25 shots were fired at him, at pretty close range; three of them hit him; another killed a young negro, his servant. They seized him, mistreated him, they led him to the village, three leagues from his home; they wanted to cut off his head; the other plantation owners could do nothing but groan about such behaviors."[52] About twenty people of color rushed to ask for M. Labadie's release, and his freedom was subsequently granted. After recounting more of these horrors in bullet points, Raimond argued that it was evident that the men of color did not deserve these atrocious persecutions; and he furthermore insisted that these violent outbursts were caused by the excessive slanders contained in the infamous letter of August 12, which had quickly circulated through the island. Raimond concluded with his repeated assertion: because of that letter, the French colonists alone were to be considered responsible for any resulting violence that might subsequently occur and "should be held in contempt for what happened to the unfortunate Ferrand."[53]

An apostrophe to Ferrand written by another of our intrepid pamphleteers, a free man of color named André Rigaud, later a French general, punctuates the now lost revolutionary *caché* that the name Ferrand de Baudière carried with it in the colony in 1789. After recalling that the free men of color were treated like "criminals and scoundrels," Rigaud said they were indiscriminately arrested while scaffolds were prepared for their execution. "The head of a friend of mankind has fallen," Rigaud lamented. "Oh, Ferrand de

Baudière! Time will never destroy your memory and your honorable name will live on forever."[54] Yet, it was not the name of Ferrand de Baudière, nor that of M. Labadie, which lived on in popular memory of the earliest days of the revolution. Instead, it was the name of Vincent Ogé, a free man of color from Dondon executed by the French colonial government in February 1791. The name Ogé resounded across Saint-Domingue and across the Atlantic Ocean to France. Ogé's death turned out to hold more significance in Haitian thought than his rebellion.

The white colonists' next move was to attempt to prevent all communication between men of color in France, like Ogé—who had appeared in Paris to testify before the Club Massiac, pleading the case of gradual emancipation, along with rights for free men of color only—and those back in Saint-Domingue. The white colonists insisted in a letter to the Chambers of Royal Commerce that people of color in France should be forbidden from returning to Saint-Domingue, lest they spark insurrection once home. Raimond cataloged the letter in his pamphlet under the title "Lettre aux chambres du commerce par les deputés des colonies" (Letter to the chambers of commerce by the deputies of the colonies). It reads: "As the security of Saint-Domingue requires that we take all possible precautions at this time to stop the disorder with which this island is threatened, we urge you to use all the means in your power to prevent all negroes and all mulattoes from embarking for the colony."[55] It is in this context of augmenting fears about free people of color, and amid attempts to repress their freedoms, that the March 8 and March 28, 1790, decrees emerged from the National Assembly. Far from clarifying the citizenship status of free men of color, the decrees led to more conflict, owing to their ambiguous resolutions that made no mention of the plight of the free people of color, and over whose implementation Ogé would be destroyed. The law ratified by the National Assembly of France on March 28, 1790, declared that "all free persons, property-owning or established for two years and paying taxes, will enjoy the voting rights that constitute active citizenship."[56] This was a compromise. An earlier version of the law spoke of "free citizens," rather than "free persons." Raimond had objected to the draft law, because he knew that the French colonists would not accept this language, since it did not specifically mention the free men of color as having the rights of "active citizenship." The original version of "Article 4 of these instructions, which laid down the qualities necessary for one to be considered an active citizen in the colonies was so vague that it could only give rise to endless quarrels between the two classes of free citizens," Raimond said. Anticipating the objections of the white French colonists, the men of color sued to Antoine Barnave, one of the most influential members of the National Assembly, to explain that it was essential to designate much more clearly in Article 4 that it covered

Prejudice   81

the people of color, "either by adding to the vague word citizen, the word free, or, that which would have been even clearer, any citizen whatever his color." The Assembly responded to this demand by observing that it did not recognize any distinction between citizens of France and "could not use terms that indicated it recognized them." "After having discussed it for a long time," Raimond explained that in the final language of the law, "we obtained from M. Barnave assurance that he would substitute for the word citizen in Article 4, the words all persons."[57] The origin of France's claims to color neutrality with respect to all its "citizens" resides in these laws, which is to say of March 8 and March 28.

Raimond only reluctantly accepted the argument that equal rights of citizenship for men of color were covered by the phrase "toute personne," or all persons. Raimond knew that the illogic of racism required acknowledging particularity as a first step toward legislating equality. If the men of color were not considered to be "people" by the white French colonists, then phrases like "all persons" could be used by the white colonists to continue to exclude those without "white" status. French universalisms, as set out in the 1789 Declaration of the Rights of Man, could not help either. These propositions were not designed to protect Black people, but in fact formed the basis of revolutionary France's argument to keep enslaving them, since enslaved Africans were not considered by the French to be *hommes* or "men." A precedent for this type of obfuscatory wording was set by the language of the U.S. Constitution, with its insistence that, without even using the word "slave," "all other Persons" would only be considered "three-fifths" of a person. Personhood, the very same language upon which slavery rested in the U.S. Constitution was as problematic in Saint-Domingue and France as it has been for the United States.[58]

Even though free men of color were not allowed to represent themselves at the Estates-General, at the urging and insistence of Raimond, who had appointed himself the spokesperson of the free men of color in Paris, in March 1790 the *hommes de couleur* did gain a Pyrrhic victory. They succeeded in getting the newly formed National Assembly to decree that the provisions of the Declaration of the Rights of Man and the new constitution did apply to the *gens de couleur libres*, under the provision "all persons." However, Raimond's suspicions were correct. The white colonists, indeed, did not accept this law and seemed to lose their minds at the very suggestion that the men of color might have equal rights with them. The white colonists obstinately maintained that the *hommes de couleur* were not covered under the provision of the words "toute personne," or "all persons." They were opposed to any resolution that would give even meager rights of citizenship (even when generically phrased as rights of "personhood") to people of color.

82   Chapter 3

Following the debates over personhood that directly resulted from the National Assembly's laws puts into bare relief the racist origins and "pretzel logic" of contemporary French universalisms, also referred to as its "color-blind" ideology, whereby the republic "does not acknowledge racial, religious, or ethnic identification," and therefore "racism cannot exist."[59] Responding to the white colonists' opposition, Raimond pointed out that Article 4's instructions did not textually exclude the "men of color from the rights of citizenship, and as a necessary consequence they had to be understood as covered under the denomination of *toute personne*."[60] White colonial deputies disagreed and outright claimed that the words "toute personne" were meant for whites only and that the assembly had not intended, with these "generic" words, for this appellation to include the people of color.[61] As a result, the primary assemblies in the colony were formed without the participation of the more than twenty thousand eligible men of color. This exclusion reigned, despite that in many parishes of the colony, the free men of color were the richest *personnes*.[62] What resulted from that first Colonial Assembly was more violence, and the birth of an independence movement on the part of the white colonists, which was wholly white supremacist in nature.

Although the March 1790 decree was not quite as clear-cut as the free men of color would have liked, it did leave the door open for the "American colonists," qua Raimond, to promote the law as legislating rights for them. It was true that French lawmakers in Paris declared that there would be no separate laws pertaining to the free people of color. According to Raimond, all the newspapers in France understood the men of color to be included in Article 4's granting of equal rights of representation to all "persons" of France. Vincent Ogé agreed. Almost immediately after the publication of the law, he attempted to travel back to the colony to try to ensure its proper implementation. Prevented by the French government from returning directly to Saint-Domingue, Ogé first went to Charleston, South Carolina, a major node in the transatlantic slave trade, before successfully landing on Saint-Domingue where he addressed himself to the other men of color. He hoped to enjoin them to his cause of forcing the white colonists to publicly acknowledge the rights of the free men of color.[63] "I must say that when the ardent Ogé deposited in their bosom the resentments of his ulcerated soul, they, like me, never ceased to exhort him to moderate his feelings," Raimond reported. "They told him that the time would come when the artifices of the whites would be unmasked, when the National Assembly would recognize the need to render complete justice to the mulattoes."[64] Raimond preferred to go the route of petitions rather than revolution. He counseled Ogé to therefore remain patient and to gather as many signatures as possible, saying that this should be the primary goal of his mission.

Ogé had distinctly personal motivations for dismissing Raimond's counsel and seeking to rebel against white colonial authority. First, there was the horrific violence following the August 12 letter; second, Ogé also had correspondence from the white colonial deputies mentioning in at least ten different places that the white colonists needed to be on guard and to "defy Ogé, [or] arrest and lock up Ogé."[65] Ogé had family reasons for rebelling as well. His brother was assassinated by one of the men he was enslaving, who had been promised his liberty by the white colonists for accomplishing this task.[66]

Ogé's first move upon returning to the colony was to ask the colonial powers to execute the March 1790 decree of the National Assembly. The white French colonists responded to his demand with a similar proscription to the one used against his brother: they put a bounty on Ogé's head and promised "liberty and a considerable sum" to any enslaved person who would bring it to them. The colonists also sent troops to find and capture Ogé, while arming enslaved individuals and entreating them to fight against the free men of color. "Every day saw more of their [the free men of color] heads fall, which were carried to Cap by the slaves who slaughtered them, to obtain the rewards that were promised to them," Raimond claimed.[67] The colonists' suspicions about Ogé were not entirely unfounded. In October 1790 Ogé rebelled with a few hundred men of color, but with what contemporary historians and eyewitnesses alike acknowledge were only ambiguous intentions and method.[68] Émile Nau painted Ogé and Jean-Baptiste Chavannes as only having reluctantly resorted to violence, for example. "They had faith in the force of the law and not in the right of force," Nau wrote.[69] Vastey recalled that Ogé had actually saved the notorious enslaver and infamous white French colonist François Mazères's life, a claim he based on a recitation of the event provided by Mazères himself.[70] Ambiguous intentions did not matter much to the colonists when they prescribed and inflicted the punishments to be suffered by Ogé, Chavannes, and their allies.

Calling Ogé a "genius" and a "Manco-Capack"—the thirteenth-century Inca ruler—Dumesle narrated the history of Ogé's revolt and execution in a way indicative of how his story came to be understood in nineteenth-century Haitian revolutionary history as a precursor to the formal beginning of the revolution in August 1791. "On the night of October 28th to 29th 1790, Ogé assembled about four hundred of his armed forces; the next day he made himself master of the borough of Dondon, and from there, he demanded the amelioration of the lot of the most unfortunate of the oppressed, and the admission of everyone into the civil and political order. His claim was based on the rights inherent to human nature." But as a "shining example of the downfall of human enterprises, after abusing everything, this nation fought its own principles!" Dumesle concluded. The colonists responded with 1,200 men

84   Chapter 3

to Ogé's few hundred. Beaten back, Ogé and his men fled to the Spanish side of the island, which was about three leagues from Dondon, and from there they solicited asylum. But the Spanish, seduced by gold, sent them back.[71] Ogé was captured by the Spanish in November and extradited from their side of the island to the French side with Chavannes and around twenty of the men of color. Before their execution in February 1791, the white colonists formally accused Ogé of several crimes, including a desire to raise the enslaved to rebellion, but none of which they had evidence for.[72] "We will never know the truth until the mulattoes of the islands can correspond freely with those of France, with their defenders, and send their grievances to the National Assembly," Raimond maintained.[73]

While in France Ogé had publicly declared that he only believed in gradual emancipation.[74] He later stated, in the famous letter he wrote to the Provincial Assembly of Cap, that when he had addressed the National Assembly back in France, "in favor of our American colonists, known under the hitherto injurious epithet of the *sang-mêlés* [mixed bloods], I never comprehended in my claims the negroes in a state of slavery." "You and my adversaries have poisoned my proceedings with this, to destroy my estimation in the minds of the honest planters. No, no, Messieurs, we have only demanded concessions for a class of free men, who have endured the yoke of your oppression for two centuries." Ogé also insisted that his current interest was solely the implementation of the March 1790 law. "We only desire the execution of the decree of March 28," he concluded.[75] What is clear from examining reportage on Ogé from the French Saint-Dominguan side, as produced in the *Affiches Américaines*, is that the French colonists and French colonial authorities considered Ogé to have engaged in nothing less than an insurrection designed to encourage if not lead to general slave revolt. On November 11, 1790, the *Affiches* reported: "Monsieur the Governor-General has spread as promptly as was possible the notice he received of the insurrection into which a young man named Ogé carried some people of color in the north." "This leader of the rebels is doubtless only an emissary of the enemies of the nation & of the colony," the article continued, "but the forces sent against him & his adherents will probably soon bring them back to their duty. The Governor-General hopes that this spirit of revolt will not spread to the western and southern parts [of the colony]. He is counting on the vigilance of these parishes to maintain public peace by means of justice, moderation, and utmost constancy." For any of the free people of color who might have been similarly inspired to use "insurrection" to force the French colonial administration's hand regarding the law of March 1790, the government issued a warning, averring that it was "relying heavily on the fidelity & submission of the people of color themselves, who have given proof of this on various occasions. They will feel that their

Prejudice 85

well-being depends on general tranquility, and they will deserve the protection of the laws which the general promises to give to all those who make no attempt on the regular order of things."[76] The idea that Ogé's was a full-blown "insurrection" was so pervasive that Castaing, a prominent free man of color, possibly the same Charles Guillaume Castaing who married into the Bonaparte family,[77] read a letter before the parish of Saint-Pierre du Terrier-Rouge effectively apologizing for Ogé's actions. "I would be pleased to believe, I would even dare to say that it is certain, that the major part of the rebels of Grande-Rivière took up arms in spite of themselves," Castaing claimed. "I mean either they were forced to or did so out of ignorance; and that if they were encouraged to return promptly with the indulgence of the province, they would abandon their unbridled leader, and would soon come to expiate, by their repentance, their contagious and barbarous conduct. Let us implore the commiseration & benevolence of our patrons for them."[78] When Lieutenant General Philibert-François Rouxel de Blanchelande gave a speech a few days later in Port-au-Prince, he claimed Ogé definitely led a rebellion and he outlined various steps Ogé allegedly took to put it into effect. "The so-named Ogé, a free mulatto, secretly landed in Cap, & not only raised the standard of revolt, but he also dared to announce it to the King's representatives, adding threats to his rationale, which the principles of sound politics show to be nil," Blanchelande said. The lieutenant general then recalled that it was only when the provincial assembly of the north asked for the usage of public forces to repress "the audacious leader of the revolt and his adherents," that troops were sent to quell the rebellion. Adopting his characteristic rhetoric of paternalism, Blanchelande finished by declaring that any free person of color who "will not disregard their duties & obligations towards the whites, their benefactors & their fathers," would be accorded the protection of the king, but "all those of you who have taken up arms, or who will have tarnished themselves, by a culpable connivance, in the projects of the so-named Ogé, & his adherents, will be delivered to all the rigor of criminal justice."[79] Public opinion on this matter was everything, and white French colonial authorities did not drag their feet to attempt to tilt it to their side.

White French officials spread their side of the story—that Ogé was a rebel of the state bent on causing a slave revolt, possibly encouraged by enemy powers—by publicizing the voices of a few key free men of color, in addition to Castaing. On December 4, 1790, several speeches and letters by other free men of color professing fealty and loyalty to France appeared in the *Affiches*. After praising Castaing's earlier condemnation of Ogé, Bonneau *aîné* told the assembly, "These rebels dare to attack the justice and benevolence of our fathers." Then, contradicting the raison d'être for Ogé's attempted revolution, racism, Bonneau opined, "They speak of a ridiculous & barbaric prejudice, but they are the ones who ensured they would experience it." Using circular logic, Bonneau claimed that Ogé and his followers justified white colonial prejudices against them by behaving in a manner that seemed to confirm that those prejudices were founded, even though their rebellion was in protest of those prejudices in the first place. In contrast, Bonneau claimed that he and his associates had never been "exposed" to color prejudices "because we have morals, honor, and we understand the laws."[80] Ogé, Chavannes, and company understood the laws, too, and one might say even more so than the government that created them. They watched how the white French colonists deliberately misinterpreted the law of March 1790, by insisting that the free men of color were not "persons," and therefore had no rights of representation.

The disingenuousness of the white French colonists vis-à-vis the *gens de couleur libres* helped set the stage not simply for France to lose the colony of Saint-Domingue, but for France to become the incoherent republic that it remains today. The very French revolutionaries in France who later created the republic were ultimately to blame for the colonists' deliberate misinterpretation of the March law. The National Assembly refused to substantively acknowledge the issue of color prejudice. They repeatedly failed to recognize how racial hierarchies structured who was considered a *personne* in the colony, just as they failed to pronounce whether the enslaved were also *hommes* in the French métropole. The National Assembly's March 1790 instructions concerning the formation of colonial assemblies further muddled the conflict. The National Assembly granted unequivocal legislative powers to the Colonial Assembly, which thrilled the colonists because they viewed this move as one that gave them almost complete autonomy. The white colonists challenged the authority of the National Assembly to make laws for Saint-Domingue, asserting they were the only ones who could do so. For Raimond, this state of affairs was simply inadmissible, as it rested on one principle only, that of color prejudice. "The white colonists allege no other reason than that of a difference in origins, for asking the National Assembly to make laws which only affect and subjugate free men of color, who are owners, taxpayers, etc. like the white colonists," Raimond wrote.[81]

It is at this moment that the Colonial Assembly, seated in Saint-Marc, frustrated that their demands were not being fully put into operation by the National Assembly, began pushing in earnest for independence from France. The Saint-Marc planters (enslavers) vowed that they would never grant political rights to the free people of color, whom they called a "bastard and degenerate race." They issued decree after decree that expressly excluded them from the primary and local assemblies. The new members of the Colonial Assembly were therefore elected without a single free person of color among them. The incoherence between the metropolitan and the colonial governments only escalated from there. The Colonial Assembly at Saint-Marc responded to the March 1790 law by issuing a strange decree declaring that its laws, like those made by the National Assembly in France, were subject only to the sanction of the king. The authors of the decree further insisted that any National Assembly law regarding colonial affairs could be vetoed *tout court* by the Colonial Assembly. On October 12, 1790, the French National Assembly responded to the radical move toward legislative independence made by the Colonial Assembly at Saint-Marc by officially dissolving it. The governor of Saint-Domingue, Antoine de Thomassin de Peynier, assembled troops led by a white Frenchman named Colonel Mauduit (Thomas-Antoine de Mauduit du Plessis) to dissolve the Colonial Assembly with violence, if necessary. The Colonial Assembly still refused to disband and told all the white citizens to arm themselves. Mauduit, for his part, was killed in March 1791 in Port-au-Prince by his own troops. Eventually outnumbered by the governor's forces, the eighty-five assembly members realized they had no choice but to capitulate. They ended their opposition by boarding a ship called the *Léopard* and subsequently sailed to France where they hoped to plead their cause before the National Assembly in person and reaffirm their right to determine the fate of the free people of color of Saint-Domingue.[82]

These conflicts led to more violence against the free people of color. After the arrival in Saint-Domingue of the vague and ambivalent March 8 decree, and the instructions about its implementation issued on March 28, blood had not ceased to flow in the colony.[83] The white colonists, as we have seen, were far from disposed to adhere to the March law. Despite the white French colonists' claims that the free men of color were on the verge of violent rebellion against the government, in a July 27, 1790, letter written by Louis Boisrond, we can clearly see that the colony's men of color were counseling one another to remain "patient and peaceful" in the face of "arbitrary humiliations."[84] To prove that the men of color never sought to foment rebellion, much less revolution (Ogé's brief exertion notwithstanding), Raimond released his *Correspondance de Julien Raimond avec ses frères, de St.-Domingue, et les pièces qui lui ont été adressées par eux* (Correspondence of Julien Raimond with his brothers, from St.-Domingue, and the documents addressed to him by them, 1793–94). The pamphlet introduced a series of letters between Raimond and other "American colonists" as evidence that the *gens de couleur libres* did not seek to raise the enslaved to rebellion or to overturn the French government. Raimond and his correspondents repeated multiple times that from 1789 to 1791 the *gens de couleur* were devoted to preserving the colony for France.[85] Raimond pointed out in one letter that it was the white colonists who sought to commit treason with what he termed their independence movement.[86] Boisrond, for his part, reported that a speech

88   Chapter 3

given by a white colonist named Bacon de la Chevalerie, who had been appointed by a "cabal" of colonists to be the first president of the Assembly in Saint-Marc, proved that the only revolution for independence underfoot in Saint-Domingue in 1790 was a white one. Bacon de la Chevalerie began his speech before the assembly by painting the inhabitants of Saint-Domingue (by which he meant only the whites) as "free and independent conquerors" (*conquérants libres et indépendants*).[87] In contrast, Boisrond said that despite the loyalty of the "American colonists," by which he meant the *gens de couleur libres*, "We are still denied here the name of citizen or inhabitant: we are recognized only under the denomination of people of color, or the insulting denomination of enemies of the public good; and we are the most peaceful and patient ones in the colonies." Peaceful and patient they were, he insisted, despite the outrageous level of violence that continued to be directed at them by the white French colonists. The patience and peace of the free people of color resulted purely from their connection to whiteness, property, and slavery. The free people of color had not yet given up on any of the three.

Among the many abuses perpetrated by the Assembly in Saint-Marc against the free men of color in the name of whiteness, property, and slavery, one particularly disastrous and disturbing example occurred during the "catastrophe at Fond-Parisien."[88] In his "Récit de l'événement du Fond-Parisien" (Narrative of the event of Fond-Parisien), Raimond told the horrific tale of a man of color and a white man who lived close to one another and who were accustomed to selling their animals to each other, respectively. This all changed when one animal escaped and went to the other habitation. The *économe* (financial administrator) from the white habitation took it into his head to go and seize several of the animals on the man of color's plantation in revenge, some of which were not among the animals that had escaped from the white colonist's plantation. The *économe* further tried to exact from the man of color "un droit de prise" or holding rights. The man of color paid him, deciding that he could get his own revenge later. The man of color then did the reverse to the white man. Subsequently, the *économe* paid him a visit and insulted him by calling him a "beggar, a mulatto, and threatening to beat him with a stick if he did not return his animals." The man of color responded by standing his ground and repeating the same imprecations against the *économe*. The white man claimed to be insulted and that he was not accustomed to being spoken to like this by a man of color. The *économe* then sought out some other white men to help him force the man of color to give back the animals he claimed belonged to his habitation. The man of color divined what the white *économe* was going to do, however, and went to round up some other men of color to provide him with support. Right at that moment ten or twelve armed whites arrived. The men of color hid in the woods "and only left two children behind, one of whom was ten years old and the other being eight."[89] After this,

> The whites arrived, caused a horrible disturbance in the house, smashed and broke the furniture, captured the scared children, and asked them where their fathers were. They said they didn't know. One of them was killed on the spot, the other was tied up and taken away by the whites. The three men of color, witnesses to these atrocities, fled to the coffee fields, and waited for the whites in a narrow path leading to the house where they had to pass by; there, they took aim at the men until several of them were spread out dead, the others, frightened took flight; they were pursued and several others were killed. The rest escaped and spread alarm throughout, saying that there were in the colored man's home an army of colored men who were going to come swooping down on the whites to slaughter them all. All the whites assembled and wrote to Cap, asking for reinforcements; and this is what gave rise to this proscription.[90]

After several more violent conflagrations with the free men of color, in spring 1791 the National Assembly was forced to clarify the meaning of the law of March 1790. On May 15, 1791, the National Assembly decreed, "the legislature will never deliberate on the political status of people of color who were not born of free fathers and mothers without the previous, free, and unprompted request of the colonies; that the presently existing Colonial Assemblies will remain in place, but that the Parish Assemblies and future Colonial Assemblies will admit the people of color born of free fathers and mothers if they otherwise have the required status." Although landowning enslavers who were free men of color like Julien Raimond viewed this law as merely another compromise—since it set up only conditional citizenship for free men of color—they were willing to accept it. The white French colonists, however, were once again not. As a result, the National Assembly was forced to include much stronger language in the May 29, 1791, instructions specifically related to "the status of Persons in the Colonies." "The National Assembly could not refuse to render this March 28 decree," the instructions read. "It cannot grant one part of the empire the ability to exclude men from active citizenship when the constitutional laws guarantee those rights in the entire empire."[91] In other words, the National Assembly was still insisting that they could not make separate laws for people of color since the laws of French citizenship required that the National Assembly not distinguish among "free" people. Another Pyrrhic victory, for the *gens de couleur libres*, at least. But what about the enslaved population? In all this talk of freedom, citizenship, personhood, and the natural rights of "man," where did the people both the *gens de couleur* and the white colonists were enslaving fit in?

Raimond repeatedly pointed out that in late eighteenth-century colonial Saint-Domingue the white French colonists were the ones who argued for a definitive rupture with France and that they were the first to use the kind of unequivocal violence usually associated with enslaved Africans in rebellion. While the Assembly of Saint-Marc had essentially decreed itself independent of the metropole, the men of color stood in stark contrast as blatant loyalists: "our only wish is addressed to Heaven and to the nation, we intend to find out if we are to be considered men and citizens."[92] For Raimond, there were two reasons for this contradictory behavior on the part of the white colonists who were betraying France by seeking independence: prejudice and slavery. While Raimond earlier separated the former from the latter, after the events of 1790–91, Raimond became painfully aware that the two were yoked together and he began to make public arguments for gradual emancipation. In his *Réflexions sur les véritables causes des troubles et des désastres de nos colonies* (Reflections on the real causes of the troubles and disasters of our colonies, 1793) Raimond offered several measures designed to conserve the new Republic of France. The French king had been sentenced to execution by the Jacobins, which they carried out in January 1793. Raimond believed that, to conserve the colony for the Republic of France, gradual emancipation of the enslaved population would be required, which he argued could be facilitated "without upheaval, without harm, either to national commerce, nor to particular fortunes."[93] In the meantime, while Raimond was busy reaching this conclusion, the white colonists were becoming even more determined to gain independence as a way to preserve slavery and thus their "particular fortunes." Dumesle pointed out that the white colonists were so determined to preserve their system of color prejudices that at the Saint-Marc Assembly a speech was pronounced linking the white colonists' independence movement, not to the Indigenous resistance of the Ayitians, but to a right of conquest related to French capture of the western third of the island in the seventeenth century during Spanish dis-settlement of Ayiti.

This first French conquest of the island was undertaken in 1630, according to the man who gave the speech, by "valorous, independent Frenchmen, who belonged to France only in their hearts, as they lived solely upon the sea." They considered the island of Saint-Domingue, "created in their own name, with their own strength," he continued, "to be their own property. They kept it to themselves for ten years under the name of *Flibustiers*. Sovereign over this territory, as uncultivated as it was at that time, they believed it could one day become very imposing, and that they were the absolute masters of giving it to whichever of the kings of Europe they believed was most worthy."[94] Reflecting upon the conclusions drawn in the speech, with its appeal to the "right of conquest," Dumesle directly countered that if any of the island's current inhabitants were the rightful inheritors of the island of Ayiti, it was present-day Haitians and, specifically, those born there:

> This is the country of our birth; our ancestors, who were removed from their native deserts by the barbarity of the Europeans are here interred; their dust is mixed with that of the primitive inhabitants of this island, whom the Europeans inhumanely massacred; that is, in fact, the first and most sacred basis of our current possession. Should we leave this country to which we are attached by the most powerful links of the human heart, in order to look for a new homeland in the wildernesses of Africa, where your greed, unjust Colonists that you are, would only pursue us again? or should we be sufficiently ignorant of the decrees of God to renounce our right to exist, to bend our debased heads under the yoke that you would like to impose upon us, to renounce the institutions that have made our glory, and unveil for the eyes of the world your bad faith and your lies? . . . Tell us, do you think that if we could ask the ashes of the ancient Aborigines of this island, and demand of them which of us they claim as their successors, do you not think that they would support this speech?[95]

Like Vastey, Dumesle awakened the ashes of the ancestors for the purposes of testimony. Yet more than asking them to testify to the evils of slavery, Dumesle requested they entertain the proposition he put forward—whether the Haitians of his day were the rightful inheritors of Ayitian land. The ghosts of the Ayitians did not disappoint. The "first Haitians" gave their response directly to the white colonists: "After having made us disappear from this land, brigands, who boast of your civilization, you depopulated Africa by the wars that your greed spewed there, to rip away its peaceful inhabitants and transport them to another hemisphere, where they were destined to replace us in forced labor." The Haitians, "the *nouveaux indigènes* (new Indigenous), were produced here after having paid the debt that nature imposed on them to break their shackles and to avenge us," the Ayitian ghosts continued. "Since they have accomplished this great design, we proclaim them our successors." This response permitted Dumesle to conclude, "There you have it, do not doubt what the oracle of the tombs would be. They would affirm the rights that we have been given from the Master of the masters of the world."[96]

To understand how and why the free people of color styled themselves as the "new Indigenous" without making a claim for independence, when this same claim would later be used by the *armée indigène* for the opposite purpose, we must sink even more deeply into the relationship between nineteenth-

92 Chapter 3

century Haitian thought and the eighteenth-century forms of testimony given not only by Raimond, but by other free people of color more closely tied to the armed struggles of the Haitian Revolution, principally Generals Toussaint Louverture and André Rigaud. The independence movement led by the white French colonists was motivated by greed and racism. The French republican antislavery movement led by Raimond, Rigaud, and Louverture, only one of whom, Rigaud, would live to see Haitian independence, though he would not participate in its making, was motivated by liberty and equality. Taken together, their writings reveal how an anti-racism movement initially created by free people of color like Raimond and Rigaud was eventually merged with an antislavery movement forged by the enslaved and formerly enslaved Africans of Saint-Domingue like Boukman, Biassou, Jean-François, Louverture, and their many allies in the mountains of the colony. It was this convergence that eventually erupted into full-fledged revolution and then into Haiti's war of independence. Letter Number 5 in Raimond's *Correspondance* reaffirmed that the men of color sought neither to raise the enslaved to rebellion nor to gain independence from France. Addressed to de Joly, president, and Raimond, *député* of the southern province of Saint-Domingue, by several prominent *hommes de couleur*, the letter was also sent to the National Assembly in Paris, dated July 27, 1790: "Whatever happens, dear compatriots of ours, we will die free and French, and we will wrap ourselves in the Flag of France, which will serve as our shroud."[97] "Free and French," there it is, first produced to support the efforts of the free men of color, this language of "free and French" will become of utmost significance in part 2, as we watch Louverture co-opt it to reaffirm the precarious first attempts of the French commissioners to legislate abolition of slavery on the island. These precarious words of "free and French" appear verbatim in the July 1801 revolutionary constitution for Saint-Domingue, signed by Louverture, as governor-general of the colony for life. Raimond was a principal contributor.

-1—
0—
+1—

PART II

Independence

-1—
0—
+1—

Chapter 4

Revolution

Vincent Ogé is the most well-known victim of the white supremacist machinations of the Colonial Assembly. Born in the city of Dondon in northern Saint-Domingue, he took up forever residence, metaphorically, *lòt bo dlo*, or on the underside of the water, like so many captive Africans, victims of the same criminal European commerce in human beings that his family profited from as enslavers. Numerous ads and other notices concerning "maroon negroes" from Dondon stamped Ogé and/or stating they belonged to the Ogé family appeared in the *Affiches Américaines* throughout the late eighteenth century. Being from a family of enslavers, as was Chavannes (sometimes spelled Chavanne) from Grande-Rivière, too, could not erase the opprobrium the French colonists attached to their color.[1] They were both gruesomely executed by the white colonists on February 25, 1791, in nearly the same spot where an enslaved Black man whom French colonial officials said was born in Africa, François Makandal, was burned at the stake thirty-three years earlier.[2] Along with the April 1802 death of Toussaint Louverture, the deaths of Makandal and Ogé mark crucial flashpoints in the history of the Haitian Revolution, as much as in Haitian revolutionary thought. Their deaths, separately and together, symbolically and materially, influenced to an unmatched degree the development of antislavery revolution in Saint-Domingue and its transformation into a war of independence for Haiti.

Recall that in October 1790, along with another free man of color named Jean-Baptiste Chavannes, Ogé led a small rebellion of a few hundred men. As *personnes* of France, they were demanding implementation of the March 1790 French law guaranteeing free men of color equal rights of representation with white French people.[3] After their extradition to French Saint-Domingue from the Spanish side of the island, Ogé, Chavannes, and around twenty other men of color were sentenced to execution on "the wheel." We have not yet exam-ined this white French colonial ritual of capital punishment. We must do so now because it relates to two other momentous events in Saint-Domingue: Makandal's execution, and the August 1791 Vodou ceremony at Bois Caïman, the latter commonly narrated in Haitian thought as having heralded the start of the Haitian Revolution. The official document describing how Ogé, Cha-vannes, and the other so-called conspirators were to be executed "on the wheel" demonstrates the pervasive evilness of "white supremacy"—a concept that existed well before Vastey formulated it into a term in 1814—and the out-sized violence that its purveyors visited upon those they used French laws to dehumanize.

The Ogé sentence stated that the "guilty" ones were to be "broken alive on the wheel," after which they were to have their heads placed on pikes to serve as a warning, as in the case of Ferrand de Baudière. The sentence further read that Ogé and Chavannes were to be led before "the executor of high justice in front of the main door of the parish church of this city, and there, barefoot and *en chemise* (long shirt dress or gown), a rope around their neck, and on their knees, each having a torch of hot wax in their hands weighing two pounds, they are to perform an *amende honorable* (public apology), declaring with a loud and intelligible voice that it was wicked, reckless and ill-advised for them to have committed the crimes of which they are convicted":

> They are to repent of them and ask forgiveness of God, of the king, and of justice: this being done, they are to be led to the Place d'Armes of this city, opposite the spot that is intended for the execution of the whites, and to have their arms, legs, thighs and loins broken while they are alive on a scaffold that will be erected for this purpose, and they are to be put by the executor of high justice on the wheel, their faces turned toward the sky, to stay there so long as it pleases God to spare their lives; after this, their heads are to be cut off and exposed on pikes, namely: that of said *Vincent Ogé* jeune on the main road which leads to Dondon, and that of *Jean-Baptiste*, called Chavanne[s], on the route to the Grande Rivière.[4]

Even in death, segregation was the order of the day. "The trial of the insurrection of people of color, who joined willingly or by force with Ogé & Chavanne[s] is over," the *Affiches Américaines* announced: "These two rebel leaders expired on the wheel on February 25. Their accomplices, guilty of murder or other violence against whites, will be executed immediately." "The secrecy necessary for the judicial process in this case prevents us from disclosing the number of people of color doomed to death. It would be impossible for us to disclose the day of their execution," the announcement finished.[5]

A crowd of witnesses watched as the two men had every bone in their bodies broken. What human mind first dreamt up such a "punishment"? What kind of human being carried it out? And what kind of people stood around and watched? I am hardly the first to wonder. On August 27, 1791, Pierre Labuissonnière, one of Julien Raimond's correspondents, wrote to him of this lamentable atrocity: "The memory of this butchery will survive in every century and will remain horrific to all of humankind; it is without example: the most ferocious cannibals have never done anything of the sort. This

98 Chapter 4

punishment, which is believed to be a way to frighten us, will on the contrary only make us more determined to succeed or die, when it comes to enjoying the freedom offered to us by our legislators, the restorers of French liberty."[6] It hardly matters whether the punishment had any analogues in human history. The shock produced upon learning that one group of human beings would treat another group of human beings in such a manner transcends time. A character named Henri in the twentieth-century French philosopher Jean-Paul Sartre's play, *Morts sans sépulture* (The unburied dead) implies that human-made tortures were an existential problem of the highest order: "Is there any reason to go on living when there exist men who will beat you until the bones in your body break?"[7] The juxtaposition I have inserted between the execution of Ogé and Chavannes and Sartre's play, which takes place during the Second World War in Nazi-occupied France, is not meant to be gratuitous. The very word "holocaust" is one that nineteenth-century Haitians used to describe the mind-numbingly everyday—in the sense that they were common—murders of enslaved Africans and other people of color in Saint-Domingue by the white French colonists. Referring directly to the bone-breaking execution of Ogé and Chavannes, Dumesle comforted himself with the thought that these "holocausts offered up to tyranny fertilized the desire for liberty."[8] The actions of the French during the Leclerc expedition sent by Bonaparte to reinstate slavery called for the resonant language of holocaust once more. Asking his audience first if they required him to "retrace the course of atrocities" committed by the French—"the massacre of the entire population of this island, meditated in the silence and coolness of the cabinet"—Dessalines issued a warning in his famous proclamation of April 28: "Tremble, tyrants, scourges, usurpers of the new world, our daggers are sharpened, your tortures are ready." He then averred that he had equipped sixty thousand men who, ready to follow his orders, "burn to offer a new holocaust to the ghosts of their slaughtered brothers."[9]

Although he never lived to see the atrocities committed during the Leclerc expedition, responding to the racist writings of Moreau de Saint-Méry, Raimond pointed out that French executions of free men of color and enslaved individuals for perceived "crimes" were nothing more than the result of a tyrannical mode of logic that prevailed whenever the question of rights for people of color, and especially for enslaved Black people, were concerned. For Raimond, white supremacy—formulated by him as "color prejudice"—was the real cause of the ensuing slave rebellion; the very one that was ongoing at the time Labuissonnière wrote to Raimond; and the very one that eventually led to Haiti's liberty and independence. Raimond said that in the colony, "When . . . oppressed men try to shake off their oppression, or to soften their plight, at the same time that furious tyrants are engaging in all kinds of crimes to prevent these acts of humanity, the guilty ones are determined not to be the tyrants; but those arguing in favor of rights for the oppressed." "Thus, when good men demand, on behalf of the *hommes de couleur,* the restitution of their rights, the whites answer them with massacres," he concluded.[10]

The mere demand for the rights of free people of color was enough for the white French colonists to justify using violence against them and any of their putative allies. One of those allies, Jacques Brissot, founder of the Société des Amis des Noirs, was similarly astonished at the level of brutality directed against Ogé. "Ogé is no more," he wrote in May 1791 for *Le Patriote français* (The French patriot): "He expired on the wheel with his fellow unfortunates; he was executed, not for crimes, but for the misfortune of having succumbed to the desire of demanding his human rights, those rights that the decrees restored to him, and that the unjust despotism of the whites denied him." "Providence, what therefore are your designs!" Brissot exclaimed. "You crown the enemies of tyranny in France; there, the heads of the tyrants are carried on pikes; but in Saint-Domingue, the heads of freedom's defenders roll on the scaffolds."[11] Brissot went further than Raimond in his defense of Ogé, whose rebellion against white French authority the famous abolitionist painted as wholly justified regardless of the methods. "Even if, in order to defend himself, Ogé had been obliged to shed blood, to burn some houses, to ransom his enemies; has not blood also stained our revolution?" Brissot asked.[12] Brissot finished by pointing out the contradictions in French revolutionary principles that would eventually lead the French state to become an incoherent republic incapable of offering true liberty and equality to its citizens. These incoherences only further contributed to the slave revolt and rebellion that broke out in Saint-Domingue just a few months later. Brissot prophesied the general rebellion of the enslaved population as both righteous and cosmological. The white colonists of Saint-Domingue might have been able to dupe the National Assembly, but they could not dupe nature: "It is she who is now preparing the punishment of the whites, who will avenge the blood of the innocent, and who will avenge the mulattoes subjected to the most heinous despotism. The intrepid Ogé said it while dying, and he will not have said it in vain: *May my ashes give birth to an avenger!* Nature gave him thousands."[13] Chanlatte, too, directly connected the persecution of Ogé not solely to the actual revolution but to the later independence of Haiti, which Brissot, who was executed by the Jacobins in October 1793, never lived to see. "But [Ogé's] punishment became an altar, and august liberty would one day become connected to it, and would soon enough affix before it, her dear daughter, independence," Chanlatte wrote.[14]

Ogé's struggle against white colonial authority has resonated across Black studies for centuries. Ogé is a central figure in the works of the Black American

100   Chapter 4

abolitionists, William Wells Brown and George Vashon; the Haitian play-wright Pierre Faubert devoted an entire play in the 1840s to Ogé's efforts with his *Ogé, ou le préjugé de couleur* (Ogé, or color prejudice), eventually published in 1856; and before penning his magisterial *Histoire des caciques*, Émile Nau drew the history of Ogé and Chavannes in his *Réclamation par les affranchis des droits civils et politiques* (The demand of freed men for civil and political rights, 1840).[15] In 1938, the Trinidadian historian, C. L. R James, too, wrote of Ogé in his famous book, *The Black Jacobins*, "It was the news of Ogé's torture and death which made France as a whole fully aware of the colonial question."[16] The execution of Ogé created a philosophical earthquake whose aftershocks rocked the Atlantic World. While Ogé's name resounded across France with a crash, its most immediate tremors were felt right there in Saint-Domingue, epicenter of the age of revolutions.

The high-profile execution of Ogé and Chavannes was directly associated with the onset of the Haitian Revolution just six months later, on the night passing from August 22 to the 23, 1791. Writing a few days after the beginning of the wide-scale freedom struggle of the enslaved men and women in the north, Labuissonnière could not help but to see a connection between the grue-some public execution of Ogé and Chavannes and the outbreak of greater slave rebellion. Of the insurrection of the enslaved population, he said to Raimond, "You know that there is a prodigious population of them [slaves] hiding in the Grand-Bois, which is to say, in the south-eastern part of this quartier, border-ing the side of the Spanish, who are facilitating them in everything; and that for now, we have not been able to subdue them. . . . I have learned that [the rebels] are currently in correspondence with those of Cul-de-Sac, of which there are a large number straying apart, since they began the insurrection, which resulted in 5 or 6 of them being executed in Port-au-Prince."[17] Rai-mond's horizon of understanding the motivation of these rebellions was just as limited as his correspondent's. Raimond believed, as did many free people of color, that the white colonists had armed the enslaved population to ad-vance their own cause of independence from the metropole.

At times, Raimond's writing, perhaps unwittingly, reflected doubts about the claim that the August general rebellion of enslaved individuals was caused by the white colonists' independence machinations rather than the enslaved population's freedom desires. Raimond reported that there were uprisings of enslaved people in Saint-Domingue long before the execution of Ogé and Cha-vannes, before the ceremony at Bois Caïman, and even before the French Revolution. Such enslaved freedom-seekers were ordinarily executed when captured. "In the month of April 1789, several blacks rebelled in Saint-Domingue, their leader was hanged," Raimond wrote.[18] Moreau de Saint-Méry painted this kind of white on Black violence as the logical consequence, not

Revolution   101

of slavery, but "of the system of the Friends of the Blacks."[19] Raimond contested this interpretation forthrightly. In his systematic attack on Moreau de Saint-Méry's racist writings about the *hommes de couleur* of Saint-Domingue, Raimond directly refuted that slave rebellions that had already occurred on Saint-Domingue were inspired by either the 1789 *Déclaration des droits de l'homme* or the budding transatlantic abolitionist movement. He knew that the enslaved were already motivated and predisposed to rebel due to the tortures and suffering to which the white colonists repeatedly subjected them. "Would it not be natural to fear that the blacks, in thinking about their own situation, would have wanted to demand their liberty?" Raimond asked.[20] Even as he acknowledged the possibility that the enslaved could conceivably be aware of and affected by the enlightenment's abolitionist doctrines, Raimond declared: "For two centuries the blacks have attempted uprisings in multiple regions; and yet there was not even a Société des Amis des Noirs."[21] While one of those revolts occurred only a month after the famous storming of the Bastille prison in July 1789, it took place before news of the French rebellion reached Saint-Domingue and before the Société des Amis des Noirs had even written one line in favor of the abolition of slavery.[22] Still, the white colonists blamed the free people of color and the free people of color blamed the white colonists. Both groups were wrong. Ultimately, it was enslaved organization that resulted in the full-scale revolt and rebellion that broke out during the third week of August 1791.

The primary people in the colony to suffer from the horrid and twisted white supremacist logic that undergirded the violence of slavery were always enslaved Black people. True to the form of relation with Ayiti inaugurated by his predecessors in Haitian thought, Dumesle called our attention to the similitude of the ceremony of Bois Caïman that unleashed the Haitian Revolution with Ayitian resistance against Spain in the early modern world and to an earlier rebellion in Saint-Domingue led by Makandal in the 1750s. The Haitian Revolution would have exploded much earlier, Dumesle said, if Makandal had not been executed by French colonial authorities. "Such was the project formed in the 16th and 17th centuries by the successors of the Aborigines in several colonies of the American archipelago," Dumesle wrote. Makandal's rebellion as a continuation of those plans, Dumesle explained, "would have enveloped every organism on this island, if Macanda[l], its restorer, a man otherwise endowed with rare intelligence, and with that character of energy that tyranny labors to destroy by making it seem odious, if I may say so, had not been arrested in the course of his design, and if the circumstances in which his conspiracy was revealed had not subjected him to the fate of an obscure conspirator."[23] Makandal, that resonant name whose evocation for so long after his death became the sign, symbol, and rhythm of rebellion in the Caribbean, was a fugitive from slavery, a maroon, who had been allegedly using poison as well as a vast network of formerly enslaved people who had liberated themselves to sow the seeds of revolution in Saint-Domingue as early as the 1750s.[24] Upon his condemnation in January 1758, Makandal, like Ogé and Chavannes, was subjected to the *amende honorable*.[25]

As recorded in the account written for the Conseil Supérieur du Cap-Français, colonial officials accused Makandal of having "corrupted" and "seduced" other enslaved individuals with "des paquets prétendus magiques," or "supposedly magical packets," which he sold with "malicious intent." Colonial officials further charged that Makandal "sold, composed, and distributed poisons of all kinds" using "sacred" materials. For this, Makandal was condemned to make the "*amende honorable, nu et en chemise*, holding a torch of hot wax of two pounds in his hands, before the main door of the parish church of this city." The executor of high justice was to transport Makandal to the spot of his execution with a sign that read, "suborner, profaner, poisoner" (*séducteur, prophanateur, et empoisonneur*). Like Ogé and Chavannes more than three decades later, Makandal was required to admit to his supposed crimes and to ask for pardon from "God, the King, and Justice." After doing so, he was to be "burned alive" while attached to a stake in the same public square in Cap-Français where the white colonists would one day execute Ogé and Chavannes.[26]

This is where the similitude between the execution of Makandal and that of Ogé and Chavannes diverges. An anonymous planter writing from Cap-Français in a letter dated June 24, 1758, reported that Makandal had been a maroon for eighteen years, after having previously been enslaved by M. Tellier, a planter in Limbé. During those eighteen years of fugitivity, the planter accused Makandal of selling various poisons that killed many enslaved people. "The number of people he caused to die during those 18 years is incalculable," the report stated. Having been condemned to his death on January 20, 1758, the anonymous author claimed that Makandal made such "prodigious efforts" to avoid the punishment that the "neck chain (*collier*) and the shackles became detached from the *poteau* (stake); such that he saved himself from the fire, his body having been partially burned."[27] The enslaved population, observing firsthand this white colonial ritual of capital punishment and Makandal's evasion, believed he escaped his execution by flying away.[28] "The Maréchaussée and the planters were careful to have the Negroes surrounding the square taken away as soon as possible," the writer recalled. "All those unfortunate people, upon leaving, shouted aloud that François Makandal was a sorcerer and incombustible; that he was right to tell them that no one

Revolution 103

was able to stop him, and that as soon as we got hold of him he would turn into a mosquito." So extraordinary was this suggestion, vision even, that "the executioner himself could not believe what he was seeing."[29] As the story was passed down from generation to generation in Saint-Domingue, and then in Haiti, it took on its own life. Some tellers of the story insisted that Makandal indeed fled as a mosquito. Makandal himself purportedly claimed that if he were ever to be captured by the white colonists he could escape by taking on a multitude of life forms. Others recalled that he transformed himself into a fly.[30] Because of the general chaos that ensued when Makandal leapt out of the fire, however, scattering the audience in multiple different directions, there were few witnesses to the actual execution. This ambiguity, coupled with French suppression of personal testimony from any perspective other than that of his executioners, has lent even more credence to the idea that no one really knows what happened to one of Saint-Domingue's most famous maroon leaders.[31]

Sébastien Courtin, sent by the French government to Cap-Français to investigate the string of "poisonings," reported that Makandal's power over the other enslaved Africans was so strong that even when confronted with his capture, they seemed to make a mockery of the entire white colonial ritual of crime and punishment. "He acquired such control over the Negroes, that they did not believe it was possible to capture him," Courtin wrote:

> And when he was brought in, I told two of the accused about it, but they did not believe it, and one of them told me that he would have to see it with his own eyes to believe it. And when they were confronted with him, they had already been condemned to being burned, and were only waiting for the moment of their own punishment. While they said they were, in a way, absorbed by the horror of their condition, nevertheless, when they were brought before him, their surprise, their bursts of laughter and their speeches, especially those of L'Éveillé, who knew him better than anyone, created the most singular scene, and convinced us to what extent they were beguiled. The Negro Jolicoeur was also astonished, and yet he was not an idiot. He had learned to read and write a little, and he was not lacking in knowledge; thus it must be admitted that François Macandal was not an ordinary Negro. He had been a leader in his country.[32]

The anonymous letter writer, who referenced Courtin's arrival and investigation, had a slightly different reading. The letter writer stated that after Makandal leapt out of the fire "the executioner threw himself at the criminal, tied up his feet and hands and threw him back into the inferno."[33] This same writer claimed that the enslavers brought back the people they were enslaving precisely so that they could witness the final execution, in person, and therefore would not continue to believe in the kinds of "magic" and "sorcery" fueling the rumor of Makandal's escape. "All the planters brought back their Negroes, who, seeing him burn, understood the falsity of what he had made them believe," the anonymous author wrote. "Since this execution," the letter continued, "we burn four or five of them every month: there have already been twenty-four enslaved Negroes or Negresses, and three free Negroes, who have suffered the same fate." These differing interpretations of the reactions of the enslaved witnesses to Makandal's capture and execution—Courtin's and the anonymous writer's—have more to tell us about the beliefs of colonial officials and other enslavers than they do about what Makandal's alleged followers and allies understood about their erstwhile companion's death. The alleged laughing, along with the mockery it suggests, does not necessarily imply disbelief on the part of the enslaved individuals so much as it might speak to the differing values the enslaved population attached to life and death in this colonial context. If slavery was a kind of living death, then would a physical death be punishment or would it be deliverance?

Despite their general inability to understand and/or decode much of what they saw in connection with Makandal, the more "poisoners" white colonial officials arrested, the more information these officials believed they gathered about what exactly a *macandal* was to the people they were enslaving and the extent of the network of "poisoning" the personnage of Makandal had allegedly formed.[34] "Whoever makes it [the macandal] is recognized as a sorcerer of the first order," Courtin wrote. To make the "macandal," this "sorcerer" "takes bones from the cemetery, preferring those of baptized infants; he adds a few nails, pounded roots of banana, *figuier maudit* (accursed fig tree), etc., holy water, holy incense, and holy bread. He ties it together with several pieces of string and forms a bundle the size of two to four inches . . . he sells it tied up like that." Courtin then explained why the enslaved called these "paquets" makandal/macandal. The sorcerer "gives it whatever name he wants, and whoever receives it is known by that name among the initiates, which explains why some of them have Macandals. Those to whom he gave the name of Charlot were of the first order." Courtin then tried to explain his understanding of what he saw as a mishmash of religious beliefs—which Courtin considered sacrilegious and profane—expressed by those initiated into the ritual of the "macandal." "The sorcerer, who composes it, says a few words during the ritual," Courtin wrote, for example, and "François Macandal, during his interrogation by the Conseil, pronounced these words, which seemed to be taken from the Turkish idiom, and where the word *alla, alla*, was repeated several times, and when he spoke in French, he said that he was invoking God and the Lord Jesus Christ." Different captives provided differing testimony about

Revolution   105

the words attached to the ritual. Courtin claimed to have learned the following from testimony given by Makandal's "wives" during the course of an interrogation: "Mercure and Brigitte, wives of François, who admitted they knew how to make macandals that can mess with a person's head, spoke of the same rituals, and said that the magic words were 'god knows what I have done, the good lord has his eyes upon what you are asking' [*bon dieu conné qui ça moi faire, bon dieu baïe yeux ça qui yeux demandé vous*]." Incredulity reigned because colonial observers like Courtin insisted upon absorbing this testimony according to their own worldview: "This good lord is undoubtedly Charlot or the Devil, this is what is no longer in doubt, as we will see later. The composing sorcerer only wraps the nails, bones, and herbs in a rag with mud, holy water, holy candles, and holy incense; saying the magic words, he strings it all together several times, soaks it in holy water. There ends his ritual."[35] The competing energies of these testimonies, drawing on the language of Ann Laura Stoler, are crucial for understanding the role the history of Makandal and macandals play in Haitian revolutionary thought.[36] As scholar Étienne Charlier has reminded us, after Makandal's public execution, "the poisonings did not decrease, and the colonists were powerless to stop them; for, the profound reason for this practice is located in the very regime of slavery."[37]

In his report, Courtin referred at several points to an interrogation of Makandal's "wives," Brigitte and Mercure. "The interrogations of Mercure and Brigitte revealed to us, unequivocally, the whole mystery of the culture of worship that these sorcerers rendered to the Devil," Courtin wrote. In particular, "Brigitte, who seemed to speak frankly during the last days of her life, said that the Macandal, consulted by her servitor, spoke to her clearly in her ears, according to her own expression, telling her the location of the *Nègre marron*, who was the thief of something for which they were condemned to death, the poisoner and the rest of them." The network of alleged poisonings based on the teachings of Makandal was extensive and hit close to home for Courtin. After having previously reported that a woman enslaved by him named Marianne was "the leader of the poisoners in Cap," Courtin wrote, "My Negress Marianne who received poisons that Macandal sent her by Brigitte, his wife, communed with them every eight days. Macandal had a crowd of devoted Negroes who covered for him, and all of whom he exposed as poisoners, during an interrogation after the questioning, whereas he never wanted to confess anything he himself did."[38] Despite his supposed reticence to confess his own crimes, Makandal was naturally a key witness in Courtin's investigation.

Courtin's summary of this testimony, and others, are worth examining at length for what they reveal about the white colonists' understanding of the methods and goals of these "poisoners." "Macandal made several very impor-

106   Chapter 4

tant declarations, from which it can be concluded that he and his confidants, who were honored to be called his valets, devastated by way of poison the quartiers of Port-Margot, Limbé, Souffrière, and Borgne, and that his network, which began in Cap, was destined to become very fatal there," Courtin claimed. "The Negro L'Éveillé agreed to have poisoned Labadie, the upholsterer, his first master, the wife of Delbos, a saddler, with whom he lived, who had been dying for a year, and Lambert, surgeon in Limonade." Many enslaved women were also involved. "It is basically proven that Mongoubert, a merchant in Cap, was poisoned by his Negress (this Negress has since been convicted and condemned), that the young lady Lespès was poisoned by her own [Negresses] (one of these Negresses was convicted and condemned)," he continued. "It is proven that Laborde, the garçon of Vatin, the wigmaker, was [poisoned] by Marianne, Jolicœur, and Michel, because he did not want to let them perform their sabbath in Vatin's kitchen. That Rodet's wife was poisoned by a Negress with whom Rodet lived, and who lived with Jolicœur, confessed to by the latter who had wanted to poison his master, Sieur Millet." Courtin's list went on and on.

The interrogations and so-called trials, in addition to producing "evidence" the colonists used to indict those they accused, unwittingly left a trace of the white colonists' awareness that the condition of slavery was conducive to producing a rebellious state of mind, even if none of the enslaved people they accused were actually using so-called poisons in protest of their condition. "We discovered a series of horrors during the trials of all the different accomplices," Courtin reported:

> The trial of the Negroes of Mr. Pillat, counselor, charged with having poisoned him is being investigated. There is a lot of evidence against the Négresse Henriette, of Dame Faveroles, who is also suspected of having poisoned her mistress (she was convicted and condemned). We have not yet been able to follow the thread of all the crimes of this kind, committed in the plain of Cap, but it will certainly come to pass, and we will prove the founded suspicions that we have concerning the deaths of several Whites and Negroes in every quartier.

Importantly, many of the charges involved the claim that those engaged in the ritual of Makandal/Macandal were poisoning other enslaved people:

> The Negro Cupid, belonging to Sieur Gôle, was convicted of having poisoned the Negro Apollo, and he confessed that he had poisoned the Negro Apollo, and he admitted that he had poisoned the two Misses Decourt, one of whom his master wanted to marry, as well as his master himself. The master is not dead. There is a lot of evidence against the

Negroes of M. Hiret, those of M. de Marquet, and of M. de la Cassaigne for having poisoned their masters. The Negress of Lady Papret, and the Negroes of Sieur Delan and Monsieur Le Prieur, are accused of the same crime. His Negro Thélémaque was condemned for having wanted to poison him with verdigris, which he put in a soup of cabbage, at the Limbé guardhouse; almost all the guests were very ill. There are a great number of Negroes, charged with having composed and distributed poison, and having killed their comrades and animals. A few have been convicted.[39]

Colonial officials gathered these testimonies from the people they enslaved, less so they could determine their innocence or guilt (the colonists already believed all the accused were guilty), and more to gather information about their accomplices and their methods, the better with which to condemn them and future freedom fighters.

After the white colonists executed Makandal, the "poisonings" increased and so did the arrests. Our anonymous letter writer admonished, "Judge for yourself when this terrible situation will end: there are currently 140 defendants in prison." The white French colonial officials used the proliferation of executions of the people they condemned as evidence of the vastness of the alleged poisoning "conspiracy" of the "Negroes" who supposedly wanted to kill all the white planters, their enslavers. Yet, at every turn we see that the accused were killed, brutally and publicly, for these "crimes," in a manner not unlike that of Ogé and Chavannes, on the strength of suspicion, assumption, and dubious testimony, much of it coerced. Amid all these interrogations little material evidence was ever presented; and these white colonial rituals of capital punishment did not produce the desired effect of deterrence. The more executions the colonists committed, the more "conspiracies" and rebellions they said took place in response. We might say, using Brissot's words about the conviction of Ogé, by killing all these Makandals/Macandals, the white French colonists believed they had created "thousands" of "avengers."

During the many interrogations, our anonymous observer said the colonists learned that the "poisonings" were much more extensive than they had imagined. In addition to poisoning other enslaved people, "some of the Negroes who had been executed claimed to have caused to die by poison 30 & 40 whites, even their own Masters with their wives and their children; others [had killed] 200 & 300 Negroes belonging to different masters."[40] In the white colonial imagination, all this could be supposedly traced to one source—François Makandal—who "discovered three types of poisons" so dangerous they could kill a dog on the spot. Others of his poisons were said to be more slow to take effect and caused the victim to "languish for five or six months, but would always kill them in the end."[41] For Moreau de Saint-Méry, writing in the 1790s, long after the story had become famous, the goal of this vast network of poisoning—aided by the "open schools" Makandal supposedly created to facilitate this "execrable art"—could not have been clearer: the elimination of the white population. Moreau de Saint-Méry concluded, "In the end, according to his vast plan, [Makandal] conceived of the infernal project of making disappear from the surface of Saint-Domingue all the men who were not black, & his successes, which were ever increasing, spread a fear which almost assured it. The vigilance of the magistrates, that of the government, nothing was able to ensure that this scoundrel could be seized, & his attempts, resulting in almost sudden death, only served to terrify everyone even more."[42] Moreau de Saint-Méry's understanding of the Makandal affair was largely drawn from Courtin's official report, called the "Mémoire sommaire," wherein the French official vividly evoked the three main populations of people on the island of Ayiti—Ayitians, Africans, and Europeans—for the purpose of creating an allegory about Makandal. "François Macandal always had a piece of canvas which he dipped in a bucket of water," Courtin wrote. "His canvas came out sometimes one color, sometimes another, and he dyed the water with all the colors. He is said to have started by pulling out the one that was olive-colored, like the former islanders, calling them the first inhabitants of the island, then he pulled out the white one, which represented those who were currently the masters. And finally, he pulled out the black one, to make known those who were to be the masters from now on."[43] Using this anecdote, Moreau de Saint-Méry and Courtin interpreted Makandal's "conspiracy" to be a bona fide rebellion with the revolutionary aim of doing away with the white colonial oligarchy.

In these white colonial readings, Makandal sought to reverse the order of white colonial domination and replace it with Black African domination. Yet, even as we simultaneously are called to read against and along the grain of the interpretation of those with a vested interested in condemning Makandal, we might recognize how Makandal created an alternative way of being in a world designed to enslave his body and kill his soul. Scholar Daina Ramey Berry has used the concept of "soul values" to explain how "enslaved people found ways to draw upon the strength of their souls to survive slavery." "This kind of resistance manifested as a deep expression of their self-worth and can be found in testimonies of the enslaved, deep analyses of their actions, and careful examinations of their internal fortitude," Ramey Berry wrote. "Such spiritual resilience represents one response to enslavement on a much larger spectrum of reactions. Recognizing the power of enslaved people's spirits and souls provides another important way to explore the complex lives of the enslaved."[44] What we learn from Makandal's stated unwillingness to be killed is not necessarily that he believed his corporeal body was unable to die, but rather that he knew his "soul values" would not, even when he was set to be burned at the stake.

The *Macanda* is today the name of a Vodou dance inspired by the life-story of François Makandal. In eighteenth-century Saint-Domingue the word Macandal continued to refer to rebellious enslaved Africans and was also adopted by freedom-seekers as a symbol of their own agency. On April 2, 1766, Saint-Domingue's newspaper, the *Affiches Américaines*, ran an advertisement for the recovery of an enslaved man on a quest for freedom: "A Negro Congo, named Eustache, & surnamed for some years Makandal, stamped Boyveau, 5 feet & a few inches tall, about 40 years old, with a red face, & missing a few front teeth, has gone maroon." "Mr. Boyveau, living in Dondon, to whom this Negro belongs, asks those who recognize him, to have him arrested & to give him notice: he will give 150 livres for the capture," the notice finished.[45] In another issue of the *Affiches*, also published in 1766, a M. Fremon, Syndic du Quartier du Limbé, published a long article refuting the idea that Limbé was not properly geographically situated for the cultivation of sugar. In so doing, he essentially blamed Makandal's "poisonings" for the fact that the quartier had not been more productive. "Now we must ward off an objection that could be made; here it is. One could say: but how can we agree that the soil of Limbé is suitable for the cultivation of sugar, and that the inhabitants work there according to the quality of their soil and the indications of nature?" Fremon asked. "It is hardly getting better with the lack of facility that we see reigning there even today. The objection will not endure for long, when we remember the immense losses that the Inhabitants suffered there due to the poisonings," he continued. Referring to what he considered to be the longitudinal consequences of having to combat Makandal and the many Macandals who came after him, Fremon wrote: "No one is unaware of the ravages wrought there by those cursed poisoners known as Macandal, their leader, who being a slave of the Quartier, had chosen [Limbé] to be the theater of his crimes; also there were few plantations where this scourge did not make itself more or less felt."[46] Makandal was a historical figure, a symbol, and metaphor, and as with Ogé, the story of his death, as it traveled through the ages, in many ways, became larger than his life.

The story lived on, in part, through subsequent efforts to portray the life of Makandal, both on the page and the stage. In 1786, the French Saint-Domingue playwright Acquaire wrote a play titled *Arlequin mulâtresse, protégé par Macanda* (The mulattress Arlequin, protected by Macanda), advertised in the *Affiches Américaines* as a "grand pantomime in two acts."[47] An eighteenth-century short story with an ironic title, "Makandal, histoire véritable" (Makandal, a true history), signed only "M. de C.," circulated widely

-1—
0—
+1—

110   Chapter 4

after it first appeared in the *Mercure de France* in September 1787, before going on to be published in the periodical, *L'Esprit des journaux*.[48] In February 1788 "Le Makandal" was translated by the London-based *Universal Magazine of Knowledge and Pleasure* as "The Negro Makandal, an Authentic History," and that same year it also appeared in German translation.[49] In 1801, the British playwright James Cartwright Cross borrowed liberally from "Le Makandal" for his drama, *King Caesar: Or the Negro Slaves* (1801), first performed on September 16, 1801, at the Royal Circus.[50]

The name and story of Makandal had lasting resonance throughout the second part of the nineteenth century too. In 1865, the French novelist, L. V. Denancé published a multivolume novel, *Makandal: ou, le noir marron* (Makandal, or the Black maroon).[51] Although Denancé used the name of the famous revolutionary, the novel, which announces its abolitionist aims in the preface, takes place in the United States and concerns a fugitive U.S. slave named Makandal. In 1892, a subsequent French novel, *Le Macandal: épisode de l'insurrection des noirs à Saint-Domingue* (The Macandal: Episode from the insurrection of the Blacks in Saint-Domingue) appeared in New Orleans, signed by Tante Marie, the pen name of Marie Josephine Augustin.[52] Augustin's novel is the most anachronistic of the literary representations, in that it places Makandal in Saint-Domingue in the 1790s as a part of the general slave rebellion. He was the one who inspired the enslaved Africans to rebel against the white French colonists:

> Men of Africa! I, Macandal, your king, declare you free like the eagle in your mountains, like the tiger in your faraway forests. All in nature is free—thunder tearing through the air, the lightning bolt striking wherever it pleases, wind howling in the tempest; birds, reptiles, beasts, all in nature demands the right to be free—then why would you, Africans, be enslaved! Chiefs of powerful tribes, Mayaca, Maouna, Biassou, through me your fetish orders you to swear the blood oath. Come, I am waiting![53]

In nineteenth-century Haitian thought, Makandal's famous resistance represented a more metaphysical rather than literal relationship to the much later general insurrection. For Dumesle, it was the spirit of Mackandal—his "soul values"—that remained for a long time a part of the general climate of opposition to colonial slavery in Saint-Domingue. According to Dumesle, in the 1770s, another large complot designed to end in liberty was formed by maroons who took the appellation Docoëns (today, Doko), "a denomination derived from the name of the place where the insurgents lived." "Having seized the mountains which surround those of Jacmel, they achieved perfect independence, which the colonial government recognized under the administration of Mr. Bellecombe, who was not able to subdue them," Dumesle wrote.[54] Recall that Julien Prévost drew a direct link between this maroon settlement and Enrique/Henri's in Bahoruco (see chapter 1 of the present volume). In Dumesle's account, this example of marronnage was evidence of an independence of spirit that was as inherent to New World African life as it was to Indigenous American life.

Ayitian resistance, Makandal's legacy, the maroons of Doko, and everyday fugitivity came to a fulcrum in mid-August 1791 when the path to full-blown revolution was blazed in the northern plain by Boukman Dutty. The French writer Antoine Dalmas was the first to report the story of the famous ceremony at Bois Caïman, which he said occurred on August 14, 1791, in a northern plain of Saint-Domingue called Morne-Rouge, near an uncultivated section of the Choiseul plantation called "le *Caïman*."[55] Most story-tellers today narrate the ceremony at Bois Caïman by describing it as one in which an enslaved man named Dutty Boukman (or Boukman Dutty) and a Black female religious leader (later identified by her grandson and granddaughter as Cécile Fatiman, a "green-eyed mulatto woman with long silken black hair, the daughter of a Corsican prince and an African woman," herself a "mambo" or a "voodoo high priestess") officiated.[56] The traditional version of the story holds that Fatiman, or another high priestess, killed a sacrificial pig and subsequently offered the blood of the animal to the adherents to drink. Boukman then reportedly delivered to his audience an exhortation to war in Creole: "The god of the white man calls him to commit crimes; our god asks only good works of us. But this god who is so good orders revenge! He will direct our hands; he will aid us. Throw away the image of the God of the whites who thirsts for our tears and listen to the voice of liberty which speaks in the hearts of all of us."[57] Dalmas's official recitation of the revolution in his *Histoire de la révolution de Saint-Domingue, depuis le commencement des troubles* (History of the revolution in Saint-Domingue, from the beginning of the troubles), though it was partly composed in 1793, was not published until 1814. All the same, it has long been recognized by scholars as the first mention of the Bois Caïman ceremony. Even before Dalmas's account was published, the importance of Boukman's leadership was known. After all, the Colonial Assembly succeeded in having Boukman's head delivered to them by a white French colonist named M. Michel who received six thousand colonial livres for assassinating the architect of the Haitian Revolution.[58] Killing Boukman was not enough to satisfy the rage of the colonists who blamed him for the entire rebellion. They decapitated and then burned his body. The white French colonists, with their veritable mania for heads on pikes, afterward exposed Boukman's in the middle of the Place d'Armes in Cap with a sign that read, "Head of Boukman, leader of the rebels." The white French colonists could see only massacre, not freedom, in the defunct leader's eyes. "Never did a severed head conserve so much expression: the open and still glistening eyes seemed to send his troops the signal to massacre," wrote one nineteenth-century chronicler.[59]

News of Boukman's radical undertaking traveled along with news of the Haitian Revolution, but in more quixotic ways than the stories of Makandal and Ogé, with each chronicler adding to, changing, or referencing the story to suit their own purposes. The unsigned manuscript of an illustrated play written in 1807 on board the British HMS *Crown* by a French prisoner captured by the British in the course of the French evacuation of Saint-Domingue, called *Le Philantrope révolutionnaire: ou, l'hécatombe à Haïti: drame historique, en 4 actes et en prose* (The revolutionary philanthropist, or hecatomb in Haiti: Historic drama in four acts and in prose), contains a character called "Boucman." However, he is not the leader of the insurrection of the enslaved population, which is led by the character called Spartacus. Antoine Métral's 1818 account of Boukman and the Bois Caïman ceremony was the first to make mention of a "young priestess, wearing a white dress," who "plunged a sacred knife into the entrails" of a "black pig." The French writer Civique de Gastine added that the ceremony took place on a stormy night with the "sound of thunder succeeding the mournful and plaintive chords occasioned by the winds blowing through reeds of broken bamboo."[60] Dumesle's *Voyage dans le nord d'Hayti*, however, is the first known written source to document the contents of Boukman's speech and contains the transcription of it still referenced by the vast majority of scholars who discuss the ceremony today.[61]

In Dumesle's retelling, the lyricism of poetry is restored to this world historical event. Eschewing with Dalmas's account, which Dumesle referenced disapprovingly,[62] the Haitian poet-historian recalled that it was "toward the middle of the month of August 1791 when cultivators, manufacturers, and artisans from several *ateliers* in northern Saint-Domingue reunited in the middle of the night. In the midst of a violent storm, they met up in the thick forest that covers the *sommet* of Morne-Rouge and formed the plan for a vast insurrection, which they sanctioned with a religious ceremony." Dumesle's account of the ceremony adds details potentially more crucial than just the speech. Here is the magnificent story as it was rendered by Dumesle into a poem:

Through the furrows by the lightning traced,
Where the glow of a hundred lights eclipsed burn,
Groups of the oppressed assemble in silence
They bow their heads invoking assistance
From the God, who, in a brilliant people awakened,
The illustrious Spartacus, that valiant slave,

Victim of destiny, but the eternal example,
Whose name and virtues deserved a temple
which no doubt would have its sublime design achieved.
If blind egoism, with a cold heart of brass and
of selfish interest, an apotheosis would not have made;
If the world had condemned these tyrants and their cause.

Although it is Toussaint Louverture who is most often connected to the narrative of the Roman rebel Spartacus,[63] here we find Boukman, whom Dumesle elsewhere refers to as "the principal leader of the congress at Morne-Rouge" (*principal formateur de la conjuration du Morne-Rouge*), fulfilling that position.[64]

Boukman seemed to command nature, whipping up a veritable chorus of rebellion, like Poseidon raising the seas:

With their plaintive tones, on these shores assembled,
The fiery sons of Eole, with lugubrious chords,
Mix their whistling sounds with the horrors of darkness;
The flexible bamboo, in these funereal concerts,
Shaken by the blows, breaks off with a roaring sound,
That reverberates far and wide with frightening resound.
Nature is troubled . . . their lamentable voices
Rise to her throne; she suspends those laws
Which from motion make harmony flourish,
And have made famous the cantor of Ausonie.
She saw the Colonist, in fits of delirium,
Engage in the transports of criminal excess;
Three centuries of slavery, outraging her clemency,
Her august presence sullied by his tortures;
And, unlucky plaything of the most cowardly furors,
The colored man groans under so many horrors.
Vengeance awakens, and the sword it does make shine
That once liberated Geneva's neighbors;
It arouses rapid surges of the heart;
That unheard of thirst, wonder of the senses;
Guide of despair and crime's precursor,
Out of necessity, becomes legitimate.

After the enslaved designees registered their storm of complaints at the altar of nature, and with Boukman residing, a calm washed over the assembly. Nature was already witness to the white colonists' many "fits of delirium" and "crimes of criminal excess." Now, nature would hear the testimony of the

114   Chapter 4

"colored man" who was made to "groan" under these endless "tortures." A moment of reflection followed. The animal victim of the sacrifice appeared, a bull, and a fire was lit:

Suddenly, calm is born, fiery north winds,
To the reign of Zephir have delivered these valleys;
Borée has fled the profound thickness of the woods;
The nymph, frightened by his escape, scolds him;
But what strikes our eyes! What is this light
That springs from a pyre in this place prepared! . . .
Has Attica transmitted its worship and its customs
To the unhappy children of these distant shores . . .
But a bull appears, and his black coloring,
This funereal apparel and its flowery fetters
Are for a sacrifice offered by innocence
To this deity that is adored by Hope.
Among the adherents a speaker arises
He has the august duty of a sacrificer
Armed with a sacred sword, his arm to the victim
Delivers the fatal blow, in the ardor that animates him.
It dies . . . At that moment he reads its entrails . . .
Prophetic delirium! . . . holocaust of blood! . . .
You unveil the fate of a noble undertaking
That makes heroes and immortalizes them! . . .
He speaks; and this language beloved by our ancestors,
That ingenious tongue that seemed made for them,
Whose naive accents, is a painting of their soul,
Lending more unction to this fiery speech
Electrifies their hearts in new transports.

Dumesle set this scene before he spoke of the "oracle" he consulted that revealed to him the contents of Boukman's speech, which the latter uttered before the "crowd . . . of the oppressed," who had gathered to hear Boukman's words of wisdom. The poem continues with Dumesle's transcription of Boukman's famous speech, the text of which appeared in *Voyage* in both French and Creole:

This God who from the sun the torch lit,
Who raises the seas and the storms makes rumble,
This God, have no doubt, hidden in a cloud,
This country he observes the infamies of the whites he sees;
Their religion encourages crime, and ours, good works.

But the supreme goodness commands vengeance
And will guide our hands; bolstered by his assistance,
Let us tread upon the idol thirsty for our tears.
Powerful Liberty! come . . . speak to every heart.

Placing particular and sustained emphasis on the ceremony, as narrated by Dumesle in his *Voyage*, allows us to trace how a poetics of Romanticism, or the notion that the poet is a "visionary, capable of piercing the mystery of the world and explaining it through symbol and allegory," became wedded to a politics of historical analyses in nineteenth-century Haitian thought.[65]

Early Haitian poets did not simply make the Haitian revolutionary past into lyric using the tenets of the Romantic school in concert with art for art's sake.[66] Dumesle referenced specific locales of the war for Haitian independence to activate a collective and corrective memory of the revolution, one that is further revealed in his extensive historical footnotes. Dumesle also called on deceased Haitian generals to act as witnesses, as well as on more germane objects of nature, such as stones, flowers, and valleys. By using these unconventional methods of historical reconstruction, Dumesle created a revolutionary romanticism for Haiti that, while designed to combat what he considered to be false and flawed representations of the country coming from the former colonists, did not rely solely, or even primarily, on the kinds of official documents ordinarily deployed to support the tone of positivist empiricism commonly found in white French colonial writing. Instead, Dumesle used a range of ethnographic, archeologic, literary, and historical artifacts, including oral testimonies, verse poetry, official colonial records, and physical relics, to turn the ceremony of Boukman into both an impressionistic romantic poem and a politically charged historical epic.

Dumesle's *Voyage* seems to tell us that relying on the Haitian ancestors as well as the Haitian earth to tell Haiti's story would better reflect the lived experiences of the Haitian revolutionaries, in contrast with the utterly prejudiced writings of former French colonists papering the world with their lies about the Haitian people, such as Drouin de Bercy, Antoine Dalmas, and Baron de Malouet. Those former white French colonists' theories of the natural world, Dumesle said, had one purpose only: "to prove the inferiority of a great portion of the human race."[67] Dumesle manifested the Haitian revolution as a war for freedom by referring to the oracle once more and the immediate consequences its prophecy of salvation delivered for the budding revolutionaries in its midst:

The oracle is proclaimed. The devouring flame
Rises in a whirl toward the shining vault,

-1—
0—
+1—

116   Chapter 4

Where a thousand diamonds with their starry fires,
Shine upon these deserts with shadows veiled
The trembling light of their pale rays.
Incense burns; and, already upon a broad litter,
The victim is offered to the vengeful god,
That this liberating god has just received.
The burning pyre is now nothing more than a pile of ashes;
They consecrate these woods; their songs are there heard.
They will turn their steps toward the next hamlet;
But their eyes are struck by a new wonder . . .
Near a smoldering stake falls an owl;
Its fall announces the hecatomb of the wicked.
The interpreter of the gods explains their plans;
All is purified in these pious hands.
Each of the conspirators, with a feather embellished,
In this frail ornament sees according to the custom
Of these various rites that defy reason,
The sacred amulet unknown to Jason,
That Europe did adore under the law of a pontiff
Fanatic rival of the indignant Caliph.[68]

Let us pause once again to consider the relationship between Haitian revolutionary thought and the language still used to describe the most gruesome oppression and suffering that occurred in the twentieth century. "Holocaust of blood," Dumesle lamented earlier in the poem. For him, a "holocaust" of enslaved Africans is what the system of slavery wrought and the Haitian Revolution was the retribution it deserved. African body after African body after African body had disappeared during "three centuries of slavery" and would now be avenged by the enslaved of Saint-Domingue. The "hecatomb of the wicked" was the general insurrection that was soon to enflame the entire northern plain.

Chanlatte provided even more distinct terminology to describe the culpability of the colonists of Saint-Domingue and the righteousness of the freedom fighters who put an end to their crimes. In 1807, as editor of the *Gazette de l'État d'Hayti*, Chanlatte wrote that the French colonial traffic in the "human race" (*de l'espèce humaine*) was a "crime against humanity" (*crime de lèse-humanité*).[69] Early nineteenth-century Haitians used this seemingly modern legalistic language of human rights a lot—crime, holocaust, extermination—to describe the attempted genocide of the French against the Haitian people, not just during the Leclerc–Rochambeau expedition of 1802–3, but during the entire period of slavery and colonialism.[70] In so doing they created a new syllabary with idioms for white supremacy and racism and, crucially, for slavery and the slave trade as crimes against humanity.

Both the slave trade and slavery were "legalized" forms of human commerce in most of the early modern and eighteenth- and nineteenth-century Atlantic World. But Haitians called this putative legality into question much earlier than previous intellectual debates over the emergence of the term "crime against humanity" have acknowledged. With forceful condemnation, they pointed to the deep immorality of laws authorizing human trafficking. To do so, they used the language of modern human rights.[71] Haitian writers and politicians created new vocabulary words and phrases for the New World forms of torture and degradation that they and their ancestors on the island of Ayiti were among the first inhabitants of the Caribbean to experience.

Although the phrase "crime de lèse-humanité" as connected to the slave trade first surfaced in Haiti in 1807 with Chanlatte, it was Baron de Vastey, who coined its more modern formulation to refer to the European practice of enslaving people. In his 1816 *Réflexions sur une lettre de Mazères*, Vastey wrote that slavery was a "crime . . . contre l'espèce humaine" or a "crime . . . against the human race." The passage is remarkable for how Vastey labels slavery and the slave trade as crimes, with racism, and white supremacy as tools the colonists used to perpetuate their "sophistic and absurd" justification for slavery. "They gave themselves the barbaric right to reduce us to perpetual slavery, and to treat us like the most vile beasts," Vastey wrote. The Haitian Revolution was atonement for these crimes. "What event is more glorious, more worthy of capturing the world's attention, than the one that overturned in fact, with still living witnesses, the entire scaffold of crimes and lies erected by them for two centuries against the human race!" Vastey exclaimed.[72] Even though the word genocide did not exist in the era of the Haitian Revolution, it is not an anachronistic term to use.[73] Genocidal acts far predate the word's mid-twentieth-century official definition, which includes "intentional destruction of a national, ethnic, racial and religious group, in whole or in part."[74] What the Haitian Revolution clearly demonstrates—in particular, the revolutionaries' development of an entire vocabulary to describe the many atrocities that fell under the umbrella of a "crime against humanity"—is that words that describe never before seen phenomena usually only emerge in the wake of the momentous events occasioning their birth.

The words for genocide that the French colonists and then the Haitian revolutionaries most often used were "destruction," "massacre," and "extermination." The Marquise de Rouvray, wife of a famous French colonist and military leader, penned a painfully detailed outline for the total "destruction

-1—
0—
+1—

118   Chapter 4

or deportation" of the free people of color in a letter to her daughter in August of 1793. She wrote that a massacre of the "white" population of Saint-Domingue was generally unavoidable unless, "we succeed in creating another way of doing things which will entail the destruction or the deportation of all free men and women of color, after having marked them on both cheeks with the letter 'L' for Libre, so that they will never be tempted to come back to Saint-Domingue." These deportations, according to de Rouvray, should be of long *durée* and have longitudinal familial consequences. Those who were born subsequently, she insisted, would at the age of seven years old be branded and deported. "If we held firm to this rule," the Marquise wrote, "we would be able to rebuild our properties in Saint-Domingue." Deportation combined with sterilization was for the Marquise the final solution: "One other measure may perhaps be more final than the one that I just described, which would be to render male and female children of color unable to reproduce . . . the men would be too weak to try anything against the whites and the women would no longer serve the latter. In the end, my dear girl, if we do not crush this caste, there will be no salvation for Saint-Domingue."[75] In 1792, the colonist Barillon also argued that every "mulatto" should be "crushed" using the bayonet. But to effect this "extermination" without having to literally kill each and every person of color, he proposed a potential alternative method of eliminating them: "their deportation to the island of Ascension . . . providing them with food for one year . . . and giving them for a bishop *that troublemaker Grégoire*, and for a mayor *that coward Brissot*." Barillon concluded that regardless of the method ultimately used, "*the first point is the deportation of the mulattoes, and the confiscation of their property in compensation [for the property] of the whites that were burned*."[76] Genocidal imaginings spanned the spectrum of the white population in the colony. Garran de Coulon recalled that a crowd of sailors, in a "recitation" signed by them, wrote that the French should "*exterminate that execrable race of mulattoes*."[77]

Exterminating the entire population of "mulattoes," free people of color, and eventually all "negroes" is alluded to constantly in French colonial writing during the Haitian Revolution. André Rigaud lamented this in a 1797 memoir, "There exists (and this is not at all in doubt), there exists a faction that tends to want the total destruction of all the citizens of color in Saint-Domingue."[78] Such horrifying imaginings vis-à-vis exterminating people of color could be found in the letters of ordinary citizens, as well as in the decrees and speeches of public officials, in the accounts of mariners and merchants, and in the publications of travel writers. The white supremacist ideologies of the colonists turned the Haitian Revolution in their imaginations into a "racial" war where the victor would not only win the contested territory but would completely eliminate their opponents from the earth.

Racism in French colonial Saint-Domingue clearly was used to support transatlantic slavery, but it was also instrumentalized by the white population to urge the implementation of eugenics and what has euphemistically been called "ethnic cleansing." Revolutionary Saint-Domingue was a world in which the idea of Black rebellion as race war was so well accepted that a language that reeked of *genocidal imaginings* was ubiquitous.[79]

The Haitian Revolution, and the 1804 Principle it brought to life, were direct responses to what Dumesle referred to as the "inhumane doctrine" of extermination proposed by the colonists. "Condemning us to eternal reprobation," Dumesle said that it was the white colonists "who forced us to take control over our civil and political existence by braving both dangers and death."[80] The blood spilled by the "juridical assassins" of Ogé and Chavannes "birth[ed] the avengers" who congregated during the Morne-Rouge assembly, and freedom manifested in revolution.[81] As eighteenth-century Saint-Domingue's free people of color had done before them, nineteenth-century Haitian intellectuals like Dumesle and Vastey linked the murder of Ogé and Chavannes directly to the general insurrection that led to the Haitian Revolution. Vastey wrote, "The blood of those martyrs, the blood of Ogé and Chavanne[s], shed ignominiously on a scaffold, was crying out for revenge, and provided the impetus for the revolution."[82] Dumesle more directly connected the deaths of these revolutionary free men of color to the beginning of the revolution.[83] Saint-Domingue was already sitting on the crater of a volcano, Dumesle said. Taking a detour to explain this overwrought, but nonetheless arresting metaphor,[84] Dumesle made the comparison by way of analogy to Pliny, the Roman naturalist and philosopher. Pliny was reportedly sitting on the edge of a volcano one day when he decided to throw a rock inside to check its depths. This action caused such agitation that the sulfur gasses within rose up and engulfed the unfortunate "observer."[85] Although Dumesle believed that the execution of Ogé and Chavannes was the rock thrown into the volcano, what follows from his account can help us to see that the volcano was located in the hearts of the enslaved and it was set to erupt long before the famous public execution of these free men of color.

For three centuries, enslaved Africans set the stage in Saint-Domingue for a spectacular revolution against the enslavers subjecting them to horrible crimes against humanity. Everyday resistance was common in the form of marronnage, but there was also outright violent opposition. The execution of Ogé and his allies merely helped to propel forward a wheel long since set in motion. Before the eighteenth century concluded, the New World revolutionaries of Saint-Domingue forced France to abolish slavery in all its overseas territories and laid the groundwork under the leadership of Toussaint Louverture for the country to gain the independence that none of the island's first revolutionary figures appear to have wanted.

In their unequivocal pronouncement in the Haitian Declaration of Independence that slavery could no longer exist alongside liberty, the post-Toussaint Haitian revolutionaries taught the world about the true meaning of not only freedom, but revolution. The larger events ordinarily narrated as central to the Haitian Revolution—the execution of Makandal, then of Ogé and Chavannes, followed by the ceremony at Bois Caïman—had active precursors that did not necessarily enter into the colonial frame in easily discernible ways. Dumesle more forcefully referenced these circumstances than either Raimond or Vastey, who both alluded to them in more subtle fashion. Dumesle linked the start of the Haitian Revolution to several seemingly small catalysts that all converged at once. "Rumors and the flight of several individuals to the woods, created a true disturbance that agitated even the simplest spectators of these scenes, and gave to the partial insurrections, which they had created, a consistency that one could judge by the rapidity of their progress," Dumesle wrote.[86] Here, he stressed that it was the many forms of resistance and enslaved *Black* organization that led to the success of Haiti's war of independence. Dumesle, who was only a child when the Haitian Revolution began, indicated that several additional clandestine meetings of enslaved people took place around the same time as the Morne-Rouge assembly. These accounts of subsequent meetings make Dumesle's *Voyage* one of the most important *Haitian* sources, a stunning flashpoint even, for the early days of the slave rebellions that turned into the full-blown Haitian Revolution. Dumesle appears, in fact, to have been the first to call Haiti's war of independence the "Haitian Revolution" (*la révolution haïtienne*).[87] Baron de Vastey, in contrast, who wrote the first full-length history of Haiti by a Haitian, referred to these events as the revolution of Haiti (*la révolution d'Hayti*), while many French authors simply called it the "insurrection in Saint-Domingue."[88] Dumesle, in contrast, gave himself the permission to name this momentous event the "Haitian Revolution" and, in so doing, he put it on par with its French and U.S. American counterparts.

Haiti's was not simply a revolution that happened in Saint-Domingue after the French and American revolutions. It was a three-centuries-long organized rebellion, which resulted in an overthrow of elite colonial authority and the establishment of an anti-racist, anti-colonial, antislavery state. As such, this event of world-historical significance was far more radical than either the U.S. American or French revolutions. The African American writer and orator James Theodore Holly, who permanently relocated to Haiti in 1861, acknowledged the disproportionate significance of the Haitian Revolution when compared to the American Revolution. "The Haitian Revolution is also the grandest political event of this or any other age. In weighty causes, and wondrous and momentous features, it surpasses the American revolution, in an incomparable degree," Holly wrote. "Never before, in all the annals of the world's history, did a nation of abject and chattel slaves arise in the terrific might of their resuscitated manhood, and regenerate, redeem, and disenthrall themselves: by taking their station at one gigantic bound, as an independent nation, among the sovereignties of the world."[89] This much was earlier recognized by Vastey, who observed that if both the U.S. American and Haitian revolutions were products of a "torrent and coincidence of events" that eventually culminated in the termination of a "bad marriage" with the metropole, there was no comparison to be made between the material conditions of U.S. Americans at the moment of independence and those of Haitians.[90] The American colonists, Vastey reminded the world, at the time of their revolution, "were themselves white Englishmen, free and propertied [who] enjoyed their natural civil and political rights, [and] no one disputed them these rights."[91] Their revolution against England was solely a question of independence, not emancipation. Any comparison between the only two independent states of the Americas and their acts of independence therefore sublimated the racial distinctions of Haiti as a country populated mostly by Africans who were, "black and enslaved, without country, without property, deprived of their natural rights." In other words, Haiti's blackness was the reason for its threatened position in the New World, and the United States' whiteness was the reason for its security.[92]

Let us now follow Dumesle as he takes us into some of the other *acts* and *deeds* that led to Haiti's remarkable revolution for *racial* freedom. Not far from that spot where the Morne-Rouge assembly occurred, Dumesle reported another ceremony took place to make a separate offering to the gods. "There, a pig was sacrificed, and a young virgin became the Pythia [oracle of Delphi] who consulted the palpitating entrails of the victim; she raised her innocent hands to the sky and exclaimed in inspired tones that the divinity was propitious for an enterprise surrounded by so many happy portents. Every person's imagination, excited to action by the reference to all the ills suffered, compelled them to no longer hesitate to run to arms."[93] Dumesle put numerous prominent female participants front and center in the myriad religious ceremonies and secret meetings that ushered in the revolution. Here, we have the introduction of a "jeune vierge" (young virgin) at a separate ceremony, along with a sacrificial pig, rather than the bull Dumesle associated with Boukman's meeting. Dalmas's initial conflation of the two gatherings is perhaps how the two stories, that of Boukman in Morne-Rouge and that of Fatiman, or the unnamed female religious leader who sacrificed a pig, became one in the narrative of the nineteenth-century Haitian historian Céligny Ardouin.[94]

C. Ardouin, brother of the much more famous nineteenth-century Haitian historian Beaubrun Ardouin and the poet Coriolan Ardouin, wrote that

122   Chapter 4

on the night of August 14, 1791, "Boukman also resorted to the influence of the magical fetish. He led those believers to the woods named Caïman . . . there, a priestess plunged a knife into the bowels of a black pig. . . . On his knees, Boukman took the terrible oath to direct the enterprise, an oath commanded by the priestess." Ardouin put this ceremony not at the Choiseul plantation in Morne-Rouge, but at the plantation of Le Normand de Mézy. Le Normand de Mézy also owned another plantation in Limbé, where he enslaved Makandal.[95] Although the two ceremonies have been often conflated, Dumesle clearly understood there to have been two distinct events, one where the actual planning of the rebellion took place, in Morne-Rouge, about which the "oracle" spoke to Dumesle to transmit Boukman's speech, and a second one, where God gave the "young virgin" the signal to begin the revolution after the pig sacrifice.[96] Dumesle's understanding is commensurate with cont emporary historians' conclusions. It has now been well established that the ceremony where the pig was sacrificed followed, and did not precede, the Morne-Rouge assembly.[97]

The consequences of both gatherings were immediate. Near midnight, the night after the second ceremony referred to by Dumesle, on the night passing from August 23 to 24, in his account, a tocsin rang out. This was the signal to act, and the insurrection exploded with furor. "Liberty" and "vengeance" were the rallying cries and the "divinities" to which all was sacrificed in the early days of the "insurrection." Elderly whites, along with white women and children, fled the plantations that just the day before were the scene of their opulence and pleasure.[98] As for the white colonists, Dumesle wrote that their own memories would have conjured up for them the reasons behind their sudden change of fortune, if they had been capable of such introspection.

A planter named Jean-Baptiste Pillet returned to Saint-Domingue from Bordeaux in August 1791, just before the outbreak of general insurrection.[99] In the manuscript called "Mon Odyssée" (My odyssey) that he penned while a refugee in the United States, which not unlike Dumesle's *Voyage* is part prose narration of his experiences and part epic poetry, Pillet recalled his horror upon seeing his family's plantation burned to the ground:

> Already, the insurrection was spreading its ravages on all sides, and we were afraid that it would very soon reach the place where we were living. News of this terrible catastrophe had already spread all over. Frightened neighbors of our family came to join us. The men armed themselves in order to face the storm head on. Mothers, spouses, and sisters groaning, gathered in haste a few precious belongings. Fear and despair were painted on every face. The sky appeared to be on fire. Rifle shots could be heard in the distance. The bells on the plantations sounded the alarm. Danger was growing. The flames, with their hideous envelopment, at

every instance, grew closer to us, and there was no time to lose: we departed. Victims fleeing the dagger joined us and thus increased the number of fugitives, and told us of the horrors to which they were witness. They had seen tortures unheard of until that moment; planters who were the most renowned for their generous treatment with respect to their slaves were torn to pieces first, and by those who had been most favored by them. Women who were young, beautiful, and virtuous had perished under the vile caresses of these brigands, among the cadavers of their fathers and their spouses. Their still pulsating tatters were dragged through the streets with the most atrocious applause. Some young children, transfixed by the point of the bayonets, were the bloody standard-bearers who followed the troops of cannibals. Alas! These portraits have not been exaggerated, and me, myself, more than one time, I was witness to this terrible spectacle![100]

Many of Pillet's reactions exemplify Dumesle's sense that there was little self-reflection on the part of the colonists, even long after the revolution was over. Pillet demonstrated a clear lack of empathy for the previous violence he admitted to using against the people he enslaved on his plantation, a violence that, had he similarly described in explicit terms, would have clearly justified what he characterized as treachery and disloyalty. Instead, Pillet inserted this poem to lament his fate:

Oh! What painter could re-create
this terrible portrait,
which at this moment offers only an image of a desert!
Those grids where the evergreen cane grew,
ashes now hide its depths!
Those vast workshops, those opulent homes,
otherwise the sites of hospitality,
furniture smashed, fuming joists
cover over the bloody marble floors.
That subdued African, who, made into a slave,
not so long ago, for his master would have shed his blood,
today, furious, he slits his throat in rage,
as well as his fearful wife and feeble child!
Oh, my country! Oh, land that was once without rival!
Crimes, misfortunes, unleashed all at once,
have come to your shores from the infernal banks;
and your sons, having escaped from the fatal hatchet
defend without hope the wreckage of their homes![101]

Professing bewilderment, Pillet asked of the enslaved in rebellion, "Why was there so much anger in their destruction? . . . It can only be out of hatred for us; they don't even know us."[102] For Dumesle, who likely witnessed much of the flight of these white planters while still a child, the white colonists were incapable of feeling remorse. In fleeing the colony, they callously wiped away, along with their tears, the traces of "the long suite of injustices, those attacks against humanity," the result of their many tyrannies.[103] "They compared their situation to the fate of the victims of their greed," Dumesle continued, "who, reduced to seeking in suicide a remedy for their painful anxieties, found in crimes contrary to the laws of nature the means of removing from their unhappy destiny, the fate to which they could bequeath only their sufferings and their chains!"[104]

Vastey asserted even more aggressively the right of those who were forced into slavery by the ex-colonists to free themselves using any available means. "I have often asked myself this question," Vastey wrote, "what right did the ex-colonists have to torture their unfortunate slaves like that?" "What? is there in this world, as in the other, a race of executioners destined to torment humankind? are the ex-colonists on earth what are the demons of hell?" he asked. Vastey then redefined and recategorized slavery in the annals not just of human crimes, but of human sins. "Slavery is the work of corrupt and wicked men," he insisted. "It is the most awful plague that has ever afflicted humankind." Whereas in other texts Vastey largely rested his case on legal arguments, which approach modern doctrines of human rights, here Vastey turned to religion and the idea that because all human beings originate, in Christian thought, from a single source, all human beings are in essence part of the same great divine family, sharing the same holy lineage to Adam and Eve, and therefore the same right to life. Appealing to the Christian sensibility of his readers, Vastey called enslavers sacrilegious since they claimed rights over other human beings that only God could possess. "What? you could deprive me of my liberty, deprive me of the most precious of all possessions; you could burden me with chains I do not deserve, and I, your brother and fellow human, I could not claim the rights that I hold from God alone, that no one can take away from me; I could not, I must say, break my chains, and overwhelm you with their own weight[?]" Vastey finished by pointing out that only the purveyors of such an "abominable logic!" evidence of a "frightful morality!" would want to "persuade men that some of them should have the right to reduce others to perpetual slavery, without the latter having the right to ever be able to free themselves from it!" The colonists' desire to continuing enslaving Black people in perpetuity was more than a perversion of biblical thought in Vastey's mind. It was also evidence that the enslavers of

Revolution 125

the Americas had adopted a "science of slavery" that entailed trying to convince the world that "freedom is evil, and slavery is good." If the white colonists truly wanted to prove the righteousness of their actions, as much as the sophisms they used to support them, all they had to do, Vastey sardonically concluded, was to "put themselves in our place."[105]

Yet, it is perhaps one of Vastey's earlier phrases in his *Réflexions sur une lettre de Mazères* that most speaks to the incoherence of white colonists who dared to call themselves Christians. "But have white people followed the spirit of the gospel vis-à-vis the unfortunate Africans and Americans?" Vastey asked. Answering in the negative, he declared, "The whites only followed the spirit of the gospel vis-à-vis whites." "Christianity, the religion of a God of peace and charity, is the pretext these men used to exterminate the unfortunate Americans," and claiming to want to "make Christians of them, the unfortunate Africans have been plunged into the most cruel slavery."[106] The way that Vastey speaks of "God," the God he believed in, if you will, brings us back to how Boukman evoked *Bondye* in his speech, and the contrasting way the white colonists used the idea of God in the punishment they served to Ogé and Chavannes. What a stark divergence from how the white colonial officials spoke of their God (the Christian one who kept Ogé and Chavannes alive so that they might suffer on the wheel, as "long as it pleases him") versus how the enslaved Black people of the Morne-Rouge gathering spoke of *Bondye*, the true God (a righteous one who labeled as a "good work" the ability of the Black people of Saint-Domingue to free themselves). This "theological orientation," in one scholar's words, closely reflects a Vodou cosmology, where there is "one true Bondje (God), who is good, the Bondje of Voudou."[107] The God of the Haitian revolutionaries begged them to seek virtuous revenge, while that of white French people was a spiteful, torturing, and punishing God, who took distinct pleasure in the suffering of others, not unlike the white colonists. There would be no absolution in suicide for colonists such as these. Their feelings of unwarranted righteousness did not compel them to give into the slaves' despair and desperate deliverance. To that end, Pillet seemed astonished by what he interpreted as an enslaved man's disregard and indifference toward life. Pillet, who was in pursuit of the man in open rebellion, alongside the French military, suddenly happened upon him, and:

> When [the man] saw that his fate had been decided, he began to laugh, sing, and banter. At times he insulted us with a furious tone, at other times, he made fun of us with an air of mockery . . . he accepted death without fear and without complaint. We found, in one of his pockets, pamphlets, printed in France, filled with commonplaces about the rights of man and the holy insurrection. In his jacket there was a big packet of

phosphoric locks. He had on his stomach a little bag filled with hair, herbs, and bones. It was what they call a fetish; with this he believed that he was sheltered from all danger; and it is without a doubt because of this amulet that our man owed the fearlessness that the philanthropists will call stoic philosophy.[108]

Whether or not this stoically executed man spoken of by Pillet carried these pamphlets, or the macandal, in his pocket is not as important as the fact that the planter believed, or sought to make others believe, that the man had them. Pillet here connected the revolt and rebellion of the enslaved of Saint-Domingue all at once to the Enlightenment, the French Revolution, and the earlier rebellion of Makandal, whose "soul values" made a mockery of the French colonial ritual of capital punishment.

For many free people of color, like Raimond, who had still not yet been willing to see that their fates were indelibly yoked to that of the people they enslaved, all of this could have been avoided if the colonists had simply granted to the *hommes de couleur* unequivocal rights of citizenship. Labuissonnière reported to Raimond, while the latter was still in France, that from every corner it was being said that the decree of May 15, 1791, would not be executed and that the colonists would prefer to lose the colony. "As for me, I'm imagining this to be a schoolboy mutiny," Labuissonnière wrote. Although the white colonists said they were superior in every way to the men of color, Labuissonnière pointed out that the men of color, at the very least, were equal in number population-wise to the white colonists.[109] Therefore, if need be, the men of color could easily assemble troops. Specifically, "all those who have been to Savannah are once again volunteering themselves, and I am proud to believe that these three thousand men . . . would be a torrent to which Lucifer could oppose nothing."[110]

A not insignificant number of the *hommes de couleur* of Saint-Domingue, including the late Chavannes himself, fought in the American War of Independence as a part of the Comte de Estaing's Chasseurs Volontaires at the Battle of Savannah in October 1779. These same men were mobilized in the wake of the affairs of Ferrand de Baudière, Ogé, and Boukman. In Dumesle's account we learn of a free woman of color whose house, after the execution of Ogé and company, became the destination for a secret assembly of the *indigènes*, Dumesle's word for those *hommes de couleur* born with free status in the colony. It was at the home of Louise Rateau, according to Dumesle, that Louis Jacques Beauvais, a principal fighter at the Battle of Savannah, was named captain general; Antoine Chanlatte, major general; Alexandre Pétion, commandant of the artillery; and Marc Borno, commandant of the cavalry.[111] A pact was also made with Rigaud, another fighter from the Savannah days, who became colonel general for Les Cayes.[112] After Rigaud's release from jail in connection with the Ogé affair, he retired to Croix-des-Bouquets, where many other free men of color were gathered. At their head were Beauvais and another free man of color, Lambert, who had been named their leaders. They chose Rigaud to second them. "We were, Beauvais and I," Rigaud wrote, "among those who, having fought in the plains of Savannah for the freedom of the peoples of America, learned to fight for our own. Enthusiastic about the French revolution, we had from then on taken the solemn oath to defend it until our last breath, and we never varied in our principles."[113] These "indigenous" men of Saint-Domingue who fought in the American revolutionary war, like Rigaud, "for so long showered with annoyances, and whom the colonial system placed outside of humanity," in Dumesle's estimation, set an "example," both abroad and at home, which would stand as "testimony against those tyrants until the final ages of the world."[114] Still, even these free men of color, the warriors of Savannah, associated liberty with France. This would only change by degrees and in increments.

The National Assembly eventually revoked the law of May 15—guaranteeing voting representation for persons born of free parents and "possessing the requisite qualifications"—in September of the same year. However, the provisions of the May 15, 1791 law, granting political rights to a few of the free Blacks and other qualified free men of color, were reinstated with a subsequent French law on April 4, 1792. This law guaranteed political equality to the men of color universally with the sanction of the king. But Louis XVI was at that point an unwitting constitutional monarch who had fled to Varennes, and who had no choice but to ratify and execute the laws passed by the Legislative Assembly. The incoherence of revolutionary and then republican France was not lost on Dumesle, who observed that it was French revolutionary contradictions— back and forth on the question of whether all human beings were "persons" who had rights to freedom and equality—that ultimately led to the loss of the colony during the Leclerc expedition. "This is how, with the help of much reticence, contradiction, and exceptional arrangements, the governments of Europe at one moment withdraw the concessions they are forced to make in another," Dumesle wrote. "We have seen that of France successively promulgate the law of April 4, and then halt its implementation: proclaim General liberty [in 1794], promising to the heavens that it would be maintained, and then decree, on May [20], 1802, *that the French Colonies would return to the regime of 1789.*"[115] It was not just the colonists of Saint-Domingue who posed a threat to the newly formed French republic. The National Assembly remained unable to fully contend with questions of liberty and equality. Raimond pointed out this very contradiction when he rhetorically addressed the French National Assembly: "If the liberty and equality which you have so sol-

128   Chapter 4

emnly decreed are not meaningless things without effect for those who have made it their religion; if you have not triumphed in vain over the whole of Europe; if the fortunes and blood of the French were not lavished on chimeras; if finally we must rely on the principles irrevocably laid down by our constitution, pronounce between the partisans of slavery and the privileged, and the men who have put all their effort and sacrificed their lives and their fortunes to fight them."[116] Regarding the September 24 revocation of the May decree, Raimond explained that Barnave, who supported this surprising reversal, had been ill informed and just repeated what the colonists had told him, "*if ever the colored men were assimilated to the whites, the slaves would revolt and the colonies would be lost.*"[117] Raimond, though still preaching moderation and patience, was indignant: "The decree of May 15, 1791 . . . seemed to all sage minds to have reconciled everything, because it established the right of citizenship for every individual born of a free father and mother."[118] This was done to reassure the colonists that they would continue to have property rights over their "slaves." The decree instead led to huge disasters because the colonists protested it. The effect of the May 15 decree's revocation, in the colonists' own words, was the slaughter of the free men of color in Cap, at least nine of them, while others were pursued in their flight "like ferocious beasts."[119] The rupture of the *concordat*, or agreement between the *hommes de couleur* and the *blancs colons* to implement the May 15 law, along with the continued rebellion of the enslaved population, led to the burning of Port-au-Prince,[120] and later Cap-Français, and subsequently forced the second set of commissioners sent by France to the island in September 1792 to "restore order"— which originally meant to maintain slavery—to instead abolish it a year later. We are still not at the moment when independence enters the horizon. The free people of color, including Toussaint Louverture, who is about to enter our story more forcefully, cannot yet see their way through the incoherence of French republicanism to Haitian sovereignty.

Chapter 5

Abolition

Following two years of general insurrection, the French government sent Léger-Félicité Sonthonax, along with two other French commissioners, Étienne Polverel and Jean-Antoine Ailhaud, to Saint-Domingue to enforce the April 4 decree guaranteeing equal rights for free men of color. Although upon their arrival the commissioners declared slavery had to endure forever, on August 29, 1793, Sonthonax stunned the colony's white inhabitants by issuing a general emancipation proclamation to the enslaved men and women of Saint-Domingue. "The French Republic wants liberty and equality to exist for all men, without distinction of color," the decree reads. "Kings are only happy when they are among slaves: it is they who, on the coasts of Africa, sold you to the whites; it is the tyrants of Europe who would like to perpetuate this infamous traffic. The REPUBLIC is adopting you among its children; kings aspire only to load you with chains or annihilate you."[1] In this preamble, Sonthonax blamed the defunct French monarchy for slavery and proclaimed the French republic to be, in stark contrast, emancipatory. The republic, diametrically opposed to monarchy, could no longer continue with the laws that governed the colonies under the *ancien régime*. "Liberty transports you from nothingness to existence," Sonthonax wrote. Then, before taking a sharp dig at the former French king, executed by the Jacobins in January 1793, Sonthonax reminded the (now) formerly enslaved and the free men of color that it was, he, Sonthonax, who was ostensibly *freeing* them. Sonthonax said that both groups—the *anciens libres* and the newly "freed"—should be wary of aligning themselves with either the British or Spanish king, especially if the latter promised them liberty. "The kings are promising freedom to you: but do you see them giving it to their subjects?" he asked. "Does the Spaniard free his slaves? No, without a doubt; he promises very well, on the contrary, to load you with irons as soon as your services become useless to him. Was it not he who delivered Ogé to his assassins? Unfortunate as you are! if France had a king once more, you would soon become the prey of the émigrés; they caress you today; [but] they would be your first executioners." For Sonthonax, kings now meant slavery and racial subjugation. The republic, in contrast, supposedly signified liberty. Sonthonax's evocation of Ogé, too, for the second time in the preamble, would have played right into the free men of colors' racial consciousnesses, as well as that of the newly liberated formerly enslaved population, for whom the memory of this lost comrade was still a motivating force.

In the emancipation proclamation, Sonthonax positioned the colonists, both the royalists and the independence strivers, as well as the Spanish, as Ogé's eternal enemies. They were therefore also the enemies of his numerous avengers, including the enslaved population, many of whom had already de facto freed themselves through rebellion. Sonthonax characterized the white French colonists as "a horde of tyrants who publicly preached that skin color was of necessity a sign of superiority or of degradation." Sonthonax also underscored that the French government sent the three Civil Commissioners, Sonthonax, Polverel, and Ailhaud, to the island specifically to put the brakes on the prejudices of "the judges of the unfortunate Ogé, the cretins and members of those infamous commissions of marshals who filled the cities with gibbets and wheels, to sacrifice Africans and men of color to their atrocious pretensions."[2] The very name Ogé repeatedly evoked in this historic document highlights the magnitude of the earthquake that his execution released, the aftershocks of which continued to shake the Atlantic World for decades.

Following the fiery preamble were thirty-three articles announcing the formal abolition of slavery in the northern province: "Men are born free and equal in rights." Every person was born free, semantically, but that freedom was physically taken away in Saint-Domingue through active violence and legal manoeuvers. The white French colonists labored for two centuries to prove that Africans and those of African descent were not quite human and therefore that any doctrines pertaining to the rights of human beings did not apply to them. Sonthonax used the Declaration of the Rights of Man as if it were an abolitionist manifesto, though its creators never intended it as such. The first article of the emancipation decree mandated, "The Declaration of the Rights of Man and the Citizen" should be "printed, published and posted everywhere"; while the second observed, "All Negroes and people of mixed blood currently enslaved are declared free to enjoy all the rights pertaining to French citizenship."

A series of complicated provisions followed. These put into question the meaning of abolition, not for the enslaved, but for Sonthonax. Article 9 mandated, "Slaves currently attached to the plantations of their former masters will be obliged to remain there and work the land." Articles 11 and 12 then laid out a system of compensation for such "laborers" who were to share a third of the plantation's revenues, equal thirds belonging to the planter and to the French government, respectively.[3] This system, called *affermage*, or leasing, is linked to the labor organization that remained in place under Toussaint Louverture's later rule, as it did in altered form under that of Dessalines, Christophe, and Boyer.

A little under a month after Sonthonax shook the island anew with his emancipation proclamation, on September 21, 1793, fellow French commissioner Étienne Polverel followed Sonthonax's lead by abolishing slavery in sections of the colony under his authority, starting in the western province. Beaubrun Ardouin wrote of this:

> And so, September 21, 1793 was marked in Port-au-Prince and in all the municipalities of the West, by the greatest act of justice that has ever been rendered in the colony of Saint-Domingue. A pompous ceremony brought together citizens of all colors on the Place d'Armes in this city: the National Guard, the Legion of Equality, European line troops, civil and military officials. There, Polverel, mounted on the altar of the fatherland, delivered a speech after which he proclaimed the general freedom of all slaves. All the owners adhered to this act of justice, and affixed their signatures to the registry opened for this purpose.[4]

Polverel began this speech so celebrated by Ardouin by reminding the inhabitants of the western part of the colony, where he lived, that he had earlier promised eventual emancipation to enslaved Africans. Stating that Sonthonax's August 29 emancipation decree moved forward his own timeline for issuing one, Polverel explained to the inhabitants of the city of Port-au-Prince that he was abolishing slavery there, not simply for the sake of the enslaved Africans, but for the good of the entire French republic and, especially, for the owners of plantations in the west. "Citizens, this is what I have done, I will not say for the Africans only, but for you as well as for them. This is what you would have done yourselves under the present circumstances, if the habit of ordering slaves around, of doing nothing for yourselves and relying only on slaves, had enabled you to properly judge your position and your true interests." Directly referencing the Declaration of the Rights of Man, Polverel then asked, "Will your ears be closed to the voice of your motherland? When she said in September 1792, I want all my children to be governed by a republican government, for the Republic to be one and indivisible in every territory that comprises the French Empire; I want Liberty and Equality to be the forever immutable foundations of this Republic; did you never hear her words? Did she not remind you of the language of human rights? 'All men are born and remain free and equal in rights'?"[5] Polverel then went straight to the contradiction at the heart of the foundation of the French republic. "Can Equality exist wherever there is a single slave?" he asked. "Isn't freedom the most important of human rights? The Africans whose blood runs in your veins, are they not also men?"[6] Although it was Louverture who later became associated with the Haitian revolution's classic tree of liberty image when he was loaded onto the ship to France that would become the vessel to his grave—

132   Chapter 5

"in overthrowing me in Saint-Domingue, you have only cut down the trunk of the tree of liberty of the blacks; but it will grow again from the roots, because they are deep and numerous"[7]—Polverel here attached the metaphor to the French Revolution. While giving the speech, Polverel approached the "altar of the fatherland" and attached to it "the national cockade with the bonnet of Liberty." "I lit the fire in the sacred vase which had been prepared on the altar," he said. Afterward, Polverel described how with "the Bonnet placed on the top of the Tree of Liberty planted in front of the altar of the Fatherland, each of the constituent bodies then came forward to decorate the sacred tree with a bouquet of flowers adorned with a tricolor cockade; during this ceremony the cries of Long live the Republic redoubled, and long live the Civil Commissioner was heard from all sides." This republican ritual can be compared to the religious one whereby Boukman and his adherents led the initial emancipation of the enslaved population in the northern plain. Instead of invoking God, Polverel continued to speak of the "tree of Liberty," saying it "will not have been planted in vain" and "this Bonnet, which crowns its summit, will not be a lying emblem." "I declare, in the name of the Republic, that I am giving freedom to all the male and female Africans, and the male and female descendants of Africans, who have hitherto belonged to the State."[8] Unlike the Declaration of the Rights of Man, with its obvious gender exclusion, Polverel deliberately specified in his emancipation decree that the rights attached to liberty and equality applied to both enslaved men and women in Saint-Domingue. In good French republican fashion, two days after Polverel issued his proclamation, he renamed Port-au-Prince, the administrative capital of the colony, Port-Républicain, "to forever remind the inhabitants of the obligations that the revolution imposed upon them."[9]

The kind of particularity within the indivisibility of the French state wished for by free people of color like Raimond in 1790, and by Olympe de Gouges, who penned *The Declaration of the Rights of Woman and the Female Citizen* in 1791, stamped Polverel's intervention into the discourse of the rights of "man." Polverel was also the authority of the southern part of the colony seated in Les Cayes, which had not been addressed by the September proclamation. To rectify this, on October 6, 1793, Polverel signed a second emancipation proclamation from Les Cayes. In this version, Polverel told his audience that it was on September 21, the first anniversary of the creation of the French republic, that he abolished slavery in the western province. "I have likewise ordered that all the external signs of slavery must disappear, that the chains of all those who only have the misfortune of being or of having been slaves be broken instantly in two and that there no longer exist any public chain other than as a monument and punishment for crimes," Polverel wrote. "Immediately all signs of slavery disappeared and the Africans attached to the government enjoyed the precious blessing of freedom." Polverel continued, "this new condition only increased their zeal for work, and the tranquility that for so long had been missing from the western province was now perfectly restored there."[10] The south was clearly still in open rebellion though, emancipation having not yet there been officially decreed. Polverel rectified this in writing laws that would be particular for them. Watch as particularity (that is, divisibility) entered into the heart of France's beloved indivisibility: "Convinced that benefiting from freedom requires the return to order and the tranquility of this province; that it alone can restore to Saint-Domingue the splendor that this colony is capable of and give to the French Republic children worthy of her and her principles. I declare freedom given, in the name of the Republic, to all Africans, male and female, and male and female descendants of Africans, who have until now belonged to the State, and who inhabit the Southern Province." Just as in the west, Polverel said that the formerly enslaved men and women of the south "will enjoy from this day forward all the rights of French citizens and will be equal in rights to all free men."[11]

While Sonthonax lived many lives in Saint-Domingue—leaving in 1794 and then returning in 1796, only to be compelled to leave by Louverture and Raimond in 1797—Polverel barely outlived the trial he underwent before the Comité de Salut Public at the urging of angry white Saint-Dominguan colonists, who had him recalled back to France in 1794. In 1795, he died of a chronic illness.[12]

In Polverel and Sonthonax's absence, the white French colonists continued to try to destroy the work of liberty first inaugurated by the enslaved freedom fighters of the northern plain and that the commissioners legally sanctioned with their emancipation decrees. Polverel, whose proclamation ran counter to planter desires to continue enslaving the African population and to the colonists' determination to exclude the *gens de couleur* from citizenship rights, had many supporters among people of color in the south and west. After the death of Vincent's Ogé's mother, Orphé Ogé, who perished on the Spanish-controlled side of the island, where she fled in exile with her late son, Polverel provided for her two daughters, Angélique and Françoise. Joseph Saint-Rémy described how the two girls "suffered in the prisons of Cap, and then found themselves in Port-au-Prince, nearly destitute." Polverel, "before leaving for the South, had them granted from the treasury of the Republic 16,500 francs, and facilitated their departure for New Orleans, where devoted friends took pleasure in making them forget their misfortunes."[13] Polverel's reputation as the defender of the destitute was seconded by André Rigaud, one of his most ardent supporters. Rigaud resurrected the ashes of Polverel to thank him for being a singular defender of the free men of color and called upon his ashes to testify on their behalf. "Shadow of Polverel!" Rigaud

134 Chapter 5

exclaimed. "Come out of the grave, come render shining homage to the truth. Tell us: have you not seen in the citizens of color, and especially in those of the Southern department with whom you have almost always lived during your stay in Saint-Domingue, have you not seen in me, (eh! Have you not seen into the depths of my Heart!) Have you not seen, I say, an inviolable attachment to France, an invincible hatred for her enemies." Referencing the accusation that the men of color joined with British invaders of the island, Rigaud called out to the grave, "Shadow of Polverel! With what eye do you see today the unjust accusation that cowardly enemies bring against them? Do you fear that we might succeed in discouraging them, or wearying their steadfastness? Be at ease, O shadow, my brothers and I, we will all perish, before any damage is done to your work."[14] With this passionate statement Rigaud promised his former collaborator in freedom that their work in legislatively abolishing slavery and encouraging putatively *free* labor in its place would not be undone by the cowardly and greedy colonists, nor by any of Rigaud's detractors.

Polverel, who did in fact paint himself as the ultimate liberator, also acknowledged that the enslaved had already in a very material sense broken their own chains and liberated themselves. In the emancipation decree pertaining to the west, Polverel referenced the earlier promise of general liberty he made to the enslaved population. He said the decree finally halted the fires set by the enslaved, in "all the *ateliers* in Gonaïves and the Artibonite which had been in full rebellion."[15] The mere promise of eventual liberty was enough to put an end both to the rebellion and to the alleged plot of "the armed brigands of the north," whom Polverel identified as Biassou, Jean-François, Guiambois, Carreau, Despinville, Jean-Pineau, and Jacinthe. The French commissioner claimed that the kind of "liberty" sought by the above-named revolutionaries involved Black domination over the white colonists, including the confiscation of their properties. Of these Black leaders, Polverel said their only designs were to "make [the enslaved] become brigands like them," to take control of the properties of the white colonists, and "divide them up among themselves." "This plan was greeted with enthusiasm by the commune of Petite Rivière," Polverel lamented. To combat this alleged plot, Polverel said he "promised General Liberty and everything returned to order." By pronouncing the "grand word, Liberty," Polverel explained, the properties of the white colonists were saved, as were the lives of the white French colonists and those of their wives and children.[16] Polverel even claimed to have "consulted with those in the *ateliers*" about whether they wished to remain in open rebellion, and therefore to put their hopes of liberty in the arms of the "brigands of the north," or to rely on the French commissioners. Polverel said he received this response, "We are very content with what the commissioners have done for us. We know that there is nothing good nor any Happiness without Labour; we are not going to put the commissioner to death after all he has done for us; we want to be made happy, we are going to wait peacefully."[17]

According to the original decree issued by Sonthonax, the obligations of the now free Black men and women of Saint-Domingue did not stop at the kind of devotion and reverence for "labor" referenced in Polverel's emancipation decree and accompanying anecdotes. The formerly enslaved were now formally required to express loyalty to and defend the French republic: "Having become citizens by the will of the French Nation, you must also be zealous observers of its decrees; you will undoubtedly defend the interests of the Republic against kings, less due to the feelings you have about your own independence, than due to gratitude for the benefits with which she has showered you."[18] Sonthonax then chided, "Show yourselves to be worthy of her: forever abjure indolence as well as brigandage: have the courage to want to be a people, & soon you will equal the European nations."[19] With these curious words, Sonthonax suggested that the people of Saint-Domingue had the possibility to become a nation that could rival those in Europe. Was Sonthonax sincerely on the side of Saint-Dominguan independence already or was he at this moment still a staunch French republican using the well-worn French colonial tactic of promising one solution while actively working toward its opposite? After emancipation, the former became the charge of, by turns, Rigaud and Louverture, and finally, belatedly, by the incredulous Raimond, who reluctantly helped Louverture send Sonthonax back to France.

According to Louverture, it was Sonthonax who first made the connection between abolition and independence. After Sonthonax returned to the colony in 1796, Louverture said Sonthonax hatched a full-blown scheme for independence, by rather boldly, and audaciously, proclaiming himself to be the sole author of the general liberty that reigned in Saint-Domingue. He told Louverture, to that end, "I am the founder of liberty."[20] Yet Louverture's most ardent rival, General Rigaud, seemed ill inclined to agree with Sonthonax's self-designation. In his *Réponse du général de brigade André Rigaud à l'écrit calomnieux du Général Toussaint Louverture* (Response of Brigadier General André Rigaud to the slanderous writing of General Toussaint Louverture), Rigaud stated forthrightly, to provide context for his war with Louverture, that it was he and the other men of color from the south who had "planted the sacred tree of liberty at the price of our own blood."[21] Yet, Sonthonax repeated to Toussaint Louverture again and again that he was "le fondateur de la liberté" (the founder of liberty). Sonthonax's insistence betrayed him. He had to insist he was Saint-Domingue's rightful hero precisely because there were so many Black freedom fighters, most of them far less prominent than Louverture, who could contest him for this label. Louverture reported that

136   Chapter 5

Sonthonax admitted to him that, without Louverture's leadership, "we would not have found an inch of earth belonging to France upon our arrival."[22] Did Sonthonax declare liberty? Absolutely. But the only reason the entire colony had not gone up in smoke with the burning plantations, or was not forcibly ceded to either the British who had invaded the south, or to the Spanish to whose side Louverture had initially defected, was because Louverture rallied the Black freedom fighters to the side of the Frech republic.

In *Ti dife boule sou istwa Ayiti* (1977) Michel-Rolph Trouillot gave chapter 5 the iconic words of the Vodou *lwa* Papa Legba, "*Louvri barye,*" or open the gate. Trouillot used a simultaneously secular and sacred evocation of Vodou to describe the process by which Sonthonax came to officially abolish slavery in colonial Saint-Domingue. "Why did he liberate the slaves?" Trouillot asked. "What could have brought him to such a decision?"[23] For Trouillot, walking through the history of how Louverture and, specifically, the enslaved Africans of Haiti, set the conditions for Sonthonax's revolutionary decision could open the gates to an entire world of thought, one that would show how it was the Haitian people who informed, shaped, and created the Haitian present, which is to say the slavery-free and independent republic where they lived.[24] Drawing as he did on two centuries of Haitian thought, Trouillot could see exactly what post-independence Haitian chroniclers saw. There was nothing surprising to the enslaved Black population about the tumultuous circumstances that led to Sonthonax's and Polverel's emancipation decrees. Chanlatte, who lived through this momentous moment, reminded his readers, "Whatever great character [Sonthonax and Polverel] displayed, they were forced, in order to keep the island in France's possession, to proclaim general liberty."[25]

Wandering through nineteenth-century Haitian thought reveals much about the multiple layers of silencing that have crowded out the Haitian people from narrating their own history, such that they appear more like historical puppets than historical actors, accidental beneficiaries of French revolutionary principles instead of creators of their own. Baron de Vastey's words, on this score, provide a poignant lesson in how failing to acknowledge both perspective and positionality can make invisible those whose lives, as much as their motives, lay outside the colonial gaze. "It was from those brave inhabitants of the forests, the real authors of liberty and independence, that we received this grand and crucial lesson," Vastey wrote, "*to never confront our enemies without weapons in our hands.*" Vastey explained that during the Leclerc expedition, unlike Louverture and many other prominent revolutionary figures, the "brave inhabitants of the mountains," that is to say the Saint-Dominguan maroons, "saw armed whites, and that was enough for them: worried about their *freedom*, they secretly procured weapons, hid themselves

Abolition   137

in the depths of the woods, and prepared for war." This foresight, Vastey concluded, showed that "the defiance of our compatriots in the mountains was more useful than our feeble *lumières*."[26] Those "real authors" of Haitian independence did not need enlightenment slogans or beautiful decrees to instinctively hold suspect the arrival of Leclerc and the French troops, who spouted the French revolutionary principles of liberty, equality, fraternity, while plotting the reenslavement of most of the island's Black population.

Nevertheless, the question of who ultimately abolished slavery in Saint-Domingue animated much of Louverture's conflict with Sonthonax. To grasp both the merits and the importance of their differing interpretations of the phenomenon of abolition, let us more fully examine the language in which Sonthonax couched his claims to radical ingenuity. Louverture said that around "the start of Nivose, in Year 5" (circa December 21, 1796), Sonthonax told him directly, "It is I who am the founder of liberty; it is I who am the sole salvation of the blacks; it is I who defended them against the colonists."[27] Sonthonax seemed to reprimand Louverture in remarking, "Without me, liberty would not have been proclaimed; I am your true, your only friend, in this you must believe."[28] Louverture recorded word for word this conversation to explain to the Directory government, which replaced the Jacobins, why he sent Sonthonax back to France in 1797. In the course of Louverture's conversation with Sonthonax deeper cracks appeared across the otherwise smooth surface of Sonthonax's claim that he bravely, and uniquely, interrupted colonial slavery. Sonthonax inadvertently admitted to Louverture that it was the enslaved in rebellion who forced him into the dramatic decision to legislatively abolish slavery. "At the time, I had to take steps toward giving freedom, because without that I would have had my throat cut," Sonthonax stated.[29] It was not out of pure benevolence that Sonthonax came to this hasty decision. It was much more out of sheer self-preservation. Polverel had intimated something similar when he credited the enslaved Africans who spared his life while they waited to see if he would make good on his promise of declaring general liberty.

The fact of striving for abolition did not always result in an anti-racist perspective. Sonthonax's prejudices are on full display in the *11 pluviôse an 6* (January 30, 1798) account he sent to the Executive Directory to explain how it was that he found himself departing from Saint-Domingue, of his volition, so he claimed.[30] He said he wanted to address his departure from Saint-Domingue, which had been "so variously interpreted," and also to discuss "the writings that are attributed on this subject to Toussaint Louverture, and especially the ridiculous accusation of independence with which they [Louverture and Raimond] dare charge me." "I freely left Saint-Domingue, on 7 Fructidor last," Sonthonax insisted. He continued by saying that he "had

138   Chapter 5

gotten wind of a plot announced by Toussaint Louverture to get rid of the Commissioners . . . and remain sole master of affairs in St. Domingue." The former commissioner claimed to have been informed of this by several Black military commanders and notably by a European *chef de brigade*. As for Louverture's ability to govern the colony, let alone to put in place a plan to effectively get rid of Sonthonax, the commissioner said, "He is incapable of designing such a project." Sonthonax said of the very man he previously exalted, "He is a narrow-minded agent, as humble as he was in his first state as a slave, guardian of animals." "He ordinarily speaks the Creole language, and barely understands French," Sonthonax continued. "Made to be governed, he is destined to be subjected to foreign control." Sonthonax's prejudices shine through in this passage, but the report is laden with even more disturbing forms of incoherence.

Sonthonax painted Louverture as at once incapable of deep thought, owing to the fact he was an "ex-slave," and a master politician whose schemes against Sonthonax revealed nothing less than the general's unceasing desire for power and control of the colony. "They have dared to accuse me of dreaming of the independence of the Colonies and the general massacre of Europeans," wrote Sonthonax. "This imputation is based on an alleged dialogue that I supposedly had on this subject with Toussaint Louverture. I have read that wretched pamphlet, a vile production of intrigue and imposture; I have only two things to say: Toussaint speaks only Creole; that he hardly understands French and is perfectly incapable of carrying on the conversation attributed to him." "I have never been accused of stupidity or baseness of soul, and yet, in this ridiculous conversation, I am portrayed as a schoolboy under the stick, spouting nonsense and being called to order by his pedagogue," Sonthonax complained. The next passage is where Sonthonax's defamation of Louverture becomes most incoherent. Louverture, in his estimation, was all at once stupid, illiterate, incompetent, and incapable of understanding French, or any complex problems, but he was also a mastermind, the architect of the entire revolution and of his own project of independence, who duped two monarchs. "Certainly, if anyone can be suspected of wanting independence, it is undoubtedly he whose political life has been nothing but a continuous revolt against France," Sonthonax charged:

Toussaint Louverture is one of the leaders of the *Vendée* of Saint-Domingue. In 1791, at the instigation of those same émigrés who surround him today, he organized the revolt of the blacks and the massacre of the white landowners. Toussaint commanded in 1793 and 1794 the army of brigands under the orders of the King of Spain; he only entered into the service of the Republic when the peace negotiations led him to conclude that Spain no longer needed him. In 1795 he negotiated with the agents of the King of England. He deceived two monarchs; he might end up betraying the Republic.[31]

It could only be expected that Sonthonax would seek to ardently defend himself against Louverture and Raimond's highly publicized accusations in the land of the guillotine, where others had been executed for far lesser charges. But Louverture had the foresight to painstakingly preserve his conversations with Sonthonax because he knew that without such evidence he could not protect himself from the kind of charges Sonthonax was making.

Louverture never professed to be a professional historian, but in the documents bearing his signature, some of which he made public in pamphlet form, he insisted that he was trying to correct the historical record in real time. Although Louverture was certainly pleased at the emancipation proclamations, he did not fail to remind Sonthonax during the earlier referenced meeting that so much bloodshed could have been avoided if Sonthonax had decreed the end of slavery at the outset of his arrival in Saint-Domingue, instead of proclaiming, as Sonthonax himself admitted in the emancipation proclamation, that slavery would endure in the colony forever. Sonthonax stated in the preamble to the emancipation decree, "Upon our arrival, we found a dreadful schism between the whites who, divided amongst themselves in interest & opinion, only agreed on one point, that of perpetuating forever the servitude of the negroes, & of also proscribing any system of freedom and even improvement of their lot. To thwart the ill-intentioned and to calm their spirits, all excited by the fear of a sudden change, we declared that we believed slavery was necessary for agriculture."[32] Sonthonax's earlier support of slavery is confirmed in the March 28, 1793, issue of the *Journal des Révolutions de la partie française de Saint-Domingue* (Journal of the revolutions of the French part of Saint-Domingue). The journal's epigraph was not drawn from any of the documents that made France a republic rather than a monarchy. Rather, it was taken from the *"Proclamations of September 24 and December 30, 1792,"* described as an *"oath solemnly pronounced in the church of Le Cap, by the Civil Commissioners."* The civil commissioners are then quoted as saying, "The colonies are part of the French empire.—We declare in its name that SLAVERY is necessary to the cultivation and prosperity of the colonies, that it is neither in the principles nor in the will of the nation to touch in this respect the properties of the colonists.—We shall die rather than suffer the execution of an anti-popular plot."[33] Louverture reminded Sonthonax of one crucial fact concerning this: Louverture said he would have not waited to rejoin the French army from the Spanish side, where he previously defected, if Sonthonax had been more sincere and trustworthy from the beginning. "If in arriving here you had proclaimed General Liberty, we would have reunited ourselves to you; but remember that you swore the contrary, eternal slavery, in front of the Supreme Being; and because of that we could not place any trust in you."[34] Moreover, it was Louverture who, prior to Sonthonax's proclamation, rallied the various Black revolutionaries, especially the *hommes de couleur*, to fight for the cause of abolition.

In the now famous letter he wrote to the free men of color, Louverture rebuked those among them who were fighting against general emancipation. He warned them, "The time has come—I tremble to announce it—when we are going to strike a great blow against all the enemies of peace. So, dear comrades, join our side."[35] Next, he laid out the distinct relationship he saw between slavery and color prejudice, which so many of the *hommes de couleur* had either been unable to acknowledge or unwilling to accept: "Freedom is a right given by Nature; equality is a consequence of this freedom that has been upheld and granted by this national assembly. You say that you . . . now want these two things. It is for me to work for them. I have been given the right to do so, because I was the first to favor a cause that I have always upheld. I cannot yield my position; having begun, I will finish. Join me and you will enjoy your rights sooner."[36] Not long after, on August 29, 1793—while Sonthonax was declaring the enslaved of the north to be emancipated—Louverture gave his equally famous speech at Camp Turel. Like Sonthonax, he did not fail to awaken the ashes of Ogé: "Brothers and Friends, . . . Do you remember, dear comrades, brave Ogé who was put to death for having taken the side of liberty? Weep. He is dead. But those who are now defending him were perhaps his judges. I am Toussaint Louverture. You have perhaps heard my name. You are aware, brothers, that I have undertaken vengeance, and that I want freedom and equality to reign in Saint Domingue. I have been working since the beginning to bring it into existence. . . . Equality cannot exist without liberty, and for liberty to exist we need unity."[37]

Was it a coincidence that on the same day Sonthonax ended up issuing the emancipation decree? It all depends on what is meant by coincidence. Certainly, Louverture's rising power, as evidenced by his ability to achieve exactly his aims with this letter, pressured the French commissioner to formally abolish slavery. In reality, African freedom fighters had already brought the plantation economy to a standstill and ended the ability of human traffickers to profit from their system of slavery. On June 21, 1793, Black freedom fighters set fire to the city of Cap, burning nearly every structure in the center of the city to the ground, with damage estimated into the billions.[38] The French general César Galbaud, brother of the infamous French general François-Thomas Galbaud du Fort (whose governorship of the colony the commissioners and the Black freedom fighters were contesting), reported that four days later, on June 25, ten thousand "negroes in revolt" came down from the mountains into the charred city to present a motion to Sonthonax to "proclaim general liberty for all the slaves in the colony." "That idea was well-received, and we expect very soon to see this proclamation," César Galbaud reported.[39] The commissioners had, in fact, already declared that any enslaved men who fought on their behalf against Galbaud, who was trying to have the commissioners arrested, would earn their liberty. The oath Sonthonax and Polverel swore to this effect constituted in fact their first attempt to legislate emancipation.[40] Yet many previously enslaved freedom fighters did not take the bait and refused to join those who fought against Galbaud. Louverture, Jean-François, and Biassou were among that number.

Louverture, as one of the six leaders of the early freedom struggle—Biassou, Jean François, Aubert, Toussaint, Mauseau, and Després—was used to standing his ground with the white colonists and French agents. In December 1791, Louverture and the above-named fighters addressed a letter to the first set of civil commissioners, Philippe Rose Roume de Saint-Laurent, Ignace Frédéric de Mirbeck, and Edmond de St. Léger. The letter demonstrates their awareness of their own agency and de facto free status. "Dear Sirs," the letter began, ". . . we are taking the liberty of expressing our gratitude to you and, at the same time, restating those points that we think are essential for re-establishing order in these critical circumstances":

> We feel compelled to inform you that you have misunderstood our position, and that you have only a vague idea of the nature of the revolution of which we, as well as the whites, are the unfortunate victims. In ordering us each to return to our homes, you are demanding something that is both impossible and dangerous. One hundred thousand men are in arms, of whom we make up no more than an eightieth part. Most of us are heads of families, and you will understand that makes us entirely dependent on the general will. That means on the will of a multitude of Negroes from Africa, most of whom scarcely know two words of French but who have been accustomed to warfare in their native countries.

The leaders then urged, "as much for our sake as for yours," that freedom be granted to a number of leaders, whom Biassou and company would be the ones to name. They averred that the "generals," whom they counted themselves to be among, were the only ones who could bring peace and a return to order "without great losses," which "a large [French] army," in contrast, "could accomplish only with great difficulty, slowly, and by causing the ruin of the planters."[41] The freedom leaders were hardly asking for general emancipation.

142   Chapter 5

Instead, they insisted on better working conditions for the enslaved, including the elimination of whipping, and on the dissolution of any distinctions among the free people of color (the *nouveaux libres*, or newly freed, from those born with free status) from the standpoint of citizenship. If the first principle of their demands were to be granted, including the emancipation of the generals and commanders, the leaders insisted that "public prosperity will be reborn from its ashes," a resonant image that would later form a part of Christophe's motto as king of Haiti.[42]

While the Spanish king was busy reinforcing his troops in Santo Domingo, the national civil commissioners of France were planning a meeting with the leaders of the freedom struggle. The leaders on the side of freedom decided that Jean-François would be the one to meet the French commissioners on the St. Michel plantation in mid-December. Although the meeting resulted in the successful release of several white prisoners, they could not agree upon a ceasefire. This is partly because the African freedom fighters were unwilling to put down their arms. They were wary that those who proclaimed themselves their leaders and who were leading the negotiations were advocating more for their own freedoms than for general emancipation.[43] Indeed, in their December 12 letter, Biassou and company had offered to help combat the African masses, as difficult as the task would be, if their demands were granted. "We cannot hide from you the fact that we will have to camp out across the different parishes for a very long time," Biassou et al. wrote. "Many Negroes will contaminate the forests, where they will hide out, and constant pursuit of them will be necessary, braving danger and fatigue."[44] It was only after Louverture became the uncontested leader of the freedom struggle that he began to insist on general emancipation more unequivocally. Troops under his command from that moment on, which included his nephew Moyse and Colonel Jean-Baptiste Sans-Soucy, declared they would not cease fighting France until universal abolition.[45]

Sonthonax and Polverel merely made official what many of the island's African freedom fighters had already conceived, if not conjured with violent insistence into reality. This much was recognized by Polverel in the October 31, 1793, decree he issued relative to the general liberty of the formerly enslaved of the south and west. "Two years of war against the African insurgents convinced the landowners that it was now impossible to maintain slavery," Polverel wrote: "Their *ateliers* were deserted, their houses or their plantations burnt or devastated. France was being drained of money; and while its armies were being annihilated in Saint-Domingue, that of the Africans was growing daily by new recruits from among those who had deserted the *ateliers*. The colonist no longer believed that his lands could ever be reclaimed, because he believed that they could only be cultivated by slaves."[46] The actions of the Black revolutionaries of the forests and mountains, whom Louverture rallied together with the *hommes de couleur* to bring to a halt the plantation economy, forced Sonthonax and Polverel to abolish slavery. Their actions had repercussions that resounded across the Atlantic Ocean.

In February 1794, the French National Convention followed in the stead of the Haitian revolutionaries and universally abolished slavery across all French overseas territories. "The National Convention declares that the enslavement of negroes in all the Colonies is abolished, as a result, it is decreed that all men without distinction of color, living in the colonies, are French citizens."[47] Louverture was right to remind the commissioner that neither Sonthonax nor France could have been brought to this decision if not for the enslaved Africans who forced the opening that Toussaint Louverture would soon walk through as leader and chief, but out of which he would only emerge as a prisoner, a captive, in the ship that was to lead him to an early death.

The intricate events that led to Louverture's treacherous arrest and sad demise are as integral to the founding of Haitian independence as they are to understanding the relationship of Louverture's revolutionary life to Haitian thought. It is to these terrible events that we must now turn to fully grasp how the colony's African freedom fighters came to view independence from France as the only way to ensure slavery would never return. Whereas, the white colonists of the Saint-Marc Assembly had once conceived of independence as the surest measure of ensuring the continuation of slavery, now the island's free Black citizens would mobilize independence to ensure its forever abolition.

———

Popular history has it that Louverture was born sometime in May 1743 on the Bréda plantation in Haut-du-Cap in Saint-Domingue.[48] However, according to Louverture's son, Isaac, who is a key source of information about his father's life, Louverture was born in the colony in 1746, the grandson of an Arada prince named Gaou-Guinou.[49] Although the white Bréda family previously claimed Toussaint as their slave, called Toussaint Bréda at the time, by 1776 we know that he had been emancipated and was working for the subsequent owner of the plantation, the Comte Louis-Pantaléon de Noé, a white Frenchman.[50] In 1782, Toussaint married an enslaved woman, Suzanne Simone Baptiste, who had at least one child, Placide, from a previous relationship.[51] Louverture, who also had a child or children from a previous relationship, and Suzanne went on to have two children together, Isaac and Saint-Jean, the latter of whom was born in 1791, the year the revolution formally began.

According to Céligny Ardouin, Louverture was present at the assembly of enslaved leaders who gathered in Morne-Rouge on August 14, 1791. At this

144   Chapter 5

meeting, Louverture, who could already read and write, was happy to let his close friends, Jean-François Papillon, Georges Biassou, Boukman, and Jeannot Bullet, assume the command. "Toussaint reserved for himself the role of intermediary between the conspirators and the secret motors of the insurrection," C. Ardouin wrote.[52] By August 1793, however, Toussaint, fighting on the side of the Spanish, was clearly a leader. Although he later acted in concert with Sonthonax, Louverture initially distrusted the French commissioner, which is one of the reasons Louverture did not rejoin the French army until May 1794, three months after the National Convention abolished slavery.

As Sonthonax began to move more ardently toward independence, Louverture, now a French general, would, at least on the surface, remain a staunch supporter of the French republic. In a letter he penned to the Directory government of France, Louverture said that at the very moment when he believed he was being recognized for his accomplishments and appreciated for his services to the republic, a speech was pronounced against him at the legislative corps' session of *10 prairial an 5* (May 29, 1797) by the infamously racist white French colonist Vincent-Marie Viénot de Vaublanc. Louverture received Vaublanc's speech by way of the United States, and he said it pained him in perusing the transcript to see that at every turn Vaublanc slandered him, while "threatening the political existence of my brothers."[53] Vaublanc, who was a member of the legislative body in France and a former enslaver from Saint-Domingue, claimed that Louverture, first, sought to massacre all the whites and, second, that he was striving for independence. In direct response to these charges, Louverture evoked the maroon treaties, not of the famous Cacique Enrique/Henri, but those closer to his own day, in the Blue Mountains of Jamaica. Louverture exhorted Vaublanc to recall that "in the heart of Jamaica, on the Blue Mountains, a small number of men were so determined to acquire liberty, that they have forced up until this day the powers that be of England to respect the rights given to them by nature and that the French Constitution guarantees to us."[54] The comparison that Louverture evoked with his own situation was perhaps too apt. As with the Trelawney Town Maroons, the Blue Mountain or Windward Maroons, under a formerly enslaved African known as Captain Quao, were compelled into a treaty with the British in 1740 that while offering them freedom and protection similarly required them "to suppress and destroy all other party or parties of rebellious negroes, that now are, or shall from time to time gather together to settle in any part of this island, and shall bring in such other negroes as shall from time to time run away from their respective owners."[55] Louverture was undoubtedly aware that the circumstances and substance of the Blue Mountain Treaty with England vis-à-vis the status of colonial Saint-Domingue with respect to France were different. Yet, the comparison he made does allow us to confront

Abolition 145

how both freedom struggles—the one in Saint-Domingue and the much earlier one in Jamaica—compelled their leaders to carve out compromised abolition in the middle (literally, in the case of the Trelawney Town and Blue Mountain Maroons) of an empire.

Abolition in colonial Saint-Domingue post-Sonthonax's and Polverel's decrees was under severe constraint and remained so under Louverture when he assumed the role of governor-general in 1801, not the least because of ongoing slavery and empire in the surrounding Caribbean and in the United States, as well as in South America. While the concessions Louverture made when he created his famous constitution of 1801, particularly in terms of labor,[56] were altogether different from the maroon concessions in Jamaica, both situations call forth questions about the capacity of marronnage (and maroons), figurative and material, to bring about unilateral abolition in the heart of a slaving empire.

Despite their problematic nature, maroon treaties with European powers continued to be a consistent and constant point of reference for people of African descent in Saint-Domingue precisely because the phenomenon of marronnage was so omnipresent in the Caribbean. The Haitian historian Étienne Charlier has written that in the eighteenth century there was a "particular upsurge [of marronnage] in the West Indies, specifically, in Grenada, in Surinam with the Sarameca rebels, and in Jamaica with the Independents of the Blue Mountains." "The militias eventually got the better of the Grenadian rebels," he continued, "but in Suriname and Jamaica, where the movement rose to the level of a general independence movement, it was necessary to bring in special forces. European troops." Many of these conflicts ended with maroon treaties of the stripe that Enrique, and the Trelawney Town and Blue Mountain Marroons, agreed to.[57] We do not need to push the comparison between Louverturian law and Jamaican maroon treaties too far in a literal direction. Putting them in relation simply provides a way to understand what happened to abolition under Louverture's governorship of the colony.

Although he believed that allying with the French republic was the best path to preserving abolition, Louverture also derived ideas about constituted freedom from his knowledge of Jamaican maroons and the de facto abolition treaties they forced the British government to concede to in order to quell armed freedom struggles. Louverture and the other Black revolutionaries had already forced France to concede to one type of maroon treaty, if you will, even if not named as such. Polverel's and Sonthonax's separate decrees, along with the French National Convention's unilateral abolition of slavery in all French territory, at first glance, seem entirely unlike maroon treaties. The Trelawney Town and Blue Mountain treaties with the British spelled out the

146   Chapter 5

relationship between the maroons who had been in open rebellion and the nation-state that claimed the physical territory upon which they lived, while requiring the so-called maroons to in effect perpetuate slavery by actively combating marronnage from other groups.[58] Both maroon communities were required, in exchange for their own independence, for example, to no longer admit runaways into their community, and in fact to help the authorities hunt them down. In contrast, the French commissioners' proclamations, as did Toussaint's constitution, declared universal emancipation, in the first case to all those still enslaved in 1793, and in the second case guaranteed that slavery could no longer exist in the entirety of Saint-Domingue/Ayiti. Yet, the freedom of the formerly enslaved population to move about as they pleased, or to change occupations, that is, to cease engaging in the work of cultivation, or farming, was severely limited in both instances.

The freedom of the formerly enslaved population was constrained by the affermage system put in place, first, by Sonthonax, Polverel, and Raimond, with assistance from Christophe, Dessalines, and other prominent Black military officers;[59] and then by reforms attempted by the French agent General Gabriel-Marie-Théodore-Joseph de Hédouville, and in the end, Louverture, who had his own nephew, Moyse, killed to protect this system of labor. Called "engagements" under Hédouville, that French agent's reforms to affermage mandated that a formerly enslaved laborer, called a cultivator, had to be "engaged for a minimum of three years" on specific plantations without the right to leave.[60] Though he also participated in enforcing affermage, or the leasing system, initially put in place by the civil commissioners, Moyse was one of Hédouville's starkest opponents because of the engagements system.[61] Hédouville consequently blamed Moyse for the armed resistance cultivators in Fort-Liberté (previously Fort-Dauphin) used to protest engagements. The conflict ended when Hédouville was forced to leave the colony. Administrators from various communes and cities in the north had received numerous petitions submitted by bands of cultivators who demanded Hédouville's recall to France. The cultivators threatened that they would refuse to work if he remained.[62] Dozens of citizens in the commune of Port-à-Piment and Terre-Neuve, for example, appeared before authorities of their municipality to assert their will, like those from other parishes. One of those citizen-cultivators was a man named Mayombé, who represented his chagrins, along with those of his fellow cultivators, "about the engagements we were forced to commit to under the law of Agent Hédouville." "We reject the said proclamation since it violates our rights to liberty," the cultivators said. "We don't need engagements to work. Our good General Toussaint Louverture, who rescued us from the hands of the Spanish and the English, has repeated to us that the free man must work." Like those from other sections of the colony, they also demanded Hédouville's recall to France and that "the brave General Moyse, whom Hédouville made an outlaw, should be restored to his rights and duties." The postscript to this letter, signed by several of the cultivators, read, "P.S. We forgot to tell you that if Agent Hédouville does not leave, our resolution has been made, we will no longer work." Another petition, from Petite-Rivière, one of the most forceful that was registered at the time, was actually read aloud, partially in Creole, to a prodigious crowd of cultivators gathered before the justice of the peace and the *commandant de la place*. "He wants to bring war again to our country" (*Li vlé faire encore la guerre dans pays-ci avec nous*), they said of Hédouville. The cultivators then told the entire story from their perspective, in Creole:

> To take away our freedom, we have also learned that they arrested two hundred of our brothers; that they took them to Cap, Citizen Hédouville disarmed them, and told them that they were going to be taken to the plantations of other masters. That is why we think that the same thing is going to happen to us since we have demanded that the brave General Moyse remain our leader and continue to fight for our rights as he has always done. His compensation for having so well defended us against the enemies of the French Republic is that today the Agent Hédouville has given an order to have him arrested and killed. We have learned that they have killed 22 of our brave officers who fought for our liberty and preserved this country for France. They arrested them and took them to Cap. Citizen Hédouville had them embarked, along with two of Moyse's brothers, they shipped one off and killed the other. We understand that this is the compensation that will be delivered to us as well. As such we are warning you, since General Moyse is condemned to death, that we will refuse to work, preferring to die, since that is the fate that awaits us. We demand action from the municipality. Hail the French Republic!
>
> —Signed on behalf of the people, Jean-Pierre, Paul-Augustin, Dominque.[63]

A nonviolent protest movement against the French agent was more than underfoot. It was taking place out in the open and in the most public of ways with the approbation and approval of colonial administrators.

It was quite a surprise to many, then, and especially to Moyse, who was not killed by the French, when in an October 1800 decree, stressing the importance of agriculture and the plantation system to the flourishing of the colony, Louverture stated that the cultivators would be subject to the same laws moving forward as the military. These laws spelled out how insubordination would be dealt with, which is to say punished, and also regulated the movements and terms of service of the cultivators. "A soldier, without incurring the most severe punishment, cannot leave his company, his battalion or his demi-brigade to pass into another, without the proper permission of his commanders," the preamble declared. "It must also be forbidden for cultivators to leave their plantations to reside in another, without legal permission." Article 3 went even further by essentially declaring mandatory labor and outlawing idleness (a law that would resurface under King Henry in 1811 with his famous Code Henry):

> All the male and female cultivators who remain idle, whether having retreated to the cities, towns, or plantations other than their own to escape the work of farming, even those who since the revolution would not have been occupied in this task, will be required to return immediately to their respective habitations. If, within eight days from the promulgation of this regulation they have not proved to the commanders or soldiers of the places where they reside that they are engaged in a useful enterprise, which provides for their existence (understand that the state of domesticity is not considered as useful), consequently, those from among the male or female cultivators who left farming to rent out their services, will be required to return to their plantations, under the personal responsibility of the people whom they are serving.

Article 3, without a doubt, recalled to the cultivators the "engagement" system that Hédouville tried to enforce, the very one that led to the rebellion in Fort-Liberté, which Moyse was accused of having planned, and that forced the departure of the French agent. Article 4, however, might have appeared threatening to inhabitants of the colony who did not work on the plantations as citizen-cultivators, too. "Any individual, male or female, whosoever, who is not a cultivator, must prove immediately that he is engaged in a useful state that provides for his subsistence and that allows him to pay taxes to the Republic," the article mandated. "Otherwise, and failing to do so, all those who will be found in contravention, will be immediately arrested, to be, if they are found guilty, incorporated into one of the regiments of the army; otherwise, they will be sent to farm, where they will be forced to work. This measure, which must be strictly enforced, will prevent vagrancy, since it will force everyone to usefully occupy themselves."[64] Louverture's legacy has been considerably tarnished in Haitian thought because of these laws. "There were men who began to say: Cousin, is this liberty? As if to say, this is not what you told us it was," Trouillot explained in *Ti dife boule*.[65] To understand how Louverture arrived here, promulgating a freedom that to many did not look like the freedom they envisioned for themselves when they took up arms in the name of liberty, will require us in chapter 6, aptly titled "Freedom," to revisit the *free* labor system laid out by Sonthonax and Polverel in the very decrees of emancipation that seemed to so radically undermine slavery.

For now, let us consider how Louverture's 1801 "free and French" constitution was both a radical reinvention of the kind of maroon treaties that had already been forced by Black revolutionaries elsewhere in the Antilles and a severe compromise with constituted power that called into question the meaning of not just freedom, but abolition. The permanent abolition of slavery in Louverture's constitution went considerably further than the eighteenth-century maroon treaties of Jamaica, and even the 1794 version issued by the National Convention, in hailing: "There can no longer exist any slaves in this land, servitude is forever abolished here. All men are here born, live, and will die free and French."[66] These three precisions were made to prevent any ambiguity. Yet, the circumstances under which the constitution was created seemed to prove the maxim that, in the age of slavery, whenever people of African descent negotiated with constituted authorities from the slaving world powers, the result was compromised freedom (emancipation, perhaps, but not necessarily liberty). By proffering a set of laws to protect Africans and their descendants in Saint-Domingue from slavery while also maintaining peace with the metropole, Louverture tried to force Bonaparte's government, which overthrew the Directory in 1799, to adopt the kind of particularism that French women and Saint-Dominguan free men of color originally sought during their negotiations with the Jacobins and the white French colonists throughout the 1790s. Louverture wanted laws that specified abolition, permanently.

Louverture also hoped the colony of Saint-Domingue might more than just coexist with the French republic. He sought to collaborate and cooperate with French metropolitan authorities to increase commerce on the island, in the hopes of maintaining his authority. Using language that eventually ended up in his 1801 constitution, Louverture previously told the Directory that he would never do anything that might "weaken in the eyes of the black generals the inviolable attachment to France and her constitution, would never make them break the oath they have taken to live free and French." There was one caveat. Louverture sought to make it clear that while the Black soldiers under his command had pledged their loyalty to the republic, "they would all prefer to bury themselves under the ruins of their country rather than to see slavery return here."[67] Both of these ideas—the permanent abolition of slavery and the concept of "free and French"—made their way into the set of laws that Louverture signed in July 1801.

Before Louverture could arrive at the constitutional ingenuity of "free and French," he had two rivals to contend with. The first was Sonthonax, who in that damning conversation Louverture recorded, claimed that the two of them

150   Chapter 5

needed to become the "Supreme leaders of the Colony."[68] When Louverture asked Sonthonax, his superior, in fact, for clarification, Sonthonax replied, "That is to say, that we will be the masters, you will be in control of all the armed forces, and I will be your counselor; I will direct you."[69] Louverture reported to the French government afterward that he responded by telling Sonthonax to no longer speak of independence: "that very word makes me shudder coming from your mouth."[70] Sonthonax continued to justify the claim that striving for independence was a necessary move. He reminded Louverture that France at that time had no marines capable of invading because the French were still at war with England. As a result, Sonthonax stated that France "would be obliged to do as England has done with respect to the United States. Afterward, France and every other nation will be so happy to be able to come and engage in commerce with Saint-Domingue, and the country will prosper even more."[71] Despite Sonthonax's persistence, Louverture still insisted that he merely wanted freedom for everyone in the colony and that he believed France wanted that too. Sonthonax disagreed. He told Louverture that his own liberty would be more certain with independence and "it will then depend on no one. You will be the master."[72]

In a passage dripping with unfortunate prescience, Louverture imagined how France would respond to an attempt by the inhabitants of Saint-Domingue to become independent. If the colony were to become independent, Louverture surmised, France would perhaps not strongly react, at first, "but here is what would happen next. France would make peace with all the other powers and say to itself: The colonists were right to say that the blacks were not worthy of enjoying the freedom and benefits of France. And France, in agreement with all the powers that do not want freedom, would bind itself to them out of revenge, and we would be lost."[73] There it is, a prophetic narration of the aftermath of the official Treaty of Amiens between England and France, and the Leclerc expedition that anticipated its formalization, captured in the remarks of one who did not foresee that he would be the one determined by Bonaparte to not be "worthy of enjoying the freedom and benefits of France."

Louverture's other most ardent rival was André Rigaud. Rigaud also positioned himself as the rival of Sonthonax. Rigaud's charge against Sonthonax was slightly different than Louverture's. Rigaud accused Sonthonax of trying to align with England, whose troops had invaded the island in 1793. "What therefore is Sonthonax's country?" Rigaud asked. "In all truth, it could be said that it is basically England."[74] Charging Sonthonax with treasonous motives provided the occasion for Rigaud to demonstrate that independence was not on his mind, or that of those so-called *hommes de couleur*. "I have proved by the facts that, from the beginning of the revolution until this day, the citizens of color of the department of the South, together with the blacks, their maternal parents, and assisted by some Europeans friends from their homeland, I have proven, I repeat, that they have constantly and invariably carried arms to defend the great and sublime principles of liberty and equality."[75] "As long as blood still circulates in my veins," Rigaud continued, "I will prove with my deeds my ardent love for the French Republic, one and indivisible, and my hatred for her enemies."[76] Rigaud's claim about equality was an important one. While he was at odds with Sonthonax over the latter's role in the English invasion—in contrast to his admiration for Polverel—Rigaud was also at odds with Louverture.

Rigaud agreed that Sonthonax merely wanted the power for himself. However, Louverture had also made a damning accusation against Rigaud by saying that the latter did not want to be ruled by a Black man. Rigaud responded to this claim with deep offense. In his 1799 *Réponse du général de brigade André Rigaud*, Rigaud charged that Louverture was jealous of his prosperity in the south and, therefore, "he wants, in electrifying all his men, to force them to serve as an instrument for his blind rage, and under the vain pretext that I have vowed a personal hatred against him, he sounds the tocsin of civil war, he wants every dagger pointed at me."[77] The footnote to this statement resonates in importance for understanding not only the ultimately *political* conflict between the two men, but how it became coded by subsequent chroniclers as instead a *racial* one.[78] Rigaud wrote that Louverture, "not content to accuse me of having avowed personal hatred for him, says that my deaf maneuvers are intended to avoid me having to obey a black man, he claims that I said that I was not made to obey him, I challenge General Toussaint to give the slightest proof of that accusation."[79] "Indeed, if I were to testify that I did not want to obey a black man, if I had the foolish presumption to believe that I was not made for that, by what right would I want the whites to obey me?" Rigaud asked.[80] Rigaud, like Louverture, was a French general and therefore some of the men over whom he commanded were likewise "white" French soldiers. Rigaud pointed out that his sense of logic was developed enough to understand that color hierarchies were false, on the one hand, and on the other, that it would be a contradiction for him to hold a position of power over a white man, if in fact he believed in them.

In a passage that upsets the idea that race is at once biological and immediately perceptible based on slight differences in skin hue, Rigaud sardonically asked:

Besides, is there such a big difference between General Toussaint's color and mine? Is a shade more or less dark than another color evidence of principles of sound philosophy, and does it have anything to do with the merit of an individual; and if one person is a little bit darker than

152 Chapter 5

another person, does it follow that the one can do anything at will to the other? I am not made to obey a black man! and all my life, from my cradle, I have been obedient to blacks. Aren't the circumstances of my birth like that of General Toussaint? Wasn't it a negress who gave birth to me? Didn't I have an older brother who was black, for whom I have always had deep respect and obedience? Who gave me the first principles of education? Wasn't it a black man who was a schoolteacher in the town of Les Cayes? I have therefore been accustomed to obey blacks, and we know full well that our first principles remain eternally engraved in our hearts; also, I have devoted my entire life to the defense of the blacks; I braved everything for the sake of their freedom, from the beginning of the revolution.[81]

Rigaud's race theorization is not commonly remarked upon in stories of his involvement in the Haitian Revolution, which he clearly identified as a revolution, rather than a mere slave rebellion. His remarks are even less analyzed as a part of Haitian thought. But his words importantly speak to how conditions of life in the colony and the onset of revolution made unwitting race theorists out of many people of color, especially those who, as Rigaud acknowledged, lived with the direct entanglements of racism and color prejudice. Free people of color like Rigaud, with genealogical ties to both the enslaved and the enslavers, were often unwittingly forced to confront head on the racial hierarchies and attending prejudices running rampant in the colony, even if they had previously benefited from their higher statuses as free and lighter skinned people of color.

Louverture did not readily discuss his family background in his reports to the French government or his printed pamphlets. Rigaud and Raimond, in contrast, not unlike Vastey after them, spoke of their family histories in their writings to support their revolutionary positions and ideologies. Vastey had a white French father from Normandy, Jean Vastey, and a free woman of color for a mother, Élisabeth Dumas, daughter of a wealthy, white planter from Marmelade. The Dumas family owned a large plantation in Marmelade, in addition to the one in Ennery where Vastey grew up.[82] Similarly, Raimond was the son of a white Frenchman named Pierre Raimond and a significantly wealthier free woman of color, also the daughter of a rich white planter, Marie Begasse.[83] The Raimond family were perhaps the richest enslavers in all the southern plain.[84] Rigaud, in contrast, was the son of a white man from Provence and Rose Bossy, a formerly enslaved African woman, some say from Arada, like Louverture's parents.[85] While Raimond stressed that his father and grandfather were white to position himself closer to *whiteness*, Rigaud wanted to make the case for his *blackness*, so he stressed that his mother

Abolition   153

was a Black woman, a "negress," without mentioning his white father, therefore eliding his own proximity to *whiteness*. Vastey, later, used the same tactic in alluding to his "African" mother, but remaining silent about his white Normand father.[86]

Of these three prominent *hommes de couleur* who used their pens for anti-racist and eventually antislavery ends, only Rigaud had a previously enslaved parent. Is this the reason that he expressed much earlier than either Raimond or Vastey—who was only ten years old when the revolution began but who fought in it at the age of sixteen—an anti-racist *and* antislavery ideology? "Besides, I am too penetrated throughout my being with ideas of human rights to believe that there is in the order of nature one color which is superior to another," Rigaud stated. "I recognize in man only man himself, and among men I only recognize republicans whom I will always take pride in obeying."[87] The smoke and mirrors of color prejudices fell away before the equality for all proclaimed by republican France, at least as far as Rigaud was concerned: "The days where color prejudices were magic have passed; only true Republicans are here known as friends."[88] To defend himself against the accusation that he was prejudiced, Rigaud charged Louverture—the son of two captives forcibly transported from the continent of Africa to Saint-Domingue to labor as slaves—with having attempted to separate him, Rigaud, from his Black brothers who "vowed to trust me." As for Louverture, Rigaud remonstrated, "He wants to cut down the tree [of liberty], believing that it will then be easier to cut off all its branches, and dig up all the roots; vain dream of a delirious imagination! He does not know that, even if death cuts short the thread of my life, there will remain many of my brothers whose talents at least equal the little that I have received from nature, as well as those that I have acquired through life, education, and experience."[89] Approaching very close to Louverture's famous, if apocryphal, tree of liberty speech, the footnote to this passage clarified: "When I speak of my brothers, I mean whites, blacks, as well as the men of color, who are republican."[90]

A hapless reader of the above pamphlet forced onto it an interesting paratextual intervention. The reader's pencil mark annotations shine a skeptic's light on received narratives about Rigaud's position as a "mulatto" vis-à-vis Louverture's as a "negro." Written on the pages of Rigaud's *Réponse du général de brigade André Rigaud* there are numerous question marks, scribbled in pencil, no doubt by an overly zealous reader. One particularly noteworthy extratextual modification by this reader appears after the quote I cited above, whereby Rigaud stated that he considered all republicans, "black and white," to be his brothers. The scribbles, which in this instance include question marks as well as underlining, appear in brackets: "Quand je dis mes frères, j'entends *les blancs* [?]; *les noirs* [?], ainsi que les *hommes de couleur* qui sont

154   Chapter 5

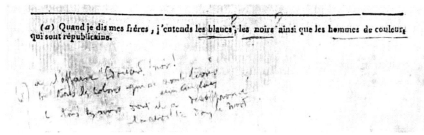

André Rigaud, *Réponse du général de brigade André Rigaud, à l'écrit calomnieux du général Toussaint Louverture*, 1799. Courtesy of Bibliothèque Nationale de France.

républicains."[91] The reader placed these question marks perhaps because he was puzzled to confront a declaration of egalitarianism coming from Rigaud or, perhaps, the reader did not consider the statements genuine, finding it hard to square an anti-racist ideology with the usual representation of Rigaud as pro-*mulatto* and anti-*Black*. But reading Rigaud's words in the passage above requires us to question historical characterizations of him as anti-Black simply because he was a "mulatto." In his 1854 speech turned pamphlet, *St. Domingo, Its Revolutions and Its Patriots*, the Black U.S. abolitionist William Wells Brown, drawing directly from John Relly Beard's *The Life of Toussaint L'Ouverture* (1853), called Rigaud a "mulatto" who was naturally one of the "haters of the blacks." Brown described Rigaud as one of the "mulattoes" who tried to "reduc[e] the land of their birth to slavery."[92] C. L. R. James, too, relying on many of the same nineteenth-century sources as Brown and Beard, fell prey to such readings when he wrote that Rigaud had a clear bias in favor of "mulattoes" against "blacks" that caused him to "ruin himself, his caste, and his country for a generation."[93] A version of Rigaud who did not outrightly express racist ideas about Black people—and who, in fact, contested them—and who did not wish for their continuous enslavement seemed not to make sense within the broader transatlantic print culture of the Haitian Revolution, where the revolution was described as a "race war" with three sides: "Black," "Mulatto" (sometimes called "Red"), and "White."

We do not know either the identity or the motives of our intrepid library scribbler. Yet one thing we do know is that men of color from Saint-Domingue like Louverture, Raimond, Rigaud, Dumesle, and Vastey, despite their different origins and connections to slavery, consistently pointed out that so seduced by the "magic" of white supremacy were the white planters (enslavers) that they believed murderously racist yearnings to be a fact of life for the Black people they were enslaving and/or otherwise subjugating with the law. In other words, because the white colonists believed they were superior to Black people on the basis of *race* or skin color, those same colonists believed it was only

Abolition   155

logical that other groups might consider themselves superior to others, especially if they had some connection to *whiteness*, like the *hommes de couleur*. The planter Vaublanc charged that a great deal of the formerly enslaved population remained in rebellion even after general emancipation because, led by Louverture, they sought to slaughter all the whites and confiscate their property. Louverture responded to this accusation by rhetorically asking, if the Blacks and men of color "had sworn a ferocious hatred to the whites, how is it that the white population of the city of Cap equals at this moment the black population and that of the men of color? How is it that among the farmers in the plain of Cap's sugar plantations, more than half of them are white? If unity and brotherhood did not reign among men of all colors, would we see whites, reds and blacks teaming up to reestablish these same sugar plantations, and living in the most perfect equality?"[94] Louverture went on to point out that a logic that pitted all white people in the colony against all the Black people was nonsensical (one of the illogics of white supremacy). Louverture had white soldiers fighting under him as a part of the French republican army. Louverture was, therefore, stunned by Vaublanc's accusations: "And then for Citizen Vaublanc to come and endeavor to stir up the passions of the men of Saint-Domingue, to re-establish barbaric prejudices, by publishing that the whites in Saint-Domingue are the only true Frenchmen; does he include in this denomination, the traitors paid by England, those who as a result of odious betrayals brought that treacherous nation onto the land of liberty?"[95] For Louverture, as for Rigaud and Raimond, the only identity that mattered was that of being a good French republican: "If the friends of liberty classify under this respectable denomination [of republican] men submissive in heart and mind to the French Constitution, to its beneficent laws, men who cherish French friends of their countries, we swear that we have and that we will always have the right to be called French Citizens."[96]

The illogic of white supremacist thought was everywhere apparent to our devoted pamphleteers from Saint-Domingue who consistently called out their enemies by explaining what was faulty in their behavior or logic, not in their skin. For Rigaud, Sonthonax was blamable for the conflict with England—the very one referenced above by Louverture—because he had seemed to betray the republican principles that Rigaud and Louverture so exalted. However, Rigaud also charged Louverture with having betrayed the putatively *color-blind* principles of the French republic. In the same 1799 pamphlet, Rigaud gave his interpretation of Louverture's treaty with the British general Thomas Maitland, which led to British evacuation of the island. "The evacuation of Saint-Domingue by the English seemed at first glance a great conquest, it seemed to irrevocably ensure for France the possession of one of its most precious and important territories, and General Toussaint did not fail at the time to loudly speak of the signal service he had just rendered to the Republic."[97] Louverture famously proclaimed, "I've been fighting for a long time, and if I must continue, I can. I have had to deal with three nations and I defeated all three."[98] Rigaud acknowledged that previously he only spoke well of Louverture and even sang his praises. However, because of Louverture's recent conduct toward England, Rigaud felt he could no longer praise the rival general.[99] "My frankness did not allow me, it is true, to use the emphatic terms of Laveaux and Perroud, in whose eyes [Louverture] was, they said, a new Spartacus, the immortal hero predicted by the abbé Raynal, who would, in the end, become the greatest man in the universe."[100]

It was in spring 1798, that the French government, fearing the growing power of Louverture, sent that additional French agent to Cap-Français, Gabriel-Marie-Théodore-Joseph de Hédouville. Hédouville was tasked with demonstrating that Saint-Domingue remained a French colony and was not under Louverture's singular rule. Unlike General Étienne Laveaux, the previous governor of Saint-Domingue who first likened Louverture to the liberating hero in Raynal's famous Black Spartacus passage of the *Histoire des deux Indes*,[101] Hédouville favored the free people of color rather than the formerly enslaved population and sought to create a distinct division between Louverture and Rigaud. Despite his attempts to drive a wedge between the two most important leaders in the colony, both Louverture and Rigaud remained suspicious of him, and Louverture eventually forced Hédouville to leave the colony, as we have seen. Louverture's sharp defeat and expulsion of Hédouville only confirmed that the Black general was indeed the only true authority in French colonial Saint-Domingue.

Of the situation with Hédouville, Rigaud accused Louverture of having chased away all the French agents, simply because they refused to listen to his "tantrums" and give in to his many caprices.[102] "Is it not Toussaint who has never wanted to recognize the laws of the Republic?" Rigaud asked.[103] In his *Réponse à la proclamation de Toussaint Louverture* (Response to the proclamation of Toussaint Louverture), Rigaud once again referred to Louverture's autonomous agreements with England and the United States. Rigaud argued that in pursuing these negotiations on his own, without approval from the Directory, Louverture had in fact directly betrayed the republic.[104] In Rigaud's analysis, Louverture violated the French constitution "with an act of sovereignty and of scission with France" by signing an autonomous trade agreement with the United States.[105] Rigaud charged that this move constituted a de facto declaration of independence from the republic. As for Louverture's evacuation treaty with the British general Thomas Maitland, Rigaud called it both "liberticidal and anti-republican."[106] "Perhaps, it is in his new capacity as an independent leader, the sovereign of

Saint-Domingue," Rigaud concluded, "that he proclaims me to be insubordinate, a traitor, and a rebel, etc."[107] It is very clear from this letter that Rigaud read his conflict with Louverture to not be one of color, even though he believed that Louverture tried to make it one when he charged Rigaud with being prejudiced against him. The two men had separate styles of governing and differing thoughts on their role in, and the future of, the republic vis-à-vis colonial Saint-Domingue.

Rigaud claimed he could no longer support Louverture because the latter failed the test of loyalty to the French republic. Rigaud's refutation of the idea that Louverture was the "Black Spartacus" demonstrates the depths of his scission with his former comrade and foretold the long reach of the trope. [108] William Wells Brown, in praising Louverture's heroism, compared him to Nat Turner, "the Spartacus of the Southampton revolt."[109] Rigaud made a much more damning comparison when he likened Louverture to the erstwhile monarchs of France: "He wants to take his place among the tyrants of the century, he wants to be powerful, he requires a throne."[110] Speaking directly to his rival, Rigaud remonstrated, "Fool! Oh, do you not know that the Republic overturns both thrones and the powerful!"[111] If Louverture sought to be a powerful monarch with a throne, a royalist, Rigaud claimed to simply want to remain a good republican.[112]

Louverture and Rigaud were engaged in more than a war of words. They fought each other with troops during the War of the South. But, in the end, Rigaud failed to solidify his command over the southern part of the colony. Louverture rallied Generals Christophe, Dessalines, and Moyse, who helped Louverture soundly defeat Rigaud, whereafter the latter was forced into exile in France. After Rigaud's exit, Louverture held virtually unrivaled power. To cement his supreme authority, Louverture issued the constitution of July 1801, which prescribed laws about everything in the colony from laboring hours to religion to the permanent abolition of slavery in any form. The constitution also made Louverture governor-general for life with the right to choose his successor. Bonaparte saw an opportunity here. He used the existence of the constitution as a pretext for sending the Leclerc expedition to Saint-Domingue. France's First Counsul wanted to get rid of Louverture so that he could more assuredly undo the work of abolition.

It was February 1801 when Louverture called forth an assembly to create a constitution for Saint-Domingue. It was completed in May and Louverture signed it in July 1801 and then sent it to Bonaparte.[113] Although the third article declared, as we have seen, that the inhabitants of Saint-Domingue would henceforth be "free and French," Bonaparte saw Louverture's naming of himself as governor-general as a distinct obstacle not simply to his own authority, but to reinstating slavery. In his memoirs, written during his second exile, on

158   Chapter 5

the island of Saint-Helena, Napoléon explained that he viewed Louverture's constitution as a declaration of war: "Toussaint knew very well that in proclaiming his constitution, he had thrown away his mask and had drawn his sword out of its sheath forever."[114]

Louverture was in Santo Domingo, on the eastern side of the island, which was ceded to France by Spain in 1795, when General Leclerc arrived off the coast of Cap in late January 1802 with nearly thirty thousand French troops. General Christophe, commander over the city, denied entry to the troops. Leclerc responded with a combination of disbelief and fury: "I have learned with indignation, citizen general," Leclerc wrote to Christophe on February 3, 1802, "that you are refusing to receive the French squadron and the army I command, under the pretext that you have not received an order to do so from the general government." Leclerc then threatened to "send 15,000 men the next day at daybreak to Fort Picolet and Fort Belair, with another 4,000 disembarking at this moment at Fort Liberté, and yet another 8,000 at Port Républican."[115] Christophe's response was similarly indignant, "General . . . I have the honor of informing you that I cannot deliver these forts and posts, over which I have been given command, before having received an order from the governor-general Toussaint-Louverture, from whom I derive my authority." Christophe sent his aide-de-camp to inform Louverture of Leclerc's arrival, but in the meantime he issued his own warning, "If you realize these threats," he wrote to Leclerc, "I will resist as an officer-general must; and . . . please understand that you will only enter the city of Cap, after having watched it be reduced to ashes. And even upon these ashes, I will fight you."[116] After Leclerc tried to gain the port anyway, Christophe ordered his men to set fire to Cap. The cities of Port-de-Paix and Saint-Marc soon also burned under the direct orders of Louverture.[117]

Louverture paid dearly for this opposition to Leclerc, both personally and politically. By mid-February, Leclerc officially decreed both Louverture and Christophe to be "outlaws."[118] By the spring, French newspapers were regularly printing articles defaming Louverture. One declared that "the cruelty and barbarity of Toussaint are without example," another offered that he was having the entire white population of the colony's major cities slaughtered, despite the fact that Louverture helped his former enslaver financially.[119] Leclerc also used Louverture's children as pawns in this game of revolutionary chess. "I received from my children the letter that you did me the honor of writing to me on the 23rd of the current month," Louverture wrote:

> I am instructed by the account that General Christophe gave to me, and by the letter that you wrote to him, of which he sent me a copy, as well as by what I saw with my own eyes and the little bit of common sense that

I have of the manner in which things unfolded on the arrival of your squadron and of the means it employed to enter Cap: firstly, I must observe to you that in every era when a squadron appears it is customary to send an aviso ahead of time to warn of its arrival; this was not done. Secondly, as news from abroad spoke of peace and I hadn't received any notice of it from the French government, I then thought that it was our enemies who might be spreading these rumors with the intention of coming to attack us: consequently, I ordered all the generals and commanders of the districts under my orders to take their precautions and to make sure that if any warships arrived, if they were French, and, if there were one or two of them, with or without troops, to admit them; but that if a squadron presented itself, they had to report it to me before allowing it entry into the Port: you therefore agree, Citizen General, that if General Christophe refused entry into the port to your squadron, it was not his fault, he did nothing more than execute the orders he had received; and you will agree that in the military order and hierarchy, superior leaders should not address subordinates but rather the commanding officer; for, this inversion of military discipline may occasion insubordination, from which then result endless misfortunes.

"I believe I have earned the title of Pacifier of Saint-Domingue, since I brought peace, abundance, happiness, and prosperity to an island that was torn apart by internal factions and whose external enemies were feuding over its shreds," Louverture continued. "At the time of your arrival the greatest order had been established, the crops here had made astonishing progress; my conscience is pure and I have not the slightest reproach of myself to make, if the haste with which you wanted to enter Cap caused the devastation of this city and its surroundings." He concluded, "I have never been foolish enough to think of fighting against France, the colony does not need to be conquered by its own arms, since we are and have never ceased to be French."[120]

After key allies, including Christophe, Clervaux, and Louverture's own brother, Paul, defected to the French army on the strength of Leclerc's insistence that he had not come to reinstate slavery,[121] Louverture begrudgingly agreed to acknowledge Leclerc's authority and, by May, Louverture officially retired from the French army and went home to his family. Still, Louverture found himself repeatedly charged with inciting insurrection among the "blacks." French newspapers, as well Leclerc's letters, constantly referred to secret missives supposedly exchanged between Louverture and commanders over regions of the colony still in open rebellion. Using the supposed existence of these letters as a pretext, Leclerc issued a warrant for Louverture's arrest. On June 7, 1802, Louverture and his whole family—including

160   Chapter 5

his 105-year-old godfather—were forced onto a ship and deported to France.[122] Louverture never saw his homeland again. The official report of his death recorded in the registry of the justice of the peace of the canton of Pontarlier in the department of Doubs, France, confirmed that Louverture was declared dead by French authorities on April 7, 1803. French doctors claimed he died from a fatal combination of pneumonia and a stroke. The autopsy recorded that both his lungs were filled with blood.[123]

It would be tempting to end this section with the ensuing victories of the Haitian Revolution that led to the creation of the first slavery-free nation in the Americas; or, to once more call upon the famous phrase that Louverture is said to have uttered while boarding the ship to his eternal captivity, "In overthrowing me, you have only cut down the trunk of the tree of liberty of the blacks; but it will grow again from the roots, because they are numerous and deep."[124] Instead let us pause on the place of Louverture (and his ashes) in Haitian thought.

In the *Manifeste du roi*, published in 1814 and signed by King Henry and Julien Prévost, the Comte de Limonade, we read, "Under the administration of Governor General Toussaint Louverture, Haiti was reborn from its ashes, and everything seemed to augur a happy future for us." Under Louverture, the *Manifeste* continued, "laws, piety, education, industry, commerce, agriculture, and good mores reigned." Yet the governor-general "favored the white colonists," the authors of the *Manifeste* claimed, even to the point of having his own nephew, General Moyse, executed for having "deviated from the orders that [Toussaint] had given for the protection of the colonists." Moyse's execution, the king's manifesto conceded, "together with the great confidence he had in the French government, were the chief causes of the feeble resistance that the French experienced on landing in Hayti, and [Louverture's] confidence in that government was so established, that he had sent the bulk of line troops to the farms." The Leclerc expedition, with its mission to reinstate slavery, was nonetheless indefensible. The authors of the *Manifeste* averred, "Posterity will find it difficult to understand that in a century of enlightenment . . . it was from within an enlightened nation that a swarm of barbarians set out with the criminal intention of destroying an entire civilized and peaceful nation, or of plunging them back into the chains of slavery forever." "It was not enough for them to come at gunpoint," the *Manifeste* continued. "It was for them still necessary, to better ensure the success of the expedition, to employ perfidious and shameful means; it was necessary to sow disunity among us and put into effect a salutary diversion to their destructive projects." French methods were as perfidious as their goals: "The leaders of both colors who were in France, even the sons of Governor Louverture, were sent back with the expedition; they were deceived, like us, by the First Consul's proclamation, a masterpiece of treachery, in which he said to us: You are all equal and free before God and before the Republic. At the same time General Leclerc had been given formal instructions to reinstate slavery." Leclerc's famous proclamation, issued in French and in Creole, in which the French commander promised that slavery was not being restored by the First Consul, as well as Bonaparte's secret instructions to him, were printed along with the *Manifeste*.[125] We will examine these documents in the next chapter. For now, let it be stated that in combating distortions of Haitian revolutionary history, Haitian writers not only provided documentary evidence, but insisted on applying a Haitian perspective. Haitians wanted to publicize the gruesome history of the French mission to restore slavery on the island of Saint-Domingue from their point of view.

After Louverture's retreat, resignation, and retirement from the French army, under the assurance that "freedom would be maintained . . . and that France would never go back on her finest laws," the French began to "put into effect their dreadful system of slavery and destruction." "To better achieve this, it was resolved to arrest Governor Toussaint Louverture," the authors of the *Manifeste* lamented. "He was accused of designs that had never entered his heart; he was removed from the Pongaudin plantation, at the moment when he believed in the faith of treaties; loaded with chains, he was thrown with his family on board the ship, *L'Héros*, and transported to France." Louverture's arrest and subsequent death could only but have taken on transatlantic significance, given that one was the precursor to French reinstatement of slavery, the most radical overturning of universal human rights the world had ever seen, and the other was evidence that Black lives did not matter to the French. "The whole of Europe is aware of how he ended his unfortunate career in the tortures and horrors of the dungeons of the Château de Joux," King Henry and Limonade concluded. "Such was the reward reserved for him for his loyalty and for the great and eminent services he had rendered to France and to the colonists."[126]

Boisrond-Tonnerre, for his part, wrote that Louverture's arrest was a "bolt of lightning for Dessalines," who subsequently rallied Christophe, Augustin Clervaux, and Alexandre Pétion to fight definitively against the French troops.[127] In his *Journal de la campagne du nord* (Journal of the northern campaign), written after the Battle of Vertières to explain how the Haitian revolutionary army forced the French army's retreat, Dessalines argued that Louverture's tragic fate demonstrated that the only thing that could combat French treachery was strength. Dessalines implied that the evidence was in Leclerc's violation of his peace with Louverture. Louverture willingly retired, but Leclerc ordered his arrest anyway. "Let France now compare the treaty of capitulation which I signed [with General Rochambeau], to that made between

162 Chapter 5

Generals Toussaint and Leclerc, but violated by the latter, because he was the stronger," Dessalines wrote. The future emperor pointed out that after his division took possession of Cap, they allowed the French army to stay for one day in the port, "on my word." Dessalines also noted that the French commandant of the naval forces obtained from him the "salvation of his division, when it could have been sunk in two hours." Unlike how the French behaved after Louverture's capitulation—engaging in a war of "extermination," their words—Dessalines behaved honorably, based on the agreement he made with General Rochambeau to allow for ten days of evacuation. Dessalines included with his report letters he exchanged with French military officers during the ten days that stood between the Battle of Vertières and the time of the agreed-upon French evacuation. Offering this evidence, Dessalines insisted, would "provide a proper idea of the loyalty and humanity that one must have, and which dictated my conduct toward a defeated army." This humanity was exercised in the wake of the most inhumane behavior. "It is true," Dessalines continued, "I had cause to reproach the murders and the horrible brigandage exercised for more than a year, against my compatriots and me." Because Dessalines intended his report to be sent to the First Consul, he did not fail to indict the deceased Leclerc's conduct. Even though Rochambeau is today most associated with the attempted genocide, in early Haitian thought, Leclerc did not escape Haitian judgment simply because he died of yellow fever before the expedition reached its most murderous heights. Leclerc was the first architect of the genocidal drownings. He had also behaved dishonorably with respect to the French army. Dessalines wanted the French consuls to know, "when I entered Cap, I discovered that Captain General Leclerc still possessed some of the richest shops , at a time when the most dreadful poverty was felt by all men."[128] Dessalines minced no words about the implications of the French army's behavior for the republic: "And if men who want to be free because they can be, are still known in France under the dreadful epithet of brigands; let [France] send back, if it is possible, to fight them, the small number of French soldiers that our climate and our humanity have spared."[129]

In Haitian revolutionary thought it is the terrible fate of Louverture and his family that taught the other revolutionary leaders that there could no longer be any meaningful negotiations for peace with France. The French continued to act bewildered by the powerful obstinance of the Black freedom fighters and their resolution to die rather than be enslaved by the French again. Leclerc famously said, "It is not enough to have gotten rid of Toussaint. Here, there are two thousand leaders to get rid of. . . . The more weapons that I get rid of, the more the taste for insurrection grows. I collected 20,000 rifles, there are just as many in the hands of the cultivators."[130] The French officer Pamphile de Lacroix used a more cerebral metaphor in writing that combating

Abolition   163

the general insurrection was like trying to combat a "hydra with one hundred heads that grow back throughout the colony with every blow we deal against it."[131] The *Gazette Royale d'Hayti*, characterized in the following way the lessons the Haitian revolutionaries learned from how the French government treated Louverture:

> Toussaint Louverture voluntarily resigned his authority and laid down his arms: having retired to his home, stripped of all his grandeur, like that famous Roman [Spartacus], he cultivated with his hands the same land he had defended with his weapons; he urged us, by his words and his example, to imitate him, to work and to live peacefully in the bosom of our families. Against the good faith of treaties, the French lured him into a trap: he was arrested, loaded with irons; his wife, his children, his family, his officers all suffered his disastrous fate. Thrown aboard French ships, they were taken to Europe to end their unhappy careers, with poison, in dungeons and in irons!

Louverture was not the only one to suffer under the French plot to exterminate. "Generals Jacques Maurepas and Charles Bélair died by torture: Maurepas was nailed alive on the main mast of the ship *Annibal*, in the presence of his wife and children; his body was thrown into the sea with those of his entire family: the unfortunate Bélair was shot with his intrepid wife; that heroine who bravely died." We further read in the *Gazette* of the fates of some of Louverture's other trusted soldiers and officers: "Thomany, Domage, Lamahotière, a host of officers and distinguished citizens experienced death as if they were scoundrels, they were hanged; those who escaped their murderous irons or gibbets, died of poison; Generals Vilate, Léveillé and Gaulard experienced that deadly fate; others were deported to be sold to the Côte-Ferme or France where they ended their careers in the galleys." Nineteenth-century Haitian writers tied the ardent war of independence that subsequently ensued directly to the terrible war the Black soldiers were forced to wage against the French army to achieve liberty. "Tired of so many crimes and punishments, we ran to arms," the same article in the *Gazette* continued. "We measured ourselves against our executioners: we fought hand to hand, man for man, with stones and iron sticks, to preserve our freedom, our existence, that of our women and our children. After shedding torrents of our blood, mingled with that of our tyrants, we remained masters of the battlefield."[132] We know that these are the words of Vastey because they are repeated in his 1816 *Ré-flexions sur une lettre de Mazères*, where he added the following justification for Haitian independence: "From whatever point of view one considers this great and important question, it will always be resolved in our favor; whether it is out of consideration for the deplorable situation in which we were plunged

164   Chapter 5

under the dreadful colonial regime; whether it is out of consideration for the circumstances that brought us to freedom, and from freedom to independence; the injustices and cruelties of all kinds that we have experienced; our sufferings and our misfortunes."[133] In his later 1819 *Essai* Vastey described Louverture's arrest as the moment that independence from France became both necessary and possible. Adding yet more detail to the scene of Louverture's arrest and deportation, Vastey wrote, "Governor Toussaint was arrested, bound, and tied up, like a criminal, to be embarked for France with his officers and his family, the instant he arrived at General Brunet's." Louverture did not submit to this arrest quietly. "You dare to arrest me; you dishonor an honorable officer," Louverture reportedly cried. "Is this how you observe in good faith treaties; you are traitors and perjurers; Heaven is just; I will be avenged." Vastey's reading of these words in relation to later independence underscores Louverture's key position in Haitian thought. "These were the last words that this great man spoke on the soil of his homeland," Vastey wrote. "On that soil he had conquered for France, and which was still resounding with his name, his services, and his exploits! He was undoubtedly avenged, but he was not given the chance to see this beautiful day of vengeance."[134]

Louverture's legacy spawned many lives. The system of life he helped create out of the French enslavers' and colonists' system of death transcended comparison to any other historical figure. "Toussaint is not comparable, as they liked to say in his time, either to Spartacus, nor to Alexander the Great, nor to Bonaparte," wrote Vergniaud Leconte, in his famous history of the Haitian Revolution and biography of Henry Christophe in 1931. "He was a unique man in quest of a unique goal; he did not bring down peoples: he raised them up; he ravished no empire: he built one of Liberty and Equality; he conquered no nation: he created a hundred." "Born on a straw mat, he died on straw," Leconte continued, "leaving our black humanity but one thought: you are all brothers; only one recommendation: live free or die!"[135]

The arrest of Louverture and many prominent soldiers from the Black army had only added to the chaos created when Bonaparte issued the damning law of May 20, 1802, sanctioned with a vote from France's Legislative Assembly, permitting slavery to exist on the French territories England returned to France at the Treaty of Amiens, namely, Martinique. To understand how and why the revolutionaries came to agree with the conclusion that the island needed independence, iterated previously by Sonthonax, the very man whom Raimond, Louverture, and Rigaud, exiled from the colony, we must also consult the intricate history of how slavery was legislated back into existence in the French republic under Bonaparte. These laws demonstrate the enduring incoherence of French republicanism and undergird the philosophy of freedom developed by the Haitian revolutionaries to combat them.

Chapter 6

Freedom

Remember Louverture's prediction? Any perceived move toward independence for Saint-Domingue would encourage France to negotiate peace with the European warring powers, which would only better facilitate the republic's ability to recapture its lost colony. *"Here is what would happen next,"* Louverture told Sonthonax in 1797, *"France would make peace with all the other powers and say to itself: The colonists were right to say that the blacks were not worthy of enjoying the freedom and benefits of France. And France, in agreement with all the powers that do not want freedom, would bind itself to them out of revenge, and we would be lost."*[1]

On November 13, 1801 (22 *brumaire an X*), amid peace talks with Great Britain, and anticipating a future and official peace accord, First Consul Napoléon Bonaparte wrote to his chief diplomat Charles-Maurice de Talleyrand-Périgord (called Talleyrand) to explain how getting rid of Toussaint Louverture would better prevent Saint-Domingue from achieving independence: "In the decision I made to annihilate the government of the blacks in Saint-Domingue, I was guided less by considerations of trade and finance than by the need to stifle in all parts of the world every germ of worry and unrest; but . . . it could not escape me that a Saint-Domingue reconquered by the Whites would be for many years a weak point that would require the support and the peace of the mother country."[2] In the paragraph preceding this, Bonaparte mused about what would happen if the French republic instead was "obliged to recognize Toussaint, to renounce Saint-Domingue and to constitute them as Black Frenchmen."[3] Listen closely to hear the incoherence that follows from the mere thought that Bonaparte would be forced to recognize Black men as truly French. Bonaparte first acknowledged that maintaining Black freedom in Saint-Domingue would place the French republic at the vanguard of the world. He wrote, "The freedom of black people recognized in Saint-Domingue and legitimized by the government [of France] would, in every way, be a fulcrum for the Republic in the New World."[4] What a torturous seduction that was never to be. It was Bonaparte's own racism that prevented him from carrying this vision into reality.

Astonishingly, Bonaparte insisted that Black freedom in the French Caribbean could facilitate the downfall of the still slaving British empire, his most ardent enemy. But Bonaparte, the man who wanted to conquer the world, could not envision such supreme power for himself, if Black freedom accompanied it. We must look to the next paragraph of the letter to understand how Bonaparte's audacious desire for white supremacy took precedence over his dream of conquering Europe. "One of the main benefits of peace at the present time for England was that it was concluded at a moment when the French government had not yet recognized the organization of Saint-Domingue and therefore the power of the Blacks," Bonaparte wrote. "In that case, the scepter of the new world would have, sooner or later, fallen into the hands of the Blacks; the shock which would have resulted from that for England is incalculable, while the shock of black control, relative to France, was simply comingled with that of the Revolution."[5] Instead of pursuing Black freedom to ruin his enemies in Britain, while extending the more radical precepts of the National Convention's unilateral abolition by making emancipation permanent, Bonaparte sought to destroy Black freedom by bringing back slavery. He sent secret instructions to his brother-in-law, General Charles-Victor-Emmanuel Leclerc, directing him to rid Saint-Domingue of Louverture. Leclerc's mission after this was to reinstate slavery.

In the confidential missive Bonaparte sent to Leclerc he wrote a phrase that he later betrayed. "The French nation will never enslave men it has recognized as free," he claimed. "Thus, all the blacks of Saint-Domingue will live like those in Guadeloupe today." Bonaparte then instructed Leclerc to overthrow Louverture in three phases, the first of which involved disarming "only those blacks who are in rebellion," while in the third, Leclerc was instructed to "disarm them all." The detailed missive laid out a plan for first "seducing" Toussaint Louverture, before arresting and deporting him in the second phase. "Win over Christophe, Clairveaux, Maurepas, Félix, Romain, Jasmin, etc., and all other blacks favorable to the whites," Bonaparte advised, before instructing Leclerc to turn on them too. "In the first phase, confirm their ranks and positions. In the third phase, send them to all to France with their ranks if they served well during the second phase." The third phase was to be unmistakably violent and had only one true goal, "If Toussaint, Dessalines, or Moyse have been captured under arms, they will be judged by a military commission within 24 hours and shot as rebels. Whatever happens, in the course of the third phase you should disarm all negroes, regardless of the party to which they belong, and return them to field work."[6] In mid-March, Bonaparte wrote to Leclerc to remind him of the goal, counseling his brother-in-law to "follow exactly the instructions, and as soon as you have defeated Toussaint, Christophe, Dessalines, and the principal brigands, and the black masses have been disarmed, send back to the continent all the blacks and men of color who played a role in these troubles."[7]

Bonaparte's actions for the legacy of the French Revolution are damning. Universal humanity was either proclaimed by the French revolutionaries in bad faith, or it was designed to exclude Black people by allowing French republican principles to be extended only to those the French considered to be *like them*, that is to say, *white*. Either everyone and everything is subjected to universalisms or nothing and no one is. And Bonaparte's decisions, coupled with the expedition he sent to destroy Louverture, Christophe, Dessalines, and their allies, illustrate how colonial racism masqueraded as universalism in the age of revolutions. The Haitian philosophy of independence was developed as a response to the contradictions of French republicanism: the French revolutionaries loudly proclaimed liberty, equality, and fraternity with humankind, while maintaining slavery, at first, and then after they abolished it, they allowed it to be unabashedly reinstated in Guadeloupe, where it persisted for forty-six long years.

Railing, in part, against French so-called universalisms, Vastey insisted that in light of what Bonaparte and the French army did in attempting to restore slavery in Saint-Domingue, "The Haitian people found themselves placed in an all-together particular circumstance, which is what forever ensured the righteousness and justice of their cause": independence. First, Vastey pointed out that the "entire world" was aware that "Republican France proclaimed *freedom* on this island." Then, "after having enjoyed under the law for ten years this good act . . . those vile republicans, without any reason whatsoever, sought to rob us of the freedom they had given us, as if man, subjected to the whims of tyrants, must discard or resume the chains of slavery, according to their wishes." Leclerc's army came not only in numbers and with force, but with the goal of tricking the Black population into believing that the French government had no desire to restore slavery. "They told us that we were all brothers and all equal before God and before the Republic," Vastey wrote, "even though they had come with the barbaric and criminal intention of exterminating us or reducing us to slavery."[8] Upon his arrival in Saint-Domingue, Leclerc circulated in both French and Haitian Creole a proclamation from Bonaparte "to the inhabitants of Saint-Domingue." Dated November 8, 1801, its first line read, "Whatever your origin and your color, you are all French, *you are all free and all equal before God and the Republic*."[9] When Vastey said Bonaparte did not have "any reason whatsoever" to try to destroy Black freedom he was playing with his words. Racism and reason were incompatible in Vasteyan thought. Racism is illogical, an absence of logic; as such, for Vastey, racism could undergird an action but could itself not be a logic or characterized as *a reason*.

Bonaparte expressed explicitly racist illogics throughout his rule, which clearly undergirded his decision to destroy Louverture so he could reinstate slavery. In a 1799 consular address, Bonaparte explained that if he had been in Martinique at the time the French lost that colony to Great Britain circa the 1794 Battle of Martinique, he would have been on the side of the British because they never dared to abolish slavery. "I am for the whites, because I am white," Bonaparte said. "I have no other reason, and this is the right one. *How could anyone have granted freedom to Africans, to men who had no civilization.*" "It is quite simple," he continued, "those who wanted the freedom of the blacks want the slavery of white people." We have already seen this simple-minded tropology of reversal in the writings of white colonists like Viénot de Vaublanc who believed that the Black people of Saint-Domingue, and other men of color, merely wanted to establish their own domination over those classified as white. Bonaparte, sharing in this illogic of white supremacy, dreamt of freedom as subjugation and could only imagine that Black people did too. Thus, the latter had to be destroyed at all costs. Bonaparte opined in the same report, "But again, do you think that if the majority of the Convention had known what it was doing and was familiar with the colonies, that it would have given freedom to the blacks? No, without a doubt; but few were able to foresee the results, and a sense of humanity still held power over the imagination." Human rights had to be crushed not just for the sake of the republic, but for all "whites like us, civilized people, our neighbors," Bonaparte insisted.[10] In 1804, the Haitian revolutionaries, with their antislavery, anti-colonial, and anti-racist Declaration of Independence, exposed French republican "universalisms" to be mere sophistry; and early Haiti's politicians, writers, and other intellectuals were determined to document the disastrous genocidal consequences of this incoherence, a mode of illogic that did not prevent the French from continuing to falsely exalt their revolution as having resulted in a "liberatory republic."[11]

What needs more elaboration is the role that white French people played in their country's violent return to slavery. Haitian histories of the French Revolution remind us that this decision did not result solely from the capricious whim of one terrible dictator. The French reinstatement of slavery in Guadeloupe and the failed attempt in Saint-Domingue could not have been carried out without the consent of large sectors of the French populace. "Who attacked us with a hundred thousand bayonets in 1802, was it not the French?" Vastey asked. To be sure, the French colonists, he insisted, were the instigators who pushed Bonaparte and the French legislature to reinstate slavery, but "the ex-colonists alone," in Vastey's words, "without the support of the government and French people, could they have attacked us?"[12] French legislators and the French army, along with large sectors of the citizenry, upheld, sanctioned, and accepted Bonaparte's decisions, ensuring the enduring incoherence of French republicanism.

Bonaparte's thoughts on restoring slavery were undoubtedly influenced by the evil sermons of white French colonists from Saint-Domingue like

Freedom   169

Vaublanc, who famously declared before the legislative body of the Directory that "the present cry" of all the "negroes" in the colony was that the "country belonged to them, that they did not want to see there a single white man. At the same time that they swear to the whites, that is to say to true Frenchmen, a ferocious hatred."[13] In his response to Vaublanc's speech, addressed to the Directory, Louverture pointed out that the goal of the revolution in Saint-Domingue was not to produce Black African domination over white French people, but was instead to create an egalitarian society, the one alluded to, but never materialized by the signers of the French Declaration of the Rights of Man. "If it was true that the blacks were so unjust as to believe that all property in Saint-Domingue belonged to them, why would they not have made themselves the masters, by chasing away men of every other color, since it would have been easy for them to gain control because of their numbers?"[14] The Black revolutionaries, Louverture pointed out, did not seek to divest the white colonists of their property. In fact, Louverture protected the property rights of the colonists, even those who initially fled and then returned, called *émigrés*.

Bonaparte, like Vaublanc and the majority of the white French colonists, was far from being an anti-racist, nor was he open to learning about and understanding the point of view of others. André Rigaud likened white French colonial racism to being under a spell cast with "the magical wand of prejudice."[15] Dealing with the deceptions and manipulations of the white French colonists taught "the men of color and the free negroes," Rigaud said, to be wary of "that great art which we call politics, an art which consists of speaking in one way, while thinking in another, in making public oaths that one denies in the recesses of his heart, and violates even more, when a supposed interest demands it." As a result, the men of color of Saint-Domingue, "at least learned not to be so gullible, they saw that it was important to their salvation to be suspicious."[16] Public declarations mismatched with private missives and vice versa were everywhere apparent in the history of France's relationship with the Caribbean during and after the French Revolution and contributed much to the incoherence of the resulting French republic. This much is evident in Bonaparte's outright, rather than implicit, overturning of French revolutionary principles at the conclusion of the Treaty of Amiens.

In addition to ending France's war with Great Britain, at the March 1802 Treaty of Amiens the British officially ceded Martinique, where slavery had never been abolished, back to the French. Suddenly Bonaparte found himself in the position of either needing to readmit Martinique into the republic as a slave colony or ending slavery there. In May of that year, the First Consul resolved the conflict by issuing the following decree, "In the colonies returned to France, by execution of the Amiens treaty . . . slavery shall be maintained in accordance with the laws and regulations in place prior to 1789." The new law also allowed the return of the slave trade.[17] The *acte* had first gone before the French tribunal before official adoption by the republic's legislative body. Admiral Eustache Bruix had pronounced a speech urging an affirmative vote. "Doubtless it is unfortunate that part of the human race is condemned by nature or social institutions to servile labor and slavery. But we will heed the lessons of our experiences and those provided by the example of our rivals," Bruix said. "Could France rely on colonies peopled primarily by free blacks?" he asked. No, was his unequivocal conclusion:

> Their interests would soon diverge from the home country's, because the Antillean negro's absent homeland is Africa. . . . If the blacks acquire land, their harvests will pass into contraband commerce. Thus, property and power must be in the hands of a few whites, and negroes, in great numbers, must be slaves. . . . Without our slave colonies, there will be no more trade with Africa, no way of increasing our fisheries. . . . In Europe, our agriculture, and industry would decline, along with our East Indian commerce; our naval power would suffer gravely from reductions in sailors and workers. All this would result from the freedom of the blacks.[18]

Many members of the tribunal agreed, not just on economic and philosophic principles, but on white supremacist ones. Averring that freedom could only be a "poisonous fruit" for Black people in the colonies, one citizen pronounced, "Let us no longer trouble the world with theories. The Constituent Assembly knows the cost of liberal ideas. . . . The Tribunal therefore must applaud the thinking of the government when it proposes to you, citizen legislators, to return to the former laws concerning the people of the colony, and to the means by which we can repopulate the class of laborers." While not missing the opportunity to paint the Jacobins as mere theorists, whose ideas of liberty and equality put the colonies in fateful peril, Bruix had more specifically focused on the skin color of the laborers as a reason to re-enslave them: "Liberty in Rome was ensconced in slavery. The difference of color, mores, habits, justifies the domination of the whites; but it is politics, preserving your greatness, and perhaps even your conservation itself, that proscribes us from breaking the chains of the blacks." An erstwhile member of the Society of the Friends of the Blacks stated even more forthrightly that the only way to save the republic was to retreat from the *theories* of freedom and equality established during the French Revolution. "Without a doubt, it is necessary, just, and honorable to regress," he said, since only the reinstatement of slavery could secure "peace, order, stability, and true glory" for the Republic of France.[19] So it was that a law reauthorizing slavery on French territory was

Freedom 171

passed with 211 assembly members voting in its favor, and only sixty-three opposing it.[20] The return of slavery was couched in language that tells on itself: the republic must regress and return to a state of political, philosophical, and metaphorical infancy.

The law of May 20 created an opening for slavery to return elsewhere on French territory and occasioned even more conflict in the Caribbean, rather than lessening it. Black people on the island of Guadeloupe fought the French troops Bonaparte sent there to subjugate them. Correctly suspecting that the French squadron that arrived on Guadeloupe on May 6 came to restore slavery, the Martinican-born freedom fighter, Louis Delgrès, like so many brave Black Saint-Dominguans, used armed resistance to try to prevent the leader of the expedition, General Antoine Richepanse, from reinstating slavery. Around May 21, 1802, Delgrès, along with four hundred men of color, locked himself in the Fort Saint-Charles for a week to prevent the French from acquiring its ammunition. On May 28, surrounded by French troops and with no hope of effectively escaping, Delgrès, in Saint-Rémy's words, "resolved not to outlive the removal of freedom from his race." With three hundred remaining men by his side, Delgrès set fire to the fort's gunpowder, committing mass suicide in the process. Suicide, a crime in Christian religions, provided salvation and deliverance in a world of slavery. Joseph Saint-Rémy, our intrepid Haitian historian, but a native of Guadeloupe, was clearly agitated when evoking the dramatic events that preceded the restoration of slavery on the island where he was born. Saint-Rémy described Delgrès's "face as completely radiant with the greatness of his oblation, setting the powder keg on fire," after which "friends and enemies alike, met each other in the air with a shock, their crushed and mutilated bodies soon covering the ravines and fields." Concluding this gruesome, sad scene with a lament, Saint-Rémy opined, "Passerby, go and tell freedom, if you find it somewhere in the world, that there died three hundred souls preferring not to live longer than its holy laws."[21]

Though the opposition led by Delgrès could not prevent French reinstatement of slavery, his attempt is an important reminder that bringing back the shameful institution was a choice made by French leaders, one that was supported at the time by large segments of the French population and most French colonists, while being implemented by vast numbers of military generals and soldiers. Guadeloupeans saw slavery officially reinstated per a subsequent decree passed by Bonaparte in July 1802. Similar to the May 20 law allowing slavery on Martinique, the July 16 decree maintained in Article 1, "The colony of Guadeloupe and dependencies would be managed like Martinique, St. Lucia, Tobago, and the oriental colonies, by the same laws that were in force in 1789." Yet unlike the prior decree, in which French legislators used euphemistic language, never outright mentioning slavery (they referred only to the laws of the *ancien régime*, or old regime), the July law was accompanied by a more specific "Plan concerning the reestablishment of slavery on Guadeloupe and dependencies" (*Projet d'arrêté concernant le rétablissement de l'esclavage à la Guadeloupe et dépendances*). In this addendum, "the Consuls of the Republic, following the report of the Minister of the Marine and the Colonies, [and] the Council of State," forthrightly explained what it meant to return to the laws that were in force "before 1789." The document provided six illogics for the republic's reinstatement of slavery:

> Consideration. 1. That the law of Pluviôse an 2 [February 1794], which accorded liberty to the blacks of Guadeloupe, has only had destructive effects,
>
> 2. That we had vainly flattered ourselves by envisioning this island fertilized increasingly by free hands; that it has been, on the contrary, deteriorating every day . . .
>
> 3. That sharing of the fruits of the plantations because of their gradual decline has become under the new system [affermage] equally insufficient for both the master and the worker [atelier].
>
> 4. That the example of the neighboring Colonies where slavery persists, offers a stark contrast in prosperity and tranquility . . .
>
> 5. . . . above all the terrible use that the blacks of Guadeloupe have made of freedom by arming their parricidal arms against the government . . .
>
> 6. . . . finally the great crimes with which these blacks have just finished soiling themselves with their rebellion.[22]

The return to slavery decreed by this law, sanctioned by the French minister of the marine and Council of State, only encouraged more rebellion in Saint-Domingue. Leclerc acknowledged in a letter he wrote to the minister of the marine: "All the blacks are persuaded that we have come here to re-enslave them and I will not be able to get them to lay down their arms without a long struggle."[23] The Haitian revolutionaries also testified about the effect the July 1802 law had on the ongoing revolution in Saint-Domingue. In his April 1804 speech, Dessalines reminded the new Haitians of the relationship between what happened in Guadeloupe and Haiti's ensuing fight for freedom and independence. While Leclerc and Bonaparte repeatedly promised not to bring back slavery, assuring that all people in Saint-Domingue regardless of skin color would remain free—Leclerc said he would even provide "a provisory constitution . . . for the colony; but that will not be definitive until it will have been approved by the French government, [which] will have as its base the liberty and equality of all the inhabitants of Saint-Domingue, without

Freedom   173

distinction of color"[24]—the French turned around and directly reinstated slavery on neighboring Guadeloupe. They sent a large army that "ransacked and destroyed," he said. And "[Guadeloupe's] ruins [are] still fuming with the blood of children, of women, of old men run through with the sword," Dessalines lamented.[25]

Opposition to the idea of slavery's return to the colony unfolded differently in Saint-Domingue. General Leclerc said to preserve Saint-Domingue and bring back slavery, the French army needed to kill all the people of color in the colony over the age of twelve and who had ever "worn an epaulette."[26] The French military gassed, drowned, and sent dogs trained to eat the revolutionaries;[27] while the French colonists openly bragged that after the "extermination" the island could simply be repopulated with Africans from the continent. Such monstrous resolve only encouraged the Black soldiers to swear they would fight for "independence or death." After defeating Bonaparte's army, and declaring their independence on January 1, 1804, Haiti, rather than France, became the first modern state to permanently abolish slavery.

No, because of his shameful legislation and white supremacist dreams, Napoléon could never be a hero to celebrate in Haiti. "Whether or not he has the qualities of a great man, hardly matters to me; he has done great things, so be it; he extended and receded the limits of his empire. Still, what interest can I take in his greatness, in his glory even?" asked Julien Prévost (the Comte de Limonade) and secretary to King Henry Christophe. "None," Prévost continued. "I see, and want to see in him, only the enemy of my country, who, through his agents, covered it with ruins, blood, dead bodies, and wreckage."[28] The history of the Leclerc expedition is damning for Napoléon, but it also implicates large sectors of French society. The nineteenth-century Haitian writer and politician Chanlatte, who helped craft Haiti's first constitution, called the "unheard-of executions" perpetrated by the French "des crimes de lèse-humanité," or "crimes against humanity." Chanlatte reserved his deepest and most profound indignation for the French soldiers who carried out the orders of their leaders, which involved the effective creation of the prototype for the gas chamber. "It is difficult to understand," he wrote, "how the more than 60,000 men involved in this expedition, could have degraded themselves to the point of simply becoming blind executioners."[29] The Black people of Saint-Domingue had little choice but to begin to fight for unqualified freedom.

———

Louverture frequently noted in the letters and statements he gave to French officials during his incarceration, as in his memoirs, that he tried to compromise with French authority and was even willing to accept some blame. In the letter to Bonaparte that he wrote aboard *Le Héros*, after his arrest,

174   Chapter 6

Louverture implored, "Citizen First Consul, I will not conceal from you my faults: I have committed several. Is any man exempt from them?" Louverture also pointed out that assured of amnesty by General Leclerc and having retired to his lands, as promised, he was tricked into a meeting and summarily arrested.[30] The French had betrayed *him*. Later, alluding to the fact that in May 1802 Bonaparte legislated the reintroduction of slavery into the French empire, but also clearly despondent over his forced estrangement from his family, Louverture told General Marie-François Auguste de Caffarelli, whom Bonaparte sent to interrogate Louverture in the Fort de Joux during his incarceration, "Saint-Domingue is a huge treasure, but to bring it to its full potential, you need . . . the peace and freedom of the blacks. But oh! General, I don't care about treasures, because I have lost things far more precious than treasures."[31]

In part because of his tragic demise, Governor-General Louverture was framed as *the* revolutionary hero in nineteenth-century transatlantic print culture.[32] But soon after independence in 1804, Dessalines's most prominent secretary, Adjutant General Louis-Félix Boisrond-Tonnerre, tried to remind the world with his own *Mémoires pour servir à l'histoire d'Haïti*—a book bearing Dessalines's stamp of approval on the cover page—that it was Dessalines who was the primary author of Haitian freedom and the founder of Haitian independence. It was Dessalines's story that needed to be retold from a national perspective to make his heroism broadly understood. Boisrond-Tonnerre felt that this could best be accomplished by comparing Dessalines to Louverture. Boisrond-Tonnerre wrote: "Toussaint owed his success [during the war against Rigaud] to this general [Dessalines] alone, which otherwise would have ended in the death of his troops, if not for the discipline that Dessalines introduced among them and without the example he gave to them by throwing himself into their ranks to lead them in combat." Boisrond-Tonnerre continued to exalt Dessalines above the other revolutionary heroes by describing him as "without ambition, modest, and blindly obedient to the orders of his leader [Toussaint Louverture]." "He seemed to have been born for war," the secretary added, "it made him a happy soldier and ended by making him a hero."[33]

While Boisrond-Tonnerre described Dessalines as a superior and gifted soldier, other contemporaries continued to exalt Louverture for his patience and moderation as governor. Writing in 1810, Chanlatte, after alluding to the "government of Toussaint Louverture," seemed to astonish himself with his own words: "Under the government, I said it, of Governor General Toussaint Louverture, this country was reborn from its ashes."[34] Chanlatte used the same language to describe Louverture that he used in the short seven-page pamphlet he produced in 1804 to characterize the later birth of independent

Haiti under Dessalines. "The Island of Hayti, like the Phoenix, after having experienced its entrails being torn apart by its own children, after having been consumed by flames," he wrote, "will be reborn from its ashes, and will emerge from its ruins, more beautiful and more glorious."[35] Later still, Chanlatte famously attached these words to the rise of King Henry Christophe, whose official motto was, "Je renais de mes cendres" or "I am reborn from my ashes." Yet, Chanlatte employed the metaphor in *Le Cri de la nature* to suggest that Louverture's 1801 Constitution for Saint-Domingue had lighted the way for independent Haiti's first constitution. Chanlatte's exclamation about the "government of Toussaint" unwittingly captures the central paradox of Haiti's ongoing freedom struggle—a by turns tragic and celebratory drama that led to the unfreedom of Louverture, his arrest and murder, but to freedom and equality for the Haitian people, their sovereignty and independence from France. Louverture's constitution did not declare independence for the island, as we have seen, but it is nonetheless a crucial step on the way to understanding how Haitian independence later emerged under Dessalines. In Prévost's words, "This great work [of independence] was of necessity the continuation of the constitution that was adopted [in 1801]."[36]

The constitution of 1801 was the most radically free set of laws the American hemisphere had ever seen since the instantiation of chattel slavery there by the British, Spanish, French, Portuguese, and Dutch. It is only fitting that we now return to this constitution, how it was formed and why, so that we may come to appreciate how, with even with its limited radicality—in that it did not create an independent state—it set the terms for Haitian freedom after independence. The colonial constitution of 1801 was the first draft for independent Haiti's constitution in 1805.

Scholars Michael Drexler and Ed White have argued that the Saint-Domingue Constitution of 1801, "following its dissemination throughout the US in fall of 1801 . . . became the most widely read piece of literature authored by an African American and may have remained so until the publication of the *Narrative of the Life of Frederick Douglass* in 1845."[37] What attracted U.S. readers to this early constitution was undoubtedly its unequivocal third article: "There can no longer exist any slaves in this land, servitude is forever abolished here. All men are here born, live, and will die free and French." The 1801 constitution, even while preserving Saint-Domingue's colonial status as *French*, "made universal freedom from slavery its radical foundation," in great contrast to the founding documents of the United States or any of the French revolutionary constitutions, as Philip Kaisary has observed. "Neither the French Constitution of 1791 nor the Jacobin Constitution of 1793 abolished slavery, while the 1799 Constitution actually paved the way for the reintroduction of slavery in the French colonies in 1802," Kaisary pointed

176   Chapter 6

out. "In fact, . . . the only French Revolutionary Constitution that contained a provision abolishing slavery was the otherwise conservative post-Thermidorian constitution of 1795."[38] Thus it was that the 1801 constitution made the Saint-Domingue of Louverture's era a "colony of citizens." "The enslaved revolutionaries challenged the racialized colonial system of the day," as Laurent Dubois has written, "deploying the language of republican rights and the promise of individual liberty against a social order based on the denial of their humanity. In winning back the natural rights the Enlightenment claimed as the birthright to all people, however, the formerly enslaved laid bare a profound tension within the ideology of rights they had made their own."[39] The tensions of freedom plaguing the emancipated French colonies were not so much resolved in the Saint-Domingue Constitution of 1801 as they were called into question, particularly surrounding the forms of *work* or *labor* that could exist in a vast section of the world that previously hinged its economic prosperity on chattel slavery. This problematic—how to transform a slave economy into a free labor economy—stamped Louverture's first constitution, just as much as its stamped Sonthonax's emancipation proclamation. The relationship between these two documents is crucial to understanding how the Haitian revolutionaries came to define freedom after independence.

The commission to create the constitution that Louverture convoked in February 1801 had only one elected person of color on it, Julien Raimond. The rest of the elected were those with white status, many of them former planters (enslavers). From the western department there was Bernard Borgella and Lacour; from the north, there was Étienne Viard (or Viart) and Raimond; from the south, there was Philippe André Collet and Gaston Nogéré; from Ozama, there was Jean Monceybo and François Morillas (who died shortly after his election to the constitution commission); and from Cibao, there was Charles Roxas and André Mugnos (Munoz). According to Thomas Madiou, Louverture's nephew Moyse was also elected in the north, but did not accept the commission.[40] The makeup of what came to be called the Central Assembly, which first met in March 1801, is not unimportant. Louverture has been subjected to charges that he "aspir[ed] to be accepted into white planter society," on the one hand, and that "it was his intention not to leave a mulatto man alive," on the other.[41] Louverture convoked, to be sure, a relatively homogeneous assembly. Still, with Borgella residing, this assembly declared unequivocal freedom for people on the island of all *colors*. Although there were no people considered *noir* sitting on the assembly, the actions, goals, and desires of the formerly enslaved population pervaded the language of the constitution. The constitution of 1801, as Trouillot reminded us, *followed* the radical taking of rights and abolition of slavery by the people in the colony called *nègre* or *noir* beginning in August 1791. The freedom fighters of Bois

Freedom 177

Caïman and the maroons of Saint-Domingue—the very ones who refused to put down arms, even when Biassou et al. were negotiating with French authorities in fall 1791—are in many ways the ghostwriters of the 1801 constitution. The constitution of 1801 described, in theory, a colony that would also become the most free state in all the Americas and Western Europe. Even with its shortsighted position on the value of complete independence, the constitution radically redefined Atlantic freedom as incompatible with chattel, that is hereditary, slavery.

Article 1 of the constitution defined the territory of the colony as the entire island of Ayiti/Hispaniola: "Saint-Domingue, in all its extent, and Samana, La Tortue, La Gonâve, the Cayemites, L'Île-à-Vache, the Saône, and other adjacent islands, form the territory of a single colony, which is part of the French Empire, but which is subject to particular laws." Although it is the antislavery clause to which we shall return in a moment, we must pause here and return to France so that we may understand how the 1801 constitution combated slavery with its opening law by inserting divisibility, that is particularity, into the heart of the putatively indivisible Republic of France. In 1799, after Bonaparte's rise to power as First Consul of France, in one of his first legislative moves, he changed the French republican constitution to allow for different laws to reign in the colonies from those in operation in France. This should recall Raimond's incessant complaint that the republic was incoherent—declaring the rights of man at home yet denying them abroad. In other words, Raimond complained about France's contradictory declarations of indivisibility, while allowing legalized divisions. Under Bonaparte, the incoherence of the republic only increased. The French republican constitution of 1795 created under the Directory officially declared that all of France's overseas colonies would be governed by the same laws that existed in metropolitan France. Since slavery had been outlawed in the metropole since the seventeenth century, it could not exist in the overseas colonies either. The French republican constitution of 1799, however, issued under Bonaparte's consulate, legally abolished the idea that France was "l'une et indivisible" or "one and indivisible." Article 91 of the 1799 constitution stated, "The form of government in the French colonies will be determined by special laws."[42] Returning to Article 1 of Louverture's constitution now allows us to see how its creators in the Central Assembly exploited this loophole by using the same language instantiated by the French government, but to antislavery ends.

The 1799 French Constitution created an opening for the reinstatement of slavery by establishing divisibility, or separatism. The creators of the 1801 Saint-Domingue Constitution exploited that opening by agreeing to separate laws for the colony, rather than protesting them, as in the past, while taking the initiative to legislate those laws on their own rather than waiting for

178   Chapter 6

Bonaparte to do so. The colony, while remaining a part of the "French empire," was to be governed by "special laws," but those laws would be made by the inhabitants of the colony and sanctioned by Toussaint Louverture. It is therefore worth looking at these laws more closely. Article 2 of the 1801 constitution for Saint-Domingue legislated the division of the colony into three separate categories: "divisions, arrondissements, and parishes." Article 3, then, permanently decreed the abolition of slavery, while restating that the island's colonial status would be preserved. This clause was as bold as it was daring for its directness in forcing the language of slavery into the legal lexicon of France, where it had previously been euphemized into before and after dates with respect to the *ancien régime*. "There can exist no slaves on this territory, servitude is forever abolished here," reads Article 3. "Every man here is born, lives, and will die free and French." The language was quite deliberate: "There can be no slaves in this land, servitude is *forever* abolished." The first three sentences of the article are not restatements of each other's provisions, but instead offer increasing precision. The sequence of statements eschews, or rather does not fall prey to, the problems attendant in the U.S. Constitution with its vagaries of "3/5th of all other persons." The U.S. Constitution famously does not mention the words slavery or slaves, creating an incoherence in U.S. society and law that continues to this day. Louverture's constitution, in great contrast, made it clear that freedom in Saint-Domingue was for all people on the territory, including the formerly enslaved, since there could effectively be no more slavery or "servitude."

Not going quite as far as Dessalines's Imperial Constitution of 1805 did in its attempt to outlaw color prejudice (a phenomenon we will explore in chapter 9), Article 4 declared, "Every man, regardless of his color, is able to be admitted to any employ." The creators of the 1801 constitution focused at every turn on the legal structures supporting color prejudice and slavery and one by one dismantled the scaffold upholding them. Article 5 offered even more specificity, still without taking the final step to legally ban racism: "There exists here no other distinction than that of virtues and talents, no other superiority than that which law provides in the exercise of a public function." The only differences between individuals that could be acknowledged in Saint-Domingue under Louverture were those resulting from a person's *deeds*. This language reflects an important revision to Article 6 of the 1789 Declaration of the Rights of Man, which stated, "All citizens, being equal in the eyes of the law, are equally eligible to all dignities and to all public positions . . . and without distinction except that of their virtues and talents." In his 1799 report to the French government, styled as a letter against André Rigaud, Louverture wrote that he was the "friend of all men, without distinction of color or of skin, I make no difference between them, other than the

Freedom   179

virtues and vices which distinguish them."[43] While the framers of the 1801 constitution did not substitute Louverture's "vices" for "talents," they did use throughout the constitution the same explicitly anti-racist language found in Louverture's report. The creators of the 1789 Declaration of the Rights of Man had failed to specify whether its words applied to people of color, opting rather for neutrality with the generic language of "man and citizen." The Declaration of the Rights of Man was not intended to apply to enslaved Black people in the colonies but, with the constitution of 1801, Louverture forced these words to take on new meaning, by asserting they applied to all the colony's inhabitants, regardless of skin color or birth. None of the myriad vagaries, ambiguities, and obfuscations that led to Ferrand de Baudière's death, Raimond's eventual arrest, along with the terrible torture of Ogé and Chavannes on the scaffold—all because the colonists were quibbling over the meanings of the words "men," "citizen," and "person"—are present in Louverture's constitution.

That freedom required the permanent abolition of slavery and color prejudice was clearly stated in the constitution of 1801, but let us now also try to understand the kind of *free* society that Louverture tried to juridically bring into existence. It does not follow that a legally free society will necessarily have eliminated color prejudices. Nor does it follow that a society without color prejudices will of necessity be egalitarian. History had shown to the Saint-Domingue revolutionaries that creating the kind of free society they imagined, one without slavery or color prejudices, required legislation that was both particular and specific. Were they the men capable of putting legislation forward that would be materially egalitarian for all? The 1801 constitution made clear that as central as eliminating color prejudice and slavery were to the creation of the free society wished for by both the *hommes de couleur* and the formerly enslaved, setting up this society was not solely about legal status. Establishing a free and egalitarian society was also about institutions, governance, equal opportunity, and labor. Outlawing slavery and replacing it with free labor was merely the first step. The Saint-Dominguan legislators also believed that bringing this egalitarian society into existence involved questions of religion, culture, class, gender, and, ultimately, the intersection of these categories with labor and the colony's relationship to the French government.

With Article 19, instead of a Colonial Assembly, Louverture set up a Central Assembly populated by people living in the colony: "The regime of the colony is determined by laws proposed by the Governor and issued by an assembly of inhabitants, who will meet at fixed times, at the center of this colony, under the title Central Assembly of Saint-Domingue."[44] Articles 22 and 23 established age requirements and term limits for members of the Central Assembly. Another section of the constitution tackled the social questions of religion and spirituality. Very quickly we see that Louverture's colony was not

-1—
0—
+1—

180   Chapter 6

to be a society with freedom of religion. Article 6, perhaps surprisingly, restated Article 3 of the wholly prejudicial French slave codes by encoding religious exceptionalism into law. Article 3 of the Code Noir, which scholar Louis Sala-Molins called the "most monstrous legal document of modern times," declared: "Let us forbid all public exercise of any religion other than the Catholic one, Apostolic and Roman."[45] Article 6 of the Saint-Domingue Constitution directly reiterated this prohibition: "The Catholic religion, apostolic and Roman, is here the only one to be publicly professed." Article 10 outlawed divorce. Article 11 followed this by echoing the paternalism found in the writings of Julien Raimond: "The estate and the rights of children born by marriage will be fixed by laws which are designed to spread and maintain social virtues, to encourage and cement family ties."[46] The articles following this dealt with the relationship between labor, class, and culture. Article 12 said, "The Constitution guarantees freedom and individual safety," while Article 13 rendered property holy, as had done the Declaration of the Rights of Man: "Property is sacred and inviolable."

The next set of articles made it clear that property owners, whose land and buildings had already been deemed "sacred," would have special rights that the laboring class, owners ostensibly only of their own bodies, would not. Article 14 therefore laid the foundation for a labor system in which property was still king. It mandated, "The colony being essentially agricultural, cannot suffer the slightest interruption in the work of farming." Article 15 characterized the relationship between laborers and property owners in a way that reeked of the very definition of colonial paternalism: "Every plantation is a factory which requires the reunion of cultivators and workers; it is the quiet refuge of an active and constant family, over whom the owner of the land or his representative is necessarily the father." Article 16 continued in this vein by setting up a form of feudalism that bound laborers to the lands they worked, while also designating them as members of the same family with the farm's proprietor: "Every cultivator and worker is a member of the family and a shareholder in the income. Any change of domicile on the part of the cultivators will lead to the ruin of the farm."[47] Article 17 was an unwitting acknowledgment of the high death rate for Africans and their New World descendants in Saint-Domingue because of the previous system of labor in force, slavery. Tackling the question of how to ensure there would be enough laborers to take on the amount of farming needed to make the colony under Louverture as prosperous as it had been under the *ancien régime*, Article 17 stated, "The introduction of cultivators essential for the reestablishment and growth of the crops will take place in Saint-Domingue; the Constitution charges the governor to take the appropriate measures to encourage and favor this increase of hands, to stipulate and balance the various interests, to ensure and guarantee

Freedom   181

the execution of the respective commitments resulting from this introduction."[48] What exactly were to be considered "appropriate measures" and what did this provision result in materially with respect to the laboring class?

The answer to this question is largely dependent upon the kind of freedom that laborers were able to exercise under the Louverturian model. Many of the provisions in the 1801 constitution bear an important relationship to the labor system (affermage or leasing) proposed by Raimond in one of his pre-emancipation 1793 pamphlets and to the labor system set up by Sonthonax with the August 1793 emancipation decree. As such, understanding what freedom meant under Louverture requires understanding its prior basis in systems proposed by Raimond and implemented by Sonthonax. For example, what kind of salary and/or share in the profits could a laborer expect on any given plantation? If we go back to Article 8 of Sonthonax's emancipation proclamation, we learn that the salaries of "workers of every kind will be fixed by mutual agreement with the contractor who employs them." What kind of freedom of movement could a formerly enslaved laborer exercise under the new labor model initially conceived of by Sonthonax but whose implementation had been largely dependent upon the cooperation of Louverture? Article 9 of Sonthonax's decree further specified, "The negroes currently attached to the dwellings of their former masters, will be required to remain there; they will be employed in the cultivation of the land." This was difficult freedom. Article 10 of the same proclamation continued, "Enlisted fighters, who serve in the camps or in the garrisons will be able to settle on the plantations by devoting themselves to farm work, & obtaining beforehand a leave from their superior or an order from us, which can only be delivered to them if they are being replaced by a willing man." Article 11 further limited the movements of the formerly enslaved: "The former farming slaves will be hired for one year, during which time they will not be able to change plantations except with permission from the justices of the peace, which will be discussed below, & in those cases which will be determined by us." But Article 12 made it clear that this labor was not slavery. Compensation was involved, which seems in principle could have been fair: "The income from each plantation will be divided into three equal portions, after taxes have been deducted, which are levied on the net sum. One third belongs to the land and the property & will remain with the owner. He will have the enjoyment of the other third for the expenses of the *fesance-valoir* [sic];[49] the remaining third will be shared among the cultivators as to be determined."[50] Article 13 explained that the *faisance-valoir* comprised the costs associated with running the farm, including tools, the animals necessary for farmwork and the transportation of goods, the construction and maintenance of the buildings, hospital and surgical fees, as well as those of the manager.

Polverel had also issued his own articles governing the labor system of the south and west on October 31, 1793. The laws he attempted to put in place were not entirely different from those Sonthonax had already decreed. Article 6 of Polverel's system mandated, "The African laborers will receive as compensation for their labor on the plantations to which they are attached, a determined portion of its revenues." As in Sonthonax's system, Article 7 mandated, "There will be deducted from the annual proceeds of each plantation, the costs of the *faisance valoir*, & taxes." What remained of the revenue after deducting all costs, according to Article 11, would be divided into three equal portions: "one of which will belong to the cultivators, to be subdivided between them in the proportions to be determined by a subsequent regulation; and the other two portions will belong to the owner."[51] Article 18 specified that the elderly, along with children under the age of fourteen years and those who were "habitually disabled," would not be counted among the cultivators.[52]

Importantly, whipping, a key element of the maintenance of slavery, was forbidden by both Polverel's and Sonthonax's labor laws. Article 27 of Sonthonax's system declared, "Punishment by the whip is absolutely over; it will be replaced, for faults of discipline, by the [punishment] of the bar for one, two or three days, according to the requirements of the case. The greatest penalty will be the loss of part or all of the wages."[53] In contrast, Polverel's labor laws while they did require similar obedience, forbade the "bar": "They will not be permitted, on pain of destitution, to exercise any command over, nor to sentence to the bar any of their subordinates."[54] This question over how the cultivators or laborers would be "punished" for alleged insubordination or other perceived faults had been central to negotiations surrounding the abolition of slavery nearly from the beginning of the revolution in Saint-Domingue. Even after legal emancipation the question of abolishing corporal punishment remained a key factor for the commissioners who hoped to quell the ongoing rebellion. To that end, a subsequent decree issued by Sonthonax on November 5, 1793, admonished the planters who sought to convince the Black laborers that the emancipation decree was false, on the one hand, and who continued to torture them with the whip, on the other. "I have learned that in almost all the still intact communes of this province [the north], and notably in Gros-Morne, the cultivators are subjected to the punishment of the whip; that my proclamation has not yet been executed there, and that, the Africans, aware of its existence, are endlessly being told that I do not have the right to grant them liberty." With this proclamation, Sonthonax both reaffirmed the original provisions of his emancipation decree and denied he did not have the authority to proclaim general liberty while combating a rumor that he only did so because he was being held captive in Cap.[55] Polverel, too, reaffirmed the provisions set out in his two proclamations for the south and west and his authority to pursue their implementation, in the same decree governing his labor system that he issued on October 31, 1793.[56]

A closer look at Sonthonax's and Polverel's legislation reveals that Louverture's feudal system of affermage was merely an extension of the one created by the two French commissioners. One often unstated flashpoint is that Polverel's and Sonthonax's systems were themselves just alternative versions of the one earlier proposed by Raimond. Although Raimond does not appear as a signatory on either Sonthonax's or Polverel's emancipation decrees, it is to his intellectual and philosophical journey, the one that led him to transform himself from an enslaver of other human beings to their ardent defender, to which we must now return to understand the early free labor system in the post-emancipation colony and how it affected freedom in Saint-Dominguan society under Louverture.

Let us walk backward in time to October 1791, when an unlikely (and brief) truce was announced by the mayor of Port-au-Prince, in favor of the rights of citizenship for free people of color. The mayor's speech pronounced on October 23, after the civil commissioners dissolved the Colonial Assembly, adds to the proliferation of confused shadows hovering over the usage of social words in the colonial context of Saint-Domingue, a confusion that led Raimond to his ultimate reversal with respect to the need for immediate emancipation. "Citizens of color, my friends, here you lose this denomination," the mayor proclaimed. "No distinction exists anymore [between you and whites], no more difference. We will only have in the future, all together, one identical title, that of CITIZEN."[57] "Friends," "citizens," "brothers": what can these terms have possibly meant in a society driven entirely by the desire of one group of people to deprive others of ever knowing what it felt like to embody any of these social positions? The mayor's last phrase, of course, was meaningless in a plantation economy where human beings could be bought and sold largely because of the color of their skin, and where all non-white "citizens" found themselves hunted down during Leclerc and Rochambeau's genocidal policy of extermination at the turn of the century.

Unfolding the relationship between Raimond's writing about gradual emancipation and the Saint-Domingue Constitution of 1801, which inscribed into law slavery's abolition, amid an incoherent republicanism, illuminates what a magnificent transformation happened between the moment when the enslaved rebelled en masse in 1791, throwing off their shackles and disrupting the slave economy, and the moment when Haiti declared independence in 1804. Understanding the momentousness of this transition requires understanding it less as a fait accompli than as a process requiring numerous

184   Chapter 6

active steps. Those steps that took place prior to independence laid the groundwork for what happened afterward. "We had not yet calculated the extent of the transition we had made," Vastey wrote, "that from the state of a colony we had passed into the state of a free and independent nation." "We had not yet imagined that, having changed our condition, relations and situation, we should also change our state of political and rural economy, and adopt a system of agriculture appropriate to our new needs and worthy of a free people!" he explained.[58] The system of agriculture that existed in independent Haiti under its first four rulers—Dessalines, Christophe, Pétion, and Boyer—is indelibly tied to that transformation. The transformation of enslaved laborers to free laborers (and its various processes and iterations) now requires our attention, so that we may come to better understand the link between Raimond's, Polverel's, and Sonthonax's initial affermage system in French colonial Saint-Domingue, Louverture's revisions to their system, and the version various rulers put in operation in independent Haiti.

We have already seen that Raimond enslaved other human beings in Saint-Domingue. Yet not every enslaver held the same views on slavery. For Raimond, slavery played a role, for ill or for good (he is the one who is not sure), in the making of the French colony. Raimond, as an enslaver, personally benefited from the way Saint-Domingue was dis-settled to favor the owners of plantations who forced the people they enslaved to cultivate them. At the same time, Raimond acknowledged that the form of slavery responsible for his very existence, as a free man of color, needed both limits and an eventual brake. The idea of limiting the future role that slavery was to play in the French republic led him to develop a plan for gradual emancipation, one that he would never see put into effect. His plan was interrupted, first, by the Black and formerly enslaved freedom fighters who refused to put down their arms, and then by Sonthonax's and Polverel's general emancipation proclamations in August and September and October 1793, respectively.

There were no humane enslavers, but that does not mean that degrees of their awfulness could not be recognized by people living in the era. In his 1791 response to Moreau de Saint-Méry, Raimond decried the practice of white enslavers who had no qualms about enslaving their own children, à la Thomas Jefferson. "The father who creates another being only to enslave him, is he not a monster?" Raimond asked.[59] While such a damning verdict indicted anyone who would claim that the Jeffersons of the age of slavery were simply "men of their time," Raimond was himself merely a different kind of man of his time. After the French Revolution of 1789, Raimond only argued tepidly for gradual emancipation, and he never could get behind the rebellion of the enslaved population, even while recognizing they were striving for freedom. After the general insurrection of 1791, Raimond counseled enslaved people to

Freedom   185

be more patient and moderate while waiting for gradual emancipation to *naturally* occur. To that end, Raimond's 1793 *Réflexions*, included an address to the French National Assembly titled, "Proclamation to be made to rebellious slaves in the French colonies" (*Proclamation à faire aux esclaves révoltés dans les colonies françaises*). The paternalistic language from this document found its way into the official affermage system iterated in Sonthonax's and Polverel's general emancipation decree, which was revised in Louverture's 1801 constitution.

In his *Réflexions*, Raimond wrote that the enslaved needed to render themselves promptly into "order" and follow the laws of France to save the republic.[60] To facilitate this, Raimond argued the Jacobin government should adopt a policy of gradual emancipation. At the time that Raimond wrote and published this pamphlet, the French Jacobins had recently executed King Louis XVI and both England and Spain had invaded the colony to try to wrest it away from a France in propitious revolutionary turmoil. To prevent total war and the loss of the plantation system, including slavery with its seemingly never-ending death rattle, Raimond counseled that the republic needed to immediately create a plan to abolish slavery: "Considering the entire population of free people and slaves as a homogeneous whole, will organically bring us to our greatest happiness, while preserving the previous relationships; that is to say that providing all the already free people with the greatest latitude of freedom that can be enjoyed in the state of sociability, requires also bringing the slaves closer to the state of freedom, so that it can be accomplished without tumult and only with means available to them through the law."[61] Once liberty was established for everyone—the free men of color and the enslaved—all inhabitants of the colony would consider defending Saint-Domingue against foreign, which is to say, non-French invaders.[62] Raimond reminded his French interlocutors that, on the contrary, caving to the desires of the white colonists, who had been trying to obtain independence from France for some time, made no sense because in continuing to deprive the free people of color of their rights, the colony would be destroyed by making eternal enemies out of erstwhile allies.

A key passage within the *Réflexions* is Raimond's acknowledgment of his own material and spiritual transformation from an enslaver to a non-enslaver and only then to an abolitionist. Raimond noted that the enslaved remained in rebellion at the time he was writing his pamphlet and that numerous plantations had been burned down.[63] Raimond, no longer an enslaver of human beings profiting from the labor of enslaved Africans, knew the kind of loss he was attempting to warn the French against. The people he enslaved were not freed by him as a result of his benevolence. Instead, they wrested themselves from his enslaving grip in the same manner that

-1—
0—
+1—

186   Chapter 6

the enslaved of the northern plain virtually forced the end of plantation slavery there.

After addressing himself to the French government, Raimond turned to address the enslaved directly: "Your souls, for such a long time, compromised by degradation and rigorous punishment, necessarily deteriorated and saw extinguished that divine fire which gives birth to and nourishes the virtues necessary for mankind, and which are indispensable to him in his state of sociability."[64] Because the state of slavery had caused an inevitable degradation that was not present in Africans before their capture by Europeans, Raimond noted that the formerly enslaved would have to deliberately "uproot vices from your souls, [and] replace them with virtues; this will be the first concern of the law. For this, it is necessary that you remain for some time yet under the tutelage of those who will be responsible for improving your lot."[65] "The first thing the law requires in the state of freedom and sociability is respect for people and property," he continued. "So you must become accustomed to respecting these vis-à-vis others, if you want to feel the happy effects of them yourselves."[66] Raimond still could not see that it was enslavers, like him, who had not respected property rights, namely, that of people to *possess* themselves, so to speak, and to live peaceably and in harmony on the lands where they were born. Raimond went on to tell the enslaved that if they wanted to be free, they needed to cultivate a love of labor to be able to one day acquire goods for their own subsistence. He also told them to examine their present state and see if they had all the mores and customs necessary to enjoy liberty. Raimond avowed an axiom that a person without property would not respect the property of another; and since the law did not allow the enslaved to acquire property, it was natural they would lack respect for it and become inclined to theft. To prevent this, the law should allow them to have some property. He wrote, "The first property you must acquire is that of yourself, which has been alienated."[67] It would be up to the French republic to create the method of furnishing the enslaved with the means of acquiring, that is to say, *purchasing*, their own *personhood* or *selfhood*. This clause could not be more important for understanding the philosophy of free labor that Raimond bequeathed to the colony.

Echoes of Raimond's ideas can also be found in the writings of André Rigaud. Rigaud's philosophy of liberty was bound up in a philosophy of work or labor, too, not unlike what we will see happen to labor under Dessalines and Christophe. "But the African, who had been crushed under the weight of the most severe labor during the reign of his tyrants, spent the first days of his freedom in limp indolence," Rigaud wrote. After general liberty was proclaimed, "I was able to make some of them understand the need for work through gentleness and persuasion, I made others comply with the proclamations of Civil Commissioner Polverel; and farming began to flourish once more."[68] The footnote to this statement is illustrative. Rigaud argued that the French colonists were lying when they complained that Saint-Domingue could never be cultivated by free Africans. Rigaud argued that nothing could be further from the truth. In so doing, he described what freedom was to him and what it was not: "The secret enemies of freedom, more adroit than the previous ones, say that true freedom is about working only as much as you want; this is the most treacherous language, it is treason, this would occasion Saint-Domingue's annihilation and freedom's tomb."[69] Then, not unlike Raimond, Rigaud rhetorically addressed the former enslaved population: "Africans! You groaned under the yoke of slavery; the French nation, that noble and generous nation has broken your chains; united to you by blood ties, my brothers and I, we will all perish, before your freedom is violated at all; but understand well this truth: freedom cannot exist without work."[70] "Africans!" he continued. "I repeat it, do you want to be free? Labor with strength, labor with courage, labor with constancy; and then your liberty will be seated on a foundation that nothing will be able to shake."[71] Rigaud clarified when he wrote that by "Africans" he meant the cultivators, in general, because almost all of them were Africans or the direct descendants thereof.[72]

An enslaved African, as Chanlatte observed, was one who was alienated by the market from his own *personhood*, it having been sold away from him or her without consent. While for Chanlatte, writing in 1810, purchasing one's own personhood was inadmissible, it was not considered as such by the far less radical Raimond in 1793. The policy of gradual emancipation that the French republic needed to adopt, Raimond therefore said, would also need to be different from the three methods by which the enslaved could already get themselves free: (1) a Black woman having a child by a white man, who could pay a considerable sum to the government; (2) the enslaved man or woman who could pay to their master a considerable sum, which was almost impossible, and when it occurred, they often had to rent their labor back to the master for an indefinite time, thus de facto remaining enslaved; and if the enslaved person died before having paid back the entire sum, the time put in was not left to the relatives as inheritance but confiscated, so to speak, by the master; (3) the third method was very rare, Raimond claimed, which was when the master compensated with freedom the enslaved person who had rendered to him long-term and signal services. Raimond said that owing to these difficulties it was very hard for an enslaved person to achieve free status, legally, in colonial Saint-Domingue and, if they did, once freed, the formerly enslaved person became the property of every white person, in theory, such that they usually depended on the government for subsistence.[73]

188   Chapter 6

To gradually emancipate the entire enslaved population, Raimond said the state would need to fix the price at which each enslaved person could incrementally repurchase themselves (*se racheter*). The price of owning oneself would shift according to age and ability. For male slaves between the ages of fourteen and forty years, the price of purchasing personhood would be 3,000 colonial livres; for women aged twelve to thirty-six years it would be 2,600 colonial livres; every year after, for both sexes, the price would decrease by one hundred colonial livres. The punishment for being talented was the near impossibility to *purchase* oneself. Enslaved people who knew specific métiers or had special talents would have to purchase themselves at the increased cost of 4,000 colonial livres. Raimond's illogic was that it must have cost their "masters" something to educate them. Working hours were also listed, including Sundays off.[74]

This policy of gradual rather than immediate emancipation was necessary, Raimond warned, to prevent the total collapse of the French republic. In a passage dripping with audacity, he told the enslaved, "You, who have by no means yet obtained this freedom, you cannot be freed without harming the interests of the nation, those of your masters and even your own, as we will prove to you." Policy was always preferable over rebellion. His disdain for the ongoing Haitian Revolution shines through in the following passage: "You revolted against your masters, instead of asking for them to be humane; you then dared to resist the national will by continuing your rebellion: are these your claims to deserving freedom?"[75] The paternalistic language ultimately turned parricidal: "But, like a loving mother, the nation knows how to punish those of her children who refuse her entreaties, to listen only to the path of vice. A code of laws will be given to you; justice, humanity and the desire to make you happy dictated it."[76] A further and clearer threat followed, "But also woe to you if, continuing to follow the treacherous advice which has led you astray, you refuse to obey the gentle and humane laws that the nation is giving to you; then, deploying all her forces against your rebellion, she will exterminate even the last of you."[77] All roads in colonial thought lead to extermination. Although he could see the incoherence of French republicanism, and all the prejudices that had been directed at him for years, Raimond still could not divest himself of the colonialist and slaving mentality that previously enriched him and his family. Independence was out of the question: "No doubt you did not conceive the foolish pride of believing that you would be able to resist national power; because, by contemplating the forces that she has deployed here, you will soon be brought back from your error, by learning that she can bring them again, if necessary, and a thousand times as many."[78] Earlier, sounding very similar to the white colonists, he rhetorically asked the enslaved, "Do you think it would be right for the nation to reward you with liberty after all the crimes and devastation you have committed?"[79]

Similar allusions to the "crimes" of the enslaved freedom fighters had already led some previously sympathetic metropolitan French writers, such as Olympe de Gouges, to argue that Black freedom fighters in the colony were equally as cruel as the white colonists. Shortly after the Haitian Revolution began, de Gouges—who was sent to the guillotine by the *white* Jacobins in 1793—wrote that the Black Saint-Dominguan revolutionaries paradoxically "justified" the actions of the colonists by imitating their "most barbaric and atrocious tortures."[80] Those already ill inclined to support the Haitian Revolution, like the writer François-René de Chateaubriand, son of a slave trafficker, characterized the Black freedom fighters as indefensibly out for blood and undeserving of the world's sympathy. In his 1802 *The Genius of Christianity* (*Le Génie du christianisme*), Chateaubriand implored, "Who would dare to plead the cause of the Blacks after the crimes they have committed?"[81] Raimond's disdain for enslaved people striving for freedom through violence was not unlike that of these white French reactionaries. There was one simple conclusion for Raimond: the enslaved needed to first repair the wrongs *they* had supposedly committed before freedom could be *given*.[82] The reason that Raimond could not see that freedom was already being *taken*, if, in fact, it had not already been *constituted*, is because chattel slavery—in great contrast to the forms of enslavement practiced across the ancient world by Europeans, native Americans, Greeks, Romans, and Africans—was designed by the colonists to be an inalienable state germane to the life of an enslaved Black person. Unlike in serfdom, chattel enslavers, through the act of enslaving, sought to deprive the enslaved individual of all social ties, kin, family, and community, to the extent that an enslaved person was not capable, in their eyes, of legally or socially freeing themselves, in mind or body. Laws in Atlantic slave societies codified an enslaved person as "entirely under someone else's power,"[83] even though the colonists were aware of abounding evidence that they did not possess this supreme authority over the people they were enslaving. In other words, in the minds of enslavers, chattel slavery was a condition into which one was born and out of which one could rarely escape. Enslavers usually considered those enslaved people engaged in marronnage to still be their slaves, for example. This is precisely what we learn by sifting through the records of plantation sales in eighteenth-century Saint-Domingue.

Walking into a European archive where colonial records are housed is largely like walking into a crime scene, but one where the criminals have unabashedly preserved, cataloged, and organized the evidence of their crimes with the utmost pride. Some of the criminals have even confessed. As I sifted through hundreds of records of plantations at the Archives Nationales d'Outre-Mer in Aix-en-Provence, and voluminous numbers of seemingly unremarkable deeds of plantation sales and exchanges, I gained a key glimpse

190   Chapter 6

into the illogic of colonial attitudes toward marronnage, which explains why Raimond believed that the enslaved in rebellion were still actually *slaves*. Fugitives from slavery who effectively freed themselves were not considered free by authorities unless their liberty was sanctioned by a corresponding *deed*. Among the list of enslaved people sold along with the land, buildings, equipment, and animals were the names of various "maroons," fugitives from slavery, who despite their absence were often included in the price of the sale of the last plantation where they were forced to labor. Consider the 1789 record of one plantation, previously owned by the colonist Clonard and left to his inheritors at his death. After the list of sixty-four men, women, and children, many openly described as being mutilated, ostensibly by their enslavers, and all described by the markings and brandings on their bodies, we observe the following clarification: "Independent of the negroes who have just been described, there are four others to be named, Jasmin, Belhumeur, Neptune, and Venus, who are engaged in marronnage, to be noted, the negro Jasmin had been so even before his entrance onto the present plantation, and the others for several days." Although the paragraph following this sentence noted that the above "negroes" were not to be considered a part of the inheritance unless they were recovered, the case of Jasmin, who was never enslaved on this plantation, is revealing. He was sold to Clonard even though he was already in a state of marronnage.[84]

The characterization of freedom-striving, fugitive, enslaved Africans as being in the wrong forcefully stamped white European, and especially U.S. American, characterizations of the Haitian Revolution as a "white massacre." Writers from Haiti's first state governments were determined to overturn this narrative using documentary evidence. Recall that in *Le Système colonial* Vastey lamented that for years Haitians were not able to counter those who denounced their revolution as unjustified.[85] In his widely read exposé, Vastey painstakingly described how the colonists of Saint-Domingue practiced some of the cruelest tortures on enslaved people in the Atlantic World. These included burning and burying them alive; severing limbs, ears, and other body parts; bleeding the enslaved to death; and nailing them to walls and trees, along with various forms of sexual assault, which Vastey called "crapulous debauchery."[86] Detailing the horrific crimes of a planter named Gallifet, Vastey reported "he was accustomed to cutting the hamstrings of his slaves," complaining that his plantation was well known for its dungeons, where enslaved people "perished lying in water, by a cold and dampness which suppressed the circulation of their blood."[87] Vastey's descriptions did lead some foreign readers to wonder who would dare plead the cause of the white colonists after the crimes *they* had committed. A review of Vastey's pamphlet in the British *Anti-Jacobin Review and Magazine* in 1818 damningly concluded, "In

Freedom 191

reading over the tract before us we have doubted whether we were in the society of men or of wild beasts; but a little reflection easily convinced us that the brutes of the field could not act as the monsters we have been placed in company with."[88] Still, such affirmations of French barbarity did little to disrupt the general arc of the sympathy-for-whites trope that abounded in nineteenth-century literature and art of the Haitian Revolution.

The strongest inducement to an unequivocally antislavery ideology for the *hommes de couleur*, meek precursor to the radical ingenuity of independent Haiti, was the unequivocal violence the white French colonists used against all people of color in the colony during the Leclerc expedition. Being hunted down by white French soldiers during the Leclerc expedition was a key moment in Vastey's defection from the side of the white French colonists, to whom he was related by birth and whose riches in slavery he personally benefited from, to the side of the Indigenous army. Both plantation and indemnity records for Saint-Domingue show that Vastey's parents, Jean Valentin Vastey and Marie Élisabeth Dumas, were the owners of at least two plantations, one of which was on an enormous plot of land located in Grande-Rivière, where coffee, cotton, and indigo were mainstays.[89] Similarly, a decisive break in Raimond's thinking happened after Sonthonax's and Polverel's emancipation decrees were published. Raimond was subsequently arrested for fourteen months. The white French colonists accused him of financial malfeasance in connection with an alleged plot of the *hommes de couleur* to strike for independence from France. The evidence they provided for his incarceration was a fraudulent letter produced by the white French colonists Pierre-François Page and Augustin Jean Brulley. Page and Brulley were determined to have falsified the letter on September 23, 1793. Nevertheless, "On the 27th of the same month," Raimond recalled, "I was imprisoned at l'Abbaye, and following that, on October 3rd, the indictment against yours truly by twenty-two colleagues was read from the convention gallery." In the report, the white French colonists claimed to have found in Raimond's correspondence proof of Brissot's corruption, along with that of other legislators back in France.[90] "When from my prison, at the Abbey, I learned of this report, I hastened to have all my correspondence printed and distributed at the convention, in order to enlighten them and to deny the slanders advanced." Raimond continued:

Well! The day after its distribution, I was taken to the Conciergerie and brought to the revolutionary tribunal to be tried there. Who does not see in this measure the hand of the colonists, especially when we know that one of them, l'archevêque Thibault [*sic*], becoming the commissionaire of Page and Brulley, went every day to the Conciergerie to see

192 Chapter 6

the bloodthirsty [Antoine-Quentin] Fouquier-Tinville to press for
my conviction, and who at the same time furnished him with voluminous
calumnies against me? These slanderous memoirs must be with the
Colonial Commission; they must surely have been handed over with
the papers which concerned my case at the revolutionary tribunal.[91]

Raimond said that Page and Brulley were so well known for this kind of sub-
terfuge that they also falsified a proclamation they claimed emanated from
Polverel and Sonthonax.[92]

Although Raimond initially went back to France after being released from
jail, he returned with Sonthonax in May 1796 to assume a new role as a formal commissioner with a mission to help increase the cultivation of the colony using free labor. Once Sonthonax began to speak and agitate for
independence, like Louverture and Rigaud, Raimond abandoned him. In fact,
recall that Raimond, even though he was a fellow commissioner at that point,
helped Louverture send Sonthonax back to France. Rigaud, Raimond, and
Louverture had many things in common: they all professed not to want
independence, they all supported and enforced affermage, and insisted that
slavery could not return. Although Raimond stands apart in that he only reluctantly accepted immediate emancipation, like Louverture he went to his
death bed insisting the colony had to remain French. Raimond reported to
the Directory in 1797 that Sonthonax's ambition had been "to split off Saint-
Domingue from the Republic, and declare the independence of this Colony,
or rather of its enslavement to his domination."[93] It is in the era of Sonthonax's
desires for independence that Raimond proffered himself as the colony's liberator and the one best positioned to conserve it for France. On the necessity
of having banished Sonthonax, Raimond wrote:

> If my indefatigable complaisance and the wisdom of General Toussaint
> had not allowed him to sleep in happy security, the lion's awakening
> would have been terrible, blood would have flowed in torrents, the flames
> of June 20th could reignite and still devour the reborn city [of Cap] and
> the riches that cover the magnificent plains that surround it: let it finally
> be known that Toussaint Louverture himself, general-in-chief of the army,
> invested with the fullness of military powers, strong in the universal
> confidence of the citizens of all colors, never dared to tempt him, and that
> he was forced, for the salvation of the Colony, to dole out the praise
> that Sonthonax begged for, or that he extorted by terror.[94]

Raimond then observed that as one of the commissioners of the republic he
was tasked with "proving that the soil of Saint-Domingue could be fertilized
by free hands and produce more wealth than when it was watered with the

sweat and blood of slaves." "Every obstacle had been placed in my way," he continued. "I overcame them all. Farming is flourishing; the cultivators are free and happy. The Colony still belongs to France. The departure of the man who was the first to proclaim general freedom was effected without shock, without reclamation, without a murmur." Raimond therefore concluded, "In a word, I swear that I saved the Colony, and that I contributed to its conservation for France."[95] He did at least acknowledge that he could not have done so alone: "You will be able to judge of this by the character and the principles of the citizens who will deliver these dispatches to you. The special account that General Toussaint Louverture, for his part, will give to you, of all that he has done to preserve this precious possession for the Republic, will leave no doubt, either of the dangers it has overcome, nor of the indispensable necessity of the measures taken to save it."[96] The unspoken master of Raimond's screed was economics, but commerce in the colony was indelibly linked to racism.

The unacknowledged people whose lives and labor are embedded within Raimond's statements about having saved the colony are the mostly Black inhabitants of the colony, the formerly enslaved Africans. Raimond referred to them with the euphemism "free hands." Raimond wrote, "I did everything to preserve the Colony for France, and consolidate the triumph of the cause of humanity, by presenting to the Universe the spectacle of this immense island, carried to the highest degree of splendor by free hands."[97] Louverture was wholly in agreement with Raimond's and Rigaud's ideas about the relationship between liberty and labor after slavery. In the response to Vaublanc that Louverture sent to the Directory, he balked at the idea that an army would be necessary to make the formerly enslaved population work. He pointed out that farming had increased, far surpassing the revenues in some regions, like Caracole, under the *ancien régime*, and he said the colony, in general, was quite prosperous.[98] "All the plantations [in the North] are leased out, and all the farmers praise the zeal of the cultivators," Louverture reported. "The proceeds of this first year, according to the accounts which have been submitted to the Government by the Commission, and which it has communicated to me itself, will amount to 25 million; the second year . . . , we hope to increase them to 70, and obtain an equal progression for the third."[99] The key to understanding how Louverture linked freedom to labor is in this fragment of a sentence: "without work, there is no freedom."[100]

As we have seen, Louverture's conflict with Rigaud had little to do with disagreeing with the abolition of slavery, affermage, or definitions of freedom. Instead, as with Sonthonax, Rigaud's and Louverture's problems had to do with who was to assume power in post-emancipation Saint-Domingue. Louverture accused Rigaud of solely wanting power at any cost: "The desire to rule has prevailed in you over fairness; from being unjust, you have started being mean."[101] Here, Louverture did not accuse his rival of prejudices, but said that Rigaud had a desire to rule, and to rule alone, which was what caused him to repeatedly betray Louverture and the Black population of the colony. Later, Louverture did accuse Rigaud of having a personal hatred for him that was about not showing deference to a "black man": "Your deaf maneuvers are only intended to escape having to obey a black man, under whose orders you say you were not made to obey, and to whom, in the end, you do not want to obey."[102] Rigaud's pride and racial prejudices led him to be parricidal, in Louverture's characterization: "You want, by arming brother against brother, son against father, to kill the Fatherland on the bloody bodies of its citizens, on the piled up ruins of their properties."[103] Referring to Rigaud as having a "fury to command," Louverture charged, "You want to rule, no matter what the cost, even over ruins."[104] Louverture's evidence was that Rigaud undermined Louverture's authority with the cultivators of Grand- and Petit-Goâve when he told them Louverture wanted to take away their freedom and return them to a state of slavery. "Where is the black man stupid enough to let himself be taken in by such crude bait, blind enough to mistake his true friend, his father, his liberator, coward enough to caress his most implacable enemy, his most cruel tyrant?" Louverture asked.[105] "The fanaticism of the priests has been overthrown, but religion has remained," Louverture continued, "and that which I profess is based on humanity and justice."[106] Louverture then reminded Rigaud that at one time he had offered him a figurative olive branch: "Nevertheless, when I ordered you to go with your troops to take possession [of the south], in the name of the Republic . . . I invited you to forget the past."[107] This question of forgetting a past of civil strife would come to structure much of Haitian thought in the nineteenth century. We find it repeated in the works of Vastey in the context of the civil war between Christophe and Pétion, and also in Émeric Bergeaud's allegorical *Stella* (1859), Haiti's first known published novel.[108] The question of revenge in connection with the past is also a salient and enduring one in the corpus of writing left behind by Louverture and Rigaud. As for Louverture, he finished by reminding Rigaud of a damning reality, "I was able to make [the republic] triumphant over enemies much more powerful than you."[109]

With Sonthonax and Rigaud by turns banished, and Raimond having died shortly after the constitution was completed, this left Louverture alone to not only govern, but to accept the blame for all that transpired in the colony post-1801, including, or perhaps, especially, the resulting labor system. In large part because of the affermage system, Louverture's reputation has suffered. Some claim he set up a form of pseudoslavery or, at the very least, a society where the freedoms and liberties outlined in his constitution did not, in fact,

Freedom   195

actually reign.[110] In *Ti dife boule,* Trouillot presented the contradictions of the Haitian Revolution, and specifically the form of liberty in post-emancipation Saint-Domingue, as a precursor to the repressions of Duvalier's Haiti. One chapter in Trouillot's book is aptly titled, to that end, "But Why Can I Not Have Freedom?"[111] Earlier in the text, using a Haitian Vodou frame of reference, Trouillot implied he was wandering through the crossroads of the history of the revolution as a series of questions and paradoxical answers—"A contradiction has three crossroads to pass through: the crossroads of establishment, the crossroads of difficulty, and the crossroads of upending"[112]—with the aim of exploring how the roots of contemporary Haiti's ills lay in the same kind of exploitation of the people that drove the slave system in the colonial era. Trouillot explained the kinds of lessons to be learned from revolutionary Saint-Domingue and the period immediately following Haitian independence: "In order for us to understand that society, our own society, we must come to understand what kind of life faded away with the three maroons from Grande'Anse. In order for us to understand the disease from which we are suffering, we must know what kind of diseases course through our blood."[113] Trouillot referred to the thirteen-year-long maroon insurrection led by Jean-Baptiste Duperrier (called Goman), who, in refusing to submit to either Haitian state after Dessalines's assassination, essentially held sovereign power over the region of Grand'Anse from 1807 until 1820, when he was finally overthrown by Jean-Pierre Boyer, precipitating, in part, the collapse of the northern kingdom.[114]

The disease coursing through Haiti's blood was that of state exploitation—"If there are no exploiters, then there are no exploited"[115]—and it was written into the code of Haitian society when Louverture failed to eliminate affermage, or plantation-based labor, from Haiti's *vèvè*. A vèvè, as Marie-José Alcide Saint-Lot explains, "is a ritual drawing" that appears on the ground and is used during a Vodou ceremony: "It represents the god who will be invoked. . . . The *vèvès . . .* are sacred," she says. "No one is allowed to step on them until the dancing reaches its peak."[116] In Trouillot's writing, the vèvè is a metaphor for a political epistemology of the state: "The first job of a state governing any society is to work on its vèvè." A society's vèvè was like a blueprint where all a country's laws and codes—replete with layers of power—were inscribed by the government. Whereas Trouillot insisted Louverture could have created a vèvè, and therefore a state, devoid of the kind of exploitation inherent in the slave economy, he instead inscribed the same inequalities by a different name. Trouillot's evidence was the Saint Domingue Constitution: "When we take the state of Saint-Domingue's fundamental text (the 1801 Constitution), we find society's contradictions inscribed in the Constitution just as the laws and statutes are inscribed in the middle of a

196   Chapter 6

vèvè. This is how curious outsiders came to say, 'The state is in contradiction with the society,' with all its dominance, which forms the vèvè of the society."[117] This conclusion—that an educated and economic elite, along with a predatory state, exploited Haiti's laboring class (the formerly enslaved) after abolition—is clearly echoed in the title of Trouillot's 1990 *Haiti, State against Nation*.[118] Trouillot believed that the root causes of such injustice were not only apparent in present-day Haiti but the same everywhere in the world.

In *Ti dife boule* Trouillot drew on Haiti's revolutionary past under Louverture to explain what is perhaps the world's most painful universalism: "In truth, in every society dog eats dog, and the social forces that politically dominate mask its contradictions," Trouillot wrote. "Louverture's party had to disguise the real nature of the society they had built so as to hide the continued economic dominance of the white planters."[119] Trouillot continued by observing:

> And this ideology has worked so well that it has continuously appeared and reappeared in the history of Haiti and it persists until today even if it has changed its Christian name. . . . We must not forget that there are certain aspects of this society that reemerged in altogether different situations, under Dessalines, under Christophe, under [Lysius] Salomon, under [Dumarsais] Estimé[120]. . . . On the one side in Haiti, as in Guadeloupe, as in Martinique, as in Africa, throughout the entire twentieth century, there are those wearing the cloak of the "Indigenists." On the other side, there has been a different ideological sector, that of the bourgeoisie, which hides its dominance under the cloak of an "Elite."[121]

These are powerful, resonant words coming from Trouillot, but it is worth taking a longer and deeper look at the meaning of Louverture's labor system in its own era, too.

Affermage was not the same as chattel slavery. However, it was a feudal system, and one not much better than what peasant Frenchmen and women were subjected to under the despotic Bourbon king they beheaded. Raimond acknowledged as much when he wrote that the labor system he originally proposed in 1793 would resemble how white men worked back in France: "Free white men in all eras, constantly worked the land in our countryside to then share the fruits with the owner of the land." "Ask your brothers who have been to France," he said, "they will tell you that many of them would prefer to endure slavery in the colonies, than to live free in France."[122] The problem with this line of illogic as justification for affermage is that proslavery apologists, particularly in the nineteenth century, consistently (even if disingenuously) claimed that white free laborers of working-class Europe and the northern United States were subjected to conditions far worse than enslaved Black people.[123] Haitian writers did not fail to notice the illogic.

After providing a long list of the crimes of the Saint-Domingue colonists—including physical torture, family separation, and rape—Chanlatte exclaimed, "You dare, after that, to argue that the lot of the slaves is better than that of day workers in Europe? Well, consult the neediest of European laborers; ask him if he would exchange his condition for that of these suffering beings, and you will soon see what wages his just indignation reserves for such zealous indiscretion?"[124] The stark differences between chattel slavery and affermage or European-style feudalism does not mean that contemporary readers, in 2023, must accept the Haitian labor system without critique (based as it was on the post-emancipation Saint-Dominguan system), even as we acknowledge that it offered far more freedom than what was previously in place. Acknowledging what readers and writers in the Atlantic World considered to be most radical or controversial, laudatory or terrible (and vice versa), about the constitution of 1801 does allow twenty-first-century readers the opportunity to sit with various tensions of freedom as they emerged in the Atlantic World in a budding age of abolition.

In its own era, the most controversial article in the 1801 constitution was not the one banning slavery. France had already done so in 1794. Instead, it was the article establishing Louverture as governor-general of the colony "for life." It was at this moment that the republican colony began to mirror the incoherence of the metropolitan republic to which Louverture yoked his future aspirations. Article 28 appointed "Citizen Toussaint Louverture, General-in-Chief of the Army of Saint-Domingue, as Governor, and in consideration of the important services that this general has rendered to the colony, in the most critical circumstances of the revolution, and per the wishes of the grateful inhabitants, he is entrusted with the reins for the rest of his glorious life."[125] The constitution also afforded Louverture the right to name his successor (per Article 30); term limits (Article 29), in contrast, would be established for all subsequent governors: "In the future, each Governor will be named for five years, and can be renewed every five years, if his administration warrants it."[126] While this might seem like a huge contradiction, it was actually extremely adherent to, even a literal interpretation of, Jean-Jacques Rousseau's *On Social Contract*. In *On Social Contract*, in a chapter tellingly called "Slavery," Rousseau argued that a given people could choose to elect a king or even to accept a king's rule for life. Rousseau found, on the contrary, that it would go beyond the realm of the social good for those same people who had chosen their own king to condemn the future inhabitants of that society, their children, to accept a hereditary ruler that they in turn did not choose. "If each man could alienate himself he could not alienate his children, they are born men and free," Rousseau wrote. "Their liberty belongs to them, no one else has a right to dispose of it." "Fathers," in keeping with the allegory, should not choose the government under which their children would live. For, in so doing, there would no longer be consent and therefore no social contract. "It would be necessary, then, in order so for an arbitrary government to be legitimate, that in each generation the people be at liberty to admit or reject it," Rousseau wrote. "Then the government would no longer be arbitrary."[127] In other words, hereditary, that is, arbitrary rule was the problem with European monarchies. Elsewhere in *On Social Contract* Rousseau explained:

> Crowns have been made hereditary in certain families; and an order of succession has been established which prevents all dispute at the death of a king—that is to say, by substituting the inconvenience of a regency for that of an election, an apparent tranquility is preferred to a wise administration, and the risk of having a child, a monster, or an imbecile for chief has been preferred to a contest over the choice of a good king.
>
> The fact that, in exposing the nation to the risks of an alternative, nearly all the chances are against it, is not taken into consideration.
>
> The reply of the younger Dionysius to his father, when reproached by him for some shameful action was very sensible, "Have I given you such an example?" said the father. "Ah!" replied the son, "your father was not a king."[128]

The commingling of French revolutionary principles with those of the autocratic rule of kings and queens (after all the French monarchy was only gradually abolished too) also existed within the colony under Louverture's rule. Article 39 established official censorship, and put limits on, if it did not outright eliminate, freedom of the press. Louverture had the power to "monitor and censor, through his commissioners, all material intended for printing on the island" and to "suppress all those coming from abroad that could tend to corrupt morals or to disturb the colony again." The governor-general also had the right to "punish the perpetrators or peddlers" of such material, "depending on the seriousness of the case."[129] This form of censorship also acted as protection from the colonists who sought to bring back slavery and often circulated seditious documents with this intent. Louverture's colony was an ultimately fragile one, as his later arrest and incarceration proved.

The most important clause of the constitution came at the end. A statement in the constitution noted that its provisions were not yet official since the document did not have the approval of the metropolitan French government, the consuls of France. Article 77 stated, "The general-in-chief Toussaint Louverture is and remains responsible for sending this Constitution to be sanctioned by the French government." As governor-general, Louverture

Freedom   199

made a direct first-person statement reiterating this clause at the very end of the decree: "After having read the Constitution, I give it my approval. The invitation of the Central Assembly is an order for me; consequently, I will pass it on to the French government to obtain its sanction."[130] This final statement supports Louverture's claim in the memoirs he penned while in the Fort de Joux. Louverture said that he meant merely to get Bonaparte's approval by sending the constitution, not to usurp the latter's authority.[131]

The mid-nineteenth-century Haitian historian, Joseph Saint-Rémy, who edited Louverture's memoirs in 1853 and published a biography of him in 1850, contended that Louverture had without doubt attempted to usurp the authority of Bonaparte when he sent his famous 1801 constitution to the first consul. For Louverture to have declared himself "governor-general for life," according to Saint-Rémy, with the right to name his own successor, "was to have, in fact, proclaimed the independence of Saint-Domingue."[132] Saint-Rémy also quoted from that section of Napoléon Bonaparte's *Mémoires* in which the exiled self-proclaimed French emperor stated outright that Louverture had declared war on him by way of his 1801 constitution.[133] In his own memoirs, Louverture argued that he did not seek to replace Bonaparte with his constitution, but merely wanted to "offer some laws, based on local customs" that would take into account "the character and morality of the inhabitants of the colony." He further insisted, "The Constitution was designed to have been submitted for approval to the [French] government, which, alone, had the right to adopt it or reject it."[134] Louverture went on to accuse Bonaparte of refusing to dialogue with him about the constitution and of sending Leclerc to the colony instead. These explanations, qua vindications, of his behavior allowed Louverture to consistently paint himself as wholly honorable—rather than vengeful—from the start of his life until the present moment. Even when he was still suffering under the terrible imposition of slavery, Louverture insisted: "I was a slave, I dare to admit it; but I never suffered the reproach of any of my masters."[135]

Louverture mentioned the fact that he was previously subjected to slavery only a few times in his correspondence with government officials. In what is perhaps the most moving mention of his life under slavery, he commingled the official account of his conduct as a French officer with the form of life-writing called the slave narrative that North Atlantic readers are more accustomed to encountering from formerly enslaved individuals. In his *Rapport au directoire exécutif* (Report to the Executive Directory), dated *18 fructidor an 5* (September 4, 1797), Louverture admitted, "Born in slavery, but having received from nature the soul of a free man, I often exhaled my sighs toward the heavens, I raised my hands every day toward him, to implore the Supreme being to come to the aid of my brothers, so that he might deign to let his mercy

200   Chapter 6

rain down upon us."[136] This fleeting autobiographical foray was deployed, like much of Louverture's writing, for the purposes of defending his own conduct and character while simultaneously proving his loyalty to the republic. Louverture affirmed his gratitude and admiration for the republic that at the time of his report seemed to uphold the liberty Louverture had implored God to bestow. "The French Republic was not mistaken when it honored me with its trust, when it sought for the faithful children of its colonies to become free," he wrote. "Filled with appreciation for the nation that was the first to raise my brothers and me to the dignity of free men, I would have been the most vile and the most atrocious of men if I had been even for one instant guilty of ingratitude and if I have ceased to be faithful to a Republic that has adopted us."[137] Consistent refrains in Louverturian thought are gratitude, honor, and fidelity to the French republic despite its prior role in enslaving Black people. All too familiar with the evil machinations of the white colonists who never accepted Black liberation, Louverture correctly predicted Bonaparte's ill-fated Leclerc expedition, although he only expected French troops to descend if the island were to openly strive for independence. Louverture never seemed to imagine that he would be the one accused of trying to bring this independence about with his constitution and, thus, that the troops would come for him.

The arrest and deportation of Louverture under Leclerc and Rochambeau forced another of Louverture's previous prophecies to come true. In his response to Vaublanc's accusations that Louverture was stoking the flames of insurrection among the formerly enslaved and striving toward independence, Louverture insisted that he would never do such a thing. He also correctly prophesied that an ardent war would be waged by the Black population of the colony if General Rochambeau were "to come back at the head of an army to enslave the blacks, because then, with the [French] Constitution in one hand, they would defend the freedom it guarantees."[138] The arrest of Louverture, an intrepid defender of a world without chattel slavery, opened the door for Leclerc and Rochambeau to restore slavery as they did in Guadeloupe. One week after Louverture's arrest, the French minister of the marine and colonies, Denis Decrès, wrote to Leclerc to transmit Bonaparte's instructions "for the conduct of the war and the restoration of slavery." "As far as the return to the *ancien régime* of the Negroes is concerned, the bloody Struggle from which you have just emerged glorious and victorious, demands the greatest consideration. It would perhaps be to reengage in it again to want to break with precipitation that idol of liberty in the name of which so much Blood has been shed up to now." To conceal their goals, Leclerc was counseled, "It is necessary that for some time to come vigilance, order, discipline, both rural and military, replace formal slavery." French colonial delusions were perhaps never more heightened than when the consuls declared, "When they [the Blacks] have felt by comparison the difference between a usurping and tyrannical yoke and that of a legitimate owner, interested in their preservation, then the time will have come to return them to their original condition, from which it has been so fatal to have extracted them."[139] In other words, the French government illogically claimed that after ten years of freedom, the formerly enslaved would accept and welcome being rechained. If Bonaparte and his ministers were possessed of logic, they would have understood that if the Black population was really open to reenslavement, as they said, the French army would not have repeatedly claimed the need to resort to genocidal tactics to subdue them.

After Leclerc died of yellow fever in November 1802, the French government and military only grew more genocidal. On January 10, 1803, Leclerc's successor, General Rochambeau, issued an order "to exterminate the negro generals, black soldiers and officers, along with the former laborers." Three and a half months later, Rochambeau wrote to the French minister of the marine that he needed even more troops to complete the extermination. "We must support the war of the whites against the two other colors in this colony, so as to create a new order. Without this, we will have to start over again every two or three years . . . I am here now . . . I understand this execrable colony . . . I believe that my plan is the only one to adopt to sail this infernal hell into port."[140] In April 1803, Rochambeau wrote to Bonaparte to request more troops to not only help him eliminate Black leaders like Dessalines and Christophe and reinstate slavery, but to bring an effective end to what he characterized as a race war. Rochambeau claimed that he needed "three strong expeditions combined and arriving nearly at the same time to combat, disarm and chain the Negroes for the future." "Slavery must be proclaimed again in these parts, and the black code made much more severe. I even think that for a time the masters must be given the right of life and death over their slaves."[141] Rochambeau's genocidal tactics only encouraged the various existing factions among the Black generals, officers, and soldiers to unite together to fight at last for independence.

At the celebrated Congress of Arcahaye in May 1803, Dessalines pronounced the words "Liberty or Death"—famous utterances used during both the U.S. and French revolutions—as he trampled underfoot the white fabric he reportedly tore out of the French tricolor flag. The Black freedom fighters did not have to fear the arrival of French troops any longer, because they had already come in tens of thousands beginning in February 1802. Later, creolizing that classic revolutionary motto to fit the circumstances of the new country over which he sought to preside, Dessalines shouted the Black army's new mission into the humid air, "Independence or Death. . . . Let these sacred words rally us, and let them be the signal of our combat and of our reunion." Chanlatte

202   Chapter 6

recalled that day by referencing "the flag that we consecrated, the one that for so long should have been the only one on display." He went on to say that Haiti's new standard would "from now on be the slender, but indestructible chain, around which a brotherly People will always be ready to rally."[142] Haitian chroniclers of these events continuously stressed that the most important element of the achievement of Haitian independence was unity—*l'union fait la force* (unity makes strength). After independence, unity was required more than ever to keep the colonists, sovereign Haiti's ultimate enemy, from ever returning to Haitian shores. "If folly and ineptitude should carry them again to our shores to avenge their defeats, and reclaim a country over which they purport to have rights, they would not find, as at the time of their first expedition, a disunited population, a portion of whom were disposed to rally to their side," Prévost explained. Haitian independence was a process based on past experiences that distinctly involved Louverture's demise. "Why, enlightened Haytians repeated, did Governor Toussaint Louverture not breathe the word? Why didn't he proclaim Hayti's independence?" Prévost asked. "I would respond that this precious fruit had to be ripened by experience and misfortune!" "Governor Toussaint was perhaps not yet aware of this necessity," Prévost concluded. "If he had spoken of independence at that time, he would have found all minds wary and formally predisposed to declare against him: even Haytians who had never known France were more attached to it than to their own country; but this predilection no longer exists."[143] Any lingering affection for France among the Black army dissipated with the French military's increasingly genocidal tactics.

By November 1803, the Indigenous army, largely unified in their goal of independence, was in control of most of the south, along with the north and western parts of the island. French troops continued to fight them on multiple fronts and controlled Cap, however, including in places highly guarded by Dessalines's troops. At the Battle of Vertières, which came to an end on November 18, 1803, the Leclerc–Rochambeau expedition Bonaparte sent to bring back slavery was effectively terminated. Under the command of General François Capoix, and aided by General Vernet (related to Toussaint Louverture by marriage), the Indigenous army forced French forces to capitulate.[144] The surviving French soldiers retreated and Rochambeau declared his surrender. On December 4, the majority of French troops sailed away from the island in exhaustion and humiliating defeat.[145]

With the French effectively kicked out of Saint-Domingue, Generals Jean-Jacques Dessalines, Henry Christophe, and Augustin Clervaux, declared the island independent from France. The preamble to the Declaration of Independence signed by these men on November 29, 1803, stated, "In the name of the black people and men of colour of St. Domingo. The independence of

Freedom   203

Heroes Monument in Vertières, Haiti, 2020. Courtesy of Samy F. Zaka.

St. Domingo is proclaimed. Restored to our primitive dignity, we have proclaimed our rights; we swear never to yield them to any power on earth: the frightful veil of prejudice is torn to pieces, and is so forever. . . . We have sworn not to listen to clemency towards all those who dare to speak to us of slavery."[146] Foreign newspapers of the time reported this development with an equal mix of awe and stupefaction.[147] The world had never seen such a move: formerly enslaved Black people declaring themselves independent from one of the fiercest colonial powers in the world. Perhaps even more surprisingly, this no longer French island in the middle of the Caribbean Sea managed to find an unlikely, but immediate, if fairweather, friend in the northern U.S. press.

The *Morning Chronicle* out of New York, just before the news of Haiti's declaration reached the United States, published an outright defense of Haitian opposition to "French Oppression." "It appears from what I have collected in different conversations, that General Leclerc committed a great fault," the author wrote. Using an analogy to the American revolutionary war, the author asked his audience to contemplate the lack of wisdom inherent in France's attempt to reestablish slavery ten years after its abolition: "Were it indeed proposed to all our generals, officers . . . to return to that state in which they were before the revolution, can anyone believe that they would willingly consent; that they would suffer themselves to be deprived of their rank . . . and that they would not take up arms to resist, and excite all their comrades to do the same?"[148] Of course, it was an imperfect comparison. The white colonists of North America had not been enslaved by Great Britain. While the U.S. Declaration of Independence had in effect been a proclamation of war against England by the white American colonists, the Haitian Declaration of Independence of 1804 narrated "Saint-Domingue's" newfound status as a fait accompli. At least, in theory.

The founding documents of Haiti eschew much of the incoherence found in France's multiple republican constitutions, and Louverture's own, while creating their own contradictions, which are perhaps germane to the genre of statecraft. Notably, the founding documents of Haiti do not set up a republic.[149] The two existing examples of modern republics in their era were republics that proclaimed liberty while enslaving people. There was no reason for Haitians to think that a republic was inherently better than a monarchy, which we learn from reading the writing of Haiti's Baron de Vastey. "One finds this institution [monarchy] in all of the most free people, the most civilized and the most enlightened on the earth," Vastey wrote.[150] That England abolished the slave trade, but not slavery, in 1807, was part of his reasoning. Also, there was a republic on the other side of the island, under Pétion, and the Haitian monarch and his allies did not fail to point out that it was the French republic under Napoléon that tried to reinstate slavery on the island. Republics were associated in the minds of northern Haitian politicians not only with slavery, but with an incoherent form of enlightenment where liberty and equality were proclaimed but did not exist. The political doublespeak that Rigaud said was germane to life under French colonial rule was confirmed when Leclerc arrived in Saint-Domingue promising that slavery would never return, while simultaneously waging war against the

Black soldiers all the while trying to conceal the fact that France had maintained slavery in Martinique and then restored it in Guadeloupe.[151] No wonder that a republic would not be an immediately attractive form of governance for two of Haiti's first rulers, Dessalines, who set up a nonhereditary empire in 1804, and Christophe, who set up a constitutional but hereditary monarchy in 1811.

Even without the *racial* incoherence of the French republic, Haiti's own particular tensions of freedom remained. Was the Black independence movement destined to turn from marronnage, to revolution, to nationalism, and then to empire? Vastey wrote of Haiti's first attempt to govern itself as an empire under Dessalines, "If we had had at that time enough experience, wisdom, and prudence, we would have founded a constitutional monarchy, and we would have created for ourselves useful institutions and a stable and regular government; how many ills and calamities would we have avoided!"[152] Moreover, Vastey traced the civil war between Christophe and President Jean-Pierre Boyer (who succeeded Pétion as president over the southern republic in 1818), which he was then living through, to Dessalines's previous failure to create an appropriate constitution—a vèvè—for Haiti. Vastey argued, first, that the "purely military government" that Dessalines created did not immediately instate a constitution and, second, that when the government finally did so, the constitution it formed was, in Vastey's words, a "political monstrosity."[153] "The empire was an electoral Republic," Vastey wrote, referring to the constitution's creation of a Council of State. Then, acknowledging the fact that the constitution paradoxically gave the Emperor Jacques I, rather than the theoretical state councilors, the right to choose his successor, Vastey continued, "but in the constitution were principles diametrically opposed to the Republic, and that could not at all be appropriate, except for a purely *despotic* government; and on the other side, with a strange overturning of ideas, the constitution consecrated the most *democratic* of principles." The 1805 constitution also stated that the theoretical councilors would be responsible for choosing the next head of state in the event of the emperor's demise, which seemed to contradict the idea that Dessalines was to name his successor before his death.[154] Ultimately, it was the Haitian people who suffered the most because of the so-called legislative errors made by Dessalines, whereby his empire was couched in, but at the same time opposed to, republican terms. "As in every country," Vastey lamented, "it is the people who are always the victims of the mistakes their lawmakers make; it is always they who are forced to pay for them with their tears, their blood, and their livelihood."[155]

In the final part of this book, I turn to early sovereign Haiti's voluminous print culture, produced under the governments of Dessalines, Christophe, Pétion, and Boyer. Examining postrevolutionary Haitian political and histori-

-1—
0—
+1—

206   Chapter 6

cal writing provides distinct keys for understanding how sovereignty in Haiti unfolded (and eventually fell apart) in the long nineteenth century after the Haitian Revolution. In *Une lecture décoloniale de l'histoire des haïtiens* (A decolonial history of the Haitians, 2018), Jean Casimir used the concept of the "counter-plantation," derived from the readings of Baron de Vastey, Beaubrun Ardouin, Thomas Madiou, and Anténor Firmon, precisely to explain "how Haitians have survived and lived in the midst of political structures that exclude all participation on their part." His thesis, in effect, is that the majority of the Haitian people, the seeming victims of a world order based on capitalism, have created their own vision of the world in negotiation with dominant governments, including their own.[156] There is a Haitian proverb that states, *se vye chodye ki kwit bon manje*, or it is the old pot that makes the best food. The early nineteenth century was, in many respects, the last time that Haiti had uncompromised sovereignty. Narrating the firm existence of sovereignty in early nineteenth-century Haiti is a fraught and painful exercise, in many ways, because the history we are discussing lies in ruins. Haiti remains under both figurative and literal foreign occupation. The memories of lost sovereignty hurt and are conjured up again and again when studying the history of early Haiti, reminding us in the words of Aimé Césaire, "and the museums . . . it would have been better not to have needed them. . . . No, in the scales of knowledge all the museums in the world will never weigh so much as one spark of human sympathy."[157] One way to work through this pain is to take it into Papa Legba's crossroads, where the living and the dead, the colonial and the decolonial, have no choice but to interrogate one another.

-1—
0—
+1—

PART III

Sovereignty

-1—
0—
+1—

Chapter 7

Anti-colonialism

Haiti's first published Declaration of Independence, dated November 29, 1803, robustly circulated around the Atlantic World, as it was reprinted in numerous British and U.S. newspapers. Dessalines seems not to have found that version adequate for the purposes of creating the new state he hoped to lead, however. In a memoir he penned, but that was only published by his son in 1864, General Guy-Joseph Bonnet, a former aide-de-camp to André Rigaud, recalled that Dessalines charged his secretary, Charéron, with composing a clearer declaration of independence. Dessalines wanted a document that enumerated French crimes and "spoke of the griefs we had against France," to "naturally establish the causes that led the Haitian people to proclaim its independence." On the evening of December 31, 1803, Charéron reportedly gave a draft of the new declaration to Dessalines's more well known secretary, Louis-Félix Boisrond-Tonnerre. Boisrond-Tonnerre evidently dismissed it at once, saying "this manifesto does not suit us at all." Later, Boisrond-Tonnerre told Bonnet that Charéron's version "was not what Dessalines needed." "I locked myself in my room," Boisrond-Tonnerre then explained. "I drank two cups of coffee and three shots of rum; the work flowed from the source." This is the story, according to Bonnet, of how and why Boisrond-Tonnerre produced the famous January 1, 1804 official declaration of the newly inaugurated Haiti's independence from France.[1]

A more apocryphal account of how Boisrond-Tonnerre came to draft the official declaration also exists. In one popular retelling, after Charéron presented his draft to Boisrond-Tonnerre, the latter said to him, "What you have done here is not in harmony with our natural dispositions; to prepare a declaration of independence, we need the skin of a white man for paper, his head for a writing desk, his blood for ink, and a bayonet as a pen." Upon hearing this, Dessalines, who was present in this version of the account, immediately demanded that Boisrond-Tonnerre pen the declaration instead.[2]

Haiti's second and official Declaration of Independence was signed on January 1, 1804, by numerous generals from the Haitian army, among whom were Dessalines, Christophe, Clervaux, and Pétion. This second version was even more strongly worded than the preliminary November 29 document. The January 1 *acte*, while announcing that the island was now called Haiti, rather than Saint-Domingue, declared in no uncertain terms that the Haitian people had "sworn to posterity, in front of the entire universe, to renounce France forever, and to die rather than live under her domination, and to fight until their last breath for independence."[3] Following the oath to independence the generals swore at the home of General André Vernet on Rue L'Ouverture in the city of Gonaïves, Dessalines reportedly had Boisrond-Tonnerre read the declaration as a speech to a crowd of formerly enslaved people and veterans of the war of independence.[4] "It is not enough to have expelled from your country the barbarians who have bloodied it for two centuries," Boisrond-Tonnerre pronounced. "We must, by a final act of national authority, assure forever the empire of liberty in the country where we were born; we must take away forever from that inhumane government, which has for so long held our spirits in the most humiliating bondage, all hope of re-enslaving us; we must live independent or die." It must have been arresting for the audience to hear these solemn words drawn from the trauma of their own experiences: "Everything here calls forth the memory of the cruelties of that barbaric people; our laws, our mores, our cities, everything still carries the stamp of the French; what am I saying? There are still Frenchmen on this island, and you believe yourselves to be free of this Republic that has made war against every nation."[5] These particular words, though far less famous than many others in the declaration, are some of the most important. They demonstrate that in the new government's mind (consisting of Dessalines and those generals who cosigned the declaration) the war with the French was not yet over. On the one hand, after the evacuation of Rochambeau, French general Jean-Louis Ferrand fled to Santo Domingo, on the eastern side of the island, which remained occupied with French troops until 1809. Santo Domingo remained under Ferrand's authority until 1808 when he committed suicide after losing a major battle to the Spanish. The Spanish officially reclaimed the eastern side of the island in 1809.[6] On the other hand, the Haitian revolutionaries were well aware that the U.S. Declaration of Independence started the American colonists' war with Great Britain and did not end it.

Haiti's official Declaration of Independence, ratified and made public on January 1, 1804, made it clear that the only enemies of the new Haitians were the French. The *acte* also detailed how Haiti's government intended to behave toward the neighboring islands where slavery still reigned. Keeping true to the idea of friendship for all those who posed no direct threat to Haiti, the declaration is laden with numerous reassurances that Haitians had no plans to export their revolution abroad, and certainly not to the other surrounding islands of the Caribbean, all of which were still powered by the painstaking labor of enslaved men, women, and children from Africa. "Let us guard against the spirit of proselytizing so that it does not destroy our efforts," the declaration reads, "let us leave in tranquil repose our neighbors,

212   Chapter 7

for we are not going to, as revolutionary firebrands, erect ourselves as legislators of the Caribbean by seeking our glory through troubling the tranquility of the other islands in our vicinity."[7] Chanlatte confirmed the anti-colonial foundations of the new Haitian state when in his 1804 pamphlet he wrote that Haitians did not intend to "immerse themselves in the affairs of the powerful neighbors of this Island." "Let us swear never to look to interfere with them in their possessions and to concern ourselves only with the necessity of our conservation," Chanlatte wrote. Haiti's leaders presented this policy as the clearest way to ensure the prosperity of the new Haitian state and its new leader, Dessalines.[8]

Though they declared their independence almost by megaphone, Haiti's leaders still needed to convince the world that their part of the island was no longer a French colony but an independent state. The task was tall because no other nation immediately recognized Haitian independence. Perhaps it is for this reason that on January 25, 1804, General Vernet, seconded by twenty generals of the army, wrote an open letter to Dessalines, imploring him to consider adopting the title of "Emperor." Previously, Dessalines was designated "governor-general" of the island, the title Louverture held. The generals believed this appellation to be inadequate for the office of Haitian head of state. "Persuaded that supreme authority cannot be shared, and that the interests of the country demand that the reigns of the administration be placed into the hands of he who inspires us with confidence," they wrote, "and considering that the title of Governor-General, heretofore bestowed upon citizen Jean-Jacques Dessalines, does not fulfill, in a satisfying manner, the wishes of the public, because it supposes a subordinate authority, dependent upon a foreign power, whose yoke we have shaken off. . . . Let us now confer upon citizen Jean-Jacques Dessalines the title of Emperor of Haiti with the right to choose and name his successor."[9] Dessalines accepted this nomination in a letter to the generals of the Haitian army dated February 15, 1804, referring to them as "the organs of the people." "If there is any consideration that justifies in my eyes the august title that your confidence bestows upon me," he said, "it is no doubt only my zeal to oversee the salvation of the Empire and the goodwill I have to consolidate our enterprise, an enterprise which will grant to us, from nations that are less friendly to freedom, not the designation that we are a horde of slaves, but the opinion that we are men who have chosen their own independence . . . which the powers that be never seek to grant to peoples who, like us, are the artisans of their own freedom." "I am a soldier," he continued. "War has always been my arena, and as long as the ferocity, barbarity, and greed of our enemies bring them to our shores, I will justify your choice, and fight at your head, I will prove that the title of your general will always remain an honor to me." While he accepted the title of emperor, Dessalines rejected the notion of a hereditary government. He opted not to exercise the kinds of laws of hereditary descent that characterized most monarchies in the era. Instead, he said that upon his demise, he would be "happy to be able to transmit my authority to those who have shed their blood for the nation." "I renounce, yes, I officially renounce," he declared, "the unjust practice of passing the power down to my family. I will never have regard for that kind of outdatedness, since the qualities required to govern well may not be found in the [hereditary] subject; often the head that contains the boiling fire of youth, can contribute more effectively to the happiness of a country, than the cold and experienced head of the old man who temporizes in moments when temerity alone is in season. It is on these terms that I am becoming your Emperor." The above letters are dated several months before Napoléon Bonaparte announced his intention to become emperor of France in May 1804. However, the January and February 1804 letters referenced above were not published in Haiti until November of the same year when they were printed in the new state-run newspaper, the *Gazette politique et commerciale d'Haïti* (Political and commercial gazette of Haiti). Notably, when Dessalines signed the nomination acceptance (which was undersigned by Boisrond-Tonnerre), he used the title governor-general.[10] Vastey, like many later historians, implied that the date of the letters, plus the designation Dessalines used, governor-general, meant he only took the title emperor, "with a spirit of imitation," after Napoléon claimed it in spring 1804, later being officially crowned on December 2, 1804.[11]

The belated publication of the documents has led more recent historians to also argue that the letters were backdated to January and February 1804 to protect Dessalines from the charge of imitation.[12] It is important to point out, however, that the tardy publication of the letters may have been because before November 15, 1804—the date that the first issue of Haiti's state-run newspaper appeared—the new Haitian state did not yet have a national newspaper to communicate with the most outlying sectors of the Haitian populace. The methods by which they could therefore spread news across the country were limited.

Not having a state-run newspaper press allowed rumors to flourish—not unlike those proclaiming Dessalines copied Bonaparte—and afforded foreign governments the opportunity to publish and circulate proclamations, decrees, and other documents before Haitian leaders could do so. The effect of not having a newspaper press had already led to internal disorder and confusion. In the first four months of independence numerous reports circulated saying that Dessalines committed so-called massacres of the entire remaining white population. In response, Dessalines issued his famous April 28, 1804 proclamation. This proclamation, undersigned by Chanlatte, was written not only to justify

214   Chapter 7

any actions taken against agitators from France but to take control of the narrative of Haitian governance and independence. Haitian leaders knew that they and their independence, their sovereignty, was on trial before the world.

The French government was papering the earth with defamatory accusations against its erstwhile colony to such an extent that Anglophone newspapers, like the *Caledonian Mercury* out of Edinburgh, sometimes cautioned their readers about news coming from France. The *Caledonian* urged other newspapers to be wary of reporting French claims as fact, as the Scottish paper said the London-based *Morning Post* recently had. "Some of the small French papers last received contain a very exaggerated account of the barbarities committed by Dessalines, in St. Domingo," the *Calendonian Mercury* stated. "It is the policy of Bonaparte to make the State of St. Domingo an object of horror in the eyes of France, and all the other nations—to efface the memory of the frightful scenes which he caused to be acted there, by an exaggerated account of present cruelties, and to make his rival tyrant more detestable, if possible than himself." Napoléon's government and the French press, which it largely controlled, had clear reasons for seeking to paint Haitians as massacring aggressors. France's gruesome actions during the Leclerc expedition were not evenly known across the world, giving the French ample room to promote their side of the story, with Haitians having few avenues for rebuttal. The article in the *Caledonian Mercury* aptly described the resulting dynamic whereby the French tried to paint themselves as the victims of both the Haitian revolutionaries and independent Haitians under Dessalines: "The French papers only publish the bad actions of this black chieftain, whom we should advise not to imitate the Corsican in anything more, and in an official *Moniteur* of St. Domingo make the world acquainted with some of the horrors committed there by Bonaparte's white slaves under the command of his brother-in-law General Leclerc."[13] The writer for the *Caledonian Mercury* deliberately advised Dessalines to publish the atrocities of the French in an official government outlet, which is precisely what Boisrond-Tonnerre and Chanlatte did when they published their 1804 memoir and pamphlet, respectively.

Refuting French versions of the last days of Saint-Domingue and the first days of independence was, along with announcing Dessalines's nomination to emperor, one of the primary aims of the first few issues of Haiti's *Gazette politique*. When independent Haiti belatedly established the *Gazette politique* on November 15, 1804, its first article condemned the despotic and murderous violence of the Leclerc expedition:

A formidable squadron and the most powerful army that any power had ever yet sent to the Antilles, came to descend upon every part of the

Anti-colonialism   215

island. At the head of such considerable forces, a general [Leclerc], with a reputation for equivocation and of an incomprehensible character, presented himself, sometimes with a threatening air, other times with the sweetest of speeches and the most brilliant promises; the most insidious proclamations and letters swarmed from his hands; he lied; he seduced, rather than defeated most of the country's leaders; and soiled, at last, with his infamous barbarity, the character of the nation he represents.

The article went on to describe how, during the Leclerc expedition, General Dessalines "already renowned because of his exploits," decided that he "did not have any longer to be the tool of such a madman." "He assembled all around him, from among the remains of the various, disparate regiments; he raised the standard of disobedience, and swore from that moment forward to be the liberator of his country, or to bury himself under its ruins; the generals of the island joined together with him; and they marched from victory to victory, and soon enough they took Cap, on the 29th of November 1803."[14] Still, the war with France—both discursive and material—was not over on November 29, any more than it was on January 1.

Haitians were still in self-defense mode in the first year of the country's existence. In the April 28 proclamation, Dessalines acknowledged that the French were still vying to "restore Saint-Domingue," which meant to reestablish their domination over the island and slavery along with it. Haitians had no choice, in his estimation, but to continue to adopt a mode of self-defense despite whatever opinion their actions might cause the world powers to form against them. "Already, at [France's] approach, the irritated genie of Haiti, emerging from the bosom of the seas, appears; his menacing regard stirs up the waves, stirs up storms, his powerful hand breaks or scatters vessels; at his formidable voice the laws of nature obey, diseases, pestilence, devouring hunger, fire, poison, follow him," Dessalines said. In his formulation it was not God's vengeance that would save the Haitian people. Haitians were responsible for saving themselves. This is why Dessalines awakened the ashes of the Haitians thrown into the seas and summoned that "irritated genie of Haiti," which was as much the land as it was the people, and the air they breathed, to defend Haitian sovereignty with their lives. "But why count on the help of the climate and the elements?" Dessalines asked, almost as if to ward off the climate myth (yellow fever, coupled with the high temperatures) of Haitian success.[15] Haiti had an army that was more than sixty thousand strong, Dessalines insisted, and their numbers were not nearly as important as those fierce warriors who constituted it. "Have I then forgotten that I command uncommon souls, nurtured in adversity?" he asked. If "hom-

216   Chapter 7

icidal cohorts" were to arrive once more from France, Dessalines resolved to "await them firmly, with a fixed eye," before noting that he would first evacuate the coasts and the towns. But as soon as any French soldier were to approach the mountains, "It would be better for him that the sea had engulfed him in its deep abysses, than to be devoured by the anger of the children of Haiti," he concluded.[16] Article 28 of Dessalines's 1805 constitution warned, to that end, "At the first shot of the warning cannon, the cities will vanish and the nation will stand up."[17] Trying to get the world to accept the ongoing state of war, whereby Haitians were the attacked, and thus on the defensive, rather than the attackers, and therefore on the offensive, remained just as important to Dessalines as proving to the world that Haiti and Haitians had created a sovereign, independent state, separate from French authority. Setting up a state newspaper press was one small step along this larger trajectory.

On October 10, 1804, the *Commercial Advertiser* out of the United States published an English translation of the full text of the Haitian army's January 25, 1804, nomination of Dessalines to emperor.[18] The article in the *Commercial Advertiser* is identical in content to the one that the state of Haiti eventually published in November. The lack of a newspaper press not only permitted U.S. journalists and editors to publish these documents before they could be published in Haiti, but also allowed them to pronounce unfavorable judgment upon this crucial development along Haiti's path to sovereignty. "Dessalines, whom we mentioned some time since as having been appointed Governor of Hayti for life, with the power of nominating his successor, is consolidating if not perpetuating his power," wrote another U.S. paper, the *New-York Herald*, on October 10, 1804. "He has at length assumed the imperial purple. He was proclaimed emperor on the 15th of Sept. . . . Capt. Sealy informs us the rejoicings and illuminations at the Cape continued for three successive days." The charges of imitation came fast and furious after reports of the nomination and corresponding proclamation were published in the international press. In the same article, Dessalines's government was charged with being "modelled after that of the French." The writer even suggested that Dessalines's coronation celebration, set for a later date, "may correspond in all respects with that of his '*dearly beloved Cousin*,'" referring to Napoléon.[19] Yet Dessalines's Imperial Constitution of 1805 set up a government and society that was nothing like France under Napoléon. Slavery still existed in French territories under Napoléon's rule while it was permanently abolished by Haiti's constitution under Dessalines.

It took the United States, Haiti's analog in New World independence, more than a decade to produce an official constitution, which was not fully ratified by all states until 1790, when Rhode Island belatedly assented.[20] Despite Vastey's critique that the new Haitian government did not produce a constitution

Anti-colonialism 217

quickly enough, Haitians worked much more swiftly than their U.S. counterparts. Haitians ratified their first constitution in May 1805, only a year and a half after their Acte d'Indépendance. The *Gazette* was the place where this new Haitian constitution, along with the newly established military penal code, was made public.

Haiti's new constitution was wholly remarkable, not only for its own time, but for the enduring principles of sovereignty after colonialism it set down for the world. Haiti set the bar extremely high when it became the first state anywhere in the world to forever outlaw slavery and declare its permanent prohibition. Like the 1801 constitution issued under Louverture and the 1804 Declaration of Independence, Haiti's first constitution attracted immediate attention from the foreign media.[21] The principles of humane sovereignty it mandated acquired a huge transnational audience, allowing the concept of anti-colonialism it inaugurated to have an outsized impact in the hemisphere. In what historian Leslie Alexander has referenced as the earliest known published response to Haitian independence by a Black person from the United States, a writer calling himself an "Injured Man of Color," defended the anti-colonial foundations of Haitian independence by comparing them to those of the United States.[22] "When you fought for your independence, when you resisted the arm of Britain, and gained the cause for which you struggled, were you not elated with your success? Were you not proud of your victory? Did not your souls spurn at the man who dared to call you rebels and traitors?" "Is not the cause for which the Haytians fought the same in principle with yours?" "If your cause was just and honorable, was not theirs the same?" he asked. The Injured Man recognized a distinct difference between the way the Black freedom fighters of Saint-Domingue and the white rebels of the British North American colonies were treated by the European powers after their respective wars of independence. Referring to slavery as "a miserable life under the lash," the Injured Man noted that Haitians had been "more oppressed" and had "even stronger stimulants to urge them on to independence" than the British North American colonists. What's more important, perhaps, about the Injured Man's ardent defense of Haitian sovereignty is the way he acknowledged the French to be extraordinary aggressors desirous of an empire, while the Haitian people, he said, were guided only by "principles of honor and justice, not a spirit of revenge."[23] Onlookers, like the so-called Injured Man, had not yet even seen the powerful work that anti-colonial legislation would do in Haiti's first constitution.

If the Haitian Declaration of Independence was the work of "many hands," so too was the constitution of 1805.[24] The constitution's preamble disclosed that it was written by a combination of former enslaved and free(d) people of color from the colonial era, and was subsequently "submitted" to be "sanctioned" by Dessalines, "his majesty, the Emperor." The constitution was signed by Dessalines on May 20, 1805, but under the emperor's signature also appeared that of Chanlatte as his "secretary-general." The practice of undersigning common in the era has led to questions about whether Dessalines can be considered the proper *author* of any of the numerous state documents issued under his name and has sparked spirited debate among academics.[25] Consulting nineteenth-century Haitian thought in many ways renders such debates moot.

In his anti-Christophe southern newspaper *L'Observateur*, a partisan of Pétion and Boyer, Charles-Hérard Dumesle, praised Boisrond-Tonnerre's contributions to early Haitian statecraft while diminishing those of rival Juste Chanlatte. Chanlatte was a prominent member of Christophean aristocracy who held the title Comte de Rosiers, and who had previously been the editor of northern Haiti's official newspaper under King Henry. In reply to this slight, the new editor of Christophe's *Gazette royale*, Baron de Vastey, pointed out that while Boisrond-Tonnerre was assuredly the person who *wrote* the Dec-laration of Independence, its composition was collaborative and its principles were derived as much from Haitian revolutionary acts and deeds as from Hai-tian revolutionary men and women. "We pay tribute to the talents as a writer of Adjutant General Boisrond-Tonnerre, secretary to the late Emperor," the *Gazette* stated. "But that illustrious assembly of warriors, educated and ener-getic men of all kinds, who valiantly fought the French, that illustrious as-sembly, I say, having at its head the immortal Dessalines, who on January 1, 1804, of eternal memory, founded the independence of his country and broke forever the ties that bound us to an unjust and barbarous metropole; was it not those warriors, those respectable citizens, who dictated this sublime act to Boisrond?" Statecraft as momentous as this could only have been the work of a collective, Vastey implied. The "Great Man" theory of human history in nineteenth-century Haitian thought gave way to a more populist understand-ing of the emergence of Haitian independence and the famous act that con-secrated it: "Oh! What criminal impartiality to attribute to a single writer, that which is the work of the concurrence of so many morals, patriotism, and wis-dom united?" The work of Haitian independence did not stop with the famous 1804 declaration. "Since that magnificent time, which will forever be the glory of our nephews," the *Gazette* asked, "was it not writers from the north," principally, "who vied with the warriors, as to who would fight our oppressors with more bravery; they have destroyed the scaffolding of the colonial system and brought down the hydra of slavery!" Haiti's writers were also revolutionaries who contributed not just to Haitian independence but to maintaining Haiti's freedom and sovereignty in a hostile world of slavery and colonialism. The writer for the *Gazette* concluded, "Was it not these same writers, led by the energy of their leaders, who enlightened the people, who stoked that fire, that sacred love of country, that inveterate hatred for our oppressors, and who have prevented our fellow citizens from falling into the many traps that partisans of the French have constantly set for them."[26] Many of Haiti's revolutionary chroniclers, who contributed to the written deeds of Haitian sovereignty, like Boisrond-Tonnerre and Chanlatte, were also officers and soldiers who fought in the war of independence. Post-1804 they became discursive warriors, who defended Haitian sovereignty by writing Haiti's history and offering novel definitions for the words freedom, equality, and, in the end, independence, which altogether differed from their usage by the slaving world powers.

Like the 1801 constitution of Saint-Domingue, and Haiti's two declarations of independence, the constitution of 1805 challenged Enlightenment humanisms,[27] as well as hierarchies of race and color, and the very meaning of freedom.[28] However, the foundational documents of Haitian sovereignty also challenged the logic and material practices of colonialism in the Atlantic World. This is not simply because these documents declared emancipation from slavery based on universal equality, and justified using violence to achieve that goal, but also because they provided a clear and direct language with which to challenge pro-colonial discourse. Acknowledging the radical nature of Haiti's anti-conquest stance in a world of colonial empires reveals Haiti's outsized influence on the trajectory of both Caribbean and African American intellectual thought.

Although Article 1 of the 1805 constitution prescribed that the country would henceforth be known "under the name of the Empire of Haiti," Article 36 contested the traditional definition of "empire" by mandating: "The emperor will never form any enterprise with the goal of conquest nor of troubling the peace or the interior affairs of foreign colonies."[29] Article 36 thus enacted into law the anti-colonial ideals first expressed in the Haitian Declaration of Independence.[30] If we can say, therefore, that Haiti's founding documents ensured that the country would never again be ruled by colonizers, these documents also mandated that Haiti's rulers could never become colonizers.

It is worth pointing out that this wholly anti-colonial constitution was issued shortly after Dessalines, Christophe, and Pétion's failed siege of Santo Domingo, whereby the Haitian army tried to wrest control of the eastern side of the island from France. The goal of this siege was to reunite the island under one government as it had been under Louverture. In May 1805, upon returning from the failed siege, Dessalines gave a speech explaining that reunification, and also protecting Haiti from potential French invaders who still occupied the other side of the island, were his primary motives. "Deter-

220   Chapter 7

mined to recognize only those borders of the island traced by nature and the seas, [and] persuaded that as long as even one enemy still breathes in this land, I still have a duty to fulfill with dignity the role to which you have elevated me," Dessalines said. "I made the decision to go and recover the entire portion of my territories, and to erase from it the last vestiges of the European idol." While the siege may not have succeeded, the sentiment motivating it persisted. Destroying colonialism meant ridding the island of its former colonizers. For the first half century of independence, Haitians tended to see the schism with the eastern side of the island as unnatural.[31] The 1805 constitution made clear that the Empire of Haiti was "one and indivisible," and that its six "integral parts" included those of the eastern side, as well as the scattered isles: "Samana, la Tortue, la Gonâve, les Cayemites, l'île à Vâche, la Saône, and adjacent islands." Boyer's 1822 reunification of Haiti and Santo Domingo was in fact predicated on the same geopolitical boundaries outlined by the 1801 and 1805 constitutions. Boyer's announcement of the "reunion" of the east and west in the official paper, *Le Télégraphe*, opened with a reprint of Article 40 from the republic's 1816 constitution: "The island of Haiti (previously called St.-Domingue) with the adjacent islands that comprise its dependencies, forms the territory of Haiti. . . . The Republic of Haiti is one and indivisible."[32] Reunification and conquest were constituted as polar opposites in Haiti.

The anti-conquest stances articulated in Haiti's founding documents were not incidental or disingenuous challenges to the colonial powers of the Atlantic World, nor were they mere relics of the fact that the words "imperial" and "empire" may not have had "the same political meanings in early nineteenth century Haiti as they did in imperial Europe of the period," in the words of scholar Anthony Bogues.[33] It might be more accurate to say that the words did not have the same meaning to Dessalines. Recall that critiquing Dessalines's nomination as emperor, Baron de Vastey explained that this was an inappropriate title since it suggested "that he who possessed it also possessed great power over large territories and peoples."[34] While finding it an insurmountable discursive contradiction, Vastey unwittingly recognized that Dessalines had in an uncanny and deliberate way become an emperor without an empire. Rather than viewing this as contradictory, let us delve further into the consequences of this move so that we may see how Dessalines provided us with a new definition of empire, one not predicated on conquest. The general principles of anti-conquest that undergird Dessalines's "empire" anticipate a postcolonial heuristic, whereby anti-colonial thought eventually became a normative political perspective across many global intellectual circles. This is true especially true in the Global South (including India and Africa) and across the Black Atlantic (primarily, the Americas and Western Europe). To glimpse the normativity of anti-colonial axioms, frameworks, and ideologies, one can look at the September 2017 controversy over an article published in the *Third World Quarterly*, which defended the historical practice of colonialism and encouraged its revival. The journal editor's decision to publish the article over the objections of the peer reviewers, who did not recommend the article for publication, led to the resignation of half the journal's editorial board.[35]

By arguing that anti-colonialism is now normative, especially in comparative Black and Global South intellectual traditions, I do not mean to suggest that all Afro-diasporic intellectuals did oppose in the past or even now unequivocally reject colonialism. Rather, I mean to point out that anti-colonialism has become essentially the default position of Black intellectuals in the Americas and Western Europe; and that for a considerable time, pro-colonialism has been considered a divergence from the norm. Deviations from the norm characterized as extraordinary can be illustrated by responses to Zora Neale Hurston's defense of the U.S. occupation of Haiti, which she referred to as a "white hope" in *Tell My Horse* (1938). Hurston's stance was contrary to that of most other Black U.S. American intellectuals of her time, and it was also opposite the official position of the National Association for the Advancement of Colored People.[36]

Raphael Dalleo has recently made a compelling case that it was the U.S. occupation of Haiti (1915–34) that foretold the rise of anti-colonial thought among such well-known Pan-Africanists as C. L. R. James, George Padmore, Marcus Garvey, Amy Jacques Garvey, Claude McKay, Eric Walrond, and Alejo Carpentier.[37] However, returning to the political and legal discourses of anti-colonialism first articulated in early sovereign Haiti points to alternative genealogies. The early constitutions of Haiti left behind a distinct legacy of anti-imperialism that would be more concretely theorized by mid- to late nineteenth-century Haitian intellectuals like Demesvar Delorme and Louis-Joseph Janvier, who were perhaps two of the earliest Black writers to connect nineteenth-century U.S. American imperialism to modern capitalism.[38] The development of this kind of radical anti-colonialism, with its explicitly anti-capitalist critique, is usually associated with later twentieth-century Pan-African thought, but has clear antecedents in Haitian revolutionary thought.[39] Rather than ruminating on the causes and consequences of the endemic suppression of nineteenth-century Haitian thought in global Black intellectual history,[40] in the pages that follow, I want us to consider how Haiti's longstanding and well-known anti-colonialism, often read as innocence in the global political sphere—merely illuminated by the occupation, rather than developed in response to it—created the possibility for the chain of anti-colonial philosophies to develop that we witness in later twentieth-century Afro-diasporic intellectual history. With even more insistence, I contend that

222   Chapter 7

comparatively reading the country's first constitutions (1805–16) positions early Haiti's global declaration of a politics of anti-conquest as elemental to the development of later nineteenth- and early twentieth-century anti-colonial movements in Europe and the United States.

———

In my prior work on Haitian intellectual history, I have observed that both the anti-conquest stance evident in Henry Christophe's 1807 constitution, and Baron de Vastey's later writings on the matter, present a challenge to current genealogies of postcolonial studies.[41] The former French colonist Pierre Victor Baron de Malouet, who was such a monstrous colonist that his name was only spoken in Haiti with horror, argued that "the revolution transferred from the whites to the blacks the question of control over the Caribbean."[42] Vastey directly contested this by explicitly noting that Haitians did not desire to create a Caribbean empire. "The revolution did not transfer from the whites to the blacks the question of control over the West Indies," Vastey countered. "Haiti is one of the islands of this archipelago and is not itself the Caribbean."[43] Nineteenth-century Haitian writers like Vastey played a primary role in defining colonialism as *bad*. An underlying assumption of postcolonial studies today is that forcefully extending the rule of law from one nation to another (regardless of any perceived benefit to the country under occupation) is the essence of colonial racism. Yet the anti-colonialism of early Haiti was certainly not shared by the only other independent nation of the American hemisphere at the time, the United States, nor was it an inevitable political position for Haitian leaders to have mandated as they developed sovereign political institutions in the Americas. This much was recognized by British parliamentarian Fowell Buxton who, on May 15, 1823, addressed the British House of Commons on the question of the abolition of slavery by first referencing Haiti's existence as a slavery-free and independent state in the Caribbean:

> What does the negro, working under the lash on the mountains of Jamaica, see? He sees another island, on which every labourer is free; in which eight hundred thousand blacks, men, women, and children, exercise all the rights, and enjoy all the blessings—and they are innumerable and incalculable—which freedom gives. Hitherto, indeed, no attempt has been made, from that quarter. The late emperor Christophe,[44] and the president Boyer, may have been moderate men; or they may have found at home sufficient employment. But, who will venture to secure us against the ambition of their successors?

Buxton then explicitly referenced Haiti's politics of anti-colonialism by way of drawing a contrast between Great Britain, Haiti, and the United States. "It would be singular enough, if the only emperor who did not feel a desire to meddle with the affairs of his neighbours should be the emperor of Hayti. Look at America," he continued. "She may send at her own leisure, and from the adjacent shore, an army to Jamaica, proclaiming freedom to all the slaves. And—what is worse still—she may do so in exact conformity to our own example; not only in the first American war, but in the recent contest of 1813."[45] Though Buxton attributes the policy of non-conquest to Christophe, it was Article 36 of the first Empire of Haiti's 1805 constitution that laid the groundwork for the later anti-meddling/anti-conquest clause issued under Christophe, which Buxton ostensibly references.

Article 36's anti-conquest mandate appeared in Dessalines's constitution only after careful scaffolding of the meaning of Black sovereignty, which was defined as much by what it was (antislavery and anti-racist) as by what it was not (colonial). The constitution made explicit Haiti's claim to sovereignty on the basis of these three positions—antislavery, anti-racist, and anti-colonial—first, by its proclamation of the essential equality of all human beings (Preamble and Article 3); second, through the granting of a new sovereign name, "the Empire of Haiti," rather than "the colony of Saint-Domingue" (Article 1); third, by the abolition of slavery (Article 2); fourth, by the constitution's delineation of who could become a citizen and therefore a Haitian (Articles 7–14); fifth, through the legal ban against color prejudice (Articles 3 and 14); sixth, through the establishment of a clearly defined territory (Articles 15 and 18); seventh, through the designation of a sovereign ruler (Article 20); and, finally, through the unequivocal declaration that the emperor had no desire or intention to pursue any "conquests" (Article 36). This patient construction of sovereignty in Haiti, as antislavery, anti-racist, and anti-colonial, forms a fundamental part of Haitian epistemology, or ways of knowing and thinking about the world, from the origins of the nation onward, but one whose contributions to Afro-diasporic intellectual traditions we have yet to fully examine.

Examining nineteenth-century Haitian writing shows that even if the anti-conquest clause can be read as pragmatic, in part designed to preserve and protect Black sovereignty in a white colonial world, it also set up the anti-colonial foundations of independent Haiti. An article signed only "By a Haitian," published in 1806 in the *Gazette politique et commerciale*, asserted, "Dessalines is not . . . a dangerous neighbor, but a strong enemy to be feared by anyone who comes to attack him." Referring to European exploration and conquest of the Americas, the anonymous author argued that unlike the British, for instance, Haiti's emperor "has never been compelled by envy to enter into a little boat; he will never leave his island, and will take care to ensure his subjects do not either; he is content to conserve his territory, which is well worth as much as any other."[46] The idea of Haiti as a pacifist neighbor echoed the words of Chanlatte, who helped to pen the constitution: "Little desirous of interfering in the affairs of the neighboring powers of this island; let us swear never to seek to trouble them in their possessions; and to concern ourselves solely with our own preservation."[47] The so-called Injured Man, too, recognized Haitians as having little "will" to bring harm to other countries, particularly the United States.[48]

News of the constitution's ratification on May 20, 1805, with its radical anti-colonial, antislavery, and anti-racist clauses, quickly reached Haiti's continental neighbor and elicited much commentary. The *Mercantile Advertiser* from New York City announced on July 13, 1805, they had received a printed copy of the constitution by way of the brig *Ann-Maria*, under the command of Captain Starbuck. "It is a curious and interesting document, comprising 16 pages," the paper reported. "The supreme command is vested in Dessalines, who is called 'Emperor 1st' but the government is not hereditary; slavery is abolished forever; no particular church establishment is acknowledged by the state; provision is made for the education of youth; and the national colours of Hayti are very appropriately declared to be black and red stripes."[49] Although the newspaper announced it intended to print the constitution in two parts, on July 15, 1805, the *Mercantile Advertiser* published the full text of Haiti's constitution in English translation.[50] Not long after, the same U.S. translation appeared in over a dozen local British newspapers, which collectively referred to Haiti's constitution as "the most curious document."[51] The national newspaper of England, *The Times*, offered more substantial commentary: "The Constitution of Hayti, which we communicated to the public yesterday, will be read by politicians with some degree of interest." The paper went on to call it "certainly the outline of an arbitrary . . . military government." But the constitution was ultimately judged by these journalists to "offer . . . a much milder system of despotism than that established by the European rival of DESSALINES," which is to say Napoléon. *The Times* found much to admire in Article 36, or the anti-conquest clause: "The declaration that the Haytians will not attempt to make conquests, or disturb the peace of the European Colonies, is both just and politic."[52] The anti-colonial definition of empire demonstrated by the existence of the emperor and Empire of Haiti, in contrast with that of the emperor and Empire of France, had a measurably positive impact on public sentiment toward Haitian sovereignty, at least as expressed in the Anglophone press.

With some of the earliest foreign commentators immediately noticing the political ingenuity of the nascent Empire of Haiti with regard to imperial desires (or lack thereof), let us now more fully explore the consequences of Haiti's anti-colonialism. How did the anti-conquest stance of Dessalines's 1805 constitution—whereby the country continued to eschew the idea, initially pronounced in the *Acte d'indépendance*, that Haitians would become "legislators of the Caribbean"—lay the foundation for anti-colonial thought to become an axiomatic proposition of the Black diaspora distinctly opposed to all forms of imperialism? Although Article 36 may have initially been created to "pragmatically" reassure "the international community that [Haitians] would not instigate rebellion abroad," the examination of subsequent constitutions issued in early Haiti allows us to trace the longitudinal consequences of independent Haiti's instantiation of an anti-colonial state.[53] All of Haiti's first constitutions not only continued to define conquest as *bad* in the nineteenth-century Atlantic World, but they helped pave the way for anti-colonialism to become an explicit stance of Pan-Africanism. Linking Article 36 of the 1805 constitution to the development of anti-colonialism that undergirds radical Black intellectual traditions—insomuch as the constitution outlawed both colonial rule and colonial racism—not only further disrupts the common misconception that "the black Atlantic is anglophone," but it connects the anti-colonial/anti-conquest stance of Afro-diasporic intellectual history to the first state(s) of Haiti.[54]

When Dessalines became emperor of Haiti in 1804 he did so in a world where neither emperors nor empires were strange. Though, of course, Vastey did point out that both Dessalines's nomination to emperor and the idea that Haiti was an empire were actually kind of strange, given the particular context of Haitian sovereignty. As secretary to André Vernet, Dessalines's minister of finance, Vastey had a front row seat to developments in Haiti and he later identified numerous contradictions couched in the constitution at the heart of which was the fact that Haiti was called an "empire." Vastey ultimately concluded that the way Dessalines politically constituted the Empire of Haiti contained the fatal errors that led to it and its emperor's demise. Recall that Vastey pointed out that even though Dessalines rectified the primary error that led him to adopt the "inappropriate" title of "governor-general," the title of emperor was similarly problematic. Perhaps more important than the head of state's nomination, Vastey argued that the constitution Dessalines's government ratified was, in effect, a "political monstrosity." While Dessalines eschewed the right to pass down his reign to his descendants, he was still appointed emperor "for life," with the right to name his successor (Article 26). Moreover, the constitution spoke of the formation of three different governmental bodies—legislative, executive, and judicial—but in the same breath stated that these "three powers . . . were reunited in one hand," that of Dessalines. Article 30 made clear that Dessalines was the highest and only authority in the land: "The Emperor makes, seals, and promulgates laws, [and] appoints and dismisses, at his will, ministers, the general-in-chief of the

226   Chapter 7

army, state councilors, generals, and other officers of the Empire, officers of the army and the sea, members of local administrations, government commissioners to the courts, judges, and other public officials."[55] "There was in name a Council of States," Vastey acknowledged, "but it was essentially null and without duties, per the constitution itself." "The empire was an electoral Republic," Vastey concluded, "and in the constitution were princi ples diametrically opposed to the Republic, and that could not at all be appropriate, except for a purely *despotic* government; and what's more, with a strange overturning of ideas, the constitution consecrated the most demo cratic of principles."[56]

While this incoherence in Haiti's first constitution was rectified in later it-erations, other incoherencies and disputes over how sovereign Haiti should be governed and by whom were soon to surface. Early Haitian sovereignty transformed in shape, as Haiti moved from empire to republic, simultaneous state and republic, to republic and monarchy, and then to a singular republic. Despite the numerous changes the constitution underwent during t hese various forms of statecraft, and under varying rulers, the anti-conquest clause remained.

Dessalines was assassinated at Pont-Rouge outside of Port- au- Prince by members of his own military on October 17, 1806. Almost immediately after the assassination, on October 21, General Henry Christophe was named pro-visory president of Haiti. On December 27, the provisory government, now comprising a formal senate, issued a new constitution that transformed the Empire of Haiti into the Republic of Haiti. On December 28, Christophe was officially elected by a self- designated council as the republic's first president. However, Christophe, who was not one of the dozens of men who signed the new constitution, was unhappy with the number of delegates from the north who were excluded from the process by Pétion's faction. Christophe believed his ascension to president under these circumstances rendered him merely a figurehead.[57] Fearing that he might suffer the same fate as Dessalines— after all, he was elected president by the very men he believed orchestrated the em-peror's assassination— Christophe refused to appear in Port- au- Prince to take office. On December 31, he unsuccessfully tried to march with an army against the republic that had just named him president.[58] Afterward, Chris-tophe set up his state in the north of Haiti at Cap-Haitïen, which he eventually renamed Cap- Henry. Rival general Alexandre Pétion stayed in Port- au- Prince and in March 1807 became Haiti's second, but simultaneous, president, over the south. In March 1811, northern Haiti stunned the world when Chris-tophe's Council of State announced their intention to make him Haiti's first king.[59]

With a republic in the south, a monarchy in the north, and a Spanish col-ony in the east, the independence of Haiti must have seemed from the outside to be more incoherent than ever. But examining the different logics of early Haitian statehood reveals that setting up a republic was not common sense in the era of Haitian independence and it especially would not have been for Black people at one time subjected to the very form of slavery that still existed in the only two other republics the modern world had yet seen, the erstwhile slaving French republic and the equally slaving Republic of the United States of America. As the "Injured Man of Color" reminded his U.S. readers, it was the supposedly "*generous* and *enlightened*" French republic that "solemnly promised, and published to the world its promise, to preserve the rights of the people of St. Domingo" and then turned around and "violated their engagements" when they "attempted to enslave and exterminate the inhabitants of that ill-fated island."[60] Because republics carried with them an aura of freedom that veiled the existence of slavery, Vastey devoted an entire chapter in his *Essai* to defending the monarchy as a system of government; and in his earlier *Réflexions politiques*, he argued that the method of government hardly mattered as long as it was "wise, just, enlightened, and benevolent, and the governees have religion, virtues and good morals!"[61] Vastey further wrote that no single form of government could suit all nations, since there were scarcely two separate peoples who were alike. To that end, Vastey paraphrased Baron de Montesquieu (Charles-Louis de Secondat) to prove that it would be an error to insist that a republican government was innately better for the development of freedom than a monarchy since "the best constitution is not the one that is most beautiful in theory, but the one that suits itself the best to the people for whom it has been made."[62] This statement was specifically aimed at the United States. Vastey said Haiti's U.S. neighbors had a democracy that was an exceptionally good form of government with "sage laws," which were specifically suited to the U.S. mindset. His point, however, was that such a democracy was not exportable for the Black citizens of Haiti.[63] The U.S. constitution permitted slavery. Vastey's work challenged developing notions of "American exceptionalism"[64] by making the radical assertion that putative democratic republics could be just as flawed and tyrannical as monarchies.

Before the division of Haiti into north and south, the Constituent Assembly (the eventual Senate) established after the assassination of Dessalines created a new constitution. This constitution maintained the abolition of slavery (Article 1) and banned conquest with nearly the same language as the constitution of 1805 (Article 2). Article 2 of the 1806 constitution inserted one small revision, however, as the new law now emanated from the state itself rather than the state's sovereign ruler, that is, "The Republic of Haiti," instead of the "Emperor of Haiti," "will never form any enterprise with the goal of conquest nor of troubling the peace or the interior affairs of foreign colonies." While

228   Chapter 7

the Imperial Constitution of 1805 was signed by twenty-two men, beginning with Christophe, the republican 1806 constitution (used by Pétion in 1807 after he was declared president of the republic and not revised by his government again until 1816),[65] was signed on December 27, 1806 by a daunting seventy-two men, including Pétion and Boyer, but not Christophe.[66] The preamble to Haiti's first republican constitution made it clear that despite the many signatories, the document, in theory, derived from the citizens of the country: "The people of Haiti proclaim, in the presence of the Supreme Being, the present Constitution."[67] This is a clear echo of an idea found in Jean-Jacques Rousseau's *Social Contract*—that a government's constitution must be a manifestation of the will of the people, who are the state, rather than their ruler. Dumesle observed, in fact, that the 1806 constitution was directly inspired by Rousseau's idea that a sovereign state should not be too closely identified with its sovereign ruler: "The constitution of 1806 wonderfully develops this political theory which distinguishes sovereignty from the sovereign. This idea that J.-J. Rousseau drew from Locke, and which he applied in the social contract, was not the basis of any of the ancient governments. The revolution of England had made it visible; that of France had seized upon it: but here again these attempts were stifled by a devouring anarchy." Pétion, in contrast, was according to Dumesle "a great man [who] has proved in these lands that Europeans call savage, that this idea is not purely an abstraction of the mind."[68] In other words, whereas the British and French, along with Christophe and Dessalines, failed to adopt Rousseau's separation of a sovereign people from its sovereign ruler, Pétion succeeded.

Yet, even as we see republican ideology in Haiti repeatedly pitted against monarchy,[69] the major principles of antislavery, anti-colonialism, and antiracism endured. Under the state's many political iterations Haitian politicians and intellectuals viewed being anti-colonial as key to maintaining early Haiti's sovereignty in a world of slavery. They also framed anti-colonialism as a fundamental characteristic of the Haitian peoples' sovereign identities.

The fact that the anti-conquest article persisted in both the 1806 republican constitution and the 1807 constitution for the state of Haiti under Christophe (while the article requiring the recognition of all Haitians as "black" did not in either, for example) indirectly points to the essential rather than incidental quality of the original 1805 anti-conquest law. Although the article requiring recognition of all Haitians as "black" did not appear in Christophe's 1807 or 1811 constitutions, the article's work in constituting Haiti as *Black* endured. "We are all black, we are happy with our color, just as white people are happy with theirs, black is . . . the generic designation for Haytians!" wrote northern Haiti's Julien Prévost in 1814.[70] The 1816 revision to the republican constitution of Haiti, while not reinserting the blackness clause either, did extend the idea of *Haitianness* (and therefore *blackness*) to white people, without explici tly excluding the French, as in Article 44. Article 39 stated, "They will be recognized as Haitians, t hose whites who are a part of the military, those who are civil servants, and those who were admitted to the Republic at the time of the adoption of the Constitution of 27 December 1806; but no other [whites], after the publication of the present revision can claim the same right, nor can they be employed, nor can they enjoy the rights of citizenship, nor can they acquire any property within the republic."[71] Taking a look at the parts of the Imperial Constitution that did and did not remain under both Christophe and Pétion reveals much about what two of Haiti's earliest rulers considered to be important for state governance.

Dessalines's constitution reversed many of the laws created by the group of men who authored the 1801 constitution: it permitted divorce (General Dispositions: Article 15) and legislated religious freedom (Articles 50–52). The 1806 constitution also allowed divorce, but while it did not completely reverse the religious freedoms established under Dessalines (Article 37), it did proclaim Catholicism to be the state religion (Article 35). In contrast, the February 17, 1807, constitution issued under Christophe's rule, after he established a separate government in the north of Haiti, immediately reversed both trends with respect to marriage and religion. Like the 1801 constitution issued under Louverture, the 1807 version re-outlawed divorce (Article 46) and declared that Catholicism was the only religion that could be professed in public, "though the practice of other religions would be tolerated" (Article 30). An ardent defender of Dessalines's empire and its laws, Christophe seemed ill inclined to accept the idea of religious freedom expressed in Haiti's first constitution, which foretold his elimination of this principle in his own version. On November 13, 1805, Christophe wrote the following letter to General Capoix, "I have been informed, general, *le Vaudoux* is being danced continuously in the quart ier of Bois-de-l 'Anse. If this is true, that quart ier needs your immediate attention, to prevent a dance so prejudicious to tranquility, and which has always been forbidden by every government. You must take, therefore, every measure necessary to prevent this dance and to arrest the performers."[72] Perhaps more tellingly, neither Christophe's 1807 constitution, nor the revised version issued in 1811 after he was declared king by his councilors of state, proscribed white property ownership, which was maintained in the 1806 version, as well as in the revision issued under Pétion in 1816 (Articles 27, 38 and 39, respectively). Claiming Pétion only retained this provision to prove that he was not prejudiced against darker-skinned Haitians, Vastey criticized the president of the republic, saying that his law "excluding all whites in general . . . was so far from being reasonable, that it was also unjust, impolitic, inconsequential, and contrary to the laws of all civilized nations."[73] Vastey said Christophe was opposed to this principle precisely because he was wholly anti-racist:

> His Majesty, the King of Hayti, often said, when he found himself in the position of having to pronounce justice among the whites, the yellows and the blacks, (and it often happens) that he was *green*, in color; he recognizes in [skin] color only the honest man from the dishonest man, which is proof of his impartiality, the precision of his justice, and his deep contempt for that absurd and odious prejudice of color! in vain would anyone accuse us of having that odious prejudice against whites, we hate the French and not their color; those who were our executioners, we hate them, but otherwise we love all men without distinction of color or nation.[74]

Despite the many differences between Christophe and Pétion—their ideas of statehood and monarchy versus republicanism, as well as the role and future of foreign diplomacy—one principle that continued in the republican constitution, and was extended in Christophe's, was the ban against conquest. Article 36 of Christophe's 1807 constitution contained an anti-empire statement that addressed the charge that Haitians allegedly sought to transfer control of the Caribbean from the "whites to the blacks."[75] The 1807 law also addressed much more specifically the idea that Haitians might try to encourage rebellion elsewhere in the Caribbean: "The government of Haiti declares to all the powers of the region, which still have colonies in our vicinity, its unshakeable resolution to never trouble the regimes by which they are governed." Article 37 then returned to the more general anti-conquest language of the 1805 and 1806 constitutions, but turned the spirit of the idea into a material fact by using the present tense rather than the conditional, and by attributing the desire for anti-conquest to Haitians themselves rather than to the head of state or the state itself: "The people of Haiti," Article 37 declared, "do not engage in conquest outside of their island, and limit themselves to preserving their own territory." Anti-conquest had gone from being constitutionally framed as the will of a ruler (1805), to the will of a state (1806), to the fact of a people (1807). "Any idea of conquest is far from our minds," explained Prévost, whom King Henry eventually appointed as minister of foreign affairs and secretary of state. "We limit ourselves only to preserving the territory we possess."[76]

Early Haiti's anti-colonial stance, which did not prohibit actively combating slavery, is also reflected in subsequent Haitian governmental interventions in the Americas.[77] These interventions included Pétion's creation of the southern Republic of Haiti as a "free soil" nation and therefore as an ostensible safe haven for all the enslaved of the world.[78] But it is Pétion's monetary and other material support of Simón Bolívar's Latin American wars of

Anti-colonialism   231

independence, which established the sovereign and eventually the slavery-free states of Gran Colombia (Venezuela, Bolivia, Colombia, Ecuador, Peru, and Panama), which most clearly demonstrates the Republic of Haiti's commitment to anti-colonialism.[79]

Pétion's assistance to Bolívar was a radical collaboration of world historical significance in the struggle against colonialism in the nineteenth century. The ingenuity of Haitian contributions to an age of South American independence that began with Bolívar is best considered from the point of view of Haitians who had a front-row seat to some of the more intricate moments of the collaboration that allowed Bolívar to eventually succeed. In the words of the publisher who printed the book on the topic written by Senator Cinna Marion (aîné), son of General Ignace Marion, Haitian revolutionary and signer of the Declaration of Independence, "Without a doubt, many people are perhaps unaware that this expedition could not have taken place without the assistance that was so generously granted by our government to General Bolívar; even fewer know what was the nature, the extent of this assistance."[80]

———

In 1815, after his defeat in Cartagena, where Bolívar established himself at the head of an insurrection aimed at overthrowing Spanish colonialism, he arrived in Les Cayes, in the Republic of Haiti. Les Cayes was in many ways an obvious choice for him. In 1813, following the December 1812 fall of the First Republic of Venezuela, in the words of one scholar, "The Haitian town of Les Cayes became a revolutionary entrepôt, hosting political agitators, revolutionary fighters, and privateers." By late 1815, the city of Les Cayes once again became a refuge for some of Cartagena's most prominent families fleeing its fall.[81] For Bolívar and his allies, though not necessarily aligned with the elite families already established in the city, the Republic of Haiti remained an anti-colonial safe haven, whose president could potentially help guide them to independence from Spain. That those under the yoke of colonialism and slavery turned to Haiti with hopeful eyes is aptly demonstrated by the words of the French abolitionist, the abbé Grégoire, who later remarked that nineteenth-century Haiti was a "lofty beacon toward which turn the eyes of the oppressors, blushing, and the eyes of the oppressed, sighing."[82]

Upon arriving in Les Cayes in December 1815, Bolívar was received, according to Senator Marion, commander over the city, "with the greatest distinction, and with extreme cordiality."[83] On January 6, 1816, about ten days after Bolívar arrived, ten ships commandeered by Captain Louis Aury, similarly disembarked in Les Cayes.[84] In Marion's retelling, the citizens of Les Cayes took great care of the South American refugees, while Bolívar left for an audience with President Pétion in Port-au-Prince. When Bolívar returned to

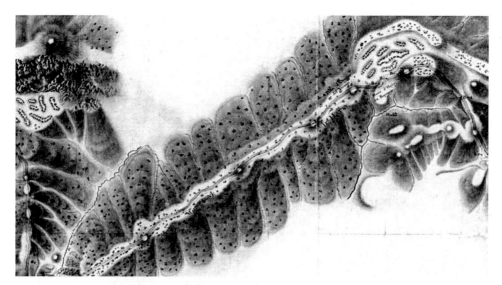

"Quartier de l'Artibonite," showing mountains called "Hayty," from "Carte générale des limites de l'Isle de Saint-Domingue entre la France et l'Espagne conformément au traité definitif conclu à l'Atalaya le 29 février année 1776, représenté en neuf feuilles numérotées et signées," by Jean-Pierre Calon de Felcourt, Marie-Gabriel-Florent-Auguste de Choiseul-Gouffier, and Joaquin Garcia, 1776. Courtesy of Bibliothèque Nationale de France.

Les Cayes a few days after the meeting, he brought a letter of recommendation from President Pétion to General Marion, the highest authority of the city. The letter averred that Bolívar's "pre-occupation with accomplishing this great social and humanitarian mission" received the highest approbation from Pétion. Before leaving Port-au-Prince, Pétion assured Bolívar that he would aid his mission to gain independence from Spain, but that he re-quired one condition in exchange: "the abolition of slavery, in the states that [Bolívar] was going to liberate."[85] Pétion did not hold this stipulation over Bolívar in vain. The Venezuelan revolutionary attempted to enact the man-date when, upon his return to the South American continent, he declared he was emancipating the enslaved Africans of Margarita, Carupano, and Ocumare, as well as those Africans he had enslaved in San Mateo. That Bolívar's newfound abolitionism was directly inspired by Pétion's intervention seems clear in the letter he penned to the Haitian president, dated June 27, 1816. "I proclaimed the absolute liberty of the slaves," wrote Bolívar.[86]

By June 1817, *Le Télégraphe*, the official newspaper of the southern Republic of Haiti, reprinted documents referencing the abuse of Bolívar's laws by some former enslavers who sought to pass off the people they were enslaving as domestics to sell them in other colonies.[87] However, Bolívar had a different

Anti-colonialism 233

"Bust of Alexandre Pétion at the entrance of the Casa Museo de Quinta de Bolívar, Bogotá," photo, 2010. Wikimedia, Creative Commons License BY-SA 3.0.

explanation for the fact that his directives were not being explicitly followed. As to why some of the enslavers from the region had yet to free the people they were keeping in bondage, Bolívar claimed in a letter to Pétion, "Many of them [the enslaved] followed the Spaniards, or boarded English ships that sold them to neighboring colonies." "Barely a hundred showed up," Bolívar continued, "while the number of f ree men who have voluntarily taken up arms is considerable."[88] A subsequent proclamation issued by Bolívar on July 6, 1816, unequivocally reiterated what Bolívar, as "Supreme Chief," previously told the Haitian president about his intent to unilaterally enforce the antislavery laws: "Our unfortunate brothers who are enduring slavery are from this moment forward declared free. The Laws of Nature and Mankind, and the government itself demand their freedom. From now on there will be only one class of inhabitants in Venezuela: all will be citizens."[89] The matter of the abolition of slavery having been agreed to by both men, Bolívar would seek Pétion's assistance once more. The Haitian president had already awarded money, ammunition, and weapons to Bolívar, who was, according to Marion, entirely devoted to the cause of South American independence.[90]

When Bolívar failed to liberate Cartagena in August 1816, the South American freedom fighter returned to Haiti to ask Pétion for more aid.[91] President Pétion had already assisted Bolívar once, which was a remarkable testimony to the anti-colonial commitment of the republic. That he did so a second time only further underscored the theoretical principles that undergirded those material deeds. "If we recall the position of the republic, which was then at war with the North, and its trade which had languished for so long, as a result of the disastrous continental system," Marion wrote, "we will be convinced that the aid given to Bolívar was an immense undertaking for the time; and that nothing more than the sacred cause and commitment of this patriotic leader to free the slaves of his country was needed to bring our government to make sacrifices."[92] P assing o ver i n s ilence t he p art w here Bolívar stopped over and received assistance from Haiti, the Haitian periodical *L'Abeille Haytienne* supplied its readers with historical context for Bolivár's independence movement, which the publication characterized as one meant to "give liberty to the slaves." Venezuelan abolition was one of the Haitian Republic's most signal accomplishments, after i ts o wn r evolution. The writers for *L'Abeille* maintained: "We have detailed the Venezuelan war like so, because it is the most important one from a political and geographical point of view."[93] Like *L'Abeille Haytienne*, the southern republic's *Le Télégraphe* praised Bolívar while remaining circumspect about Pétion's involvement. *Le Télégraphe* reported the positive results of Bolívar's renewed efforts to liberate Cartagena from the Spanish on several occasions in 1817, without mentioning Pétion or the Haitian government's involvement.[94]

Marion offered an explanation for this seeming silencing of the Republic of Haiti's contribution:

> The President recommended guarding the utmost secrecy in the deliveries made to Bolívar: and this was for several reasons: first, to be consistent with this system of apparent neutrality that he wanted to observe; and second, to deprive malicious actors of the opportunity to spread their slander in public, to say, as they always do, that the government is sacrificing the interests of the country in favor of that of foreigners; which would perhaps have produced unfortunate impressions among the people, who are not always capable of being brought to understand, albeit in their own interests, the political logic that determines the decisions of the government; which Pétion wanted above all to avoid. Regardless of all this, he knew that in general people do not like to see what belongs to their country sent abroad. We might say these are sentiments of national selfishness, a feeling from which even the most enlightened people cannot always defend itself.[95]

The material assistance the Republic of Haiti offered to Bolívar had been considerable. On January 26, 1816, Pétion directed General Marion to provide Bolívar with "two thousand shot guns and their bayonettes," along with "as many cartridges and rifle bullets as you can, keeping only a small amount of the cartridges for us." The Haitian republic also provided food, shelter, and money to Bolívar and his men. The republic was evidently all in for the cause of Venezuelan independence, but not publicly so. All of this had to be done "in a manner so as not to be perceived," Pétion warned.[96] It seems Pétion's government also did not want to publicly profess that they had permitted—by "closing their eyes"—a significant number of soldiers, marines, and other important members of society to board Bolívar's ships, "to strengthen those few hundred men," and sail with the expedition back to South America for the cause of freedom.[97]

If Haitian officials from Pétion's early nineteenth-century republic were loath to speak of their encouragement of revolution, independence, and abolition abroad, Haitians of the later nineteenth century felt no such qualms. The later nineteenth-century medical doctor Louis-Joseph Janvier insisted that Pétion exhibited the utmost willingness to materially intervene in world affairs when he gave "weapons, money, and soldiers to Bolívar," which "helped the Colombian patriot to deliver his country from Spanish rule." The ricocheting and longitudinal anti-imperial and antislavery consequences of the Haitian president's collaboration with Bolívar were clear for Janvier: "It is the independence of Colombia and Venezuela that led to that of Peru and Bolivia."[98] Janvier's contemporary, Demesvar Delorme, also evoked Haiti's

236   Chapter 7

historical commitment to combating colonialism and slavery in the Americas when he spoke of the role that the Haitian people played in nineteenth-century South American struggles for independence: "Right next door to us, in America, on the southern continent, there are people who have, like us, rendered themselves independent from their European metropole, who accomplished this feat a long time after we did, and for whom our fathers, already leaders here at home, still went to fight."[99] Yet, it is the Haitian ethnographer Anténor Firmin who is probably the most well known of later nineteenth-century Haitian writers to have linked Pétion's government to the Latin American age of independence. In his *De l'Égalité des races humaines* (1885) Firmin wrote that "the illustrious Bolívar, liberator and founder of five republics in South America," desperate and out of resources, turned to "the black republic in order to request help from it to complete the work of liberation."[100] Quoting this very passage, the late nineteenth-century U.S. Black historian, T. G. Steward observed, "Bolívar's first expedition with his Haytian volunteers was a failure; returning to the island he procured reinforcements and made a second descent which was brilliantly successful." "Haytian arms, money, and men turned Bolivar's disasters to victory," Steward concluded, "and the spirit of Western liberty marched on to the redemption of South America. The liberation of Mexico and all Central America, followed as a matter of course."[101]

Bolívar, like many Haitians and later Black writers, also assigned primary significance to the role that Haiti under Pétion played in Venezeulan independence. Bolívar wrote to Pétion in February 1816, while he was still residing in Les Cayes, "I don't know, I sometimes ask myself, if I should name you as the author of our freedom. I ask Your Excellency to express your will to me in this regard."[102] Not openly publicizing Haitian involvement was politically strategic and geopolitically necessary from Pétion's point of view. His logic of silence, in other words, his desire for his radical intervention in facilitating Venezuelan freedom *not* to be publicized, emphasizes not simply an enduring philosophy of anti-colonialism, but an activist commitment to independence movements. Although writers from Christophe's kingdom were much more vocal about their contributions to anti-colonialism and transatlantic abolitionism (a dynamic to be explored in chapter 8), the situation with Bolívar demonstrates that being antislavery and anti-colonial was as deeply held a belief of Pétion's as it was for Christophe in the north. Pétion responded to Bolívar's question by writing,

> You are aware, General, of my feelings for what you must with your heart defend, and as for you personally, you must deeply understand how much I desire to see emerge from under the yoke of slavery those who

still groan under it, but motives that relate to the consideration I owe to a nation [Spain], which has not pronounced against the Republic in an offensive manner, obliges me to beg you not to declare anything within the limits of the Republic, nor to associate my name with any of your actions; and I am counting, in this regard, on your characteristic good faith.[103]

When he returned to the republic for the second time, Bolívar addressed Pétion with another letter of thanks. This time, he exalted Pétion for his "twenty-five years of sacrifices" in the name of freedom and independence. "Your Excellency possesses a faculty which is above that of any empire, that of beneficence," Bolívar wrote. "It is the President of Haiti alone who governs for the people," he continued. "It is he alone who commands for his equals." Bolívar then directly compared Pétion, "Leader of the republic in perpetuity," to the "great [George] Washington," whose memory Pétion far surpassed. Bolívar presented as another foil "the hero of the North," Henry Christophe, whose "greatest triumph," Bolívar said, "was only that of his own ambition."[104]

It was one thing to profess admiration for the Republic of Haiti privately and quite another to do so publicly. Despite such laudatory and admirable language, in the words of Marion, "this same Bolívar forgot the effective hospitality that he had received among us," when "at the Congress of Panama that he organized [in 1826], to form an amphictyony of all the independent states of the New World, he did not invite Haiti."[105] By that time, Bolívar had succeeded in creating the independent state of Gran Colombia, which helped accelerate the Latin American age of independence that Pétion's assistance enabled. The purpose of the congress, which also included Mexico, was to determine the future shape and direction of the South and Central American republics. According to Marion, the Republic of Haiti, now reunified under President Boyer, was specifically excluded because it was *Black*. Marion located racism as the reason for the exclusion when he sardonically asked, "Is it because our fathers and mothers were in the recent past slaves?" Marion pointed out that the United States' obstinacy vis-à-vis recognizing Haitian independence had something to do with it as well. Despite being a slaving American republic, the United States was invited to the Congress, although one of its two delegates evidently died en route and the other did not make it in time to participate.[106]

Haiti's proposed participation in the Congress was a subject of fervent debate on the floor of the U.S. Senate and seems to have contributed to the country's exclusion from the convening in Panama. Senator Robert Y. Hayne of North Carolina delivered the most heated remarks when he argued that the subject of recognizing Haiti, in any diplomatic fashion, especially at the Congress of Panama, was out of the question. "Our policy, with regard to Hayti, is plain," he said. "We never can acknowledge her independence.—Other States will do as they please—but let us take the high ground, that these questions belong to a class, which the peace and safety of a large portion of our Union forbids us even to discuss. Let our government direct all our Ministers in South America and Mexico to *protest* against the Independence of Hayti. These are subjects not to be discussed any where. There is not a nation on the globe with whom I would consult on that subject, and least of all with the new Republics."[107] The U.S. Congress's hostility to recognizing Haitian independence was well known, leading Marion to wonder, "Did Bolívar, as head of state, capitulate to the demands of the deputies of the American Union who refused to sit with the black and yellow deputies of our country?" Slavery was still king in the United States, and racism was the name of its foreign policy. "Whatever [Bolívar's] motive may have been, Haiti will condemn it forever," Marion concluded. "The politics of statehood do not excuse him for having forgotten that Pétion was the author of the freedom of the people over whom he presided."[108] This occasion was not the first, nor would it be the last, time that Haitians were subject to U.S. racism and/or exclusion from Latin American geopolitical formations.

It is impossible to understand the history of Latin America, and the formulation of such a geopolitical term, without first understanding the Haitian Revolution and Haitian independence. Yet, despite Haiti's position as a "beacon" for other states striving for freedom, Haitians experienced what Marion called a "strange destiny!" of exclusion vis-à-vis the history of those American states that sought liberty after them. It was not just in Latin America that Haiti's revolution served as a beacon for freedom while its independence was used as a cautionary tale. "Everyone rails against the revolution, while everyone benefited from it," Vastey wrote.[109]

Despite the scorn of a world that had no problem philosophically benefiting and materially profiting from a nation they claimed not to recognize, the Haitian people were serving a higher, systemic purpose with the 1804 Principle undergirding their sovereign state. Marion reminded his readers that despite Bolívar's betrayal of Haitian revolutionary principles, and perhaps even because of this, the underlying anti-colonial, antislavery, and antiracist logics of Haitian independence prevailed. They could not be overturned by diplomatic nonrecognition. The state of Gran Colombia was conjured into existence solely because of the assistance of Pétion. "In 1816 we witnessed the *indigènes* of Haiti, known under the denomination of blacks, reach out to whites, owners of slaves, who being oppressed in their turn, recognized the legitimacy of our revolution, and felt strongly, surrounded by persecutors, all that is odious in slavery," Marion wrote. Even if Bolívar betrayed Haiti, many enslaved individuals in South America still achieved their freedom. Marion concluded, therefore, "Bolívar's dealings with Pétion brilliantly highlights the sanctity of the cause that brought about our independence."[110] Without Pétion's insistence on the abolition of slavery, Bolívar might not have made the decision to liberate those still enslaved by the planters of Gran Colombia. The effect of the Haitian 1804 Principle reverberated across South America in the freedom of all the formerly enslaved people who were now longer enslaved, hardly a small thing.

Haitian support of freedom movements around the world was both longitudinal and race neutral, but eliminating chattel slavery was a driving factor. While the Republic of Haiti was willing to put itself at risk to defend liberty and to spread anti-colonial ideas in the Americas, their material support seems to have been limited to areas of the world under the yoke of chattel slavery. Consider, for example, the case of President Jean-Pierre Boyer and the rumor that he sent Haitian soldiers to fight in the Greek war of independence. Before Pétion died in March 1818, he reportedly handpicked Boyer to be his successor. This choice was ratified by the senate in Port-au-Prince and Boyer took immediate office.[111] After Christophe committed suicide on October 8, 1820, Boyer, as the president of the Republic of Haiti, reunited at last the northern and southern sides of the island. Soon enough, he, too was involved in supporting independence movements in another part of the world. In a letter he wrote to Greek revolutionaries in January 1822 Boyer demonstrated his discursive support for their freedom. The letter reveals Haiti's commitment to independence movements outside the Americas, and is thus worth reproducing at length:

To the citizens of Greece
Korais, K. Polychroniades, A. Bogorides and Ch. Klonaris
In Paris

Before I received your letter from Paris, dated last August 20, the news about the revolution of your co-citizens against the despotism which lasted for about three centuries had already arrived here. With great enthusiasm we learned that Hellas was finally forced to take up arms in order to gain her freedom and the position that she once held among the nations of the world.

Such a beautiful and just case and, most importantly, the first successes which have accompanied it, cannot leave Haitians indifferent, for we, like the Hellenes,[112] were for a long time subjected to a dishonorable slavery and finally, with our own chains, broke the head of tyranny.

240   Chapter 7

Wishing to Heavens to protect the descendants of Leonidas,[113] we thought to assist these brave warriors, if not with military forces and ammunition, at least with money, which will be useful for acquisition of guns, which you need. But events that have occurred and imposed financial restrictions onto our country absorbed the entire budget, including the part that could be disposed by our administration. Moreover, at present, the revolution which triumphs on the eastern portion of our island is creating a new obstacle in carrying out our aim; in fact, this portion, which was incorporated into the Republic I preside over, is in extreme poverty and thus justifies immense expenditures of our budget. If the circumstances, as we wish, improve again, then we shall honorably assist you, the sons of Hellas, to the best of our abilities.

Citizens! Convey to your co-patriots the warm wishes that the people of Haiti send on behalf of your liberation. The descendants of ancient Hellenes look forward, in the reawakening of their history, to trophies worthy of Salamis.[114] May they prove to be like their ancestors and guided by the commands of Miltiades,[115] and be able, in the fields of the new Marathon, to achieve the triumph of the holy affair that they have undertaken on behalf of their rights, religion and motherland. May it be, at last, through their wise decisions, that they will be commemorated by history as the heirs of the endurance and virtues of their ancestors.

In the 15th of January 1822 and the 19th year of Independence

BOYER[116]

Although a rumor circulated that a ship with one hundred Haitian volunteers left Haiti for Greece to aid in the revolution but sank along the way, it seems clear from Boyer's letter that no such operation was carried out. In fact, Boyer clearly stated that it was the reunification of Haiti with the eastern side of the island, or Santo Domingo, which was effectively completed later that same year, which prevented Haiti from offering financial assistance to Greece.

The letter's unwitting confirmation that Haiti did not send troops to Greece, at that time, takes us down an important side street to the story of Haiti's long-standing anti-colonialism. Neither Haitians nor Santo Domingans saw Boyer's efforts to bring the eastern side of the island back into the republic as a "conquest."[117] However, at least one rival government characterized it as such. Ironically, this characterization is found in documents from the French government where its officials contemplated the best method to re-conquer Haiti. In 1822, Louis XVIII attempted to set up a spying operation on the Republic of Haiti. Ministers of the French king proposed using as a pretext Toussaint

Louverture's "adopted" son's demand to return to Haiti. Placide Séraphin Louverture had been living in Agen, France, since his family's arrest and deportation in 1802.[118] The French government ultimately deferred responding to Placide's request to return to Haiti, hoping that in so doing they might be able to use Placide to open negotiations that might then lead to the "restoration of Saint-Domingue." The official letter from the French government stated: "Your Majesty's Council, occupied solely with the political inclinations of France, persuaded that the current influence of people of color in Saint-Domingue offers us more opportunities than that of the blacks, whose reestablishment Placide could attempt, is of the opinion that it is advisable to evade the authorization requested by him, or even to approach Boyer, who has become very powerful due to recent conquests, by deferring to him the request of Toussaint Louverture's son."[119] The reference to Boyer having "become very powerful," coupled with the mention of "recent conquests," referred to Boyer's reunification of the island of Ayiti under one government that same year. This development seems to only have heightened France's interest in undertaking its own conquest of its erstwhile colony, which had at that point been free of French domination for eighteen years.

While the Haitian government did not seem to have been able to materially aid the Greek revolutionaries, the Haitian newspaper *Le Télégraphe* reprinted articles from around the world detailing the Greek movement for independence from the Ottoman Empire throughout 1821.[120] Senator Marion wrote of the interest of the Haitian populace in events taking place in Greece, "When Greece uttered its cry of pain, and armed itself against its exterminators, all generous hearts were moved." He then added the detail that the Greek revolutionaries reached out to Boyer for assistance. "They addressed to President Boyer . . . a touching and sublime letter, the reading of which could only move and inspire us. They asked him, if not for battalions, at least for some of those brave warriors who had so brilliantly defended the cause of [our] freedom." In concert with Haiti's growing reputation as a bastion of liberty, Marion seemed to lament what he interpreted as the Haitian government's regrettable refusal to assist the Greeks. "A wonderful opportunity to fulfill a pious duty to liberty eluded us," he complained. "Perhaps if Haiti would have been forced to make some sacrifices; certainly our veterans and our young volunteers would have shed with joy all their blood for such a noble cause, and for the glory of their country, whose name would have been spread throughout the countries of the East."[121] Bolívar's later exclusion of Haiti from the Congress at Panama might have affirmed as the correct move Boyer's reticence to take money from Haitian coffers and put it toward an independence movement whose leaders could turn around and try to exclude, ignore, or isolate Haiti. Senator Marion did not make the connection between Bolívar's later betrayal of Haiti and Boyer's preference to concern himself with affairs closer to home. Marion did wonder in a footnote to the brief passage where he discussed Greek i ndependence, however, if it would have been "possible, appropriate even, for Haitians to go to another world, to travel more than 2000 leagues from their homeland, to fight for a cause in which they were only indirectly interested, especially when they could contribute so many things to their own country?"[122] Even though the Haitian government under Boyer was reticent to send troops to Greece, Haitians found other ways to support i ndependence movements closer to home, particularly where questions of racism and slavery were involved.

Later in the mid-nineteenth century, after the schism that separated Haiti from the Dominican Republic, following the 1843 coup d'état that unseated Boyer, the Haitian people provided aid to Santo Domingo, on the eastern side of the island. Spain, which still maintained slavery in Puerto Rico and Cuba, was interested in reestablishing its authority over the eastern side of the island after its disunification with Haiti. In concert with Haitian claims that the people of the island belonged under one government, Faustin Sou-louque I, who became the second emperor of Haiti in April 1849, two years after being elected president, went on a brief, but failed, campaign to once again reunify Dominicans and Haitians. Soulouque's efforts were opposed by many in the Dominican elite and were later used to bolster anti-Haitian sentiment by those who claimed that Haitians had attempted to colonize the eastern side of the island. Still, after Soulouque was dethroned and sent into exile, the Haitian people supported Dominican opposition to Spain's brief annexation of the eastern two-thirds of the island, despite President Fabre Geffrard's declared position of neutrality.[123]

Yet while Haitian newspapers, at the orders of Geffrard, published mandates declaring they would return Dominican rebels over to the Spanish, "there were also limits" to Geffrard's "cooperation with Spain." Particularly, after Abraham Lincoln's preliminary abolition of slavery in the United States on 1 January 1863—the 59th anniversary of Haitian independence—support among the Haitian people for Dominican freedom especially in Cap-Haïtien, began to swell. Geffrard had to be careful since his "stance of studied neutrality," in the words of historian Anne Eller, was in opposition to the "overwhelming popular support" of Haiti's citizens for Dominican i ndependence from Spain.[124] So ingrained was anti-colonialism into the people of Haiti that they pursued its precepts even in opposition to their own government. By January 1865, various pressures, including a growing independence movement led by rural Dominicans, newfound support from Haiti's president, and the involvement of several Caribbean antislavery and anti-colonial activists such as Ramón Emeterio Betances from Puerto Rico and Cirilo Villaverde from

Cuba, helped "Domincans [to] challenge . . . Spanish authority" and achieve independence, Eller concluded.[125]

In 1870, Betances, during his own exile in Haiti, gave a speech at the Masonic Lodge of Port-au-Prince in which he acknowledged Haiti's ongoing commitment to independence movements in the Americas. He directly implored Haitians to help Cubans end slavery and obtain their independence from Spain:

> Where are the people, who more than any other, have the right to take into their own hands the defense of the oppressed? Your heart has already told you: they are in Haiti; it is you . . . you are Haitians, you are men of equality, you are the sons of those first great citizens who knew how to achieve, for their race, civil and political rights. You are therefore suited to understand better than any other people, this valiant Liberating Army [of Cuba], which is composed of all the races mixed together, and which fights to proclaim, by supporting Cuba against Spain, the honor of raising the same standard of liberty that you made triumphant in Haiti against the power of France.[126]

In the United States, what connected nineteenth-century U.S. African American writers and artists to Haiti was a grammar of solidarity against slavery and colonialism inspired by knowledge of the Haitian Revolution. U.S. African American writers continuously pointed out that Haitian independence exposed an embarrassing truth about the American Revolution. The Haitian revolutionaries used the same violence, physically and discursively, to declare their independence. Yet, unlike the white British colonists of North America, Haitians legislated the U.S. Declaration of Independence's putatively "self-evident" phrase "all men are created equal." While the U.S. founders, most of whom were enslavers, were by turns too cowardly, depraved, or self-interested to end slavery, Haiti's founders saw "liberty" and "equality" as more than just pretty slogans.

The Haitian definition of "liberty" remains the most significant development in the history of modern democracy, and the 1804 Principle undergirding it continues to define contemporary political ideas about what it means to be free. Because he saw Pétion as a public-facing symbol of the spread of the Haitian revolutionary principles of anti-colonialism, anti-racism, and antislavery, Senator Marion wished to see his favorite president's likeness appear in stone in Gran Colombia. "In the National Palace of Santa-Fé in Bogotá, should Pétion not be raised on a pedestal bearing these words from Bolívar: You are the author of our freedom."[127] Of the meaning of the word liberty and Pétion's specific role in helping to spread it across the American hemisphere, Marion concluded, "Pétion's glory reflects on all of Haiti. This was a time when there was no such thing as true liberty anywhere in the New World, aside from in Haiti, America's second independent state. We say true liberty because we cannot refer to as a free country in the 19th century, one whose fields are covered with endlessly tortured slaves. The word liberty, proudly traced by the flag of the United States of America, cannot fill our hearts with enthusiasm, for it is an illusion."[128] What these examples suggest is that nineteenth-century Haiti had not only "taught the world the danger of slavery and the value of liberty," to use the words of Frederick Douglass, but it had demonstrated to that same world that national sovereignty did not need to entail overseas expansion.[129] In one of his letters to General Marion, Pétion reminded him that although the republic was assisting Bolívar, it should "not lose sight of how important it is that the system of perfect neutrality that we profess be followed exactly, and to avoid any misunderstanding which could give concern to any other government, which is for us of the utmost importance."[130]

Various Haitian governments of the nineteenth century, as well as the Haitian people themselves, seemed to have understood sliding scales of difference between seeking to help liberate other enslaved Africans, or attempting to unify the island of Ayiti under one government, and desiring to colonize the other islands of the Caribbean through conquest.[131] There was surely a desire in Haiti to unify the north and the south under Christophe and Pétion, and even the eastern part of the island, as Vastey noted in an 1819 letter to the British abolitionist Thomas Clarkson, but there was not a wish to expand the borders of the country beyond the limits of Ayiti;[132] nor was there any effort to make war on other nations under the guise of transferring the Haitian ideals of universal emancipation and liberty for all human beings to other countries in accordance with the U.S. American government's ideology that it has to the right to "violently export" its democracy to other countries.[133]

Even if Article 36 of the 1805 constitution may have partially been inserted "pragmatically" because of various international pressures, its ideological and philosophical importance appears to be much more longstanding. Except for a brief period of reunification with what is now the Dominican Republic under the presidency of Jean-Pierre Boyer, from 1822 to 1843, Haiti has never occupied any other territory than the one in which it now sits.[134]

Part of U.S. African American outrage at the Wilson administration's occupation of Haiti from 1915 to 1934 appears to have stemmed precisely from the fact that Haiti had not only never colonized any other nation, but it had never declared war against any other country. This made the occupation an indefensibly aggressive act on the part of the United States, as James Weldon Johnson reminded readers of the U.S. magazine, *The Nation*. Johnson

Anti-colonialism 245

observed that Haiti had "never slaughtered an American citizen, it never molested an American woman, it never injured a dollar's worth of American property."[135] W. E. B. Du Bois, too, framed the U.S. occupation as the "violation of a sister state," precisely because Haitians, despite his acknowledgment of their domestic political problems, could be characterized as internationally pacifistic. He wrote, "Here, then, is the outrage of uninvited American intervention, the shooting and disarming of peaceful Haytian citizens."[136]

Even though the anti-conquest ban did not appear again in Haiti after the overthrow of Boyer in 1843, when a new constitution was issued, we do find Haitian intellectuals throughout the nineteenth century such as Pierre Faubert, Demesvar Delorme, Louis-Joseph Janvier, Frédéric Marcelin, and Anténor Firmin continuing to criticize imperialism and collaborating with anti-colonial and antislavery activists from across the Americas, such as Betances and José Martí, which will be a subject of concern in the final chapter of the present volume.[137] If we can clearly see how the existence of an independent Haiti in the nineteenth century ushered in "alternative practices and conceptions of freedom"[138] with respect to slavery, one important legacy of Haitian thought is that it provided the grammar for a politics of anticolonialism to become a virtual universalism among radical intellectuals of the Americas.

Chapter 8

Antislavery

After declaring independence from France, Haitians built a sovereign nation on the 1804 Principle by permanently outlawing slavery and formally banning imperial rule. By establishing a land of freedom in a world of slavery and colonialism, independent Haiti's legislators challenged the contradictions of the Western European Enlightenment, whose proponents intended liberty and equality to be only for white men. The fact of Haitian independence and the instantiation of their antislavery state pushed and held the door wide open for the wholesale destruction of chattel slavery in the Western Hemisphere.

Nineteenth-century Haitian writers were very aware of the ingenuity of the Haitian revolutionaries who fought for their freedom and the longitudinal theoretical implications and material consequences of the resulting fact of Haitian independence. In the words of the nineteenth-century Haitian politician, medical doctor, historian, and novelist, Louis Joseph Janvier, "It is the independence of Haiti that led to the emancipation of the slaves in the English colonies, to the founding of Liberia, and to the emancipation of slaves in Martinique and later, in the United States. It was our independence, which had an influence that has not even been acknowledged." Janvier reminded his readers that the legislative abolition of slavery elsewhere in the Americas only came in the wake of the physical revolution in Saint-Domingue. The existence of an independent, sovereign, and slavery-free state in the middle of the Caribbean had put the Atlantic World powers in an embarrassing position. If "Haiti is an argument . . . that is embarrassing and displeasing," as Janvier wrote, this is because the Haitian revolutionaries exposed an uncomfortable truth about the age of Enlightenment.[1] Haiti's founders believed in the putatively "self-evident" phrase of the U.S. Declaration of Independence, "all men are created equal," more than the author of those words, Thomas Jefferson; and the Haitian people implemented the French Declaration of the Rights of Man's designation of the "natural and imprescriptible rights of man" to be "liberty, property, security, and resistance to oppression," when the French would not. The white legislators of France and the United States were by turns too invested in white supremacy and the economics of slavery to permanently and unilaterally end slavery after their respective revolutions, but Haitian legislators felt no such quandary. For them, victims of more than one hundred years of torture at the hands of white European colonists and enslavers, "liberty" and "equality" were not just republican talking points. They were independent Haiti's signal accomplishment.

As the nineteenth century wore on, the world powers were increasingly compelled by slave rebellions, insurrections, and abolitionist activism to follow in Haiti's lead. Janvier concluded, "It was the independence of Haiti and the sovereignty of Haiti that put an advantageous pressure on certain governments and that led to the emancipation of slaves in Puerto Rico and Brazil."[2] As Michel-Rolph Trouillot pointed out in *Silencing the Past*, powerful actors in the North Atlantic—including heads of state, foreign governments, and academic institutions—worked for two centuries to occlude, suppress, and undermine the radical implications of not just Haiti's revolution but sovereign Haiti's contributions to modern democracy and universal human rights. As emperor, Dessalines demonstrated that he was far more *enlightened* than his U.S. counterpart, President Jefferson. The 1805 Imperial Constitution of Haiti, with its clear antislavery *and* egalitarian mandate—"Slavery is forever abolished . . . equality in the eyes of the law is incontestably acknowledged"[3]— lay bare a damning contrast: it was infinitely possible to eliminate slavery in the declaration of U.S. independence, but Jefferson and the other U.S. founders chose not to. Indeed, the fact that the state of Vermont took early steps toward abolishing slavery in 1777, and that in an earlier draft of the declaration Jefferson railed against the evils of slavery while hardly proposing its abolition, demonstrates just how determined to preserve actual slavery were the U.S. founders, in the end.[4] Although Benjamin Franklin had previously been an enslaver, at the end of his life, while the making of the U.S. constitution and the Bill of Rights was underway, he sent a petition to the U.S. Congress asking for the end of slavery. Franklin counseled the U.S. Senate to "devise means for removing the Inconsistency from the Character of the American People," and to "promote mercy and justice toward this distressed Race." The petition was immediately attacked by pro-slavery congressmen. Afterward, the U.S. Congress claimed not to have the authority to act to abolish or limit slavery until 1808, the year of the proposed ban on the international slave trade.[5] The U.S. republic was therefore founded on principles designed to preserve slavery for as long as possible, in contrast with the Empire of Haiti, which was founded on principles designed to uphold and spread freedom.

When Dessalines died in 1806, the principle of antislavery, like the principle of anti-conquest, did not go with him. The antislavery mandate was repeated in Christophe's 1807 constitution: "Slavery in Haiti is forever abolished."[6] And in great contrast to the U.S. republic, both of President Alexandre Pétion's constitutions for the southern Republic of Haiti, issued in 1806 and 1816, respectively, stated forthrightly, "There cannot exist any slaves in the territory of the Republic; slavery is forever abolished here."[7] In the nine-

248   Chapter 8

teenth century, Haiti, in its many political iterations, became the land of the free and home of the brave to which other freedom fighters in the hemisphere, like Simón Bolívar, looked for inspiration. The persistence of antislavery politics under many forms of government in Haiti proved without a doubt that there was nothing inherently more egalitarian about a republic than an empire or a kingdom. Napoléon had presided over a republic, and yet, his claim to fame is being the only head of state to restore slavery after it was previously abolished. As for President Jefferson, when he had the opportunity to support the Haitian revolutionaries—whom he once called "cannibals of the terrible republic"—and their newfound sovereignty, he did the opposite. Jefferson so feared Haiti's antislavery egalitarianism would spread to U.S. shores that he tried to cut off contact by instituting a trade embargo.[8]

Despite the United States' hostility and continuous threats of reconquest from France, early nineteenth-century Haiti largely thrived. In 1808 President Christophe, during a celebration marking the fifth year of Haitian independence, spoke to the Haitian people about the robust and profitable industry, commerce, and agricultural production of northern Haiti. The president even boasted of ongoing trade with other countries, including the United States. He bragged about the United States' inability to prohibit their citizens from trading with Haiti despite the embargo. In Christophe's words, "You have even seen the citizens of a country whose unjust laws forbid trade with you, hasten, in spite of their Government, to bring us supplies of all kinds, and to become for us one of our most important branches of commerce."[9] Haitian prosperity, as much as Haitian independence, put enormous pressure on slaving empires around the world. The slaving powers, led by the United States and France, did everything they could, short of declaring outright war against Haiti, to disrupt the spread of the 1804 Principle, while commercially benefiting from it.

The Haitian Revolution marked the beginning of the end of what we might aptly call the age of slavery. The Haitian Revolution ushered in an age of abolition that spanned almost the entire nineteenth century. Following the Haitian revolutionaries' permanent abolition of slavery in 1804, Haitian president Jean-Pierre Boyer, as a part of reunification of the island in 1822, abolished slavery on the eastern side of Ayiti, Santo Domingo (present-day Dominican Republic). Great Britain finally abolished slavery in 1833 (with full implementation in 1838). Mexico fully outlawed slavery in 1837. France definitively did so in 1848. Most of South America saw slavery's end by 1850, and the Netherlands declared abolition in 1863, with its full implementation by 1873. The United States, in contrast, only decreed unilateral emancipation after a long and bloody Civil War in 1865, beating just Puerto Rico (1873), Cuba (1886), and Brazil (1888).

Despite their belated willingness to join the age of abolition, French, British, and U.S. abolitionists have been unduly associated with the eventual destruction of the transatlantic slave trade and the elimination of Atlantic slavery. The Trinidadian historian Eric Williams complained about this in his groundbreaking 1944 book *Capitalism and Slavery* when he wrote of the "humanitarians" who helped "spearhead the onslaught which destroyed the West Indian system and freed the Negro": "their importance has been seriously misunderstood and grossly exaggerated by men who have sacrificed scholarship to sentimentality and, like the scholastics of old, placed faith before reason and evidence."[10] In the Haitian case, we must stress that the revolutionaries spearheaded (pardon the pun) the end of slavery with their physical acts and deeds before they turned to legislating abolition in the new state they proclaimed. The "humanitarians" of Great Britain and France who helped to bring about legislative abolition for their respective countries thus followed the lead of the Haitian revolutionaries.

Haiti's fight to end slavery in the Americas did not cease when the Haitian revolutionaries declared victory over France in 1804. Yet, the nineteenth-century French antislavery humanitarian and historian Victor Schoelcher ignored Haiti's ongoing fight for abolition when he suggested that the Haitian people were not using their freedom to help end slavery elsewhere in the Americas. "Is it not a shame that you have not taken any part in the efforts of Europe for emancipation, that you have not even sent any statement of solidarity or sympathy to the friends of emancipation, and that in this republic of emancipated slaves, there is not even a society of abolition?" he asked.[11] Schoelcher was of course deeply mistaken. The entire country of Haiti was an abolitionist society. The 1804 Acte d'Indépendance, Dessalines's April 28 speech, and all early sovereign Haiti's first constitutions reiterated the principles of antislavery, anti-racism, and anti-colonialism upon which the country was founded. These documents, which were translated and published in various international newspapers, were as powerful examples of abolitionist thought as any of the pamphlets, petitions, or speeches of Thomas Clarkson and William Wilberforce. Moreover, many of early Haiti's professional writers decried and deconstructed slavery's many illogics in their historical and political writings.

The two professional writers from early nineteenth-century Haiti who were most known in the Atlantic public sphere were Baron de Vastey and Juste Chanlatte. They both penned antislavery pamphlets, newspaper articles, and books that circulated around the world.[12] Chanlatte addressed his 1810 *Le Cri de la nature* directly to the famous French abolitionist the abbé Grégoire, whose name appears in the full title of the work: *Le Cri de la nature, ou, hommage haytien au très-vénérable abbé H. Grégoire, auteur d'un ouvrage nou-*

-1—
0—
+1—

250   Chapter 8

veau, intitulé De la littérature des Nègres, ou, Recherches sur leurs facultés individuelles, leurs qualités morales et leur littérature; suivies de notices sur la vie et les ouvrages des négres qui se sont distingués dans les sciences, les lettres et les arts.[13] In the opening pages, Chanlatte explained both his logic for dedicating the pamphlet to Grégoire, author and editor of the book referenced in Chanlatte's title, *De la littérature des nègres* (On the literature of Negroes, 1808), and Christophe's reaction to reading Grégoire's book: "President H. Christophe's heart trembled at the voice of justice, and in one of those transports that arise only due to the virtue of feeling and inspiration, he cried out: 'I doubted there was still a man among them.' A New Diogenes, with my lantern in hand, I searched for him amidst the corruption of a century; I finally found him."[14] Amid his discourse on the origins of color prejudice Chanlatte attributed to the Virgin Mary a statement that he said guided his reflections, "I am black, but I am beautiful."[15] Chanlatte also remonstrated against the white colonists and their consorts who "turned man into a material thing, to legitimate and perpetuate their odious tyranny."[16] "Yes! Undoubtedly, there would have to be criminal pretexts from shameless individuals to justify trafficking in one's fellow man," Chanlatte wrote. Using the metaphor of "lifting the veil" that so distinctly characterizes Vastey's later work, Chanlatte added that the colonists legislated color prejudice to uphold slavery and "disavowed with respect to us the unity of the species, in order to, in fact, propose that we are morally inferior, all to somehow legitimate the traffic of those sellers of human flesh and in principle constitute the law of slavery."[17]

Chanlatte's powerful antislavery contributions were recognized by many who read his book and wanted his words to travel even further. The French writer Auguste-Jean-Baptiste Bouvet de Cressé edited and reissued *Le Cri de la nature* in 1824 under the title *Histoire de la catastrophe de Saint-Domingue* (History of the catastrophe of Saint-Domingue). In his preface to the work, Bouvet de Cressé wrote that for him, Chanlatte, as "orator, historian and poet," could be considered "one of the most distinguished writers of the New World."[18] In evaluating Chanlatte's work more directly, the antislavery activist Antoine Métral wrote of *Le Cri de la nature*, "Since the dominant passion of the Haitian people is their love of freedom and independence, the main source of their literature derives from that feeling that they cherish all the more because, on the one hand, they look back with nothing but fear in their eyes on the bondage from which they emerged, and, on the other hand, because they have preserved fond memories for Africa, their homeland. Nothing is more favorable to eloquence than this situation admirably traced in the following text by Juste Chanlatte."[19] Haitians were lovers of freedom, and they continued to fervently condemn not just the fact of slavery, but any person, institution, and nation-state that continued to engage in it. Haiti's thinkers and legislators acquired distinct reputations as vanguards of antislavery discourse.

Vastey's name was familiar to U.S. African American and French antislavery activists as well. Several of Vastey's antislavery book-length pamphlets were translated and reviewed across Western Europe and North America, for example;[20] and excerpts of his *Réflexions sur une lettre de Mazères* (1816) appeared in English translation in the first U.S. African American newspaper, *Freedom's Journal*, on December 12, 1828, and February 7 and 14, 1829, respectively.[21] Yet it is actually Vastey's earlier *Le Système colonial dévoilé*—which circulated heavily in its original French throughout the early United States but was only fully translated into English in 2014[22]—that demonstrates the world historical reach of the Haitian Revolution against slavery and its Haitian chroniclers.

In *Le Système*, Vastey argued that Haitians were the only revolutionaries to have created a sovereign anti-colonial, anti-racist, and antislavery state after colonial upheaval. It was the anti-colonial, anti-racist, and antislavery principles of the Haitian Revolution that made it, and not the U.S. or French revolutions, the "triumph of humanity."[23] Vastey more specifically inserted independent Haiti into the philosophical discourses and activist traditions of transatlantic abolitionism when he wrote, "I hope that Haiti will serve as the point of departure for the philanthropists who can here stake the powerful lever that will be required to lift up the moral world against the enemies of humankind."[24] The "enemies of humankind" were of course the enslavers and colonists. Haiti was at a very different moment with both Europe and the rest of the Americas at that historical juncture, which made it possible for Vastey to imagine a world where Haiti was not the recipient of the world's benevolence, but rather where Haiti provided a space from which to spread antislavery and anti-colonial ideals and actions. It was because of the example that Haiti set and the meaning of Haitian freedom that Vastey proclaimed in his later *Réflexions politiques* (1817), "the cause of the Haitian people" "involves all of humankind."[25] For him, it behooved humanitarians around the world to support not just the end of slavery but the creation of Black sovereignty in its stead.

Vastey argued that Black sovereignty was the natural and desirable outcome of abolition. There are two kinds of sovereignty evident in Vastey's works—personal sovereignty and political sovereignty. For Vastey, both were fundamental to promoting racial justice, but only one had the capacity to do so from an institutional perspective and with a longitudinal, ricocheting outlook. Only political sovereignty could change the status of every enslaved person. In the United States before 1865, political sovereignty was not really an option, even for the free people of color, who could not become citizens.

Vastey therefore highlighted a difference between the form of individual sovereignty in the U.S. fight against slavery, which later became popular to narrate in the U.S. African American slave narrative (autobiographies of fugitives from slavery like William Wells Brown, Frederick Douglass, Harriet Jacobs, etc.), and the forms of political sovereignty mandated in Haiti's founding documents (the texts that abolished slavery in all of Haiti and established Haitian independence). Haitians were free and independent regardless of personal inclination, that is, one person's ability (even within a larger network like the Underground Railroad) to render themselves individually free from chattel slavery, or for the person enslaving them to offer freedom. It is precisely because of the difference between personal and political sovereignty that Vastey believed the goal of transatlantic abolition needed to be the creation of more political institutions in which Black people would play a central part.

Vastey's writing remained vital in the international Black community well into the nineteenth century, as observed by James McCune Smith's high-profile reference to *Le Système* in his own "Lecture on the Haytien Revolutions," given at the Stuyvesant Institute on February 24, 1841 and reprinted in the *Colored American* on August 7, 1841.[26] In 1851, Henry Bibb also referenced *Le Système* in his Upper Canada newspaper, *Voice of the Fugitive*. For Bibb, Vastey's writing helped to make the case for not only the triumphant meaning of the Haitian Revolution but the equality of the human *races*. "Here it will be observed," Bibb wrote of Vastey, "that one of our calumniated race shows himself capable of entering the arena and vindicating his claim to an equality with the whites, in a diction as polished, and with ideas as forcible as have been elicited on the opposite side of the question."[27] Bibb thus extended Vastey's sense of the Haitian revolutionaries' profound impact on world history to Haitian authors too.

Vastey's writings were also central to how U.S. Black writers thought and wrote about the history of slavery and the ongoing fight for racial justice after abolition. I have elsewhere written about Vastey's influence on W. E. B. Du Bois, Mercer Cook, and Alain Locke.[28] We can add to the list of famous Black readers of Vastey's works from the United States, Eric Walrond and Arturo Schomburg. In the April 22, 1922 edition of the famous Harlem Renaissance era magazine, *The Negro World*, Walrond recalled a visit to the library of the Puerto Rican American bibliophile, collector, and scholar Arturo Schomburg in New York City. Walrond, who was accompanied by then graduate student Zora Neale Hurston, described Schomburg's excitement as he presented several rare books and other documents before his young visitors. Among those texts was Baron de Vastey's *Le Cri de la patrie* (1815), a pamphlet whose title Schomburg translated as "Cry of the Fatherland in the Interest of All Haytians," and which Schomburg called, "of course a very valuable work."[29]

Antislavery   253

Later, in his celebrated 1925 essay, "The Negro Digs Up His Past," Schomburg wrote that Baron de Vastey's *Cry of the Fatherland*, "the famous polemic by the secretary of Christophe," formed a part of a larger body of writing by diasporic American Blacks, which included Julien Raimond, so impressive as to become "evidence . . . of scholarship and moral prowess" "too weighty to be dismissed as exceptional."[30] Schomburg's sense that the Haitian Revolution *and* its writers deserved a distinct place in Black American history and in the annals of world history repeatedly surfaced in U.S. African American analyses of the impact of Haitian independence. Haiti's homegrown antislavery had provided the backbone of the philosophical, legal, and material efforts of U.S. Black Americans to spread the Haitian Revolution's principles of freedom and equality in the hopes of ending slavery in the United States.

Aside from circulating documents useful for abolishing slavery, Haitian authors from across the long age of abolition sent both direct and indirect antislavery statements to Black people around the world still subjected to slavery. In his *Mémoires pour servir à l'histoire d'Haïti* (1804), Louis-Félix Boisrond-Tonnerre wrote that the revolutionary history of Dessalines was itself a mandate for the inevitable liberty and undeniable humanity of "slaves" everywhere: "Haitians, whom the bravery of a true hero has lifted out of the anathema of prejudice, in reading these memoirs, you will be able to see with your own eyes the abyss from which he has rescued you. And you, slaves of all nations, you will learn from this great man [Dessalines], that every person naturally carries liberty in his heart, and the keys to that liberty are in his own hands."[31] Boisrond-Tonnerre stands in a long line of Haitian politicians, historians, and other thinkers from Haiti, including Dessalines, who discussed Haitian independence as the beginning of a revolutionary consciousness that could only lead to universal emancipation across the Atlantic World.

In his famous April 28, 1804 proclamation, recall that Dessalines called out to the "unfortunate Martinicans!" whom the French colonists were still torturing with slavery. "If only I could fly to your aid and break your chains!" Dessalines said, before suggesting that Haiti's revolutionary principles might travel to Martinique like embers through the air: "Perhaps a spark from the fire that ignites us, will alight in your soul; perhaps at the sound of this commotion, awakened with a start from your lethargy, you will claim, weapons in hand, your sacred and imprescriptible rights!"[32] Note here that Dessalines took the word "imprescriptible" that appeared in the 1789 Declaration of the Rights of Man, alongside the phrase "resistance to oppression," to remind Haiti's Martinican neighbors that they held the keys to their own liberty. The message was clear. Haiti was more than an example. It was a blueprint. Dessalines was hardly the only Haitian thinker of the nineteenth century to say so. The

254   Chapter 8

later nineteenth-century Haitian poet Emmanuel F. Édouard dedicated his book of poems published in 1882, *Le Panthéon haïtien* (The Haitian pantheon), "to the negro slaves of Cuba, the negro slaves of Brazil, [and] the youth of Haiti." In his letter to the Haitian minister of education that Édouard included in his volume, he said, "It is to us that consoled humanity owes, definitively, its considerable progress toward the abolition of slavery in the Americas, with Brazil and Cuba being exceptions, which shamefully cannot endure for too much longer."[33] Édouard shared Janvier's sense that Haiti remained a decisive player, not at all a bystander, in the ongoing struggle for the liberation of enslaved people across the hemisphere, especially in Cuba and Brazil.[34]

After the French belatedly abolished slavery in 1848, mid-nineteenth-century Haitian authors praised their abolitionist counterparts in the antebellum United States for continuing to attack slavery in multivalent ways. Joseph Saint-Rémy dedicated his publication of Toussaint Louverture's memoirs, *Mémoires du général Toussaint-L'Ouverture, écrits par lui-même* (1853), to the U.S. abolitionist, "Ms. Harriet Beecher Stowe, author of the philanthropic novel *La Case de l'Oncle Tom, ou Vie des Nègres Aux Etas-Unis* [Uncle Tom's cabin, or negro life in the United States]."[35] In his dedication, Saint-Rémy said to Stowe that her novel would help the United States to "attack slavery" and in effect "succeed in vanquishing that monster." This was because the abolitionists, in Saint-Rémy's estimation, had "the truth" and Stowe herself—"daughter of the heavens"—on their side.[36] The Haitian dramatist and poet Pierre Faubert also praised Stowe's *L'Oncle Tom* in a note accompanying the publication of his play, *Ogé, ou le prejugé de couleur* (1856). Faubert wrote that while a seemingly endless production of pro-slavery novels were being circulated around the world, he was comforted by Stowe's contribution to abolitionist thought and called her epic, "that little volume that moved the two worlds."[37] Faubert's claim that the two hemispheres of the world could be moved to humanitarian action by abolitionist writing like Stowe's, as equally as by his own, demonstrates a conception widely shared among nineteenth-century Haitian authors that Haitians had a duty to intervene in international antislavery efforts, both materially and discursively. If Europeans used the printing press to support slavery and colonialism, Haitians recognized the press to be a very powerful technology that the enslaved and formerly enslaved could also use to maintain and spread their own sense that freedom, equality, and the end of slavery required Black sovereignty.

Schoelcher's admonition that Haitians sent no antislavery statements abroad thus rings hollow, both in the era in which his complaint was issued and in the years that followed. His biases led him to silence the radical ingenuity and ongoing possibilities of Haitian sovereignty. It is not enough to merely expose Schoelcher's ignorant refusal to recognize the longitudinal significance and ongoing contributions of Haitian independence and the Haitian people to the transatlantic abolitionist movement with which he, himself, is more closely associated in the annals of world history than any of the Haitian writers mentioned here. Not only did Schoelcher write his book after visiting Haiti in 1841, but he also evinced knowledge of Haiti's constitutional principle of anti-conquest, which prevented the Haitian state from exhibiting aggression to other states through "meddling." Schoelcher had done the reading, but he seemed to lacked understanding. Even in acknowledging that Haiti was an antislavery state precariously surrounded by slaving empires, Schoelcher deliberately elided Haiti's contributions to antislavery thought. In so doing, he willfully silenced the radicality of Haitian sovereignty. "What role does Haiti play in the middle of the Antilles, where it could, where it should impose great influence?" Schoelcher asked. "None at all." His professed knowledge of Haitian literature and laws make his dismissal of the individual acts of protest evident in nineteenth-century Haitian acts and deeds even more curious:

> The constitution, I know, forbids you from doing anything of a nature that might overshadow the other powers with respect to the regime of their colonies, and the executive power cannot be blamed for having forbidden Haitian merchants from going to the islands that have slaves or to the Carolinas in the United States. Haiti, not being in a state to enforce its pavillion, it is wise not to expose the country to insults that it would not be possible to avenge. But, without taking the risk of being compromised, couldn't you, with some individual act, protest against the system of absolute isolation adopted by your government? [President Boyer] seems to be determined to make the rest of the universe forget Haiti. Shouldn't you oblige the world to speak about you?[38]

Haitians did far more than oblige the world to incessantly talk about their country.[39] The world powers felt compelled, in both good and bad ways, to react to Haitian sovereignty throughout the nineteenth century.[40] The Haitian Revolution and Haitian independence led directly to Great Britain's abolition of the international slave trade in 1807.[41] Haiti's *Gazette officielle* reprinted the for and against debates that led to Great Britain's abolition of the slave trade, which included reference to the "example of Saint-Domingue."[42] The Haitian Revolution inspired slave revolts and rebellion across the Americas too and served as an incessant talking point in the transatlantic abolitionist movement.[43]

Moreover, every Haitian state, from Dessalines to Boyer, interfered with the slave trade both discursively—in individual and collective acts of protest—and materially. These interventions had the world talking. On January 14,

-1—
0—
+1—

256   Chapter 8

1804, Dessalines issued the following statement, "Considering that a great number of negroes and people of color from this island, are found at present on the American continent, in a state of extreme misery, because they lack the means to return to their country, it is decreed: 'Article 1: There will be allocated to captains of American ships a bonus of 40 dollars (200 francs) for each individual designated above who they can return to their country. Article II. The present decree will be printed, published, and posted, and a copy will be addressed to the congress of the United States.'"[44] This policy was more than just a quixotic and ultimately ignored intervention. The letter from the "Injured Man" that we examined in the previous chapter reveals that U.S. readers were distinctly aware that Dessalines had written a letter to U.S. American merchants requesting the return of any Black people from Haiti (Saint-Domingue) who might have been transported to U.S. shores. Of this, the "Injured Man" wrote, "To you, O Haytians! who are on this continent . . . embrace the offer of your Chiefs: accept their invitation to return to your home . . . accept the opportunity which Divine Providence has so bounteously placed in your hands, to reclaim your rights and maintain your country's cause: convince the world that you are not without courage, and that life is not worth your care when deprived of your original inherent rights."[45] An article published in the *Journal de Paris* derided Dessalines's statement and commented on what the writer characterized as the audacity of Haiti's then governor-general to believe that he could treat with the United States as "one power to another power."[46] The article from the *Journal* previously appeared in the United States, where it was printed in both its French original and in English translation in the *New York Herald* on March 31, 1804.[47] While it is not clear if any Haitians were ever returned under this particular incentive of Dessalines's, sometime in late 1805 or early 1806, Dessalines sent Christophe two men with French names who had recently arrived from the United States. Although Christophe did not mention how the men came to Haiti or reveal anything about their origins or skin colors, he observed that he followed the emperor's orders to have the two men, Jean Colar and Auguste, incorporated into the first and twenty-seventh demi-brigades, respectively.[48]

Although Pétion was much more circumspect than Dessalines about his own involvement in antislavery activities in Venezuela via Bolívar—recall that Pétion expressly did not want the press to report on his interventions—his "free soil" policy was a different story. Pétion's attempt to expand freedom to fugitives from slavery in the United States was highly publicized, with ministers from Pétion's government even issuing public statements formally inviting free Black people from the United States to emigrate to the Republic of Haiti. On October 17, 1818, the *Niles Weekly Register* belatedly published the text of a November 1817 letter from Haiti's secretary-general B. Inginac to a Mr. James Tredwell, inviting the "coloured people in America to emigrate to that country." The antislavery Tredwell had previously traveled to Haiti and subsequently published the text of Inginac's letter in his book, *The Constitution of the Republic of Hayti* (1818). The article from the *Niles Weekly*, titled "People of Color," opened with a preamble: "The following official communication from the secretary general of the Haytian republic is highly interesting to all whom it may concern in the United States. The communication was made in reply to an enquiry—*What privileges people of color might expect who should emigrate thither from America.*" In Inginac's letter, as reprinted in the *Niles Weekly*, the Haitian secretary-general said he "communicated to H.E. the president of Hayti, the verbal message which [Tredwell] brought me from your fellow countrymen, the black and colored men of the city of New York, who groan under the dominion of a barbarous prejudice, and desire to become partakers of those blessings which the constitution we have given ourselves affords." Inginac then reminded his interlocutor that the Haitian people had "sacrificed twenty-eight years of their life, in order to efface the traces of a yoke to which other men, who pretend to virtue and justice, had too long enchained them." "Men, women, and children, of our color," Inginac continued, "let them come, we will receive them with pleasure, and we wait for them with open arms." Going on to describe the many benefits that the "colored" emigrants would enjoy in the free Republic of Haiti, in contrast to the United States' slave republic, Inginac ended the letter by saying, "I shall be flattered, sir, if this statement of facts, this genuine picture, which you can present to our unhappy fellow countrymen, shall determine a great number of them to come and console themselves beneath the protection of our laws. . . . The government will pay the passage of those who have no means, at the rate of forty dollars per head for men and women, and half that sum for children from three to twelve years of age."[49] The article in the *Niles Weekly* concluded with four laws from the Haitian Constitution of 1816, issued at the time Pétion was declared to be "President for life" of the Republic of Haiti. Article 44 contained the "free soil" policy: "All Indians, Africans, and their descendants, born in the colonies or elsewhere, who shall hereafter reside in this republic, shall be acknowledged as Haytians; but they shall not enjoy the rights of citizenship until they shall have resided one year within the limits of the republic."[50] Also included was Article 1, which would have been of utmost interest to the audience for the *Niles Weekly*, since it offered a life of freedom to any of those "Indians, Africans, and their descendants," who might take the Haitian government up on its offer: "There cannot exist any slaves on the territory of the republic; slavery being forever abolished." In the nineteenth-century Americas, this provision made all of Haiti, even with its stark division of a republic in the south and a monarchy in the north, a land where freedom and equality were universal. Article 38, which was later interpreted by U.S. politicians as a white property exclusion clause, also appeared in the *Niles Weekly*, but with something other than a literal translation. The *Niles Weekly* printed: "No white man, of whatever nation he may be, shall ever set his foot on this territory under the title of *master* or *planter*." A more faithful translation of Article 38 would be: "No white man, of whatever nation he may be, shall ever set his foot on this territory under the title of master or property owner (*propriétaire*)."[51] The choice of the *Niles Weekly* to translate the word "propriétaire" as "planter," with the double resonance that word has with slavery, may have been an effort to soften the charge that Haitians were isolationist and even themselves prejudiced. More likely, it was tacit recognition of something the most honest and astute foreign interpreters of Haitian law knew: Article 38 was about forbidding the white ex-colonists from returning to Haiti, yes, those enslavers who euphemistically called themselves *planters*.[52]

It did not take long for pro-slavery politicians in the United States to misinterpret the law in service of preserving slavery and isolating Haiti. When Inginac, under President Boyer, invited the United States to be "the first New World republic" to recognize Haitian independence, President James Monroe responded to the request during a session of the U.S. Senate on February 26, 1823. Monroe remarked that formal recognition of Haiti was out of the question since it was a land where "provisions . . . prohibit the employment in the government of all white persons who have emigrated there." Monroe said there were also laws that prohibited the "acquisition by such persons of the right of citizenship or to real estate in the island . . . [which] evinces distinctly the idea of a distrust of other nations."[53] Some nineteenth-century Haitian writers also criticized Articles 44 and 38. Article 44, in particular, contributed to the *guerre de plume* between the north and the south because of Christophe's and Pétion's differing interpretations of what it meant to operate with "neutrality" in the hemisphere. This had already been an issue when the kingdom became aware of Pétion's relationship with, and assistance to, Bolívar. The *Gazette royale* reported the kingdom's disapproval: "We can affirm that Carthaginian corsairs are not frequenting the ports of the kingdom; that Haitians, far from wanting to expatriate themselves in order to serve as instruments for any [foreign] faction whatsoever, are determined to remain peacefully at home, where they have enough to do to consolidate their freedom and independence, without needing to go and imprudently throw themselves into enterprises contrary to the laws of their countries, and to their natural inclinations, and they have strongly pronounced that they will never abandon their native soil."[54] In much the same vein, Vastey explained the kingdom's problem with the more overtly public "free soil" policy of the republic: "Now, with article 44, you have made a direct appeal to the black and yellow population of the colonies of foreign countries, to come and settle in the Republic, you offer them the right of asylum, which is sacred and inviolable in the Republic, according to article 3 of the constitution, and the prospect of being able to enjoy the rights of citizenship after one year of residence; which tends directly to disturb the peace and the internal regime to which those colonies of foreign countries are subject."[55] Vastey vehemently argued against the slave trade and the horrors of colonialism in his *Reflexions sur une lettre de Mazères*, *Le Système*, and *Notes à M. Le Baron de V.P. Malouet*, but simultaneously affirmed that Haitians were not going to meddle in the affairs of the other countries in the hemisphere. On this account, Vastey pointed out (and as Schoelcher repeated) that Christophe's codes, as Dessalines's 1805 constitution had already done, expressly prohibited Haitians from interfering with "affairs outside of our island."[56] Even if we view Vastey's (and by extension Christophe's) opposition to the article as more political than philosophical, later Haitian authors similarly worried about the effects of such laws. Of Article 38, which was not officially off the Haitian law books until the U.S. occupation in the early twentieth century, the anti-Boyer Saint-Rémy wrote, "This system, in continuing a fatal antagonism among members of humanity—who are all unified among one another—will retard the moral and intellectual development of men who have a black face like me."[57] Writing in 1851, decades after the law was instated, and divorced from the original context in which it was mandated, it is easy to see how Saint-Rémy arrived at this critique. The world seemed to fear Haiti and Haitians and brought punishment to them repeatedly for their elimination of slavery and creation of a sovereign Black state. Saint-Rémy's mistake was his inability to see that pre-1825 Haitian laws, issued before the indemnity agreement, were reflections of that reality.

Not long after the Louisiana Purchase in 1803, the relationship between independent Haiti and the United States considerably cooled. An article published in the October 17, 1804, issue of Haiti's *Gazette politique et commerciale* and written by Joseph Rouanez provided a prescient analysis of the more metaphysical meanings, rather than the purely material effects, of the change that U.S.–Haitian trade relations underwent once the pro-slavery Thomas Jefferson became president. Rouanez wrote that the United States would one day inevitably "occupy a distinguished rank among the masters of the Sea." The justification for this prophecy now seems so clairvoyant that it is worth quoting from the piece at length. Averring the inevitable decline of France and England, the article reads: "The same thing will befall the powers that are presently dominant; they will undergo an unmistakable decline, while the

260 Chapter 8

United States will assume the rank to which it is destined. But this era will become deadly for the Caribbean. It will simply change masters. It will come under the yoke of the United States." The Caribbean was not in danger of being overrun by Haitians. The real danger, according to Rouanez, was the United States. Rouanez found it was obvious that the United States had designs to take over the whole continent. Louisiana was a case in point. As for ongoing U.S. slavery, "in the states of the south, [it] is a fire that smolders under the ashes, the eventual explosion of which will one day make tremble the hardened and deaf masters who still maintain it, despite the prudent advice of their fellow citizens of the north." Like Boisrond-Tonnerre, who urged that the "keys to liberty" were already in the hands of the enslaved people across the Americas, Rouanez, who likewise fought in the Haitian Revolution, warned that one day "some audacious avengers will reclaim with interest their natural rights that have been violated." While most Haitians believed that France was their greatest enemy, with this article the Haitian people were asked to not discount the much more serious danger next door in North America:

> [France's] attempts will come crashing down like the waves of the sea at the foot of the rock of our independence, and from the mountains our rescue squad will descend upon them. But a more hidden danger, and one far less apparent, as it is still distant for now, threatens us anyway; it will not be from Europe that our ills must come, if we are to ever experience them, it will come from the continent of the United States: their too close proximity, the constant comings and goings of their citizens in our ports, the expectations that they will bring with them, if our government does not restrict them, must open our eyes to the plots that they may one day attempt against us.

"It is not at all my intention," Rouanez finished, "to attempt to place a cloud over the conduct of the Americans, nor do I think at all that, either the present government or the individuals who are linked to it through commercial relations with that country, have thus far had any plans to dominate us, nor to meditate on our enslavement." Yet, he said, "it is no less true that the possibility of such a combination could arise from a concurrence of circumstances, if ever the United States were to erect itself to become a maritime power."[58]

The U.S. trade embargo against Haiti did not completely end all commercial exchange between the two countries, but it did reflect the multipronged nature of attacks on Haitian sovereignty in the first three decades of independence.[59] Not only were the French at least partly responsible for the increasingly cold and distant relationship between Haiti and the United States, but Napoléon had not entirely given up his designs of regaining control of the entire island. The fact that the French were at first still in possession of Santo Domingo and therefore had military ships constantly in the vicinity of Haiti presented distinct perils. In March 1806, French corsairs captured three Haitian *caboteurs*, or coasting ships, and subsequently kept some of the men in their possession. The French eventually released eight of the men and two of the ships, but not before having dismantled and otherwise destroyed them. Christophe was greatly distressed when he learned of this event from General Paul Romain. Consequently, he urged Dessalines to take every measure possible to stop such sabotage. Otherwise, "I foresee that every kind of evil might arise," he said. "The war that we are in with the French being eternal to the death, our ships, since they are weaker, should rather crash into the side of these corsairs and the indigenous should prefer to drown themselves than to allow themselves to be captured."[60] The words "Liberty or Death" stamped so prominently atop Dessalines's April 1804 proclamation were not a chimeric banner, but a part of the difficult reality of trying to remain free and sovereign in a world of slavery.

The threats to newly sovereign Haitians were the cause of and the logic behind the property proscriptions in both Dessalines's and Pétion's constitutions. Beaubrun Ardouin explained this in a publication directed at the French abolitionist Antoine Isambert in 1842. Ardouin wrote that the law was a protection against certain "traveling friends" who came to "encourage discord" and "give the most perfidious advice" to Haitian leaders.[61] Such "perfidious advice" had abounded since Haitian independence and was particularly characteristic in the Kingdom of Haiti, which was populated by many foreigners.

———

Turning the Kingdom of Haiti into a safe haven for the enslaved of the world, qua Pétion's republic, was a bridge too far for Christophe. Yet writers from the kingdom were just as active as writers from the republic in corresponding and engaging transatlantic abolitionists to come to Haitian shores. Pétion famously entertained abolitionist Stephen Grellet,[62] both Pétion and Christophe corresponded with William Wilberforce, and Christophe employed Prince Saunders and kept up a robust correspondence with Thomas Clarkson.[63] But if President Pétion measurably interrupted Spanish colonialism when he assisted Bolívar, it was Christophe, first as president and then as king, who committed Haiti to disrupting a primary node of transatlantic slavery: the Middle Passage. On Christophe's directive, his soldiers contributed multiple times to antislavery struggles by seizing slaving vessels and liberating their captives.[64]

262   Chapter 8

The most famous and widely cited of Haiti's liberation operations occurred in October 1817 in the Kingdom of Haiti. The *Royal Gazette of Hayti* reported that a Haitian warship captured a Portuguese frigate near the port of the northern city of Cap-Henry. The ship was on its way from Cape Verde, off the western coast of Africa, to Havana when officials from the Kingdom of Haiti took control of it and set free 145 Africans, "victims of . . . the odious traffic in human flesh." The captives, the account noted, were in "an awful state," many had already perished and the survivors "looked like ghosts ready to die of misery and starvation." Once ashore in Haiti, they were greeted by a crowd who assured them that "they were free and among brothers and compatriots."[65] Seven years earlier, the northern Haitian military captured a different Portuguese slaver carrying two Hausa-speaking children. These "nouveaux *haytiens*," as they were called, were as stunned to hear their native language spoken in Haiti as they were surprised to find some of their "former countrymen" already living there. "It was as if they were meeting once again the parents from whom they had been ripped away."[66] It was not unusual to find recently arrived Africans from the continent in Haiti. The northern military previously intervened to stop the slave trade on February 2, 1811 when they captured a Spanish ship, the *Santa Ana*, and liberated 205 Africans shackled in the hold.[67] But out of revenge, Spanish and Portuguese slavers began to attack Haitian merchant ships and engage in raids on Haitian beaches, seizing men, women, and children to sell into slavery. In 1812, a schooner from Cuba captured a Haitian brig, the *Poule d'Or*, and sold its captain, Azor Michel, and two children aboard in Trinidad. Azor and the children were only returned after Christophe intervened to request "the return of all Haitian subjects who are or may still be detained by Cuba."[68]

Such operations did also take place under Pétion's presidency, especially in the Bolívar era, and, again, under the presidency of Boyer after Pétion's death in 1818. In 1819 a southern Haitian warship, aptly titled the *William Wilberforce*—architect of the 1807 ban on the slave trade in Great Britain—captured a Spanish slaving ship, headed for Cuba, and subsequently released everyone on board.[69] Boyer demonstrated even more stern opposition to slavery in connection with Haiti's "free soil" laws. An article published in the *Anti-Slavery Record* offered an anecdote about Boyer protecting two Jamaican fugitives from slavery in the era before Great Britain abolished slavery. Noting that the two individuals fled from Jamaica in a sloop, the paper said they subsequently reached Haiti and hid in its mountains. "Boyer immediately informed the Governor of Jamaica of the fact and offered to return the sloop as soon as it should be properly claimed," the paper continued. Yet when a British ship captain arrived in Haiti to inquire about the "runaways,"

Boyer had the sloop relinquished to them, but refused to release the "fugitive slaves," it being a "very 'delicate' matter" to ask this of "the President of a 'free negro' republic." Boyer reportedly said to the ship captain, "I have heard that slaves sometimes escape from the colonies to England, will you please to inform me whether they are delivered up on a claim of their masters?" The captain replied, "Every man is free in England; the law allows no slavery there, nor can the master recover his slave there." To which Boyer responded, "Well, tell your king it is just so in Hayti." In other words, the Republic of Haiti was an unequivocal free soil republic—and could not therefore put a free person back in chains—just as metropolitan England was supposed to be a free soil kingdom.[70]

The commitment of the republic to abolition endured throughout Boyer's presidency, and he even sent a member of his cabinet to attend British Antislavery Society meetings in London.[71] The Haitian people seemed just as committed as their president. In January 1843 when the Spanish demanded damages of two thousand dollars for Spanish vessels captured and being held in the republic and an "apology to the Spanish flag," the Haitian newspaper *Le Manifeste* responded with more than a threat. "Let the governor of the island reflect and abandon his outrageous pretensions," the newspaper stated. "A very narrow channel separates us from Cuba. We can reach there in one night, deliver that colony up to blood and fire, and while avenging ourselves, become the liberators of our race, which languishes there in slavery." The next passage of the article illustrates Haitians' own sense of their power and might when it came to their country's antislavery reputation: "This would for Haiti be an enterprise so glorious, that at the slightest manifestation of hostility on the part of the Spanish authorities, the *elite* of our youth would clammer to form part of the expedition that would plant in Cuba the tree of liberty!"[72] Notice here the extension of the Franco-Haitian grammar of solidarity to enslaved people in Cuba. Recall that after General Leclerc's army arrested Toussaint Louverture he reportedly said, "In overthrowing me in Saint-Domingue, you have only knocked down one trunk of the tree of the liberty of the blacks; but it will grow again from the roots, because they are deep and numerous."[73] Dessalines had redeployed this figurative language in his famous April 28, 1804 proclamation, to "striking effect," in the words of scholar Deborah Jenson.[74] Before planting the tree of liberty, the Haitian people, "sacredly armed," had taken an axe to "the ancient tree of slavery and prejudices."[75]

Another Boyer-era Haitian newspaper, *Le Patriote*, had a drastically different response to the conflict with Cuba that speaks to the ongoing fractures in Haitian society and, particularly, to the difficulties facing Boyer as he tried to maintain Haitian sovereignty in a threatening Atlantic World. "These demands being rejected, the corvette returned to Havana," *Le Patriote* reported.

"Not, however, because she was ordered off by this government. The more disagreeable this affair is, the more does it concern our interest and dignity to speak of it with moderation and caution, and not give way to bravados that might be construed into fresh offense."[76] The dance continued. Haiti needed to appear self-sufficient, powerful, and accommodating at the same time. Still, President Pétion's, President Boyer's, and King Henry's protection of Haitian citizens shows that despite the precarious position of both Haitian states in the early nineteenth century, their leaders were not mere figureheads who could be pushed around by the colonial powers. Shortly after the assassination of Dessalines, in fact, the *Gazette politique* approved a stern warning by the British historian, James Stephen: "[Stephen] considers that the position of the island of Haiti, located in the center of the Antilles, and from which the destruction of all the surrounding colonies could extend, would be extremely formidable, if ever the spirit of conquest entered into the system of its government, irritated by the obstacles that might be placed on its independence . . . nothing would prevent it from becoming the queen of the Antilles."[77] Haiti's posture of self-defense was a direct response to continuous foreign aggression. The existence of freedom and independence in Haiti terrified enslavers, colonists, and heads of state throughout the slaving Atlantic World and brought economic punishment to Haiti and repeated threats of war. This is how the *National Anti-Slavery Standard* continuously reported about Haitian conflicts with Cuba. "A war between these two islands was lately threatened," said an article in the December 29, 1842, issue. The immediate cause of concern was that a "small armed vessel [from Haiti] cruising about," was captured after it docked in Puerto Rico, "slave-holding islands having, for obvious reasons, great dread of their free colored neighbors." "Soon after, two Spanish ships, laden with flour, were captured by a Haytien corvette," the article continued. "The Spanish government supposed this to be an act of retaliation and were highly indignant." After this, a Spanish squadron sailed to Port-au-Prince to make their demands of restitution from the Haitian government.[78]

The larger background to this episode with Cuba is that many Haitians were suffering under Boyer, in the wake of the devastating May 7, 1842, earthquake that practically leveled the city of Cap-Haïtien. In seemingly one fell swoop, all the opulence of the Christophean years dissipated, giving way to generalized famine and poverty. The earthquake, whose tremors were felt as far away as Arkansas, crumbled the former kingdom's capital and unleashed a deadly tsunami. Nearly ten thousand people died and virtually every structure suffered catastrophic damage.[79] The Haitian novelist and historian, Demesvar Delorme, was only eleven years old at the time, but he recalled that around dusk, "a deafening thud, a distant, mournful rumbling, as if emerging from a deep abyss was heard." "The bell tower of the Cathedral began to sway in the air, the bell's chimes were ringing in full blast, sinisterly, without rhythm; a horrible death knell," he continued. "Then the bell tower crumbled, the upper part first. Then the Church came down altogether, and all the surrounding houses, and all the houses for as far as I could see; and all the streets came down afterward, and finally the whole city."[80] Following the conflict with the Spanish in Cuba, the *New Orleans Bee* subsequently reported that Haitians had been "driven to this act of piracy," not because of ongoing slavery on the Spanish-claimed island, but because "they were perishing of hunger, as the late earthquake had destroyed everything they possessed."[81] Delorme associated the upheaval caused by the quake with the eventual overthrow of President Boyer in 1843. "This event had produced in our spirits a commotion difficult to name. In Cap, we were almost as stunned as we were by the earthquake."[82] Unlike the earthquake, the coup d'état was a positive development. "President Boyer had been in power for twenty-five years, he governed the entire island," Delorme wrote. "He was the most perfect personification of authority that had ever been known in this country, and that we could know in this country. This president of the Republic was a king." Delorme insisted that all that was missing from Boyer's reign was the concept of "heredity," and that while his "power had the appearance of being determined by a constitution, his power was in reality without limit." "[King] Louis Philippe [of France] was more of a president than Jean-Pierre Boyer," Delorme concluded.[83]

Part of the reason for Delorme's ire was the 150 million francs that Boyer pledged to France as the price of recognition. Although the colonists claimed the indemnity agreement struck between Charles X and Boyer would only cover one-twelfth the value of their lost "properties," the original agreed upon amount was nearly twice the eighty million francs (fifteen million U.S. dollars) the United States paid Bonaparte for the Louisiana Territory.[84] The 828,000 square miles of the Louisiana Territory (now comprising fifteen U.S. states) span the Mississippi River to the Rocky Mountains and doubled the size of the United States. In contrast, Haiti does not even comprise 2 percent of the Louisiana Territory. Haiti has a meager 10,700 total square miles, making it roughly the size of Massachusetts, the seventh smallest U.S. state.[85] Nevertheless, in his address to the Haitian people, Boyer framed his treaty with France as a success. Betraying the principles of Haitian sovereignty, he claimed the treaty "add[ed] the formality of law to the political existence you had already acquired," saying it "legalizes, in the eyes of the world, the rank in which you have placed yourselves, and to which Providence has called you."[86] Yet, the Haitian people suffered the brunt of the consequences of this "agreement." Boyer levied draconian taxes against Haiti's rural population with his *Code Rural* to pay back the thirty million francs he borrowed to make the first two payments.[87] Given the outrageous sum, it was hardly a surprise

266   Chapter 8

when Haiti eventually defaulted altogether. In 1838, the new French king, Louis Philippe, sent another expedition with twelve warships to address the lack of payment. The 1838 revision between Louis Philippe and Boyer, inaccurately labeled "Traité de Paix et d'Amitié"—or "Treaty of Peace and Friendship"—reduced the outstanding amount owed to sixty million francs, for a total indemnity of ninety million instead of 150 million, but the Haitian government was once again forced to take out crushing loans to pay the balance. With interests and fees from successive loans, from 1825 until 1947 Haiti paid approximately 560 million in today's dollars, with losses to the Haitian economy of more than 21 billion dollars.[88]

After news of this superseding treaty reached England and the United States, foreign newspapers reported that the war between Haiti and France had been narrowly avoided.[89] Already, in 1831 France had threatened to send five hundred thousand soldiers "ready to fight" to collect the rest of the payments.[90] Both the "Haytian Government and people are in consternation in consequence of the peremptory demand of the indemnity due the French Government," one U.S. paper reported. "Boyer would find it extremely difficult, if not impossible to raise such a sum from his black subjects, and there was a good deal of alarm on the subject," it concluded.[91] There were protests and criticisms in Haiti of the indemnity from the beginning. Some of Haiti's high functionaries in Port-au-Prince, who watched the country's gold and silver stores emptied to make the first payments, marched through the streets crying, "You see! How can we alleviate your misery, when we are forced to give everything to France?"[92] Delorme reported that at the time of the earthquake, the city of Cap-Haïtien remained politically strong and was "filled with former soldiers, officers, and influential generals from the war of Independence," who had "only accepted with great difficulty the Treaty between Boyer and Charles X." "Owing to their national pride," Delorme said, they believed the treaty should have "at least stipulated in a separate act that the republic itself was offering the indemnity in its benevolence to dispossessed colonists."[93] In other words, these "influential" Capois citizens wanted the government rather than the people to be responsible for the payments. Opposition to the indemnity was protested even more profoundly among the rural population.[94]

Boyer's *Code Rural* was based on a similar style of feudalism as existed under Louverture, Dessalines, and Christophe with affermage (adapted from the system imposed by Sonthonax, Polverel, and Raimond). But the *Code Rural* now redefined Haitian citizenship. The majority of Haitians were required to become agricultural workers and were "obligated to cultivate the land" and "forbidden from leaving the countryside." In addition to the high taxes Boyer levied, these reforms were meant to generate resources to cover the cost of the loans Boyer contracted.[95] "To pay the French debt, the masses,

"Deux-gourdes notes, circulated 'en vertu de la loi du 16 Avril 1827,'" example of paper money that circulated under the reign of President Jean-Pierre Boyer. Courtesy of the Connecticut Historical Society.

composed mostly of the black population who worked the land, were alone overloaded with an indirect tax on the exportation of coffee [a staple product of Haitian foreign trade], made worse by an issue of paper money which prevented the farmer from knowing exactly what the exchange value offered to him would be for the product of his labors," explained Firmin.[96] Compounding the problem was that, facing deficits, the Boyer administration started printing paper bank notes, which because they were not backed by gold, led to the rapid devaluation of the Haitian gourde in the international market.[97]

By many accounts, Boyer's repressive practices in service of this debt were a primary cause of his downfall. The consequences for the Haitian people were far greater though. For the more than twenty-five years of his reign, while the United States and Europe were investing in "agricultural machinery capable of lightening the load of working the land," Firmin wrote, "the black farmer had to draw from his own capacities, with ancient tools from the time of slavery to produce the same results that the European or American farmer derived from mechanical instruments."[98] Progress in the agricul-

268   Chapter 8

tural realm was not the only industry to have suffered because of Boyer's limited capacity to envision a Haiti not dependent on the approval of the United States and the Western European powers. While Christophe had been busy developing a national school system during his reign, under Boyer, such projects were not only put on hold, but they were completely dismantled.[99]

The year 1825 marked the end of a period of prosperity and the beginning of Haiti's long economic and political decline. Up until that time, Haiti prospered despite international nonrecognition and its continued state of war with France. "On January 1, 1804, in Gonaïves—the holy city—a new state was born into the world," Janvier wrote. "And—an amazing thing!—it was a black state." "To preserve the flag they had chosen for themselves in Arcahaie, on May 18, 1803, Haitians remained in arms until 1825, thinking little of finalizing the order of things, since they were determined to burn everything should a foreign invader return, and to all die rather than renounce their independence." After the indemnity, what Janvier called Haiti's "era of prosperity" ended. "From 1825 to 1881 we were crushed under the burden of a far too considerable debt, a debt granted to compensate the former colonists of Saint-Domingue," Janvier explained. At the same time, Janvier acknowledged that Haiti's political upheavals before Boyer's reign had also created political instability. However, Haiti's pre-1825 political problems paled in consequence to the economic deprivation brought on by Boyer's 1825 consent to the indemnity. In Janvier's estimation, "The absence of political tranquility from 1804 to 1825 and that devotion of Haitian capital [to France], from 1825 until today, for the payment of territorial indemnity, has largely shaped the political struggles that have desolated the country since that time." "Haitian capital has not had time to grow," he lamented. "This is why industry has not yet emerged and this is, basically, the true reason why Haitians have been so restless and so impatient in their search of social betterment." "I will surprise many people by saying that the revolutions and revolts of which Haiti has been the theater, have almost always been generated by an economic crisis, or a social crisis, rather than by purely political ideas or due to simple competition among contenders for power," Janvier finished. Janvier's analysis of the role the indemnity played in the political, economic, and social instability of the post-1825 Haitian republic is key to understanding the contest between state and nation in Haiti that was only exacerbated under every subsequent Haitian ruler after Boyer.

By the time President Boyer signed the 1825 indemnity agreement, the French had been openly plotting to "exterminate" the Haitian populace in the name of restoring slavery for two decades. That history of planned genocide is essential to understanding the threat of violent warfare, not merely financial exploitation, that nineteenth-century Haitians lived with because, in the words of Dessalines, they "dared to be free." Dozens of manuscripts and pamphlets from early nineteenth-century France show that what the French really wanted in their negotiations with Haiti up until 1825 was not money. Rather what the French sought, in their words, was to "restore Saint-Domingue," which meant to bring back slavery. The French began planning reconquest soon after the Haitian Declaration of Independence on January 1, 1804, and threatened the new nation under all its first leaders, from its founder Emperor Jacques I to both King Henry and President Pétion. In 1806, Saint-Domingue's former head of finance addressed a detailed plan for reinstating slavery to Napoléon. While neither ruling out deporting or exterminating the entire population, the official argued the first step was to assassinate Haiti's leader. "As long as Dessalines exists," he wrote, "we will never attain our goal." General François-Marie Perichou de Kerversau, stationed in Saint-Domingue during the Leclerc expedition, also sent detailed reconquest plans to Napoléon. Like his predecessors, Kerversau spoke of the need to "exterminate" the entire population, including the children. No conciliations for the "negroes" should be made at all, Kerversau warned. "They want to be free," but "the honor of the French name, the security of the West Indies and indignantly outraged humanity cannot allow it," he said. "The aura that once guaranteed the safety of the master and allowed one man to live in peace among two hundred slaves is gone," Kerversau concluded. "The black man knows today that a *blanc* is only a man."

Napoléon's Bourbon successors similarly wasted no time trying to come up with schemes to reinstate slavery. In 1814, Baron de Malouet, the French minister of the marine under Louis XVIII, sent three spies to coerce Haiti's leaders to surrender. One of the spies, Dauxion-Lavaysse, threatened Président Pétion that if the Haitian people did not submit they would be "treated as barbarous savages and hunted down like maroon negroes."[100] This same spy also sent a letter to King Henry that unabashedly revealed that France was ready "to replace the population of Haiti, which . . . would be totally annihilated by the forces sent against it."[101] Despite all the political changes that France underwent in the nineteenth century, its politics toward Haiti remained largely the same: enslave, crush, or destroy. It is for this reason that Vastey railed against those from France or elsewhere who would say, "It was Bonaparte who had done everything; it was Bonaparte who we should be talking about"; or that if one wanted to talk about the "crimes of the French," more broadly, "it was the ex-colonists who had done all the harm, [and] it was against them that it was necessary to thunder." "The French government has changed hands; Bonaparte has fallen," Vastey acknowledged. But "the new government and the new sovereign who governs France, have they changed their system?" he asked. The Haitian people, in Vastey's words, were experi-

270   Chapter 8

encing the "same treatment under the legitimate Bourbon government as they had already experienced under that of Bonaparte." "It hardly matters to us if we fall under the blows of Bonaparte, Louis XVIII, or the ex-colonists," Vastey averred. "We are still falling under the blows of the French!"[102] It was only after realizing that Haitians would rather fight a war to the death than see the return of slavery and French rule—the *Gazette royale* reads, "*if the French must come, let them come only once! the more who come, the more we will kill!*"—that the French settled for economically enslaving them.[103]

In the early 1820s, with the obstacle of Christophe gone, President Boyer repeatedly tried to negotiate France's recognition of Haitian independence for an indemnity, as Pétion first proposed in 1814.[104] These missions failed because Louis XVIII was determined to gain at least suzerainty over the island—which would have made Haiti a protectorate of France. Only one month before Louis XVIII died his ministers rebuked the two commissioners Boyer sent to Paris to try to negotiate in exchange for recognition a "pecuniary indemnity."[105] After Boyer's delegates returned to Haiti, the government printed a pamphlet summarizing France's various demands. "In 1814, they wished to impose upon us the absolute sovereignty of France," the pamphlet began. "In 1816, they were satisfied with constitutional sovereignty; in 1821, they demanded only a simple suzerainty." Then, "in 1823, during their negotiations with General Boyer, they confined themselves to asking for, as a sine qua non, the indemnity, which we had previously offered." The editor of the pamphlet questioned therefore why the French were now asking for external suzerainty again. "Through what kind of return to a spirit of domination, do they want, in 1824, to subject us to an external sovereignty? What then is this external sovereignty?" he asked. "It is composed, in our view, of two kinds of rights: one which is restricted to a protectorate; which is the one presented to us: the other, which extends to external relations, either political or commercial, and which subsequently they would not fail to enforce." The editor concluded by clarifying that Haitians did not intend to give up their all-important sovereignty for any reason, to any power, or in any way: "But from whatever side we consider this suzerainty it seems to us injurious or contrary to our security: that is why we reject it."[106] Nine months before he signed the indemnity, Boyer issued a circular denouncing as an "incredible" "pretention" the French government's belief that they had the right to "suzerainty" over Haiti. Boyer told the people to remember his prior orders for all Haitians to help prepare the country for war. "Hurry to finish all the necessary work," the president wrote, "ensuring the weapons are in order, maintaining good condition of the artillery, and the preparation of ammunition of all kinds." "Put in requisition the workmen of the [military] corps, and even, if necessary, private individuals, for the prompt execution of the cannon mounts," he continued. "Make sure, finally, in case of invasion by the enemy, that you are not behind on any of these things."[107] It was not long after Louis XVIII's death that his brother Charles X, the new French king, caving to the pleas of the ex-colonists, decided to accept the offer of indemnity. The nonnegotiable conditions required Haiti to agree to not only pay the exorbitant sum of 150 million francs but to give France most favored nation status, which ended up hurting Haiti's lucrative trade with Great Britain.[108]

France's economic war against Haiti long predated the indemnity. Bonaparte's government had similarly structured its dastardly dreams about restoring "Saint-Domingue" around the idea of Haiti paying reparations to France. Dumesle wrote in *Voyage*, "It must be remarked upon that our eternal detractors, the ex-colonists, requested, in 1805, that after the conquest of Haiti (an easy thing according to them), 700,000,000 francs be delivered to them gradually, and as a loan fixed on national credit, for the restoration of properties." When not dreaming of an indemnity four and a half times the amount of the one mandated in 1825, the French were trying to strangle independent Haiti through commerce.

The French wanted to trade with Haiti under King Henry without recognizing Haitian independence. This state of affairs was both incomprehensible and unacceptable to the Haitian king and his administrators who recognized that, just as in the French colonial era of slavery, it was "by way of commerce that our tyrants count on being able to insinuate themselves among us, to corrupt us, to disunite us and to arrive at the means of subjugating or exterminating us."[109] King Henry's November 20, 1816, official ban against trading with the French, even via another country, such as England or Germany, was designed to prevent the French government, and the French people, from continuing to benefit from Haitian commerce, either directly or indirectly, while disavowing Haiti's independence.[110] "Since the French intended to destroy us by way of commerce," Vastey wrote in 1817, "when we outlawed French trade, we destroyed all their hopes, and their chimerical edifice crumbled." King Henry was willing to take his ban against French commerce even further. "If France continues its system of insults and aggression against Haiti, if it stubbornly refuses to recognize our full and entire independence, which is the one and only guarantee we can have against it," Vastey wrote, "we would do well, after banning ships under its flag and individuals from that nation from our territory, to proscribe its goods also." Citing a proverb, Vastey remarked "that one must know how to lose an egg to gain an ox; and in politics, which deals with the existence of peoples . . . we must know how to lose a day to gain centuries."[111] Vastey was correct. France's most terrible weapon turned out to be economics, and the war of extermination was to come by means other than the cannon.

272   Chapter 8

After King Henry committed suicide in 1820, France's greatest obstacle to imposing its will on Haiti might have just as well been buried under limestone at the Citadelle along with Christophe's body. Baron de Mackau, whom Louis XVIII's brother and successor King Charles X sent to deliver the economic ultimatum to President Boyer, arrived in Haiti in July 1825, accompanied by a squadron of fourteen brigs of war carrying more than five hundred cannons.[112] In the instructions the French minister of the marine gave Mackau he reminded the French diplomat that his task was merely that of a messenger. "My mission to the people of our former colony is not a negotiation," Mackau wrote. "I am limited to explaining to them on what conditions His Majesty [of France] consents to grant their independence, fully and entirely." "I lack the powers to make the slightest modification to the proposals of which I am the bearer." The directive, marked "very secret," stated that if Haiti "did not demonstrate gratitude for what His Majesty deigns to do for them," Mackau was to "announce to the leaders of that government that henceforth they will be treated as enemies of France; that already a squadron is ready to establish the most rigorous blockade in front of the ports of the island; that this squadron will soon be reinforced by other vessels sent from our ports; and that the interruption of all maritime commerce will cease for Saint-Domingue only after this island will have submitted, without conditions, to the domination of France."[113] The French abolitionist and antislavery activist Schoelcher passed harsh judgment on Boyer for allowing himself to be intimidated by the French king's fleet. "It is clear that Boyer, by allowing Charles X to grant recognition to Haiti, did not know how to protect or support national honor. He was afraid of the French fleet, and that is precisely why the patriots [of Haiti] have condemned his pusillanimity and have never forgiven him for the way he behaved during this negotiation."[114]

Even if Boyer consented to the indemnity less out of fear of war than because it served his own economic interests,[115] by what right could Boyer force the Haitian people to also consent, and to consign away their futures and that of their children and grandchildren to paying an illegitimate independence tax? "Our independence act, our constitutions, our laws, logic, and our interests, all compel us never to consent to pay any tribute, any contribution, and even less, to cede any islands, towns, or stronghold, or even an inch of land to the French, under any title, condition or pretext whatsoever," Vastey had insisted.[116] Writing more than three decades later, Schoelcher could not but react against the illogic of the idea that it was the Haitian people who owed the French compensation. "Haitians angrily say, and we agree completely agree with them, that they owed nothing to the property owners of Saint-Domingue," Schoelcher wrote. "To impose an indemnity on slaves who conquered their masters, in fact, is to make them pay with money what they already paid for with their blood." Long before contemporary debates about reparations for slavery for the descendants of formerly enslaved peoples, the French abolitionist could see that it was clearly the Haitian people who deserved compensation from the French. "Is it not, moreover, within the firmest scales of justice that the freed slaves could have established a compensation between what they took from the masters and what the masters had taken from the slaves?" he asked. "The riches of Saint-Domingue, who created them? Was it not with the hands of slaves?" Because the enslaved laborers of Saint-Domingue had worked without compensation for the enslavers, Schoelcher could not help but ask if it were "necessary to have dispensed with logic to not admit that they themselves [the formerly enslaved] had more right to demand from the colonists the balance of this debt, than the colonists had to come and claim the price of a land from which they were chased after having defiled it using violence and crime." "France could, if it was pleased to do so, compensate the colonists, but Haiti owed them nothing," Schoelcher concluded.[117]

Even if the indemnity also served the interests of Haiti's economic elite in the nineteenth century, the indemnity and the loans Boyer committed Haiti to impoverished the country and only changed the state of war that existed between France and Haiti from a physical one to an economic one.[118] In 1838, the *Catholic Miscellaney* reported of French king Louis Philippe's delegation to Haiti, "The French fleet consisting of 14 vessels, left Martinique on the 20th of January for Hayti. President Boyer, it is said, acknowledged the justice of the French claim, but alleges the inability of the island to pay, and calls upon the inhabitants to make war to extermination rather than submit to subjugation to France."[119] Yet when that fleet arrived, Boyer signed the fatal treaty rather than go to war.

Boyer is undoubtedly the most unpopular of Haiti's leaders who fought in the revolution, but in both past and present foreign writing about Haiti (that is, writing from non-Haitians), Louverture, Dessalines, and Christophe—who reigned separately over a colony, an empire, and a kingdom—are the most likely to find themselves charged variously with reinstating slavery and oppressing their own people. Pétion and Boyer, who ruled separately over the republic, and are responsible for the idea and fact of an indemnity agreement, have largely escaped these accusations, most likely because of the mistaken association of republicanism with universal freedom and equality. Yet in a chapter about the work that Haitian antislavery thought and deeds have performed in the world, this assumption must be addressed. We must come to terms with this idea that it was nineteenth-century Haitian rulers who reinstated slavery. The charge here rests with Christophe since, to a large extent, he is the one who had the most opportunity to extend and transform the colonial plantation model of affermage first dreamed up by Sonthonax, Pol-

274   Chapter 8

verel, and Raimond. Louverture remained governor-general for only a handful of years and Dessalines ruled for less than three. Christophe, in contrast, first, as president, then as king, ruled for thirteen years, and the majority of claims about the putative reinstatement of slavery involve his reign.

Claims that Christophe reinstated slavery were ardently repeated in the nineteenth century not only by the king's enemies in the republic, but by some of the very foreigners whom Christophe had variously entrusted and allowed to live among the Haitian people. Their testimony is key to understanding how one of the world's most storied defenders of freedom and equality for Black people came to be instead characterized in world history as their enslaver. Dealing with the position of Christophe in both Haitian and foreign thought opens a window onto the sovereign state he dreamed of building. It also sheds light on what were the most obvious and unequivocal mistakes of Pétion and Boyer, in hindsight, with respect to the Haitian indemnity, which placed a new pressure on Haitian sovereignty, an economic one. In the words of historian Sudhir Hazareesingh, "First they come in armies, then they come in economics."[120]

————

During his lifetime, the king of Haiti was something of a hero to British abolitionists like Thomas Clarkson and William Wilberforce, but soon after his death in 1820, Christophe was accused of effectively re-enslaving the Haitian people. According to Schoelcher, while Pétion's most grave misdeed was being "useless" and "loving power merely for the sake of power," Christophe was the "tyrant of the north who oppressed his brothers."[121] Schoelcher was hardly a fan of either Haitian ruler, nor was he a disinterested observer. "Instead of combating Christophe with better institutions, [Pétion] found it easier to keep the people close to him with the prospect of *far niente*," Schoelcher claimed. He clarified what he meant by this in writing, "While the king of the north used violent and barbaric means to curb indiscipline, suppress theft, restore agriculture, raise up the ruins, establish manufacturing, and provide his kingdom with free schools, for which he appointed foreign professors, Pétion used the false freedom of disorder to oppose that iron despotism, which was at least orderly."[122] Having never traveled to Haiti while either Pétion or Christophe was alive, Schoelcher was an armchair observer of Haiti's first republic and its only kingdom. He therefore relied on the accounts of many of those whom Ardouin derogatively called Haiti's "traveling friends."[123]

In 1828, James Franklin, a British traveler who lived in Haiti for a time, published a book called *The Present State of Hayti*. In it, Franklin accused Christophe of having forced his people "to perform that labour which ought to have been performed by brutes." Franklin's allegations were not motivated by humanitarian rights or benevolence. "To place the slaves in the British colonies upon a footing with the free labourers in Hayti, or with the largest proportion of the people in that country, would be a work of easy accomplishment," Franklin concluded. "But the effect would be, to cause them to exchange a state of comparative plenty and comfort, for one in which every species of tyranny and oppression, with their concomitants, disease and want, are most lamentably conspicuous."[124] In 1842, the British Quaker John Candler accused Christophe of having "compelled" "bands of men and women . . . to labour under insufficient rations of food," causing "vast numbers" of them to die.[125] These grave charges were consistently heaved at the king of Haiti but, notably, most of these accusations were published only *after* his death. After visiting Haiti in 1833, thirteen years after Christophe's suicide, the U.S. traveler Jonathan Brown criticized the Haitian king with his two-volume *The History and Present Condition of St. Domingo* (1837). Brown wrote that to build his famous palace Christophe used "despotic power and a portion of the prospective ambition of the ancient Egyptian kings." "Christophe employed vast multitudes of his subjects, gathered from every district of his kingdom, to accomplish the stupendous undertaking which he had planned."[126] Claiming to have based his account on firsthand testimonies, Brown continued, "When measures of public necessity or public embellishment required it, the whole laboring population of a district was called out en masse, and made to continue their toil until the work was finished."[127] Writing in the 1840s and relying on many of the same accounts, the Haitian historian Thomas Madiou also described Christophe as having mandated "forced labor" when he ordered that farmworkers be "attached to the glebe," meaning that laborers could not leave the habitations where they were employed. Furthermore, Madiou wrote, "The proceeds of this forced labor were used largely to cover the expenses of his government. Property owners were no longer the masters of their income; tax officials seized [their revenues] to fill government coffers."[128]

Let us examine this charge that the king instituted at the very least a form of pseudoslavery so we do not the make the mistake, like our predecessors, of confusing feudalism and affermage with chattel slavery. To start, we shall return to Christophean thought. "In history power begins at the source," wrote Trouillot in *Silencing the Past*. We must return to contemporaneous Haitian narrations of the story of the kingdom if we want to understand how the dire charge of having re-enslaved the Haitian people could have been launched against the first and last king of Haiti.

In 1812 Christophe issued a complex series of labor laws called the Code Henry.[129] Yet even with its titular echo of both Louis XIV and Napoléon's draconian Code Noir and Code Napoléon, respectively, initially many foreigners recognized Christophe's code not as a blueprint for a form of forced labor that was simply slavery by another name, but as the greatest work of legislation governing the rights and duties of workers that the world had ever seen. "In lieu of wages," the third article stated, "the labourers in plantations shall be allowed a full fourth of the gross product, free from all duties."[130] The code, in fact, described an elaborate system of compensation similar to the state-run affermage of Dessalines's era.

Christophe had been an integral part of Dessalines's system of affermage. On July 24, 1805, André Vernet, as the newly appointed minister of finance and the interior, issued a decree spelling out to the public—and, in effect, to the world—how the labor system in the Empire of Haiti worked. The decree included information about who would be employed on the plantations and who would oversee the work and be entitled to profits. Referring to abuses taking place in the empire, particularly with regard to the former plantations of the white colonists, the decree's stated aim, as articulated in its preamble, was to ensure that rightful property owners were enjoying the peaceful possession of their lands and to stop illegal possessions of both state and privately owned plantations. The first article required all property owners to present themselves to the Office of Finance, furnished with their titles of ownership. These would then be verified and formally registered by the state. Article 5 of the decree is in some senses the most historically significant. It reaffirmed the name for the empire's labor system, which was formally called "affermage," as in post-emancipation colonial Saint-Domingue, and contained a detailed description of how the plantations owned by the state were to be accounted for. The six division generals were in charge of registering the plantations. The land registers had to include "the name of the farmer, that of the plantation, the type of product, farm, and the number of laborers." These registers were also needed to help the state complete its population statistics and to provide clarity about the "empire's revenues."[131] The state did not plan to keep all of the seized land that previously belonged to the former white French colonists. In February 1804, the government set up a system allowing military officers to make claims for and take possession of various confiscated plantations.[132] Christophe was closely involved in the assignation of coffee and cotton farms to various military officials.[133]

While private property did exist in the empire, as indicated in the article, it was also true that the government owned many plantations and other estates. The revenues from these state-run farms, under the system of affermage, were according to the *Gazette*, "immense, surpassing by a lot even certain countries in Europe, without even counting what was received from customs, which comprises an always fruitful method for a government to enrich itself." Foreign trade, too, was reportedly robust, despite no other country having officially recognized Haitian independence. The article, written on behalf of the government, labored to convince the Haitian people that this lucrative international commerce would eventually trickle down and contribute to the "prosperity . . . and opulence of all citizens."[134]

Of Christophe's modifications to this system with the Code Henry, the British naturalist Joseph Banks wrote, "It is without doubt in its theory, . . . the most moral association of men in existence; nothing that white men have been able to arrange is equal to it." Banks explained that the code could prevent the alienation of workers, both Black and white: "To give the labouring poor of the country a vested interest in the crops they raise, instead of leaving their reward to be calculated by the caprice of the interested proprietor, is a law worthy to be written in letters of gold, as it secures comfort and a proper portion of happiness to those whose lot in the hands of white men endures by far the largest portion of misery." Banks hoped that in time, Christophe's code could help to "conquer all difficulties, and bring together the black and white varieties of mankind under the ties of mutual and reciprocal equality and brotherhood."[135] William Hamilton, another British botanist and resident of Haiti, translator of Vastey's writings, also praised Christophe as a legislator and for his social vision. The "code of laws which bears his name, the wholesome regulations he has established in the administration of the state, . . . and above all, the institutions he has founded for diffusing the light of moral and intellectual improvement throughout his dominions," Hamilton wrote, "are so many splendid monuments of the extent of his genius."[136] The French antislavery historian Antoine Métral echoed the admiration. He referred to Henry's laws as "original beauties"; and the Black American abolitionist Prince Saunders was so enamored that he had portions of the code printed in English translation in his *Haytian Papers* (1816), before he relocated to northern Haiti to start a school in Port-de-Paix.[137]

It was precisely because of his commitment to both antislavery activism and what we might call racial uplift that Christophe was in regular contact with fellow British abolitionist Thomas Clarkson. On February 5, 1816, Christophe explained to the renowned abolitionist his plan to institute a public school system. "For a long while my intention, my dearest ambition, has been to secure for the nation which has confided to me its destiny the benefit of public instruction," Christophe wrote. "I am completely devoted to this project. The edifices necessary for the institutions of public instruction in the cities and in the country are under construction."[138] To that end, Christophe set up a Royal Chamber of Instruction, appointed a minister of education, and issued an edict mandating the development of schools throughout northern Haiti. To facilitate national education, Christophe created a program to sponsor foreign artists, scientists, musicians, and mathematicians, as well as

278   Chapter 8

English teachers, to come to the kingdom to instruct Haitian students, both boys and girls, though their schools were to remain segregated by gender.[139]

That education would be available to citizens of both sexes was not designed to be a mere illusion but formed a part of the kingdom's egalitarian dreams. Baron de Vastey wrote that female education was just as important as male education: "The benefits of education must necessarily extend equally to both sexes," he said. "Young ladies of noble families, who by their birth are destined one day to appear at court, must they remain at home with their parents, deprived of the means to receive a deliberate education?" Vastey asked. "Domestic mores influence public mores," he continued. "The education of women affects more immediately than one might believe the education of men, and it would be in vain for us to desire good mothers of families, who are wise, thrifty, active and hard-working, without the assistance of education, religion, and mores."[140] The kingdom's program of "equal" education for both sexes was designed to correct a long-standing historical problem whose origins reached back into the age of slavery. Vastey observed, "The education of this half of humankind has always been completely abandoned in Hayti; as in all islands peopled with slaves."[141] The kingdom's greatest contribution to Haitian sovereignty was in many respects its visionary antislavery culture. The kingdom's writers claimed that the aim of the king was to overturn every single element of social life in existence under the colonial regime of slavery. Promoting freedom under sovereignty meant doing the opposite of what the enslavers did under colonialism. In place of the colonial system of death, the kingdom brought a system of life.

Even Schoelcher, who was not at all a fan of the Haitian king, admired the progressiveness and ingenuity of Christophe's desire to educate the entire Haitian citizenry and the institutions he built to support that endeavor. Pétion and Boyer's inability to do the same for the republic was the French abolitionist's primary reproach at the time he wrote *Colonies étrangères et Haïti*. "What have you done for the young nation you were charged with leading?" Schoelcher asked. "No more schools: the ones Toussaint and Christophe had opened, you voluntarily closed them; no more roads, no more trade, no more industry, no more agriculture, no more relations with Europe, no more order, no more society, no more anything, there is nothing left."[142] Schoelcher admitted, in contrast, that there was much to admire about Christophe's dreams: "It is impossible to deny that Christophe was of a higher order of mind. The country under his harsh reign was marching rapidly toward civilization." He continued:

> People worked. The ports of Cap were filled with ships that came to exchange fine merchandise for sugar and coffee; schools were established

in all the towns and received large numbers of pupils; a chair of medicine and anatomy, where hygiene and surgery were taught, was established in the capital of the kingdom; entire books were published in three still active printing presses, and the royal almanac of 1820 contains several meteorological observations made at Cap-Henri [*sic*] in 1819, by Mr. Moore, professor of mathematics at the Royal College of Cap. Let us not forget that public education was entirely in English. This is a characteristic that speaks strongly to Christophe's genius. He had guessed that one always possesses the spirit of the language that one speaks and that the influence of language on ideas and mores is felt even in the most remote generations. He therefore wanted to drive out the idiom of the hated masters from Haitian soil.[143]

Christophe not only sought sovereignty over the historical record of Haiti and its future political enterprises. He also sought to create linguistic mastery over it as well. To escape from the prison of linguistics the French colonists left behind when the revolutionaries drove them out of Saint-Domingue, Christophe desired to change the language of Haiti from French to English.

Establishing sovereignty over independent Haiti meant many things to its various early nineteenth-century rulers. For Christophe, the remnants of French rule, and therefore slavery, needed to be attacked from multiple angles: politically, linguistically, educationally, physically, economically, and philosophically. Christophe was very interested in letting the world know about the antislavery culture he was creating. The privy council Christophe tasked with creating the Code Henry, and which included Vastey and Prévost, explained that to create these laws "it was necessary to create a new edifice, to invent a new process, which is still without example among nations; it was necessary to establish entirely new principles, to erase from the pages of our legislation even the last vestiges of an odious system, which we have reprobated forever."[144] On October 17, 1816, an article in the *Gazette royale* praised the king's Code Henry by claiming that it had effectively eliminated to the "very last vestige" all remaining remnants of French colonial codes of law:

Up until now, in the absence of our own laws, justice was administered according to the rules and ordinances of our tyrants: the creation of the Code Henry completely changed the face of things, and made disappear the very last vestiges of the colonial regime: if this code were to be the only lasting work of Henry, it would be enough to immortalize his name! during the deliberations, he used his wisdom to avoid falling into the traps of our implacable enemies; he knew how to thwart their guilty plans and reject with horror their odious proposals; and through his energy and courage, he raised the glory of the Haitian people!

280   Chapter 8

In regard to "Public instruction," we read that its establishment was entirely "with a view toward the blessings it will spread to the Haitian people." Haitian writers associated denial of education with slavery.[145] The kingdom therefore constituted the creation of an education system as germane to freedom. "Already national schools are being established according to the Lancaster method," the article explained. "Soon the Royal College of Hayti will be established, where our young people will be able to take up the hard sciences. Already an academy of drawing and painting has been established in the city of Sans-Souci. Honorable appointments have been fixed by the government for the teachers and schoolmasters who come to devote themselves to the instruction of the young." Going on to compare the king of Haiti to other historical "benefactors of their people," the article said that Henry I's goal is to "introduce into the kingdom theater and the arts." "He wants to give us the best present the King can give to his people, that of education and enlightenment!" This was consonant with King Henry's efforts to change the culture of his country from one of slavery to one of freedom.

Haitians were emerging under Christophe's rule, said the *Gazette royale*, as different "men" and a different "people" than they were in 1789, or even than they were immediately after independence in 1804:

> Everything has vanished, the face of everything has changed! The Haitian man of 1789 cannot be found, and we barely recognize the one from the first year of our independence! Our mores, our manners, our customs, are no longer the same; these are no longer the same men, nor is it the same government, nor are we the same people: everything has been transformed; everything has been perfected, everything has been consolidated; we no longer recognize that unhappy people, stupefied under the weight of ignorance and slavery; in their place we find today good fathers of families, hard-working farmers, practicing good manners and social virtues; here can also be found the family of a magnanimous sovereign, a hereditary nobility, generals, magistrates, a large and seasoned army; all of this, in the end, out of a people, once so humiliated, so degraded: what a lesson for the world![146]

Christophe viewed making broad inroads into the makeup of the military to be a method of serving the antislavery position of the state, inasmuch as it strengthened the contrast between Haitian sovereignty and colonial slavery. In the same article from the *Gazette* that praised the Code Henry, we learn that striving toward gender equality, at least theoretically, also extended to the military: "The army was put on a formidable footing, and the entire population received weapons." The Republic of Haiti also saw women involved in combat, particularly during its civil war with the kingdom. Dumesle

Antislavery 281

explained that when Christophe's troops began to gain on those of Pétion during the civil war in 1808, "We then saw that so interesting portion of humanity, women . . . animated by the sentiments that had set us ablaze, forget the weaknesses of their sex, brave every danger, and at the risk of being crushed under the rubble that the bullet and the bomb piled up on all sides, devote their delicate hands to the work for which man seemed only to be exclusively destined."[147]

The kingdom had its own standing corps of female soldiers called the "Amazones," but they were not known for participating in combat. Usually made up of noble women, the Haitian newspaper, *Le Propagateur Haïtien* printed a letter from a foreigner who had lived in the kingdom to explain that the Amazones were "a singular troop commanded by the Queen of Haiti: it was made up of 50 women, dressed as Amazones, armed with bows, arrows and sabers." "I never saw them," the author wrote, "but I was assured that their costume was particularly rich and beautiful." The letter continued, "These ladies were not destined for active service, but existed simply to increase the entourage of the queen. This troop was stationed in Sans-Souci. They were ordinarily only ladies of quality. I have heard a lot about the beauty of their horses, selected from all over the kingdom."[148] Dumesle wrote more disapprovingly of these "Amazones," but he did say that it was "Madame Christophe" who suggested the creation of the corps to bring back "an ancient American institution." Dumesle's comments, perhaps in an unintended manner, suggest the influence of Queen Marie-Louise on the developing culture of Haiti under the reign of her husband. "She gave herself the task of forming this corps of new heroines; and thus they appeared." Dumesle concluded, in any event, that "they had none of the qualities that distinguished the Amazones; they were just shapeless and disfigured copies of them."[149] The Haitian Amazones, even if simply for show, became a distinct part of the antislavery culture that Christophe constructed in the Kingdom of Haiti.

During the August 1816 celebration of the annual fête of Queen Marie-Louise, which lasted for twelve days and had 1,200 people in attendance, the Amazones formed a part of the royal court. An article published in the *Gazette royale* on August 20 reads: "Their Majesties, the King and the Queen mounted on horseback, and went to spend the day at Bande-du-Nord, at the Dahomet Bridge, previously called Port Français; the whole court was on horseback; the ladies were remarkable for the elegance of their costumes; they were all dressed as Amazones, wearing little hats of the latest fashion, adorned with ostrich feathers, and mounted on superb horses; these souls appeared to the eye of any observer as the most beautiful sight ever presented."[150] Chanlatte also wrote about these women in a way that indicates the performative and cultural role they played and the antislavery messages they could carry.

282   Chapter 8

An "Amazone" appears in Chanlatte's 1818 opera, *L'Entrée du roi en sa capitale,* to credit Henry Christophe with being one of the founders of Haitian independence: "Our mothers had cried out, our fathers had trembled, our husbands were swimming in their own blood, everything seemed finished in our sad homeland, when a hero, the great Henry extended a helping hand to us, and on the debris of the odious scepter of the French raised this Column to Independence." Going on to call King Henry "that powerful genius who saved us all," the Amazone tells the children of Haiti to "live to serve and worship him." "If we were to be deprived of the aid of this great man," she continued, "we would soon recognize just how much we were in need of this great man's assistance."[151]

The column of independence was not metaphorical. An August 1816 issue of the *Gazette royale* announced the king's intention to create a monument to Haiti's freedom: "In the middle of the Place d'Armes of the Citadelle Henry, there will be erected a Column to Liberty and Independence!" According to the article, the column would contain engraved on the bronze the entire Acte d'Indépendance with the names of each signer, with the exception of all those persons deemed traitors to the kingdom, whose names were to be "erased." On the tenth anniversary of the assassination of Dessalines, the October 17, 1816, issue of the *Gazette royale*, while proclaiming the construction of the Citadelle to be a physical monument to Haitian independence, further described the "column of independence" and how it was meant to honor the Haitian revolutionaries: "The King satisfied the nation's debt by decreeing that a granite column to liberty and independence would be erected in the middle of the Citadelle Henry's square!" Christophe desired to create monuments in Haiti that could rival those of old Europe, and in homage to the king's efforts, the *Gazette* praised him: "You have just raised a column to freedom and independence! If you continue, your glory will not be lacking! What? we see monuments, obelisks, triumphal arches rising all over the world, to call forth the memory of a battle or of an ordinary event, and we who have glorious memories to perpetuate, we who are free and independent, we did not yet have a monument, nor any column, which would attest for centuries to come to the memory of this glorious event!"[152] In these lines there is a strikingly modern theory of monuments that fills a void expressed by some later Caribbean writers. In his poem "The Sea Is History" Derek Walcott grieves that the greatest Caribbean monument is the Atlantic Ocean itself:

> Where are your monuments, your battles, martyrs?
> Where is your tribal memory? Sirs,
> in that grey vault. The sea
> has locked them all. The sea is history.[153]

Commemorating those lost to the transatlantic slave trade, to be sure, was less important for Christophe than combating ongoing (legalized) human trafficking. At the same time, Christophe desired to create a physical monument to Haitian sovereignty and freedom that could also memorialize those who lost their lives fighting in the revolution. The creation of this kind of monument, he knew, could be of world historical significance.

The Battle of Vertières, which ended the Haitian Revolution and led to Haitian independence, was of signal importance like the Battle of Austerlitz or the Battle of Yorktown. As the kingdom's writers pointed out, however, until Henry erected the Citadelle, several arcs de triomphe at the Palace of Sans Souci, and this column of independence, there were no Haitian monuments to visually represent Haitian victory and its simultaneously triumphant and tragic meaning. "O bitter pain!" we read in the *Gazette*, "the scattered bones of the warriors who died for independence in the fields of Crête-à-Pierrot, la Tannerie, Haut-du-Cap, on the plain of Cul-de-Sac, in the mountains of Petit-Goâve and the Tiburon, have become whitened into dust, without a monument raised in national recognition, to collect their ashes!" Present-day Haitians were the ones to benefit from the sacrifice of their ancestors who died on the battlefields. The least they could do was honor the ashes of their predecessors in stone:

> We are their brethren, and we are enjoying the fruits of the blood they shed! O Henry, magnanimous and generous prince! raise to your glory this immortal column where the names of the illustrious founders of independence will be engraved on bronze; the names of the traitors who betrayed this sublime and sacred cause will be erased; a cruel lesson, but a just punishment for those who have renounced honor and country! . . . Raise, I say, this immortal column within the walls of this formidable Citadelle that your genius created for the defense of independence; it is by embracing and forming around him a rampart with our bodies that we will be invincible; that one day, just as at the Olympic Games, the father, leading his son there, can say to him while looking at that monument: Do you see in what kind of country you were born, we honor everything that is great here; and you too will one day deserve to be honored by your country.[154]

The Haitian monument was undoubtedly an homage to the deceased revolutionaries who lost their lives fighting to end slavery. It was also a symbol of the sovereignty and power of the king and the antislavery Kingdom of Haiti. Christophe clearly desired to be considered one of history's "great men." The August 26, 1816, issue of the *Gazette royale* stated, to that end, "History dem-

284   Chapter 8

onstrates that no people has ever done anything great entirely by themselves; it is only ever in collaboration with the great men who become elevated in their midst that they raise themselves up to the glory of accomplishing extraordinary deeds."[155]

Walcott did acknowledge King Henry's attempt to create monuments for the Caribbean in Haiti. "There was only one noble ruin in the archipelago: Christophe's massive citadel at La Ferrière," he said. For Walcott, however, the Citadelle was not to be admired: "It was a monument to egomania, more than a strategic castle; an effort to reach God's height."[156] But Walcott's analysis offers limited purview. The monument represented all at once the radical history of Haiti's revolution, a memorial to the lost fighters of the revolution, and the sign and symbol of Haitian sovereignty in a still slaving world. In *Le Cri de la nature*, Chanlatte hypothesized the testimonial work of memory and history that the culture of Haiti could do, "if ever we have our own painters, poets, sculptors and historians," while saying to the French, "how our monuments will be shameful for you, if your crimes are therein faithfully traced."[157] The crimes of the colonists had to be recorded and preserved for the sake of historical posterity, so Haitians would never forget all the obstacles their ancestors overcame for freedom and independence, but colonial culture and art also needed to be uprooted and discarded. One issue of the *Gazette* decried the fact that foreigners had brought into the kingdom for sale "an infinite number of tableaux depicting the Bourbon family," "testaments of Louis XVI, [and] French hearts of Louis XVIII." Christophe responded by ordering the seizure of all images "carrying the French imprint and that could remind them of their odious domination." "Orders have also been given in the customhouses, to prevent the introduction into the kingdom, of objects of the above description, under penalty of confiscation and fine," the *Gazette* warned, before concluding, "not having been able to make us listen to them through letters and insidious proclamations, they wanted to speak to us in paintings."[158]

King Henry was continuously portrayed by northern writers as the founder, if not of Haitian independence, then of Haitian sovereignty. The Duke de L'Avancé said of him: "Divine Providence, in its immutable decrees, ordered that Your Majesty should regenerate the Haytian people; a more skillful pilot than those who have preceded you in this honorable task, it was reserved for the great Henry, the Founder of our Moral and Warlike Institutions, to put the finishing touches on the edifice you have erected. Continue, Sire, your glorious career and complete the operation of the happiness of the Haitian nation. Penetrated with the keenest gratitude for such great blessings, it will raise its voice to heaven, and implore its blessings on Your Majesty."[159] The palace at Sans-Souci, erected by Christophe around the same time as the

Citadelle, was also a monument to independence and sovereignty. In 1815, the *Gazette royale* described several inscriptions newly etched onto the facade of the palace at Sans-Souci meant to consecrate Christophe's power in a visibly scribal manner. These inscriptions were sufficiently infused with antislavery statements to make them serve a dual purpose: "On the principal facade of the palace, we read one of t hose verses that seemed to be written just for Haitians: *Injustice, in the end produced Independence.*" At the bottom of the palace facade, there was also a "Cross of the Royal and Military Order of Saint-Henry," which was sixteen feet high and contained the motto: "*Henry, Founder.*" Next to that was "a star of the same size with the motto: *cost of warlike valor.*" In front of the wings of the palace were two painted crowns, each one standing at six feet tall. "At the bottom of the crown placed in front of the right wing of the palace was this inscription: *To First Monarch Crowned in the New World.* At the bottom of the crown, placed in front of the left wing, was yet another inscription: 'Cherished Queen, reign forever over our hearts'; in front of the facade of the Palace of the Council we read this verse: *To reign is his duty, To govern, his virtue.*"[160] Christophe's most lasting legacy may just be the culture he left behind in these marvelous architectural monuments, which outlived his antislavery monarchy.

Christophe's agricultural reforms were also designed to be inherently antislavery. While exports—indigo, coffee, sugar, and tobacco—of the kingdom's staples were strong, King Henry also urged Haitians to cultivate wheat and other grains. The goal was to make Haiti less dependent upon imports: "Producing our own means of subsistence, is the safest and most powerful way to increase and maintain the growing population."[161] The Comte de Limonade's *Instructions pour les établissemens et la culture des habitations caféyères de la couronne* (Instructions for the establishment and cultivation of the Crown's coffee plantations, 1818) described how the kingdom's agricultural system worked. We read in the section titled "On Cleared Lands," "Only bananas, peas and corn will be planted in the *bois neuf* [cleared lands] among the rows of coffee trees, but rice, yams, potatoes, and other foods, which could harm the cultivation of coffee, w ill n ot b e p lanted t here." I n t he s ection after "On the Harvesting of Coffee," the decree clarified that subsistence crops could be planted, but "care must be taken to separately prepare the plots where can be planted food like rice, cassava, potato, *tayau*, yams, which are not compatible and thus cannot be planted alongside the cultivation of coffee."[162]

Consulting the Baron de Vastey's *Réflexions politiques* produces not simply evidence of a policy friendly to and dependent on subsistence crops, but also a logic and theory to support it. Vastey continued the tradition of both philosophical and material upheaval that undergirded the creation of the antislavery Code Henry when he linked the necessity of planting *vivres*, or

286 Chapter 8

everyday foodstuffs, in independent Haiti to the fact that the enslaved were largely forbidden from planting *vivres* for their own subsistence in colonial Saint-Domingue: "Wheat, barley, oats have already been sown and harvested, and we have definitive proof that if we have not been able to enjoy these substantial products for a long time, it has only been due to the malice and the combined interests of the ex-colonists with their metropole; the Carthaginians, the better to impose their yoke on the Sicilians, forbade them on pain of death to sow wheat; in the Colonial Regime, it was similarly forbidden in Saint-Domingue, to cultivate wheat and vines to make wine, under the most severe penalties." "Continue to produce the means for your livelihood, say all economists, and you will see men grow and multiply!" Vastey exclaimed. "That eminently wise and political calculation, designed to increase the population of a country, could not be permitted to enter into the minds of the ex-colonists."[163] Vastey claimed that food dependency was dangerous because it could lead to other kinds of dependency. "A people must become sufficient with respect to their principal needs," he wrote. "If they depend on foreigners for their subsistence, they will no longer be the masters of their own existence; but would have abandoned themselves."[164] The kingdom's creation of agricultural policies designed to support life necessitated overturning colonial agricultural policies that, if not designed to produce Black death, were at the very least indifferent to Black life.

The British botanist and translator of Vastey's writings, William Hamilton, praised Christophe's agricultural policies. Quoting the passage above from Vastey, Hamilton noted that preventing wheat from being grown in the "tropics" was especially prejudicial and designed to support enslaving Black people in the Americas: "Other causes appear to have concurred with the African Slave Trade, in excluding not only the culture of the Cerealia, but likewise the manufacture of wine and other objects of European industry, from Haiti, under the Colonial Regime, which are fully explained in the following passage extracted from the 'Reflexions Politiques' of my talented and lamented friend, Baron de Vastey."[165]

Although in popular history, Pétion usually gets associated with friendly land policies, in the latter 1810s, Christophe further extended his land grant program, previously only available to the aristocracy and the military, to the entire Haitian population. Now, every Haitian could apply to acquire the erstwhile farms of the French planters. The aim was "for every Haytian, indiscriminately, the poor as well as the rich, to have the ability to become the owner of the lands of our former oppressors."[166]

Some of the world's most storied antislavery advocates admired the Kingdom of Haiti, but many of northern Haiti's foreign inhabitants questioned whether the king's codes benefited the average Haitian citizen. William

Wilson, a British teacher who worked in Cap-Henry and acted as a tutor to Christophe's son, Prince Victor, wrote to Clarkson shortly after the king's suicide, "They owed him all that they had. As the founder of their most beneficial institutions, he had done everything for them." But "if he made good laws, he was the first to violate them," Wilson explained. "In a word, he was a *philosopher*."[167] Dumesle also claimed that though the code described the plan for a remarkably novel society, it was one that lamentably, "only existed on paper."[168] For Dumesle, who referred to Christophe as "the monster who desolated the beautiful north," the kingdom's greatest sin was the putatively antidemocratic principles undergirding it.[169] "As I turned my eyes to the countryside, I saw that despite the display of splendor derived from exploitation of northern sugar factories, despite all appearances, those dwellings produced labor only through violence," Dumesle continued. "There was extreme inequality between the products produced for export and the agricultural ones." Agriculture for subsistence was the "very real foundation of the power of empires which fertilizes industry and gives life to commerce" and "produced an advantage in favor of the democratic state."[170] In other words, Dumesle said that in the kingdom, in contrast to the republic, there was a striking imbalance between the goods produced for export and those produced for subsistence. Dumesle claimed this imbalance did not exist in the republic because the latter was formed on so-called democratic principles. These principles were designed to serve the people rather than to use the people to produce products for the state. Christophe's downfall had therefore been inevitable in Dumesle's estimation because the people were treated as a means to an end.

The way "the people" appear primarily as laborers in the voluminous print culture of the Kingdom of Haiti provides clues to their otherwise mysterious absence in the forms of Haitian thought that cohered under Christophe. In March 1818, the *Gazette* announced, "All the idle people in the towns and villages have been rounded up and sent to the countryside to engage in the work of farming." The Haitian people were assured that preventing "idleness" was merely proof that "our august and beloved Sovereign is taking every care to ensure the prosperity of agriculture and commerce."[171] Some of the king's foreign supporters claimed this harsh hand of "kingly power," as the U.S. journalist Caleb Cushing wrote, was necessary to preserve Haiti's freedom from slavery and independence from colonial rule in a world determined to see the descendants of Africans fail.[172] Such a conclusion might have been directly drawn from reading Christophean publications. In a speech from November 1806, but not printed in the *Gazette officielle de l'état d'Hayti* until May 1807, a few months after Christophe was established as president of a separate state in the north of Haiti, the future king told the people of his country, "Remember

288 Chapter 8

that the government that will from now on guarantee your rights and assure your rights to independence, demands of you obedience, and the precise maintenance of order and unity, respect for your leaders, a commitment to military discipline and execution of the laws; these are the conditions without which it will be impossible for us to begin to step forward in the new world that has opened up for us."[173] Writers from the Kingdom of Haiti made it their mission not only to combat the lugubrious image of Haiti being produced in the Western European and U.S. literary and historical imaginations, but to highlight the industry and devotion to work of the Haitian citizenry and show off the magnificent culture of Black freedom they were creating.

Later Haitian historians like Madiou forcefully disputed the claim that Black feudalism could secure Black freedom. According to Madiou, workers on northern farms received almost no compensation and the farmers, because they had to pay such high taxes to the state, could only keep a small portion, one-fourth of their revenue. For Madiou, this was not the kind of liberty and equality promised by the Caribbean's first and only modern king,[174] the one who swore at his coronation "to never allow, under any pretext, the return of Slavery nor of any feudal system contrary to liberty and the exercise of the civil and political rights of the people of Haiti."[175] Yet without being able to examine testimony of Christophe's subjects themselves, it is difficult to determine their attitudes about his labor system. Dumesle, for his part, believed that the proof of the northern populace's disdain for Christophe resided not in their so often reported cries of "vive le roi," or "long live the king." These "acclamations," Dumesle wrote, "are not the most faithful testimony of the feelings of a people." Instead, Dumesle located the perspective of northern Haitians in Christophe's downfall: "Tired of the excesses of tyranny to which they had been victim for fourteen years, the people were simply waiting for the moment to overthrow him; they had made several attempts, the vicissitudes of which caused conjecture, and the deceptive calm that followed proved the state of impassability into which a nation falls when its energy has been exhausted."[176] Although for Dumesle, Christophe's downfall was inevitable simply because he was a king in a world trending toward republics, understanding the consequences of King Henry's death for the Haitian people requires consciously avoiding the sense of historical inevitability that pervades Dumesle's rendering.

In the *Gazette royale d'Hayti*, dated October 28, 1819, the editor, Baron de Vastey, responded directly to Dumesle's claim, in his newspaper, *L'Observateur*, that "a sinister calm reigns in that capital [Cap-Henry]." The editor of the *Gazette* went on to contest Dumesle's assertion that "the people are under oppression, trade is languishing, foreigners only approach that city with fear, like a place affected by the plague," and that "there are no institutions." Pointing out that Dumesle's report of life in the kingdom was written in armchair

Antislavery   289

fashion, "from the depths of his office in Les Cayes," the editor of the *Gazette* stated, to the contrary, that the many foreigners who actually lived in the north and experienced life there "have been persuaded that freedom reigns here, but without license." "They see that people and property are respected here," the writer clarified. "That all men, rich and poor, noble and townspeople, as well as simple citizens are entitled to rights, and are punishable before the same laws, and the same judges; and if liberty reigns, equal rights also reign." To combat Dumesle's claim that King Henry reinstated slavery, the *Gazette* declared: "Oh! How could it be that oppression, tyranny, and slavery reign in the midst of a people who have won their freedom and their rights at the cost of their blood? If it could be so, wouldn't it be the height of human extravagance and madness, and could it last? These people who expelled their tyrants, proud and protective of their freedom, could they admit others with their own hearts? Wouldn't they hasten to claim their rights?"[177] We might be tempted to conclude that this passage ended up being prophetic in that the people of the kingdom did eventually turn on the king and demand their rights. However, this would be making quite a far leap. Christophe was overthrown by a conspiracy of elites, led by the Duc de la Marmelade, Jean-Pierre Richard, and not one of farmers from the countryside or "simple citizens."[178] All the same, there are things we might infer about the king's treatment of his subjects. Writing from Cap on December 8, 1820, exactly two months after the suicide, Christophe's personal physician, a Scotsman by the name of Duncan Stewart, told Thomas Clarkson what he no doubt already knew: "King Henry died by his own hands; finding himself reduced to a helpless state by paralytics and deserted by all his troops, he shot himself through the heart." Reporting that he was nearly always by the king's side since his August 1820 stroke, Stewart claimed Christophe was in good spirits at the time he learned of the rebellion forming against him. The king seemed "quite collected to the last, and sometimes quite cheerful," Stewart wrote. "I used often to converse with him for hours," the doctor added. "He seemed sensible that he had used his people harshly and that he ought to have been more liberal to his soldiers."[179]

Though Boyer proclaimed himself to be the liberator of the Haitian people when he reunified the north and south into the Republic of Haiti immediately after Christophe's death,[180] the lives of farmers, who were technically classified as noncitizens under the Code Rural, and who did not have the freedom to change locales or profession, seemed to get worse.[181] Moreover, we must not assume that all the citizens of the north, especially the farmers, shared the opinions of the southern and northern elites who wanted Christophe gone, mostly so they could assume power for themselves; and, furthermore, that the lack of first-person testimonials from those living under Christophe does not present a historical conundrum, even though the his-

290   Chapter 8

torical profession has now become far more accustomed to considering artifacts other than print as containing narrative capacity. The fact of the matter is that the majority of the Haitian populace, that is to say narration of their actual lives and individuality, are missing even from narratives of Christophe's downfall penned by his enemies, other than their reports that the people replaced their cries of *vive le roi!* (i.e., King Henry) with those of *vive le président! or vive la république!* (i.e., Boyer).[182] This shift in political cheer, while not necessarily untrue, was obviously self-serving for those in power narrating it. Those Boyer-era writers from Haiti who chronicled the king's downfall sought to prove that their favored leader had the support of the people as supposedly evidenced by these chants, which Dumesle has already warned us against reading as faithful evidence of the feelings of a populace, not least in the context of King Henry's rule.[183]

We might say, in the end, the Citadelle Laferrière and the Palace at Sans-Souci, today World Heritage UNESCO (United Nations Educational, Scientific and Cultural Organization) sites, transcend the difficult history that brought them into being and remain antislavery monuments, as much as they are emblems of anti-colonialism. Walcott, for his part, still found it difficult to admire all that the Haitian king tried to build, saying King Henry's enormous fortress marked "the slave's emergence from bondage," at the same time as it suggested "the slave had surrendered one Egyptian darkness for another."[184] Yet, France's continuous aggression against its lost colony, culminating in a disastrous indemnity as the price of freedom, proves its leaders were far more Pharaoh-like than Christophe. In the early nineteenth century, Napoléon was overthrown twice, and both times, Louis XVIII—who was restored as French king in 1814 and 1815, respectively—following the urges of the former colonists, attempted to "restore Saint-Domingue" and bring back slavery. Vastey wrote that this merely proved "twenty-five years of misfortune and experience have failed to correct the irascibility of the ex-colonists":

> They have not let go of one iota of their iniquitous and barbaric system; they
> have not ceased to provoke the cabinet of Louis XVIII, to lead it, like
> that of Bonaparte, into sending a similar expedition against us; they have
> not only advised it, but they have also offered, just like the first time,
> pecuniary means for it to be undertaken; first, they sent us spies, then
> commissioners, all of them ex-colonists, to insult us and offer us the
> choice between slavery or death; they conceived of plans of attacks, plans
> of extermination in their writings and pamphlets, which make nature
> tremble, and which violate all the laws of religion, justice, morality, and
> humanity; finally, they have proposed to exterminate our entire popula
> tion, even suckling babies.[185]

View of Citadelle Henry from below, 2020. Courtesy of Samy F. Zaka.

Understanding the kind of state Christophe, and all of Haiti's first rulers, tried to create means understanding that the world they lived in was one where the liberty of Black people was everywhere under threat. To deny that diplomatic nonrecognition, ongoing French slavery in the Caribbean, and various threats of war, embargo, the indemnity, and other kinds of interference made governing Haiti complicated, is to contest the very force and power of slavery

View of Palace at Sans-Souci, 2020. Courtesy of Samy F. Zaka.

and colonialism. The specter of Black freedom and self-government in the Americas was so frightening to the slaving nations of the Atlantic World that its realization brought punishment to Haiti again and again. At the same time, the insidiousness of Atlantic World slave economies was so great that even though he did not reinstate slavery, the king of Haiti still profited from it. By trading with the colonial powers, the break with the capitalist order sparked by the initial slave rebellion in Saint-Domingue dissipated into the air.

Even though the king's rule was full of the kinds of contradictions facing every modern state, paradoxically, the end of the Christophean era led to a Haiti that was far less free than the one King Henry left behind. No one knows how things might have turned out had Christophe lived, but we do know how things turned out without him. In contrast to Pétion and Boyer, Christophe was adamantly against paying any reparations to the French. His death left the door wide open for France to extort Haiti for millions as the price of the very liberty that the Haitian people had already spilled so much of their blood to secure.

Chapter 9

Anti-racism

Haiti's victory over France upset the very idea of the superiority of *whiteness*, which the French colonists wielded with their swords as much as with their words to justify their enslavement and colonization of Africans and their descendants in the Americas. Tiny Haiti's ability to defend itself against one of the largest and fiercest armies in the world could not but upset the white supremacist illogics of colonialism, slavery, and racism. In the wake of Haitian independence, the ex-colonists of Saint-Domingue threw a seemingly endless number of discursive tantrums. François Mazères, a notorious enslaver from the Quartier Morin neighborhood in Petite-Anse, wrote a racist and wholly white supremacist diatribe in response to a pamphlet written by the Genevan abolitionist, Jean Charles Léonard Simonde de Sismondi, who had defended Haitian sovereignty and praised life in the Kingdom of Haiti. In Mazères's reply, which Vastey quoted from at length, the ex-French colonist confirmed that he previously declared that Haitians did not deserve freedom since the "negro is a big child . . . who has neither energy of the mind or spirit."[1] Baron de Vastey, in his reply to Mazères, pointed out a simple contradiction that Haitian defeat of French forces made obvious. "If Mazères were capable of logic," Vastey wrote, "he would have recognized that he was reducing himself and the former colonists to the bottom rung of humanity; because, alas, those overgrown, ignorant, simple-minded children . . . defeated them in battle, loathe them, and have sworn an implacable hatred for them."[2] Vastey correctly located "the pride, prejudices, and greed of the planters" as the illogic undergirding Mazères's attempt to "make of the *black* man, a particular and distinct species from the *white* man."[3] Colonists like Mazères used this "sophistic and absurd rationale," Vastey said, less to prove the inferiority of the people they had tried to "reduce to perpetual slavery," than to justify their continued desire to do it.[4] What naturally followed from Mazères's illogical conclusion that "negroes are inferior to whites" was a self-serving denial of Haitian independence. In one breath, Mazères charged, "There cannot be found in all of Christophe's kingdom ten men in a state to read fluently," adding that "there are certainly not more of them to be found who are educated enough to understand the meaning of the words *tactic, military, geography, mathematics, fortifications*"; while in another breath, Mazères exhaled his resentment against Sismondi for "recognizing as legitimate" "that ridiculous sovereign that no European power has yet recognized." "You quite formally declare the colony of Saint-Domingue independent by law as well as in fact," Mazères continued, "and you sanction at the same time a blithe brigand at the expense of the forfeiture of the legitimate sovereign of France's claim to the colony." All roads in colonial thought lead to extermination, indeed. In the last sentence of his reply, Mazères wrote that King Henry's government was so "horrible" that "with eyes of reason," "English writers themselves are advising their own [government] to unite with France, to annihilate that foyer of barbarism."[5] To save face, from Mazères's perspective, Haiti had to be either punished (returned to slavery and the colonial yoke) or destroyed.

Casting aside Mazères's desire to destroy the Haitian people, Vastey knew that Haitians had the moral high ground. The ex-colonists could not rely on Christianity to support their claims to the island, since the fact of the Haitian Revolution and Haitian independence had a coherent rationale and a logic that was cosmological in nature. Speaking directly to "Grand Dieu," Vastey called the Haitian Revolution one of God's "greatest works." "From within the heart of a herd of slaves, your almighty power formed the elements necessary to avenge your divine laws!" Vastey exclaimed. "You breathed into our hearts the divine fire of liberty; suddenly our chains were broken, our oppressors disappeared from our soil, and their prejudices and their pride were confounded forever!"[6] Vastey's metaphor of a Grand Dieu breathing freedom into a crowd of enslaved people also resonates with the Bon Dieu (or *Bondye*) evoked in the story of the Morne-Rouge assembly that heralded the start of the revolution. Haiti's existence was therefore not "a political fiction," but a divine fact.[7] Destroying Haiti to preserve slavery across the Americas and uphold the idea of white supremacy could therefore be framed as trying to destroy the work of God.

The "basis of the colonial system," as Vastey wrote in his *Essai sur les causes de la révolution*, "rests on slavery and color prejudices with the goal of preserving the supremacy of whiteness, which the ex-colonists jealously guard."[8] Napoléon had been at war with the whole of Europe essentially from the beginning to the end of his reign, but one thing all the European slaving powers he fought could agree on was not recognizing Haitian sovereignty. "The course of the revolution showed us that the whites, our enemies, from all parties, divided among themselves in political opinions, were perfectly in agreement when it came to the question of destroying the Haytians," Vastey wrote. "The cause of the French whites was *unique*, I am saying that of the Haytians, although divided in opinion, must also be *unique*, for their preservation," he continued. "Mutual salvation has demanded, and still demands, that we should always remain united and indissolubly attached."[9] Independent Haiti's various states—as the country moved in the nineteenth century from empire to republic to kingdom and back to empire and then finally to a republic again—collectively offered to the world an instruction manual about how to destroy slavery and colonialism not only through revolution but with the law. Despite the many forms of statecraft that marked nineteenth-century Haiti, the 1805 Imperial Constitution remained fundamental with its anti-colonial, anti-slavery, and anti-racist clauses.

The preamble to the 1805 constitution developed an anti-racist philosophy that set the stage for the later dismantling of color prejudice contained in its numerous articles and provisions. Referencing the idea that human diversity was a spiritual and natural phenomenon, the constitution began by stating that it reflected the will of the Haitian populace and was being proclaimed "in the presence of the Supreme Being, before whom all mortals are equal, and who has spread so many different kinds of creatures over the face of the globe, for the purpose of manifesting his glory and his power, through the diversity of his oeuvre."[10] The purpose of the colonial theory of white supremacy was to justify slavery. The purpose of the Haitian theory of human diversity was to promote freedom. Anténor Firmin called the racism of the colonists, in contrast, "that fiction which subalternizes a man to the point of making him into a thing." Early modern European enslavers invented a new form of racism, white supremacy, purely to justify such *thingification*. "From the point of view of pure logic," Firmin continued, "a reason had to be found to legitimize that institution, and never was a reason made to seem more plausible than the intellectual and moral inferiority that was legally presented as the natural basis for slavery."[11] The nineteenth-century Haitian novelist Émeric Bergeaud also criticized the fiction of color prejudice in an actual fiction, *Stella* (1859), the first Haitian novel. Bergeaud wrote that color prejudices were contrary to divine laws, containing "a proposal of which the simple enunciation is absurd." "The rationales for slavery and the prejudices that hideously form its cortège are well known," Bergeaud continued:

> They come solely from insatiable greed. To torture the miserable Africans without remorse, the masters, veiling their crimes with sophistry, have purported that they were inferior to all the other individuals of the human race, and solely because they were black. Many of them, not even having been slave owners—without a doubt to their chagrin—have also said this and written it. But this inferiority is so little proven that we are convinced that even those who have espoused it do not even really believe that it exists. Is there a color that is privileged in nature? Where is the animal that can be judged based on the appearance of its fur?[12]

Haitians used the natural diversity of humankind—a diversity that reflected God's will—to shoot enormous holes into the theory of white supremacy.

Vastey wrote that white people, in asserting for themselves the right to dominate Black people, were "revolting against the views of the creator, who wanted for there to be different varieties of men on this earth, as with animals."[13] Chanlatte, perhaps most forcefully, used the fact of human diversity, coupled with the idea of divinity, to rebuke the theory of white supremacy:

> No, no, let us no longer suffer from that disgraceful [idea of] privilege; when the Lord spread various races over the earth, he did not claim that one particular species should destroy another. The French think they are insulting us, they think they are allowed to do anything to us by calling us negroes: well, then! Let us be vain, let us show them that those they despise surpass them in courage, greatness of soul, and above all in loyalty; let them, in their homeland, slaving away today under an unjust and ambitious master, learn from a savage people the secret to being free.[14]

Sovereign Haitians had much to teach a world plagued by Napoléon's despotic and murderous wars about the "secret to being free." An acceptance and embrace of diversity was axiomatic to the principles the Haitian revolutionaries set down in 1804 before the "foreign powers" and the "entire universe."[15] Through its first constitution, sovereign Haiti extended the ideology of anti-slavery and anti-colonialism inscribed in the Declaration of Independence to include anti-racism.

The constitution for the Empire of Haiti encoded anti-racism into the law in both material and philosophical ways. Article 14 is the most important on that score: "All distinctions of color among children of the same family, of whom the head of State is the father, needing to necessarily cease, Haitians will be known from now on only under the generic denomination of blacks."[16] This meant that all citizens of Haiti, regardless of their actual skin color, were to be considered and called Black. The idea that all Haitians from that moment forward were "Black" has been the subject of fascinating debate for scholars. Sibylle Fischer has written that Article 14 "disrupts any biologistic or racialist expectations" by allowing for white women, Germans, and Polish people to attain citizenship, rendering "'black' a mere implication of being Haitian and thus a political rather than a biological category."[17] Jean Casimir has suggested that "this new 'black'" demonstrated Haiti's essential diversity, as it "encompassed the various ethnic groups that had been involved in the struggle against the Western vision of mankind. Victory in adversity gave birth to this new character," Casimir wrote, "which was a synthesis not only of Ibos, Aradas, and Hausas but also of French, Germans, and Poles."[18] Anthony Bogues has added, "By making all Haitians black the Constitution reversed the colonial hierarchical status of human being."[19] But for our purposes, we are more interested in the first part of the law, the clause which has so much to tell us about the legacy and influence of Haiti's revolutionary attempt to legislate anti-racism. By declaring that "all distinctions of color" had to "*necessarily* cease," Haiti became the first state not only to permanently outlaw slavery and to ban imperial rule, but to try to criminalize color prejudice. Article 14 constituted a legal attempt to prevent color prejudice by erasing the possibility of Haiti's lawmakers and citizens to create, recognize, or give nomination to the kinds of color distinctions, with their implied hierarchies, that the white colonists of Saint-Domingue used to justify the oppression of the Black people they enslaved (*nègres*) and to exclude the *hommes de couleur* (*mulâtres*) from citizenship rights.

To understand this remarkable move, a nineteenth-century head of state's unprecedented attempt to legally ban color prejudice, we must take a look at earlier articles that set the context. Researchers have been mainly interested in Articles 12–14 for reasons other than the idea that it banned color prejudice. Article 12, which we examined briefly in chapter 7, became quite infamous, historically speaking, because it seemed to forbid white property ownership: "No white man, whatever his nationality, will set foot on this territory with the title of master or proprietor and can never, even in the future, acquire any property." Yet, as Fischer reminded us, Article 13 undid what, at first glance, appeared to be a contradiction of the later anti-racism clause in Article 14 by describing which whites could own property anyway. Article 12 did not apply, for example, to "white women," "Poles," and "Germans," who could become Haitian and, therefore, "Black" through marriage. Blackness was as theoretical as whiteness in the Empire of Haiti. The constitution's creators implicitly recognized race as a social construct, a fiction of the highest magnitude. As such, inclusion in one or another "race" could be constructed in a number of diff erent ways that might shift and change over time.

The laws in the Haitian Constitution of 1805 upended whiteness as the legal basis for property ownership on the island (including the Africans the white colonists were permitted to claim as property), which had been encoded in Louis XIV's edict of 1685. As such Haiti's laws of 1805 are of distinct relevance to the framework of critical race theory that brought us Cheryl Harris's groundbreaking "Whiteness as Property." Haiti's preliminary laws about property and race disrupted what Harris called, in the context of the antebellum United States, the "property interest in whiteness." Harris explained:

> Slavery linked the privilege of whites to the subordination of Blacks through a legal regime that attempted the conversion of Blacks into objects of property. Similarly, the settlement and seizure of Native American land supported white privilege through a system of property rights in land in which the "race" of the Native Americans rendered their

first possession rights invisible and justified conquest. This racist formulation embedded the fact of white privilege into the very definition of property, marking another stage in the evolution of the property interest in whiteness. Possession—the act necessary to lay the basis for rights in property—was defined to include only the cultural practices of whites. This definition laid the foundation for the idea that whiteness—that which whites alone possess—is valuable and is property.[20]

The Haitian Constitution of 1805 interrupted the idea of whiteness as *intangible* property that could give rights to *tangible* property, by legally forbidding the white settler colonial practice of taking possession of people, places, and things, *in the name of whiteness.*

In his April 28 proclamation, Dessalines explained beforehand the historical context that was to undergird the so-called white property exclusion in the constitution. Dessalines pointed out that he was not at all like his predecessor, "the ex-general Toussaint Louverture," because while Louverture let the white property owners (the former enslavers!) return, at his own peril, and at that of the future Haitian people, "I have been faithful to the promise I made to you when I took up arms against tyranny, and as long as there is a single breath left in me, I will keep this oath." The oath followed in the next sentence: "No colonist or European will ever set foot on this territory, as master or owner." It must be noted that here Dessalines used the very specific identity marker "colonist," but this was changed in the constitution. In his first formulation of the law, Dessalines said nothing about whiteness as a criterion, though he may have assumed that his audience would consider all colonists and Europeans to be *blancs.* Nevertheless, Dessalines continued by explaining, "This resolution shall henceforth be the fundamental basis of our constitution." The historical sequence of events narrated in the proclamation provides further context. The white property exclusion was conceived of only after the white ex-colonists who remained on the island after January 1 tried to overthrow the newly minted Haitian government. "Should I remind you again of the plots recently hatched in Jérémie?" Dessalines asked. "The terrible explosion that was to result from it, despite the generous pardon granted to those incorrigible beings at the expulsion of the French army; their emissaries imitated them in all the cities in order to stir up a new internecine war." Seeming to foreshadow or at least to preconceive the imminence of his own death, and the possibility that his legacy might be tarnished, Dessalines asked, "What does it matter to me the judgments that will be pronounced upon me by contemporary and future races?" Dessalines had before him the examples of Louverture and Rigaud, both jailed by the French at the Fort de Joux, while professing their utter devotion to the Republic of France.[21] Still, the future emperor of Haiti seemed to sense that his time on the physical earth might be short and that his successors might make different choices with respect to the ongoing war with the French: "If other leaders, after me, dig their own graves and those of their fellow men, by adopting a conduct diametrically opposed to mine, you will have only to accuse the inevitable law of fate that will have prevented me from ensuring the happiness and salvation of my fellow citizens; but may my successors follow the path that I will trace for them! It is the system best calculated to consolidate their power; it is the most worthy homage they can pay to my memory."[22] Examining the trajectory of foreign invasion and occupation in Haiti to the present day would make us hard pressed to disagree with Dessalines. His seemingly draconian policy proscribing foreign property ownership no longer seems so drastic. Perhaps, it was merely an oracle professed by a man who was before his time.

To understand the further development of this law, and its consequences for Haitian revolutionary thought, let us turn to a much less examined section of the 1805 constitution, which clarified the white property clause in important ways. Under the heading "General Dispositions," Article 12 declared, "Any property that previously belonged to a white Frenchman is irrevocably and legally confiscated for the profit of the state." Even as the constitution decoupled whiteness and property, it was not the color of the landowner that mattered most, but the nationality. This did not prevent critics from interpreting Article 12 under its many iterations in later Haitian constitutions as mandating blanket white property exclusion, as we have already seen. Some of those critics came from nineteenth-century Haiti. Recall that Vastey was a huge critic of the idea of banning white property ownership, as it appeared in Pétion's 1816 constitution (Article 38), and which was included in every Haitian constitution except Christophe's until 1918.[23] Vastey believed that Article 38 should have maintained its origins in both the Haitian Declaration of Independence and in the constitution of 1805. He wrote that a better law for the Republic of Haiti under Pétion would have been, "No *French* person whatever his color can set foot on this territory for any reason at all until the French government has recognized the independence of Haiti." As Vastey pointed out, "the declaration of independence only effectively excluded the French from the territory of Haiti," not white people altogether.[24] With this clarification, Vastey hoped that the other foreign powers might break the tacit agreement they seemed to have formed with the French government not to recognize Haitian independence.

In the early nineteenth century, Napoléon, and later the Bourbon kings and their ministers, along with the ex-colonists, continually and openly threatened Haiti's sovereignty. Just as in the era of the Treaty of Amiens, the French hoped that the interest of the other Western European powers and the United

300　Chapter 9

States in preserving slavery would continue to ally them together in the cause of destroying Black sovereignty in Haiti. Vastey saw Louis XVIII's appointment of Pierre Victor Malouet, called the Baron de Malouet, to the position of minister of the marine as a shot fired across the Atlantic directly at Haiti. In 1802, while the Haitian Revolution was still ongoing, Baron de Malouet pled with the European powers to create "a confederation of their interests" based on a "preponderance of their color," meaning white people, who could fight against the Black revolutionaries of Haiti, whom Malouet said were "their natural enemies."[25] Malouet wanted the other slaving states of the Atlantic World to join together with France to help restore slavery in Saint-Domingue, and he used the shared idea of European *whiteness* as the illogic for this proposed coalition. Writing ten years after France definitively lost its most prized possession, Vastey noticed that the French government remained open to cooperating with its most storied enemies—England and Spain—in the name of whiteness, just as it was similarly open to those enemies at the time of the Peace of Amiens in 1802. Vastey wanted to remind the world that the reason Haitians could not trust Minister Malouet not to attack their sovereignty was his previous proposal that Europeans create a coalition of "white" states specifically to restore slavery in Saint-Domingue. Vastey had no reason to think that Malouet had changed his mind since that time, and so he asked: "Why are you calling for the creation of a confederation of powerful European states to work against the Haitian people? What interests would these other powers have in allying themselves with you? . . . What would be the benefit of them helping you in this unjust enterprise? . . . Why would we be their natural enemies? Have we ever tried to invade their territories? Have we ever troubled the peace or the happiness of our neighbors by ransacking their capitals? Have we ever involved ourselves directly or indirectly in their domestic or foreign policies?"[26] Vastey finally asked, "Have black people ever crossed the seas in order to invade, enslave, and destroy whites?"[27]

Even though before his downfall Napoléon had been busy fighting wars around the world and seemed to lose sight of Saint-Domingue, Vastey was correct to remain wary that he might try to bring back slavery by organizing another expedition. However, that dishonor went to the Bourbons, who managed to be even more delusional in this regard than Napoléon. After Napoléon was forced to abdicate his throne to the Bourbons, for the first time, in spring 1814, Louis XVIII, brother of Louis XVI, became king and immediately began to plot a reconquest of France's erstwhile colony. The official reconquest instructions issued by the Baron de Malouet, whom Louis XVIII appointed as minister of the marine, mandated the return of slavery and the wholesale extermination of most of the country's population.[28] Vastey decried this attempt on Haitian freedom using a powerfully poetic language, distinctive of his numerous condemnations of France's continuous plans to restore slavery. "The colonial hydra troubles us once again," Vastey lamented. "Its roars have crossed the vast expanse of these seas and have reached us . . . it multiplies and transforms itself, taking on diverse appearances in order to defeat us."[29] The colonial hydra would indeed arrive, but its head would soon be cut off, only to grow back once again. Christophe ultimately foiled Louis XVIII's plot, not once, but twice. Louis XVIII tried again in 1816 after the second Bourbon restoration. On January 9, 1817, the *Royal Gazette of Hayti* published an account of Louis XVIII's various plots. These exposés were meant to prove to the Haitian people and to the world that the French government desired and was blatantly attempting to reconquer "Saint-Domingue," which meant to bring back slavery. Publishing these descriptions allowed the editor of the newspaper to justify the fact that "from the South to the North, from the East to the West, in light of the new insults of the French, one sole and lone cry can be heard once again: Liberty, Independence, or Death; war to the French, and all their allies!"[30]

Early Haitian writers and politicians repeatedly narrated Haiti's revolutionary history to remind the populace that the French had always been the biggest threat to Haitian freedom and sovereignty. Recalling the divisions that the French agent Hédouville stoked between Rigaud and Louverture, a writer who signed his or her name A. L. D. in a May 1824 article in *Le Télégraphe* opined in Creole, "The one who burns the mother pig, is the same one who burns all her children." In other words, the same people who killed their ancestors, still wanted to kill them. Citing also at length passages from Chanlatte's *Le Cri de la nature*, the writer for *Le Télégraphe* reminded readers of the thirty thousand members of "our population" killed by the French during the Leclerc expedition. The article's writer concluded by observing that the French had the same murderous intentions vis-à-vis Haiti in 1824 as they did in 1802: "For what do these wicked men hope? to have this country as a colony!" Using another Haitian Creole phrase, the writer warned, "my dear friends, isn't it better to be wary than to be sorry?" (*chers amis nous yo, pringa miore passé pardon?*), lest Haitians be deceived once more by Frenchmen like Leclerc and Hédouville, whose treacherous deeds the author enumerated in gruesome detail.[31] The writer finished by using language worthy of Dessalines, Boisrond-Tonnerre, or Vastey: "Eternal war, therefore, to the colonists! have nothing to do with them except with arms in hand. Defiance against our enemies! Indissoluble unity among the children of Haiti."[32]

The Haitian Revolution forced the Atlantic World powers, as much as those in their public spheres, to openly confront and debate whether they were committed more to the liberty and equality they shouted in republican constitu-

-1—
0—
+1—

302   Chapter 9

tions, declarations, and party slogans or to upholding white supremacists' illogics to preserve chattel slavery. Those conversations in many ways revolved around Haiti as an anti-colonial, antislavery, anti-racist state. What happened in Saint-Domingue could happen in the French or British colonies or on U.S. shores. In the nineteenth century, the independence of Haiti constituted the most immediately visible attempt of Black people to destroy en masse the foundations of racism that white people were using to justify and explain the slave regime they continued to perpetuate. In their writings, Haitian writers and politicians exposed not only the dire political consequences of color prejudice but also its dire material consequences, not just for Haitians but for the world. Prévost marveled at the lack of humanity evident in the Leclerc expedition as much as in French attempts at reconquest. "It is hard to believe, and one would not want to believe, that men who announced themselves as apostles of liberty, who continually had that sacred word in their mouths, could have profaned it, made themselves the instruments of a handful of beings alien to all human feeling, and with joy, without any reason, as if without any motive, have braved the perils and dangers of the ocean, to destroy, to annihilate a population whose only crime, after having tasted that same liberty, which had been taken away from them, was to cherish it!"[33] The Haitian revolutionaries had the moral high ground because, unlike the French, they used violence to fight for liberty, not to take it away. "The bosom of slaves sometimes bore the most intrepid and proudest defenders of freedom. Toussaint Louverture, and so many others, are the proof," Prévost remarked. "Where did they draw that energy, that indomitable courage, which made them triumph over every obstacle, to establish and consolidate the great oeuvre toward which all their hopes were drawn?" Prévost answered his own question: "In the school of adversity!"[34] Prévost wished "eternal honor on the first founders, and peace to the ashes of the virtuous Haitians who perished for such a beautiful cause."[35] The idea that there could be something beautiful, useful, or at least instrumental about Haiti's long suffering was far easier to pose in the era of the Kingdom of Haiti, a time of relative prosperity and protection from the predatory Atlantic powers.

Despite the interior political problems that Haitians faced throughout the rest of the nineteenth century—following Boyer, from 1843 to 1847 alone, *unified* Haiti saw five different presidents—it is remarkable to consider how Haitian writers and politicians, many writing from the sad position of forced overseas political exile, continued to insist that the anti-racism of their republic best positioned them as Haitians to materially and discursively spread the principles of liberty and equality upon which their country was founded. It was precisely because of all they and their ancestors suffered and continued to suffer in the name of Black freedom that Haitian thinkers argued they were best positioned to offer advice to the world about how to use the original principles of Haitian sovereignty to destroy slavery and colonialism, wherever they continued to exist, and to erect forms of humanism capable of recognizing the innate *racial* equality of all human beings.

Writing in the late nineteenth century, Firmin argued that Haitian victory was clear proof of the equality of the human races. "Can the proof of racial equality ever be better, nor more eloquently demonstrated?" he asked. Like his predecessors in early Haiti, Firmin argued that the Haitian revolutionaries were possessed of a morally superior spirit to have triumphed after experiencing the tortures and abuses of the colonists and then the French army. "All that display of military skill in the trappings of war, supported by the most moving bravery, however," Firmin continued, "is absolutely nothing compared to the strong dose of morality that those men needed to believe in, to continue that bitter struggle, and from whence was to emerge for them the most glorious of conquests, that of freedom and of a country!"[36] The same moral fortitude they drew upon to fight for the end of slavery required Haitians to aid the rest of the world. Firmin argued that teaching the world about racial justice may have been the cosmological destiny of the Haitian people when he said that Haiti's greatest act of participation in "the flourishing of progress, will be, above all, to develop a sense of justice with more force, and at the same time, more generosity" than the Europeans: "The more that we have suffered, the more that we are prepared to understand and practice justice. And really, we do not even know how wonderful will appear before the eyes of the philosopher and the thinker this family of men emerging from the most profound intellectual and moral misery, having been brought up under the influence of hardened prejudices; but having engendered, in any case, a flower of virtue made of courageous strength and ineffable kindness, two qualities that tend at the same time toward promoting and tempering justice."[37] The idea of Haiti as the philanthropic nation is a distinct reversal of the situation that now exists in most people's minds: a Haiti dominated by and dependent on the world system. Haitians are the ones who are repeatedly imagined, if not forced, to need the world's assistance. Even with all their internal problems and external threats and pressures, nineteenth-century Haitians were still immediately concerned with disrupting the very forms of white supremacy that had kept slavery alive for so long in their new biggest threat: the United States.

Following French recognition of Haitian independence (at a steep price!) in 1825, Haiti's most immediate threat of physical invasion shifted to the United States. This shift stamped the way later nineteenth-century Haitian writers and politicians wrote about their revolution, independence, and sovereignty, and how they framed their ongoing struggle against colonialism, slavery, and racism. Boyer believed that recognition from France would lead to recognition from the rest of the world.[38] That did not happen. Racism and empire were stronger pulls than democracy or diplomacy. Great Britain did not recognize Haitian independence until after slavery was fully abolished there in law and in fact in 1838 (England did send a consul in 1826, which was one step toward general recognition), and the United States did not do so until 1862, one year after the Civil War began. The rest of the world may have been slow to catch up to Haiti, but Haitian authors kept their eye on dismantling the pseudoscientific theories of race that undergirded slavery in the Atlantic World, all the while staving off new threats of imperialism coming from the United States.

Examining the political theories and material practices developed in Haiti from the mid-nineteenth century onward (when the country saw numerous different administrations, including the return to an empire under Faustin Soulouque I), highlights how Haitian intellectuals continued to use Haitian revolutionary history and the fact of Haitian sovereignty in service of anti-racism, while distancing themselves at times from state power, foreign and domestic. Haitian writers in the first half of the nineteenth century often explicitly wrote on behalf of the state, or even as the state, making state and nation one, philosophically and ideologically, under Dessalines, Christophe, Pétion, and Boyer. This is one reason why there is remarkable anti-colonial, anti-racist, and antislavery coherence as much in state-produced newspapers, laws, and other decrees, as in popular poetry, plays, short stories, or historical and political books, pamphlets, and essays. Boyer's 1825 indemnity interrupted the monologue of Haitian sovereignty as a fait accompli when he signed the treaty that called into question Haiti's a priori existence and encouraged French writers, journalists, and artists to promote Charles X, rather than Dessalines, or any other Haitian revolutionary, as Haiti's veritable founder. After the treaty, it was not uncommon to see headlines in France, the United States, and England touting the "emancipation" of "Hayti." Some foreign journalists offered more circumspection. In the words of one British writer, "One effect of this foolish treaty—foolish only on the part of Boyer—is, that by purchasing the acknowledgment of what was before an undisputed fact, he has brought the fact itself into question, for he has afforded room to doubt, that Haiti had the means of keeping that which she had begged herself to buy."[39] Indeed, there is a famous French engraving that circulated in France in 1825 titled, "His Majesty Charles X, the beloved, recognizing the independence of St. Domingue," which depicts the French king on his throne bestowing freedom on a chained Black person kneeling before him.[40]

Some Haitian writers also contributed to this specious new narrative of Haitian independence. The most surprising is certainly the case of Juste

Chanlatte. Though he was from a huge family of enslavers on both his mother's and his father's side, Chanlatte was one of the most highly visible trumpeters of Haitian independence from the start.[41] His 1804 pamphlet, published immediately after the Declaration of Independence, finished with unequivocal support for Haiti's new leader, Dessalines: "Long live Haitian independence! Long live the Governor-General!"[42] After Dessalines's assassination, Chanlatte joined ranks with Christophe and praised him throughout his reign as the "august leader" of the Haitian people, dedicating many poems and plays to court life.[43] Yet, immediately after the king's suicide, Chanlatte began publishing nasty diatribes, in verse and prose, about the late Haitian king, whom he called an "absolute tyrant" who "sullied and massacred" "my dear country."[44] Worse still, Chanlatte discursively betrayed everything he wrote in *Le Cri de la nature* to defend Haitian sovereignty when at a formal dinner in January 1826 that Boyer gave to welcome the newly appointed French consul general to Haiti, Chanlatte ventriloquized Boyer's talking points about the indemnity. In a song he composed for the occasion Chanlatte praised Charles X, of the still slaving France, as a "philosopher," a lover of "liberty," who with the 1825 treaty put his "immutable seal" on Haitian rights. Chanlatte finished by singing the lines, "It is only by plowing these fields, That we can remain free."[45]

As the nineteenth century progressed, Haitian writers continued to develop a philosophy of blackness as freedom, even though the compromises Boyer, and successive Haitian rulers, placed on Haitian sovereignty detached Haiti's public intellectuals increasingly from the state. After Boyer's ouster in 1843, many Haitian writers found their ideas in direct opposition to Haiti's successive heads of state and sought exile abroad in France or elsewhere in the Caribbean. For the most part they avoided the United States. Worried about U.S. government encroachments on Haitian sovereignty, Haitian writers also feared the consequences for the collective Black struggle against white supremacy of the U.S. government's denial of true citizenship rights and equality to American Blacks after slavery. At the same time, Haitians correctly predicted the United States was trying to become an imperial power in their shared hemisphere.

———

In his 1866 book, *La Démocratie et le préjugé de couleur aux Étas-Unis/Les Nationalités américaines et le système Monroë* (Democracy and color prejudice in the United States/American nationalities and the Monroe system), Demesvar Delorme observed that the end of the U.S. Civil War (1861–65) did little to disrupt the racism that had impeded *American* democracy from the origin of the U.S. nation onward. "The blacks," he explained, "cannot become

306   Chapter 9

citizens. They are a separate and inferior race. That is the sacramental explanation of the contradiction of color prejudice in the United States. . . . And this self-serving fiction has helped them to perpetuate the prejudices whereby the black man, even when liberated from slavery, lives without the rights of citizenship within American democracy."[46] For Delorme, the fact that the United States did not immediately outlaw distinctions based on color after the Civil War, as Haiti did in its first constitution in 1805, issued one year after i ndependence from France, signaled a lack of seriousness about integrating formerly enslaved Africans into the nation. Delorme wrote that despite "a long and fierce c ivil w ar,"[47] t he elimination of color prejudice had "not been accomplished by the great struggle that the government of the Union has just so gloriously supported against the States of the South, in the name of the liberty of the blacks."[48] Delorme argued that eliminating slavery would not be enough to rid the United States of its corresponding "slavery of color prejudice."[49] Equality needed to be supported by an actual legal policy requiring it. Alongside this observation, Delorme identified ongoing domestic racism as indelibly connected to U.S. colonial conquest. The title of Delorme's book affirmed that U.S. color prejudices had to be understood alongside U.S. expansionism in the Americas, racism and empire being mutually enforcing.

Delorme's entwining of racism ("le préjugé de couleur") and imperialism ("le système Monroë") as corollaries to capitalism's threat to democracy (the subject of Delorme's l ater 1873 *La Misère au sein des richesses* [Poverty in the heart of wealth]) intersects with earlier critiques by radical intellectuals like Haiti's Baron de Vastey, as well as with l ater nineteenth-century writings penned by anti-colonial activists like Puerto Rico's Ramón Emeterio Betances. The strategy of discourse analys is used by nineteenth-c entury Caribbean and Latin American writers like Delorme set the stage, in many ways, for the works of l ater twentieth-century Caribbean writers like Aimé Césaire, whose *Discourse on Colonialism* (1950) is considered one of the foundational texts of anti-colonial theory.

The seemingly commonsense idea espoused by today's postcolonial theorists that anti-i mperialism and anti-racism are humanistic imperatives was inaugurated by revolutionary Haiti's refusal to engage in racist empire-building. Delorme contrasted Haiti's long-standing anti-i mperial stance to the white U.S. American nativism and hemispheric imperialism associated with the so-called Monroe Doctrine. Although Delorme's faith that European and U.S. American adherence to their own Enlightenment values could bring about an end to both racial and imperial domination was unduly optimistic, his critical analysis of the way domestic racism and colonial expansion were indelibly intertwined remains relevant in our own age of empire, where structural racism at home in the United States (police killings of Black people, as one example) reinforces global police action elsewhere (i.e., until very recently, continuous U.S.- and United Nations-backed foreign intervention, if not outright occupation of Haiti). As James Baldwin wrote in his 1967 essay, "The War Crimes Tribunal," "A racist society can't but fight a racist war—this is the bitter truth. The assumptions acted on at home are also acted on abroad."[50] In contrasting nineteenth-century Haiti with the racism that had at that point been fundamental to U.S. democracy (rather than contradictory), Delorme implied that Haitians, as members of the first state in the Americas to outlaw slavery, color prejudice, and imperialism, could offer crucial lessons to the world, and specifically to the United States, about how to implement both a spirit of democracy and laws appropriate to its true fruition. The Haitian Revolution and the subsequent political theories that Haiti's earliest leaders inscribed into law definitively linked anti-Black racism with imperial domination by decidedly forswearing both.

Like most Haitian authors of his era, Delorme drew upon the legacy of the Haitian Revolution and the ingenuity of Haitian independence (the 1804 Principle). To Haitian writers, there was an obvious contrast between Dessalines's radical legislation mandating universal equality and the United States' disastrous continuation of white supremacy under its own laws long after the formal end of slavery. This dynamic is underscored by the words of the twentieth-century Haitian author, Fernand Hibbert, in his novel *Les Thazar* (1907), in which a character remarks at one point with fury: "Again, a negro lynched in Georgia! . . . And at every instance, our brothers are hanged, crushed, exterminated over the least founded accusations, outside of all the rules of the most elementary justice, all that in a country that calls itself civilized! When will providence, whose intentions are impenetrable, bring forth a Dessalines in North America to grant true liberty . . . ?"[51] Dessalines is here yoked to the U.S. struggle against racial terror. Yet the victory of a latter-day "Dessalines in North America" would have meant more than a successful end to the fight against color prejudice. It would also have meant the implementation of a decidedly anti-imperialist policy. Although Dessalines's Haiti positioned its past under colonial domination in direct opposition to any future potential as an empire, according to Delorme, the United States, under President James Monroe, exhibited a more fraught relationship between its past as a colony and its future as an empire. In his December 1823 presidential message to Congress, Monroe gave a speech asserting, as Dessalines had earlier done, that "European world powers" should abandon any imperial designs on the Americas,[52] claiming that the United States would actively resist such incursions not only on its own territory, but anywhere in the Americas.[53]

Although Monroe's words are often cited as evidence of early national U.S. imperialism, the speech did not become the mantra for either westward expansion or U.S. American hemispheric protectionism until closer to the middle of the century. In 1845, President James Polk used Monroe's words to "defend the rights of the United States to the Oregon territory."[54] From that point forward, Monroe's speech had lasting influence in the U.S. political sphere. Its longitudinal implications for the intellectual history of the Haitian Revolution, however, can be glimpsed in the continuous engagement of Caribbean writers like Delorme with the suspect phrase, "America for the Americans," which has become a synecdoche for the kinds of racial-imperial policies associated with the speech.[55] Delorme's book constitutes perhaps one of the earliest responses from the Caribbean to the speech, which Delorme saw as evidence of an "equivocal laconism that troubles Europe and America at the same time: *America for the Americans*," even though Monroe did not utter those words in the speech.[56]

Although the phrase Delorme attributes to Monroe does not appear in the U.S. president's speech, tracing the genesis of this set of words that have had lasting resonance and power illuminates how and why Delorme came to associate Monroe with the phrase.[57] An early instance of the phrase appeared in an article published in the *Times-Picayune* on June 25, 1851, which used "America for Americans" as a title and reported that "the [U.S.] Secretary of State is about to make a proposition to England and France for a joint protectorate of Central America and Hayti."[58] An article in the *Christian Inquirer* dated July 29, 1854, also used "America for Americans" as a title, making the argument that the two biggest threats to the United States were "slavery" and "the Foreign and Catholic element."[59] The phrase appeared in a slightly different context in an article titled, "Ireland in America," published in Boston-based *Littel's Living Age* on May 6, 1854.[60] One of the most telling early uses of the phrase in the United States appeared in an 1855 article published in *Putnam's Monthly*, which similarly took the imperial slogan as its title. In the anonymously authored article, a slightly different version of the phrase— "America belongs to Americans"—is attributed to a scurrilous fellow, "mythical or real," writing under the pseudonym Sam, said to have been publishing questionable political diatribes in mid-nineteenth-century U.S. newspapers.[61] The author seemed to want to counter the nativist implications of the phrase, arguing that tolerance was crucial to the nation's future: "Nor is there any danger that threatens our country now—scarcely excepting slavery—more subtle or formidable than the danger which lurks in those ill-suppressed hatreds of race and religion."[62] It should be noted here that "race" is a stand-in for nationality, rather than skin color. As such, the author advocated the integration

Anti-racism   309

of "aliens," such as "the Germans and the Irish, and all the Swiss, English, French, Scotch, Swedes and Italians," into the United States as full citizens.[63] Even in acknowledging that slavery was a blight for the United States, the *Putnam's* essay still managed to ignore racism against people of African descent and to limit the status of "American" to those of European descent. This limitation continued more aggressively in subsequent uses of the phrases, especially by white nativist groups in the postbellum era and beyond. In the mid-1930s, for example, a San Diego based group called the National Club of America for Americans "petitioned the Los Angeles City Council to pass an ordinance barring 'non-naturalized aliens from working in the Los Angeles area,'" a move specifically targeted at California's growing immigrant population from Mexico.[64]

Juxtaposing Delorme's 1866 analysis of the idea of "America for the Americans" with its application in the *Putnam's* article reveals the sharp gap between U.S. understandings of democracy and Delorme's own. In place of *Putnam's* facile extension of the phrase to a range of European immigrants, Delorme offered a sardonic critique of its hemispheric implications, one that eventually characterized subsequent Latin American and Caribbean interpretations.[65] "Since the citizens of the United States call themselves simply Americans," he wrote, "Monroe's maxim might be an attempt to affirm exclusive control of the United States over the rest of America: America for the United States."[66] Not only had U.S. democracy been stunted by continuous application of the "sacrilege" of color prejudice, Delorme asserted, but U.S. imperialism extended the threat of racism to the very idea of democracy itself. Delorme called imperialism "that fatal idea of universal domination [that] has already plagued many societies, many thinkers, and has always destroyed them."[67]

Delorme's critique anticipates Césaire's prophetic condemnation of European imperialism in his famous treatise, *Discourse on Colonialism*. Césaire wrote that unless Europe could put into practice a politics of human rights "founded on respect for peoples and cultures," "it will have deprived itself of its *last chance*, and with its own hands, drawn up over itself the pall of mortal darkness."[68] With his more tempered language, inflected with all the romance of the post-Enlightenment Atlantic World, Delorme similarly predicted the downfall of the United States if it refused to renounce its imperial (racist) inclinations: "Universal domination is impossible," Delorme said, "The momentum of the world is opposed to it. Nature condemns it. And the impiety of such an attempt is always met with the most cruel of punishments."[69] Yet the two men differed significantly in their view of the prospects for change on the part of the United States. Even though Césaire was writing in the aftermath of two world wars and in the context of France's

310   Chapter 9

violent occupation of Vietnam, he imagined that Western Europe could still make the choice to mitigate the effects of its devastating colonial history. His vision of U.S. imperialism, considering the U.S. occupation of Haiti from 1915 to 1934, on the contrary, was irremediably grim: "American domination," Césaire famously wrote, "the only domination from which one never recovers. I mean from which one never recovers unscarred."[70]

In an editorial for *Crisis* magazine W. E. B. Du Bois said of the U.S. occupation that there was "absolutely no adequate excuse" for the United States to have "made a White Admiral sole and irresponsible dictator of Hayti." "The anarchy in Hayti is no worse than the anarchy in the United States at the time of our Civil War," Du Bois continued. "The lynching and murder in Port-au-Prince is no worse than, if as bad as, the lynching in Georgia." Delorme, who wrote long before the United States had, in the words of Du Bois, "violated the independence of a sister state," was uncannily optimistic about the United States' ability to reverse its tendency toward "domination" and aim toward humanism.[71] Delorme conjectured that "America for the Americans" could become the mantra of U.S. humanitarian rather than imperial interests: "Glory and commerce legitimately call [the United States] to exercise itself as an arbiter to the other American nations in their differences with one another and above all in their relationships with European powers." "It is through a politics of this nature," he continued, "that [the United States] can exercise a veritable and salutary influence in America and in the world."[72] What the United States needed, but continued to lack, was not only an acceptance of its existing geographical borders but, crucially, an embrace of difference in place of U.S. racism and white supremacy.[73]

At the end of the first part of *La Démocratie*, Delorme signaled the importance of the "virtue" of tolerance for democratic progress: "Tolerance is the doctrine of the nineteenth century," he wrote, "and tolerance signifies the destruction of prejudices, the fusion of religious beliefs into benevolent work, the reunification of the races into a pacifistic and reconciliatory humanity."[74] Delorme's optimistic embrace of tolerance as a radical democratic virtue, and as the missing link in any real political democracy, may well have influenced the Puerto Rican nationalist and novelist Ramón Emeterio Betances, who countered the so-called Monroe Doctrine with his own iconic phrase, "The Antilles for the sons of the Antilles,"[75] which he uttered for the first time at a speech he gave at a masonic lodge in Port-au-Prince.[76] Betances used the iconic phrase in French ("Les Antilles pour les fils des Antilles"), before he went on to make it famous in Spanish ("Las Antillas para los Antillanos"). Betances became acquainted with the works of Delorme while he lived in exile in Jacmel, Haiti from 1870 to 1872. Perhaps their encounter inflected Betances's decision to have the eponymous character in his 1890 short story, "Voyages de Scaldado," revise Benjamin Franklin's "Thirteen Moral Virtues" by adding tolerance as the fourteenth.[77] Delorme fundamentally believed that, though materially untested, democracy as a form of governance could exist without the capitalism that made the inequalities of domestic and colonial racism axiomatic for the imperial powers. For Delorme, tolerance, or what Glissant called "diversity," that is, "accepted difference," was ever possible.

Like Delorme, Janvier also located Haiti at the center rather than to the margins of a Caribbean world system that not only included the entire archipelago of the Caribbean and the broader continent of South America, but an Atlantic World that included Western Europe and the United States. Both writers envisioned Haiti as a central part of an interconnected intellectual tradition that I have elsewhere referred to as Black Atlantic humanism. Black Atlantic humanism, which derives from the eighteenth century, describes how Black thinkers from the Americas like Ottobah Cugoano and Olaudah Equiano theorized and historicized ways to eradicate the human-made problems of racism and slavery. In the case of nineteenth-century Haitian writers and politicians, the eradication of color prejudice and the elimination of empire could be brought about using the principles of Haitian independence.

In the early nineteenth century, producing a *Haitian* Atlantic humanism entailed affirming the 1804 Principle, with the Haitian revolutionists' radical exhortation to fight for "liberty or independence," and in so doing to "avenge America" like Dessalines, thereby ensuring the growth and spread of Toussaint Louverture's apocryphal "tree of liberty" throughout the world, each of these being iconic phrases repeated throughout nineteenth-century transatlantic abolitionist literature.[78] For Janvier and Delorme, Haiti was more than an important symbol to be proverbially evoked by the oppressed of the Atlantic World. In Delorme's and Janvier's respective theorizations, Haitian intellectuals remained decisive players in the ongoing struggle for the liberation of enslaved people across the hemisphere, especially in Cuba, where Janvier lamented that in 1883 slavery was, "unfortunately," still in existence.[79] Delorme saw himself as exposing the continuation of domestic racism on U.S. soil after the Civil War when he wrote that after he traveled to "North America," "where for a long time slavery in name has no longer existed," he was forced to confront the fact that "men of our race are obliged to resign themselves to living in that country as the Jews had everywhere lived in the middle ages, tolerated, but persecuted."[80] Demesvar Delorme dreamed that Haiti and Haitians could help end such racism: "And who knows, when prosperous, and capable of producing the same economic output that has made other countries powerful, what humanitarian destinies Providence will lead us toward in this archipelago of the Caribbean where we are at the center!"[81]

Even though both Delorme and Janvier argued that Haiti represented the very sign and symbol of Black American sovereignty in a white world of imperialism, neither suggested Haitians should alienate themselves or divorce their ideas from the United States and Western Europe. Janvier, who lived most of his life abroad,[82] had this to say about "noble France":

> I give thanks to noble France, that teat of the world, which has nourished my brain for about six years, and has made it possible to this day for me to pick up the pen in defense of my country, of my race, which is being attacked, injured, and slandered by a few men from the middle ages who evidently find themselves lost among us here in the nineteenth century, and by several individuals who do not wish to understand that just as the sun cannot be forced to retreat, neither can the sublime French revolution, nor can Haiti, daughter of the one, and godchild of the other, nor can the black race, which is awakening and emerging at last from the intellectual and physical prison where it has been trapped for centuries.[83]

Delorme, too, while highly critical of the United States' continuous attempts to seize the Dominican Republic's Bay of Samana, counseled U.S. politicians to follow the example of George Washington and Benjamin Franklin, who Delorme claimed did not have such imperial designs.[84] The United States, looking to secure a naval station in the Caribbean, attempted to lease the bay from the Dominican Republic in 1868. Haitians widely viewed the United States' presence in the region, and their later attempt to acquire Haiti's Môle St. Nicholas, as foreboding U.S. imperial interests. "That was not what Franklin and Washington desired," Delorme wrote. "They wanted, these men, to create a great country for themselves out of independence; but they said at the same time that this should not be done by despoiling the others."[85] If J. Michael Dash has observed that Firmin's *Letters from Saint Thomas* "belong to a new geographic imaginary where metropolitan France and postindependence Haiti" as well as "postcolonial Haiti are no longer opposed," the same could be said to characterize the works of Delorme and Janvier, particularly, in relation to the United States.[86] Neither Haitian writer saw any contradiction in defending against European and U.S. American imperial attempts in the West Indies by critiquing and praising France or lauding and lambasting the United States. Janvier praised the citizens of the United States, speaking to the fiction of "Anglo-Saxon blood," in one breath, while in another he provided a damning critique of what he described as a U.S. imperial mindset.[87] According to Janvier, Americans had "only one fault: that of believing that all of America should be one big colony or outpost of the United States."[88] In the works of both Haitian writers, France and the United States could be venerated in the service of arguing for Latin America's—and specifically

Haiti's—right to sovereignty and critiqued in concert with the larger goal of combating color prejudice around the world. Delorme acknowledged, in fact, that the 1867 constitution for the Republic of Haiti was "roughly the same" as the U.S. Constitution,[89] even though he later lamented, "In that country [the United States], things do not have the same meaning that they have elsewhere: for them, in other words, republic and democracy do not mean what they mean in other nations. There is, we know only too well, a strange but very great difference between what we call Republicans and Democrats and what is meant by these denominations in their country. There, freedoms and rights are not for all, but only for some. Justice is limited by ethnic considerations. Reason is circumscribed by prejudice."[90] The Haitian Atlantic, in contrast, or in Janvier's words "the irregular triangle formed by the Atlantic, the Caribbean Sea, the Lucayes, and the Gulf of Mexico,"[91] while necessarily opposed to the imperial "French Atlantic triangle"[92] and the imperialist striving United States, was at the same time where ideas of democracy and republicanism ordinarily associated with Europe and the United States could be restored to the more metaphysical meanings they held for Haitians, rather than distinctly French enlightenment or U.S. national ones. As interpreted through the works of Janvier and Delorme, once wrested free of their racist and imperialist implications, democracy and republicanism could be put into the service of Black sovereignty as well as inter-American and transatlantic political and economic alliances.

Although both Janvier and Delorme theorized a simultaneously hemispheric and Afro-diasporic Americas long before such thinking became common in more modern scholarly circles, neither Haitian writer has readily been associated with Pan-American or Pan-African thought. Jean Price-Mars, for example, whom Robert Cornevin eulogized as "in the black world, the equivalent of what Dr. William Burhardt Du Bois is for anglophone black people,"[93] regularly collaborated with Marcus Garvey, Claude McKay, and Réné Maran on *Le Cri des nègres*.[94] Price-Mars referenced the influence that the writings of Booker T. Washington had on his own agricultural theories in *La Vocation de l'élite* (1919), and the Haitian ethnographer described having collaborated for at least a fortnight with the "powerful American orator" in the early years of the twentieth century. Price-Mars praised Washington when he said, "At last, the American negroes have produced the most powerful orator of our time: Mr. Booker T. Washington."[95] Referring to what he perceived as an enviable "social solidarity" that stretched across lines of class among Black people living in the United States, Price-Mars claimed Haiti could learn from such cross-class unity.[96] Specifically, the Haitian ethnologist believed that Haiti's educated class needed to play a formative and collaborative role in the country's agricultural industry, and vice versa,

314   Chapter 9

merging the work of Du Bois and Washington in an unusually complementary rather than diametrical way.[97] Janvier predated Price-Mars, however, in arguing that Haiti needed to recognize its *cultivateurs*, or farmers, as intellectuals.

For Janvier, a farmer, was already a type of intellectual, who, with the proper education, could become a politician or civil functionary and contribute to Haiti's governance. A national education available to people in Haiti from all walks of life was the key, Janvier said, to making social fluidity possible on a broader scale. "For thirty years the Haitian worker—that of the big cities—has always sat somewhat next to the bourgeois one, both in primary school and in Masonic lodges," Janvier wrote. "Since our independence, the worker of the small town has constantly found himself standing on the battlefield next to the bourgeois man or laying in the bivouacs very close to him. They exchange their ideas, they speak fraternally, and the distance that exists between them is slight. Besides, we are not very far from 1804 and we all know where we come from," Janvier explained. "The Haitian worker knows that it is up to him to rise through the ranks in the great social army and to become, through his good behavior and his labor, general, minister, district commander, professor, etc., and this contributes not a little to the fact that he demands a little education for his son and enough independence for himself." Janvier linked the transformation from worker to politician or intellectual, a process he believed was incomplete in Haiti, to the trajectory of several U.S. presidents: "President Lincoln was successively a lumberjack, postman, lawyer; President Grant is the son of a tanner—and he brags about it;—President Garfield, who has just died so unfortunately under the bullet of the assassin Guiteau and whose premature death all honest people regret, President Garfield was the son of a peasant and was a boatman before becoming a professor of ancient languages and philosophy, although at the age of fourteen he could not yet read." An egalitarian education system was the key to preventing the creation of an elite divorced and alienated from the larger working classes, à la European aristocracy. "The Haitian worker, when primary education becomes compulsory—and it will soon be the case—will certainly become one of the finest workers not only of his race, but in all of America," Janvier concluded.[98]

Before Price-Mars's simultaneous creolization of Washington's agricultural theories and co-optation of Du Bois's idea of the "talented tenth," Janvier proffered an internationalist political vision that would make Haitians, rather than Black U.S. Americans, the leaders of a broader social justice movement for not only the "Africano-Américains" of the United States, but for "negroes" and other "Americans" of color across the hemisphere. "For the black race, Haiti is the sun rising over the horizon," Janvier wrote. "Shame upon anyone, whatever his nationality may be, who, having even a single drop of the noble and generous blood of an African, would attempt to deny this; and blinded, three times blinded, would be any Africano-Américain who would not have the eyes to recognize this."[99] Aside from providing a very distinct precursor to the contemporary term, African American, Janvier envisioned people of African descent around the globe as linked to one another not only because he believed they shared the same skin color or "race," but because they shared the same interest in combating colonialism and slavery, and, therefore, the same interest in Haitian sovereignty. Janvier argued that all Black people in the Americas were the figurative, or rather political, descendants of Toussaint Louverture, and Janvier admonished people of color around the world "to learn to live among and speak with respect about the grandchildren of Toussaint-Louverture to whom . . . you owe so much, all of you, the children of Africa, living in America."[100]

Despite Janvier's own conception of what Césaire later referred to as "our condition as Negroes,"[101] such linkages among nineteenth-century Haiti and Europe, the United States or the broader circum-Caribbean have been ordinarily tied to twentieth-century Haitian writers like Jacques Roumain, whose novel *Gouverneurs de la rosée* (1944) was famously translated into English in 1947 as *Masters of the Dew* by Mercer Cook and Langston Hughes.[102] In many respects, Janvier and Delorme were just as connected to an Afro-diasporic and inter-American world of activism as Firmin, Jose Martí, Price-Mars, and Roumain. Janvier, for example, was a French-trained medical doctor who was part of a burgeoning Parisian Latin American expatriate community, which included Betances, also a medical doctor. Betances translated U.S. abolitionist Wendell Phillips's famous speech, "Toussaint Louverture," into Spanish in 1869;[103] and in 1882 a letter from Betances appeared in a collection of essays published in Paris and coedited by Janvier, *Les Détracteurs de la race noire et la République d'Haïti* (Detractors of the Black race and the Republic of Haiti, 1882). In this volume, Betances defended Haiti against the charge from its racist "detractors" that what had resulted from the Haitian Revolution was only "sterility."[104] In March 1874, Betances, who was known under the pseudonym *El Antillano*, the moniker he used to sign the above-mentioned letter, reviewed Delorme's *La Misère au sein des richesses* for the Parisian journal *El Americano*.[105] Betances translated the title into Spanish as "Miseria entre riquezas" and went on to call the work "an important volume published by a Haitian," referring to Delorme himself as a "bueno américano."[106]

Betances's later idea of "Confederación Antillana" also coincided with an idea of Delorme's, at the same time as it was wholly contrary to the racist alliance of white supremacist European states proposed by France's late minis-

316   Chapter 9

ter, the Baron de Malouet, and to the United States' clear attempts to take possession of more and more of the Americas. Delorme theorized in *La Misère* that a "North American Confederation" could be conceived of less in terms of the nation-state and more in terms of a full-scale inter-American political organism that could benefit all the Americas, rather than just the United States. Delorme wrote, "The citizens of the great Republic of the United States should not allow themselves to become drunk on their own prosperity. Wisdom consists largely in not getting a big head amid success. The role of the mighty North American Confederation should be, instead of coveting the territory of these young nations that have formed themselves next to it in the New World, to protect, defend, and form with them a great confraternity of societies in solidarity in an independent America."[107] Delorme's desire for separately sovereign yet connected states is not entirely dissimilar to the inter-Caribbean political organizations imagined, first, by the Puerto Rican writer Eugenio María de Hostos, then extended by Betances, and further modified by Janvier.

The Caribbean Confederation Hostos and Betances first imagined was one where the alliance would comprise the three Spanish-speaking Caribbean islands, Cuba, Santo Domingo (the Dominican Republic), and Puerto Rico, in concert with Hostos's novel *La Peregrinación de Bayoán* (The pilgrimage of Bayoán, 1863) where political solidarities are metaphorically represented in characters personified as Cuba, Santo Domingo, and Puerto Rico, respectively. As Betances continued to develop his own idea for a "Confederación Antillana," the vision for this alliance became more inclusive, to the point where Betances imagined an alliance with Haiti (unlike in Hostos's vision, or Bolívar's congress).[108] Betances's now characteristic motto—"the Antilles for the sons of the Antilles"—was a call for inter-Caribbean solidarity in the face of U.S. attempts to annex various islands in the Caribbean even before the war of 1898. Such a cross-pollination of ideas that led from Haiti to Cuba to Puerto Rico and back to Haiti can be immediately glimpsed in the title of Janvier's *Haïti aux Haïtiens* (Haiti for Haitians, 1884). Janvier was almost certainly influenced in this titular position by the works of his contemporary Delorme and by Betances's exhortation in the Delorme review that Haiti was an absolutely central player in "our archipelago," specifically when it came to preserving "The Antilles for the Antilleans" (*Las Antillas, para los Antillanos*).[109] Janvier explained the seemingly nationalist logic behind his phrase "Haïti aux Haïtiens" by speaking directly to the Haitian people: "What is important above all is that in autonomous, independent Haiti, Haitians remain the only ones in charge. Anything contrary to this doctrine represents only danger or chimera."[110] In other words, the most important thing was for Haiti and Haitians to remain sovereign.

Anti-racism   317

The intertextual similarities to be found among the writings of Betances, Delorme, and Janvier are perhaps unsurprising when we consider that each was educated in Paris and lived there in exile, a situation that was common among Latin American *émigrés* in the late nineteenth century. Scholar Paul Estrade observed, "Paris had become a site of meetings and exchanges between Latin Americans, and it was also a kind of 'center of operations' where politically, economically, culturally, North American incursions in Latin America could be thwarted in the interest of Latin America."[111] The Latin American Paris described by Estrade is the locale where Delorme wrote and published almost all of his major works. The more common story told of Delorme's Paris is that in the 1870s he frequented the salons of French writers Alphonse de Lamartine and Victor Hugo, as well as Alexandre Dumas.[112] The innermost circle of Janvier is similarly described as having been made up of primarily French writers, such as Charles Leconte de Lisle, Judith Gautier, François Coppée, and Stéphane Mallarmé.[113] It is perhaps the linkage of both men to a circle of French Parisian literati, rather than a Latin American one, that has made less visible both Haitian writers' involvement in Latin American and hemispheric-American intellectual circles.

Both Delorme and Janvier wrote novels that have been used as examples of what Price-Mars called a *bovarysme des collectivités* (collective bovarysme) or a collective imitation of French forms and subject matter in Haiti.[114] However, instead of viewing their veneration for France and usage of the French language (which was not at all dissimilar from Betances's in both regards) and their penchants for classical forms in their fiction as examples of *bovarysme*, perhaps we should see their claims that Haiti's history, literature, culture, and politics were indelibly intertwined with that of France, and Europe in general, as a part of the tensions involved in creating transnational Black sovereignty *through* Haiti in a hostile Atlantic World. Neither writer sought to isolate Haiti from its European past or to isolate it from a future that might include collaborating with the United States. This tendency to turn simultaneously toward and away from colonialist powers might reflect, as Raphael Dalleo has written, "the shifting tension between these two demands—of being oppositional to power yet representing the nation," which he says "is crucial to periodizing Caribbean literature."[115] Dalleo has argued, "The persistently peripheral location of the Caribbean in relation to the centers of global power means that one consistent structural element of the Caribbean public sphere is the contradictory push and pull of consolidation and oppositionality."[116] Part of what makes the work of Delorme and Janvier so critical for thinking about the relationship of nineteenth-century Haiti to a Latin American age of independence is the argument that Haiti stood at the "center," not at the periphery, of the archipelago of the Caribbean.[117] This strategic placement in the middle of North and South America, Africa, and Europe meant that Haiti had just as much to teach as it had to learn from transnational cultural, political, and intellectual histories. In describing the language of Haiti, Janvier wrote that while it was officially French, "among the people we speak a patois that is a mixture of words from the French, English and Spanish languages, along with words from various African dialects. In our schools we also teach English and Spanish."[118] The strength of Haiti was that even while its citizens were determined to preserve the sovereignty of their republic as a separate and distinct nation from any other in the Americas or Europe, the country remained creole like the Atlantic. The Haitian anthologist and poet, Louis Morpeau, seconded this idea when he described "the Haitian soul" as "a moral mosaic . . . like the popular dialect of Creole . . . is a linguistic mosaic where we find, in great part, the old French of the 17th century mingled or mixed together with African locutions and onomatopeias, Spanish and English, Caribbean and indigenous words."[119]

In their famous 1989 manifesto, "Éloge de la créolité" (In praise of Creoleness), written in part as a diatribe against negritude, Jean Bernabé, Patrick Chamoiseau, and Raphaël Confiant criticized twentieth-century Haitian indigenist literature and philosophy. Bernabé et al. wrote that Caribbean life "ought not to be described ethnographically, nor ought there to be a census-taking of Creole practices after the fashion of the Haitian indigenists, instead we ought *to show what, in these practices, bears witness to both Creoleness and the human condition.*"[120] The trio explained that "Creoleness encompasses and perfects Americanness because it involves a double process:—*the adaptation of Europeans, Africans, and Asians to the New World; and—the cultural confrontation of these peoples within the same space, resulting in a mixed culture called Creole.*"[121] While Bernabé, Confiant, and Chamoiseau, as subjects of France, each of them hailing from Martinique, have the luxury of operating with an affective statelessness, defined by them as *créolité*, all the while enjoying citizenship rights as ancillary members of a powerful nation-state, no such position was available to nineteenth-century Haitians. Haitians lived and continue to live in a state of material precariousness that makes giving recourse to the aesthetic imaginings of a conglomerate and utopian state of *créolité* much less attractive, let alone useful.

In a more contemporary milieu in which such transnational citizenship has not only been loudly proclaimed as liberatory, but regarded as the only path toward moving beyond what Bernabé et al. conceived as the limitations of *négritude, Americanness,* and *Caribbeanness,* it is easy to see why Haitian authors like Janvier and Delorme can so often be left out of accounts of the critical intellectual and historical trajectory of *créolité*. Janvier minced no words when it came to the protection of Haitian sovereignty. Observing U.S.

Anti-racism   319

imperial designs in the West Indies, Janvier repeated Delorme's interpretation of the Monroe Doctrine by saying it amounted to one thing: "America for the Americans, *which means America for the United States*."[122] Even before the publication of his 1884 *Haïti aux Haïtiens*, Janvier's response to this was, "if the Yankees voluntarily say: America for the Americans," "let us Haitians never forget to shout even louder: 'Haiti for Haitians!'"[123]

Janvier published in haste his short forty-three-page *Haïti aux Haïtiens* to express his displeasure at the news that at the 1884 Republican National Convention in Chicago the Republicans chose as their candidate for the U.S. presidency, James G. Blaine, former secretary of state under U.S. president James Garfield.[124] Janvier's dismay with the Republican nominee was directly related to Blaine's attempt to strengthen and extend the so-called Monroe Doctrine. Blaine's most characteristic "creed," according to those who knew him well, was "America for the Americans."[125] Of Blaine's nomination, Janvier wrote, "M. Blaine, former secretary of state, has always shown himself to be one of the greatest advocates of the hegemony of the United States over all of America." "He is the author of the Republican plan accepted in Chicago and that has translated the words of Monroe and Adams to mean: *America for the Americans*."[126] Janvier clearly understood Blaine's co-optation of the phrase to mean that the United States sought control over the entire American hemisphere. However, even "westernized Haitians," Janvier said, "do not want anything in the world to do with the idea that Haiti would become a colony or even a state [of the United States]."[127] "To whom should the Haitian people abdicate?" he asked. "Our fathers, so it seems to me, created the Haitian nation by themselves, all alone, without loans, which they paid for with the gold that they procured through the sweat of their labor, precisely in order to have the right to live independently; they left us this little corner of the earth so that there would be at least one place on the globe where no one could spit upon the black race with impunity."[128] If Janvier wanted "Haiti for Haitians" as a protection against U.S. imperialism and global white supremacy, Delorme went even further in his criticism by warning Haitians not to be seduced by the ostensive stability that could be offered by the United States if Haiti were to become its protectorate, and thus a part of its empire of racism. Delorme wrote, "Now, we must admit that we are aware that those who oppose our sovereignty have been stating *very loudly* that our country has not been productive in the realm of agriculture in order to challenge our autonomy by questioning our ability to govern ourselves."[129] But if Haiti were to become a protectorate of the United States, not only would Haitians lose their national sovereignty, but they would be subject to the kinds of racism experienced by all people of color in the United States. Delorme warned, to that end, "They will have nothing but scorn for you, they will mistreat you, just as they scorn and mistreat all the men of our race who live in the United States."[130]

Delorme did not just fear that the Haitian government might consent to U.S. "protection." He also feared that Haitian citizens might want to emigrate to the United States. Warning them away from such a fatalist project that he said would doom them once again to subjugation, Delorme critiqued U.S. racism and imperialism by way of capitalism. Delorme argued that the term civilization itself had merely monetary, rather than philosophical or humanistic, meaning for U.S. Americans: "Everywhere else, civilization means humanity striving toward its moral, intellectual, and physical improvement all at once; in [the United States], civilization means money. It's all about making dollars; no matter the cost." Delorme was even more insistent when he observed that in the United States, "Every idea of justice and duty is subordinated to this dominant idea: having millions. A person is appreciated, esteemed, considered of value, if he does not have black skin, of course, according to the sum of money that he has in his possession." He continued, "Of a man who has sixty thousand dollars, it is said: *He is worth sixty thousand dollars*. He is worth, that is to say the amount by which he is valued. The language of a people reveals its spirit."[131] This drive to have more and more, and therefore to be *worth* more and more, led Delorme back to U.S. imperialism. Delorme described imperialism as an outgrowth of the same sense of capital that dominated U.S. American life when he likened it to a desire to possess geographical and political sovereignty over more and more regions of the world. He asked why the United States, with a large part of an entire continent to itself, constantly sought to extend its borders: "You have become a great power, one of the richest, most powerful countries in the world," he wrote. "You have all to yourselves almost the entire northern continent of America, essentially half of a world; and that is not enough for you; you would like to take from a small people who have done nothing to harm you the tiny part of the earth that belongs to them!"[132] Echoing Vastey, Delorme returned to the philanthropic project of racial uplift and solidarity that informs so much of his predecessor's work by asking, "Is it in the name of justice that you crossed the sea in order to attack the rights of the inhabitants of Hispaniola?"[133] This passage presciently questioned what would become the logic of U.S. imperialism throughout the rest of the nineteenth century and continuing today: spreading U.S. notions of democracy and capitalism to places ravaged by forms of dictatorship, political unrest, and poverty that can very often be directly linked to the political machinations of the United States and other world powers. Janvier noted as much when he wrote, "If we were truly to look into the matter, behind every insurrection that has taken place in Haiti from 1843 until now, we would always see that a foreign hand has been pulling the strings and making the puppets dance."[134] Instead of pursuing the enlargement of its territories, Delorme wondered why the United States did not just settle for being a beacon for the other states of the Americas. He wrote that if the United States were to follow his advice to be content with the already magnificent largesse of its terrain, the country "could become, like its president has said he desires, *the star that will guide* the other Republics."[135]

Firmin went even further than Vastey and Delorme to posit the still greater morality of the pacifistic stance of the Haitian people vis-à-vis the rest of the world, and their desire to maintain good relations with the Atlantic World powers, even after all they had suffered because of them. "Yes, we must repeat it again, of all the human races the black race is the only one that has presented the example of a multitude of men plunged into the most cruel servitude, but who kept in their souls the energy necessary to break their chains and turn them into so many avenging weapons of the law and freedom," Firmin wrote. "All of this is forgotten, and systematically. Is there anything that will not be forgotten when pride and interest unite to stifle the truth? Yet this truth must triumph; for it is stronger than all the savants, stronger than all prejudices."[136] The Haitian nation represented the longest running attempt at creating an egalitarian society in the Americas since the Europeans arrived on Ayitian lands with their violent follies of slavery and colonialism. Haitian independence introduced another possible trajectory for the Americas, one that could interrupt white European domination over Black American subjects. Firmin concluded, "The island of Haiti has been, for about eighty years, the most beautiful field of observation that has ever existed to study this famous question of the equality of human races."[137] The success of Haiti's experiment with liberty and equality could be plainly seen in the fact of the survival of the Haitian people and their enduring commitment to the 1804 Principle. "As for me, I admit quite frankly that I cannot help being proud of my fathers, when I think back to that time of misery when, bound to an infernal existence, with their bodies broken by the whip, fatigue, and chains, they moaned in silence, but retained in their panting breasts the sacred fire that was to produce a superb explosion of freedom and independence!" "But there is much more," Firmin continued. "Barely two generations after the proclamation of black freedom in Haiti, a complete transformation had taken place in the nature of these men. It was in vain that everything seemed to condemn them to live eternally in the state of inferiority to which they were reduced and which was getting worse every day."[138] While in the larger course of his study Firmin sought to prove how far Black people in Haiti had advanced in the arts, sciences, mathematics, astronomy, etc., the greatest feat, to him, was that they were able to achieve independence, in the first place, after all they

322 Chapter 9

suffered in slavery. Firmin pointed out that no white people in the same condition were able to perform such an arduous miracle: "Considering the moral part of their conduct, it seems to me that in the face of history and philosophy, these Africans are above all praise. No tribute can match their magnanimity."[139] In his own comparison of white U.S. citizens to Black Haitians, Janvier did not miss the opportunity to point out that it was not just a past history of being enslaved that separated their destinies. Part of the United States' "strength" was it did not have to pay an "indemnity" to its former colonizers.[140]

For Firmin, as for Janvier, white supremacy was the tool that the colonialists of old Europe used to justify slavery and expand their empires in the new world of capitalism they created in the Americas. Firmin wrote, "The result has been that all the European nations, of the white race, are naturally inclined to unite together in order to dominate the rest of the world and the other human races."[141] "Finding too small the soil where they were born and must live, they seek, with an insatiable ardor, vaster territories, where their dreams can be realized of deploying to infinity their immense resources to increase their riches more and more," Firmin complained.[142] The Europeans invented the scientific-sounding doctrine of the "inequality of the human races" to produce and then support colonization, slavery, and other forms of white domination, such as economic imperialism, even after slavery. "The majority of those who pedantically proclaim that the human races are unequal—that blacks, for example, will never succeed in achieving the most elementary civilization, unless they are made to bow under the rule of whites— have formulated these notions most feverishly in times of regret, when they were thinking of a colony that had escaped them." "One does not easily renounce the former exploitation of man by man," Firmin explained. "That is nevertheless the main motive for all colonization, supported by the need that the great industrial nations feel to constantly extend their radiuses."[143] In being anti-colonial, Haiti had no need for greater territory, and in being anti-slavery, Haiti had no need for the pseudoscientific doctrine of the inequality of the human races (racism). Although early Haitian authors did engage in the kinds of conversations about "civilization" common in white European and U.S. American justifications for imperialism, Haitian nationalism, as it was developed beyond the mid-nineteenth century, was defined not as a desire to be imperial, but as its opposite. Janvier, Firmin, and Delorme believed that Haitians could remain Haitian and be good citizens of the world since making Haiti, unlike making the United States, did not mean becoming an imperialist state. What their contributions to nineteenth-century Haitian thought teach us is that a policy of nationalities may not be at odds with the *créoliste*'s dream of global citizenship, after all.

Delorme had no problem with the existence of the United States as a sovereign nation, and we might say he even admired it. "It is in the United States of America that the system of republics has been practiced on the widest of scale. Never has a country with such a great expanse, with such a numerous population and with such considerable material riches, been ruled by democratic institutions," Delorme wrote. To perfect the concept and implementation of a republic by eliminating color prejudice, Delorme then said, "is the task, the most beautiful of them all, that can be accomplished by the United States."[144] This statement urges us to think anew about Haiti as a laboratory or an experiment. Michel Rolph Trouillot once remarked, "[Haiti] represents the longest neocolonial experiment in the history of the West."[145] We might let ourselves be prompted now to think about a formulation for the United States whereby it is also a laboratory, but for democracy, with experiments so far having gone very wrong.

Delorme's romance of racial democracy challenged ideas about the greatness of the United States' political democracy being put forward in the general era by writers like the United States' most famous democratic poet, Walt Whitman. In his 1883 *Speciman Days*, Whitman wrote, "The advent of America, the history of the past century, has been the first general aperture and opening-up to the average human commonalty, on the broadest scale, of the eligibilities to wealth and worldly success and eminence, and has been fully taken advantage of; and the example has spread hence, in ripples, to all nations."[146] For Delorme, the United States' foundations in slavery, ongoing color prejudice, and its continued desire to become an imperial power were the primary obstacles to the United States' full realization of its democracy. "At this sonorous word of eternal truths, [democracy], the pen hesitates and stops," Delorme lamented. "Has the republic of the United States generally respected its sacred principles outside of which there is only violence, lies, iniquity? It must be said no, in spite of the sympathies that we nourish, at bottom, for this people in terms of liberty and legality, no, then, alas, because there is no equality."[147] Firmin reached a similar conclusion: "One cannot proclaim the universal fraternity of mankind without at the same time proclaiming its equality."[148] Firmin still believed that Haiti's independence was the answer to the problem of white supremacy. "It can be argued that the proclamation of Haiti's independence positively influenced the fate of the entire Ethiopian race, living outside Africa," Firmin concluded. "At the same time, it changed the economic and moral regime of all the European powers with colonies; its achievement also put pressure on the domestic economy of all American nations maintaining the system of slavery."[149]

Thinking back to Hibbert's call for a "Dessalines in North America," we can see now that it reflects the more radical vision of social change found in

324   Chapter 9

early nineteenth-century Haitian thought, but one inflected with all the failures of nineteenth-century post-Enlightenment democratic republics, like the United States and France, to eliminate both racism and imperialism. The belief that only awakening the ashes of Dessalines could counter the inevitable violence of racism's empire underscores a growing pessimism in Haitian thought at the turn of the twentieth century about the relationship of white democracy to Black freedom.

Epilogue

In 1983, Jacquelin Dolcé, Gérard Dorval, and Jean Miotel Casthely published an intellectual history of Haiti titled *Le Romantisme en Haïti: La vie intellectuelle, 1804–1915* (Romanticism in Haiti: The intellectual life). In this book, they described how the particularities of Haiti's history since independence, coupled with its unique relationship to both the French language and its French colonial past, led the country's intellectuals to develop a national romanticism that extended beyond the boundaries of traditional western European or U.S. American periodizations of the "romantic movement."[1] Dolcé, Dorval, and Casthely started from the premise that "Haitian romanticism" endured from the year of independence from France in 1804, to the beginning of the U.S. occupation of the country in 1915.[2] What made Haitian romanticism "particular" (their word) and distinct from its European counterpart was the fact that all art in Haiti produces a "call to action": "No, art and literature are not the vain products of indolence. How many struggles are translated by a simple epigraph! How many constraints and oppressions does even the most impersonal poem reveal: how many troubles, how much powerlessness is expressed by even the shortest verse?"[3] Haitian romanticism ended with the U.S. occupation because that invasion effectively meant the loss of Haitian sovereignty, on the one hand, and the exposure of the illusory quality of freedom (that it was a romantic idea, nonexistent in the real world), on the other. Post-indemnity Haitian rulers, even while supporting the radical anti-colonial, antislavery, and anti-racist ideals of 1804, failed to adequately protect Haitian sovereignty.

The United States finally recognized Haiti in 1862, a year after the U.S. Civil War began. All the same, throughout the mid-nineteenth century the United States repeatedly encroached on Haitian territory, using gunboat diplomacy to seek territory for naval bases.[4] From 1915 to 1934, the United States staged its full-blown occupation of Haiti. Although U.S. diplomats framed the occupation as a response to the assassination of Haiti's president Vilbrun Guillaume Sam, the fundamental goal was to force Haiti to pay loans and fees associated with the French indemnity, in which American banks had a fiduciary interest. In 1914 the United States had impounded $500,000 in gold from Haiti to ensure payments were made.[5]

Haitians, naturally, protested the presence of U.S. forces. In 1919, the Haitian nationalist Charlemagne Péralte led a rebellion against the occupiers. U.S. soldiers responded with a harsh crackdown, killing Péralte and afterward circulating a picture of his body positioned in a crucified pose as a warning.[6] During the occupation, more than fifteen thousand Haitians were killed by U.S. soldiers. Haitians viewed this violent quashing of all protest as a decisive turning point away from the country's revolutionary principles of freedom and independence and toward autocratic rule. In 1929, the Haitian historian and diplomat Dantès Bellegarde complained in a book addressed to President Herbert Hoover that many Haitians now had a "general scorn" for the law, obeying it only "in order to escape its severe sanctions, decreed and applied by brutal force."[7] The economist Emily Greene Balch, who later received the Nobel Peace Prize, led a delegation to Haiti in 1926 and observed, "The Americans are training not police, but soldiers." She wondered what the effect of such a force would be after U.S. withdrawal. "One possible result," she surmised, "is self-maintenance of power of whomever has control of this force, subject only to the development of a situation where, like the Pretorian guard, the soldiers sell themselves to the highest bidder."[8] During the occupation, U.S. soldiers helped establish the puppet presidency of the pro-U.S. politician Philippe Sudré Dartiguenave, paving the way for the United States to play a role in installing, deposing, or influencing the election of all subsequent Haitian presidents.

Dolcé, Dorval, and Casthely asked, "Is it possible that 'Romanticism' might merely be a certain method of seeing and translating reality? A particular mode that would disappear once the contingencies that brought it into existence were no longer present before the writer?" In other words, perhaps focusing their literature, broadly speaking, on the heroic past of the Haitian Revolution, which furnished the material and subject matter for so many of nineteenth-century Haiti's novelists, storytellers, playwrights, and poets, could not endure after the U.S. marines arrived on Haiti's shores.[9] Could the poets romantically celebrate Dessalines's proclamation of Haitian independence when Haiti was no longer fully independent? Maybe not, but still Haitian authors wrote and wrote. The U.S. occupation ushered in a realist strain that, while making it difficult for Haitians to romanticize their revolution whose world-historical significance U.S. occupiers were making a mockery of, provided opportunity to reflect on Haiti's sovereign past with a more critical lens. Turning his pen to theorizing and historicizing Haiti's lost sovereignty, Price-Mars wrote, "It is obvious that American intervention in our affairs was bound to bring about a confrontation between two doctrines and effect the substitution of one for the other." On the one side there was "the idea we had of the *State*." "We conceived of it as a very high abstraction, giving to it the attributes of a Divinity: omnipotence and omniscience," he explained. "We instinctively felt, one day, eventually, the State would finally and definitively constitute us." Despite all the civil dissensions and political upheaval of the past, "all the same, our ultimate hope was that one day the One would arrive and bring to fruition our most chimerical hopes and our most extravagant aspirations," ushering in a "new era" of "adaptation to progress, to modern civilization." But, on the other side, "one immediate result of the dramatic adventure of 1915 was it put us face to face with another conception of the State: one that, pushed to its most idealist extremes, consequently restrains and limits the actions of [state] Power to certain conditions and in determined domains and leaves to the activity of the individual the most complete fulfilment." Different conceptions they were, but both unrealized dreams all the same in a world of imperialism and capitalism. Price-Mars could see the more immediate, affective changes the presence of U.S. marines brought to everyday Haitian life too. On the morning of January 15, 1917, not long after he returned to occupied Haiti from France, Price-Mars noticed a once "familiar landscape had changed in tone." "Heavy clouds of a dirty grey were prowling across the sky and over the mountains. There was not a sound," he wrote. "It was the calm of the sepulcher. Suddenly, several bugle calls burst forth, calls such as I have heard, at other times, when there were fires in Port-au-Prince, calls for help. Then came the mournful sound of the bells: the tocsin." His sadness overtook him as he realized what those sounds were: "Involuntary tears sprang from my eyes, a sob rose to my throat. For that was the rhythmic step of the American officers on our ancestral soil."[10]

From the nineteenth to the mid-twentieth century, Haiti produced more books in proportion to its population than any other state in the Americas aside from the United States.[11] Explaining Haiti's vast literary output, Louis Morpeau wrote, "Haitians have written splendid poems, pages and pages of history shot through with elements of the epic, novels, and works of theatre, where slices of our lives are represented." Haitian authors, he said,

> Despite charges to the contrary, and according to the rhythms of their own spirits, have understood how to mingle [into their poetry] the blue skies of Haiti, along with a little bit of the melancholies of our terrible suffering, a little bit of the sweetness of our breezes, a bit of the purple of our glory, some of the gold from our sunlight, some of the indecisiveness of our spellbinding dawns, a little bit of the charms of the masters of the moonlight, which "flows across the blue roofs of our homes," a little bit of the grandiose dreams of our souls from the 120 years of our independence, but not of our liberty.[12]

Even if twentieth-century Haitian thinkers were determined to break with the romantic idealism of their nineteenth-century counterparts, there are so many lessons in the poetics of the past not to be forgotten. In Bergeaud's 1859 novel of the Haitian Revolution, after the two revolutionary brothers, Romulus and Rémus, mistakenly believe they killed the white colonist who enslaved them, and therefore that they metaphorically eliminated slavery from all of Saint-Domingue, their deceased African mother appears with this counsel:

> My children, there are cases when a man must distrust himself as if he were his own worst enemy. What he has seen often does not exist, and what he has not seen does exist. It is therefore necessary that he remain on guard against himself so as not to fall into his own ambushes, he must neglect no means of assuring himself of the truth when he can . . . go and interrogate the ruins of the *Colon*'s burnt-out dwelling; search through the rubble where his remains are supposed to be. If they are not there, come back, sharpen your cuffs and axes again, consolidate your ramparts and stand sentry: otherwise, woe to you.[13]

The brothers, becoming estranged from one another, did not follow their African mother's advice to fully sweep the white colonist's ashes from the island, and he returned again and again to harm them until the brothers reunited to proclaim Haitian independence. The *Colon* who plagued the island of Ayiti since 1492 has returned in manifold forms throughout the country of Haiti's more than two-hundred-year history, soiling with his "sacrilegious foot," as Dessalines once warned should not be permitted, "the territory of freedom."[14] "In every society dog eats dog," Trouillot told us, the oppressors merely change their "Christian name": for, "on the one side in Haiti, as in Guadeloupe, as in Martinique, as in Africa, throughout the entire twentieth century, there are those wearing the cloak of the 'Indigenists'" and "on the other side," there is "a different ideological sector, that of the bourgeoisie, which hides its dominance under the cloak of an 'Elite.'"[15] The U.S. occupation meant the masters, or the elite, had merely changed their cloaks once more.

A statement printed in the Kingdom of Haiti's *Gazette royale* provides an apt metaphor for this same changing of the guard that is as true as it was in 1816, when these words were first written, as it was in 1919 when Price-Mars published *La Vocation de l'élite*, as it remained in 1977 when Trouillot circulated *Ti dife boule*, and as it is today:

> Since the dawn of the revolution, two distinct parties have formed in Hayti, the party of France, composed of the white ex-colonists and a few free men of color and *anciens libres* blacks, dominated by prejudice and

governed above all keenly by their own interests, and the patriotic party composed of the majority of the population, blacks and yellows. The latter wanted freedom; the former wanted slavery; today the one wants to maintain the independence of the country, as the only means of preserving its political and individual existence; the other wants to bring the country back under the domination of France, as the only means of re-establishing, in time, the old order of things, by gradually bringing the mass of the population back under the yoke of slavery. . . . From the beginning . . . there has been a permanent fight between the patriots and the partisans of the French; the latter, have always hidden behind the curtains in every phase of the revolution, using every effort, either directly or indirectly, to stop or to hinder the march of the government and the Haitian people toward freedom and independence.[16]

We have never been as "steeped in history," indeed.[17] One thing is clear from examining the long tissue of successive foreign interventions in Haiti, and the deliberate destruction of Haiti's sovereignty from many corners, and by many actors, both internal and external to the country, over many years, leading up to the present day. The Haitian Revolution did not fail the world. The world failed the Haitian Revolution.

Acknowledgments

So many friends, family members, colleagues, and institutions supported this work over many years. Beginning with my immediate family, Samy F., Samy M., and Sébastien F., you are my light and my loves. Your endless energy and enthusiasm blazes a path for me every day. I would be lost without the humor, wit, and critiques of Julia Gaffield, Grégory Pierrot, and Chelsea Stieber. My world became small during the Covid-19 pandemic, and I am forever grateful to Laura Wagner for taking time to read multiple parts of this book (and to help with thorny Creole translations) and to Claire Payton and Anne Eller, who offered patient critique of much of the material that went into the introduction. Presenting this research overseas would not have been nearly as interesting without Kaiama Glover and Laurent Dubois, whose conversation and advice, always inspirational, leaves me wanting to run to my computer to jot down ideas. My best friend Maxine has been with me on this journey since the fourth grade and I can't imagine it without her. My parents, siblings, and my large extended family mean everything: Leydy, Rod, Don, Martha, Rodney II, Tatiana, Austin, Deshano, Anna, Veronica, Erika, Daniels, David Samy Sr., Chantal, Roselinde, and Dean. Many thanks also to various colleagues who have allowed me to bend their ears over the years: Leslie Alexander, Chris Bongie, Yarimar Bonilla, Eric Brandt, Brandon Byrd, Jean Casimir, Nathalie Cérin, Nadège Clitandre, Michel DeGraff, Daniel Desormeaux, Etant Dupin, Robert Fatton Jr., Ada Ferrer, Carolyn Fick, Alex Gil, Alida Goffinski, Alyssa Goldstein-Sepinwall, Cynthia Hoehler-Fatton, Régine Jean-Charles, Deborah Jenson, Jessica Marie Johnson, Sara E. Johnson, Celucien Joseph, Annette Joseph-Gabriel, Jonathan Katz, Mary Caton Lingold, Widlore Mérancourt, Claudine Michel, Nadine Mondestin, Matthew J. Smith, and Nadine Zimmerli. Miriam Franchina and Henry Stoll shared issues of nineteenth-century Haitian newspapers located in archives in Germany, Colombia, and Italy, and I am ever grateful. Thanks also to mentors Julia Douthwaite, Glenn Hendler, Cyraina Johnson-Roullier, Karen Richman, and Ivy G. Wilson. I would have been like a boat adrift with no port at the University of Virginia without the collaboration, energy, friendship, and encouragement of Anna Brickhouse, Njelle Hamilton, Carmen Lamas, Anne Garland Mahler, Charlotte Rogers, and Jennifer Sessions. Deborah McDowell lighted the path as department chair. My new colleagues at Yale University in the departments of French and African American Studies have been nothing short of welcoming, and I look forward to charting new intellectual journeys with you all. Special gratitude goes to Elaine Maisner of UNC Press for sustaining this work with her intellectual curiosity and generosity over many years and to all the editors and staff at UNC Press who made this book possible. Thank you also to all my students, new and old. Your questions sustain me. Never stop asking them.

This research was supported with an ACLS Fellowship and a NEH Grant, along with funds from the School of Arts and Sciences and the Carter G. Woodson Institute at the University of Virginia.

-1—
0—
+1—

Notes

Prologue

1. Baron de Vastey (Jean Louis de), *Le Système colonial dévoilé* (Cap-Haïtien: P. Roux, 1814), 35.

2. Baron de Vastey (Jean Louis de), *Réflexions sur une lettre de Mazères: ex-colon français, adressée à M. J.C.L. Sismonde de Sismondi, sur les noirs et les blancs, la civilisation de l'Afrique, le royaume d'Hayti* (Cap-Haïtien: P. Roux, 1816), 91.

3. Sarah McIntosh, *Pursuing Justice for Mass Atrocities: A Handbook for Victim Groups* (Washington, DC: United States Holocaust Museum, 2021), accessed March 10, 2023, https://www.ushmm.org/m/pdfs/USHMM-Pursuing-Justice-for-Mass-Atrocities.pdf.

4. Baron de Vastey (Jean Louis de), *Réflexions politiques sur quelques ouvrages et journaux français concernant Hayti* (Sans-Souci, Haiti: Royal Imprint, 1817), xvi–xvii.

5. Vastey, *Réflexions sur une lettre*, 112.

6. Louis-Félix Boisrond-Tonnerre, *Mémoires pour servir à l'histoire d'Haïti, par l'adjutant général Boisrond-Tonnerre* (Dessalines: De l'Imprimerie centrale du gouvernement, 1804), 13.

7. Boisrond-Tonnerre, *Mémoires*, 5.

8. Boisrond-Tonnerre, *Mémoires*, 92–93.

9. Vastey, *Réflexions sur une lettre*, 95, 97.

10. Boisrond-Tonnerre, *Mémoires*, 4.

11. Vastey, *Le Système*, 90.

12. Jean-Jacques Dessalines, "Le général en chef au peuple d'Haïti," in Louis-Félix Boisrond-Tonnerre, *Mémoires pour servir à l'histoire d'Haïti*, ed. Joseph Saint-Rémy (Paris: France Libraire, 1851), 3–4.

13. Boisrond-Tonnerre, *Mémoires*, 93.

14. Juste Chanlatte, *Le Cri de la nature* (Cap-Haïtien: P. Roux, 1810), 16.

15. Chanlatte, *Le Cri*, 53.

16. Chanlatte, *Le Cri*, 19.

17. Chanlatte, *Le Cri*, 27.

18. Marie-Antoinette Menier, "Comment furent rapatriés les greffes de Saint-Domingue, 1803–1820," *La Gazette des archives* 100 (1978): 13–29.

19. Julien Raimond, *Véritable origine des troubles de S.-Domingue: et des différentes causes qui les ont produits* (Paris: Bailly, 1792).

20. Anténor Firmin, *De l'Égalité des races humaines: Anthropologie positive* (Paris: F. Pichon, 1885), 110–11.

21. Firmin, *De l'Égalité*, 109.

22. Firmin, *De l'Égalité*, 310.

23. Louis Joseph Janvier, *La République d'Haïti et ses visiteurs (1840–1882): réponse à M. Victor Cochinat (de la Petite presse) et à quelques autres écrivains* (Paris: Marpon et Flammarion, 1883).

24. Émile Nau, *Histoire des caciques d'Haïti* (Port-au-Prince: T. Bouchereau, 1855), ii.

25. Nau, *Histoire des caciques*, vi.

Introduction

1. Michel-Rolph Trouillot, *Ti difé boulé sou istoua Ayiti* (Brooklyn, NY: Kóleksion Lakensièl, 1977). This was the original spelling. The subsequent edition was issued under the modern Creole orthography as *Ti dife boule sou istwa Ayiti* (see note 3 below).

2. Nathalie Pierre, "*Ti dife boule sou istwa Ayiti* as Haitian Civic Education," *Cultural Dynamics* 26, no. 2 (2014): 213. See also Mariana Past, "Toussaint on Trial in *Ti difé boulé sou istoua Ayiti*, or The People's Role in the Haitian Revolution," *Journal of Haitian Studies* 10, no. 1 (2004): 87–102; Carolle Charles, "New York 1967–71, Prelude to *Ti difé boulé*: An Encounter with Liberation Theology, Marxism, and the Black National Liberation Movement," *Journal of Haitian Studies* 19, no. 2 (2013): 152–59; Mariana Past and Benjamin Hebblethwaite, "*Ti dife boule sou istoua Ayiti*: Considering the Stakes of Trouillot's Earliest Work," *Cultural Dynamics* 26, no. 2 (2014): 149–61.

3. Lionel Trouillot, introduction to *Ti dife boule sou istwa Ayiti*, by Michel-Rolph Trouillot, rev. ed. (Port-au-Prince: Edisyon KIK, 2012), 4. All citations are to the 2012 revised edition, which uses an updated orthography that eliminates, among other letters and diacritics, the French accent aigu (´). Unless otherwise indicated, all translations are mine.

4. A fourth sibling, Jocelyne, is a writer and educator.

5. L. Trouillot, introduction, *Ti dife boule*, 4.

6. Michel-Rolph Trouillot, *Silencing the Past: Power and the Production of History* (New York: Beacon, 1995), 55. In 2015, Beacon Press published a twentieth-anniversary edition of *Silencing the Past*, with a new foreword by Hazel V. Carby. On Haitian Creole, see also Albert Valdman, "The Linguistic Situation of Haiti," in *Haiti Today and Tomorrow: An Interdisciplinary Study*, ed. Charles Robert Foster and Albert Valdman (Lanham, MD: University Press of America, 1984), 77–99; Michel DeGraff, "Demystifying Creolization, Decolonizing Creole Studies," in *Different Spaces, Different Voices: A Rendezvous with Decoloniality*, ed. Sayan Dey (Mumbai, India: Becomeshakespeare.com, 2018), 64–92.

7. See Maximilien Laroche, *L'Avènement de la littérature haïtienne* (Port-Au-Prince: Éditions Mémoire, 2001), 162–74.

8. Philippe Thoby-Marcelin, quoted in Carolyn Fowler, *Philippe Thoby-Marcelin, écrivain haïtien et Pierre Marcelin, romancier haïtien* (Québec City: Naaman, 1985), 17.

9. Trouillot, *Silencing the Past*, 55–56.

10. Trouillot, *Ti dife boule*, 56. On the language of the Haitian Revolution, see Annette K. Joseph-Gabriel, "Creolizing Freedom: French–Creole Translations of Liberty and Equality in the Haitian Revolution," *Slavery and Abolition* 36, no. 1 (2015): 111–23.

11. L. Trouillot, introduction, *Ti dife boule*, 5.

12. An English translation of *Ti dife boule* by Mariana Past and Benjamin Hebblethwaite was recently published as *Stirring the Pot of Haitian History* (Liverpool, UK: Liverpool University Press, 2021). Past and Hebblethwaite previously published a sample English translation of chapters 1 and 2: see "The English Translation of a Major Haitian Creole Text by Michel-Rolph Trouillot," accessed March 1, 2019, https://ufdcimages.uflib.ufl.edu/AA/00/01/32/60/00001/Michel-Rolph_Trouillot_Sample_Translation.pdf.

13. *Viv*, or *vivres*, the French word from which the Creole term is derived, is a play on words. In the colonial era *vivres* were everyday foodstuffs planted for subsistence, while *danre*, or *denrées*, in French, were the commodities, sugar and coffee, etc., the enslaved were forced to cultivate for the enrichment of the enslavers.

14. Trouillot, *Ti dife boule*, 96.

15. Bob Corbett, review of *Silencing the Past: Power and the Production of History*, by Michel-Rolph Trouillot, H-Net Online, July 30, 1996, https://lists.h-net.org/cgi-bin/logbrowse.pl?trx=vx&list=h-oieahc&month=9607&week=e&msg=k55chU133UoKFpi4SRmRQg&user=&pw=.

16. Bob Corbett, "A Haitian Odyssey," World History Archives, last modified 1995, www.hartford-hwp.com/archives/43a/067.html.

17. Laurent Dubois, "Éloge pour Michel-Rolph Trouillot," *Transition* 109 (2012): 26–27.

18. Michel-Rolph Trouillot, quoted in Drexel G. Woodson and Brackette F. Williams, "In Memoriam: Dr. Michel-Rolph Trouillot, 1949–2012," *Caribbean Studies* 40, no. 1 (2012): 156.

19. Michel-Rolph Trouillot, *Global Transformations: Anthropology and the Modern World* (Basingstoke, UK: Palgrave Macmillan, 2003), 8.

20. L. Trouillot, introduction, *Ti dife boule*, 4.

21. Trouillot, *Silencing the Past*, xvii. Trouillot's notable relatives include his father Ernst Trouillot, a politician and famous television host; his stepmother Ertha Pascal-Trouillot, who became interim president of Haiti in 1990; his uncle Hénock Trouillot, a formidable scholar in his own right and the former director of the National Archives of Haiti; and his siblings Lyonel, Évelyne, and Jocelyne. See Yarimar Bonilla, "Burning Questions: The Life and Work of Michel-Rolph Trouillot, 1949–2012," *NACLA* 46, no. 1 (2013): 82–84, https://nacla.org/article/burning-questions-life-and-work-michel-rolph-trouillot-1949%25E2%2580%25932012.

22. See, as another example, Charles, "New York 1967–71."

23. Susan Buck-Morss, "Hegel and Haiti," *Critical Inquiry* 26, no. 4 (Summer 2000): 821–65.

24. See Marlene L. Daut, *Baron de Vastey and the Origins of Black Atlantic Humanism* (New York: Palgrave Macmillan, 2017); Marlene L. Daut, "The 'Alpha and Omega' of Haitian Literature: Baron de Vastey and the U.S. Audience of Haitian Political Writing, 1807–1825," in *Haiti and the Early United States*, ed. Elizabeth Maddock Dillon and Michal Drexler (Philadelphia: University of Pennsylvania Press, 2016), 287–313; Marlene L. Daut, "'Nothing in Nature is Mute': Reading Revolutionary Romanticism in *L'Haïtiade* and Hérard Dumesle's *Voyage dans le nord d'Hayti* (1824)," *New Literary History* 49, no. 4 (2018): 493–520.

25. Anténor Firmin, *De l'Égalité des races humaines: Anthropologie positive* (Paris: F. Pichon, 1885), 289–90.

26. See Léon-François Hoffmann, "Lamartine, Michelet et les Haïtiens," *Revue d'histoire littéraire de la France* 85, no. 4 (1985): 669–75.

27. Liautaud Ethéart, "Origine et Influence du Théâtre," in *Les Miscellanées* (Port-au-Prince: Impr. J. Courtois, 1855), ii–iii.

28. John R. Beard, *Toussaint L'Ouverture: A Biography and Autobiography*, ed. James Redpath (Boston: James Redpath, 1863).

29. See, Charles, "New York 1967–71."

30. Quoted and translated in Wulf D. Hund, "Marx and Haiti: Note on a Blank Space," *Journal of World Philosophies* 6, no. 2 (2021): 78–79 and 88.

31. For discussions of this dynamic, see Celucien Joseph, "The English Language Does Not Humanize the Haitian People," Haiti: Then and Now, May 22, 2022, https://haitithenandnow.wordpress.com/2022/05/22/day-22-in-haitian-heritage-month-the-english-language-does-not-humanize-the-haitian-people/; and Chelsea Stieber, "Why the Lab?" RSHHGG Lab, January 4, 2021, http://rshhgglab.com/why-a-lab/.

32. Celucien Joseph, "The Haitian Turn: An Appraisal of Recent Literary and Historiographical Works on the Haitian Revolution," *Journal of Pan African Studies* 5, no. 6 (2012): 37.

33. Trouillot, *Silencing the Past*, 69.

34. "Karl Marx is Trouillot's main source of inspiration in the study of world history," wrote Drexel Woodson, claiming also that *Silencing the Past* "reflects lessons learned from an international, multidisciplinary cohort of predecessors including [Sidney] Mintz, Eric R. Wolf, [Richard] Price, David W. Cohen, Immanuel Wallerstein, Fernand Braudel, C. L. R. James, Antonio Gramsci, Jean-François Lyotard, Michel de Certeau, and Hayden White." Drexel G. Woodson, "Trouillot, Michel-Rolph," in *International Encyclopedia of the Social Sciences*, ed. William A. Darity Jr. (Farmington Hills, MI: Thomson Gale, 2008), 457–58, www.encyclopedia.com/social-sciences/applied-and-social-sciences-magazines/trouillot-michel-rolph. See also Jean Jonassaint, "Haitian Literature in the United States, 1948–1986," in *American Babel: Literatures of the United States from Abnaki to Zuni*, ed. Marc Shell (Cambridge, MA: Harvard University Press, 2002), 438; and Charles, "New York 1967–71."

35. Trouillot, *Silencing the Past*, 55.

36. Trouillot, *Silencing the Past*, 55–56.

37. Trouillot, *Silencing the Past*, 56. In the 1940s, F. Louis Déroche (who signed his name F. Loui Deroch) published a short children's history of Haiti under the title *Abréjé istoua Daiti, 1492–1945* (Port-au-Prince, Haiti: Imprimerie du Nazaréen, 194?).

38. Trouillot, *Silencing the Past*, 56.

39. Past and Hebblethwaite, "The English Translation of a Major Haitian Creole Text," 1.

40. Trouillot, *Silencing the Past*, 57.

41. Past and Hebblethwaite, "*Ti dife boule*," 153.

42. Jean-Jacques Dessalines, "Le général en chef au peuple d'Haïti," in Louis-Félix Boisrond-Tonnerre, *Mémoires pour servir à l'histoire d'Haïti*, ed. Joseph Saint-Rémy (Paris: France Libraire, 1851), 3.

43. Henry Christophe, "Royaume d'Hayti: Proclamation," *Gazette royale d'Hayti*, January 9, 1817, 2, all issues consulted at https://lagazetteroyale.com.

44. Baron de Vastey (Jean Louis de), *Essai sur les causes de la révolution et des guerres civiles d'Hayti* (Sans-Souci, Haiti: L'Imprimerie Royale, 1819), 222.

45. Juste Chanlatte, *L'Entrée du roi en sa capitale* (Cap-Henry, Haiti: P. Roux, 1818), 6.

46. See Marlene Daut and Karen Richman, "Are They Mad? Nation and Narration in *Tous les hommes sont fous*," *Small Axe* 12, no. 2 (2008): 133–48.

47. Maximilien Laroche, *L'Avènement*, 92–93.

48. Jacques Pierre, "Traduction de l'Acte d'Indépendance d'Haïti en Créole Haïtien," *Journal of Haitian Studies* 17, no. 2 (2011): 168–80.

49. Jean L. Dominique, "Une langue pour le développement: Le Créole," *Le Petit Samedi Soir*, February 8, 1973. Many thanks to Claire Payton for sharing this document with me.

50. "Débats sur le Créole," *Le Petit Samedi Soir*, February 19, 1973; Émile Célestin-Mégie, "Défense et illustration de la langue Créole: Koléksyon Koukouy," *Le Petit Samedi Soir*, November 20, 1974. Many thanks to Claire Payton for sharing this document with me.

51. Trouillot, *Silencing the Past*, 56.

52. Jean Price-Mars, *So Spoke the Uncle*, trans. Magdaline W. Shannon (Washington, DC: Three Continents, 1983), 178.

53. Trouillot, *Ti dife boule*, 8–9.

54. Karl Marx, *The Eighteenth Brumaire of Louis Bonaparte* (1851–52), chap. 1, trans. Saul K. Padover (from the 1869 German ed.), www.marxists.org/archive/marx/works/1852/18th-brumaire.

55. Louis Joseph Janvier, *Les Constitutions d'Haïti (1801–1885), avec le portrait de l'auteur et une carte d'Haïti* (Paris: C. Marpon and E. Flammarion, 1886), ii.

56. Trouillot, *Ti dife boule*, 9, ellipses in original.

57. See the speech as reprinted in "Défection et suicide de Christophe," *L'Abeille haytienne* (June 15 to October 31, 1820): 73.

58. Camille Large, "Goman et l'insurrection de la Grand'Anse," in *Portraits et itinéraires*, ed. Michel Soukar (1939; Port-au-Prince: Parténaire Principal, 2014), 22–31.

59. Trouillot, *Silencing the Past*, 28–29.

60. Trouillot, *Silencing the Past*, 28.

61. Trouillot, *Silencing the Past*, 28.

62. Beaubrun Ardouin, *Études sur l'histoire d'Haïti: suivies de la vie du Général J.-M. Borgella*, 11 vols. (Paris: Dezobry and E. Magdeleine, 1853), 1:3.

63. Trouillot, *Silencing the Past*, 28, 67.

64. Ardouin, *Études*, 1853, 1:5.

65. Michel Foucault, quoted in "Film and Popular Memory: An Interview with Michel Foucault," trans. Martin Jordin, *Radical Philosophy* 11, no. 1 (1976): 25. The interview was conducted by and originally published in *Cahiers du cinéma* (July–August 1974): 251–52.

66. Ardouin, *Études*, 1853, 4:132.

67. Thomas Madiou, *Histoire d'Haïti*, vol. 1, *1492–1799* (Port-au-Prince: Éditions Deschamps, 1989), iv. The five other volumes Madiou wrote were published posthumously by Éditions Deschamps in the 1980s.

68. Tzvetan Todorov, *The Conquest of the Americas: The Question of the Other*, trans. Richard Howard (Norman: University of Oklahoma Press, 1999), 5, 4.

69. Trouillot, *Silencing the Past*, xix.

70. Ardouin, *Études*, 1853, 1:1.

71. Trouillot, *Silencing the Past*, 48.

72. Trouillot, *Silencing the Past*, 73.

73. Trouillot, *Silencing the Past*, 48.

74. Trouillot, *Silencing the Past*, 89.

75. Laurent Dubois, "An Enslaved Enlightenment: Rethinking the Intellectual History of the French Atlantic," *Social History* 31, no. 1 (2006): 1–14.

76. Vastey, *Essai*, 1.

77. Vastey, *Essai*, 2, 1.

78. Trouillot, *Silencing the Past*, 9.

79. Baron de Vastey (Jean Louis de), *Le Système colonial dévoilé* (Cap-Haïtien: P. Roux, 1814), 35.

80. Benedict Anderson, *Imagined Communities: Reflections on the Origin and Spread of Nationalism* (London: Verso, 2006), 202.

81. Anderson, *Imagined Communities*, 202–3, italics in original.

82. Marlene L. Daut, "Monstrous Testimony: Baron de Vastey and the Politics of Black Memory," supplementary essay in Baron de Vastey (Jean Louis de), *The Colonial System Unveiled*, trans. and ed. Chris Bongie (Liverpool: Liverpool University Press, 2014), 197.

83. Vastey, *Le Système*, 35, second quote from front matter.

84. See Vastey, *Le Système*, vii.

85. Baron de Vastey (Jean Louis de), *Réflexions politiques sur quelques ouvrages et journaux français concernant Hayti* (Sans-Souci, Haiti: Royal Imprint, 1817), xi–xii.

86. See Frederick Krantz, ed., *History from Below: Studies in Popular Protest and Popular Ideology in Honour of George Rudé* (Montréal: Concordia University Liberal, 1986).

87. See Marlene L. Daut, "Un-silencing the Past: Boisrond-Tonnerre, Vastey, and the Re-writing of the Haitian Revolution," *South Atlantic Review* 74, no. 1 (2009): 35–64.

88. Édouard Glissant, *The Poetics of Relations*, trans. Betsy Wing (Ann Arbor: University of Michigan Press, 1997), 11.

89. Trouillot, *Silencing the Past*, 2.

90. "The 1619 Project," *New York Times Magazine*, ed. Nikole Hannah-Jones, August 14, 2019, www.nytimes.com/interactive/2019/08/14/magazine/1619-america-slavery.html.

91. Geraldo Cadava, "Cuba and the U.S.: Necessary Mirrors," Public Books, April 13, 2022, https://www.publicbooks.org/cuba-ada-ferrer-1619-project-nikole-hannah-jones-slavery/.

92. Sean Wilentz, "A Matter of Facts," *Atlantic*, January 22, 2020, https://www.theatlantic.com/ideas/archive/2020/01/1619-project-new-york-times-wilentz/605152/.

93. See Édouard Glissant, *Caribbean Discourse: Selected Essays*, trans. J. Michael Dash (Charlottesville: University Press of Virginia, 1989).

94. Trouillot, *Silencing the Past*, 2–3.

95. Trouillot, *Silencing the Past*, 3.

96. Georg G. Iggers and Q. Edward Wang, *A Global History of Modern Historiography*, with contributions from Supriya Mukherjee (Harlow, UK: Pearson Education, 2008), 9.

97. Iggers and Wang, *Global History*, 75.

98. Firmin, *De l'Égalité*, 110.

99. Michel-Rolph Trouillot, "The Odd and the Ordinary: Haiti, the Caribbean, and the World," *Cimarrón* 2, no. 3 (1990): 3–12.

100. Jules Michelet, *La Femme*, 4th ed. (Paris: Hachette, 1863), 213–14.

101. Firmin, *De l'Égalité*, 290–91.

102. Firmin, *De l'Égalité*, 203.

103. Jules Michelet, "Préface de 1869," *Histoire de France* (Paris: Imprimerie Internationale A. Lacroix et Cie., 1876), n.p.; Project Gutenburg, accessed March 12, 2023, https://www.gutenberg.org/cache/epub/47969/pg47969-images.html; for Michelet's tomb, see https://upload.wikimedia.org/wikipedia/commons/f/f8/P%C3%A8re-Lachaise_-_Jules_Michelet_01.jpg.

104. Trouillot, *Silencing the Past*, 29.

105. Michelet, "Préface de 1869."

106. Baron de Vastey (Jean Louis de), *Le Cri de la conscience* (Cap-Henry, Haiti: P. Roux, 1815), 10.

107. Antoine Métral, "De la littérature haïtienne," *Revue encyclopédique* (1819), 1:528–29; Daina Ramey Berry, *The Price for Their Pound of Flesh: The Value of the Enslaved, from Womb to Grave, in the Building of a Nation* (Boston, MA: Beacon, 2017), xiii.

108. Vincent Brown, *The Reaper's Garden: Death and Power in the World of Atlantic Slavery* (Cambridge, MA: Harvard University Press, 2010), 6.

109. See Marc Bloch, *The Historian's Craft* (New York: Vintage, 1953), 47.

110. Arlette Farge, *The Allure of the Archives* (New Haven, CT: Yale University Press, 2015), 55.

111. Alessandra Benedicty, "Questions We Are Asking: Hegel, Agamben, Dayan, Trouillot, Mbembe, and Haitian Studies," *Journal of Haitian Studies* 19, no. 1 (2013): 7.

112. Juste Chanlatte, *Le Cri de la nature* (Cap-Haïtien: P. Roux, 1810), 53–54.

113. Dessalines, "Le général en chef," 4.

114. Jean-Jacques Dessalines, "Proclamation: Jean-Jacques Dessalines, Gouverneur-Général, aux Habitans d'Haïti," April 28, 1804, in *Dessalines Reader*, ed. Julia Gaffield, https://haitidoi.com/2015/10/30/dessalines-reader-28-april-1804/.

115. For other elements of "Dessalinean critique," see Chelsea Stieber, *Haiti's Paper War: Post-Independence Writing, Civil War, and the Making of the Republic, 1804–1954* (New York: New York University Press, 2020), 6.

116. Hérard Dumesle, *Voyage dans le nord d'Hayti: ou, Révélations des lieux et des monuments historiques* (Aux Cayes, Haiti: De l'Imprimerie du Gouvernement, 1824), 199, 34.

117. Michelet, "Préface de 1869."

118. Dumesle, *Voyage*, 211–13 and 5.

119. Dumesle, *Voyage*, 29.

120. Dumesle, *Voyage*, 222.

121. Dumesle, *Voyage*, 276–77.

122. Dumesle, *Voyage*, 198, 197.

123. Dumesle, *Voyage*, 199.

124. Dumesle, *Voyage*, 199.

125. Dumesle, *Voyage*, 367–68 fn. uu; Claude-Pierre-Joseph Le Borgne de Boigne, *Nouveau système de colonisation pour Saint-Domingue* (Paris: Dondy Dupré, 1817). Baron de Vastey's refutation of Le Borgne de Boigne's writings can be found in his *Réflexions politiques*, cited above.

126. Dumesle, *Voyage*, 199.

127. Trouillot, *Silencing the Past*, 36; Trouillot quotes Vastey, *Essai*, 201.

128. Pierre, "*Ti dife boule*," 213.

129. Joan Wallach Scott, "The Evidence of Experience," in *The Historic Turn in the Human Sciences*, ed. Terence J. McDonald (Ann Arbor: University of Michigan Press, 1996), 382.

130. Trouillot, *Silencing the Past*, 71–72.

131. See Chelsea Stieber, "Beyond Mentions: New Approaches to Comparative Studies of Haiti," *Early American Literature* 53, no. 3 (2018): 974.

132. Trouillot, *Global Transformations*, 10.

133. Dumesle, *Voyage*, 225 (italics in original).

134. Jean Casimir, *The Haitians: A Decolonial History*, trans. Laurent Dubois (Chapel Hill: University of North Carolina Press, 2020), xvii.

135. Matthew Arnold, *Culture and Anarchy: An Essay in Political and Social Criticism* (1869), www.gutenberg.org/cache/epub/4212/pg4212.html.

136. Alfred Nemours, *Haïti et la guerre d'indépendance Américaine* (1952; Port-au-Prince: Éditions Fardin, 2012), x.

137. Nemours likely refers to the Christmastime Rebellion of 1521, which occurred twenty years after 1501, when the Spanish first brought enslaved Africans to Ayiti for the purposes of chattel slavery. During the 1521 rebellion, enslaved Africans led a generalized, but swiftly crushed, revolt against the Spanish. For more information on this, see chapter 1 of the present volume; on 1501 as the beginning of European slave trafficking to the island, see Alex Borucki, David Eltis, and David Wheat, "Atlantic History and the Slave Trade to Spanish America," *American Historical Review* (April 2015): 433 fn. 1, www .institutomora.edu.mx/Documentos_RHITMO/Atlantic-History-and-the-Slave-Trade-to -Spanish-America.pdf.

138. Nemours, *Haiti*, vi.

139. Nemours, *Haiti*, xi.

140. Louis Joseph Janvier, *La République d'Haïti et ses visiteurs (1840–1882): réponse à M. Victor Cochinat (de la Petite presse) et à quelques autres écrivains* (Paris: Marpon et Flammarion, 1883), i–ii.

141. See Trouillot, *Global Transformations*, 1–28.

142. Janvier, *La République*, 123.

143. Émile Nau, *Histoire des caciques d'Haïti* (Port-au-Prince: T. Bouchereau, 1855), 37.

Chapter 1

1. Émile Nau, *Histoire des caciques d'Haïti* (Port-au-Prince: T. Bouchereau, 1855), iii.

2. Baron de Vastey (Jean Louis de), *Le Système colonial dévoilé* (Cap-Haïtien: P. Roux, 1814), 92–93.

3. Quoted in Vastey, *Le Système*, 4–6.

4. Nau, *Histoire des caciques*, 328–29.

5. Nau, *Histoire des caciques*, 322.

6. Nau, *Histoire des caciques*, 329.

7. Nau, *Histoire des caciques*, 329–30.

8. José I. Castro, "On the Origins of the Spanish Word 'Tiburón,' and the English Word 'Shark.'" *Environmental Biology of Fishes* 65 (2002): 249–53.

9. William F. Keegan and Corinne Hofman, *The Caribbean before Columbus* (Oxford: Oxford University Press, 2016), 12–13, 240–47.

10. Keegan and Hofman, *Caribbean before Columbus*, 259.

11. Edmundo S. O'Gorman, *The Invention of America: An Inquiry into the Historical Nature of the New World and the Meaning of Its History* (Bloomington, IN: University of Indiana Press, 1961).

12. Nau, *Histoire des caciques*, iv.

13. Nau, *Histoire des caciques*, ii–iii.

14. Nau, *Histoire des caciques*, iv.

15. Nau, *Histoire des caciques*, ii.

16. Hérard Dumesle, *Voyage dans le nord d'Hayti: ou, Révélations des lieux et des monuments historiques* (Aux Cayes, Haiti: De l'Imprimerie du Gouvernement, 1824), 355–56 fn. dd.

17. Émeric Bergeaud, *Stella, par E. Bergeaud (Des Cayes, Haïti)* (Paris: E. Dentu, 1859), 317.

18. Jean-Jacques Dessalines, "Proclamation. Jean-Jacques Dessalines, Gouverneur-Général, aux Habitans d'Haïti," April 28, 1804, in *Dessalines Reader,* ed. Julia Gaffield, https://haitidoi.com/2015/10/30/dessalines-reader-28-april-1804/; "Constitution du 20 mai 1805," Digithèque MJP, https://mjp.univ-perp.fr/constit/ht1805.htm.

19. Joseph Saint-Rémy, *Pétion et Haïti: étude monographique et historique,* vol. 4 (Paris: Auguste Durand, 1857), 12 fn. 1.

20. Baron de Vastey (Jean Louis de), *Essai sur les causes de la révolution et des guerres civiles d'Hayti* (Sans-Souci, Haiti: L'Imprimerie Royale, 1819), 43, italics in original.

21. Vastey, *Le Système,* 11–12.

22. Nau, *Histoire des caciques,* 329.

23. Vastey, *Le Système,* 8 fn. 1.

24. Marlene L. Daut, "The Wrongful Death of Toussaint Louverture," *History Today* 70, no. 6 (June 2020): 28–39.

25. Nau, *Histoire des caciques,* 329.

26. Henri Chauvet, *Les Quisqueyennes: fille du Kacik, drame en cinq actes et en vers* (Paris: Imprimerie Vve. Victor Goupy, 1894), 8.

27. Chauvet, *Les Quisqueyennes,* 138–39.

28. Chauvet, *Les Quisqueyennes,* 113 n. 4. In the section, "De la Langue et de la littéraure des aborigènes d'Haïti," Émile Nau contested the idea that we could know for certain what the first Ayitians meant by this phrase, since it was recorded and given meaning by European travelers and missionaries. See Nau, *Histoire des caciques,* 334.

29. Edgar La Selve, *Histoire de la littérature haïtienne, depuis ses origines jusqu'à nos jours, suivie d'une anthologie haïtienne* (Versailles: Imprimerie et Stéréotypie Cerf et Fils, 1875), 21–22.

30. Nau, *Histoire des caciques,* 331. See also, Jean Fouchard, *Langue et littérature des aborigènes d'Ayiti* (Port-au-Prince: Éditions Henri Deschamps, 1988), 80.

31. Nau, *Histoire des caciques,* 332.

32. Nau, *Histoire des caciques,* 217.

33. Leclerc to Bonaparte, October 7, 1802, in Paul Roussier, *Lettres du Général Leclerc* (Paris: Société de l'Histoire des Colonies Françaises, 1937), 256.

34. Baron de Vastey, *Réflexions sur une lettre de Mazères: ex-colon français, adressée à M. J.C.L. Sismonde de Sismondi, sur les noirs et les blancs, la civilisation de l'Afrique, le royaume d'Hayti* (Cap-Haïtien: P. Roux, 1816), 96–97. For étouffoir, see the speech of Alexandre Pétion, reprinted in Vastey, *Essai,* Appendix, 32; and Victor Schoelcher, *Vie de Toussaint Louverture* (Paris: Paul Ollendorff, 1889), 372.

35. Quoted in Dumesle, *Voyage,* 208.

36. Juste Chanlatte, *Le Cri de la nature* (Cap-Haïtien: P. Roux, 1810), 52.

37. Nau, *Histoire des caciques,* v–vi; 244–45.

38. Beaubrun Ardouin, *Études sur l'histoire d'Haïti, 11 tomes réunis en 3 volumes,* vol. 1 (Port-au-Prince: Éditions Fardin Collection du Bicentennaire Haïti, 2004), 49; David Geggus, "The Naming of Haiti," *New West Indian Guide* 71, no. 1/2 (1997): 49.

39. Ardouin, *Études,* 2004, 1:49.

40. Julien Prévost, *Relation des glorieux événemens qui ont porté leurs majestés royales sur le trône d'Hayti, suivie de l'histoire du couronnement et du sacre du roi Henry 1er, et de la reine Marie-Louise* (Cap-Henry: P. Roux, 1811), xxi–xxii, xxiii.

41. Prévost, *Relation*, xxvii–xxviii.

42. La Selve, as reprinted in Émile Nau, *Histoire du Cacique Caonabo,* ed. Christophe Charles (Port-au-Prince: Éditions Choucoune, 2007), 33. Nau does not specifically mention Vastey but refers only to "Les lettrés de la cour du roi Henri Christophe." See Nau, *Histoire des caciques*, 334.

43. Vastey, *Le Système*, 92–93.

44. Quoted in Vastey, *Le Système*, 10.

45. Vastey, *Le Système*, 4.

46. Vastey, *Le Système*, 4.

47. Vastey, *Le Système*, 4.

48. Vastey, *Le Système*, 94–95.

49. Vastey, *Le Système*, 3.

50. See Keegan and Hofman, *Caribbean before Columbus.*

51. Nau, *Histoire des caciques*, iv–v.

52. Nau, *Histoire des caciques*, 293; African rebellion began in 1501, shortly after the Spanish forcibly transported the first captive Africans to the island, see "The Early Trans-Atlantic Slave Trade: Nicolas Ovando," in *African Laborers for a New Empire: Iberia, Slavery, and the Atlantic World*, accessed March 15, 2023, https://ldhi.library.cofc.edu/exhibits/show/african _laborers_for_a_new_emp/early_trans_atlantic_slave_tra#:~:text=A%20letter%20from%20 Spanish%20monarchs,de%20Indias%2C%20Sevilla%2C%20Spain; see also, Alex Borucki, David Eltis, and David Wheat, "Atlantic History and the Slave Trade to Spanish America," *American Historical Review* (April 2015): 433 fn. 1, www.institutomora.edu.mx/Documentos _RHITMO/Atlantic-History-and-the-Slave-Trade-to-Spanish-America.pdf.

53. Nau, *Histoire des caciques*, 288.

54. Anthony Stevens-Acevedo, *The Santo Domingo Slave Revolt of 1521 and the Slave Laws of 1522: Black Slavery and Black Resistance in the Early Colonial Americas* (New York: CUNY Dominican Studies Institute, 2019), 10.

55. Reprinted and translated in Anthony Stevens-Acevedo, "Appendix 4: Translation, Decree by Viceroy Diego Colón Including Ordinances on Blacks and Slaves of La Española and Puerto Rico, January 6, 1522," in Stevens-Acevedo, *Santo Domingo Slave Revolt*, 23–29.

56. Stevens-Acevedo, *Santo Domingo Slave Revolt*, 5.

57. Stevens-Acevedo, *Santo Domingo Slave Revolt*, 10.

58. "Articles of Pacification with the Maroons of Trelawney Town, Concluded March the First, 1738," Cyberjam: Maroon Sovereignty Project, accessed October 1, 2022, https:// cyber.harvard.edu/eon/marroon/treaty.html.

59. Quoted and translated in Ida Altman, "The Revolt of Enriquillo and the Historiography of Early Spanish America," *Americas* 63, no. 4 (April 2007): 605.

60. Altman, "Revolt of Enriquillo," 605.

61. Quoted in Nau, *Histoire des caciques*, 305.

62. Nau, *Histoire des caciques*, 290–91.

63. Nau, *Histoire des caciques*, 311.

64. Quoted and translated in Altman, "Revolt of Enriquillo," 606.

65. Altman, "Revolt of Enriquillo," 607.

66. Altman, "Revolt of Enriquillo," 608.

67. Nau, *Histoire des caciques*, 307.

68. Nau, *Histoire des caciques*, 315.

69. Dumesle, *Voyage*, 313–14.

70. Dumesle, *Voyage*, 313–14.

Chapter 2

1. See a digital image of the letter from Spanish monarchs to Ovando, dated September 16, 1501, in *African Laborers for a New Empire: Iberia, Slavery, and the Atlantic World*, accessed March 15, 2023, https://ldhi.library.cofc.edu/exhibits/show/african_laborers_for_a _new_emp/early_trans_atlantic_slave_tra#:~:text=A%20letter%20from%20Spanish%20 monarchs,de%20Indias%2C%20Sevilla%2C%20Spain; see also, Alex Borucki, David Eltis, and David Wheat, "Atlantic History and the Slave Trade to Spanish America," *American Historical Review* (April 2015): 433 fn. 1, www.institutomora.edu.mx/Documentos _RHITMO/Atlantic-History-and-the-Slave-Trade-to-Spanish-America.pdf.

2. Baron de Vastey (Jean Louis de), *Le Système colonial dévoilé* (Cap-Haïtien: P. Roux, 1814), 13.

3. Vastey, *Le Système*, 14.

4. Vastey, *Le Système*, 16.

5. Vastey, *Le Système*, 17.

6. Vastey, *Le Système*, 17.

7. Juste Chanlatte, *Le Cri de la nature* (Cap-Haïtien: P. Roux, 1810), 10.

8. P. Gabrielle Foreman et al., "Writing about Slavery/Teaching about Slavery: This Might Help," community-sourced document, accessed March 15, 2023, https://docs .google.com/document/d/1A4TEdDgYslX-hlKezLodMIM71My3KTNozxRvoIQTOQs /mobilebasic.

9. Baron de Vastey (Jean Louis de), *Réflexions politiques sur quelques ouvrages et journaux français concernant Hayti* (Sans-Souci, Haiti: Royal Imprint, 1817), 87 fn. 1.

10. Quoted in Baron de Vastey (Jean Louis de), *Notes à M. le Baron de V.P. Malouet, Ministre de la Marine et des Colonies . . . en réfutation du 4ème volume de son ouvrage, intitulé: Collection de Mémoires sur les colonies et particulièrement sur Saint-Domingue* (Cap-Henry, Haiti: P. Roux, 1814), 7.

11. Vastey, *Notes*, 7.

12. Lurline V. Simpson, "Doubleheaders: Ce qui n'est pas clair n'est pas français," *French Review* 17, no. 3 (1944): 154–56.

13. Jean Fouchard, *Les Marrons du syllabaire: Quelques aspects du problème de l'instruction et de l'éducation des esclaves et affranchis de Saint-Domingue* (Port-au-Prince: H. Deschamps, 1988), 85.

14. Vastey, *Le Système*, 36.

15. Vastey, *Le Système*, 37.

16. "Supplique et pétition des citoyens de couleur des isles et colonies françoises," December 2, 1789, University of Maryland Special Collections, https://colonyincrisis.lib .umd.edu/1789/12/02/request-and-petition-from-the-citizens-of-color-of-the-french-isles -and-colonies-december-2-1789/, italics in original.

17. Chanlatte, *Le Cri*, 8.

18. Chanlatte, *Le Cri*, 13.

19. Quoted in Hérard Dumesle, *Voyage dans le nord d'Hayti: ou, Révélations des lieux et des monuments historiques* (Aux Cayes, Haiti: De l'Imprimerie du Gouvernement, 1824), 128.

20. See Jean-François Niort and Jérémy Richard, "L'Édit royal de mars 1685 touchant la police des îles de l'Amérique française dit 'Code Noir': Comparaison des éditions anciennes à partir de la version 'Guadeloupe,'" *Bulletin de la Société d'Histoire de la Guadeloupe* 156 (2010): 73–89.

21. Quoted in Dumesle, *Voyage*, 127.

22. Aimé Césaire, *Discourse on Colonialism*, trans. Joan Pinkham (New York: Monthly Review Press, 2000), 42.

23. Vastey, *Le Système*, 31.

24. Vastey, *Le Système*, 67.

25. Chanlatte, *Le Cri*, 11.

26. Vastey, *Le Système*, 66.

27. Dumesle, *Voyage*, 333 fn. a.

28. Dumesle, *Voyage*, 151, 197.

29. Baron de Vastey (Jean Louis de), *Essai sur les causes de la révolution et des guerres civiles d'Hayti* (Sans-Souci, Haiti: L'Imprimerie Royale, 1819), 203.

30. Dumesle, *Voyage*, 151.

31. "racism, n.," OED Online, accessed March 1, 2023, Oxford University Press, https://www-oed-com.yale.idm.oclc.org/view/Entry/157097?redirectedFrom=racism.

32. For 1902 as origin in English, and for Spanish and French genealogies, see Nathan G. Alexander, "Towards a History of the Term Racism," *Monitor: Global Intelligence on Racism* (May 2019), http://monitoracism.eu/towards-a-history-of-the-term-racism/.

33. Vastey, *Le Système*, 71.

34. Orlando Patterson, *Slavery and Social Death: A Comparative Study, with a New Preface* (Cambridge, MA: Harvard University Press, 2018); Vastey, *Réflexions politiques*, 49–50.

35. Vastey, *Le Système*, 40–41.

36. Vastey, *Le Système*, 41 fn. 1.

37. Vastey, *Le Système*, 41–42 fn. 1.

38. Thomas Thistlewood Papers, Yale Beinecke Library, OSB MSS 176.

39. Portuguese money made of minted gold from Brazil, which constituted one of the major and preferred, because most highly valuable, currencies of Saint-Domingue. See Robert Lacombe, *Histoire Monétaire de Saint-Domingue et de la République d'Haïti jusqu'en 1874* (Paris: Éditions Larose, 1958), 20–21, 14.

40. For Castonnet des Fosses, see "Députés à la Constituante: Larchevesque-Thibaud," *G.H.C.* 29 (July–August 1991): 359, http://www.ghcaraibe.org/bul/ghc029/p0359.html.

41. Vastey, *Le Système*, 43–44.

42. "Esclaves en maronage," *Supplément aux Affiches Américaines* (December 3, 1783): 4.

43. Vastey, *Le Système*, 48–49.

44. Joseph Saint-Rémy, *Mémoires du Général-Toussaint L'Ouverture, écrits par lui-même* (Paris: Pagnerre, 1853), 58 fn. 1.

45. Frantz Fanon, *The Wretched of the Earth*, trans. Constance Farrington (New York: Grove, 1963), 61.

46. Baron de Vastey (Jean Louis de), *Réflexions sur une lettre de Mazères: ex-colon français, adressée à M. J.C.L. Sismonde de Sismondi, sur les noirs et les blancs, la civilisation de l'Afrique, le royaume d'Hayti* (Cap-Haïtien: P. Roux, 1816), 103.

47. Vastey, *Le Système*, 49–50, quotes 50 fn. 1.

48. Vastey, *Le Système*, 60–61.

49. Vastey, *Le Système*, front matter.

50. Vastey, *Réflexions sur une lettre*, 91.

51. Alfred N. Hunt, *Haiti's Influence on Antebellum America: Slumbering Volcano in the Caribbean* (Baton Rouge: Louisiana State University Press, 1988); Ashli White, *Encountering Revolution: Haiti and the Making of the Early Republic* (Baltimore, MD: Johns Hopkins University Press, 2010); James Alexander Dun, *Dangerous Neighbors: Making the Haitian Revolution in Early America* (Philadelphia: University of Pennsylvania Press, 2016).

52. Vastey, *Le Système*, 35.

53. Jean-Paul Sartre, *Qu'est-ce que la littérature?* (Paris: Gallimard, 2015), 164; Theodor Adorno, "Commitment," in *Aesthetics and Politics: The Key Texts of the Classic Debate within German Marxism*, ed. Theodor Adorno, Walter Benjamin, Ernst Bloch, Bertolt Brecht, and Georg Lukacs, trans. Ronald Taylor (London: Verso, 1980), 189.

54. Vastey, *Le Système*, 39.

55. Vastey, *Le Système*, 40.

56. Marlene L. Daut, *Baron de Vastey and the Origins of Black Atlantic Humanism* (New York: Palgrave Macmillan, 2017), 29.

57. Vastey, *Le Système*, 70–71.

58. Vastey, *Le Système*, 47, 49.

59. Quoted in Vastey, *Le Système*, 24; Vastey borrowed this quotation from the abbé Raynal, see Chris Bongie, tr. and ed., *The Colonial System Unveiled* (Liverpool, UK: Liverpool University Press), 156 fn. 37.

60. Vastey, *Le Système*, 66.

61. Vastey, *Le Système*, 66 fn. 1—Vastey cites from the "Arrêt" as published in volume 3 of a compliation edited by Médéric Louis-Élie Moreau de Saint-Méry, *Loix et constitutions des colonies françoises de l'Amérique sous le Vent* (Paris: Chez l'Auteur, 1784–1790), 3:399.

62. "Copie d'une lettre d'un capitaine," A Colony in Crisis, September 17, 1791, University of Maryland Special Collections, https://colonyincrisis.lib.umd.edu/1791/11/15/copy-of-a-letter-from-a-captain-presently-in-cap-francais-sent-via-the-ship-named-the-cap-francais-which-arrived-in-nantes-after-31-days-on-november-15-1791-addressed-to-paris-to-m-w/.

63. "Reflections on the Code Noir, and the Denunciation of an Atrocious Crime Committed in Saint-Domingue: Addressed to the National Assembly by the Society of the Friends of Blacks, Paris, August 1790," A Colony in Crisis, August 15, 1790, University of Maryland Special Collections, https://colonyincrisis.lib.umd.edu/1790/08/15/reflections-on-the-code-noir-and-denunciation-of-an-atrocious-crime-committed-in-saint-domingue-addressed-to-the-national-assembly-by-the-society-of-the-friends-of-blacks-paris-august-1790/.

64. Vastey, *Le Système*, 71–72.

65. Vastey, *Le Système*, 72.

66. Michel-Rolph Trouillot, *Silencing the Past: Power and the Production of History* (New York: Beacon, 1995), 18.

67. Vastey, *Le Système*, 90.

68. T. S. Winn, *Emancipation: Or Practical Advice to British Slave-Holders: With Suggestions for the General Improvement of West India Affairs* (London: W. Phillips, 1824), 57; "white supremacy, n.," OED Online, accessed March 1, 2023, Oxford University Press, https://www-oed-com.yale.idm.oclc.org/view/Entry/421025?redirectedFrom=white+supremacy.

69. Henry Bevan, *Thirty Years in India; Or, A Soldier's Reminiscences of Native and European Life in the Presidencies, from 1808 to 1838, in two volumes* (London: Pelham Richardson, Corhill, 1839), 2:299.

70. Georges Pigeonneau, "La Question nègre aux Etas-Unis," in *Annales de l'École Libre des Sciences Politiques* (Paris: Félix Alcan, 1891), 649.

71. Vastey, *Le Système*, 89.

72. Vastey, *Le Système*, 74.

73. Vastey, *Le Système*, 83 fn. 1.

74. Vastey, *Le Système*, 83–84 fn. 1.

75. Vastey, *Le Système*, 84 fn. 1.

76. Vastey, *Le Système*, 85.

77. Vastey, *Le Système*, 86–87.

78. Vastey, *Le Système*, 86; for how the French royal edicts governing slavery became a "guarantee of tyranny," on the part of the white French colonists, see Joan [Colin] Dayan, *Haiti, History and the Gods* (Berkeley, CA: University of California Press, 1998), 207.

79. Quoted and translated in Malick W. Ghachem, *The Old Regime and the Haitian Revolution* (Cambridge: Cambridge University Press, 2012), 158–61.

80. Vastey, *Le Système*, 90.

81. Vastey, *Le Système*, 89.

Chapter 3

1. Hérard Dumesle, *Voyage dans le nord d'Hayti: ou, révélations des lieux et des monuments historiques* (Aux Cayes, Haiti: De l'Imprimerie du Gouvernement, 1824), 362 fn. 00.

2. Julien Raimond, *Observations sur l'origine et les progrès du préjugé des colons blancs contre les hommes de couleur: sur les inconvénients de le perpétuer: la nécessité, la facilité de le détruire: sur le projet du Comité colonial, etc. par M. Raymond, homme de couleur de Saint Domingue* (Paris: Chez Belin, 1791), 3 fn. 1, 28.

3. Raimond, *Observations sur l'origine*, 3 fn. 1; see also, *Édit du Roi, Touchant la Police des Isles de l'Amérique Française* (Paris, 1687), https://revolution.chnm.org/d/335/.

4. Quoted in Nemours, *Haïti et la guerre d'indépendance Américaine* (1952; Port-au-Prince: Éditions Fardin, 2012), viii.

5. Julien Raimond, *Réponse aux considérations de M. Moreau, dit Saint-Méry, député à l'Assemblée nationale, sur les colonies: par M. Raymond, citoyen de couleur de Saint-Domingue* (Paris: De l'Imprimerie du Patriote François, May 12, 1791), 52.

6. Raimond, *Réponse aux considérations*, 54.

7. *Édit du Roi.*

8. In several pamphlets and letters Raimond described being one of the only men of color who could afford to fund the activism required to agitate for their rights in Paris, among them, "Première lettre écrite dans la partie de l'Ouest," October 21, 1791, Bibliothèque nationale de France, https://gallica.bnf.fr/ark:/12148/bpt6k58038278/f9.item.

9. Julien Raimond, *Observations adressées à l'Assemblée nationale, par un député des colons Amériquains* (1789), 1.

10. Raimond, *Observations adressées*, 5–6.

11. Julien Raymond, baptismal record, État Civil for Baynet, December 31, 1744, Archives Nationales d'Outre Mer, Aix-en-Provence, France (hereafter ANOM). All records from

these civil registers consulted at http://anom.archivesnationales.culture.gouv.fr/caomec2/recherche.php?territoire=SAINT-DOMINGUE.

12. See note 11 listing baptismal record, and also death record for Pierre Raymond, État Civil de Aquin, June 19, 1772, ANOM.

13. Julien Raimond, *Réponse aux considérations de M. Moreau, dit Saint-Méry, député à l'Assemblée nationale, sur les colonies: par M. Raymond, citoyen de couleur de Saint-Domingue* (Paris: De l'Imprimerie du Patriote François, May 12, 1791), 16; see also, Raimond, *Observations sur l'origine*, 42–43.

14. See marriage record for Pierre Raymond and Marie Begasse, État Civil for Baynet, July 2, 1726, ANOM.

15. Julien Raimond, *Correspondance de Julien Raimond avec ses frères de Saint-Domingue, et les pièces qui lui ont été adressées par eux* (Paris: De l'Imprimerie du Cercle Social, 1793), vi fn. 1.

16. Raimond, *Observations adressées*, 7.

17. *Déclaration des Droits de l'Homme et du Citoyen de 1789,* August 26, 1789, https://www.legifrance.gouv.fr/contenu/menu/droit-national-en-vigueur/constitution/declaration-des-droits-de-l-homme-et-du-citoyen-de-1789; Baron de Vastey, *Le Système colonial dévoilé* (Cap-Haïtien: P. Roux, 1814), 30.

18. Statistics from the March 26, 1785, issue of the *Affiches Américaines* list the ratio of white men to white women as three to one, also noting that the stable population, that is not travelers, military, or merchants, was actually ten to one. See "État des baptêmes, mariages, & sépultres, dans les différentes paroisses de la Colonie, pendant l'anné 1783," *Affiches Américaines* (March 26, 1785): 2–3.

19. Raimond, *Observations sur l'origine*, 2.

20. Raimond, *Observations sur l'origine*, 4.

21. Raimond, *Observations sur l'origine*, 4.

22. Raimond, *Observations sur l'origine*, 5.

23. Raimond, *Observations sur l'origine*, 6.

24. Raimond, *Observations sur l'origine*, 7.

25. Raimond, *Observations sur l'origine*, 8.

26. Vastey, *Le Système*, 75–77 fn. 1.

27. John Garrigus, *Before Haiti: Race and Citizenship in French Saint-Domingue* (Basingstoke, UK: Palgrave Macmillan, 2006), 211.

28. *Édit du Roi.*

29. Raimond, *Observations sur l'origine*, 8–9.

30. Marlene L. Daut, *Tropics of Haiti* (Liverpool, UK: Liverpool University Press, 2015), 220–21.

31. Raimond, *Observations sur l'origine*, 9, 10.

32. Raimond, *Observations sur l'origine*, 10.

33. Raimond, *Réponse aux considérations*, 4.

34. Raimond, *Réponse aux considérations*, 60.

35. Raimond, *Observations sur l'origine*, 28.

36. Raimond, *Observations adressées*, 13.

37. Raimond, *Observations adressées*, 1–5.

38. Raimond, *Réponse aux considérations*, 6, italics in original; the part about "Americans" needing to fly to the defense of their country is missing in the version Raimond

reprinted in his *Véritable origine des troubles de S.-Domingue, et des différentes causes qui les ont produits; par M. Julien Raimond, Député des citoyens de coueur* (Paris: Desenne, 1792), 6–8.

39. Raimond, *Véritable origine des troubles*, 7–8, italics in original.

40. Raimond, *Réponse aux considérations*, 9–11.

41. Raimond, *Réponse aux considérations*, 19.

42. Raimond, *Observations sur l'origine*, 39; Raimond, *Réponse aux considérations*, 19.

43. Raimond, *Réponse aux considérations*, 20.

44. Raimond, *Réponse aux considérations*, 20.

45. Raimond, *Réponse aux considérations*, 20–21.

46. Raimond, *Réponse aux considérations*, 21.

47. Raimond, *Réponse aux considérations*, 21–22.

48. Raimond, *Réponse aux considérations*, 22.

49. Raimond, *Réponse aux considérations*, 9.

50. Raimond, *Réponse aux considérations*, 10.

51. Raimond, *Réponse aux considérations*, 11.

52. Raimond, *Réponse aux considérations*, 22.

53. Raimond, *Réponse aux considérations*, 23.

54. André Rigaud, *Mémoire du général de brigade André Rigaud* (Aux Cayes, Haiti: L'Imprimerie de Lemery, 1797), 4.

55. Raimond, *Véritable origine des troubles*, 20.

56. Quoted and translated in "The National Assembly: Law on the Colonies, with an Explanation of the Reasons That Have Determined Its Content," in *Slave Revolution in the Caribbean, 1789–1804: A Brief History with Documents*, ed. Laurent Dubois and John D. Garrigus, 2nd ed. (Boston: Bedford/St. Martin's, 2017), 71.

57. Raimond, *Véritable origine des troubles*, 22–23.

58. Jan Ellen Lewis, "What Happened to the Three-Fifths Clause: The Relationship between Women and Slaves in Constitutional Thought, 1787–1866," *Journal of the Early Republic* 37, no. 1 (2017): 1–46.

59. Chelsea Stieber, "Who's Afraid of Antiracism?" March 29, 2021, Public Books, www.publicbooks.org/whos-afraid-of-antiracism/.

60. Raimond, *Réponse aux considérations*, 37.

61. Raimond, *Véritable origine des troubles*, 23–24.

62. Raimond, *Véritable origine des troubles*, 24.

63. Raimond, *Réponse aux considérations*, 28.

64. Raimond, *Réponse aux considérations*, 29.

65. Raimond, *Réponse aux considérations*, 32 fn. 1.

66. Raimond, *Réponse aux considérations*, 32.

67. Raimond, *Véritable origine des troubles*, 25–26.

68. John D. Garrigus, "'Thy Coming Fame, Ogé! Is Sure': New Evidence on Ogé's 1790 Revolt and the Beginnings of the Haitian Revolution,' in *Assumed Identities: The Meanings of Race in the Atlantic World*, ed. John Garrigus and Christopher Morris (College Station: Texas A&M University Press, 2010), 19–45.

69. Émile Nau, *Réclamation par les affranchis des droits civils et politiques: Ogé et Chavannes* (Port-au-Prince: T. Boucherau, 1840), 46–47.

70. Baron de Vastey, *Réflexions sur une lettre de Mazères: ex-colon français, adressée à M. J.C.L. Sismonde de Sismondi, sur les noirs et les blancs, la civilisation de l'Afrique, le royaume d'Hayti* (Cap-Haïtien: P. Roux, 1816), 1; M. Mazères, *De l'Utilité des colonies, des causes intérieures de la perte de Saint-Domingue et des moyens d'en recouvrer la possession* (Paris: Renard, 1814), 77–79.

71. Dumesle, *Voyage*, 75, 77–80.

72. Raimond, *Réponse aux considérations*, 33.

73. Raimond, *Réponse aux considérations*, 34.

74. Vincent Ogé, *Motion faite par M. Vincent Ogé, jeune à l'Assemblée des Colons, habitants de St-Domingue, à l'Hôtel de Massiac, Place des Victoires* (Paris, 1789), Bibliothèque nationale de France, département Philosophie, histoire, sciences de l'homme, 8-LK12-1156.

75. "Lettre de M. Ogé le jeune au président de l'assemblée provinciale du Nord," *Gazette nationale, ou Le Moniteur universel*, December 29, 1790.

76. "Avis du gouvernement," *Affiches Américaines* (November 11, 1790): 1.

77. Garrigus, "Thy Coming Fame, Ogé!," 30, 43 fn. 67.

78. "Copie du discours de Castaing, mulâtre libre," *Affiches Américaines* (November 13, 1790): 4–5.

79. "Proclamation de M. le Lieutenant-général au gouvernement, concernant les troubles actuels de la colonie, en date du 12 novembre 1790," *Affiches Américaines* (November 18, 1790): 1.

80. "Extrait des minutes de l'assemblée de la commune section du quartier de l'Islet-à-Pierre-Joseph; séans [*sic*], MM. les maires et echevins de la municipalité de la paroisse du Cap-Dame-Marie, en date de ce jour quinze novembre mil sept cent quatre-vingt-dix, après midi," *Affiches Américaines* (December 4, 1790): 4–5.

81. Florence Gauthier, *L'Aristocratie de l'épiderme: Le combat de la Société des Citoyens de Couleur, 1789–1791* (Paris: CNRS Éditions, 2007), 141–52; Raimond, *Observations sur l'origine*, 25.

82. Carolyn E. Fick, *The Making of Haiti: The Saint-Domingue Revolution from Below* (Knoxville: University of Tennessee Press, 1990), 80–84, 121.

83. Raimond, *Réponse aux considérations*, 17.

84. Raimond, *Correspondance*, 17.

85. Raimond, *Correspondance*, 18.

86. Raimond, *Correspondance*, 15 fn. 2.

87. Raimond, *Correspondance*, 16.

88. Raimond, *Correspondance*, 17.

89. Raimond, *Correspondance*, 36–37 fn. b.

90. Raimond, *Correspondance*, 37 fn. b.

91. "The National Assembly Law on the Colonies with an Explanation of the Reasons That Have Determined Its Content, 1791," repr. and trans. in Dubois and Garrigus, *Slave Revolution in the Caribbean*, 70–71.

92. Raimond, *Correspondance*, 19–20.

93. Raimond, *Correspondance*, v fn. 2.

94. Dumesle, *Voyage*, 354–55 fn. dd.

95. Dumesle, *Voyage*, 355 fn. dd.

96. Dumesle, *Voyage*, 355–56 fn. dd.

97. Raimond, *Correspondance*, 34.

Chapter 4

1. For example, "Nègres Marons," *Supplément aux Affiches Américaines* (February 17, 1776): 81; "Nègres Marons," *Supplément aux Affiches Américaines* (December 28, 1771): 578; "Liste des Nègres Épaves, qui conformément à l'Ordonnance du Roi du 18 novembre 1767, doivent être vendus à la Barre du Siège Royal du Cap, le 12 juillet prochain, à la requête de Me Blanchet, Notaire du Roi & Receveur de ce droit," *Supplément aux Affiches Américaines* (May 17, 1777): 239; for Chavannes, see Stewart King, "Chavannes, Jean-Baptiste (1748–1791) Haitian Revolutionary," in *Dictionary of Caribbean and Afro-Latin American Biography*, ed. Franklin W. Knight and Henry Louis Gates Jr. (Oxford: Oxford University Press, 2016), https://www-oxfordreference-com.yale.idm.oclc.org/view/10.1093/acref/9780199935796.001.0001/acref-9780199935796-e-480.

2. "Du Cap-Français," *Affiches Américaines* (March 5, 1791): 117.

3. See John D. Garrigus, "'Thy Coming Fame Ogé! Is Sure': New Evidence on Ogé's 1790 Revolt and the Beginnings of the Haitian Revolution," in *Assumed Identities: The Meanings of Race in the Atlantic World*, ed. John D. Garrigus and Christopher Morris (College Station: Texas A&M University Press, 2010), 19–45.

4. Reprinted in Lieutenant-Général Baron Pamphile de Lacroix, *Mémoires pour servir à l'histoire de la révolution de Saint-Domingue*, 2 vols. (Paris: Pillet Aine, 1819), 1:63–64.

5. "Du Cap-Français," 117.

6. Julien Raimond, *Correspondance de Julien Raimond avec ses frères de Saint-Domingue, et les pièces qui lui ont été adressées par eux* (Paris: De l'Imprimerie du Cercle Social, 1793), 58–59.

7. Jean-Paul Sartre, *Morts sans sépulture: Pièce en trois actes* (Lausanne: Éditions Marguerat, 1946), 184.

8. Hérard Dumesle, *Voyage dans le nord d'Hayti: ou, Révélations des lieux et des monuments historiques* (Aux Cayes, Haiti: De l'Imprimerie du Gouvernement, 1824), 82.

9. Jean-Jacques Dessalines, "Proclamation: Jean-Jacques Dessalines, Gouverneur Général aux Habitants d'Haïti," April 28, 1804, Haiti and the Atlantic World, https://haitidoi.com/2015/10/30/dessalines-reader-28-april-1804/.

10. Julien Raimond, *Réponse aux considérations de M. Moreau, dit Saint-Méry, député à l'Assemblée Nationale, sur les colonies: par M. Raymond, citoyen de couleur de Saint-Domingue* (Paris: De l'Imprimerie du Patriote François, May 12, 1791), 23.

11. Originally published in *Le Patriote Francais* on May 1, 1791. Quoted in Raimond, *Réponse aux considérations*, 41 fn. 1.

12. Quoted in Raimond, *Réponse aux considérations*, 42–43.

13. Quoted in Raimond, *Réponse aux considérations*, 44.

14. Juste Chanlatte, *Le Cri de la nature* (Cap-Haïtien: P. Roux, 1810), 29.

15. William Wells Brown, *St. Domingo, Its Revolutions and Its Patriots: A Lecture Delivered before the Metropolitan Athenaeum, London, May 16, and at St. Thomas' Church, Philadelphia, December 20, 1854* (Boston: B. Marsh, 1855); George Boyer Vashon, "Vincent Ogé" (Auburn, NY: Alden, Beardsley and Co., 1854); Pierre Faubert, *Ogé, ou le préjugé de couleur* (Paris: Librairie de C. Maillet-Schmitz, 1856); Émile Nau, *Réclamation par les affranchis des droits civils et politiques* (Port-au-Prince: T. Bouchereau, 1840).

16. C. L. R. James, *The Black Jacobins: Toussaint L'Ouverture and the San Domingo Revolution* (New York: Vintage Books, 1989), 75.

17. Raimond, *Correspondance*, 60.

18. Raimond, *Réponse aux considérations*, 23.

19. Raimond, *Réponse aux considérations*, 24.

20. Raimond, *Réponse aux considérations*, 12.

21. Raimond, *Réponse aux considérations*, 12.

22. Raimond, *Réponse aux considérations*, 24.

23. Dumesle, *Voyage*, 85–86.

24. David Geggus has written that Makandal's name "derives from a Kongo word for an amulet or magical charm." See "Macandal the Poisoner," in *The Haitian Revolution: A Documentary History*, trans. and ed. David Geggus (Indianapolis, IN: Hacket, 2014), 19; see also Christina Frances Mobley, "The Kongolese Atlantic: Central African Slavery and Culture from Mayombe to Haiti" (PhD diss., Duke University, 2015), 218.

25. Monique Allewaert, "Super Fly: François Makandal's Colonial Semiotics," *American Literature* 91, no. 3 (2019): 467.

26. "Macandale, chef des noirs révoltés, arrêt de condamnation par le Conseil Supérieur du Cap-Français à Saint-Domingue 1758," http://anom.archivesnationales.culture.gouv.fr /osd/?dossier=/collection/INVENTAIRES/Ministeres/SEM/E/&first=241_458A/FRCAOM 06_COLE_241458A_0210&last=241_458A/FRCAOM06_COLE_241458A_0214&title=Ma candale,+chef+des+noirs+r%C3%A9volt%C3%A9s,+arr%C3%AAt+de+condamnation+pa r+le+Conseil+sup%C3%A9rieur+du+Cap-Fran%C3%A7ais+%C3%A0+Saint-Domingue +1758.

27. "Relation d'une conspiration tramée par les Negres: dans l'Isle de S. Domingue; défense que fait le Jésuite Confesseur, aux nègres qu'on suplicie [*sic*], de révéler leur fauteurs & complices," (June 24, 1758), 2–3, Library of Congress, https://dl.wdl.org/14720/service /14720.pdf.

28. Allewaert, "Super Fly," 461.

29. "Relation d'une conspiration tramée," 3–4.

30. M. L. E. Moreau de Saint-Méry, *Description topographique, physique, civile, politique et historique de la partie française de l'isle Saint-Domingue. Avec des observations générales sur sa population, sur le caractère & les moeurs de ses divers habitans; sur son climat, sa culture, ses productions, son administration, &c. &c, accompagnées des détails les plus propres à faire connaître l'état de cette colonie à l'époque du 18 octobre 1789; et d'une nouvelle carte de la totalité de l'isle*, 2 vols. (Philadelphia: Chez L'Auteur, 1791), 1:652–53.

31. Allewaert, "Super Fly," 461–62.

32. Sébastien Jacques Courtin, "Mémoire sommaire sur les prétendus pratiques magiques et empoisonnements prouvés au procès instruit et jugé au Cap contre plusieurs nègres et négresses dont le chef nommé François Macandal a été condamné au feu et exécuté le vingt janvier mille sept cents cinquante huit," F/3/88, January 20, 1758, Archives Nationales d'Outre Mer, Aix-en-Provence, France (hereafter ANOM).

33. "Relation d'une conspiration tramée," 4.

34. Contemporary scholars have questioned whether Makandal poisoned anyone since, as Geggus has written, the colonists may have confused "epidemic disease with poison"; while Mobley observes, "there is no evidence that Makandal was guilty of a conspiracy to poison the white population of the colony"; and Burnard and Garrigus have argued that

Courtin did not prove Makandal was "a poisoner in the toxicological sense," saying "he had no evidence that Macandal distributed [poisonous] powders, just charms," noting that even "when other slaves testified about these macandals, they claimed the talismans could not cause death or even illness." See Geggus, "Macandal the Poisoner," 19; Mobley, "Kongolese Atlantic," 288; Trevor Burnard and John Garrigus, *The Plantation Machine: Atlantic Capitalism in French Saint-Domingue and British Jamaica* (Philadelphia: University of Pennsylvania Press, 2016), 110.

35. Courtin, "Mémoire sommaire."

36. Ann Laura Stoler, *Along the Archival Grain: Epistemic Anxieties and Colonial Commonsense* (Princeton, NJ: Princeton University Press, 2010), 53.

37. Étienne Charlier, *Aperçu sur la formation historique de la nation haïtienne* (Québec: Les Éditions Dami, 2009), 60.

38. Courtin, "Mémoire sommaire."

39. Courtin, "Mémoire sommaire."

40. "Relation d'une conspiration tramée," 4.

41. "Relation d'une conspiration tramée," 5.

42. Moreau de Saint-Méry, *Description topographique*, 652.

43. Courtin, "Mémoire sommaire."

44. Daina Ramey Berry, "Soul Values and American Slavery," *Slavery & Abolition* 42, no. 2 (2021): 201.

45. "Avis Divers," *Affiches Américaines* (April 2, 1766): 124.

46. "Observations de M. Fremon, Syndic du Quartier du Limbé, sur l'Article concernant ce Quartier inséré dans le Journal de Janvier," *Supplément aux Affiches Américaines* (February 12, 1766): 67.

47. "Spectacles," *Affiches Américaines* (March 4, 1786): 1.

48. M. de C., "Makandal, histoire veritable," *Mercure de France* (September 15, 1787): 102–14.

49. "Account of a Remarkable Conspiracy Formed by a Negro in the Island of St. Domingo," ed. Duncan Faherty and Ed White, Common-Place, accessed January 5, 2021, http://jto.common-place.org/wp-content/uploads/sites/2/2016/01/Makandal-text-JTO-version.pdf.

50. "James Cartwright Cross," in *Haitian Revolutionary Fictions: An Anthology*, ed. Marlene L. Daut, Grégory Pierrot, and Marion C. Rohrleitner (Charlottesville: University of Virginia Press, 2022), 254.

51. "L.V. Denancé," in Daut et al., *Haitian Revolutionary Fictions*, 273.

52. Tante Marie [Augustin], *Le Macandal: épisode de l'insurrection des noirs à Saint-Domingue* (New Orleans: Imprimerie Geo. Müller), 1892.

53. "Marie Augustin," in Daut et al., *Haitian Revolutionary Fictions*, 86.

54. Dumesle, *Voyage*, 349 fn. f*; Guillaume de Bellecombe was governor of Saint-Domingue from February 14, 1782, to July 3, 1785.

55. Antoine Dalmas, *Histoire de la révolution de Saint-Domingue; depuis le commencement des troubles, jusqu'à la prise de Jérémie et du Môle S. Nicolas par les Anglais; suivie d'un mémoire sur le rétablissement de cette colonie* (Paris: Chez Mame Frères, 1814), 1:117–18; David Geggus, "The Bois Caiman Ceremony," in *The Haitian Revolution: A Documentary History* (New York: Hackett, 2014), 78–79.

56. Carolyn Fick, *The Making of Haiti: The Saint-Domingue Revolution from Below* (Knoxville: University of Tennessee Press, 1990), 93; Charlier, *Aperçu sur la formation*, 102 fn. 7.

57. Boukman Dutty, quoted in Fick, *Making of Haiti*, 93.

58. "Extrait de la séance du 16," *Moniteur général de la partie française de Saint-Domingue*, December 22, 1791, 154–55.

59. [Charles-Yves] Cousin d'Avallon, *Histoire de Toussaint-Louverture chef des noirs insurgés de Saint-Domingue; Précédée d'un coup d'oeil politique sur cette colonie, et suivie d'anecdotes et faits particuliers concernant ce chef des noirs, et les agens directoriaux envoyés dans cette partie du Nouveau-Monde, pendant le cours de la révolution* (Paris: Chez Pillot, frères, 1802), 19–20 fn. 2; Aimé Césaire, *Toussaint Louverture, la révolution française et le problème colonial* (Paris: Présence Africaine, 1961), 179; Jean Fouchard, *Les Marrons de la liberté, Éditions revue, corrigée et augmentée* (Port-au-Prince: Éditions Henri Deschamps, 1988), 415.

60. See Laurent Dubois, *Avengers of the New World: The Story of the Haitian Revolution* (Cambridge, MA: Harvard University Press, 2004), 100–101; "The Revolutionary Philanthropist," in Daut et al., *Haitian Revolutionary Fictions*, 30–37; Dalmas, *Histoire de la révolution*, 117; Antoine Métral, *Histoire de l'insurrection des esclaves dans le nord de Saint-Domingue* (Paris: F. Scherff, 1818), 15; Civique de Gastine, *Histoire de la Republique d'Haïti, ou, Saint-Domingue, l'esclavage et les colons* (Paris: Plancher, 1819), 105; "Le Philantrope révolutionnaire: ou, l'hécatombe à Haïti: drame historique en 4 actes et en prose" (Portsmouth, England, 1811), in Daut et al., *Haitian Revolutionary Fictions*, 30–37.

61. See Dubois, *Avengers*, 101; and Doris Y. Kadish and Deborah Jenson, eds., *Poetry of Haitian Independence*, trans. Norman R. Shapiro (New Haven, CT: Yale University Press, 2015), 225.

62. Dumesle, *Voyage*, 349 fn. e*.

63. Grégory Pierrot, *The Black Avenger in Atlantic Culture* (Athens: University of Georgia Press, 2018), 9.

64. Dumesle, *Voyage*, 85–86, 300.

65. Dumesle, *Voyage*, 86–88; Léon-François Hoffmann, *Haitian Fiction Revisited* (Pueblo, CO: Passeggiata Press, 1999), 217.

66. Jacquelin Dolcé, Gérald Dorval, and Jean Miotel Casthely, *Le Romantisme en Haïti (la vie intéllectuelle, 1804–1915)* (Port-au-Prince: Éditions Fardin, 1983), 15. See also the introduction to Kadish and Jenson, *Poetry of Haitian Independence*, xxi–xliii.

67. Dumesle, *Voyage*, 257, 333–34 fn. b.

68. Dumesle, *Voyage*, 86–89, trans. Marlene L. Daut and Grégory Pierrot for Daut et al., *Haitian Revolutionary Fictions*, 316–20.

69. "Avis," *Gazette royale d'Hayti*, May 7, 1807, 2. All issues consulted at https//lagazette royale.com.

70. Chanlatte, *Le Cri*, 62 fn. 1.

71. See examples of common eighteenth-century U.S. pronouncements against slavery and the slave trade as an "inhuman trade," in Adrien Wing and Diane Marie Amann, "Slave Trafficking as a Crime against Humanity," *Proceedings of the Annual Meeting (American Society of International Law)* 101 (March 28–31, 2007): 277–79.

72. Baron de Vastey, *Réflexions sur une lettre de Mazères: ex-colon français, adressée à M. J.C.L. Sismonde de Sismondi, sur les noirs et les blancs, la civilisation de l'Afrique, le royaume d'Hayti* (Cap-Haïtien: P. Roux, 1816), 86–87.

73. Ben Kiernan, "Is 'Genocide' an Anachronistic Concept for the Study of Early Modern Mass Killing?" *History* 99, no. 336 (July 2014): 530–48.

74. William A. Schabas, "Convention for the Prevention and Crime of Genocide," United Nations Audiovisual Library of International Law, United Nations, 2008, https://l egal. un .org/avl/pdf/ha/cppcg/cppcg_e.pdf.

75. Reprinted in Laurent François Le Noir de Rouvray, *Une Correspondance familiale au temps des troubles de Saint-Domingue, Lettres du Marquis et de la Marquise de Rouvray à leur fille. Saint-Domingue-Étas Unis (1791–1796),* ed. M. E. McIntosh and B. C. Weber (Paris: Société de l'Histoire des Colonies Française et Librairie Larose, 1959), 102–3.

76. Reprinted in J. P. Garran de Coulon, *Rapport sur les troubles de Saint-Domingue* (Paris: Imprimerie nationale, 1797–99), 3:36–37, italics in original.

77. Quoted in Garran de Coulon, *Rapport,* 3:440, italics in original.

78. André Rigaud, *Mémoire du général de brigade André Rigaud* (Aux Cayes, Haiti: L'Imprimerie de Lemery, 1797), iii–iv.

79. Marlene L. Daut, "Genocidal Imaginings in the Era of the Haitian Revolution," *Age of Revolutions* (blog), January 25, 2016, https://ageofrevolutions.com/2016/01/25/genocidal -imaginings-in-the-era-of-the-haitian-revolution/.

80. Dumesle, *Voyage,* 84.

81. Dumesle, *Voyage,* 83, 85.

82. Baron de Vastey, *Essai sur les causes de la révolution et des guerres civiles d'Hayti* (Sans-Souci, Haiti: L'Imprimerie Royale, 1819), 8.

83. Dumesle, *Voyage,* 85.

84. See, for example, J.-Félix Carteau, *Soirées Bermudiennes, ou Entretiens sur les évène-mens qui ont opéré la ruine de la partie française de l'île Saint-Domingue, ouvrage où l'on ex-pose les causes de ces évènemens, les moyens employés pour renverser cette colonie; les reproches faits à ses Habitans, et les calomnies dont on les a couverts; enfin . . .* (Bordeaux: Chez Pellier-Lawalle, 1802), 43, 49; B. B., "A Tale of St. Domingo," *Atkinson's Gasket: Gems of Literature, Wit, and Sentiment* (Philadelphia: Samuel C. Atkinson, 1833), 205; for more recent application of the metaphor, see Alfred N. Hunt, *Haiti's Influence on Antebellum America: Slumbering Volcano in the Caribbean* (Baton Rouge: Louisiana State University Press, 2006), 121.

85. Dumesle, *Voyage,* 345 fn. a*.

86. Dumesle, *Voyage,* 85.

87. Deborah Jenson and Doris Kadish have claimed that Dumesle's use of the term "la révolution haïtienne" rather than "la révolution d'Haïti," may mark the first usage in French of the distinctive phrase "Haitian Revolution." Kadish and Jenson, *Poetry of Haitian Independence,* 225.

88. Vastey, *Essai,* 2.

89. James Theodore Holly, *A Vindication of the Capacity of the Negro Race for Self-Government, and Civilized Progress, as Demonstrated by Historical Events of the Haytian Revolution: And the Subsequent Acts of That People since Their National Independence* (New Haven, CT: African American Printing Co., 1857), 7–8. Holly, who is considered to be the first African American bishop of the Protestant-Episcopal Church, made several trips to Haiti before permanently relocating there in the summer of 1861. The dedication page of *A Vindication* notes that the contents were first given as a lecture in New Haven, Connecticut, "after my return from Hayti in the autumn of 1855." Holly, *Vindication,* 3.

90. Baron de Vastey, *Réflexions politiques sur quelques ouvrages et journaux français concernant Hayti* (Sans-Souci, Haiti: Royal Imprint, 1817), 31, 49.

91. Vastey, *Réflexions politiques,* 49.

92. Vastey, *Réflexions politiques*, 49.

93. Dumesle, *Voyage*, 89.

94. For a female participant, see Métral, *Histoire*, 15.

95. Quoted in Beaubrun Ardouin, *Études sur l'histoire d'Haïti, 11 tomes réunis en 3 volumes*, vol. 1 (Port-au-Prince: Éditions Fardin Collection du Bicentennaire Haïti, 2004,), 51.

96. Historian David Geggus has discussed these conflations in *Haitian Revolutionary Studies* (Indianapolis: Indiana University Press, 2002), 83–89. See also the work of Aisha K. Finch, "Cécile Fatiman and Petra Carabalí, Late Eighteenth-Century Haiti and Mid-Nineteenth-Century Cuba," in *As If She Were Free: A Collective Biography of Women and Emancipation in the Americas*, ed. Erica L. Ball, Tatiana Seijas, and Terri L. Snyder (Cambridge: Cambridge University Press, 2020), 293 fn. 2.

97. Carolyn Fick, "Appendix B: Bois-Caïman and the August Revolt," in *Making of Haiti*, 260–63; Dalmas also puts the Morne-Rouge assembly on Le Normand de Mézy's plantation slightly before the Bois Caïman ceremony took place on the Choiseul plantation, see Dalmas, *Histoire de la révolution*, 117; see also, Geggus, *Haitian Revolutionary Studies*, 84–86.

98. Dumesle, *Voyage*, 89–90.

99. Bernadette Rossignol and Philippe Rossignol, "'Mon odyssée': l'auteur et sa famille," http://ghcaraibe.org/articles/2012-art09.pdf.

100. "Jean-Baptiste Pillet," in Daut et al., *Haitian Revolutionary Fictions*, 693.

101. "Pillet," in Daut et al., *Haitian Revolutionary Fictions*, 694.

102. Jean-Baptiste Pillet, *Mon odyssée: l'epopée d'un colon de Saint Domingue*, ed. Anja Bandau and Jeremy Popkin (Paris: Société Française d'Étude de dix-Huitième Siècle, 2015), 120.

103. Dumesle, *Voyage*, 90.

104. Dumesle, *Voyage*, 90–91.

105. Vastey, *Réflexions sur une lettre*, 92–93.

106. Vastey, *Réflexions sur une lettre*, 51–52.

107. Boukman's speech, as printed in Dumesle's *Voyage*, is also a contemporary Vodou song called "Lapriyè Boukmann." For the song and Vodou cosmology, see "Benjamin Hebblethwaite, *Vodou Songs in Haitian Creole and English* (Philadelphia: Temple University Press, 2012), 47–48.

108. "Pillet," in Daut et al., *Haitian Revolutionary Fictions*, 695.

109. Raimond, *Correspondance*, 62.

110. Raimond, *Correspondance*, 63; numerous men of color from Saint-Domingue, including the future king of Haiti, Henry Christophe, fought at the Battle of Savannah during the American Revolutionary War in 1779. See T. G. Steward, *How the Black St. Domingo Legion Saved the Patriot Army in the Siege of Savannah, 1779* (Washington, DC: Published by the Academy, 1899), 12; see also Vastey, *Essai*, 160 fn. 1.

111. Dumesle, *Voyage*, 107.

112. Dumesle, *Voyage*, 108.

113. Rigaud, *Mémoire*, 8.

114. Dumesle, *Voyage*, 112.

115. Dumesle, *Voyage*, 356–57 fn. ee, italics in original.

116. Julien Raimond, *Preuves complettes [sic] et matérielles du projet des colons pour mener les colonies à l'indépendance, tirées de leurs propres écrits; ouvrage présenté à la Commission des colonies* (Paris: De L'Imprimerie de l'Union, 1795), 28.

117. Julien Raimond, *Véritable origine des troubles de S.-Domingue, et des différentes causes qui les ont produits; par M. Julien Raimond, Député des citoyens de couleur* (Paris: Desenne, 1792), 40, italics in original.

118. Raimond, *Preuves*, 24.

119. Raimond, *Preuves*, 24–25.

120. Raimond, *Preuves*, 26.

Chapter 5

1. "Émancipation des esclaves: proclamation du 29 août 1793," Digithèque MJP, https://mjp.univ-perp.fr/constit/ht1793.htm.

2. "Proclamation du 29 août 1793."

3. "Proclamation du 29 août 1793."

4. Beaubrun Ardouin, *Études sur l'histoire d'Haïti* (Paris: Dezobry et E. Magdeleine, Lib.-éditeurs, 1853), 2:258.

5. Étienne Polverel, "Proclamation relative à l'émancipation des esclaves appartenant à l'État dans la province de l'Ouest, à l'émancipation volontaire de leurs esclaves par les propriétaires et à la promesse de la liberté Générale," reprinted in "Aux origines de l'abolition de l'esclavage," *Revue d'histoire des colonies*, 36, no. 127–28 (troisième et quatrième Trimestres, 1949): 364. (Hereafter referred to as "Proclamation relative [a].")

6. Polverel, "Proclamation relative [a]," 365.

7. Quoted in Lieutenant-Général Baron Pamphile de Lacroix, *Mémoires pour servir à l'histoire de la révolution de Saint-Domingue*, 2 vols. (Paris: Pillet Aine, 1819), 2:203–204.

8. Polverel, "Proclamation relative [a]," 366–67.

9. Ardouin, *Études*, 1853, 2:259.

10. Polverel, "Proclamation [relative à l'émancipation des esclaves appartenant à l'État dans la province Sud]," reprinted in, "Aux origines de l'abolition de l'esclavage," *Revue d'histoire des colonies* 36, no. 127–128 (troisième et quatrième Trimestres, 1949): 369. (Hereafter referred to as "Proclamation relative [b]"). The National Convention abolished the French monarchy on September 21, but dated the official start of the Republic of France as September 22, 1792.

11. Polverel, "Proclamation relative [b]," 370.

12. Hérard Dumesle, *Voyage dans le nord d'Hayti: ou, Révélations des lieux et des monuments historiques* (Aux Cayes, Haiti: De l'Imprimerie du Gouvernement, 1824), 150.

13. Joseph Saint-Rémy, *Pétion et Haïti: étude monographique et historique* (Paris: Chez L'Auteur, 1854), 1:217 fn. 2.

14. André Rigaud, *Mémoire du général de brigade André Rigaud* (Aux Cayes, Haiti: L'Imprimerie de Lemery, 1797), 17.

15. Polverel, "Proclamation relative [a]," 363.

16. Polverel, "Proclamation relative [a]," 363–64.

17. Polverel, "Proclamation relative [a]," 364.

18. "Proclamation du 29 août 1793."

19. "Proclamation du 29 août 1793."

20. Toussaint Louverture, *Extrait du rapport adressé au Directoire exécutif par le citoyen TOUSSAINT LOUVERTURE, général en chef des forces de la République Française à*

Saint-Domingue (September 4, 1797), 5, Bibliothèque nationale de France, Paris, France (hereafter BN), https://gallica.bnf.fr/ark:/12148/bpt6k9788606r.texteImage.

21. André Rigaud, *Réponse du général de brigade André Rigaud à l'écrit calomnieux du Général Toussaint Louverture* (Aux Cayes, Haiti: Chez Lemery, June 8, 1799), 8.

22. Louverture, *Extrait du rapport*, 38.

23. Michel-Rolph Trouillot, *Ti dife boule sou istwa Ayiti*, rev. ed. (Port-au-Prince: Edisyon KIK, 2012), 50–51.

24. Trouillot, *Ti dife boule*, 8.

25. Juste Chanlatte, *Le Cri de la nature* (Cap-Haïtien: P. Roux, 1810), 31.

26. Baron de Vastey, *Essai sur les causes de la révolution et des guerres civiles d'Hayti* (Sans-Souci, Haiti: L'Imprimerie Royale, 1819), 23, 24, italics mine.

27. Louverture, *Extrait du rapport*, 5.

28. Louverture, *Extrait du rapport*, 5.

29. Louverture, *Extrait du rapport*, 6.

30. "Paris, le 11 Pluviôse, l'an 6 (January 30, 1798) . . . Le représentant du peuple Sonthonax ex-agent particulier du Directoire exécutif, au Directoire exécutif de la République Française," Archives Nationales de France, Paris, France (hereafter AN), AF/III/210.

31. "Paris, le 8 Pluviôse, an 6 (January 27, 1798) . . . Observations présentées au Directoire exécutif sur mon départ de St. Domingue, et sur les écrits qu'on publie sous le nom de Toussaint Louverture," AN, AF/III/210.

32. "Proclamation du 29 août 1793."

33. *Journal des Révolutions de la partie française de Saint-Domingue, dédié à la république du 20 Septembre 1792*, March 28, 1793, 1, AN, D/XXI/115, italics in original.

34. Louverture, *Extrait du rapport*, 6.

35. Reprinted in David Geggus, *The Haitian Revolution: A Documentary History* (New York: Hackett, 2014), 123–24.

36. Reprinted in Geggus, *Haitian Revolution*, 124.

37. Reprinted in Geggus, *Haitian Revolution*, 125–26.

38. Ch. Warin, "Plan de la ville du Cap Français dans l'Isle de Saint Domingue, sur lequel sont marqués en teinte noire les ravages du premier incendie; et en rouge les Islets, parties de l'islets, édifices &c qui existent encore. Le 21 Juin 1793," BN, accessed February 7, 2022, https://gallica.bnf.fr/ark:/12148/btv1b55005281x.r=Cap%20Fran%C3%A7ais.

39. "Copie de la lettre de l'adjutant Général Cezar [*sic*] Galbaud au Général Galbaud, son frère," August 28, 1793, Box 29, Rochambeau Papers, University of Florida Libraries.

40. Saint-Rémy, *Pétion et Haïti*, 1:193–200; Jeremy Popkin, *You Are All Free: The Haitian Revolution and the Abolition of Slavery* (Chicago: University of Chicago Press, 2010), 15.

41. Letter to the Civil Commissioners signed by Jean François, Biassou, et al., December 12, 1791, reprinted in *The Haitian Revolution: A Documentary History*, ed. and trans. David Geggus (Indianapolis, IN: Hackett, 2014), 87–88.

42. Letter to the Civil Commissioners signed by Jean François, Biassou, et al., December 12, 1791, 87–88.

43. "The Negotiations Break Down," in Geggus, *Haitian Revolution*, 89.

44. Letter to the Civil Commissioners signed by Jean-François, Biassou, et al., December 12, 1791, 87–88.

45. Response of the officers of the army of General Toussaint rejecting cease-fire proposed by the Civil Commissioners, June 27, 1793, AN, D/XXV/20, no. 199. Many thanks to Julia Gaffield for sharing this document with me.

46. Polverel, "Proclamation relative [b]," 372–73.

47. "Décret de la Convention Nationale, du seizième jour de pluviôse, l'an deuxième de la République française une et indivisible," February 4, 1794, https://www.assemblee-nationale.fr/histoire/esclavage/d%C3%A9cret_1794.pdf.

48. Madison Smartt Bell, *Toussaint Louverture: A Biography* (New York: Vintage Books, 2007), 58–60.

49. Isaac Louverture, "Notes Divers d'Isaac sur la Vie de Toussaint Louverture," in *Histoire de l'expédition des Français, à Saint-Domingue, sous le consulat de Napoléon Bonaparte, par Antoine Métral: suivie des mémoires et notes d'Isaac Louverture, sur la même expédition, et sur la vie de son père; ornée du portrait de Toussaint et d'une belle carte de Saint-Domingue* (Paris: Fanjat ainé, 1825), 325–26; Bell, *Toussaint Louverture*, 60.

50. Sudhir Hazareesingh, *Black Spartacus: The Epic Life of Toussaint Louverture* (London: Allen Lane, 2000), 31.

51. Hazareesingh, *Black Spartacus*, xix; Bell, *Toussaint Louverture*, 76; Jean-L ouis Donnadieu, "La famille 'oubliée' de Toussaint Louverture," *Bulletin de la Société Archéologique et Historique du Gers* 401, no. 3 (2011): 357–65.

52. Quoted in Ardouin, *Études*, 1853, 1:228–29.

53. Toussaint Louverture, *Réfutation de quelques assertions d'un discours prononcé au Corps législatif, le 10 prairial, an cinq, par VIENOT VAUBLANC*, October 29, 1797, 1, BN, https://gallica.bnf.fr/ark:/12148/bpt6k91032688.

54. Louverture, *Réfutation*, 11.

55. "An Act for Confirming the Articles Executed by Colonel Robert Bennett, and Quao the Commander of the Rebels, for Paying Rewards for Taking Up and Restoring Runaway Slaves . . . ," in *The Laws of Jamaica: Comprehending All the Acts in Force, Passed between the Thirty-Second Year of the Reign of King Charles the Second, and the Thirty-Third Year of the Reign of King George the Third, to Which Is Prefixed, a Table of the Titles of the Public and Private Acts Passed during That Time* vol. 1, 2nd ed. (St. Jago de la Vega, Jamaica: Alexander Aikman, 1802), 278.

56. Paul Berman, "*Toussaint Louverture: A Revolutionary Life*, by Philippe Girard," review, *New York Times*, December 9, 2016, https://www.nytimes.com/2016/12/09/books/review/a-biography-reveals-surprising-sides-to-haitis-slave-liberator.html.

57. Étienne Charlier, *Aperçu sur la formation historique de la nation haïtienne* (Québec: Éditions Dami, 2009), 53.

58. Ed Baptist, "Overview Essay: Maroons in Jamaica," in *Slave Resistance: A Caribbean Study*, accessed March 17, 2023, https://scholar.library.miami.edu/slaves/Maroons/maroons.html.

59. Under Raimond's direct authority, Christophe was listed as "chef de brigade and inspector" in the north. "État de l'habitation Mazères que nous envoyons au Citoyen Commandant Raymond," *15 thermidor an 5* (August 2, 1797), Archives Nationales d'Outre-Mer, Aix-en-Provence, France (hereafter ANOM), 10 DPPC 167; for the more than two dozen plantations leased by Dessalines, see ANOM, 10 DPPC 190 and 191.

60. "Arrêté concernant la police des habitations et les obligations réciproque des propriétaires et fermiers et des cultivateurs: extrait du registre des délibérations de l'Agence

358   Notes to Chapter 5

du Directoire Exécutif à Saint-Domingue," *6 thermidor an 6* (July 24, 1798), AN, AF/ III/210.

61. For plantations Moyse leased, see the dossier "Moyse," ANOM, 10 DPPC 131.

62. For the petitions, see, "Arrêtés des différentes communes de la colonie de Saint-Domingue, adressées à l'agent particulier du Directoire, au général en chef et à l'administration municipal du Cap," AN, AF/III/210.

63. "Arrêtés des différentes."

64. Reprinted in Ardouin, *Études*, 1853, 4:248–53.

65. "Kouzen, eskè se sa libète a? . . . Komkidire se pa sa ou te di nou," Trouillot, *Ti dife boule*, 93.

66. "Constitution du 3 juillet 1801," Digithèque MJP, https://mjp.univ-perp.fr/constit /ht1801.htm.

67. Louverture, *Réfutation*, 30–31.

68. Louverture, *Extrait du rapport*, 6.

69. Louverture, *Extrait du rapport*, 6.

70. Louverture, *Extrait du rapport*, 7.

71. Louverture, *Extrait du rapport*, 7.

72. Louverture, *Extrait du rapport*, 7.

73. Louverture, *Extrait du rapport*, 7–8.

74. Rigaud, *Mémoire*, 46.

75. Rigaud, *Mémoire*, 61.

76. Rigaud, *Mémoire*, 63.

77. Rigaud, *Réponse du général*, 6.

78. See David Nicholls, *From Dessalines to Duvalier: Race, Colour and National Independence in Haiti* (New Brunswick, NJ: Rutgers University Press, 1979), 32.

79. Rigaud, *Réponse du général*, 6 fn. b.

80. Rigaud, *Réponse du général*, 6 fn. b.

81. Rigaud, *Réponse du général*, 6 fn. b.

82. Marlene L. Daut, *Baron de Vastey and the Origins of Black Atlantic Humanism* (New York: Palgrave Macmillan, 2017), 29; for the Dumas family plantations, see the dossier Dumas at ANOM, 10 DPPC 102.

83. Saint-Rémy, *Pétion et Haïti*, 1:42. For Raimond's parentage, see chapter three of the present volume.

84. John Garrigus, *Before Haiti: Race and Citizenship in French Saint-Domingue* (Basingstoke, UK: Palgrave Macmillan), 182.

85. Saint-Rémy, *Pétion et Haïti*, 1:83 fn. 1. The marriage record for André Rigaud and his wife Anne Villeneuve lists Rigaud's parents, André Rigaud and Rose Bossy, as "both deceased, native to this department [Les Cayes], on one side." Marriage record for André Rigaud and Anne Villeneuve, État Civil des Cayes, *17 prairial an 7* (June 5, 1799), ANOM.

86. Baron de Vastey, *Réflexions sur une lettre de Mazères: ex-colon français, adressée à M. J.C.L. Sismonde de Sismondi, sur les noirs et les blancs, la civilisation de l'Afrique, le royaume d'Hayti* (Cap-Haïtien: P. Roux, 1816), 31.

87. Rigaud, *Réponse du général*, 6 fn. b.

88. Rigaud, *Réponse du général*, 9.

89. Rigaud, *Réponse du général*, iii.

90. Rigaud, *Réponse du général*, iii fn. a.

91. Rigaud, *Réponse du général*, iii fn. a. This version is held by the Bibliothèque Nationale de France and appears on the library's digital platform Gallica.

92. William Wells Brown, *St. Domingo, Its Revolutions and Its Patriots: A Lecture Delivered before the Metropolitan Athenaeum, London, May 16, and at St. Thomas' Church, Philadelphia, December 20, 1854* (Boston: B. Marsh, 1855), 20.

93. C. L. R. James, *The Black Jacobins: Toussaint L'Ouverture and the San Domingo Revolution* (New York: Vintage Books, 1989), 207.

94. Louverture, *Réfutation*, 16.

95. Louverture, *Réfutation*, 16–17.

96. Louverture, *Réfutation*, 17.

97. Rigaud, *Réponse du général*, i.

98. Quoted in Laurent Dubois, *Avenger of the New World: The Story of the Haitian Revolution* (Cambridge, MA: Harvard University Press, 2004), 223.

99. Rigaud, *Réponse du général*, 2.

100. Rigaud, *Réponse du général*, 2.

101. In the proclamation where Governor-General Laveaux named Louverture his lieutenant-general, Laveaux evoked Louverture as the "New Spartacus" from Raynal's famous *Histoire des deux Indes*: "Let us admire this great man in him that Father Raynal tells us that nature owes to her children who have been oppressed for so many centuries. No doubt he will appear, he will raise the standard of liberty, at that venerable signal the companions of his misfortune will gather around him; everywhere we will bless the name of the Hero who will have restored the rights of the human species; everywhere we will erect trophies to his glory." "Proclamation d'Étienne Laveaux, général en chef et Gouverneur de Saint-Domingue," *12 germinal an IV* (April 1, 1796), Archivo General de Indias, ESTADO, 5B,N.127; for an analysis of this proclamation in relation to Raynal's book, see chapter 3 in Grégory Pierrot's *The Black Avenger in Atlantic Culture* (Athens: University of Georgia Press, 2018).

102. André Rigaud, *Réponse du général de brigade André Rigaud, à la proclamation de l'agent Roume, en date du XV Messidor L'An VII* (Aux Cayes: Chez Lemery, July 19, 1799), 7.

103. Rigaud, *Réponse du général . . . à la proclamation de l'agent Roume*, 7.

104. André Rigaud, *Réponse à la proclamation de Toussaint Louverture, datée, au Port-au-Prince, le 20 brumaire an VIIIème* (Aux Cayes: Chez Lemery, 1799), 1–2.

105. Rigaud, *Réponse à la proclamation*, 3.

106. Rigaud, *Réponse du général*, ii.

107. Rigaud, *Réponse à la proclamation*, 4.

108. Rigaud, *Réponse du général*, 2.

109. Brown, *St. Domingo*, 23.

110. Rigaud, *Réponse du général*, 12.

111. Rigaud, *Réponse du général*, 12.

112. Rigaud, *Réponse du général*, iii.

113. "Au Cap Français, le 27 messidor, l'an 9 de la République Française. . . . Toussaint Louverture, gouverneur de Saint-Domingue, au citoyen Bonaparte, Premier Consul de la République française," July 16, 1801, AN, AF/IV/1213; Louis Joseph Janvier, *Les constitutions d'Haïti, 1801–1885* (Paris: C. Marpon et E. Flammarion, 1886), 2.

114. Quoted in Joseph Saint-Rémy, ed., *Mémoires du général Toussaint-L'Ouverture écrits par lui-même* (Paris: Pagnerre, 1853), 87 fn. 1.

115. "Le Général en Chef de l'Armée de Saint-Domingue, Capitaine Général de la Colonie, au Général Christophe, commandant au Cap [February 3, 1802]," reprinted in *Lettres du général Leclerc, commandant en chef de l'armée de Saint Domingue en 1802*, ed. Paul Roussier (Paris: Société de l'histoire des colonies françaises, Ernest Leroux, 1937), 61.

116. Henry Christophe to General-in-Chief Leclerc, *13 pluviôse an 10* (February 2, 1802), reprinted in Henry Christophe and Julien Prévost, *Manifeste du roi* (Cap-Henry, Haiti [1811]), 21–22; see also the same letter reprinted in Chanlatte, *Le Cri*, 81–83. In the Haitian sources, both Leclerc's and Christophe's letters were sent on 13 pluviôse or February 2.

117. *Le Moniteur universel*, May 22, 1802, 998; see also, Stéphen Alexis, "Le Crépuscule d'un Dieu: Quelques Scènes des derniers moments de Toussaint Louverture au Fort de Joux," *Cahiers d'Haïti*, no. 9 (April 1944): 3.

118. "Proclamation au quartier général du Cap, le 28 pluviôse, an X . . . Leclerc, général en chef de l'Armée de Saint-Domingue . . . aux Habitants de Saint-Domingue [February 17, 1802]," reprinted in Roussier, *Lettres du Général Leclerc*, 99.

119. *Le Moniteur universel*, May 22, 1802, 998; *Le Moniteur universel*, May 28, 1802, 1022; Hazareesingh, *Black Spartacus*, 125.

120. "Aux Verettes le 25 pluviôse an 10 [February 14, 1802]: Toussaint Louverture au citoyen LeClerc, général en chef au Cap," AN, AB/XIX/5002.

121. Duraciné Vaval, "Le roi d'Haïti Henri Christophe: l'homme et son oeuvre de gouvernement," *Revue de la société d'histoire et de géographie d'Haïti* 2, no. 3 (June 1931): 6.

122. "Arrestation et renvoi en France de Toussaint-L'Ouverture et de toute sa famille," *Le Citoyen français*, *25 messidor an X* (July 15, 1802); Georges Le Gorgeu, *Études sur Jean-Baptiste Coisnon: Toussaint Louverture et Jean-Baptiste Coisnon* (Paris: Pedone-Lauriel, 1881), 33.

123. Autopsie Cadavérique, *17 germinal an 11* (April 7, 1803), C-2, Alfred Nemours Archive of Haitian History, University of Puerto Rico, Rio Piédras.

124. Quoted in Pamphile de Lacroix, *Mémoires*, 2:203–204.

125. Henry Christophe and Julien Prévost, *Manifeste du roi* (Cap-Henry, Haiti [1811]), 3–5.

126. Christophe and Prévost, *Manifeste du roi*, 6.

127. Louis-Félix Boisrond-Tonnerre, *Mémoires pour servir à l'histoire d'Haïti, par l'adjutant général Boisrond-Tonnerre* (Dessalines: De l'Imprimerie centrale du gouvernement, 1804), 48–49.

128. Jean-Jacques Dessalines, *Journal de la campagne du nord* (Cap, Haiti: Chez P. Roux, an 12), 10, National Archives of the UK, CO 137/111.

129. Dessalines, *Journal de la campagne*, 10.

130. "Le Général en Chef au Ministre de la Marine [August 25, 1802]," repr. in Roussier, *Lettres du général Leclerc*, 217.

131. Pamphile de Lacroix, *Mémoires*, 2:148.

132. "Fin du coup-d'œil politique sur la situation actuelle du Royaume d'Hayti," *Gazette royale d'Hayti*, October 17, 1816, 3–4.

133. Vastey, *Réflexions sur une lettre*, 104.

134. Vastey, *Essai*, 27–28.

135. Vergniaud Leconte, *Henri Christophe dans l'histoire d'Haïti* (Paris: Éditions Berger-Levrault, 1931), 165.

Chapter 6

1. Toussaint Louverture, *Extrait du rapport adressé au Directoire exécutif par le citoyen TOUSSAINT LOUVERTURE, général en chef des forces de la République Française à Saint-Domingue* (September 4, 1797), 7–8, Bibliothèque nationale de France, Paris, France (hereafter BN), https://gallica.bnf.fr/ark:/12148/bpt6k9788606r.texteImage, italics mine.

2. Napoléon Bonaparte to Citizen Talleyrand, Ministre des Relations Extérieures, *22 brumaire an X* (13 November 13, 1801], *Correspondance de Napoléon Ier, publiée par ordre de l'empereur Napoléon III*, vol. VII (Paris: Imprimerie Impériale, 1861), 407.

3. Napoléon to Citizen Talleyrand, *Correspondance de Napoléon*, 7:407.

4. Napoléon to Citizen Talleyrand, *Correspondance de Napoléon*, 7:407.

5. Napoléon to Citizen Talleyrand, *Correspondance de Napoléon*, 7:407.

6. Reprinted in Rafe Blaufarb, ed., *Napoleon, Symbol for an Age: A Brief History with Documents* (New York: Bedford/St. Martin's, 2008), 162–64.

7. Napoléon Bonaparte to Captain-General Leclerc, Commandant en Chef l'Armée de Saint-Domingue, *25 ventôse an X* [March 16, 1802], *Correspondance de Napoléon*, 7:525–26.

8. Baron de Vastey (Jean Louis), *Réflexions sur une lettre de Mazères: ex-colon français, adressée à M. J.C.L. Sismonde de Sismondi, sur les noirs et les blancs, la civilisation de l'Afrique, le royaume d'Hayti* (Cap-Haïtien: P. Roux, 1816), 94.

9. "Extrait des Registres des Délibérations des Consuls de la République: Paris, le 17 Brumaire, an dix . . . Proclamation. Le Premier Consul Aux Habitants de Saint-Domingue," reprinted in Comte de Limonade (Julien Prévost) and King Henry Christophe, *Manifeste du roi* (Cap-Henry: P. Roux, 1814), 19, italics in original; see the Creole version, along with the French, reprinted in *Lettres du général Leclerc, commandant en chef de l'armée de Saint Domingue en 1802*, ed. Paul Roussier (Paris: Société de l'histoire des colonies françaises, Ernest Leroux, 1937), 62–65.

10. Reprinted in Jean Baptiste Honoré Raymond Capefigue, *L'Europe pendant le consulat et l'empire de Napoléon* (Bruxelles: Société Belge de Librairie, 1840), 5:234 fn. 1.

11. Tyler Stovall, "The Myth of the Liberatory Republic and the Political Culture of Freedom in Imperial France," *Yale French Studies*, no. 111 (2007): 89–103.

12. Baron de Vastey, *Réflexions politiques sur quelques ouvrages et journaux français concernant Hayti* (Sans-Souci, Haiti: Royal Imprint, 1817), 147.

13. Quoted in Toussaint Louverture, *Réfutation de quelques assertions d'un discours prononcé au corps législatif, le 10 prairial, an cinq, par VIENOT VAUBLANC* (October 29, 1797), 14.

14. Quoted in Louverture, *Réfutation*, 15–16.

15. André Rigaud, *Mémoire du général de brigade André Rigaud* (Aux Cayes: L'Imprimerie de Lemery, 1797), 8.

16. Rigaud, *Mémoire*, 10.

17. "Loi relative à la traite des noirs et au régime des colonies," May 20, 1802, Archives Nationales d'Outre-Mer in Aix-en-Provence, France (hereafter ANOM), 1 LEG 1.

18. Reprinted in Blaufarb, *Napoleon*, 159.

19. Quoted in Joseph Saint-Rémy, *Pétion et Haïti: étude monographique et historique* (Paris: Chez L'Auteur, 1855), 3:47–50; for original, see "Corps-Législatif: Suite de l'addition à la séance du 30 Floréal," *Gazette nationale, ou, le Moniteur universel*, May 23, 1802.

20. Reprinted in Antoine-Clair Thibaudeau, *Mémoires sur le consulat, 1799 à 1804, par un ancien conseiller d'état* (Paris: Chez Ponthieu, 1827), 210.

21. Saint-Rémy, *Pétion et Haïti*, 3:70–71.

22. "Arrêté consulaire du 27 messidor an X (16 juillet 1802)," Papiers de la secrétairerie d'État impériale, Archives Nationales de France (hereafter AN), AF/IV/379.

23. Quoted in Carolyn Fick, "La Résistance populaire au corps expéditionnaire du Général Leclerc et au rétablissement de l'esclavage à Saint-Domingue (1802–1804)," in *Rétablissement de l'esclavage dans les colonies françaises, 1802: Ruptures et continuités de la politique coloniale française aux origines d'Haïti: actes du colloque international tenu à l'université de Paris VIII les 20, 21 et 22 juin 2002*, ed. Yves Bénot and Marcel Dorigny (Paris: Maisonneuve & Larose, 2003), 139.

24. Reprinted in Joseph Élisée Peyre-Ferry, *Journal des opérations militaires de l'armée française à Saint-Domingue pendant les années 1802 et 1803 sous les ordres des capitaines-généraux Leclerc et Rochambeau* (Paris: Les Éditions de Paris, 2006), 263.

25. Jean-Jacques Dessalines, "Proclamation: Jean-Jacques Dessalines, gouverneur général aux habitants d'Haïti," April 28, 1804, Haiti and the Atlantic World, https://haitidoi.com/2015/10/30/dessalines-reader-28-april-1804/.

26. Leclerc to Bonaparte (October 7, 1802), reprinted in Roussier, *Lettres du général Leclerc*, 256.

27. Sara E. Johnson, "'You Should Give Them Blacks to Eat': Waging Inter-American Wars of Torture and Terror," *American Quarterly* 61, no. 1 (March 2009): 65–92.

28. Comte de Limonade (Julien Prévost), *Relation des glorieux événemens qui ont porté Leurs Majestés Royales sur le trône d'Hayti; suivie de l'histoire du couronnement et du sacre du roi Henry 1er, et de la reine Marie-Louise* (Cap-Henry: P. Roux, 1811), x–xi.

29. Juste Chanlatte, *Le Cri de la nature* (Cap-Haïtien: P. Roux, 1810), 54.

30. "A bord du héros, le premier Thermidor, an 10, le Général Toussaint Louverture, au Général Bonaparte, Premier Consul de la république française," AN, AF/IV/1213.

31. Quoted in Stéphen Alexis, "Le Crépuscule d'un Dieu: Quelques Scènes des derniers moments de Toussaint Louverture au Fort de Joux," *Cahiers d'Haïti*, no. 9 (April 1944): 4.

32. Grégory Pierrot, "'Our Hero': Toussaint Louverture in British Representations," *Criticism* 50, no. 4 (2008): 581–607.

33. Louis-Félix Boisrond-Tonnerre, *Mémoires pour servir à l'histoire d'Haïti, par l'adjutant général Boisrond-Tonnerre* (Dessalines: De l'Imprimerie centrale du gouvernement, 1804), 7.

34. Chanlatte, *Le Cri*, 32.

35. [Juste Chanlatte], *À Mes concitoyens* (Port-au-Prince: De l'Imprimerie du gouvernement, [1804]), 6.

36. Prévost, *Relation*, xxiii.

37. Michael Drexler and Ed White, "The Constitution of Toussaint: Another Origin of African American Literature," in *A Companion to African American Literature*, ed. Gene Andrew Jarrett (Hoboken, NJ: Wiley-Blackwell, 2013), 59.

38. Philip Kaisary, "Hercules, the Hydra, and the 1801 Constitution of Toussaint Louverture," *Atlantic Studies* 12, no. 4 (2012): 399–400.

39. Laurent Dubois, *A Colony of Citizens: Revolution and Slave Emancipation in the French Caribbean, 1787–1804* (Chapel Hill: University of North Carolina Press, 2004), 3.

40. Louis Joseph Janvier, *Les Constitutions d'Haïti, 1801–1885* (Paris: C. Marpon et E. Flammarion, 1886), 2; Thomas Madiou, *Histoire d'Haïti*, vol. 2 (Port-au-Prince: Éditions Deschamps, 1989), 118–19.

41. Philippe R. Girard and Jean-Louis Donnadieu, "Toussaint before Louverture: New Archival Findings on the Early Life of Toussant Louverture," *William and Mary Quarterly* 70, no. 1 (2013): 59; Bryan Edwards, *The History, Civil and Commercial, of the British Colonies in the West Indies*, vol. 4 (Philadelphia: James Humphreys, 1806), 232.

42. "Constitution of the Year VIII: December 13, 1799 (23 Frimaire, Year VIII)," Napoleon Series, accessed March 20, 2023, www.napoleon-series.org/research/government /legislation/c_constitution8.html.

43. *Déclaration des Droits de l'Homme et du Citoyen de 1789*, August 26, 1789, https://www .legifrance.gouv.fr/contenu/menu/droit-national-en-vigueur/constitution/declaration-des -droits-de-l-homme-et-du-citoyen-de-1789; Toussaint Louverture, *Réponse du citoyen Toussaint Louverture, général en chef de l'armée de St-Domingue, aux calomnies et aux écrits mensongers du général de brigade Rigaud, commandant le département du sud* (1799), 2, BN, https://gallica.bnf.fr/ark:/12148/bpt6k9103177w.

44. "Constitution du 3 juillet 1801," Digithèque MJP, https://mjp.univ-perp.fr/constit /ht1801.htm.

45. Louis Sala-Molins, *Le Code noir, ou, le calvaire de Canaan* (Paris: Presses universitaires de France, 1987); *Le Code noir, ou édit du roy, servant de règlement pour le gouvernement & l'administration de justice & la police des isles françoises de l'Amérique, & pour la discipline & le commerce des nègres & esclaves dans ledit pays: Donné à Versailles au mois de mars 1685. Avec l'Édit du mois d'Aoust [sic] 1685, portant établissement d'un conseil souverain & de quatre sièges royaux dans la coste de l'Isle de S. Domingue* (Paris: Chez Claude Giraud, 1735), 4.

46. "Constitution du 3 juillet 1801."

47. "Constitution du 3 juillet 1801."

48. "Constitution du 3 juillet 1801."

49. "Émancipation des esclaves: proclamation du 29 août 1793," Digithèque MJP, https:// mjp.univ-perp.fr/constit/ht1793.htm.

50. "Proclamation du 29 août."

51. Étienne Polverel, "Proclamation [relative à la liberté générale dans l'ouest et dans le sud]," reprinted in "Aux Origines de l'abolition de l'esclavage," *Revue d'histoire des colonies* 36, no. 127–28 (troisième et quatrième trimestres, 1949): 378–79.

52. Polverel, "Proclamation," 380.

53. "Proclamation du 29 août."

54. Polverel, "Proclamation," 382; in colonial lexicon, "The bar is an instrument of punishment which consists of two superimposed pieces of wood, held together by means of two iron bolts or two wooden pegs which pass through them. The lower piece of wood is securely fastened to one end of a cot; it is, as with the upper piece of wood, indented with semicircular indentations, so that when the pieces of wood are fitted together, these indentations have circular gaps. . . . These holes are called leggings. When a slave is condemned to the bar, he is made to sit on the cot, and each of his legs being placed in one of the holes of the piece of wood fixed to the end of the cot, the bar is closed, and the captive is thus fastened to the cot." Quoted in "Barre," *Le Petit lexique colonial: L'esclavage et la colonisation en lecture*, accessed December 22, 2022, https://lepetitlexiquecolonial.wordpress.com /2014/11/22/barre/.

364   Notes to Chapter 6

55. "Commission Civile: Au nom de la République. Léger-Félicité Sonthonax commissaire-civil de la République, délégué aux isles françaises de l'Amérique sous le vent, pour y rétablir l'ordre et la tranquilité publique, à tous les Français de Saint-Domingue," November 5, 1793, Library of Congress, Early State Records Project.

56. Polverel, "Proclamation," 372.

57. "Speech Given October 23, 1791, by M. the Mayor of Port-au-Prince, Following the Peace Treaty between the White Citizens and the Citizens of Color from the Western Province of the French Section of Saint-Domingue," University of Maryland, Special Collections, https://colonyincrisis.lib.umd.edu/1791/10/23/speech-given-october-23-1791-by-m -the-mayor-of-port-au-prince-following-the-peace-treaty-between-the-white-citizens -and-the-citizens-of-color-from-the-western-province-of-the-french-section-of-sain/.

58. Vastey, *Réflexions politiques*, 110–111.

59. Julien Raimond, *Réponse aux considérations de M. Moreau, dit Saint-Méry, député à l'Assemblée nationale, sur les colonies: par M. Raymond, Citoyen de couleur de Saint-Domingue* (Paris: De l'Imprimerie du Patriote François, May 12, 1791), 56.

60. Julien Raimond, *Réflexions sur les véritables causes des troubles et des désastres de nos colonies, notamment sur ceux de Saint-Domingue; avec les moyens à employer pour préserver cette colonie d'une ruine totale; adressées à la Convention nationale, par Julien Raymond, colon de Saint-Domingue* (Paris, 1793), 19, BN, https://gallica.bnf.fr/ark:/12148 /bpt6k54615242.texteImage.

61. Raimond, *Réflexions*, 12–13.

62. Raimond, *Réflexions*, 13–14.

63. Raimond, *Réflexions*, 15.

64. Raimond, *Réflexions*, 19.

65. Raimond, *Réflexions*, 20.

66. Raimond, *Réflexions*, 20.

67. Raimond, *Réflexions*, 20–21.

68. Rigaud, *Mémoire*, 25.

69. Rigaud, *Mémoire*, 25 fn. a.

70. Rigaud, *Mémoire*, 26.

71. Rigaud, *Mémoire*, 26.

72. Rigaud, *Mémoire*, 26 fn. a.

73. Raimond, *Réflexions*, 21–23.

74. Raimond, *Réflexions*, 24–25.

75. Raimond, *Réflexions*, 23.

76. Raimond, *Réflexions*, 30.

77. Raimond, *Réflexions*, 31.

78. Raimond, *Réflexions*, 31.

79. Raimond, *Réflexions*, 24.

80. Olympe de Gouges, *L'Esclavage des noirs, ou l'heureux naufrage, drame en trois actes, en prose* (Paris: la veuve Duchesne, la veuve Bailly et les marchands de nouveautés, 1792), 4–5.

81. François-Auguste René de Chateaubriand, *Le Génie du christianisme*, 2 vols. (Paris: Hachette, 1872), 1:547.

82. Raimond, *Réflexions*, 24.

83. David Graeber and David Wengrow, *The Dawn of Everything: A New History of Humanity* (New York: Farrar, Straus, & Giroux, 2021), 187.

84. "Baille à ferme de l'habitation des héritiers Clonard à Joseph Macé," ANOM, 6 DPPC 3.

85. Baron de Vastey, *Le Système colonial dévoilé* (Cap-Haïtien: P. Roux, 1814), 95.

86. Vastey, *Le Système*, 89.

87. Vastey, *Le Système*, 64.

88. "Le Système Colonial Dévoil[é]," *Antijacobin Review; True Churchman's Magazine; and Protestant Advocate* 55 (November 1818): 243.

89. Dossier for Vastey, Jean Valentin, ANOM, 10 DPPC 686.

90. Julien Raimond, *Correspondance de Julien Raimond avec ses frères de Saint-Domingue, et les pièces qui lui ont été adressées par eux* (Paris: De l'Imprimerie du Cercle Social, 1793), i, iv; Julien Raimond, *Lettre d'un citoyen détenu pendant quatorze mois, et traduit au tribunal révolutionnaire, au citoyen C. B***, représentant du peuple, en réponse sur une question importante (an III de la République)* (Paris, 17 thermidor, an 3 de la république française [August 4, 1795]), 10.

91. Raimond, *Lettre*, 10–11 fn. 2.

92. Raimond, *Lettre*, 10–11.

93. Julien Raimond, *Rapport de Julien Raimond, commissaire délégué par le gouvernement français aux Isles-sous-le-vent, au ministre de la marine* (Au Cap Français: P. Roux, 1797), 31.

94. Raimond, *Rapport*, 62.

95. Raimond, *Rapport*, 63.

96. Raimond, *Rapport*, 2.

97. Raimond, *Rapport*, 8.

98. Louverture, *Réfutation*, 3, 11.

99. Louverture, *Réfutation*, 4.

100. Louverture, *Réfutation*, 11.

101. Louverture, *Réponse*, 5.

102. Louverture, *Réponse*, 5.

103. Louverture, *Réponse*, 5–6.

104. Louverture, *Réponse*, 6.

105. Louverture, *Réponse*, 7.

106. Louverture, *Réponse*, 13.

107. Louverture, *Réponse*, 14.

108. See Marlene L. Daut, *Tropics of Haiti* (Liverpool, UK: Liverpool University Press, 2015), 416–18.

109. Louverture, *Réponse*, 17.

110. See Johnhenry Gonzalez, *Maroon Nation: A History of Revolutionary Haiti* (New Haven, CT: Yale University Press, 2019), 68–69.

111. Michel-Rolph Trouillot, *Ti dife boule sou istwa Ayiti*, rev. ed. (Port-au-Prince: Edisyon KIK, 2012), 48.

112. Trouillot, *Ti dife boule*, 13.

113. Trouillot, *Ti dife boule*, 8; see also Camille Large, "Goman et l'insurrection de la Grand'Anse," in *Portraits et itinéraires*, ed. Michel Soukar (Port-au-Prince: Parténaire Principale, 2014), 17–32.

114. Large, "Goman et l'insurrection," 17–32.

115. Trouillot, *Ti dife boule*, 12.

116. Marie-José Alcide Saint-Lot, *Vodou, a Sacred Theatre: The African Heritage in Haiti* (Coconut Creek, FL: Educavision, 2003), 105.

117. Trouillot, *Ti dife boule*, 107.

118. Michel-Rolph Trouillot, *Haiti, State against Nation: Origins and Legacy of Duvalierism* (New York: Monthly Review, 1990); see also, J. Michael Dash, review of *Haiti, State against Nation: The Origins and Legacy of Duvalierism*, by Michel-Rolph Trouillot, *Social and Economic Studies* 40, no. 3 (1991): 199–202.

119. Trouillot, *Ti dife boule*, 118–19.

120. Salomon was president of Haiti from 1879 until 1888; Estimé was president of Haiti from 1946 until 1950.

121. Trouillot, *Ti dife boule*, 119.

122. Raimond, *Réflexions*, 27.

123. Wilfred Carsel, "The Slaveholders' Indictment of Northern Wage Slavery," *Journal of Southern History* 6, no. 4 (November 1940): 504–20.

124. Chanlatte, *Le Cri*, 15.

125. "Constitution du 3 juillet 1801."

126. "Constitution du 3 juillet 1801."

127. Jean-Jacques Rousseau, *The Social Contract, or the Principles of Political Rights*, trans. Rose M. Harrington, ed. Edward L. Water (New York: G. P. Putnam's Sons, 1893), 11.

128. Rousseau, *Social Contract*, 115.

129. "Constitution du 3 juillet 1801."

130. "Constitution du 3 juillet 1801."

131. Toussaint Louverture, *Mémoires du général Toussaint-L'Ouverture écrits par lui-même*, ed. Joseph Saint-Rémy (Paris: Pagnerre, 1853), 87.

132. Louverture, *Mémoires*, 87 fn. 1.

133. Quoted in Louverture, *Mémoires*, 87 fn. 1. Discussion of Louverture's quote is in chapter 5.

134. Louverture, *Mémoires*, 87.

135. Louverture, *Mémoires*, 90.

136. Toussaint Louverture, *Rapport au directoire exécutif, au Cap-Français, le 18 fructidor, an 5 de la République française, une et individisible*, 2, AN, AF/III/210.

137. Louverture, *Rapport*, 1.

138. Louverture, *Réfutation*, 10–11.

139. Denis Decrès to Leclerc, *25 prairial an 10* (June 14, 1802), Document 29, *Catalogue of the Unpublished Papers of Generals Leclerc and Rochambeau during the War of Independence in Haiti 1802–3*, Donatien Marie Joseph de Vimeur, vicomte de Rochambeau Papers relating to the French West Indies, GEN MSS 1576 Box 32, Beinecke Rare Book & Manuscript Library, Yale University.

140. Quoted in Józef Kwaterko, "'Ces Brigands qui chantent la Marseillaise . . .': Les lettres des militaires polonais et la guerre d'indépendance haïtienne (1802–1804)," *Revue d'Histoire Haïtienne*, no. 1 (2019): 255 fn. 14.

141. "Au quartier du Port-au-Prince, le 24 Germinal, an 11: Le Général en chef, au Premier Consul de la République Française," April 14, 1803, Dossier 6: Pièces Divers et Mémoires, AN, AF/IV/1213.

142. Saint-Rémy, *Pétion et Haiti*, 3:182–85; Chanlatte, *À Mes concitoyens*, 5; see a slightly different version of the quote in Louis Bro, *Mémoires du général Bro (1796–1844)*,

recueillis, complétés et publiés par son petit-fils, le Baron Henry Bro de Comères (Paris: Librairie Plon, 1914), 21: "Il faut enfin l'indépendance ou la mort" (we must at last have liberty or death).

143. Prévost, *Relation*, xxii–xxiii.

144. Boisrond-Tonnerre, *Mémoires*, 50 fn. 1; for Vernet's relationship to Louverture, see also Philippe R. Girard and Jean-Louis Donnadieu, "Web Supplement for Philippe R. Girard and Jean-Louis Donnadieu, 'Toussaint before Louverture: New Archival Findings on the Early Life of Toussaint Louverture,'" *William and Mary Quarterly* 70, no. 1 (January 2013), https://oieahc-cf.wm.edu/wmq/Jan13/GirardDonnadieu/GirardDonnadieu _table%201.pdf.

145. Saint-Rémy, *Pétion et Haïti*, 3:243–44; see also report in "West Indies," *Scots Magazine* (February 1, 1804), 147–49; and *Rapport des évènements qui se sont passés au Cap Français, Isle St. Domingue depuis le 20 brumaire an XII jusqu'aux 8 frimaire (12–30 novembre 1803) suivant adressé par le général La Poype au ministre de la guerre*, reprinted in "Vertières: suite de l'ultime bataille de l'armée," *Bulletin de l'Ispan* (November 2020), accessed March 20, 2023, https://ispan.gouv.ht/wp-content/upload/2017 /09/BULLETIN%20DE%20L%27ISPAN%20-Numero%20special%20Novembre%20%20 2020.pdf.

146. David Geggus, "The 29 November 1803 Declaration of Independence," March 3, 2013, Haiti and the Atlantic World, https://haitidoi.com/2013/03/03/the-29-november -1803-declaration-of-independence-post-by-david-geggus/.

147. "St. Domingo," *The Times*, February 6, 1804, 3, Times Digital Archive, accessed October 30, 2020, https://link-gale-com.proxy01.its.virginia.edu/apps/doc/CS51258950 /TTDA?u=viva_uva&sid=TTDA&xid=d24cc7bc.

148. "French Oppression," *Morning Chronicle* (New York), no. 388, January 2, 1804, 2, **Readex: America's Historical Newspapers**, https://infoweb-newsbank-com.proxy01.its .virginia.edu/apps/readex/doc?p=EANX&docref=image/v2%3A109C85FD5B008190%40 EANX-10AA294AC6C9EE28%402379958-10AA294B1E5E8940%401-10AA294CB5A513F8 %40French%2BOppression.

149. For more on this, see Stieber, *Haiti's Paper War: Post-Independence Writing, Civil War, and the Making of the Republic, 1804–1954* (New York: New York University Press, 2020), 2.

150. Baron de Vastey, *Essai sur les causes de la révolution et des guerres civiles d'Hayti* (Sans-Souci, Haiti: L'Imprimerie Royale, 1819), 153.

151. Lieutenant-Général Baron Pamphile de Lacroix, *Mémoires pour servir à l'histoire de la révolution de Saint-Domingue*, 2 vols. (Paris: Pillet Aine, 1819), 2:226–27.

152. Vastey, *Essai*, 49.

153. Vastey, *Essai*, 43, 48.

154. Vastey, *Essai*, 48. For an overview of the civil wars in Haiti, see Stieber, *Haiti's Paper War*, 2020.

155. Vastey, *Essai*, 49.

156. Jean Casimir, *Une Lecture décoloniale de l'histoire des haïtiens: du Traité de Ryswick à l'occupation américaine* (Port-au-Prince: L'Imprimeur S.A., 2018), 38–39.

157. Aimé Césaire, *Discourse on Colonialism*, trans. Joan Pinkham (New York: Monthly Review Press, 2000), 71–72.

Chapter 7

1. Edmond Bonnet, ed., *Souvenirs historiques de Guy-Joseph Bonnet, général de division des armées de la République d'Haïti, ancien aide de camp de Rigaud. Documents relatifs à toutes les phases de la révolution de Saint-Domingue, recueillis et mis en ordre par Edmond Bonnet* (Paris: Auguste Durand, 1864), 128–29.

2. Joseph Saint-Rémy, *Pétion et Haïti: étude monographique et historique*, vol. 4 (Paris: Auguste Durand, 1857), 18.

3. "Acte d'indépendance," January 1, 1804, Digithèque MJP, https://mjp.univ-perp.fr /constit/ht1804.htm. All translations mine unless otherwise noted. For an English translation of the 1803 version, see David Geggus, "The 29 November 1803 Declaration of Independence," March 3, 2013, Haiti and the Atlantic World, https://haitidoi.com/2013/03/03 /the-29-november-1803-declaration-of-independence-post-by-david-geggus/.

4. Saint-Rémy, *Pétion et Haïti*, 4:10–16.

5. "Acte d'indépendance."

6. Beaubrun Ardouin, *Études sur l'histoire d'Haïti, 11 tomes réunis en 3 volumes* (Port-au-Prince: Éditions Fardin Collections du Bicentenaire, 2004), 2:57; 67–68 (vol. 7 in original sequence).

7. "Acte d'indépendance."

8. [Juste Chanlatte], *À Mes concitoyens* (Port-au-Prince: De l'Imprimerie du gouvernement, [1804]), 6.

9. "Empire d'Haïti, Du Cap, le 21 novembre," *Gazette politique et commerciale d'Haïti*, November 22, 1804, 7.

10. "A Dessalines, le 15 février, 1804," *Gazette politique et commerciale d'Haïti*, November 22, 1804, 7–8.

11. Baron de Vastey, *Essai sur les causes de la révolution et des guerres civiles d'Hayti* (Sans-Souci, Haiti: L'Imprimerie Royale, 1819), 47.

12. Thomas Madiou, *Histoire d'Haïti, 1803–1807* (Port-au-Prince: Éditions Deschamps, 1989), 3:216–19; Chelsea Stieber, *Haiti's Paper War: Post-Independence Writing, Civil War, and the Making of the Republic, 1804–1954* (New York: New York University Press, 2020), 42–43.

13. "London: July 18," *Caledonian Mercury*, July 21, 1804.

14. "Empire d'Haïti," *Gazette politique et commerciale d'Haïti*, November 15, 1804, 2.

15. See Julia Gaffield, "Five Myths about the Haitian Revolution," *Washington Post*, August 4, 2021, https://www.washingtonpost.com/outlook/five-myths/five-myths-about-the -haitian-revolution/2021/08/04/1cf7be4e-f3c1-11eb-a49b-d96f2dac0942_story.html.

16. Jean-Jacques Dessalines, "Proclamation: Jean-Jacques Dessalines, gouverneur général aux habitants d'Haïti," April 28, 1804, Haiti and the Atlantic World, https://haitidoi .com/2015/10/30/dessalines-reader-28-april-1804/.

17. "Constitution du 20 mai 1805," Digithèque MJP, http://mjp.univ-perp.fr/constit/ht1805 .htm.

18. "Nomination of Emperor of Hayti, J.J. Dessalines," *Commercial Advertiser*, October 10, 1804.

19. *New-York Herald*, October 10, 1804.

20. "Observing Constitution Day," National Archives of the United States, accessed March 21, 2023, www.archives.gov/education/lessons/constitution-day/ratification.html

#:~:text=On%20September%2017%2C%201787%2C%20a,they%20had%20labored%20since%20May.

21. Deborah Jenson, "Dessalines's American Proclamations of the Haitian Independence," *Journal of Haitian Studies* 15, no. 1&2 (2009): 77.

22. Leslie Alexander, *Fear of a Black Republic: Haiti and the Birth of Black Internationalism in the United States* (Urbana-Champaign: University of Illinois Press, 2022), 17–21.

23. "Mr. Editor," *Commercial Advertiser*, May 25, 1804.

24. Julia Gaffield and David Armitage, "Introduction: The Haitian Declaration of Independence in an Atlantic Context," in *The Haitian Declaration of Independence: Creation, Context, and Legacy*, ed. Julia Gaffield (Charlottesville: University of Virginia Press, 2016), 13.

25. Jenson, "Dessalines's American Proclamations," 77; David Geggus, "Haiti's Declaration of Independence," in Gaffield, *Haitian Declaration of Independence*, 27; and Chris Bongie, "The Cry of History: Juste Chanlatte and the Unsettling (Presence) of Race in Early Haitian Literature," *MLN* 130, no. 4 (September 2015): 809.

26. "De Sans-Souci, le 25 octobre," *Gazette royale d'Hayti*, October 28, 1819, 2–3.

27. Laurent Dubois, "An Enslaved Enlightenment: Rethinking the Intellectual History of the French Atlantic," *Social History* 31, no. 1 (February 2006): 7.

28. Marlene L. Daut, *Baron de Vastey and the Origins of Black Atlantic Humanism* (New York: Palgrave Macmillan, 2017), xxii.

29. "Constitution du 20 mai 1805."

30. "Acte d'indépendance."

31. "Adresse de sa majesté l'empereur aux habitants de l'île d'Haïti, à son retour de la campagne de Santo-Domingo," *Gazette politique et commerciale*, May 30, 1805, 97; see also Stieber, *Haiti's Paper War*, 161; and Anne Eller, *We Dream Together: Dominican Independence, Haiti, and the Fight for Caribbean Freedom* (Durham, NC: Duke University Press, 2016), 4.

32. "Constitution du 20 mai 1805"; "Intérieur: Réunion de la partie orientale d'Haïti aux autres parties de la République," *Le Télégraphe*, January 16, 1822, 1.

33. Anthony Bogues, "The Dual Haitian Revolution and the Making of Freedom in Modernity," in *Human Rights from a Third World Perspective: Critique, History and International Law*, ed. José-Manuel Barreto (Newcastle, UK: Cambridge Scholars Publishing, 2013), 221.

34. Vastey, *Essai*, 47.

35. Colleen Flaherty, "Resignations at Third World Quarterly," *Inside Higher Ed*, September 20, 2017, www.insidehighered.com/news/2017/09/20/much-third-world-quarterlys-editorial-board-resigns-saying-controversial-article.

36. Dorothea Fischer-Hornung, "An Island Occupied: The Interpretation of the U.S. Marine Occupation of Haiti in Zora Neale Hurston's *Tell My Horse* and Katherine Dunham's *Island Possessed*," in *Holding Their Own: Perspectives on the Multi-Ethnic Literature of the United States*, ed. Dorothea Fischer-Hornung and Heike Raphael-Hernandez (Tubingen, Germany: Stauffenberg, 2000), 153–68.

37. Raphael Dalleo, *American Imperialism's Undead: The Occupation and the Rise of Caribbean Anticolonialism* (Charlottesville: University of Virginia Press, 2016), 2–19.

38. For Delorme's and Janvier's association of imperialism with capitalism, see Marlene L. Daut, "Caribbean 'Race Men': Louis-Joseph Janvier, Demesvar Delorme, and the Haitian Atlantic," *L'Esprit créateur* 56, no. 1 (Spring 2016): 9–23.

39. Dalleo, *American Imperialism's Undead*, 3.

40. For an analysis of this nature, see Marlene L. Daut, "Beyond Trouillot: Unsettling Genealogies of Historical Thought," *Small Axe* 25, no. 1 (64) (March 2021): 132–54.

41. Daut, *Baron de Vastey*, 22.

42. Baron de Malouet, *Collection de mémoires sur les colonies et particulièrement sur Saint-Domingue*, vol. 4 (Paris: Baudouin, 1802), 32; for the horror of Malouet's name, see Chevalier de Prézeau, *Réfutation d'un écrit des ex-colons, réfugiés à la Jamaïque, intitulé: Exposé de l'État actuel des choses dans la colonie de Saint-Domingue* (Cap-Henry: P. Roux, 1815), 10.

43. Baron de Vastey, *Notes à M. le Baron V.P. de Malouet* (Cap-Henry, Haiti: Chez P. Roux, 1814), 7.

44. Henry Christophe became king of the northern part of Haiti in March 1811, but many foreign commentators mistakenly referred to him as an emperor.

45. Fowell Buxton, "Abolition of Slavery," House of Commons Debates, May 15, 1823, vol. 9, cc257–360, https://api.parliament.uk/historic-hansard/commons/1823/may/15/abolition-of-slavery.

46. "De Londres, le 8 juin 1804," *Gazette politique et commerciale*, March 27, 1806, 48.

47. Chanlatte, *À Mes concitoyens*, 6.

48. "Mr. Editor."

49. Reprinted in "New-York, July 13," *Aurora General Advertiser*, July 16, 1805.

50. "Translated for the Mercantile Advertiser, Constitution of Haiti," *Mercantile Advertiser*, July 15, 1805.

51. "Foreign Official Papers," *Cobbett's Weekly Political Register*, August 24, 1805; "Friday's Post," *Ipswich Journal*, August 24, 1805.

52. "Lord NELSON Attended Yesterday Morning at the Admiralty . . . ," *The Times*, August 24, 1805, 2.

53. Julia Gaffield, *Haitian Connections in the Atlantic World: Recognition after Revolution* (Chapel Hill: University of North Carolina Press, 2015), 57, 73–74.

54. Deborah Jenson, "Before Malcolm X, Dessalines: A 'French' Tradition of Black Atlantic Radicalism," *International Journal of Francophone Studies* 10, no. 3 (2007): 330.

55. "Constitution du 20 mai 1805."

56. Vastey, *Essai*, 48.

57. "[Benjamin Blanchet] Le Secrétaire d'État de la République d'Haïty [*sic*], à Monsieur Peltier à Londres, July 31, 1807," National Archives of the United Kingdom (hereafter TNA), WO 1/79; see also the notice that Christophe had been "confirmed to be the first magistrate of the State, in being named to preside over the Haitian Republic," in Cezar-Télémaque et al.'s "Adresse du Sénat, au peuple et à l'armée," January 24, 1807, PAIRS Spanish Archives, Archivo General de Indias, ESTADO, 4, n.13.

58. "État d'Hayti. Proclamation. Au Peuple et à l'armée [January 14, 1807]," *Gazette de l'état d'Hayti*, June 4, 1807, 19–20.

59. "Le Conseil d'État, Au Peuple et à l'Armée de Terre et de Mer de Hayti," April 4, 1811, TNA, WO 1/79; see also, Comte de Limonade (Julien Prévost), *Relation des glorieux événemens qui ont porté Leurs Majestés Royales sur le trône d'Hayti; suivie de l'histoire du couronnement et du sacre du roi Henry 1er, et de la reine Marie-Louise* (Cap-Henry: P. Roux, 1811), 45, 60–61; and Vastey, *Essai*, 144–49.

60. "Mr. Editor," italics in original.

61. Baron de Vastey, *Réflexions politiques sur quelques ouvrages et journaux français concernant Hayti* (Sans-Souci, Haiti: Royal Imprint, 1817), 73.

62. Vastey, *Essai*, 147–48.

63. Baron de Vastey, *Réflexions politiques*, 32–33.

64. Donald Pease, "Exceptionalism," in *Keywords for American Cultural Studies*, ed. Glenn Hendler and Bruce Burgett (New York: New York University Press, 2007), 108.

65. The provision against empire appeared in Article 5 of the 1816 constitution but disappeared in the 1843 constitution that named Charles Hérard provisory president. See Louis-Joseph Janvier, *Les Constitutions d'Haïti (1801–1995)* (Paris: C. Marpon et E. Flammarion, 1886), 73, 112, 154, 185.

66. After the death of Pétion in March 1818, Jean-Pierre Boyer, also a former general, became president of the southern republic.

67. "Constitution du 27 décembre 1806," Digithèque MJP, http://mjp.univ-perp.fr/constit/ht1806.htm.

68. Hérard Dumesle, *Voyage dans le nord d'Hayti: ou, Révélations des lieux et des monuments historiques* (Aux Cayes, Haiti: De l'Imprimerie du Gouvernement, 1824), 336 fn. e.

69. For more on this, see Stieber, *Haiti's Paper War*, ch. 3, 91–127.

70. Comte de Limonade (Julien Prévost), *Le Machiavélisme du Cabinet Français* (Cap-Français: P. Roux, 1814), 16.

71. "Constitution du 2 Juin 1816," Digithèque MJP, https://mjp.univ-perp.fr/constit/ht1816.htm.

72. Henry Christophe to General Capoix, November 13, 1805, Copie de lettres (manuscript) 1805–6, FCO Historical Collection FOL. F1924 HEN, King's College, London; for Christophe's constitution, see "Constitution du 17 février 1807," Digitèque MJP, https://mjp.univ-perp.fr/constit/ht1807.htm

73. **Vastey, *Essai*, 318.**

74. Vastey, *Réflexions politiques*, 21 fn. 1.

75. Malouet, *Collection de mémoires*, 32; see also, Vastey, *Notes*, 7.

76. Prévost, *Relation*, xxv.

77. *Gazette royale d'Hayti*, October 10, 1817, 3.

78. Ada Ferrer, "Haiti, Free Soil, and Antislavery in the Revolutionary Atlantic," *American Historical Review* 117, no. 1 (February 2012): 40–66.

79. Anténor Firmin, *De l'Égalité des races humaines: anthropologie positive* (Paris: Librairie Cotillon, 1885), 586.

80. [Cinna] Marion, *Expédition de Bolívar, par le Senateur Marion aîné* (Port-au-Prince: Jh. Courtois, 1849), 3.

81. Edgardo Pérez Morales, *No Limits to Their Sway: Cartagena's Privateers and the Masterless Caribbean in the Age of Revolutions* (Nashville, TN: Vanderbilt University Press, 2018), 110–11.

82. Henri Grégoire (abbé de), *De la Noblesse de la peau, ou Du préjugé des blancs contre la couleur des Africains et celle de leurs descendans, noirs et sang-mêlés* (Paris: Baudouin Frères, 1826), 45.

83. Marion, *Expédition*, 23.

84. Marion, *Expédition*, 24.

85. Marion, *Expédition*, 25.

86. **Marion, *Expédition*, 25 fn.; quote from 39.**

87. "Palais du gouvernement à Pampator le 17 Mai 1817," *Le Télégraphe*, June 29, 1817, 2.

88. Simon Bolívar to Alexandre Pétion, June 27, 1816, reprinted in Marion, *Expédition*, 39–40.

89. "Proclamation, quartier-général d'Ocumare," July 6, 1816, reprinted in Marion, *Expédition*, 41.

90. Marion, *Expédition*, 28–29.

91. Marion, *Expédition*, 41 fn.; Sibylle Fischer, "Bolívar in Haiti," in *Haiti and the Americas*, ed. Carla Calargé, Raphael Dalleo, Luis Duno-Gottberg, and Clevis Headley (Jackson: University of Mississippi Press, 2013), 26.

92. Marion, *Expédition*, 29.

93. "Sommaire de la révolution de Venezuela," *L'Abeille Haytienne*, no. 7 (November 1, 1817), 14.

94. See, for example, *Le Télégraphe*, April 6, 1817.

95. Marion, *Expédition*, 29.

96. "Alexandre Pétion to General Marion," January 26, 1816, reprinted in Marion, *Expédition*, 32.

97. Marion, *Expédition*, 30.

98. Louis-Joseph Janvier, *La République d'Haïti et ses visiteurs (1840–1882), Réponse à M. Victor Cochinat (De la Petite Presse) et à quelques autres écrivains* (Paris: Marpon et Flammarion, 1883), 16 fn. 1.

99. Demesvar Delorme, *La Misère au sein des richesses, réflexions diverses sur Haïti* (Paris: E. Dentu, 1873), 97.

100. Firmin, *De l'Égalité*, 586.

101. T. G. Steward, "How the Black St. Domingo Legion SAVED THE PATRIOT ARMY IN THE Siege of Savannah, 1779," 1899, www.gutenberg.org/files/31256/31256-h/31256-h .htm#:~:text=Henri%20Christophe%20received%20a%20dangerous,by%20bravely%20cov ering%20the%20retreat.%E2%80%9D.

102. Simón Bolívar to Alexandre Pétion, February 8, 1816, reprinted in Marion, *Expédition*, 42.

103. Alexandre Pétion to Simón Bolívar, February 18, 1816, reprinted in Marion, *Expédition*, 43.

104. Simón Bolívar to Alexandre Pétion, October 9, 1816, reprinted in Marion, *Expédition*, 43–44.

105. Marion, *Expédition*, 44.

106. Andrew R. L. Cayton, "The Debate Over the Panama Congress and the Origins of the Second American Party System," *The Historian* 47, no. 2 (1985): 235–36.

107. Robert Young Hayne, *Speech of Mr. Hayne, Delivered in the Senate of the United States, on the Mission to Panama, March 1826* (Washington City: Gales & Seaton, 1826), 21.

108. Marion, *Expédition*, 45.

109. Marion, *Expédition*, 45; Vastey, *Réflexions politiques*, 23.

110. Marion, *Expédition*, 45; Slavery was not officially abolished throughout Gran Colombia until 1821, and full enforcement was repeatedly delayed by the obstinance of enslavers. See Harold A. Bierck, "The Struggle for Abolition in Gran Colombia," *Hispanic American Historical Review* 33, no. 3 (1953): 365–86.

111. "Intérieur," *L'Abeille Haytienne*, April 3, 1818, 6–8; Vastey, *Essai*, 386–87.

112. Name the ancient Greeks called themselves. See "Greece: Secrets of the Past," Canadian Museum of History/Musée Canadien de l'Histoire, accessed December 2, 2022, https://www.historymuseum.ca/cmc/exhibitions/civil/greece/gr1010e.html#:~:text=The%20Greeks%20called%20their%20land,to%20describe%20his%20own%20country.

113. Famous king of Sparta who valiantly led the Greeks through the Battle of Thermopylae in 480 B.C.E. See Mark Cartwright, "Leonidas I of Sparta," *World History Encyclopedia*, May 12, 2013, https://www.worldhistory.org/Leonidas_I/.

114. The Greeks famously won the Battle of Salamis, which took place between Greek and Persian forces in the Saronic Gulf in September 480 B.C.E., after losing the Battle of Thermopylae (see note 113 above). See Mark Cartwright, "Battle of Salamis," *World History Encyclopedia*, May 12, 2013, https://www.worldhistory.org/Battle_of_Salamis/.

115. A Greek general from Athenia who defeated Persian forces at the Battle of Marathon in 490 B.C.E. See Mark Cartwright, "Miltiades," *World History Encyclopedia*, February 23, 2016, https://www.worldhistory.org/Miltiades/.

116. Jean-Pierre Boyer to the Citizens of Greece, reprinted and trans. in E. G. Sideris and A. A. Konsta, "A Letter from Jean-Pierre Boyer to Greek Revolutionaries," *Journal of Haitian Studies* 11, no. 1 (Spring 2005): 167–71.

117. Throughout 1822, *Le Télégraphe* reported the "reunion" between the east and west, printing numerous letters of support from various Santo Domingan military officers. See, for example, "Intérieur: L'Île d'Haïti ne reconnaît plus qu'un seul et même gouvernement," *Supplément extraordinaire au No. V. du Télégraphe*, January 27, 1822; and José Nunez de Caceres, "Fidèles Domingois et chers Compatriotes," reprinted in *Le Télégraphe*, March 10, 1822, 3–4; see also, Eller, *We Dream Together*, 5.

118. "Rapport au conseil des ministres," Paris, October 19, 1822, Archives Nationales d'Outre-Mer in Aix-en-Provence, France (hereafter ANOM), 1 LEG 6.

119. "Rapport au roi," Paris, October 30, 1822, ANOM, 1 LEG 6.

120. See "Affaire de la Grèce (Lettre d'un correspondant)," *Le Télégraphe*, August 26, 1821, 3–4; "Nouvelles étrangères," *Le Télégraphe*, November 18, 1821, 3; "Guerre de la Grèce," *Le Télégraphe*, December 23, 1821, 1–2.

121. Marion, *Expédition*, 46.

122. Marion, *Expédition*, 46 fn.

123. See Eller, *We Dream Together*, 52, 196.

124. Eller, *We Dream Together*, 196–97, 199.

125. Eller, *We Dream Together*, 207–18.

126. Ramón Emeterio Betances, "AL.G.D.P.A.D.L.U," in *Betances*, ed. Luis Bonafoux (San Juan, Puerto Rico: Inst. de Cultura Puertoriqueña, 1970), 113.

127. Marion, *Expédition*, 43.

128. Marion, *Expédition*, 43.

129. "Speech of Frederick Douglass, Haitian Pavilion Dedication Ceremonies at Chicago World Fair, 1893," World's Fair, Jackson Park, January 2, 1893, https://canada-haiti.ca/sites/default/files/Douglass%201893.pdf.

130. Alexandre Pétion to General Marion, January 30, 1816, reprinted in Marion, *Expédition*, 33–34.

131. For debates about the meaning of early Haiti's actions in this regard, see Gaffield, *Haitian Connections*, 50–58; Deborah Jenson, *Beyond the Slave Narrative: Politics, Sex,*

374   Notes to Chapter 7

and Manuscripts in the Haitian Revolution (Liverpool, UK: Liverpool University Press, 2011), 176; and Bogues, "Dual Haitian Revolution," 221–22.

132. Paul Farmer, *The Uses of Haiti* (Monroe, ME: Common Courage Press, 1994), 69; Earl Leslie Griggs and Clifford H. Prator, eds., *Henry Christophe and Thomas Clarkson: A Correspondence* (Oakland: University of California Press, 1952), 180–81.

133. Fred Moten, "Democracy," in *Keywords for American Cultural Studies*, ed. Bruce Burgett and Glenn Hendler (New York: New York University Press, 2007), 77.

134. Eller, *We Dream Together*, 5.

135. James Weldon Johnson, "Self-Determining Haiti," *The Nation*, August 28, 1920, https://www.thenation.com/article/archive/self-determining-haiti/.

136. W. E. B. Du Bois, "Hayti," *The Crisis* 10, no. 6 (October 1915): 291.

137. See Pierre Faubert's anti-imperial poem, "Aux Haïtiens" in *Ogé, ou le préjugé de couleur* (Paris: C. Maillet-Schmitz, 1856), 143–46. An excerpt was translated and published by Jesse Fauset for *The Crisis* in September 1920. See reprint in Jesse Fauset, *The Chinaberry Tree: A Novel of American Life & Selected Writings* (Boston: Northeastern University Press, 1995), 359. For Martí and Haiti, see Brenda Gayle Plummer, "Firmin and Martí at the Intersection of Pan-Americanism and Pan-Africanism," in *José Martí's "Our America": From National to Hemispheric Cultural Studies*, ed. Jeffrey Grant Belnap and Raul A. Fernández (Durham, NC: Duke University Press, 1998), 210–27.

138. Bogues, "Dual Haitian Revolution," 212.

Chapter 8

1. Louis Joseph Janvier, *La République d'Haïti et ses visiteurs (1840–1882), Réponse à M. Victor Cochinat (De la Petite Presse) et à quelques autres écrivains* (Paris: Marpon et Flammarion, 1883), 55–56, 123.

2. Janvier, *La République*, 56.

3. "Constitution du 20 mai 1805," Digithèque MJP, http://mjp.univ-perp.fr/constit/ht1805.htm.

4. "Vermont 1777: Early Steps against Slavery," National Museum of African American History and Culture, Washington, DC, accessed March 22, 2023, https://nmaahc.si.edu/explore/stories/vermont-1777-early-steps-against-slavery; Julian Boyd, "Declaring Independence: Drafting the Documents, Jefferson's 'Original Rough Draught' of the Declaration of Independence," U.S. Library of Congress, Washington, DC, accessed March 22, 2023, https://www.loc.gov/exhibits/declara/ruffdrft.html.

5. "Benjamin Franklin's Antislavery Petitions to Congress," February 12 and 15, 1790, National Archives of the United States, Washington, DC, accessed March 24, 2023, www.archives.gov/legislative/features/franklin.

6. "Constitution du 17 février 1807," Digithèque MJP, https://mjp.univ-perp.fr/constit/ht1807.htm.

7. "Constitution du 27 décembre 1806," Digithèque MJP, http://mjp.univ-perp.fr/constit/ht1806.htm; "Constitution du 2 Juin 1816," Digithèque MJP, https://mjp.univ-perp.fr/constit/ht1816.htm.

8. Thomas Jefferson to Aaron Burr, February 11, 1799, Founders Online, https://founders.archives.gov/documents/Jefferson/01-31-02-0015; Thomas Jefferson to Rufus King, July 13, 1802, Jefferson Monticello, https://tjrs.monticello.org/letter/1741; Julia Gaffield, "'Outrages

on the Laws of Nations': American Merchants and Diplomacy after the Haitian Declaration of Independence," in *The Haitian Declaration of Independence* (Charlottesville: University of Virginia Press, 2016), 167.

9. "ÉTAT D'HAYTI. Du Cap, le 20 Janvier," *Gazette royale d'Hayti*, January 21, 1808, 10. All issues of the *Gazette royale* consulted at https://lagazetteroyale.com.

10. Eric Williams, *Capitalism and Slavery* (Chapel Hill: University of North Carolina Press, 1944), 178.

11. Victor Schoelcher, *Colonies étrangères et Haïti, résultats de l'émancipation anglaise*, vol. 2 (Paris: Pagnerre, 1843), 242–43.

12. Chanlatte's younger brother, François Desrivières Chanlatte, who lived in the southern republic, was also somewhat known in the Atlantic public sphere due to several pamphlets he published and an antislavery article he penned for *Le Télégraphe*, inviting free Black people from the United States to emigrate to Haiti. See "Vues politiques sur le sort des personnes libres, mais non blanches qui se trouvent aux Étas-Unis d'Amérique ou ailleurs" (Political views on the fate of free people who are not white found in the United States of America or elsewhere). See *Le Télégraphe*, August 4, 1822, 1–3.

13. Translation: The cry of nature, or, Haitian homage to the very venerable Abbé H. Grégoire, author of a new work, entitled The Literature of Negroes, or, research on their individual faculties, their moral qualities and their literature; followed by notices on the life and works of Negroes who have distinguished themselves in the sciences, letters and the arts.

14. Juste Chanlatte, *Le Cri de la nature* (Cap-Haïtien: P. Roux, 1810), 5.

15. Chanlatte, *Le Cri*, 7.

16. Chanlatte, *Le Cri*, 8.

17. Chanlatte, *Le Cri*, 9.

18. A. J. B. Bouvet de Cressé, "Avertissement de l'auteur," in *Histoire de la catastrophe de Saint-Domingue [par J. Chanlatte], avec la correspondance des généraux Leclerc, . . . Henry Christophe, . . . Hardy, Vilton, etc., . . . publiées par A.-J.-B. Bouvet de Cressé* (Paris: Librairie de Peytieux, 1842), i fn. 1.

19. Antoine Métral, "De la littérature haïtienne," *Revue encyclopédique, ou analyse raisonné* (Paris, 1819): 1:527.

20. See Marlene L. Daut, *Baron de Vastey and the Origins of Black Atlantic Humanism* (New York: Palgrave Macmillan, 2017), xv–xvii.

21. "Extracts from the Baron De Vastey's work in answer to the ex-colonist Mazeres and other [*sic*]," *Freedom's Journal* (December 12, 1828): 293–94; "Africa: Extract from Baron de Vastey," *Freedom's Journal* (February 7, 1829): 349–50; "Africa: Extracts from Baron de Vastey," *Freedom's Journal* (February 14, 1829): 357–58; *Freedom's Journal* reprinted translations from *Reflexions on the Blacks and Whites, Remarks upon a Letter Addressed by M. Mazères . . . to J. C. L. Sismonde de Sismondi, Containing Observations on the Blacks and Whites, the Civilization of Africa, the Kingdom of Hayti, Translated from the French of the Baron de Vastey*, trans. William Hamilton (London: J. Hatchard, 1817).

22. See Baron de Vastey (Jean Louis), *The Colonial System Unveiled*, trans. and ed. Chris Bongie (Liverpool, UK: Liverpool University Press, 2014).

23. Baron de Vastey, *Le Système colonial dévoilé* (Cap-Haïtien: P. Roux, 1814), vi.

24. Baron de Vastey, *Réflexions sur une lettre de Mazères: ex-colon français, adressée à M. J.C.L. Sismonde de Sismondi, sur les noirs et les blancs, la civilisation de l'Afrique, le royaume d'Hayti* (Cap-Haïtien: P. Roux, 1816), 4.

25. Baron de Vastey, *Réflexions politiques sur quelques ouvrages et journaux français concernant Hayti* (Sans-Souci, Haiti: Royal Imprint, 1817), 1.

26. James McCune Smith, *A Lecture on the Haytien Revolutions: With a Sketch of the Character of Toussaint L'Ouverture, Delivered at the Stuyvesant Institute, (for the Benefit of the Coloured Orphan Asylum,) February 26, 1841* (New York: Daniel Fanshaw, 1841); "'Haytien Revolutions.' Lecture on the Haytien Revolutions with a Sketch of the Character of Toussaint L'Ouverture, Delivered at the Stuyvesant Institute, Feb. 24, 1841, by James McCune Smith," *Colored American*, August 7, 1841, 1.

27. Henry Bibb, "To Our Old Masters, No. 2," *Voice of the Fugitive*, February 12, 1851, 2.

28. Daut, *Baron de Vastey*, xvii.

29. Eric Walrond, *Winds Can Wake Up the Dead: An Eric Walrond Reader*, ed. Louis J. Parascandola (Detroit: Wayne State University Press, 1998), 59–60.

30. [Arturo] Arthur Schomburg, "The Negro Digs Up His Past (1925)," in *African American Poetry (1870–1926)*, ed. Amardeep Singh, https://scalar.lehigh.edu/african-american-poetry-a-digital-anthology/arthur-a-schomburg-arturo-schomburg-the-negro-digs-up-his-past-1925.

31. Louis-Félix Boisrond-Tonnerre, *Mémoires pour servir à l'histoire d'Haïti, par l'adjutant général Boisrond-Tonnerre* (Dessalines: De l'Imprimerie centrale du gouvernement, 1804), 93.

32. Jean-Jacques Dessalines, "Proclamation à Gonaïves, 28 April 1804," October 30, 2015, Dessalines Reader, ed. Julia Gaffield, https://haitidoi.com/2015/10/30/dessalines-reader-28-april-1804/.

33. Emmanuel F. Édouard, *Le Panthéon Haïtien*, 2nd ed. (Paris: Auguste Ghio, 1885), 5, 11.

34. Janvier, *La République*, 89.

35. Joseph Saint-Rémy, ed., *Mémoires du général Toussaint-L'Ouverture écrits par lui-même* (Paris: Pagnerre, 1853), 5.

36. Saint-Rémy, *Mémoires*, 6.

37. Pierre Faubert, *Ogé, ou le préjugé de couleur* (Paris: Librairie de C. Maillet-Schmitz, 1856), 41.

38. Schoelcher, *Colonies étrangères et Haïti*, 2:242.

39. Ada Ferrer, "Talk about Haiti: The Archive and the Atlantic's Haitian Revolution," in *Tree of Liberty: Cultural Legacies of the Haitian Revolution in the Atlantic World*, ed. Doris L. Garraway (Charlottesville: University of Virginia Press, 2008), 21–40.

40. See examples and analyses from around the world in: Julius S. Scott, *The Common Wind: Afro-American Currents in the Age of the Haitian Revolution* (London: Verso, 2018); David P. Geggus and Norman Fiering, eds., *The World of the Haitian Revolution* (Bloomington: Indiana University Press, 2009); Alfred S. Hunt, *Haiti's Influence on Antebellum America: Slumbering Volcano in the Caribbean* (Baton Rouge: Louisiana State University Press, 1988); Laurent Dubois, *Haiti: The Aftershocks of History* (New York: Picador, 2012); Sibylle Fischer, *Modernity Disavowed: Haiti and the Cultures of Slavery in the Age of Revolution* (Durham, NC: Duke University Press, 2004); Sara Johnson, *The Fear of French Negroes: Transcolonial Collaboration in the Revolutionary Americas* (Berkeley: University of California Press, 2012); Julia Gaffield, *Haitian Connections in the Atlantic World: Recognition after Revolution* (Chapel Hill: University of North Carolina Press, 2015); Matthew J. Smith, *Liberty, Fraternity, Exile: Haiti and Jamaica after Emancipation* (Chapel Hill: University of North Carolina Press, 2014); Cristina Soriano, *Tides of Revolution: Information,*

Insurgencies, and the Crisis of Colonial Rule in Venezuela (Albuquerque: University of New Mexico Press, 2018); Ada Ferrer, *Freedom's Mirror: Cuba and Haiti in the Age of Revolution* (Cambridge: Cambridge University Press, 2014); see also Anne Eller, *We Dream Together: Dominican Independence, Haiti, and the Fight for Caribbean Freedom* (Durham, NC: Duke University Press, 2016); Edgardo Pérez Morales, *No Limits to Their Sway: Cartagena's Privateers and the Masterless Caribbean in the Age of Revolutions* (Nashville, TN: Vanderbilt University Press, 2018).

41. Robin Blackburn, "Haiti, Slavery, and the Age of the Democratic Revolution," *William and Mary Quarterly* 63, no. 4 (2006): 662.

42. "Parlement Impérial. Chambres des pairs. Suite des discours prononcés à l'appui du bill portant abolition du Commerce des Esclaves," *Gazette royale d'Hayti*, May 28, 1807, 13–14.

43. See the collection of essays in *The Haiti Issue: 1804 and Nineteenth-Century French Studies*, ed. Deborah Jenson, special issue, *Yale French Studies* 107 (2005); and Elizabeth Maddock Dillon and Michael Drexler, eds., *The Haitian Revolution and the Early United States: Histories, Textualities, Geographies* (Philadelphia: University of Pennsylvania Press, 2016).

44. "Nouvelles etrangères: gouvernement d'Hayti," *Journal de Paris* (29 *floréal an XII*/ May 19, 1804): 1.

45. "Mr. Editor," *Commercial Advertiser*, May 25, 1804.

46. "Nouvelles etrangères," 1.

47. "Legislative Acts/Legal Proceedings," *New York Herald*, March 31, 1804.

48. Henry Christophe to Jean-Jacques Dessalines, January 25, 1806, and Henry Christophe to Colonel Raymond, January 25, 1806, Copie de lettres (manuscript) 1805–6, FCO Historical Collection, FOL. F1924 HEN, King's College, London (hereafter Copie de lettres).

49. "People of Color," *Niles Weekly Register* (October 17, 1818): 117–18; James Tredwell, *The Constitution of the Republic of Hayti, to Which Is Added Documents Relating to the Correspondence of His Most Christian Majesty, with the President of Hayti, Preceded by a Proclamation to the People and the Army* (New York: James Tredwell, 1818), 4–7.

50. Original in "Constitution du 2 juin 1816."

51. "Constitution du 2 juin 1816."

52. "People of Color," 117–18.

53. Quoted in John E. Baur, "Mulatto Machiavelli, Jean Pierre Boyer, and the Haiti of His Day," *Journal of Negro History* 32, no. 3 (July 1947): 324–25.

54. "Du Cap-Henry, le 10 octobre," *Gazette royale d'Hayti*, October 17, 1816, 2.

55. Baron de Vastey, *Essai sur les causes de la révolution et des guerres civiles d'Hayti* (Sans-Souci, Haiti: L'Imprimerie Royale, 1819), 320–21.

56. Vastey, *Réflexions politiques*, 36. For an intriguing argument about Dessalines's desire to export the revolution in Haiti to the other colonies, see Deborah Jenson, "Before Malcolm X, Dessalines: A 'French' Tradition of Black Atlantic Radicalism," *International Journal of Francophone Studies* 10, no. 3 (2007): 340.

57. Joseph Saint-Rémy, introduction to *Mémoires pour servir l'histoire d'Haïti, par Boisrond-Tonnerre, précédés de différents actes politiques dus à sa plume, et d'une étude historique et critique* (Paris: France, Libraire, 1851), xxi.

58. [Joseph Rouanez], "Du Cap," *Gazette politique et commerciale*, October 17, 1805, 175–76; Christophe confirmed Rouanez as the author in a letter he wrote to Dessalines. See Henry Christophe to Jean-Jacques Dessalines, October 31, 1805, Copie de lettres.

378 Notes to Chapter 8

59. Gaffield, *Haitian Connections*, 152.

60. Henry Christophe to Jean-Jacques Dessalines, March 20, 1806, Copie de lettres.

61. Beaubrun Ardouin, *Réponse du sénateur B. Ardouin à une lettre de M. Isambert, conseiller à la cour de cassation de France, membre de la Chambre des Députés* (Port-au-Prince: Pinard, 1842), 16.

62. "Letters While Visiting Haiti," Stephen Grellet papers, HC.MC-967, File Box 1, Havorford Library, Bryn Mawr College.

63. Earl Leslie Griggs and Clifford H. Prator, eds., *Henry Christophe and Thomas Clarkson: A Correspondence* (Berkeley: University of California Press, 1952).

64. According to the exiled French journalist Jean-Gabriel Peltier, working to secure British recognition for Haiti on Christophe's behalf, immediately upon assuming the presidency Christophe offered "to buy any negroes that the English might procure in trading with Affrica in order to people Haiti in that case those negroes would become free," Handwritten note from Peltier, June 8, 1807, St. Domingo Foreign Agents 1807 to 1811, National Archives of the United Kingdom, WO 1/79. Many thanks to Julia Gaffield for sharing this box with me.

65. *Gazette royale d'Hayti*, October 10, 1817, 2–3.

66. "Fin du détail sur le voyage de S. A. S.: monseigneur le président," *Gazette officielle de l'état d'Hayti*, January 3, 1811, 2–3.

67. See José Luciano Franco, *Comercio clandestino de esclavos* (Havana: Editorial de Ciencias Sociales, 1996), 106.

68. Franco, *Comercio clandestino de esclavos*, 107.

69. Edgardo Pérez Morales, "Tricks of the Slave Trade: Cuba and the Small-Scale Dynamics of the Spanish Transatlantic Trade in Human Beings," *New West Indian Guide* 91, no. 1–2 (January 2017): 18; Blackburn, "Haiti," 671; for Pétion in this regard, see, Ada Ferrer, "Haiti, Free Soil and Antislavery in the Revolutionary Atlantic," *American Historical Review* 117, no. 1 (February 2012): 62–65.

70. "Anecdote of Jean Pierre Boyer, President of Hayti," *Anti-Slavery Record* (December 1, 1836): 160.

71. "British Antislavery Society," *Liverpool Mercury*, May 20, 1842.

72. Quoted in "General Items: Cuba and Haiti," *National Anti-Slavery Standard*, January 19, 1843.

73. Quoted in Lieutenant-Général Baron Pamphile de Lacroix, *Mémoires pour servir à l'histoire de la révolution de Saint-Domingue*, 2 vols. (Paris: Pillet Aine, 1819), 2:203–204.

74. Deborah Jenson, "Dessalines' American Proclamations of the Haitian Independence," *Journal of Haitian Studies* 15, no. 1&2 (2009): 77.

75. Dessalines, "Proclamation à Gonaïves."

76. Quoted in "General Items: Cuba and Haiti."

77. "Isle d'Haïti, Du Cap, le 14 novembre," *Gazette politique et commerciale*, November 13, 1806.

78. "General Items: Cuba and Haiti," *National Anti-Slavery Standard*, December 29, 1842.

79. "Le Dimanche, 22, l'on a publié la proclamation suivante: Proclamation. *Jean Pierre BOYER, Président d'Haïti*," *Feuille du Commerce*, May 29, 1842; "Intérieur," *Feuille du Commerce*, June 5, 1842; for earthquake felt in Arkansas, see "Philadelphia, May 29. [From Our Own Correspondent]," *Morning Chronicle*, June 15, 1842; and "The Earthquake in St. Domingo," *Morning Post*, June 16, 1842.

80. Demesvar Delorme, *1842 au Cap: Tremblement de terre* (Cap-Haïtien: Impr. du Progres, 1942), 2; "United States," *Morning Chronicle*, June 15, 1842.

81. Referenced in "Cuba and Hayti-War," *Baltimore Sunday Visiter* [sic], December 17, 1842, 2.

82. Delorme, *1842 au Cap*, 33.

83. Delorme, *1842 au Cap*, 33–34.

84. The United States paid sixty million francs ($11,250,000), plus canceled French debts amounting to twenty million francs ($3,750,000), for a total of eighty million francs or fifteen million dollars. "Louisiana Purchase Treaty (1803)," National Archives of the United States, accessed March 24, 2023, https://www.archives.gov/milestone-documents /louisiana-purchase-treaty; for French claims, see Désiré Dalloz, Philippe Dupin, Joseph-Élisabeth-George Merlhie de Lagrange, and Antoine Louis Marie Hennequin, *Consultation de MM. Dalloz, Delagrange, Hennequin, Dupin jeune et autres jurisconsultes pour les anciens colons de Saint-Domingue* (Paris: Hennequin, 1829), 60–61; and Liliana Obregón, "Empire, Racial Capitalism and International Law: The Case of Manumitted Haiti and the Recognition Debt," *Leiden Journal of International Law* 31, no. 3 (September 2018): 597–615.

85. "Louisiana Purchase Treaty (1803)."

86. "Proclamation au peuple et à l'armée," *Le Télégraphe*, July 17, 1825, 5.

87. M. R. Lepelletier de Saint-Rémy, *Saint-Domingue: Étude et solution nouvelle de la question haïtienne* (Paris: A. Bertrand, 1846), 2:121.

88. "Traités entre Hayti & La France: Au Nom de la Très Sainte et Indivisible Trinité," *L'-Union, recueil commercial et littéraire*, February 15, 1838, 1–2; A. M. *Emprunt d'Haïti, Réclamation des porteurs d'annuités, 31 octobre 1831* (Paris: Imprimerie de Sétier, 1831), 2; Catherine Porter, Constant Méhut, Matt Apuzzo, and Selam Gebrekidan, "Haiti 'Ransom' Project," *New York Times*, November 16, 2022, https://www.nytimes.com/spotlight/haiti.

89. [London dates to January 4], *New Hampshire Sentinel*, February 15, 1838; "Latest from England," *New Bedford Mercury*, February 2, 1838; "Important from Hayti," *Philadelphia National Enquirer*, March 15, 1838; for the unpopularity of the indemnity, see "West Indies," *Shepherd of the Valley*, December 20, 1833, 3; and "Hayti and France," *Zion's Watchman*, April 7, 1838, 56.

90. Porter et al., "Haiti 'Ransom' Project."

91. "West Indies."

92. Quoted in Benoît Joachim, "L'Indemnité coloniale de Saint-Domingue et la question des rapatriés," *Revue historique* 246, no. 2 (October–December 1971): 362.

93. Delorme, *1842 au Cap*, 22.

94. Joachim, "L'Indemnité coloniale," 362.

95. *Code Rural de Boyer, avec les commentaires de: Roger Petit-Frère, Jean Vandal, Georges, E. Werleigh*, ed. Roger Petit-Frère, Jean Vandal, and Georges E. Werleigh (Port-au-Prince: Coédition Archives Nationales d'Haïti/Maison H. Deschamps, 1992), 74.

96. Anténor Firmin, *M. Roosevelt, président des Étas-Unis et la République d'Haïti* (Paris: F. Pichon and Durand-Auzias, 1905), 325.

97. Schoelcher, *Colonies étrangères et Haïti*, 2:276.

98. Firmin, *M. Roosevelt*, 327.

99. Schoelcher, *Colonies étrangères et Haïti*, 2:197–98, 281.

100. Janvier, *La République*, 90-91; Dessalines, "Acte d'indépendance," January 1, 1804, Digithèque MJP, https://mjp.univ-perp.fr/constit/ht1804.htm; François-Marie Perichou de Kerversau, "Observations Politiques et Militaires sur la Colonie de St. Domingue et sur

380 Notes to Chapter 8

les moyens les plus analogues aux circonstances de venir à son secours," Archives Nationales de France (hereafter AN), AF/IV/1213, dossier 9; "Letter from General Dauxion Lavaysse to the President of Hayti," September 6, 1814, reprinted in Baron de Vastey, *An Essay on the Causes of the Revolution and Civil Wars of Hayti Being a Sequel to the Political Remarks upon Certain French Publications and Journals Concerning Hayti*, trans. William Hamilton (Exeter, UK: Western Luminary Office, 1823), Appendix B, no. 1, xv.

101. "Letter from General Dauxion Lavaysse, dated Kingston, the 1st of October, and addressed 'To His Excellency General Christophe, Supreme Chief of the Government of the North of Hayti'," in Vastey, *Essay on the Causes*, Appendix F, no. 2, xcviii.

102. Vastey, *Réflexions politiques*, 143–45, 146–47.

103. "Royaume d'Hayti. Du Cap-Henry, le 20 Novembre," *Gazette royale d'Hayti*, November 19, 1814, 4.

104. "Alexander Pétion, President of Hayti, to His Excellency General Dauxion Lavaysse," reprinted in Vastey, *Essay on the Causes*, Appendix B, no. 7, xxviii–xxix.

105. "France and Hayti," *Niles Weekly Register*, October 9, 1824, 85.

106. *Pièces officielles relatives aux négociations du gouvernement français avec le gouvernement haïtien, pour traiter de la formalité de la reconnaissance de l'indépendance d'Haïti* (Port-au-Prince: Imprimerie du gouvernement, 1824), 83–84; see also Obregón, "Empire, Racial Capitalism," 597–609.

107. "Port-au-Prince, le 6 Octobre 1824 . . . Circulaire. Jean-Pierre Boyer, Président d'Haïti, Aux Commandants d'Arrondissement," *Le Télégraphe*, October 9, 1824, 1.

108. "Recognition of the Independence of the Republic of Hayti by the French Government," *American Monitor* (London: 1824–1825), 2:268; see also, Julia Gaffield, "The Racialization of International Law after the Haitian Revolution: The Holy See and National Sovereignty," *American Historical Review* 125, no. 3 (June 2020): 841–68.

109. Hérard Dumesle, *Voyage dans le nord d'Hayti: ou, Révélations des lieux et des monuments historiques* (Aux Cayes, Haiti: De l'Imprimerie du Gouvernement, 1824), 339–40 fn. 0; Vastey, *Réflexions politiques*, 132.

110. Reprinted in Vastey, *Réflexions politiques*, 136.

111. Vastey, *Réflexions politiques*, 135–36, 141.

112. "Recognition of the Independence," 2:276–77.

113. *Ministère de la marine et des colonies: cabinet du ministre (très secrete)*, Paris, 17 Avril 1825, Archives Nationales de France, Paris, France, AP/156/I/20.

114. Schoelcher, *Colonies étrangères et Haïti*, 2:167.

115. Alex Dupuy, *Rethinking the Haitian Revolution: Slavery, Independence, and the Struggle for Recognition* (New York: Rowman & Littlefield, 2019), 114.

116. Vastey, *Réflexions politiques*, 128.

117. Schoelcher, *Colonies étrangères et Haïti*, 2:167–68, 169.

118. Dupuy, *Rethinking*, 114.

119. "Hayti," *U.S. Catholic Miscellany*, 1838; in 1833, the U.S.-based newspaper, *Shepherd of the Valley*, reported the French government sent an ultimatum to Haiti about the indemnity earlier that year. See, "West Indies."

120. Sudhir Hazareesingh, Bocas Lit. Festival, Port-of-Spain, Trinidad, April 2021.

121. Schoelcher, *Colonies étrangères et Haïti*, 2:233.

122. Schoelcher, *Colonies étrangères et Haïti*, 2:239–40.

123. Ardouin, *Réponse du Sénateur B*, 16.

124. James Franklin, *The Present State of Hayti (Saint Domingo), with Remarks on Its Agriculture, Commerce, Laws, Religion, Finances, and Population* (London: John Murray, 1828), 214, 9.

125. John Candler, *Brief Notices of Hayti* (London: Thomas Ward, 1842), 32.

126. Jonathan Brown, *The History and Present Condition of St. Domingo*, vol. 2 (Philadelphia: William Marshall Co., 1837), 186–87.

127. Brown, *History and Present Condition*, 2:205.

128. Thomas Madiou, *Histoire d'Haïti*, vol. 3 (Port-au-Prince, Impr. de J. Courtois, 1848), 419.

129. *Code Henry* (Cap-Henry, Haiti: P. Roux, 1812).

130. Reprinted and trans. in Prince Saunders, *Haytian Papers: A Collection of the Very Interesting Proclamations, and Other Official Documents: Together with Some Account of the Rise, Progress, and Present State of the Kingdom of Hayti* (London: W. Reed, 1816), vii–viii.

131. "Le Ministre des finances et de l'intérieur," *Gazette politique et commerciale*, August 15, 1805, 144.

132. "Empire d'Haïti: décret relatif aux testaments et autres actes portant donation de biens fonds," *Gazette politique et commerciale*, October 2, 1806, 152.

133. Henry Christophe to Col. Raymond, February 4, 1805, Copie de lettres.

134. "Du Cap, le 21 août," *Gazette politique et commerciale*, August 22, 1805, 147.

135. Reprinted in Prince Saunders, *A Memoir Presented to the American Convention for Promoting the Abolition of Slavery, and Improving the Condition of the African Race, December 11th, 1818: Containing Some Remarks upon the Civil Dissentions of the Hitherto Afflicted People of Hayti, as the Inhabitants of That Island May be Connected with Plans for the Emigration of Such Free Persons of Colour as May be Disposed to Remove to It, in Case Its Reunion, Pacification and Independence Should be Established: Together with Some Account of the Origin and Progress of the Efforts for Effecting the Abolition of Slavery in Pennsylvania and Its Neighbourhood, and throughout the World* (Philadelphia: Dennis Heartt, 1818), 18–19.

136. William Hamilton, "Advertisement by the Translator," in *An Essay on the Causes of the Revolution*, iii.

137. For Saunders, Wilberforce, and smallpox in Haiti, see "Introduction de la vaccine à Hayti," *Gazette royale d'Hayti*, February 8, 1816, 4; for Métral, see "De la littérature haïtienne," 1:530.

138. "King Henry to Thomas Clarkson: February 5, 1816," in Griggs and Prator, *Henry Christophe*, 91.

139. "Royaume d'Hayti. Proclamation: le roi, aux Haytiens," *Gazette royale d'Hayti*, January 9, 1817, 1–3; "Ordonnance du roi," *Gazette royale d'Hayti*, December 28, 1818, 1–3; see also, Marie-Louise Vendryes, introduction to *The Armorial of Haiti: Symbols of Nobility in the Reign of Henry Christophe*, ed. Clive Cheesman (London: College of Arms, 2007), 5.

140. Vastey, *Réflexions politiques*, 96.

141. Vastey, *Réflexions politiques*, 96–97. There were several small pensions for *white* female students in Cap-Français. For instance, in June 1780 a pension for "Jeunes Démoiselles" was established by Madame Sommavert in Cap. Located on the Rue Saint-Louis, the price was 1,500 colonial livres for a year of room and board. However, the ad for the pension noted that it was the parents who would have to find teachers for their daughters.

382 Notes to Chapter 8

Later, in February 1782, after relocating to the Rue Espagnole, Sommavert took out an ad to explain that her pension would from then on employ its own teachers to instruct young girls in geography, history, writing, arithmetic, art, music, and dance. Her school was popular enough that to "satisfy repeated demands," by November 1785, she opened it to female students at half-pension. See "Avis divers," *Affiches Américaines* (June 6, 1780): 2; "Avis divers," *Supplément aux Affiches Américaines* (February 13, 1782): 1; "Suite des avis divers," *Supplément aux Affiches Américaines* (November 9, 1785): 4.

142. Schoelcher, *Colonies étrangères et Haïti*, 2:242.

143. Schoelcher, *Colonies étrangères et Haïti*, 2:153–54.

144. *Code Henry*, vi.

145. "Fin du Coup-d'œil Politique sur la Situation actuelle du Royaume d'Hayti," *Gazette royale d'Hayti*, October 17, 1816, 2; Jean Price-Mars, *La Vocation de l'élite (Reproduit aux Ateliers Fardin pour compte de l'Inter-Philo, 1976–1977)* (Port-au-Prince: Imprimerie E. Chenet, 1919), 184–85.

146. "Fin du coup-d'œil politique sur la situation actuelle du Royaume d'Hayti," *Gazette royale d'Hayti*, October 17, 1816, 2–3.

147. Hérard Dumesle, *Voyage dans le nord d'Hayti: ou, Révélations des lieux et des monuments historiques* (Aux Cayes, Haiti: De l'Imprimerie du Gouvernement, 1824), 16.

148. "Christophe et ses admirateurs," *Le Propagateur haïtien* (October 15, 1823): 15.

149. Dumesle, *Voyage*, 245. Using the name Amazone to refer to warrior women stems from ancient Greek mythology and has also been associated with a body of mythical female soldiers in South America, which is what Dumesle likely refers to with the phrase "ancient American institution." However, in the nineteenth century, as Hélène d'Almeida-Topor has written, "Europeans called the female soldiers of the king of Dahomey" the "amazones." Given the fact that King Henry's personal guards were called the Royal Dahomets, the kingdom's "Amazones" were thus likely named after this female corps of Fon soldiers, which existed since the seventeenth century. Hélène d'Almeida-Topor, *Les Amazones: Une armée de femmes dans l'Afrique précoloniale* (Bescançon, France: Éditions La Lanterne Magique, 2016), 13, 16–17.

150. "Suite de la fête de S.M. La Reine," *Gazette royale d'Hayti*, August 24, 1816, 1–4.

151. Juste Chanlatte, *L'Entrée du roi en sa capitale, Opéra vaudeville en un acte* (Sans-Souci, Haiti: De l'imprimerie royale, 1818), 32–33.

152. "Ordonnance du roi," *Gazette royale d'Hayti*, August 26, 1816, 3; "Fin du Coup-d'œil Politique," 3.

153. Derek Walcott, "The Sea Is History," *Paris Review* 74 (Fall/Winter 1978), www.theparisreview.org/poetry/7020/the-sea-is-history-derek-walcott.

154. "Fin du coup-d'œil politique," 3.

155. "Coup d'oeil politique sur la situation actuelle du Royaume d'Hayti," *Gazette royale d'Hayti*, August 26, 1816, 4.

156. Derek Walcott, *What the Twilight Says: Essays* (New York: Farrar, Straus and Giroux, 1998), 13.

157. Chanlatte, *Le Cri*, 26.

158. "Au Cap-Henry, le 5 Juin 1816," *Gazette royale d'Hayti*, June 6, 1816, 1.

159. "Fête de l'indépendance: de Sans-Souci, le 3 janvier," *Gazette royale d'Hayti*, January 4, 1815, 1–2.

160. "Royaume d'Hayti," *Gazette royale d'Hayti*, July 19, 1815, 4.

161. "De Sans-Souci, le 28 mars," *Gazette royale d'Hayti*, March 31, 1818, 3; on Christophe's efforts to prevent food dependency, see also William Hamilton, *Memoir on the Cultivation of Wheat within the Tropics* (Plymouth, UK: Henry H. Heydon, 1840), 9–10.

162. Comte de Limonde (Julien Prévost), *Instructions pour les établissemens et la culture des habitations caféyères de la couronne* (Sans-Souci, Haiti: De L'Imprimerie Royale, 1818), 4–5.

163. Vastey, *Réflexions politiques*, 108–9.

164. Vastey, *Réflexions politiques*, 112.

165. Hamilton, *Memoir*, 10.

166. Reprinted in Thomas Madiou, *Histoire d'Haïti: 1811–1818*, vol. 5 (Port-au-Prince: Éditions Henri Deschamps, 1988), 431; to see how the system worked to allow any Haitian to purchase a farm by theoretically borrowing from its future revenues to take possession in advance of payment, see "Suite du RAPPORT fait au ROI, par le Grand Conseil d'État et Motifs du Projet de Loi sur la Vente des Biens Domaniaux du Royaume," *Gazette royale d'Hayti*, June 19, 1817, 4.

167. "William Wilson to Thomas Clarkson: December 5, 1820," in Griggs and Prator, *Henry Christophe*, 215, italics in original.

168. Dumesle, *Voyage*, 233.

169. Dumesle, *Voyage*, 336 fn. d.

170. Dumesle, *Voyage*, 272–73.

171. "Réflexions de l'éditeur," *Gazette royale d'Hayti*, March 31, 1818, 2–3.

172. Caleb Cushing, "Article VI: Hayti. Reflexions politiques sur quelques ouvrages et journaux Français," *North American Review and Miscellaneous Journal* 3, no. 1 (January 1821): 119.

173. See "Adresse au peuple et à l'armée," *Gazette officielle*, May 14, 1807, 8.

174. Madiou, *Histoire d'Haïti: 1811–1818*, 5:430.

175. Quoted in Comte de Limonade (Julien Prévost), *Relation des glorieux événements qui ont porté leurs majestés royales sur le trône d'Hayti* (Cap-Henry, Haiti: P. Roux, 1811), 153.

176. Dumesle, *Voyage*, 247–48.

177. "De Sans-Souci, le 25 octobre," *Gazette royale d'Hayti*, October 28, 1819, 2. Many thanks to scholar Henry Stoll for sharing this issue with me, the original of which can be found in the Archivo General de la Nación, Colombia, "Ministerio de lo Interior y Relaciones Exteriores" (1819), file 148, folio 547.

178. William Wilson to Thomas Clarkson, November 4, 1820, Clarkson and Christophe Manuscript Correspondence, British Library, London, UK (hereafter BL), MS. 41266.

179. Duncan Stewart to Thomas Clarkson, December 8, 1820, Clarkson and Christophe Manuscript Correspondence, BL.

180. Jean-Pierre Boyer, "Ordre du Jour," *Le Télégraphe*, October 22, 1820, 3.

181. *Code Rural de Boyer*, 71, 89.

182. "De la chute de Christophe (suite de l'article inséré au no. 9)," *Le Propagateur haïtien*, no. 11 (June 15, 1823): 11.

183. See "Port-au-Prince: addresse au peuple et à l'armée," *Le Télégraphe*, November 5, 1820, 1–2.

184. Walcott, *What the Twilight Says*, 13.

185. Vastey, *Réflexions politiques*, 55.

Chapter 9

1. Quoted in Baron de Vastey (Jean Louis), *Réflexions sur une lettre de Mazères: ex-colon français, adressée à M. J.C.L. Sismonde de Sismondi, sur les noirs et les blancs, la civilisation de l'Afrique, le royaume d'Hayti* (Cap-Haïtien: P. Roux, 1816), 105; original in [François] Mazères, *Lettre à M. J.-C.-L. Sismonde de Sismondi, sur les nègres, la civilisation de l'Afrique, Christophe et le comte de Limonade* (Paris: Chez Renard, 1815), 5; see also J. C. L. Simonde de Sismondi, *De l'Intérêt de la France à l'égard de la traite des nègres* (Geneva: J. J. Paschoud, 1814); for Mazères as "planter" from Quartier-Morin, see "Effets Perdus," *Les Affiches Américaines* (March 2, 1768): 76; Mazères placed numerous ads for "nègres marrons" who escaped his plantation in the *Affiches Américaines* from 1766 to 1772. Most of the issues have been digitized by LLMC Digital and can be accessed on their website, https://llmc.com /titledescfull.aspx?type=2&coll=145&div=410&set=31772.

2. Vastey, *Réflexions sur une lettre*, 105–06.

3. Vastey, *Réflexions sur une lettre*, 86, italics in original.

4. Vastey, *Réflexions sur une lettre*, 86–87.

5. Mazères, *Lettre*, 11, 36, 38, 56.

6. Vastey, *Réflexions sur une lettre*, 86–87.

7. Baron de Vastey, *Réflexions politiques sur quelques ouvrages et journaux français concernant Hayti* (Sans-Souci, Haiti: Royal Imprint, 1817), 28.

8. Baron de Vastey, *Essai sur les causes de la révolution et des guerres civiles d'Hayti* (Sans-Souci, Haiti: L'Imprimerie Royale, 1819), 4.

9. Vastey, *Essai*, 127–28, italics in original.

10. "Constitution du 20 mai 1805," Digithèque MJP, http://mjp.univ-perp.fr/constit/ht1805 .htm.

11. Anténor Firmin, *De l'Égalité des races humaines* (Paris: F. Pichon, 1885), 210.

12. Émeric Bergeaud, *Stella* (Paris: E. Dentu, 1859), 134–35.

13. Baron de Vastey, *Réflexions politiques*, 18.

14. [Juste Chanlatte], *À Mes concitoyens* (Port-au-Prince: De l'Imprimerie du gouvernement, [1804]), 4.

15. "Acte d'indépendance," January 1, 1804, Digithèque MJP, https://mjp.univ-perp.fr /constit/ht1804.htm.

16. "Constitution du 20 mai 1805."

17. Sibylle Fischer, *Modernity Disavowed: Haiti and the Cultures of Slavery in the Age of Revolution* (Durham, NC: Duke University Press, 2004), 232–33.

18. Jean Casimir, "Prologue," in *The World of the Haitian Revolution*, ed. David Patrick Geggus and Norman Fiering (Bloomington: Indiana University Press, 2009), xv.

19. Anthony Bogues, "The Dual Haitian Revolution and the Making of Freedom in Modernity," in *Human Rights from a Third World Perspective: Critique, History and International Law*, ed. José-Manuel Barreto (Newcastle, UK: Cambridge Scholars Publishing, 2013), 229–30.

20. Cheryl Harris, "Whiteness as Property," *Harvard Law Review* 106, no. 8 (June 1993): 1721.

21. Comte de Limonade (Julien Prévost), *Relation des glorieux événements qui ont porté leurs majestés royales sur le trône d'Hayti* (Cap-Henry, Haiti: P. Roux, 1811), 23–24.

22. Jean-Jacques Dessalines, "Proclamation à Gonaïves, 28 April 1804," October 30, 2015, Dessalines Reader, ed. Julia Gaffield, https://haitidoi.com/2015/10/30/dessalines-reader-28-april-1804/.

23. Julia Gaffield, *Haitian Connections in the Atlantic World: Recognition after Revolution* (Chapel Hill: University of North Carolina Press, 2015), 90–91; in 1867, there was a change of wording regarding the ban of "whites," which was replaced by the word "foreigners." See Claude Moïse, *Constitutions et luttes de pouvoir en Haïti (1804–1987)* (Montréal: CIDIHCA, 1988), 32.

24. Vastey, *Essai*, 318, 320, italics mine.

25. Quoted in Baron de Vastey, *Notes à M. le Baron de V.P. Malouet, ministre de la marine et des colonies . . . en réfutation du 4ème volume de son ouvrage, intitulé: Collection de mémoires sur les colonies et particulièrement sur Saint-Domingue* (Cap-Henry, Haiti: P. Roux, 1814), 8.

26. Vastey, *Notes*, iii, 9–10.

27. Vastey, *Notes*, 13.

28. "Instructions for MM: Dauxion Lavaysse, de Médina and Dravermann, published by order of King Henry," reprinted in Vastey, *An Essay on the Causes of the Revolution and Civil Wars of Hayti Being a Sequel to the Political Remarks upon Certain French Publications and Journals Concerning Hayti*, trans. William Hamilton (Exeter, UK: Western Luminary Office, 1823), Appendix C, no. 1, xxxiii–xxxix.

29. Vastey, *Essai*, iii–iv.

30. "Royaume d'Hayti. Proclamation: le Roi, aux Haytiens," *Gazette royale d'Hayti*, January 9, 1817, 2. All issues consulted at https://lagazetteroyale.com.

31. In modern Creole orthography this would be written, "Chè zamni nous yo, pinga miyò pase padon," and is likely an early iteration of the Haitian proverb, "evite miyò pase mande padon," meaning it is better not to make a mistake than to be sorry. Many thanks to Laura Wagner for her assistance with this translation.

32. A. L. D., "Discours deux. Les Français. De supplices. Sur les supplices," *Le Télégraphe*, May 9, 1824, 1–3.

33. Prévost, *Relation*, xiii–xiv.

34. Prévost, *Relation*, xii.

35. Prévost, *Relation*, xiv–xv.

36. Firmin, *De l'Égalité*, 542.

37. Firmin, *De l'Égalité*, 655–56.

38. See "Haïti reconnue indépendante," *Le Télégraphe*, July 17, 1825, 1. A copy of the "Ordonnance" from the French king Charles X is reprinted on p. 5 of the same issue.

39. "Recognition of the Independence of the Republic of Hayti by the French Government," *American Monitor* (London, 1824–1825): 270.

40. See, for example, Joseph Joachim Victor Chauvet's poem *Haïti, chant lyrique* (Paris: Chez de la Forest, 1825); [Nicholas] Vigor-Renaudière, *Le Chant haïtien: Hommage à S.M. Charles X; à l'occasion de l'émancipation d'Haïti* (Paris: Chez Tous les Libraires Blancs ou Noirs, 1825); and for the engraving, "S.M. Charles X, le bien-aimé, reconnaissant l'indépendance de St. Domingue," 1825, Bibliotheque Nationale de France, Paris, France, QB-1 (1825-10)-FOL, https://images.bnf.fr/#/detail/1338144/1.

41. There are numerous ads for "maroon negroes" stamped Chanlatte, Chanlat, Chanlate, or some variation thereof, in the *Affiches Américaines*. See, for example, "Nègres Ma-

rons," *Affiches Américaines* (May 26, 1778): 162; and perhaps most notably on October 5, 1782, an ad described group marronage from the Chanlatte plantation in Mont-Rouis when the month before "five maroons" tried to escape by canoe. "Esclaves en Marronage," *Supplément aux Affiches Américaines* (October 5, 1782): 4. For Chanlatte's family history, see Grégory Pierrot, "Juste Chanlatte: A Haitian Life," *Journal of Haitian Studies* 25, no. 1 (Spring 2019): 39–65; for a discussion of the common phenomenon of group marronage, see Crystal Nicole Eddins, *Rituals, Runaways, and the Haitian Revolution: Collective Actions in the African Diaspora* (Cambridge: Cambridge University Press, 2022), 180–81.

42. Chanlatte, *À Mes concitoyens*, 6.

43. Chanlatte, *Le Cri de la nature* (Cap-Haïtien: P. Roux, 1810), 5.

44. Juste Chanlatte, "Les vingt premiers jours du mois d'Octobre 1820 an 17: Est-ce un rêve?" *Le Télégraphe, gazette officielle*, November 5, 1820, 4; Juste Chanlatte, *Henry Christophe* (Cap-Haïtien: Imprimerie du Gouvernment, 1820), Moorland-Spingarn Research Center, Howard University. This item has been miscatalogued as written by Chanlatte's brother, François Desriviers Chanalatte [*sic*], but it is signed "le général Chanlatte aîné," which is the appellation Juste used, and not that of his younger brother François. See also Pierrot, "Juste Chanlatte."

45. "Le Général Chanlatte a chanté les suivans," *Le Propagateur haïtien, journal littéraire, commercial et politique* (January 15, 1826): 7–8.

46. Demesvar Delorme, *La Démocratie et le préjugé de couleur aux Étas-Unis d'Amérique/Les Nationalités américaines et le système Monroë* (Brussels: H. Thiry-Van Buggenhoudt, 1866), 19–20.

47. Delorme, *La Démocratie*, 18.

48. Delorme, *La Démocratie*, 24.

49. Delorme, *La Démocratie*, 24.

50. James Baldwin, "The War Crimes Tribunal," *Freedomways* 7, no. 3 (Summer 1967): 244.

51. Fernand Hibbert, *Les Thazar* (Port-au-Prince: Éditions H. Deschamps, 1988), 84.

52. All quotations from this speech taken from "Monroe Doctrine," 1823, National Archives of the United States, Washington, DC, https://www.archives.gov/milestone-documents/monroe-doctrine#:~:text=President%20James%20Monroe's%201823%20annual, nations%20of%20the%20Western%20Hemisphere.

53. For an analysis of this speech see Gretchen Murphy, *Hemispheric Imaginings: The Monroe Doctrine and Narratives of U.S. Empire* (Durham, NC: Duke University Press, 2005), 6.

54. Murphy, *Hemispheric Imaginings*, 27.

55. An article titled "German Rage at the Monroe Doctrine," for example, begins, "The Monroe Doctrine is founded on the catch-phrase 'America for the Americans,'" *Literary Digest* 44 (May 11, 1912): 978–99.

56. Delorme, *La Démocratie*, 44.

57. There are at least three books called *America for the Americans*, but none fully accounts for the genealogy of the phrase. See Edward P. Crapol, *America for the Americans: Economic Nationalism and Anglophobia in the Late Nineteenth Century* (Westport, CT: Greenwood Press, 1973); Dale T. Knobel, *"America for the Americans": The Nativist Movement in the United States* (New York: Twayne Publishers, 1996); and, more recently, Erika Lee, *America for Americans: A History of Xenophobia in the United States* (New York: Basic Books, 2019).

58. "America for Americans," *Times-Picayune*, June 25, 1851, 2.

59. "America for Americans," *Christian Inquirer* (July 29, 1853): 2.

60. "Ireland in America," *Littel's Living Age* (May 6, 1854): 5.520: 259.

61. "America for the Americans," *Putnam's Monthly* (1855): 533.

62. "America for the Americans," *Putnam's Monthly*, 536.

63. "America for the Americans," *Putnam's Monthly*, 536, 538.

64. See Natalia Molina, *Fit to Be Citizens? Public Health and Race in Los Angeles, 1879–1939* (Berkeley: University of California Press, 2006), 176.

65. See Hiram Bingham, "The Latin American Attitude toward the Monroe Doctrine," *Proceedings of the American Society of International Law at Its Annual Meeting* 8 (April 22–25, 1914): 186.

66. Delorme, *La Démocratie*, 45.

67. Delorme, *La Démocratie*, 46.

68. Aimé Césaire, *Discourse on Colonialism*, trans. Joan Pinkham (New York: Monthly Review Press, 2000), 77–78, italics in original.

69. Delorme, *La Démocratie*, 47.

70. Césaire, *Discourse on Colonialism*, 77.

71. W. E. B. Du Bois, *The Crisis* 10, no. 6 (October 1915): 290–92. The "White Admiral" Du Bois references was Major Smedley Butler, who commanded the newly formed Haitian gendarmerie and used the *Code Rural* to impose a large corveé on the Haitian people to repair the country's roads, the better to achieve more complete "military control of the country." See Kate Ramsey, *The Spirits and the Law: Vodou and Power in Haiti* (Chicago: University of Chicago Press, 2011), 125; see also the more recently published biography by Jonathan M. Katz, *Gangsters of Capitalism: Smedley Butler, the Marines, and the Making and Breaking of America's Empire* (New York: St. Martin's Press, 2022).

72. Delorme, *La Démocratie*, 48, 49–50.

73. For Delorme on the U.S. border, see Marlene L. Daut, "Caribbean 'Race Men': Louis Joseph Janvier, Demesvar Delorme, and the Haitian Atlantic," *L'Esprit créateur* 56, no. 1 (Spring 2016), 9–23.

74. Delorme, *La Démocratie*, 25.

75. Ramón Emeterio Betances, "AL.G.D.P.A.D.L.U," in *Betances*, ed. Luis Bonafoux (San Juan, Puerto Rico: Inst. de Cultura Puertoriqueña, 1970), 111.

76. Silvio Torres-Saillant, *An Intellectual History of the Caribbean* (New York: Palgrave Macmillan, 2016), 144.

77. Jossianna Arroyo, *Writing Secrecy in Caribbean Freemasonry* (New York: Palgrave Macmillan, 2013), 74, 82.

78. Marlene L. Daut, "Before Harlem: The Franco-Haitain Grammar of Transnational African American Writing," *J19: The Journal of Nineteenth-Century Americanists* 3, no. 2 (Fall 2015): 387–89.

79. Louis Joseph Janvier, *La République d'Haïti et ses visiteurs (1840–1882): réponse à M. Victor Cochinat (de la petite presse) et à quelques autres écrivains* (Paris: Marpon et Flammarion, 1883), 89.

80. Demesvar Delorme, *La Misère au sein des richesses, réflexions diverses sur Haïti* (Paris: E. Dentu, 1873), 124, 127.

81. Delorme, *La Misère*, 133.

82. Yves Chemla, "Louis Joseph Janvier," *Île en île*, June 12, 2005, updated April 25, 2021, https://ile-en-ile.org/janvier/

83. Janvier, *La République*, xvi.

84. See Patrick Bellegarde-Smith, "Overview of Haitian Foreign Policy and Relations: A Schematic Analysis," in *Haiti: Today and Tomorrow: An Interdisciplinary Study*, ed. Charles Foster and Albert Valdman (Lanham, MD: University Press of America, 1984), 265–81; and G. Pope Atkins and Larman C. Wilson, *The Dominican Republic and the United States: From Imperialism to Transnationalism* (Athens: University of Georgia Press, 1998), 16–24.

85. Delorme, *La Misère*, 131.

86. J. Michael Dash, "Nineteenth-Century Haiti and the Archipelago of the Americas: Anténor Firmin's Letters from St. Thomas," *Research in African Literatures* 35, no. 2 (2004): 50.

87. Janvier, *La République*, 92–93.

88. Janvier, *La République*, 105.

89. Delorme, *La Misère*, 81–82.

90. Delorme, *La Misère*, 127.

91. Janvier, *La République*, 120.

92. Christopher Miller, *The French Atlantic Triangle: Literature and Culture of the Slave Trade* (Durham, NC: Duke University Press, 2008).

93. Robert Cornevin, "L'Oncle n'est plus: Jean Price-Mars (1876–1969) Champion de la Négri-tude," *France-Eurafrique* 205 (1969): 5.

94. René Depestre, "An Interview with Aimé Césaire," in Césaire, *Discourse on Colonialism*, 86.

95. Jean Price-Mars, *La Vocation de l'élite (Reproduit aux Ateliers Fardin pour compte de l'Inter-Philo, 1976–1977)* (Port-au-Prince: Imprimerie E. Chenet, 1919), 177–78.

96. Price-Mars, *La Vocation*, 89.

97. Price-Mars, *La Vocation*, 40–41.

98. Janvier, *La République*, 90–93.

99. Janvier, *La République*, 57.

100. Janvier, *La République*, 56.

101. Quoted in Depestre, "An Interview," 85.

102. See Martha Cobb, *Harlem, Haiti, and Havana: A Comparative Critical Study of Langston Hughes, Jacques Roumain, Nicolás Guillén* (New York: Three Continents Press, 1979); and Vera Kutzinski, *The Worlds of Langston Hughes: Modernism and Translation in the Americas* (Ithaca, NY: Cornell University Press, 2012).

103. Janvier quoted from Betances's translation (i.e., Janvier's own French translation of Betances's Spanish) in *La République*, 454–58.

104. Ramón Emeterio Betances, "Lettre de M. le Dr. Betances," in *Les Détracteurs de la race noire et de la République d'Haïti* (Paris: Marpon et Flammarion, 1882), 5–10.

105. Paul Estrade, *Les Écrits de Betances dans la presse latino-américaine de Paris* (Paris: Publications de l'Équipe de Recherches de l'Université de Paris VIII, 1988), iv.

106. Reprinted in Estrade, *Les Écrits*, 11, 15.

107. Delorme, *La Misère*, 131.

108. Arroyo, *Writing*, 84–85, 161.

109. Reprinted in Estrade, *Les Écrits*, 16.

110. Louis Joseph Janvier, *Haïti aux Haïtiens* (Paris: Imprimerie A. Parent, A. Davy, 1884), 18.

111. Estrade, *Les Écrits*, vii.

112. Yves Chemla, "Démesvar Delorme," Île en île, updated April 25, 2021, http://ile-en -ile.org/delorme/. See also Raphaël Berrou and Pradel Pompilus, *Histoire de la littérature haïtienne illustrée par les textes*, 3 vols. (Port-au-Prince: Édition Caraïbes, 1975–77), 1:546–50.

113. Yves Chemla, "Louis Joseph Janvier, écrivain national," *Francofonia* 49 (Autumn 2005): 8–9.

114. Jean Price-Mars, *Ainsi, parla l'oncle* (Montréal, Québec: Leméac Collection Caraïbe, 1973), 46; Chemla, "Louis Joseph Janvier," 30.

115. Raphael Dalleo, *Caribbean Literature and the Public Sphere: From the Plantation to the Postcolonial* (Charlottesville: University of Virginia Press, 2011), 5.

116. Dalleo, *Caribbean*, 8.

117. Delorme, *La Misère*, 133.

118. Janvier, *La République*, xxi.

119. Louis Morpeau, *Anthologie d'un siècle de poésie haïtienne, 1817–1925, Avec une étude sur la muse haïtienne d'expression française et une étude sur la muse haïtienne d'expression créole* (Paris: Éditions Bossard, 1925), 1.

120. Jean Bernabé, Patrick Chamoiseau, and Raphaël Confiant, "In Praise of Creoleness," trans. Mohamed B. Taleb Khyar, *Callaloo* 13, no. 4 (Autumn 1990): 898, italics in original.

121. Bernabé et al., "In Praise of Creoleness," 894, italics in original.

122. Janvier, *La République*, 240, italics in original.

123. Janvier, *La République*, 122.

124. Janvier, *Haïti aux Haïtiens*, 19.

125. "Mr. Sprague of Monson," in *Memorial Addresses on the Life and Character of James Gillespie Blaine* (Augusta, ME: Burleigh and Flynt, 1893), 42.

126. Janvier, *Haïti aux Haïtiens*, 20, italics in original.

127. Janvier, *Haïti aux Haïtiens*, 22.

128. Janvier, *Haïti aux Haïtiens*, 30.

129. Delorme, *La Misère*, 119, italics in original.

130. Delorme, *La Misère*, 124.

131. Delorme, *La Misère*, 128, italics in original.

132. Delorme, *La Misère*, 130.

133. Delorme, *La Misère*, 130–31.

134. Janvier, *La République*, 18.

135. Delorme, *La Misère*, 132, italics in original.

136. Firmin, *De l'Égalité*, 495.

137. Firmin, *De l'Égalité*, 530.

138. Firmin, *De l'Égalité*, 533.

139. Firmin, *De l'Égalité*, 543.

140. Janvier, *La République*, 92.

141. Firmin, *De l'Égalité*, 566.

142. Firmin, *De l'Égalité*, 567.

143. Firmin, *De l'Égalité*, 569–70.

144. Delorme, *La Démocratie*, 7, 24.

145. Michel Rolph Trouillot, "The Odd and the Ordinary: Haiti, the Caribbean, and the World," *Cimarrón: New Perspectives on the Caribbean* 2, no. 3 (1990): 7.

146. Walt Whitman, *Complete Prose Works: Specimen Days and Collect, November Boughs and Good Bye My Fancy*, Project Gutenberg, last updated June 2, 2013, www.gutenberg.org/files/8813/8813-h/8813-h.htm.

147. Delorme, *La Démocratie*, 10.

148. Firmin, *De l'Égalité*, 598.

149. Firmin, *De l'Égalité*, 590.

Epilogue

1. In his article "Rethinking Romanticism," Jerome McGann summarized the debates about when the romantic period began and ended with the longer end of the spectrum spanning from 1789 to 1837. McGann also distinguished between "the romantic period," as a "particular historical epoch," and "romanticism" as a "set of cultural/ideological formations that came to prominence during the romantic period." Jerome McGann, "Rethinking Romanticism," *English Literary History* 59, no. 3 (1992): 741, 735.

2. Jacquelin Dolcé, Gérard Dorval, and Jean Miotel Casthely, *Le Romantisme en Haïti: La Vie intellectuelle, 1804–1915* (Port-au Prince: Éditions Fardin, 1983), 5–9.

3. Dolcé et al., *Le Romantisme*, 6.

4. Ludwell Lee Montague, *Haiti and the United States* (Durham, NC: Duke University Press, 1940), 94; Hans Schmidt, *The United States Occupation of Haiti, 1915–1935* (New Brunswick, NJ: Rutgers University Press, 1995), 31.

5. "Secretary of Legation Davis to the Secretary of State," January 12, 1916, Papers Relating to the Foreign Relations of the United States, with the Address of the President to Congress, December 5, 1916, Office of the Historian of the United States, Washington, DC, file no. 838.00/1375, https://history.state.gov/historicaldocuments/frus1916/d352; Patrick Bellegarde-Smith, *In the Shadow of the Powers: Dantès Bellegarde in Haitian Social Thought* (Nashville, TN: Vanderbilt University Press, 2019), 19.

6. "An Iconic Image of Haitian Liberty," *New Yorker*, July 28, 2015, https://www.newyorker.com/culture/photo-booth/haiti-u-s-occupation-charlemagne-peralte; see also Yveline Alexis, *Haiti Fights Back: The Life and Legacy of Charlemagne Péralte* (New Brunswick, NJ: Rutgers University Press, 2021).

7. Quoted in Kate Ramsey, *The Spirits and the Law: Vodou and Power in Haiti* (Chicago: University of Chicago Press, 2011), 125.

8. Emily Greene Balch, ed., *Occupied Haiti: Being the Report of a Committee of Six Disinterested Americans Representing Organizations Exclusively American, Who, Having Personally Studied Conditions in Haiti in 1926, Favor the Restoration of the Independence of the Negro Republic* (New York: Writers Publishing Company, 1927), 131.

9. Dolcé et al., *Le Romantisme*, 30; Doris Y. Kadish and Deborah Jenson, eds., *Poetry of Haitian Independence*, trans. Norman Shapiro (New Haven, CT: Yale University Press, 2015); and *Haitian Revolutionary Fictions: An Anthology*, ed. and trans. Marlene L. Daut, Grégory Pierrot, and Marion Rohrleitner (Charlottesville: University of Virginia Press, 2022).

10. Jean Price-Mars, *La Vocation de l'élite (Reproduit aux Ateliers Fardin pour compte de l'Inter-Philo, 1976–1977)* (Port-au-Prince: Imprimerie E. Chenet, 1919), ii–iii, 29.

11. Editorial Staff, "Classical Books on Haiti: Introspection into the 'Unknown': Critical Works in Haitian and Social Literature by Haitians and Others," *Journal of Haitian Studies* 10, no. 1 (2004): 188–89.

12. Louis Morpeau, ed., *Anthologie d'un siècle de poésie haïtienne, 1817–1925, Avec une étude sur la muse haïtienne d'expression française et une étude sur la muse haïtienne d'expression créole* (Paris: Éditions Bossard, 1925), xiv.

13. Émeric Bergeaud, *Stella* (Paris: E. Dentu, 1859), 57.

14. "Acte d'indépendance," January 1, 1804, Digithèque MJP, https://mjp.univ-perp.fr /constit/ht1804.htm.

15. Michel-Rolph Trouillot, *Ti dife boule sou istwa Ayiti*, rev. ed. (Port-au-Prince: Edisyon KIK, 2012), 118, 119.

16. "Suite du Coup-d'œil Politique sur la Situation actuelle du Royaume d'Hayti," *Gazette royale d'Hayti*, August 27, 1816, 2–3.

17. Michel-Rolph Trouillot, *Silencing the Past: Power and the Production of History* (New York: Beacon, 1995), xix.

Index

Note: Page numbers in italics refer to illustrations.

L'Abeille Haytienne, 235

abolition of slavery, 130–65; by Bolívar, 233, 235; in Brazil, 248–49; in Cuba, 249; doctrines/meaning of, 102, 131; emancipation decrees by Sonthonax and Polverel, 56, 130–38, 140–44, 146–47, 150, 183–86; by France, 5, 49, 56, 120, 129–30, 141, 150, 249–50, 255; in Gran Colombia, 233, 235, 240, 373n110; by Great Britain, 205, 249–50, 256, 263–64; Haitian Revolution's influence on, 26; Haiti's role in, 250; and independence, 136–37, 144; in Jamaica, 145–46; labor following (*see* affermage labor system); leaders of the struggle, 93, 120, 135–37, 141–45 (*see also* Black freedom fighters); in Martinique, 247; by Mexico, 249; Michelet on, 19; in the Netherlands, 249; in Puerto Rico, 248–49; removing the signs/remnants of slavery, 133–34, 280–81, 286; in South America, 249; in the U.S., 243, 247, 249–50, 255–56; in Venezuela, 235; in Vermont, 248; white colonists' reactions to, 134

Acquaire, M.: *Arlequin mulâtresse, protégé par Macanda,* 110

Acte d'Indépendance. See Declaration of Independence (Haiti)

Adorno, Theodor, 63

affermage (leasing) labor system: chattel slavery, 198; establishment of, 131; vs. feudalism, 197–98; of Toussaint Louverture, 147–49, 182, 185, 193–96; paternalistic language of, 186; of Polverel, 135–36, 147, 183–85; punishment of laborers, 183, 364n54; of Raimond, 147,

182, 184–85, 193–94; resistance to, 147–49; revenues from state-run farms under, 277; of Sonthonax, 147, 182–85. *See also* Code Henry

Affiches Américaines, 59–60, 85, 97–98, 110

A. L. D. (anonymous writer), 302

Alexander, Leslie, 218

Alexander, Nathan G., 56

Almeida-Topor, Hélène d', 383n149

Althusser, Louis, 4

Altman, Ida, 47–48

Amazones, 282–83, 383n149

American exceptionalism, 228

American Revolution, 121–22, 244

American War of Independence, 127, 355n110

À Mes concitoyens (J. Chanlatte), 175–76, 213, 215, 306

Amiens, Treaty of (1802), 151, 170–71, 300–301

Anacaona, Queen, 31, 36–40, 48, *48*–49

Anderson, Benedict, 17; *Imagined Communities,* 16

anti-colonialism, 211–46; anti-capitalist, 222; Bolívar's anti-colonial mission, 232–33; Buxton on, 223–24; consequences of, 225–26; of the Constitution of 1805, 220–21, 225–26; defining colonialism as bad, 223; first constitutions' (1805–16) influence on, 222–23; of the Haitian Declaration of Independence, xviii–xix, 121, 211–13, 218–21, 226; and Haitian interventions in the Americas, 231–33, 235–36; in Haiti vs. the U.S., 218, 253; of intellectuals of the Americas, 222, 246; normativity of, 221–22, 226; of Pan-Africanism, 226; of radical Black

anti-colonialism (*continued*)
  intellectual traditions, 226; reunification efforts vs. conquest, 241–42, 245; sovereignty as key to, 229; and the U.S. occupation of Haiti, 222. *See also* 1804 Principle
anti-imperialism, 222, 307
anti-racism, 294–325; anti-racism movement, 93; of Delorme, 306–12; disruption of white supremacy, 295–97, 304; of Firmin (see *De l'Égalité des races humaines*); of Haitian writers, 303–5; human diversity argument, 296–97; as a humanistic imperative, 307; of Michelet, 18–20; revolutionary history and Haitian sovereignty in service of, 305
antislavery, 247–93; Juste Chanlatte's contributions to, 250–51; Christian argument, 125–26; Constitution of 1805 on, 223, 225, 248; Constitution of 1806 on, 228, 248; Constitution of 1807 on, 248; culture of, 279–80, 282, 286; Benjamin Franklin's petition to end slavery, 248; free soil policy, 257–60, 263–64; Haitian authors' antislavery statements disseminated, 254–55; and Haitian independence, 247–48, 254–56 (*see also* Haitian independence; Haitian Revolution); Haitian interference with the slave trade, 256–58; Haitian people's commitment to, 264; Haitian Revolution's influence on, 249–52, 254–56, 376n12; Haiti as a safe haven for the enslaved of the world, 257–58, 262; Haiti transformed from a slave society to a living society, 65–66, 279; newspaper coverage of antislavery efforts, 257–59, 263–66; proposed ban on the international slave trade, 248; relations with transatlantic abolitionists, 262; in republics vs. empires, 249; slave ships captured, 262–63, 265, 379n64; Stowe's *Uncle Tom's Cabin*, 255; U.S. Black Americans' efforts, 254; in the U.S. vs. Haiti, 247–48. *See also* abolition of slavery; 1804 Principle
Anti-Slavery Record, 263

Anti-slavery Society, 264
Arawaks, 32
Ardouin, Beaubrun: on the abolition of slavery, 132; *Études sur l'histoire d'Haïti*, 5, 12–13; as a historian, xix, 12; influence of, xvii, 27, 207; influences on, xvii–xviii; on maroons as precursors to revolutionaries, 41; on property proscriptions, 262; on travelers' accounts of Haiti, 275
Ardouin, Céligny, 122–23, 144–45
Ardouin, Coriolan, 122–23
Arlequin mulâtresse, protégé par Macanda (Acquaire), 110
"Articles of Pacification with the Maroons of Trelawney Town" (Jamaica, 1738), 46
Aubert, M., 142
Augustin, Marie Josephine (*pseud.* Tante Marie): *Le Macandal*, 111
Aya, bombé ("Let us die, let us die free"), 38
Ayiti. *See* Haiti; Indigenous period
Aztecs, 39

Bacon de la Chevalerie, M., 89
Balch, Emily Greene, 327
Baldwin, James, 308
Banks, Joseph, 278
Baptiste, Jean, 60, 64
the bar (a punishment), 183, 364n54
Barillon, M., 119
Barnave, Antoine, 81–82, 129
Barrionuevo, Francisco de, 46–47
Bastille, storming of (1789), 76–77, 102
Beard, John Relly, 155
Beauvais, Louis Jacques, 127–28
Begasse, Marie, 72, 153
Bélair, Charles, 164, 167
Bellegarde, Dantès, 327
Benedicty-Kokken, Alessandra, 21
Bercy, Drouin de, 116
Bergeaud, Émeric: *Stella*, 34, 195, 296, 329
Bernabé, Jean: "Éloge de la créolité," 319
Betances, Ramón Emeterio, 243–44, 307; "the Antilles for the sons of the Antilles" motto of, 311, 317; on a Caribbean Confederation, 317; on Delorme, 316; in Paris, 318; "Voyages de Scaldado," 311–12

394   Index

Bevan, Henry: *Thirty Years in India*, 66
Biassou, Georges, 93, 111, 135, 142–43, 145, 178
Bibb, Henry, 253
Black Atlantic humanism, 312
Black freedom fighters, 136–37, 141–44, 163, 164, 190, 202, 218. *See also* Haitian Revolution
The Black Jacobins (James), 6, 101
Black sovereignty, 252, 255, 313–14, 318
Blaine, James G., 320
Blanchelande, Philibert-François Rouxel de, 86
Blue Mountain (Windward) Maroons, 145–46
Blue Mountain Treaty, 145–46
Bogues, Anthony, 221, 297
Bois Caïman ceremony (1791), 44, 97, 101–2, 112–16, 120–23, 126, 177–78, 295
Boisrond, Louis, 79, 88–89
Boisrond-Tonnerre, Louis-Félix: antislavery stance of, 261; vs. Chanlatte, 219; Declaration of Independence written by, 211–12, 219; as a historian, xix; on Toussaint Louverture's death, 162; *Mémoires pour servir à l'histoire d'Haïti*, xii–xiii, xv, 175, 215, 254; on Napoléon, xiv; on remembering colonialism's violent history, xiv
Bolívar, Simón: anti-colonial mission of, 232–33; on Christophe, 238; Congress of Panama organized by, 238–39, 242; Gran Colombia created by, 238–39; Haitian aid to, xx, 231–33, 235–40, 244–45, 259; Haitian antislavery's influence on, 249; Haiti betrayed by, 238–40, 242–43; independence movement of, 231–32, 235–38; in Les Cayes, 232–33; slaves emancipated by, 233, 235, 240
Bondje (or Bondye; God), 126
Bonneau, M., 86–87
Bonnet, Edmond, 211
Bonnet, Guy-Joseph, 211
Borgella, Bernard, 177
Borno, Marc, 127
Bossy, Rose, 153
Boukman, Dutty (or Boukman Dutty), xix, 93, 112–16, 122–23, 126–27, 133–34, 145, 355n107. *See also* Bois Caïman ceremony

Bourbons of France, 197, 270–71, 285, 300–302. *See also* Charles X, King; Louis Philippe, King; Louis XIV, King; Louis XVI, King; Louis XVIII, King
Boussole, 58
Bouvet de Cressé, Auguste-Jean-Baptiste: *Histoire de la catastrophe de Saint-Domingue*, 251
bovarysme, 318
Boyer, Jean-Pierre, 25; agricultural system under, 185; attempts to renegotiate the French debt, 271; authority/power of, 266; vs. Christophe, 206; conflicts under, 11; Constitution signed by, 229; free soil policy of, 263–64; on French recognition of Haiti, 305; Goman overthrown by, 196; government documents produced under, xviii; indemnity treaties with France, 266–69, 273–75, 291, 305; independence movements supported by, 240–41; labor system of, 131; overthrow of, 243, 246, 266, 268, 306; as president of the southern republic, 206, 240, 372n66; on reparations to the French, 293; reunification by, 11, 220, 238, 240–42, 245, 290; as self-proclaimed liberator of Haiti, 290; slavery abolished in Santo Domingo by, 249
Bréda family, 144
Brigitte (Makandal's wife), 106
Brissot, Jacques, 100, 119, 192
Brown, Jonathan: *The History and Present Condition of St. Domingo*, 276
Brown, Vincent, 20
Brown, William Wells, 100–101, 158, 253; *St. Domingo, Its Revolutions and Its Patriots*, 155
Brulley, Augustin Jean, 192–93
Bullet, Jeannot, 145
Burnard, Trevor, 352n34
Butler, Smedley, 311, 388n71
Buxton, Fowell, 223–24

Caffarelli, Marie-François Auguste de, 175
Caledonian Mercury, 215
Candler, John, 276

Caonabo/Kaonabo, 31, 36–40, 37, 48–49

Cap, burning of (Saint-Domingue), 129, 141–42, 159

Cap-Haïtien, 265–67

capitalism: and democracy, 307, 312; and imperialism, 222, 321, 323, 328; spread of, 321

Capoix, General, 22, 203, 230

Caribbean Confederation, 317

Caribs, 32

Carpentier, Alejo, 222

Carreau, M., 135

Casimir, Jean, 297; *Une lecture décoloniale de l'histoire des Haïtiens*, 25, 207

Castaing, Charles Guillaume, 86

Casthely, Jean Miotel: *Le Romantisme en Haïti*, 326–27

Castonnet des Fosses, Louise Catherine de, 59

Castries, Charles Eugène Gabriel de la Croix (marquis de), 79

Castro, José I., 31

Catholic Miscellaney, 274

Célestin-Mégie, Émile: "Defense and Illustration of the Creole Language," 10

Central Assembly (Saint-Domingue), 177–78, 180, 200

Césaire, Aimé, 55, 207, 316; *Discourse on Colonialism*, 307, 310–11; *Une Tempête*, 38

Chamoiseau, Patrick: "Éloge de la créolité," 319

Chanlatte, Antoine, 127

Chanlatte, François Desrivières, 376n12, 387n44

Chanlatte, Juste: on the Amazones, 282–83; anti-colonialism of, 213; antislavery of, 250–51; vs. Boisrond-Tonnerre, 219; vs. Boyer, 306; vs. Christophe, 176, 306; on color prejudice, 251; Constitution signed by, 219; on crimes against humanity, 55, 174; on Dessalines, 175–76, 306; on the emancipation decrees, 137; on the genocide against the Ayitians, 39–40, 174; as a historian, xix; on the impact of Vincent Ogé's death, 100; on independence, 202–3; influence of, xviii;

on Toussaint Louverture, 175; on monuments, 285; on slavery, 51, 54, 117, 188, 198

Chanlatte, Juste, works by: *À Mes concitoyens*, 175–76, 213, 215, 306; *Le Cri de la nature*, xvi, 21, 176, 250–51, 285, 302, 306; *L'Entrée du roi en sa capitale*, 9, 283; *Henry Christophe*, 306, 387n44

Chanlatte family as enslavers, 306, 386n41

Charéron, M., 211

Charles X, King, 266, 272–73, 305–6

Charlier, Étienne, 106, 146

Chasseurs Royaux, 74

Chasseurs Volontaires, 127

Chateaubriand, François-René de: *The Genius of Christianity*, 190

Chauvet, Henri, 9; *Fille du Kacik*, 36–38

Chavannes, Jean-Baptiste, 84–85, 87, 97–99, 101, 103, 108, 120–21, 126–27

Christian Inquirer, 309

Christmastime Rebellion (Santo Domingo, 1521), 26, 44–46, 340n137

Christophe, King Henry I: accused of reinstating slavery, 274–76, 290, 293; agricultural policies of, 185, 286–89; as anti-racist, 231; antislavery activism of, 278; antislavery culture under, 279–80, 282, 286; Bolívar on, 238; vs. Boyer, 206; brutality of, 24; Citadelle built by, 276, 283–86; and Clarkson, 278; conflicts under, 11; constitutional hereditary monarchy established by, 206; Declaration of Independence signed by, 211; education promoted by, 278–79, 281; and Enrique, 40–42; as a founder of Haitian independence, 283, 286; on the French capture of Haitian ships, 262; on French language, 8; French troops fought by, 158, 162; government documents produced under, xviii; on Grégoire, 251; on Haitian prosperity, 249; independence declared by, 203; influence of, xx; as king of northern Haiti, 227, 371n44; labor system of, 131, 147, 149, 278, 280, 286–89 (*see also* Code Henry); land grant program of, 287, 384n166; vs. Leclerc, xvi,

396 Index

159; legacy in Haitian thought, 176; *Manifeste du roi*, 161–62; motto of, 143, 286; Napoléon's plot against, 167–68; newspaper of (see *Gazette royale d'Hayti*); overthrow of, 289–91; vs. Pétion, 227, 275 (*see also* civil war [Haiti, 1808]); as president, 227, 288–89, 371n57; progressiveness and ingenuity of, 279–81; on religious freedom, 230; on reparations to the French, 293; revolutionary thought of, xix; Sans-Souci Palace built by, 284–86; Schoelcher on, 279–80; in the siege of Santo Domingo, 220; suicide of, 11, 25, 240, 273, 290; on trade with France, 272; on trade with the U.S., 249

Cibao (Maguana, Haiti), 31

Citadelle Laferrière (also Citadelle Henry), 24, 276, 283–86, 291, 292

civil war (Haiti, 1808), 195, 206, 281–82, 307

Civil War (U.S., 1861–65), 249, 305–7, 312

Clarkson, Thomas, xx, 245, 250, 262, 275, 278, 288, 290

The Class Struggle in France (Marx), 5

Clervaux, Augustin, 22, 160, 162, 167, 203, 211

Clonard, M., 191

Code Henry, 149, 276–77, 278, 280–81, 286–88

Code Napoléon, 276–77

Code Noir, 54–55, 68–71, 181, 276–77, 298

Code Rural, 266–67, 290, 388n71

Collet, Philippe André, 177

Colón, Diego, 44–45

Colonial Assembly (Saint-Marc, Haiti), 83, 88–91, 96–97, 112, 144, 184

colonial paternalism, 181

Colonies étrangères et Haïti (Schoelcher), 279–80

color prejudice, 70–93; and American vs. French colonists, 72; banned by the Constitution of 1805, 179, 223, 296–98; emergence of, 73–74; against free people of color, 34, 71–72, 86–87; French refusal to recognize, 82–83, 86–87; Haitian writers on the consequences of, 303; as leading to revolution, 71–72, 86–87; Vincent Ogé's role in, 81, 83–84; slavery linked to, 141;

in the U.S., 307. *See also* free people of color; racism; white supremacy

Columbus, Christopher, xx, 31–32, 38–40, 44

Comité des Cayes, 79

Confiant, Raphaël: "Éloge de la créolité," 319

Congress of Arcahaye (1803), 202

Congress of Panama (1826), 238–39, 242

The Conquest of America (Todorov), 13

Constituent Assembly, 228

Constitution (France, 1791), 176

Constitution (France, 1793), 176

Constitution (France, 1795), 177

Constitution (France, 1799), 176–78

Constitution (Haiti, 1805): anti-colonialism of, 220–21, 225–26, 296; anti-conquest clause, 223, 225–27, 229, 231; anti-racist clause, 225, 296–98; antislavery clause, 223, 225, 248, 296; on Catholicism as the state religion, 230; on citizenship, 223; color prejudice outlawed by, 179, 223, 296–98; on Dessalines's authority, 226–27; on Dessalines's successor, 206, 226; dissemination of, 218; on divorce, 230; on "Emperor of Haiti," 228–29, 372n65; on equality, 308; first draft of (*see* Constitution [Haiti, 1801]); French property exclusion in, 300; on Haitians as Black, 229, 297; Haitian territory defined in, 223; on Haiti as an empire, 226; on human diversity, 296; newspaper coverage of, 225; preamble to, 229, 296; ratification of, 217–18, 225; renaming of Haiti in, 35, 220, 223; signing of, 218–19, 229; sovereignty claim of, 223; on the territory of Haiti, 220; Vastey on, 206, 217–18, 226–27; white property exclusion in, 298–300; will of the people as source of, 229; writing of, 218–19

Constitution (Haiti, 1806), 228–30, 231, 248, 300

Constitution (Haiti, 1807), 223, 229–31, 248

Constitution (Haiti, 1811), 229–30

Constitution (Haiti, 1816), 221, 229–30, 248, 258–59

Constitution (Haiti, 1843), 246

Constitution (Haiti, 1867), 314, 386n23

Constitution (Haiti, 1987), 9
Constitution (Saint-Domingue, 1801):
anti-racist language of, 179–80;
antislavery clause, 146–47, 176–80; on
censorship vs. freedom of the press, 199;
on the Central Assembly, 180; Central
Assembly's creation of, 177–78; colonial
status preserved by, 179; color prejudice,
180; dissemination of, 176; on the
division of the colony into separate
categories, 179; divorce outlawed by, 181;
France's approval of, 199–200; on a free
and egalitarian society, 179–80; "free and
French" language of, 93, 150, 158, 176, 179;
and independence, 176; on labor, class,
and culture, 181; on laborers/cultivators,
181–83; Toussaint Louverture appointed
governor-general for life by, 198–200;
"man and citizen" language of, 180;
paternalistic language of, 186; on
property, 181; as a radically free set of
laws, 176; on religion and spirituality,
180–81, 230; signed by Toussaint
Louverture, 93, 150, 158–59, 176; society's
contradictions inscribed in, 196–97; and
Sonthonax's emancipation proclamation,
177; territory of the colony defined by,
178; on transforming a slave economy
into a free labor economy, 177
Constitution (U.S.), 82, 179, 217–18,
228, 314
The Constitution of the Republic of Hayti
(Tredwell), 258
constitutions, first (Haiti), xviii, 4,
222–23, 226. *See also specific*
constitutions
Les Constitutions d'Haïti (Janvier), 11
Cook, Mercer, 253, 316
Cooper, James Fenimore, xx
Cope, John, 58
Corbett, Bob, 3
Cornevin, Robert, 314
Correspondance de Julien Raimond avec ses
frères (J. Raimond), 88, 93
Cortés, Hernán, 39
Coulanges, Jean, 1

Coulon, Garran de, 59–60, 119; *Rapport sur*
les troubles de Saint-Domingue, 60
counter-plantation, 207
Courtin, Sébastien, 104–7, 109, 351n32
Creoleness, 319
Cric?Crac! (Sylvain), 9
Le Cri de la conscience (J. L. Vastey), 20
Le Cri de la nature (J. Chanlatte), xvi, 21,
176, 250–51, 285, 302, 306
Le Cri de la patrie (J. L. Vastey), 253–54
Le Cri des nègres (Price-Mars), 314
critical race theory, 298
Cross, James Cartwright: *King Caesar*, 111
Cuba, 243–44, 249, 264–66, 312
Cudjoe, Captain, 46
Cugoano, Ottobah, 312
Cushing, Caleb, 288

Daguin, 54–55
Dalleo, Raphael, 222, 318
Dalmas, Antoine, 116; *Histoire de la*
révolution de Saint-Domingue, 112–13
Dartiguenave, Philippe Sudré, 327
Dash, J. Michael, 313
D'Auberteuil, René-Michel Hilliard, 35
Dauxion-Lavaysse, M., 270
The Declaration of the Rights of Woman
and the Female Citizen (de Gouges), 133
Declaration of Independence (Haiti, 1803),
211
Declaration of Independence (Haiti, 1804),
14, 174; anti-colonialism of, xviii–xix, 121,
211–13, 218–21, 226; on France as the
enemy of Haiti, 212; influence/
dissemination of, 4, 211–12, 218; on liberty,
xix; on naming of Haiti, 211; newspaper
coverage of, 218; preamble to, 203–4;
ratification of, 212; on relations with
neighboring islands, 212–13; revolutionary
writers' influence on, 219–20; signing of,
211–12; on slavery, racism, and
colonialism, xviii–xix, 121, 218, 250;
translation into Creole, 9; vs. the U.S.
Declaration of Independence, 205, 217;
use in the emancipation proclamation,
131–32; writing of, 211, 219–20

Declaration of Independence (U.S., 1776): "all men are created equal," 244, 247; continued war with Great Britain following, 212; on freedom and equality, xviii; vs. the Haitian Declaration of Independence, 205, 217; slavery not addressed in, 248

Declaration of the Rights of Man (France, 1789): applied to American colonists of Saint-Domingue, 72; enslaved Africans not considered "men" by, 82, 180; gender exclusion of, 133; incoherent principles in, 76; on liberty, equality, and independence, xviii, 26, 73, 179; on the natural and imprescriptible rights of man, 247, 254; and personhood debates, 82–83, 87; on property, 181; white colonists' opposition to Article 4, 82–83

Decrès, Denis, 201

"Defense and Illustration of the Creole Language" (Célestin-Mégie), 10

Dehais, 62

de Joly, Étienne, 77, 93

De la Littérature des nègres (Grégoire), 50, 251

De l'Égalité des races humaines (Firmin), xx, 19–20, 237

Delgrès, Louis, 21–22, 172

De l'Inégalité des races humaines (Gobineau), 19–20

Delorme, Demesvar: Afro-diasporic/inter-American activism of, 316; on Boyer, 266–67; on democracy, xx, 308, 311–12, 324; *La Démocratie et le préjugé de couleur aux États-Unis/Les Nationalités américaines et le système Monroë*, 306–7, 309–11; on the earthquake of 1842, 265–66; on Haitian anti-colonialism, 236–37; on the Haitian Constitution of 1867 vs. the U.S. Constitution, 314; as a historian, xix; on imperialism, 222, 246, 313, 321–22; influence of, 311–12; *La Misère au sein des richesses*, 307, 316–17; on a North American Confederation, 317; in Paris, 318; on protecting Haitian sovereignty, 320–21; on tolerance, 311; on U.S.

imperialism, 310–11; on U.S. racism, 306–8, 312, 324

democracy: and capitalism, 307, 312; spread of, 321; in the U.S., 228, 245, 306–8, 310, 324; white, and Black freedom, 325

La Démocratie et le préjugé de couleur aux Étas-Unis/Les Nationalités américaines et le système Monroë (Delorme), 306–7, 309–11

Denancé, L. V.: *Makandal: ou, le noir marron*, 111

Déroche, F. Louis (F. Loui Deroch), 336n37

Descourtilz, Michel Étienne, 60–61

Desdunes family, 60–61, 64

Despinville, M., 135

Desprès, M., 142

Dessalines, Jean-Jacques (Emperor Jacques I), xiii; accused of reinstating slavery, 274; agricultural system under, 185; anti-colonialism of, 223–24; antislavery stance of, 254; April 28 proclamation by (1804), 21, 35, 99, 217, 254, 299; assassination of, 42, 196, 227, 248, 265, 270; conflicts under, 11; Constitution signed by, 219; on the Declaration of Independence, 211–12; as emperor, 213–14, 221, 226; on the French capture of Haitian ships, 262; on French language, 8; French troops fought by, 158, 162–63; government documents produced under, xviii; as governor-general, 213–14; historical methodology of, 21–22; independence declared by, 203; independence emerges under, 176, 219, 254; "Independence or death" exhortation of, 38, 174, 202; *Journal de la campagne du nord*, 162; labor system of, 131, 147, 277; vs. Leclerc, 162–63; legacy in Haitian thought, 175–76; "Liberty or Death" pronouncement by, 202, 262; Napoléon's plot against, 167–68; nonhereditary empire established by, 206, 214; regions/cities associated with, 22; on remembering colonialism's violent history, xiv; on reunification, 220–21; revolutionary thought of, xix; in the siege of Santo Domingo, 220–21; on slavery's

Index 399

Dessalines, Jean-Jacques (*continued*)
restoration in Guadeloupe, 174; state
documents issued under his name, 219;
on threats to Haitians for daring to be
free, 269–70; on the tree of liberty, 264;
on the U.S. slave trade, 257; on
vengeance, xiv, 21–22, 34–35, 99; on white
property owners, 299–300

*Les Détracteurs de la race noire et la
République d'Haïti* (Janvier), 316

Dézafi (Frankétienne), 10

Diay, Fatine, 60

Die deutsche Ideologie (Marx and Engels), 5

Discourse on Colonialism (Césaire), 307,
310–11

discursive justice, 21

Dolcé, Jacquelin: *Le Romantisme en Haïti*,
326–27

Dominican Republic, *37*, 41, 243, 245, 313,
317. *See also* Santo Domingo

Dominique, Jean, 10

Dorval, Gérard: *Le Romantisme en Haïti*,
326–27

Douglass, Frederick, xx, 18, 63, 245, 253;
*Narrative of the Life of Frederick
Douglass*, 176

Drexler, Michael, 176

Dubois, Laurent, 3, 14, 177

Du Bois, W. E. B., xx, 246, 253, 311, 314–15,
388n71

Dubuisson, M., 64

Ducoeurjoly, S. J., 35, 50

Dumas, Alexandre, 318

Dumas, Élisabeth Marie ("Mimi"), 63,
153, 192

Dumas, Pierre, 63

Dumesle (Charles Hérard-Dumesle): on the
birthright of Haitians, 92; on the Bois
Caïman ceremony, 113–17, 121, 123; on
Boisrond-Tonnerre vs. Chanlatte, 219;
on ceremonies that ushered in the
revolution, 122; on Christophe, 288–90;
on the Code Henry, 288; on the colonists'
genocidal imaginings, 120; on the
Docoëns, 111–12; on French revolutionary
contradictions, 128–29; on the Haitian

Revolution, 102; as a historian, xix; on
indigènes, 127; influence of, xviii, 24, 27;
on Makandal, 102–3, 111; *L'Observateur*,
219; on Vincent Ogé and Chavannes, 84,
120; on Rochambeau vs. Cortès, 39; on
silences, 25; on slavery, 54; on sovereignty
vs. sovereign ruler, 229; testimonies of
the dead used by, 23, 92; on ultra racism,
55; use of "Haitian Revolution," 121,
354n87; *Voyage dans le nord d'Hayti*,
22–25, 48–49, 56, 113–17, 121; on the white
colonists' independence movement, 91;
on white colonists' reaction to the
revolution, 125; on women in the
military, 281–82

Dumontellier, 61

Durand, Oswald, 9

Dutty, Boukman. *See* Boukman, Dutty

Duvalier, Jean-Claude, 1–2, 10–11, 196

earthquake and tsunami (Haiti, 1842),
265–67

Édouard, Emmanuel F.: *Le Panthéon
haïtien*, 254–55

egalitarianism, 170, 179–80

1804 Principle, xviii, 14, 120, 239, 244, 247,
249, 308, 312, 322. *See also* Declaration of
Independence (Haiti)

Eighteenth Brumaire (Marx), 10

Eller, Anne, 243–44

"Éloge de la créolité" (Bernabé,
Chamoiseau, and Confiant), 319

*Emancipation: Or Practical Advice to British
Slave-Holders* (Winn), 66

Engels, Friedrich: *Die deutsche Ideologie*, 5

Enlightenment, 177, 220, 247, 307

Enrique/Henri, 31, 37, 39–42, 44, 46–48, 112,
146

L'Entrée du roi en sa capitale (J. Chanlatte),
9, 283

equality: Constitution of 1805 on, 308;
Declaration of the Rights of Man on,
xviii, 26, 73, 179; French Revolution on,
76, 138, 168, 171; Haitian definition of,
244; Haitian experiment with, 322, 324;
National Assembly on, 128–29; Rigaud on,

400 Index

151–52; U.S. Declaration of Independence on, xviii; vs. white supremacy, debates by Atlantic world powers, 302–3

Equiano, Olaudah (aka Gustavus Vassa), 58, 63, 312

Essai sur les causes de la révolution et des guerres civiles d'Hayti (J. L. Vastey), 14–15, 165, 206, 228, 295

Estaing, Comte de, 127

Estrade, Paul, 318

Étienne (man enslaved by Poncet), 58

Études sur l'histoire d'Haïti (B. Ardouin), 5, 12–13

evidence of experience, 24

evite miyò pase mande padon (it is better not to make a mistake than to be sorry), 386n31

Fanon, Frantz, 61

Farge, Arlette, 20–21

Fatiman, Cécile, xix, 112, 122. *See also* Bois Caïman ceremony

Faubert, Pierre, 5, 246, 255; *Ogé, ou le préjugé de couleur*, 101

Ferrand, Jean-Louis, 212

Ferrand de Baudière, M., 78–81, 98, 127, 180

Fille du Kacik (Chauvet), 36–38

Firmin, Anténor: on colonialism, 323; on the debt to France, 267–68; *De l'Égalité des races humaines*, xx, 19–20, 237; on Douglass, xx, 18; on Haitian independence, 324; on Haitian pacifism, 322; Haitian revolutionaries as morally superior, 304; on Haiti's experiment with liberty and equality, 322; as a historian, xix; on imperialism, 246; influence of, 207; *Letters from Saint Thomas*, 313; on Madiou, Ardouin, and Saint-Rémy, xvii, 18; on Michelet, 4–5, 18–19; on Pétion's link to the Latin American independence movement, 237; on the racism of the colonists, 296

Fischer, Sibylle, 297–98

forgetting the past, 195

Foucault, Michel, 12, 27

Fouchard, Jean, 52

Fouquier-Tinville, Antoine-Quentin, 192–93

France: accusations against Haiti by, 215; color prejudice not recognized by, 82–83, 86–87; Haiti recognized by, 304–5; Haiti's sovereignty threatened by, 261–62, 265, 267, 269–70, 273, 291, 300–302; indemnity treaties with Haiti, 266–69, 273–75, 291, 305; interest in re-conquest of Haiti, 241–42; peace talks with Britain, 166; plans to reconquer Haiti and reinstate slavery, 261–62, 269–70, 291, 301–3; reparations to, 272, 293; trade relations with Haiti, 272; Vietnam occupied by, 310–11. *See also* French Revolution

Frankétienne: *Dézafi*, 10

Franklin, Benjamin, 248, 311–13

Franklin, James: *The Present State of Hayti*, 275–76

freedom: and color prejudices, 180; Constitution of 1801 on, 179–80; and egalitarianism, 180; from France (*see* Haitian independence); in French colonies, tensions of, 177; gradual emancipation, 81, 91, 184–86, 188–89; of laborers, 182–83, 194; as subjugation, 169; transforming a slave economy into a free labor economy, 177, 184–89, 193–94 (*see also* affermage labor system). *See also* abolition of slavery

free people of color: affranchis vs. citizens of color, 71–73; in the American War of Independence, 127–28, 355n110; citizenship of, 72, 81–83, 89–90, 127–29, 184, 298; color prejudice against, 34, 71–72, 86–87; conscription of men of color, 74; and the Fond-Parisien conflagration, 89–90; as "free and French," 93, 150, 158, 176, 179; Toussaint Louverture's letter about emancipation, 141; the "new Indigenous," 92–93; population of, 70–71, 74, 127; racism toward, 67–69, 74–76, 152–53; rebellion/violence eschewed by, 88–89, 93; representation at the French National Assembly, 76–77; rights of, 70, 74–75, 81–83, 87, 99–100, 128–29; slaughtered by slaves, 84; and slavery, 52, 67; warned against rebelling,

Index   401

free people of color (*continued*)
85–86; wealthy, 74, 83; white colonists' plots/violence against, 76–80, 84, 88–89, 347n38; whites' relationship with, 70, 73–74
Fremon, M., 110
French republicanism, incoherence of, 76, 128–29, 132, 165, 168–70, 178, 205–6
French Revolution: on color prejudice, 34, 73; grievances submitted following, 76–77; vs. the Haitian Revolution, 121; incoherence of, 73; on liberty, equality, and fraternity, 76, 138, 168, 171; on "man" and "persons," 72; principles/universalisms of, 26, 167–69; Rigaud on, 128

Galbaud, César, 141–42
Galbaud du Fort, François-Thomas, 141–42
Gallifet, M., 191
Gaou-Guinou, 144
Garcilaso de la Vega, 35
Garfield, James A., 315
Garrigus, John, 351n34
Garvey, Amy Jacques, 222
Garvey, Marcus, 222, 314
gas chambers, 174
Gastine, Civique de, 113
Gaulard, General, 164
Gazette officielle de l'état d'Hayti, 256
Gazette politique et commerciale d'Haïti, 214–16, 218, 224, 260–61, 265, 277–78
Gazette royale d'Hayti, 164, 219–20, 259, 263, 271, 280–86, 288, 289–90, 302, 329–30
Geffrard, Fabre, 243
Geggus, David, 351n24, 351n34
genealogies, 10
The Genius of Christianity (Chateaubriand), 190
genocide, 36–37, 39–40, 42, 117–20, 174, 184, 202, 269–70, 291
Gérard (Deputy), 79–80
Glissant, Édouard, 17, 312
Global Transformations (M-R. Trouillot), 3, 25
Gobineau, Arthur de: *De l'Inégalité des races humaines*, 19–20

Gogo (Sannite), 58
Goman (Jean-Baptiste Duperrier), 11, 196
Gouges, Olympe de, 190; *The Declaration of the Rights of Woman and the Female Citizen*, 133
Gouverneurs de la rosée (Roumain), 316
gradual emancipation, 81, 91, 184–86, 188–89
Gramsci, Antonio, 4
Gran Colombia, 233, 235, 238–40, 373n110
Grande Brigitte, xix
Grant, Ulysses S., 315
Great Britain: abolition of slavery by, 205, 249–50, 256, 263–64; evacuation of Saint-Domingue, 156–57; Haiti recognized by, 305; peace talks with France, 166
Great Man theory, 219, 284–85
Greece, 240–43, 374nn112–15
Grégoire, Henri, xx, 119, 232, 250–51; *De la Littérature des nègres*, 50
Grellet, Stephen, 262
Guadeloupe, 21, 168–69, 172–74, 201, 206
Guiambois, M., 135

Haiti (Ayiti): agriculture in, 268–69; Black people's achievements in, 322–23; British evacuation of, 156–57; chattel slavery opposed by, 240; Corbett's email list of, 3; debt to France, 266–69, 271–74, 291, 293, 305; economic and political decline of, 269, 274; education in, 278–79, 281, 315, 382–3n141; European names for, 32; exclusion from Congress of Panama, 238–39, 242; experiment with liberty and equality in, 322, 324; as first modern state to permanently abolish slavery, 174; freedom movements supported by, 231–33, 235–40; French plans to reconquer and reinstate slavery, 261–62, 269–70, 291, 301–3; French threats to sovereignty, 261–62, 265, 267, 269–70, 273, 291, 300–302; French trade relations with, 272; governance of (*see* Central Assembly; Colonial Assembly; National Assembly); independence movements supported by, 240–41, 243–44; language of, 319; Leclerc-Rochambeau expedition to, xvi, 23, 39, 99, 128, 151, 158–62, 167–68, 173–74, 203; literary output of, 328; map of mountains of, *233*; massacres in, 78; meaning of the name, 35; pacifism of, 246, 322; paper money issued in, 268, *268*; as a philanthropic nation, 304; prosperity of, 249, 269; relations with neighboring islands, 212–13, 224–25; renaming of, 34–35, 211, 220; reunification of, 11, 220–21, 238, 240–42, 245, 290, 374n117; size of, 266; vs. the Spanish in Cuba, 265–66; state-run newspaper press in, 214 (see also *Gazette politique et commerciale d'Haïti*; *Gazette royale d'Hayti*); U.S. occupation of, 222, 245–46, 260, 311, 326–29, 388n71; U.S. threat to, 304–6, 313; U.S. trade relations with, 260–61; white women in, 73–75, 347n18. *See also* Indigenous period in Haiti

Haiti, State against Nation (M.-R. Trouillot), 197

Haitian Atlantic humanism, 312. *See also* 1804 Principle

Haitian Creole: debates about, 9–10; first novel in, 10; vs. French, 1–2, 7–9; literacy in, 2–3, 9; as an official/primary language of Haiti, 8–9; as an oral language, 9; as a written language, 9

Haitian historical writing/documentation: on the Ayitian anti-colonial rebellion, 33; circulation/influence of, 4; colonial histories refuted by, 23–24; on the French mission to restore slavery, 162; French removal of colonial documents, xvi; Haiti's laws and constitutions, xviii; and history from below, 3–4, 22; on morality of slavery and colonialism, xvi; recordkeeping by Haitians, xvi–xvii; *Recueil général des lois et actes du gouvernement d'Haïti*, xvii; silencing of, 5–6; talking to and for the dead, xi, 15–16, 20–23; travel-guide historical methodology, 24. *See also individual historians*

Haitian independence, 166–207; and the abolition of slavery, 136–37, 144, 247;

anti-colonial, antislavery, and anti-racist ideas of, xviii (*see also* anti-colonialism; antislavery); commemorating (*see* Citadelle Laferrière; Sans-Souci Palace); "first Haitians" (Ayitians) linked to, 27, 32–35, 41–43, 48–49; and French republicanism's incoherence, 129, 165, 168–69, 178; and the genocidal goals/ tactics of colonists/French, 174, 202–3, 269, 291; as a human right, xi–xii; newspaper coverage of, 204–5, 214–16; populist understanding of emergence of, 219; recognition of, xx, 24, 213, 238–39, 259, 295, 300, 304–5, 326, 379n64; and republics, Haitians' attitudes toward, 205–6; transition from rebellion, 184–85; unity's importance to, 203; Vastey on, xi–xii, 42–43, 164–65. *See also* Declaration of Independence; 1804 Principle; Haitian Revolution

Haitian nationalism, 323

Haitian Revolution, 97–129; abolition influenced by, 26; vs. American Revolution, 121–22; anti-colonial, antislavery, and anti-racist ideas of, xviii, 24–26, 39, 169, 249, 252, 303; antislavery movement's role in, 93; as atonement for crimes against humanity, 118, 120, 125, 174; Bois Caïman ceremony (1791), 44, 97, 101–2, 112–16, 120–23, 126, 177–78, 295; Boisrond-Tonnerre on, xii–xiii; burning of Port-au-Prince and Cap-Français, 129; ceremonies that ushered in, 122–23 (*see also* Bois Caïman ceremony; Morne-Rouge assembly); color prejudice as leading to, 71–72, 86–87; commemorating (*see* Citadelle Laferrière); egalitarian goals of, 170; embodied historiography of, 14; end of (*see* Vertières, Battle of); European vs. Haitian writings on, 14–15; first use of term, 121, 354n87; French lies about, xvii; General Revolt (1791), 26, 120, 130, 185–86; as God's work, 295; historical writing/documentation during vs. after, xix; history of (*see* Ti *difé boulé sou istoua Ayiti*); impact of deaths of

Haitian Revolution (*continued*)
Toussaint Louverture, Makandal, and Vincent Ogé, 97, 100–102, 120–21, 127; impact of slavery's restoration in Guadeloupe, 173; influence and historical significance of, 4–6, 121–22; leaders associated with regions of Haiti, 22–23; and liberty/equality vs. white supremacy debates by Atlantic world powers, 302–3; Marx on, 5–6; onset of, 101–2; "poisonings" leading to, 103–10, 112, 351–52n34; political thresholds crossed by, 14; as transforming Haiti from a slave society to a living society, 65–66; transition from rebellion to independence, 184–85; tree of liberty image, 132–33, 312; U.S. African American writers on, 244; as a war of independence, 34, 69, 97 (*see also* Haitian independence); white colonists' anticipation of, 77–78; white colonists' reactions to, 123–27; as a white massacre, perception of, 191–92

Haitian romanticism, 326

Haitian turn, 6, 8

Haïti aux Haïtiens (Janvier), 317, 320

Hamilton, William, 278, 287

Hannah-Jones, Nikole: "The 1619 Project," 17

Harris, Cheryl: "Whiteness as Property," 298–99

Hayne, Robert Y., 238–39

Hazareesingh, Sudhir, 275

Hebblethwaite, Benjamin, 7–8

Hédouville, Gabriel-Marie-Théodore-Joseph de, 147–49, 157, 302

Hegel, Georg Wilhelm Friedrich, 4, 18

Henry Christophe (J. Chanlatte), 306, 387n44

Henry I, King. *See* Christophe, King Henry I

Heureuse, Marie-Claire Félicité Bonheur, 61

Hibbert, Fernand, 324–25; *Les Thazar*, 9

Higuemota, 31, 36, 40

Hispaniola. *See* Haiti

Histoire de la catastrophe de Saint-Domingue (Bouvet de Cressé), 251

Histoire de la révolution de Saint-Domingue (Dalmas), 112–13

Histoire de la révolution française (Michelet), xi

Histoire des Caciques (E. Nau), xxi, 27, 31–33, 38–40, 43–44, 101

Histoire des deux Indes (Raynal), 157, 360n101

Histoire d'Haïti (Madiou), 4, 13

Historia natural y general de las Indias (Oviedo), 46

historical writing/documentation: archives, use of, 20–21; bias in, xv; by French colonial writers, 23–24; and geography, 22; historical consciousness in, 18; historical resurrection in, 20; origins claims (genetic sentences) in, 16–18. *See also* Haitian historical writing/documentation

The History and Present Condition of St. Domingo (J. Brown), 276

history from below, xi, 3–4, 16, 22

Holly, James Theodore, 121–22, 354n89

Holocaust, 62–63

holocausts, 99, 117

Hoover, Herbert, 327

Hostos, Eugenio María de: *La Peregrinación de Bayoán*, 317

Hughes, Langston, 316

Hugo, Victor, 318

human rights language, 117–18, 125, 132

Hund, Wulf D., 5

Hurston, Zora Neale, 222

Iggers, Georg G., 18

Imagined Communities (Anderson), 16

imperialism: and capitalism, 222, 321, 323, 328; Delorme on, 222, 246, 310–11, 313, 321–22; Haiti as first to ban, xviii; of the U.S., 222, 260–61, 307–11, 313–14, 319–22

Indigenous army, 34, 48, 69, 92–93, 192, 203

Indigenous period, 31–49; Africans linked with Indians, 32–33; Ayitian poetry, 37–39; Ayitians, Spanish genocide against, 39–40, 42; Ayitians' physical remains, 43; Columbus's arrival and encounters with the Ayitians, xx, 31–32, 38–40, 44;

404 Index

European invaders' destruction of Ayitian culture, 38–39; "first Haitians" (Ayitians) linked to Haitian independence, 27, 32–35, 41–43, 48–49; French atrocities and conquest, 91–92, 99; inhabitants of the principalities, 31; insurrection of enslaved Africans, 44; maroon societies established, 40–42 (*see also* maroons); naming customs, 31–32; Spanish atrocities, 35–36; Spanish colonizers, 31–32; Spanish repression of slave rebellions, 44–48; Xaraguans, 31; Xaraguans, Spanish genocide against, 36–37, 40, 42

Inginac, B., 257–59

Injured Man of Color (anonymous writer), 218, 225, 228, 257

Instructions pour les établissemens et la culture des habitations caféyères de la couronne (Limonade), 286

Isambert, Antoine, 262

Jacinthe, M., 135

Jacobins, 100, 130, 138, 150, 171, 176, 186, 190

Jacobs, Harriet, 63, 253

Jacques I, Emperor. *See* Dessalines, Jean-Jacques

James, C. L. R., 222; *The Black Jacobins*, 6, 101

Janvier, Louis Joseph: Afro-diasporic/ inter-American activism of, 316; on Americans, 313; *Les Constitutions d'Haïti*, 11; on the debt to France, 269; *Les Détracteurs de la race noire et la République d'Haïti*, 316; on education, 315; on emancipation of slaves, 247–8; on farmers, 315; on France, 313; on Haitian independence's influence, xx, 247–48; on Haitians as social justice leaders, 315–16; on Haiti as inconvenient to the West, 27; *Haïti aux Haïtiens*, 317, 320; on Haiti's importance to the struggle for liberation, 312; as a historian, xix; on imperialism, 222, 246; on Toussaint Louverture, 316; on meddling foreigners, xxi; on Michelet, 19; in Paris, 318; on Pétion's aid to Bolívar aided by, 236; on protecting Haitian

sovereignty, 319–20; *La République d'Haïti et ses visiteurs*, 26, 27

Jarnac, M. de, 79

Jean-François, General, 22, 93, 135, 142–43

Jean-Pineau, M., 135

Jean Révolte (Méry), 56

Jefferson, Thomas, 185, 247–49, 260

Jenson, Deborah, 264, 354n87

Jewish expulsion from French colonies, 70

Johnson, James Weldon, 245–46

Joseph, Celucien, 6

Journal de la campagne du nord (Dessalines), 162

Journal de Paris, 257

Journal des Révolutions de la partie française de Saint-Domingue, 140

Kadish, Doris, 354n87

Kaisary, Philip, 176–77

kalinda (an Afro-Caribbean dance), 7

Kerversau, François-Marie Perichou de, 270

King Caesar (Cross), 111

Kóleksion Lakansièl, 1

Labadie, M., 80, 107

Laborde, M., 107

Labuissonnière, Pierre, 98–101, 127

Lacour, M., 177

Lacroix, Pamphile de, 163–64

La Española. *See* Haiti; Indigenous period

Lakansièl, 1

Lamarre, General, 22

Lamartine, Alphonse de, 5, 318

land grants, 287, 384n166

Laplaine, Marie-Louise, 75

Larchevesque-Thibaud, Gabriel-Jean-Baptiste, 59–60, 192–93

Laroche, Maximilien, 9

Las Casas, Bartolomé de, 35, 40–41

La Selve, Edgar, 38, 42

Latortue, Paul: *Un épisode de l'indépendance d'Haïti*, 9

L'Avancé, Duke de, 285

Laveaux, Étienne, 157, 360n101

leasing system of labor. *See* affermage labor system

Le Borgne de Boigne, Claude-Pierre-
Joseph, 23
Leclerc, Charles: death of, 202; expedition
to Saint-Domingue, xvi, 23, 39, 99, 128,
151, 158–62, 167–68, 173–74, 203; expedition
to Saint-Domingue, death toll from, 302;
genocidal goals of, 39, 117–18, 174, 184;
promises not to reinstate slavery, 21, 160,
162, 168, 173–74, 205–6; slavery reinstated
by, 201
Leconte, Vergniaud, 165
*Une lecture décoloniale de l'histoire des
Haïtiens* (Casimir), 25, 207
Le Normand de Mézy, M., 123, 144–45
Léogâne (Haiti), 48
Leonidas, 241, 374n113
Les Cayes (Haiti), 232–33
Letters from Saint Thomas (Firmin), 313
*Lettre d'un citoyen détenu pendant quatorze
mois* (J. Raimond), 192
Léveillé, General, 164
Lhérisson, Justin, 9
liberty: Declaration of the Rights of Man
on, xviii, 26, 73, 179; French Revolution
on, 76, 138, 168, 171; Haitian Declaration
of Independence on, xix; Haitian
definition of, 244–45; Haiti's experiment
with, 322, 324; "Liberty or Death"
pronouncement, 202, 262; National
Assembly on, 128–29; Sonthonax as
self-proclaimed founder of, 136–38; tree
of, 132–33, 154, 264, 312; in the U.S., 244–45;
vs. white supremacy, debates by Atlantic
world powers, 302–3
Limonade, Comte de. *See* Prévost, Julien
Lincoln, Abraham, 243, 315
Littel's Living Age, 309
Locke, Alain, 253
Locke, John, 229
Louisiana Purchase, 260–61, 266, 380n84
Louis Philippe, King, 266–67, 274
Louis XIII, King, 70
Louis XIV, King, 54, 70, 74, 276–77, 298
Louis XVI, King, 68, 76, 87, 91, 128, 130, 186,
285
Louis XVIII, King, 241–42, 271, 285, 291, 301–2

Louverture, Isaac, 144
Louverture, Placide Séraphin, 144, 241–42
Louverture, Saint-Jean, 144
Louverture, Toussaint, 14; accused of
reinstating slavery, 274; anti-racism of,
156, 179; antislavery movement led by, 93,
120, 136–37, 141–45, 150; arrest, deportation,
and death of, 36, 40, 97, 144, 160–65, 167,
174–75, 199, 201; association with
Spartacus, 114, 157–58, 164–65, 360n101;
authority/power of, 150, 157–58, 164, 195;
background/lineage of, 144; on the
British evacuation of Saint-Domingue,
156–57; and Caonabo, 36–67; Central
Assembly convoked by, 177; colonists'
property rights protected by, 170;
conflicts under, 11; Constitution signed
by (1801), 93, 150, 158–59, 176; on the
French republic, 200–201; government
documents produced under, xviii; as
governor-general, 93, 158, 198–200; on
Haitian Revolution's egalitarian goals,
170; on independence, 150–51, 193; labor
system of, 131, 147–49, 182, 185, 193–96 (*see
also* affermage labor system); vs. Leclerc,
xvi, 159–63; legacy in Haitian thought,
149, 161–65, 175–76, 316; letter to Napoléon
after arrest, 174–75; Moyse executed by,
147, 161; vs. Napoléon, 151, 158–59, 166–68,
199–200; on Vincent Ogé, 141; prophecies
of, 201; revolutionary thought of, xix; vs.
Rigaud, 136, 151–52, 154–58, 194–95; under
slavery, 200–201; on slavery's link to color
prejudice, 141; vs. Sonthonax, 136, 138–41,
150–51; speech at Camp Turel (1793), 141;
tree of liberty speech of, 132–33, 154, 264,
312; U.S.–Saint-Domingue trade policies
influenced by, xx; vs. Vaublanc, 145, 156,
170, 194, 201; in the War of the South, 158;
white property owners allowed to return
by, 299
Luzerne, César Henri Guillaume (comte de
la), 79

Macanda (a Vodou dance), 110
Le Macandal (Augustin), 111

406   Index

macandals, 62, 104–11, 351–52n34

Mackau, Baron de, 273

Madiou, Thomas: on Christophe's use of forced labor, 276, 289; *Histoire d'Haïti*, 4, 13; as a historian, xix; influence of, xvii, 207; influences on, xvii–xviii; on the members of the Central Assembly, 177; and Michelet, 4–5, 18

Mainguy, M., 65

Maitland, Thomas, 156–57

Makandal, François, xix; accusations against, 103; enslavement by Le Normand de Mézy, 123; execution of, 97, 103, 108, 121; execution of, reported escape of, 103–5; influence of, 103–6; Macanda inspired by the life of, 110; origin of his name, 351n24; poisonings by, alleged, 103–10, 112, 351–52n34; portrayals of his life, 110–11; public apology by, 103; rebellion by, 102–3; wives of, 106

"Makandal, histoire véritable" (M. de. C.), 110–11

"Le Makandal," 111

Makandal: ou, le noir marron (Denancé), 111

Malouet, Baron de (Pierre Victor), 51, 116, 223, 270, 301, 316–17

man, definition of, 72

Le Manifeste, 264

Manifeste du roi (Christophe and Limonade), 161–62

Maran, Réné, 314

marasa (twins), 7

Marathon, Battle of, 241, 374n115

Marcelin, Frédéric, 9, 246

maréchaussées, 55, 64, 103

Marie-Louise, Queen, 282

Marion, Ignace (General), 232–33

Marion, Cinna, *aîné* (Senator), 232, 235–36, 238–40, 242–45

Marmelade, Duc de la (Jean-Pierre Richard), 290

maroons: ads for, 386–87n41; as authors of independence, 137–38; Caribbean marronnage as omnipresent, 146; colonists' attitudes toward marronnage, 64, 190–91; death in rebellion or in suicide of, 64–65; Docoëns (Doko), 111–12; establishment of, 40–42; insurrection by, 11, 196; of Jamaica, 145–47, 150; map of regions where they hid, 28; *maréchaussée* pursuit of, 55, 64; petit marronnage, 64; as precursors to revolutionaries, 41–42; revolutionary thought of, xix, 3; treaties with, 46, 145–47, 150. *See also* Enrique/ Henri; Makandal, François

Martí, José, 246, 316

Martinique, 22, 170–72, 254

Martinique, Battle of (1794), 168–69

Marx, Karl: *The Class Struggle in France*, 5; *Die deutsche Ideologie*, 5; *Eighteenth Brumaire*, 10; on the Haitian Revolution, 5–6; on historical consciousness, 18; influence of, 27; influence on Michel- Rolph Trouillot, 4–6, 8, 336n34

Mauduit du Plessis, Thomas-Antoine de, 88

Maurepas, Jacques, 164

Mauseau, M., 142

Mayflower, 17

Mayombé, M., 147–48

Mazères, François, 84, 294–95

McGann, Jerome, 391n1

McKay, Claude, 222, 314

Mémoires pour servir à l'histoire d'Haïti (Boisrond-Tonnerre), xii–xiii, xv, 175, 215, 254

Mémoires (Napoléon), 200

Mémoires du général Toussaint L'Ouverture (Saint-Rémy), 5, 200, 255

Mencia, 31

Mercantile Advertiser, 225

Mercure (Makandal's wife), 106

Méry, Gaston: *Jean Révolte*, 56

Métral, Antoine, 113, 251, 278

Michel, Azor, 263

Michel, M., 112

Michelet, Jules, 4–5, 16–20, 22, 27; *Histoire de la révolution française*, xi

Milhet, Catherine, 75

military, women in, 281–83, 383n149

Mill, James Stuart, 18

Miltiades, 241, 374n115

Minis Azaka, 7

Mirbeck, Ignace Frédéric de, 142

La Misère au sein des richesses (Delorme), 307, 316–17

monarchy vs. republicanism, 205–6, 227–29, 231, 258–59

Monceybo, Jean, 177

Mongoubert, M., 107

Monroe, James, 259, 308–10

Monroe Doctrine, 307, 311, 319–20

Montesquieu, Secondat Baron de (Charles Louis de), 228

Moreau de Saint-Méry, Aménaïde, 75

Moreau de Saint-Mery, Médéric Louis-Élie, 35, 75, 77, 99, 101–2, 109, 185

Morillas, François, 177

Morne-Rouge assembly, 112, 114, 120–23, 126, 295, 355n97

Morning Chronicle, 205

Morning Post, 215

Morpeau, Louis, 319, 328

Morts sans sépulture (Sartre), 99

Moyse, General, 143, 147–49, 158, 161, 167, 177

Mugnos, André (or Munoz), 177

Mukherjee, Supriya, 18

NAACP (National Association for the Advancement of Colored People), 222

Napoléon Bonaparte: attempts to reinstate slavery, xiii–xiv, xvi, 39, 99, 158, 161–62, 167–70, 205; on Black freedom in the French Caribbean, 166–67; and the Constitution of 1801, 159, 178, 199–200; death of, 40; defeat in Saint-Domingue, 174; Directory overthrown by, 150; as emperor, 214; French republic's incoherence under, 178; Leclerc sent to Saint-Domingue by, xvi, 158; Louisiana Territory bought from, 260–61, 266, 380n84; vs. Toussaint Louverture, 151, 158–59, 166–68, 199–200; *Mémoires*, 200; overthrow of, 291, 301; plans to retake Haiti, 261–62; promises not to reinstate slavery, 21, 173; racism of/desire for white

supremacy, 166–71, 174; restoration of slavery, instructions for, 201–2; slavery reinstated on Martinique by, 165; wars waged by, 295, 297, 301

Narrative of the Life of Frederick Douglass (Douglass), 176

National Anti-Slavery Standard, 265

National Assembly (France), 76–77, 81–82, 87–88, 90, 93, 128–29, 186

National Association for the Advancement of Colored People (NAACP), 222

National Club of America for Americans, 310

National Convention (France, 1794), 49, 56, 144

Nau, Émile: on the Ayitian anti-colonial rebellion, 33; on Chavannes, 84; on Columbus vs. Napoléon, 40; on Enrique, 47–48; *Histoire des Caciques*, xxi, 27, 31–33, 38–40, 43–44, 101; historical methodology of, 43–44; on the insurrection of enslaved Africans, 44–45; on Vincent Ogé, 84; *Réclamation par les affranchis des droits civils et politiques*, 101

Nau, Ignace, xx, 9

"The Negro Digs Up His Past" (Schomburg), 254

Nemours, Alfred, 26, 340n137

New Orleans Bee, 266

New York Herald, 257

Niles Weekly Register, 257–59

Noé, Comte Louis-Pantaléon de, 144

Nogéré, Gaston, 177

Notes à M. Le Baron de V.P. Malouet (J. L. Vastey), 260

L'Observateur, 219

Observations adressées à l'Assemblée nationale (J. Raimond), 72

Observations sur l'origine et les progrès du préjugé des colons blancs contre les hommes de couleur (J. Raimond), 71, 102

Ogé, Angélique and Françoise, 134

Ogé, Orphé, 134

Ogé, ou le préjugé de couleur (Faubert), 101

408 Index

Ogé, Vincent: accused of fomenting slave rebellion, 85–87; advocacy for free men of color, 83, 85; on emancipation, 81, 85; execution of, 81, 84, 97–98, 100–101, 103, 120–21, 126, 130–31; failed rebellion by, 84–85, 97; influence of, 100–101; Mazères saved by, 84; public apology by, 98, 103; and Raimond, 83–84; on rights of free men of color, 81

On Social Contract (Rousseau), 198–99, 229

Ovando, Nicolás de, 36, 39–40, 50

Oviedo, Gonzalo Fernández de: *Historia natural y general de las Indias*, 46

Padmore, George, 222

Page, Pierre-François, 192–93

Pan-Africanism, 222, 226, 314

Le Panthéon haïtien (Édouard), 254–55

Papa Legba's crossroads, 7, 207

Papillon, Jean-François, 145

Paris, 318

Pascal-Trouillot, Ertha, 335n21

Past, Mariana, 7–8

Le Patriote, 264–65

Patterson, Orlando, 57

Paul (man enslaved by Poncet), 58

Paul, Cauvin, 1

Peltier, Jean-Gabriel, 379n64

Péralte, Charlemagne, 327

La Peregrinación de Bayoán (Hostos), 317

person, definition of, 72

Pétion, Alexandre: agricultural system under, 185; as anti-slavery, 231–33, 237–38; Bolívar aided by, xx, 231–33, 235–40, 244–45, 259; bust of, 234; vs. Christophe, 227, 275 (*see also* civil war (Haiti, 1808)); conflicts under, 11; Constitution signed by, 229; death of, 372n66; Declaration of Independence signed by, 211; Dumesle on, 229; free soil policy of, 257–58; French threats to, 270; French troops fought by, 162; government documents produced under, xviii; land policies of, 287; linked to the Latin American independence movement, 237; as president of the southern republic, 205–6, 258; regions/

cities associated with, 22; on reparations to the French, 293; revolutionary thought of, xix; role in the revolution, 127; in the siege of Santo Domingo, 220; vs. Jean Louis de Vastey, 230–31

Le Petit Samedi Soir, 10

Peynier, Antoine de Thomassin de, 88

Le Philantrope révolutionnaire, 113

Phillips, Wendell: "Toussaint Louverture," 316

Pierre, Jacques, 9

Pierre, Nathalie, 1, 24

Pigeonneau, Georges: "La Question nègre aux Étas-Unis," 66

Pillet, Jean-Baptiste, 126–27; "Mon Odyssée," 123–25

Pliny the Elder, 120

Poe, Edgar Allen, xx

poetry, 37–39, 116

point of view, xv, 13

Polk, James, 309

Polverel, Étienne: death of, 134; as a defender of the destitute and free men of color, 134–35; emancipation decrees by, 56, 130, 132–35, 138, 142–44, 146–47, 150, 184–86; labor system of, 135–36, 147, 183–85 (*see also* affermage labor system); returns to France, 134; on the tree of liberty, 133; on the creation of the French republic, 133, 356n10

Poncet, M., 57–58

Port-de-Paix, burning of (Haiti), 159

Port-Républicain (*formerly* Port-au-Prince), 133

positivist empiricism, 116

Poule d'Or (ship), 263

Poulin, Bailly, 28

Poulantzas, Nicos, 4

power, 13, 276

Pradine, Jean-Baptiste Symphor Linstant de, xvii

prejudice. *See* color prejudice; racism

The Present State of Hayti (J. Franklin), 275–76

Preuves complettes et matérielles du projet des colons (J. Raimond), 129

Index   409

Prévost, Julien (Comte de Limonade): as anti-conquest, 231; Code Henry co-created by, 280; on the Constitution of 1801, 176; on Enrique, 41–42; on Haiti as Black, 229; influence of, xviii; *Instructions pour les établissemens et la culture des habitations caféyères de la couronne*, 286; on Leclerc expedition and French attempts at reconquest, 303; on Toussaint Louverture, 303; *Manifeste du roi*, 161–62; on maroons as precursors to revolutionaries, 41; on Napoléon, 174; on unity, 203

Price-Mars, Jean, 10, 316; on collective bovarysme, 318; *Le Cri des nègres*, 314; on Haiti's lost sovereignty, 327–28; on the State, 327–28; *La Vocation de l'élite*, xx, 314, 329

Proclamations of September 24 and December 30, 1792, 140

Putnam's Monthly, 309–10

Quao, Captain, 145

"La Question nègre aux États-Unis" (Pigeonneau), 66

racism: Blacks as property, 298–99; coining and use of term, 56; domestic, and colonial expansion, 307–8; "first Haitians" (Ayitians) and anti-racism, 34; toward free people of color, 67–69, 74–76, 152–53; of Gobineau, 19–20; introduced in Ayiti (Haiti) by Spanish colonizers, 32; masqueraded as universalism, 168; of Napoléon, 166–71, 174; ultraracism, 55–56; in the U.S., 17, 239, 306–8, 310–12, 320–21. *See also* anti-racism; white supremacy/ white supremacists

Radio Haïti-Inter, 10

Raimond, Julien: advocacy for free men of color, 81–83, 90–91, 129; on American colonists' rights, 72, 77; anti-racism of, 69, 71, 82; as antislavery advocate, 71, 73, 76, 93, 184, 186–87, 346n8; arrests/ imprisonment of, 192–93; background/ lineage of, 72–73, 153; on the Central Assembly, 177; on color prejudice, 70–74, 87, 99; death of, 195; on the Declaration

of the Rights of Man, 73; elite status/ wealth of, 72–73, 346n8; emigrates to France, 73; as an enslaver, 185; on enslaving one's children, 185; "free and French" letter to the National Assembly, 93; on French colonists' violence toward people of color, xvii; on French declarations of indivisibility, 178; on the French National Assembly, 76–77; on gradual emancipation, 91, 184–86, 188–89; as a historian, xix; on independence, 189, 193–94; influence of, xviii; labor system of, 147, 182, 184–85, 187, 193–94, 197 (*see also* affermage labor system); and Vincent Ogé, 83–84; on racist laws, 75–76; on rebellion, 99–100, 101–2, 189–91; Schomburg on, 254; Sonthonax returned to France by, 136, 193; on the white colonists' independence movement, 88, 91, 186; on white colonists' plots against free people of color, 79–80, 129; on white women in Saint-Domingue, 73–74

Raimond, Julien, works by: *Correspondance de Julien Raimond avec ses frères*, 88, 93; *Lettre d'un citoyen détenu pendant quatorze mois*, 192; *Observations adressées à l'Assemblée nationale*, 72; *Observations sur l'origine et les progrès du préjugé des colons blancs contre les hommes de couleur*, 71, 102; *Preuves complettes et matérielles du projet des colons*, 129; *Réflexions sur les véritables causes des troubles et des désastres de nos colonies*, 91, 186; *Réponse aux considérations de M. Moreau*, 99, 101–2, 185; *Véritable origine des troubles de S.-Domingue*, 347–48n38

Raimond, Pierre (or Raymond), 72, 153

Raimond family, 153

Ramey Berry, Daina, 20, 109

Ranke, Leopold von, 18

Rapport sur les troubles de Saint-Domingue (Coulon), 60

rasanbleman (gathering together), 7

Rateau, Louise, 127

Raynal, Guillaume: *Histoire des deux Indes*, 157, 360n101

410 Index

rebellion: Christmastime Rebellion, 26, 44–46, 340n137; by the enslaved, 26, 44–48, 57, 61–62, 84, 101–2, 340n137 (*see also* Haitian Revolution); General Revolt (1791), 26, 120, 130, 185–86; against white supremacy/white supremacists, 99–100

Réclamation par les affranchis des droits civils et politiques (E. Nau), 101

Recueil général des lois et actes du gouvernement d'Haïti, xvii

Réflexions politiques (J. L. Vastey), 126, 252, 286–87

Réflexions sur le code noir, 64–65

Réflexions sur les véritables causes des troubles et des désastres de nos colonies (J. Raimond), 91, 186

Réflexions sur une lettre de Mazères (J. L. Vastey), xi–xiii, 118, 228, 252, 260, 264–65

Remoussin, M., 64

Réponse à la proclamation de Toussaint Louverture (Rigaud), 157

Réponse aux considérations de M. Moreau (J. Raimond), 99, 101–2, 185

Réponse du général de brigade André Rigaud (Rigaud), 136, 152, 154–55, *155*

republicanism: antislavery in republics vs. empires, 249; French, incoherence of, 76, 128–29, 132, 165, 168–70, 178, 205–6; Haitians' attitudes toward independence and republics, 205–6; meanings of, 314; vs. monarchy, 205–6, 227–29, 231, 258–59; slavery associated with, 205–6, 228

La République d'Haïti et ses visiteurs (Janvier), 26, 27

revenge, xiv–xv; Boukman on, 112, 126; in connection with the past, 195; Dessalines on, xiv, 21–22, 34–35, 99; by the enslaved, colonists' fears of, 62; for Ogé and Chavannes, 120, 126; as a soul value of formerly enslaved peoples, 20–21

Richepanse, Antoine, 172

Rigaud, André: antislavery movement led by, 93, 135, 154; background/lineage of, 153–54; on the British evacuation of Saint-Domingue, 156–57; on the colonists' genocidal imaginings, 119; on color

prejudice/racism, 152–55, 170; on equality, 151–52; exiled in France, 158, 195; on Ferrand de Baudière, 80–81; on freedom, 188; as a historian, xix; imprisonment of, 299; on labor, 187–88, 193; vs. Toussaint Louverture, 136, 151–52, 154–58, 194–95; on politics, 170; on Polverel, 134–35; racism of, 195; regions/cities associated with, 22–23; *Réponse à la proclamation de Toussaint Louverture*, 157; *Réponse du général de brigade André Rigaud*, 136, 152, 154–55, *155*; role in the revolution, 127–28; vs. Sonthonax, 136, 151–52, 156

Rivaroli, Antoine ("Rivarol"), 51

Rochambeau, Donatien, 39, 162–64, 201–93

Romain, Paul, 262

romanticism, 116, 326–27, 329, 391n1

Le Romantisme en Haïti (Dolcé, Dorval, and Casthely), 326–27

Rouanez, Joseph, 260–61

Roumain, Jacques: *Gouverneurs de la rosée*, 316

Roume de Saint-Laurent, Philippe Rose, 142

Rousseau, Jean-Jacques: *On Social Contract*, 198–99, 229

Rouvray, Marquise de, 118–19

Roxas, Charles, 177

Royal Chamber of Instruction, 278

Royal Dahomets, 383n149

Royal Gazette of Hayti. See *Gazette royale d'Hayti*

Rudé, George, 16

Ryswick, Treaty of (1697), 51–52, 70–71

Saint-Domingue. *See* Haiti

Saint-Lot, Marie-José Alcide, 196

Saint-Marc, burning of (Saint-Domingue), 159

Saintonge (man enslaved by Poncet), 58

Saint-Rémy, Joseph: on Delgrès, 172; on the free soil policy, 260; as a historian, xix; influence of, xvii; influences on, xvii–xviii; on Toussaint Louverture as governor-general for life, 200; *Mémoires du général Toussaint L'Ouverture*, 5, 200, 255; on the Ogé daughters, 134; on slavery's restoration, 172; on Stowe, 255

Index 411

Salamis, 241, 374n114

Salamis, Battle of, 374n114

Sala-Molins, Louis, 181

Sam (anonymous writer), 309–10

Sam, Vilbrun Guillaume, 326

Sans-Souci Palace (Haiti), 24–25, 284–86, 291, 293

Sans-Soucy, Jean-Baptiste, 143

Santa Ana (ship), 263

Santo Domingo, 143, 212, 220–21, 241, 243, 249, 262, 317. *See also* Dominican Republic

Sartre, Jean-Paul, 62; *Morts sans sépulture*, 99

Saunders, Prince, 262, 278

Savannah, Battle of (U.S., 1779), 127–28, 355n110

Schoelcher, Victor, 250, 255–56, 273–75; *Colonies étrangères et Haïti*, 279–80

Schomburg, Arturo: "The Negro Digs Up His Past," 254

Schomburg, Arturo (Arthur), 253

Scott, Joan, 24

"The Sea Is History" (Walcott), 283

se vye chodye ki kwit bon manje (it is the old pot that makes the best food), 207

Silencing the Past (M-R. Trouillot), 5–6; on the Alamo massacre, 15; audience for, 7–8; Corbett's review of, 3; footnotes, 4; on Foucault, 12; on the Haitian Revolution's significance as occluded, 13–14, 25, 248; Haitian sources for, 13, 15; on historians, 10, 13; on historical resurrection (talking to and for the dead), 20; on history and power, 12–13; influence of, 27; influences on, 6, 336n34; on the source of power, 276; "The Three Faces of Sans Souci," 6–7, 24; vs. *Ti dife boule*, 2–3, 8, 10, 27; on Todorov, 13

Simone Baptiste, Suzanne, 144

Simonde de Sismondi, Jean Charles Léonard, 294

"The 1619 Project" (Hannah-Jones), 17

slave narratives, 200, 253

slavery and the enslaved, 50–60; Africa depopulated by the slave trade, 50–51; Africans linked with Indians and Black Haitians, 32–33, 50; antislavery movement, 93; Blacks as property under, 298–99; black/slave codes, 44–47, 181; branding, 52; chattel slavery, 190, 198, 240; Christmastime Rebellion (1521), 26, 340n137; Code Noir, 54–55, 68–71, 181, 276–77, 298; colonists' accounts of, 58–59; colonists' fears of vengeance, 61–62; colonists' marriage to women they enslaved, 70; color prejudice linked to, 141; as commercializing/materializing humankind, 52, 54–55; in Cuba, 243–44, 264, 312; death in rebellion or suicide as escape from slavery, 21–22, 64–65, 172; dehumanizing language of, 51; under Dessalines vs. Napoléon, 217; edict of 1685 establishing heritable slave status, 54, 70–71, 73–76, 298; "first Haitians" (Ayitians) and the antislavery movement, 34; and free people of color, 52, 67; free status vs. slave status, 52; French, 51–52, 55–58, 249; French reinstatement of slavery, 162, 169, 171–74 (*see also under* Napoléon Bonaparte); General Revolt (1791), 26, 120, 130, 185–86; in Guadeloupe, 21, 168–69, 172–74, 201, 206; Haiti as first to outlaw, xviii; vs. Haiti's morality, xviii; introduced in Haiti by Spanish colonizers, 32–33; living conditions, 52; Louis XIII's establishment of slavery, 70; marronnage (fugitivity from slavery) (*see* maroons); in Martinique, 22, 170–72, 254; the Middle Passage, 50, 262–63; Émile Nau on, 32–33; number of enslaved people, 53*t*; personhood of the enslaved, 54, 82, 87; plantations, 51–52, 61, 65; plantation sales records, 190–91; in Puerto Rico, 243; punishments, 183, 364n54; rebellions, 26, 44–48, 57, 61–62, 84, 101–2, 340n137 (*see also* Haitian Revolution); refuting mythologies of and faulty arguments for, xv–xvi; religious justification, 70; reparations for, 274; republics associated with, 205–6, 228; slave patrols, 55; slavery as a crime against humanity, 117–18, 120; slave ships, 50; social death, 57; soul values,

20–21, 109–10; by Spain, 243; Spanish and Portuguese invention of the transatlantic slave trade, 50; torture, rape, and death, 56–61, 63–65, 70, 191–92, 198; in the U.S., 17, 228, 239, 249, 257, 261, 304; use of the dead as testimony against, xi, xv–xvi; Vastey on, 49–51, 55–65, 118, 125–26, 192. *See also* abolition of slavery; antislavery

Smith, James McCune, 253

Social Contract (Rousseau), 198–99, 229

Société des Amis des Noirs, 64–65, 100, 102, 171

Sommavert, Mme, 382–83n141

Sonthonax, Léger-Félicité: on color prejudice, 131; emancipation decree by, 56, 130–32, 136, 140–44, 146–47, 150, 177, 183–86; on independence, 151, 165, 193; labor system of, 147, 182–85 (*see also* affermage labor system); vs. Toussaint Louverture, 136, 138–41, 150–51; on Vincent Ogé, 130–31; prejudices of, 138–39; returns to France, 134, 136, 193, 195; vs. Rigaud, 136, 151–52, 156; as self-proclaimed founder of liberty, 136–38; slavery supported by, 130, 140–41; on white French colonists, 131

Sophie (an enslaved wetnurse), 59

sorcerers, 105

Soulouque, Faustin, I, Emperor, 5, 243, 305

sovereignty: anti-colonialism's dependence on, 229; Black, 252, 255, 313–14, 318; personal vs. political, 252–53; vs. sovereign ruler, 229. *See also* anti-colonialism; Haitian independence

Spartacus, 114, 157–58, 164–65, 360n101

St. Domingo, Its Revolutions and Its Patriots (W. W. Brown), 155

Stella (Bergeaud), 34, 195, 296, 329

Steward, T. G., 237

Stewart, Duncan, 290

Stirner, Max, 5

Stirring the Pot of Haitian History (M-R. Trouillot). See *Ti dife boule sou istoua Ayiti*

St. Léger, Edmond de, 142

Stoler, Ann Laura, 21

Stowe, Harriet Beecher: *Uncle Tom's Cabin*, 255

Sylvain, Georges: *Cric?Crac!* 9

Le Système colonial dévoilé (J. L. Vastey), xi–xii, 260; on the anti-colonial, anti-racist, and antislavery principles of the Haitian Revolution, 252; on Black sovereignty, 252; on colonists' brutality and resistance by the enslaved, 15–16, 60–62, 191–92; on color prejudice/white supremacy, 66; enslavers named in, 57; historical methodology of, 63; influence of, 252; publication, translation, and dissemination of, 35, 252

Taínos, 32

Talleyrand (Charles-Maurice de Talleyrand-Périgord), 166

Le Télégraphe, 235, 302, 374n117

Tellier, M., 103

Une Tempête (Césaire), 38

Les Thazar (Hibbert), 9

Thermopylae, Battle of, 374nn113–14

Third World Quarterly, 221–22

Thirty Years in India (Bevan), 66

Thistlewood, Thomas, 58–59

Thoby-Marcelin, Philippe, 1–2

Tiburon (Xaragua, Ayiti), 31

Ti dife boule sou istoua Ayiti (M-R. Trouillot): on the abolition of slavery by Sonthonax, 137; on affermage, 149; audience for, 7–8; bibliography, 4, 6–7; on Boyer, 11; on the crossroads of the revolution's history, 196; on Duvalier, 10–11, 196; on the economic dominance of white planters, 197; in English, 2; on the enslaved and *vivres*, 2, 335n13; on freedom, 196; in Haitian Creole, 1–2, 7, 9; on the history of the Haitian Revolution, 2; influences on, 6, 10–11; language barrier to, 2; meaning of the title, 1; publication of, 1; relationship to *Silencing the Past*, 8, 10; revised edition (2012), 1–2; vs. *Silencing the Past*, 2–3, 8, 10, 27; typographical features and organization of, 7–8

The Times (England), 225

Times-Picayune, 309

Todorov, Tzvetan: *The Conquest of America*, 13

tolerance, 311–12

torture: under the Code Noir, 70; of Toussaint Louverture, 36; of Vincent Ogé, 81, 84, 97–98, 100–101; slave trade as, 16, 51, 56–58, 59, 61–65, 69–70; Jean Louis de Vastey on, 51, 57–58, 63–65, 69, 191–92; the wheel, 97–99, 126

Toussaint Louverture (Lamartine), 5

"Toussaint Louverture" (Phillips), 316

Tredwell, James: *The Constitution of the Republic of Hayti*, 258

Trinidad, 263

Trouillot, Ernst, 335n21

Trouillot, Évelyne, 1, 335n21

Trouillot, Hénock, 335n21

Trouillot, Lyonel (or Lionel), 1–2, 6, 335n21

Trouillot, Michel-Rolph: on Ardouin, 12; on the Constitution of 1801, 196–97; *Global Transformations*, 3, 25; *Haiti, State against Nation*, 197; on Haitian historiography's language barrier, 7; on Haiti as a neocolonial experiment, 324; intellectual formation of, 4, 335n21; *Lakansièl* co-created by, 1; Marx's influence on, 4–6, 8, 336n34; on origins claims (genetic sentences), 17–18. See also *Silencing the Past*; *Ti dife boule sou istoua Ayiti*

Trouillot family, exile of, 1–2, 12

Turner, Nat, 158

"Twa Fey/Twa Rasin," 7

Uncle Tom's Cabin (Stowe), 255

United States: abolition in, 243, 247, 249–50, 255–56; "America for the Americans," 309–11, 320; democracy in, 228, 245, 306–8, 310, 324; expansionism/imperialism of, 222, 260–61, 307–11, 313–14, 319–22; Haitian independence recognized by, 238–39, 259; Haiti occupied by, 222, 245–46, 260, 311, 326–29, 388n71; Haiti recognized by, 305, 326; Haiti's trade relations with, 260–61; Haiti threatened by, 304–6, 313; origins claims about, 17; racism in, 17, 239, 306–8, 310–12, 320–21; slavery in, 17, 228, 239, 249, 257, 261, 304; white supremacy in, 17, 308, 311

Valençuela, 40–41

Vashon, George, 100–101

Vassa, Gustavus (aka Olaudah Equiano), 58, 63, 312

Vastey, Baron de (Jean Louis de), 307; on abolition/antislavery, xx, 250, 252; anti-racism of, 168, 294; on Ayitian resistance to Spanish domination, 33, 35–36, 42; background/lineage of, 35, 153–54, 192; Black writers influenced by, 253–54; on Caonabo, 36; on the civil war between Christophe and Boyer, 206; Code Henry co-created by, 280; on the Code Noir, 68–69; colonial histories refuted by, 23–24; on colonialism, 223, 295; on color prejudice/white supremacy, 66–68, 295, 297; on the Constitution of 1805, 206, 217–18, 226–27; on creolization in his works, 8–9; on the Declaration of Independence, 219; on Dessalines's title of emperor, 214, 221, 226; on Dumesle, 289–90; as editor (see *Gazette royale d'Hayti*); on the education of women, 279; on Enrique, 40–2; on free people of color, 67–8; on the free soil policy, 259–60; on French attempts to reinstate slavery, 168–9, 291; on French exclusion from Haiti, 300; on French oppression of Haitians, 270–1; on the French threat, 301–2; on French trade, 272; on Haitian independence, xi–xii, 42–3, 164–5; on the Haitian Revolution, 118, 239, 295; on the Haitian vs. American revolution, 121–2; as a historian, xix, 35, 63; on the indemnity treaties with France, 273; influence of, xviii, 15, 27, 207, 252–53; on Toussaint Louverture's arrest, 165; on the maroons and independence, 137–38; on marronnage, 64; on Mazères, 294; on monarchy, 205–6, 228; on Vincent Ogé and Chavannes, 84, 120; on personal vs. political sovereignty, 252–53; vs. Pétion,

230–31; on the physical remains of the "first Haitians," 43; on the population of Haiti, 56–57; on public opinion, xii; on remembering colonialism's violent history, xiv, 42–43; on renaming Saint-Domingue, Haiti, 35; on republics, 228; on restitution, reparation, and compensation, xii; on reunification, 245; on slavery, 49–51, 55–65, 118, 125–26, 192; on the transition to independence, 185; on U.S. democracy, 228; use of the dead as anti-slavery testimony, xi, 15–16, 61; veil metaphor used by, 251; on *vivres* and food dependency, 286–87; on the white property exclusion, 230–31, 300

Vastey, Baron de, works of: *Le Cri de la conscience,* 20; *Le Cri de la patrie,* 253–54; *Essai sur les causes de la révolution et des guerres civiles d'Hayti,* 14–15, 165, 206, 228, 295; *Notes à M. Le Baron de V.P. Malouet,* 260; *Réflexions politiques,* 126, 252, 286–87; *Réflexions sur une lettre de Mazères,* xi–xiii, 118, 228, 252, 260, 264–65 (see also *Le Système colonial dévoilé*)

Vastey, Jean Valentin, 153, 192

Vaublanc, Vincent-Marie Viénot de, 145, 156, 169–70, 194, 201

Venezuelan independence, 231–32, 235–38

vengeance. *See* revenge

Véritable origine des troubles de S.-Domingue (J. Raimond), 347–48n38

Vernet, André, 203, 212–13, 226, 277

Vertières, Battle of (1803), 162–63, 203, *204,* 284

vèvè *(sacred Vodou drawing),* 7, 196–97

Viard, Étienne (or Viart), 177

Vilate, General, 164

Villaverde, Cirilo, 243–44

Villevert, Jean-François Reynaud de, 74

vivres, 2, 286–87, 335n13

La Vocation de l'élite (Price-Mars), xx, 314, 329

Vodou ritual/cosmology, 126, 196–97, 355n107

Voyage dans le nord d'Hayti (Dumesle), 22–25, 48–49, 56, 113–17, 121

"Voyages de Scaldado" (Betances), 311–12

Walcott, Derek, 285, 291; "The Sea Is History," 283

Walrond, Eric, 222, 253

Wang, Q. Edward, 18

War of the South (Saint-Domingue), 158

Washington, Booker T., xx, 314–15

Washington, George, 238, 313

Welch, 62

wheat, 286–87

wheel (torture device), 97–99, 126

whipping, 183

White, Ed, 176

"Whiteness as Property" (Harris), 298–99

white supremacy/white supremacists, xvi; of the Code Noir, 54; Haiti's victory over France as a threat to, 294; human diversity and divinity as undermining, 296–97; illogic of, 155–56, 169, 294; independence movement of, 83, 88–89, 91, 93, 101, 186; vs. liberty/equality, debates by Atlantic world powers, 302–3; Napoléon, 166–71, 174; and pure origins, 6; on a racial war, 119–20; racist laws to preserve, 74; rebellion against, 99–100; slavery justified by, 66–67, 118, 155–56, 171, 296, 304, 323; in the U.S., 17, 308, 311; use of term, 66–67; violence by, 97–98, 102. *See also* Colonial Assembly; colonialism; racism; slavery and the enslaved

Whitman, Walt, 324

Wilberforce, William, 250, 262–64, 275

Williams, Eric, 250

William Wilberforce (ship), 263

Wilson, William, 287–88

Wilson, Woodrow, 245

Winn, T. S.: *Emancipation: Or Practical Advice to British Slave-Holders,* 66

Woodson, Drexel, 336n34

Xaraguans, 31, 36, 40, 42

-1—
0—
+1—